Brandeis and *Frankfurter*

By Leonard Baker

THE JOHNSON ECLIPSE:
A PRESIDENT'S VICE PRESIDENCY

BACK TO BACK: THE DUEL BETWEEN
FDR AND THE SUPREME COURT

THE GUARANTEED SOCIETY

ROOSEVELT AND PEARL HARBOR

BRAHMIN IN REVOLT

JOHN MARSHALL: A LIFE IN LAW

DAYS OF SORROW AND PAIN:
LEO BAECK AND THE BERLIN JEWS

BRANDEIS AND FRANKFURTER:
A DUAL BIOGRAPHY

LEONARD BAKER

Brandeis and Frankfurter

A Dual Biography

1817

HARPER & ROW, PUBLISHERS, New York
Cambridge, Philadelphia, San Francisco, London
Mexico City, São Paulo, Sydney

To Howard and Raci Brawer

FIRST EDITION

Designed by Ruth Bornschlegel

Library of Congress Cataloging in Publication Data

Baker, Leonard.
   Brandeis and Frankfurter.

   Bibliography: p.
   Includes index.
   1. Brandeis, Louis Dembitz, 1856–1941. 2. Frank-
furter, Felix, 1882–1965. 3. Judges—United States—
Biography. I. Title.
KF8744.B27 1984   347.73′2634 [B]   83-48319
ISBN 0-06-015245-1   347.3073534 [B]

84 85 86 87 88 10 9 8 7 6 5 4 3 2 1

Contents

Illustrations follow page 216.

Suppose [Brandeis] has been the subject of some undiscriminate praise. He is worthy of the urge which led to it. Suppose he had his vanities and was not proof against the constant drip of adulation. . . . All that is so minor and unimportant, so irrelevant to what he did, to what he stood for, to the effect which he had upon the times in which he lived. There is nothing here to expose. There is no sham, or pretense, or hypocrisy lurking in the background.

—Dean Acheson to Charles E. Wyzanski, Jr.,
February 27, 1956

There will be enough of Felix, the myth, in all that is said and written. He is good enough to warrant telling the story straight and true.

—Dean Acheson to Alexander M. Bickel,
September 13, 1965

BOOK
ONE

Knight Errant

1

Before the Supreme Court

In 1908 the Supreme Court of the United States met in the Capitol, in the semicircular room known by its former activity as the Old Senate Chamber. This had been the Court's home since 1860; before that the justices shuffled from one room to another, once meeting in a former Capitol Hill tavern. The nine justices sat on a raised platform, behind them were an arched doorway, a gilded American eagle, and marble columns. Lawyers stood in front of the justices' bench and spectators sat in a semicircle of wooden seats. Red drapes and carpets, as well as busts of the former chief justices, added to the room's splendor.

To the justices, the Old Senate Chamber was not all that splendid. Charles Evans Hughes, who served on the Court beginning in 1910, described its facilities as "very slender." The justices donned their robes across the hall, in a room also used for their luncheon. Below was the conference room and library, small and cluttered, Hughes continued, "where we crowded about the conference table. As some of the justices objected to open windows, the room became overheated and the air foul during our long conferences, not conducive to good humor."

In these spartan facilities, in this foul-smelling conference room, the Supreme Court had, during the previous two decades, written new definitions of law, definitions benefiting the employer, the mill owner, the steel magnate. The justices had declared that property not only was a tangible, such as a house or stocks or machinery, but was also an intangible. The right to contract then became, by the justices' decree, the right of the employer to deal with each employee regarding wages, hours worked, and safety—with each employee separately. As a result, a state generally could not impose safety, health, or economic conditions on the work site except under dire circumstances.

On Wednesday afternoon, January 15, 1908, Louis Dembitz Brandeis, lawyer from Boston, stood before the Supreme Court, this institution which had done much to benefit the owners of American industry, to ask that Court to change its thinking, jettison its definitions. Specifically, he wanted the Court to uphold a law limiting to ten hours the working day for women laundry workers in Oregon. The law had been enacted by that state's legislature and upheld by that state's highest court as a means to protect the women from thirteen-, fifteen-, and eighteen-hour work days.

Nineteen states had similar laws, but more was involved than women laundry workers in Oregon and workers in those nineteen states. The lawyers opposing Brandeis summed up the issue well, arguing, "The question involved is far-reaching. If such legislation may be sustained and justified merely because the employee is a woman, and if such employment in a healthy vocation may be limited and restricted in her case, there is no limit beyond which the legislative power may not go."

Changes in American law come neither swiftly nor easily, but only after painstaking research, years of experience, and many arguments in courts. The changes begin slowly. A footnote in one opinion is seized upon by a justice, expanded to become the basis of a dissent, and then, later, becomes the basis of a majority opinion. One decision, even within the narrowest framework, begins a process of ever-broadening legal interpretation; a remark grows into a concept spawning decisions in future decades. That is what Louis Brandeis was attempting this day. Seizing upon the remarks in earlier opinions, building them into a rationale, he was attempting to persuade the Court to funnel those diverse remarks into a decision which, in turn, would influence other decisions. He was arguing for women laundry workers in Oregon, but when he finished, he hoped all would understand, as his opponents had said, that "there is no limit beyond which the legislative power may not go."

Louis Brandeis had come to Washington from Boston early in the week, and then waited for his case to be called. He traveled much in those days but did not enjoy it. The previous evening he had written to his wife, "Our case will not be reached until two or a little earlier tomorrow and it is questionable whether I shall be able to leave before Thursday afternoon. Of course I long to be back."

He was a tall man, thin, his shoulders hunching forward when he spoke, giving him a stooped appearance. His hair then (he was fifty-one), was a blue-gray mop framing his gaunt, Lincoln-like face. He spoke in a southern drawl, a relic of his early years in Louisville, Kentucky. As he stood before the nine justices in his frock coat and striped trousers, he was known as a brilliant lawyer, certainly the equal of any of the nine before him. From a lucrative law practice, he was wealthy, more so than some of these nine.

Yet he stood before them as an outsider.

It was not because they wore the black robes of justices and he wore the civilian garb of the advocate. Rather, where they had developed the Supreme Court into a bastion of private capital, he had become the "people's advocate." The institutions the Supreme Court defended, he opposed.

As Brandeis prepared to begin his arguments, these nine men looked august, dignified, sound, wise. There was another opinion. The next year President William Howard Taft expressed a general view when he described the Supreme Court justices as "pitiable," continuing: "Yet those old fools hold on with a tenacity that is most discouraging." He described Chief Justice Melville W. Fuller as "almost senile," said Associate Justice John Marshall Harlan "does no work" and David J. Brewer was "so deaf that he cannot hear and has got beyond the point of the commonest accuracy in writing his opinions," and added that Brewer and Harlan "sleep almost through all the arguments."

Four of these nine whom Brandeis faced that Wednesday afternoon had been born in the 1830s, when America was more wilderness than civilized nation. Four had been born in the 1840s, when bitter rivalries between North and South were formalizing. Only one had been born in the 1850s, the decade of Brandeis's birth, and had come to maturity as he had with the nation's industrial expansion.

The Chief Justice, Melville Weston Fuller, was a few weeks shy of his seventy-fifth birthday. His ancestry traced back to the *Mayflower*. His was a typical American success story. After opening a Chicago law practice, he had married a bank president's daughter and, through her family's connections, made a fortune in commercial law and real estate. Most people had never heard of him when he was appointed to the Court in 1888, but businessmen later applauded him as he helped transform the Court into an agency striking down state laws such as the Oregon law before him this day.

Associate Justice John Marshall Harlan was the senior member of the Court. Only a few months younger than Fuller, a Kentuckian like Brandeis, Harlan was from a family long involved in politics. He had led Kentucky's delegation to the Republican national convention of 1876, where he swung his delegation behind Rutherford B. Hayes. When Hayes was subsequently elected, he paid his debts—Harlan was Hayes's first appointment to the Supreme Court. A conservative on property matters, Harlan was a liberal in other areas. He had fought for the Union in the Civil War, although his family owned slaves, and had dissented thirteen years earlier when his brethren on the Court had declared the separate but equal doctrine constitutional when applied to blacks. Harlan was a question mark this day.

David Brewer was next in seniority. Now in his early seventies, Brewer had been born in Smyrna, Asia Minor; his father had been a Congregational minister from New England. Brewer had been brought up to believe that the might of tradition and wealth made right. He attacked "alien" ideologies spreading "the black flag of anarchism, flaunting destruction of property." There was not much uncertainty about his position today.

Edward Douglass White, in his early sixties, born and raised in the South, had fought for the Confederacy, and later acknowledged Ku Klux Klan membership. More important this day, however, was his inconsistency on the issue before the Court. Three years earlier he had joined the Court's minority in *Lochner* v. *New York* to support a law limiting the working day for bakers to eight hours. But that same year he had voted to invalidate a federal law requiring some supervision over company contracts. The first time freedom of contract had not been interfered with but the second time it had, he explained; only he seemed to understand the difference.

Rufus W. Peckham, sixty-nine years old, like the other Court members—except one—was from a well-established family. He had followed his father into Albany, New York, politics, prospered, connected with the right contacts, and was appointed to the Supreme Court by his fellow New Yorker, President Grover Cleveland. He had disappointed none of his friends; he had written the majority decision striking down the eight-hour restriction on working hours for bakers in New York.

Joseph McKenna, at sixty-four one of the younger men on the Court, was the only justice whose family could not be traced back in America for many generations. A Catholic like Justice White, McKenna was the son of Irish immigrants who settled in Philadelphia but then traveled to California to escape the anti-Catholic, anti-Irish feelings rampant in Philadelphia in the years before the Civil War. In the House of Representatives, however, McKenna, although a child of immigrants, favored restrictions on Chinese immigrants. After his appointment to the Supreme Court, he returned to law school because he realized he needed additional legal training. He had an inconsistent record on the issue before him today, sometimes supporting governmental actions, sometimes opposing.

Then there was Oliver Wendell Holmes, Jr., sixty-six, sometimes described as a "liberal," sometimes a "conservative" on specific issues before the Court. He was neither. He believed that legal issues could not be determined without an awareness of the world outside the courtroom. "The life of the law has not been logic; it has been experience," he had written in what is one of the most famous sentences in American legal history. He did not believe that the justices had the right to impose any particular economic theory on the nation, urging in the New York bakers' case that the state be allowed to work out its own problems, explaining that "The Fourteenth Amendment does not enact Mr. Herbert Spencer's Social Statics." Holmes and Brandeis had been friends for almost three decades. This week Brandeis had been a guest of the Holmeses—"We are at home on Monday afternoon and if you have nothing better to do, you will give much pleasure to me and Mrs. Holmes if you look in about five-thirty."

William R. Day, in his late fifties, came from a family of lawyers and judges. Prominent in politics and as a judge, he generally was considered "safe" for business and property interests although he had voted on the other side a few times. Another question mark today.

The ninth member of the Court was William H. Moody, fifty-four. The only member of the Court born in the 1850s, he had been Theodore Roosevelt's Attorney General and earned a reputation as a trustbuster. His nomination had almost been defeated in the Senate—the Senators being more anxious to defend trusts than to bust them.

Now the case of *Muller* v. *Oregon* was in process, and it was Louis Brandeis's turn. "May it please the Court," he began.

The case had origins beyond specific events in Oregon. The industrial revolution after the Civil War had not only transformed the American dream, from one of turning a rough-hewn log cabin into a country estate to that of moving from a tenement to a Fifth Avenue mansion, but it also had changed the rules. The farmer was the self-employed entrepreneur, from the beginning of his career to its end, whether he succeeded in transforming his log cabin into the hoped-for mansion or not. The new industrial society, in contrast, brought the age of the wage earner.

This was a new experience for the Americans. To work became romantic, to work for someone else. Churchmen extolled the glories of long and arduous labor, castigated the idle. Horatio Alger wrote the same novel many times and under many different titles: the young man who through loyalty, honesty, industry, and subservience at last succeeds. Currier & Ives depicted a United States without sweatshops, mines, or factories. Money equaled virtue. To be "rich as Rockefeller" was the dream.

Some were aware that the romance was not the reality. One was Florence Kelley, whom Felix Frankfurter described as the "woman who had probably the largest single share in shaping the social history of the United States during the first thirty years of this century." Dignified in appearance, big-bosomed, she would have looked natural attending a society salon, or as a housemother for female college students. But her moral indignation at the sights she saw in the workplace had led her to other occupations. For almost forty years she fought—and what she did can only be described as fighting, the tough verbal and legal scratching and clawing that people must do to accomplish their ends—to help the worker. She took personal abuse in those years, some of it stated publicly but much of it said in sneers and in winks by males who knew what woman's place and position should be. But she continued her work.

Her indignation had brought Louis Brandeis to the Supreme Court this day.

She had begun her work in Illinois, where she had forced some limitations on employers, including a law restricting the work day for women to eight hours. Then the Illinois State Supreme Court, in 1895, declared the law invalid. "There is no reasonable ground," said that court, "at least none which has been manifest to us in the argument of counsel, for fixing eight hours in one day as the limit." That case, *Ritchie* v. *People,* was a defeat for Florence Kelley, but in that sentence, although not realized at the time, was potential for victory: "no reasonable ground" had been presented, but what if reasonable grounds, so reasonable that they could not be refuted, were presented?

Florence Kelley became head of the National Consumers' League. Headquartered in New York City, the League was dedicated to improving working conditions; part of its work was what a later generation called public relations, publicizing state efforts to improve the workplace, and urging consumers not to purchase sweatshop goods. The League also supported laws on behalf of the worker.

One such law was a New York prohibition against night work for women. When the law was challenged, the Consumers' League relied on the state to defend the law in court. That was a mistake. Mrs. Kelley was furious. "No representative of the Attorney General's office was present in the court. The defendants moved to submit. The people were thus deprived of their right to have the case argued. . . . There was no presentation of the law of the case. The brief was prepared— for the People—by the Third Assistant Attorney General." If the case, *People* v. *Williams,* was a disaster for the cause of the National Consumers' League, it also had taught them not to rely on the third assistant attorney general.

In the court's decision was this sentence: "I find nothing in the language of the section which suggests the purpose of promoting health except as it might be inferred that for a woman to work during the forbidden hours of the night would be unhealthful." There it was again, as it had been in the Illinois case a few years earlier, almost a plea for some reasonable basis for such a law, so that judges could do more than merely "infer." Perhaps the time would come when that point could be seized upon. It did.

In 1903 the Oregon state legislature had enacted a law forbidding the employment of a woman "in any mechanical establishment, or factory, or laundry in this state more than ten hours during any one day." In laundries, work days of seventeen hours and sometimes work weeks of seven days were common. Curt Muller, owner of the Grand Laundry in Portland, Oregon, directed his overseer, Joe Haselbock, to require a female employee, a Mrs. E. Gotcher, to work more than ten hours on September 4, 1905—Labor Day. Muller was charged with violating the law, found guilty, and fined $10. Backed by the state's laundry owners association, he appealed. When the state's highest court affirmed his conviction, he then appealed to the United States Supreme Court.

Mrs. Kelley and her associates knew this was *the* case. The issue was clear: Could a state regulate working conditions for reasonable cause? The next question was: Would the Oregon Attorney General allow the National Consumers' League to bring in a lawyer to develop the reasonableness argument?

Mrs. Kelley had been away from New York on a speaking trip when the Consumers' League received Oregon's favorable response. In her absence, the League's governing board made an appointment for her to see a prominent member of the American bar—Joseph H. Choate of New York City. His fame as an advocate was so widespread that the Oregon attorney general had requested the League invite him to participate in the case.

"I have never represented a client until convinced that his cause was entirely just," Choate once said. When his friend Theodore Roosevelt criticized corporation lawyers for using courtroom machinations to block law enforcement, a shocked Choate said, "If there are any such lawyers, I don't know who they are."

Mrs. Kelley was appalled. She knew of Choate's ability, his reputation, his generosity with charities; but she also knew that he could not represent the Consumers' League.

In 1895 Joseph Choate had successfully argued against a federal income tax law before the Supreme Court, calling the proposal to take 2 percent of incomes over $20,000 communistic and socialistic.

In 1905, speaking in England before the Political and Social Education League, he had defended an employer's right to require any number of hours of an employee, pay any salary no matter how low, and provide any working conditions no matter how unsafe. The authors of the Constitution and the people of the United States, he said, "believe that the States ought not to be permitted to intervene between the parties to a contract."

There was another factor. Choate's lifestyle demanded that he oppose legislation such as the Oregon ten-hour law. He had a summer home, a twenty-six-room mansion, in Stockbridge, Massachusetts, called Naumkeag. Servicing the house were fifteen to nineteen servants; they brought breakfast to the bedrooms, heated the water for tea, coffee, or hot chocolate. They trimmed the lawns, made certain the laundry and table linens were clean, always ready. The house operated smoothly; if Joseph Choate or his guests wanted something, it was there. They did not care how it came to be there; they only cared that it was there. That kind of lifestyle, not unusual then for those with property and wealth, could not continue for many of them in a time of maximum hours and minimum wages, of employer liability and health insurance. Joseph Choate could not be the advocate for the National Consumers' League; he was the enemy.

The morning after her return to New York, accompanied by an associate, Josephine Goldmark, Mrs. Kelley was ushered into Choate's private office. He was gracious; he remembered Mrs. Kelley's father, an Illinois Congressman. However, after a few moments he made clear that he did not understand why he was being involved with the Oregon law, and he was—as all men of his position were—pressed for time.

Florence Kelley usually had little difficulty finding the right words but this moment was not easy for her. Her answers were confused, almost incoherent. Finally, she explained the details, the issues in the case. Choate was aghast. He could see no reason why "a great husky Irish woman should not work in a laundry more than ten hours in one day, if her employer wished her to do so."

"Why not, indeed?" replied Mrs. Kelley. A few more words, and she and Josephine Goldmark left. "That's over, thank God," Florence Kelley said. "Tomorrow we'll go to Boston."

Louis Brandeis was not a stranger. Josephine Goldmark was his sister-in-law. Also Brandeis and Mrs. Kelley had mutual friends, and Mrs. Kelley's daughter had lived for several years with a woman who was a Brandeis family neighbor.

They met Brandeis in the library of his small house on Otis Place. It was not a grand room. "If you look about his home," said a sketch of Brandeis,

you will find few material evidences of wealth. Some things may have a sentimental value, but the furnishings are not conspicuous for comfort or beauty. They seem somewhat austere and rather incidental. It is as if Brandeis said, "Why buy new chairs? These do well enough for sitting." He abstains from smoking, drinking and heavy meals, not as an ascetic, but simply because he cares nothing about them. . . . He enjoys his friendships and the pursuit of intellectual problems.

Brandeis listened as Florence Kelley and Josephine Goldmark stated their case, then he stared out the window toward the Charles River for a few moments. "Yes," he finally said, "I will take the defense."

He would not accept a fee, and he insisted that he be invited by the Oregon attorney general to represent the state. Official participation in the case rather than as a friend of the court, the alternative, he believed, would strengthen his position and his argument. Mrs. Kelley was able to arrange this through League friends in Oregon.

Then they went to work.

Louis Brandeis's success as an advocate was based on three factors. First, he took on a cause—and at this point in his life he was taking on more causes than cases—only if he believed strongly in its righteousness. And he believed that the time had come to redivide the economic pie. When Elbert H. Gary of the United States Steel Corporation gave Mrs. Gary a $500,000 pearl necklace, Brandeis described the gift as extortion from the men working for United States Steel. Again and again he pounded that theme, that men of property could give away expensive baubles only because people worked long hours for salaries deliberately manipulated to the lowest point possible. Brandeis was a lawyer, an economic theorist, and also a moralist.

Second, he used the law creatively, imaginatively. He not only worked with the tools available, he picked from the bits and pieces of past decisions to build new tools. This day reasonableness was his tool.

The Supreme Court had upheld a Utah law prohibiting miners from working more than eight hours a day, saying that the right of contract was subject to reasonable limitations which the state could impose to protect "health and morals." But the gains made by that decision seemed lost when the Supreme Court handed down the New York bakery workers' decision in 1905. The Court ruled against the eight-hour day, saying there was "no reasonable foundation for holding this to be necessary or appropriate as a health law."

No reasonable foundation. The key then to Supreme Court affirmation, Brandeis realized, was to create a case based so heavily on reasonableness that it could not be denied.

Brandeis's third strength was his experience as an advocate. He had argued his first case before the Supreme Court more than eighteen years earlier. He had not expected to appear that day in November 1889; he had helped prepare the brief, and when the senior counsel did not arrive, Brandeis, borrowing a frock coat, stood in for him before the Court. The case involved a question of whether a railroad owed taxes to a Wisconsin county; Brandeis, appearing for the railroad, persuaded the Court to go along generally with his client's position.

There had been many cases since that one; Brandeis enjoyed appearing before the Supreme Court, relishing the tough questioning, the give-and-take with the justices, give-and-take rare in the lower courts. His style in these presentations was straightforward, factual. As he had explained some years earlier, "Remember, to succeed you must . . . not appear fanatical."

His brief in the laundry workers' case, filed in advance with the Court, was that way: straightforward, not fanatical. Actually there were two briefs filed for the state of Oregon. The first, twenty-four pages long, was signed by representatives of the state and Brandeis. This was a traditional brief, based on existing law and precedents. It claimed the law limiting hours was within the state's police power, that the Muller argument in opposition was the "same old hue and cry" about interference with the right of contract. "Of course [the law] works a hardship on somebody: such a result occurs from the very nature of the act." The law, the state continued, was consistent with other laws governing medical practice and zoning, restricting possession of explosives, and regulating transportation—"Such laws are the price of our advanced civilization."

This brief dealt with the law's specifics; the state had the power to impose restrictions—"the price of our advanced civilization"—if reasonableness could be demonstrated.

In the second brief, Louis Brandeis determined to demonstrate reasonableness.

When he had met with Florence Kelley and Josephine Goldmark in the library of his Boston home, he had told them he needed facts about the relationship of hours to efficiency and health. Such data were hard to come by in the United States; the profession of industrial medicine barely existed in America then. The ladies had two weeks. They returned to New York and they began.

They enlisted help from their friends, mostly women who, like themselves, had never known poverty; who, like themselves, could have retired behind the teas, the dances, the accepted social flirtations of the time. They sought help from those who, like themselves, would be derided as "do-gooders," criticized for going into areas, both physical and psychological, where women did not enter. They were a small army, perhaps at the height of their strength no more than ten or a dozen. The library at Columbia University and the New York Public Library were their battlegrounds. Josephine Goldmark recalled them sweeping through the few existing American reports, those of the British factory inspectors and British medical commissions, as far back as 1833. There were other reports from France, Germany, Italy, and Belgium—friends were hastily recruited to translate. The data grew. Did it make a difference to work eight hours a day? Twelve hours a day? Fifteen? If so, was it "reasonable" for the state then to set limits?

The women returned to Boston. Could the data be turned into a brief acceptable to the Supreme Court? Although Justice Holmes had written that the life of the law had been experience, few of his fellows on the Court had indicated agreement with him. Brandeis waved aside the doubts; the time had come to affirm reasonableness.

And so he began his presentation before the Supreme Court. According to the outline in his brief, he insisted that the single question was whether an hours-limitation law violated the Fourteenth Amendment statement that no state shall "deprive any person of life, liberty, or property, without due process of law"—deny the laundry the right to contract for labor as it wished. Brandeis acknowledged that the Fourteenth Amendment protected the right to sell or purchase labor, but insisted that such right is subjected to a "reasonable restraint of action."

Citing the history of those restraints in both Europe and the United States, Brandeis argued they had "not been the result of sudden impulse or passing humor," but had "followed deliberate consideration, and been adopted in the face of much opposition."

Then Brandeis came to his main point. The review of the law and the constitutional argument had covered ten pages in the brief. The next section covered ninety-six pages, and when Brandeis finished with this section, a new era had begun in constitutional law and in American life.

Machinery is increasingly speeded up, the number of machines tended by individual workers grows larger, processes become more and more complex as more operations are performed simultaneously. All those changes involve correspondingly greater physical strain upon the worker.

Accidents to working women occur most frequently at the close of the day, or after a long period of uninterrupted work.

The effect of overwork on morals is closely related to the injury to health. Laxity of moral fibre follows physical debility.

That is what Brandeis spoke about—higher accident rates, strain upon the worker, the "inevitable neglect" of children. To buttress his arguments, he then presented the information that Josephine Goldmark and her friends had found.

From France: "When I ask, when we ask, for a lessening of the daily toil of women, it is not only of the women that we think . . . it is of the whole human race."

From the United States Industrial Commission report of 1901: "Lessening of hours leaves more opportunity and more vigor for the betterment of character, the improvement of the home."

From an 1833 report by an English doctor: "From fourteen upwards, I would recommend that no individual should, under any circumstances, work more than twelve hours a day; although if practicable, as a physician, I would prefer the limitation of ten hours for all persons who earn their bread by industry."

From an 1872 report by the Massachusetts Bureau of Statistics of Labor: "Much of the work [in laundries] is very fatiguing . . . few are able to endure the labor from month to month."

On and on, statement after statement, report after report, expert after expert, all adding up to an indictment of excessive hours and to an argument for the state to impose reasonable restraints on working hours. As industrial medicine developed in the following decades, the data compiled by Josephine Goldmark and her friends and turned into a brief by Louis Brandeis were considered modest, even naïve. At the time, however, the information was virtually unique, collected and transformed into a shape that the Supreme Court could not ignore. Whatever the Court's decision on this particular case, the "Brandeis brief," as this type of argument came to be called, has become part of the American legal system. Felix Frankfurter said later that the "Brandeis brief" had "very little to do with what are called questions of law," but such a brief has much to do with the essence of law. Oliver Wendell Holmes, Jr., had argued that experience even more than logic was the life of the law, and on January 15, 1908, Louis Brandeis argued that concept before the Supreme Court. It did not mean that law could be changed arbitrarily, cases decided to suit a moment's whim. Rather, the concept meant that law, without losing sight of its purpose and its past, must always grow.

Muller's legal team led by William Fenton, a prominent corporation lawyer, offered a traditional defense. The restriction on hours did not deprive the employer but the employee, the Muller lawyers said, arguing in a thirty-two-page brief that since a laundry is not considered "immoral or dangerous," restricting the number of hours a woman worked there placed her under a disability "when women in all other useful vocations may contract freely as to the hours of service."

Cases of national interest usually produce decisions by the Chief Justice, but Melville Fuller was a modest man and assigned to others cases that attracted national attention. This case was assigned to David Brewer, the justice who had warned against "the black flag of anarchism, flaunting destruction of property." On February 24, one month and nine days after the case had been argued, David Brewer spoke for a unanimous Court.

The nine justices went with Brandeis. Oregon could have its law limiting working hours, and so, most likely, could the other states with similar laws. Brewer based his decision on the concept that establishing special rules for women in the workplace was not a violation of the Constitution. "The two sexes differ in structure of body, in the functions to be performed by each, in the amount of physical strength, in the capacity for long-continued labor, particularly when done standing, the influence of vigorous health upon the future well-being of the race," he wrote.

The reasonableness argument had been accepted. Brewer acknowledged that the Court previously had ruled against establishing regulations for the workplace, saying that such regulations violated the Fourteenth Amendment's "freedom of contract," but then Brewer added, and in this addition was the seed from which much of the law regulating working conditions for both men and women was to grow: "yet it is equally well settled that this liberty is not absolute and extending to all contracts, and that a State may, without conflicting with the provisions of the Fourteenth Amendment, restrict in many respects the individual's power of contract."

There was no question but that the Court was responding specifically to the arguments Brandeis had made in his second brief. "It may not be amiss," said Brewer's opinion, "in the present case, before examining the constitutional question, to notice the course of legislation as well as expression of opinion from other than judicial sources. In the brief filed by Mr. Louis D. Brandeis . . . is a very copious collection of all these matters, an epitome of which is found in the margin." The "epitome" was a footnote, a full page long, summarizing Brandeis's argument about the ill effects of the lengthy work day.

William Fenton, the lawyer for Muller, appreciated the decision's significance, saying it "will have the effect of sustaining this trend in lawmaking and will probably go far toward establishing a general eight- or ten-hour law."

The decision was a stunning victory for Josephine Goldmark and her "do-gooders," for Florence Kelley and the National Consumers' League, and for Louis Brandeis. The decision, said a press report, "may put heart in those who believe that ultimately we shall make industry for the sake of humanity and not regard humanity as existing for the sake of industry."

After *Muller* v. *Oregon*, Brandeis was frequently asked to defend laws restricting working hours or imposing other conditions. And in the ensuing years he traveled from state capital to state capital, always declining compensation for his work. "The matter is of such a nature that I should be unwilling to accept any compensation if it were possible for me to act," he explained.

During the nine years he remained as counsel to the National Consumers' League, according to Josephine Goldmark, no case went against the League when he either participated in the oral argument or supervised the preparation of the brief.

One of his victories was particularly gratifying to Florence Kelley. In 1895, in *Ritchie* v. *People*, the Illinois supreme court had overruled that state's working-hours legislation, a law shepherded to enactment by Mrs. Kelley. Following the *Muller* victory, the Illinois legislature enacted a new working-hours law. Ritchie, the same person who had successfully challenged the 1895 law, challenged the new law. Louis

Brandeis defended this new law before the Illinois court in Springfield.

It was midwinter 1910 and Brandeis was involved in a major congressional investigation at the time, but he received a three-day adjournment to travel to Illinois. Again, he argued that experience be acknowledged. The right to liberty of contract, he insisted, is "subject to the restraints necessary to secure the common welfare." The opposition presented the same argument as had Muller's lawyers. A law restricting working hours is unconstitutional because it "deprives those upon whom it operates of a valuable property right guaranteed them by the constitution of this state."

This time the Illinois court supported the restriction on working hours, reversing its 1895 position. "What we know as men," said the court's decision, "we cannot profess to be ignorant of as judges." In Illinois also experience had become the life of the law.

But if Louis Brandeis was the darling of the National Consumers' League and the other advocates of assisting the working person, he had made enemies because of his work in the *Muller* case and similar activities; he was "thoroughly hated by most of the leaders of the bar," recalled a lawyer named George W. Alger.

One of the leaders of the bar was Joseph Choate, the lawyer unable to understand the value of a law prohibiting Irishwomen from working more than ten hours a day in a laundry.

"I shall never forget the first occasion when I saw or heard Louis D. Brandeis," George Alger continued. "He was being introduced to speak on savings bank insurance, obviously an alarming topic, at the State Bar Association, by Joseph H. Choate, its president. It was the coldest introduction I ever listened to, the studied courtesy of one performing a most disagreeable duty in the grand manner."

Louis Brandeis was a graduate of the Harvard Law School, like many of the leaders of the bar; a successful corporation lawyer. He had made considerable amounts of money, also like the best of them. Why did he rush around the country arguing for laundry women, attacking institutions of power and wealth that people like Choate knew with certainty were America's greatest strength?

Who was this Louis Brandeis? Where had he come from?

2

Origins

When you look at people and see how they work and struggle to make a fortune, you might think you were living among merely greedy speculators. But this is not true. It is not; it is not the actual possession of things but the achievement of getting them that they care for. I have often thought that even the hard work of these people is a kind of patriotism. They wear themselves out to make their country bloom, as though each of them were commissioned to show the despots of the old world what a free people can do.

The writer of that 1848 letter was a young German émigré to the United States named Adolf Brandeis. In the United States only a few months, he had applied for citizenship and wanted to tell his relatives, friends, and fiancée still in Europe of the new land he had come to love.

The name Brandeis is found on tombstones dating from 1539 in the old Jewish cemetery in Prague. Adolf had attended the Technical School of Prague, hoping to become an architect, but decided to leave the old world for the new. Europe had too many people to feed, too little land to produce food, too few jobs, and too much violence. Frederika Dembitz, his fiancée, recalled that in 1848, while she was preparing to join Adolf, her family was caught in the revolutionary uprising. "One bomb landed on the house," she wrote, "but only in the garden and did no damage."

Adolf Brandeis and Frederika were like many German citizens of the Austro-Hungarian Empire. In 1847, 50,000 had come to the United States and by 1850 Germans made up 26 percent of America's foreign-born population. When the Dembitz family and the remainder of the Brandeis family came in 1849, there were twenty-five in the party, plus a governess, furniture (including two grand pianos), china, silver, and a copper warming pan. Josephine Goldmark later collected the family reminiscences and wrote:

The impedimenta carried along were worthy of the hegira. . . . Altogether there were twenty-seven great chests or package boxes, formidable in the eyes of the astonished midwesterners when the clan moved to a little town on the Ohio. . . . One of the dowry chests fell off the wagon and burst open as it was being carried into the house, displaying to the amazement of the neighbors, as they afterward said, what seemed the contents of a prospective linen store.

Adolf Brandeis established a wholesale grain business in the Kentucky-Indiana area among a number of German-speaking farmers. He settled first in Madison, Indiana, but then in 1851 moved to Louisville. Located on the Ohio River, a natural waterway for the steamboats to move goods, Louisville was already the tenth-largest city in the United States and fast becoming the center of the grain industry. Its boom times really began, however, when the Louisville & Nashville Railroad was built in the 1850s shortly after the Brandeis family settled there.

The Brandeis story is a typical one. The established Americans had grown tired, protective of what they had, reluctant to try new ideas; then these new people had come in, willing to accept challenge, work hard, and take risks. They succeeded. Once again America was invigorated by the coming of new people.

Another attraction for the Brandeises—Samuel Brandeis, Adolf's brother and a physician, and Adolf's family; he had married Frederika and eventually they had two sons and two daughters—was the large German community in Louisville. There had been Germans in Louisville since its founding in 1780. They, in turn, attracted other Germans. As had every other immigrant group, they hid their dimes and quarters in jars, old socks, in bags they carried around their necks; when there were enough dimes and quarters, they sent for their wives and their children, their mothers and their brothers. And more came. By 1850 there were more than 7,500 persons identified as German immigrants in Louisville, and several German-language newspapers.

Adolf went into business in Louisville with a man named Crawford, and the partnership was successful for many years. Samuel Brandeis prospered as a physician. Frederika's brother, Lewis Naphtali Dembitz, a lawyer, devised Louisville's tax-collection system and was the author of *Kentucky Jurisprudence, Land Titles in the United States,* and *Law Language for Shorthand Writers.* A prominent Republican, he was one of the nominators of Abraham Lincoln for President in 1860.

In 1856, Adolf Brandeis and his family lived in a large, comfortable house on Center Street (later renamed Armory Place), between Chestnut and Walnut streets. There on November 13 of that year, Louis

Brandeis was born. He was named Louis Dembitz Brandeis, in honor of his uncle, the lawyer, and to carry on his mother's maiden name.*

Louis Brandeis's family, as its financial fortunes improved, moved to larger houses, to First Street and then to Broadway, the most elegant of the residential areas in the city then.

The Civil War was part of Louis Brandeis's youth. Although Kentucky was a slave state and there was sentiment for the Confederate cause in Louisville, the state did not secede, and the people of Louisville were hospitable to the Union troops, especially the German immigrants there. Having come to the United States seeking political freedom for themselves, the Germans could not support denial of political freedom to others and opposed slavery. Louis Brandeis's earliest memories were of helping his mother carry food and coffee to the northern soldiers— "The streets seemed full of them always." Many times the southern forces neared, and the Brandeis family feared their city would become a battleground; once they avoided a threatened attack by escaping across the Ohio River to Indiana.

Because of the Civil War and the Republican party's support for homesteading to open up new farm land for immigrants and other settlers, the Brandeises became Republicans—Louis also; it was part of his family heritage.

By the 1860s Louisville was growing toward a population of 100,000, of which about a third either were German immigrants or descendants of German immigrants. While they were proud of their new land and of their contributions toward it, the Germans determined they would be good Americans without losing their German identity. With their German-language newspapers, they had their fraternal societies, and German-language instruction in the local schools. When this had been proposed, the Know Nothing Party, opposed to "foreign" and "Catholic" influences, campaigned against it. But the Germans were fighters, and by the mid-1850s German was taught in four schools. After 1862, the practice was to offer German instruction in a school if fifty pupils requested it.

The Germans also established their own German-language elementary school. In the mid-1860s, Adolf Brandeis was one of the school's four directors, helping to raise $25,000 to buy a lot and build a new

*There is a tradition, frequently reported, that he was born Louis David Brandeis but then, when an adult, changed his middle name to honor his uncle. A record of his birth does not exist, but his early school records, his Harvard records, and his records as a young lawyer in Boston show his name as Louis Dembitz Brandeis.

school building. Louis attended this German and English Academy, as it was called. He received top grades in Deportment, Home Study, English, German Composition, Geometry, Algebra, American History, Geography, and Natural History. When he finished elementary school, the note on his records stated: "Louis deserves special commendation for conduct and industry." His youth was not all good grades in school. He studied the violin, and one story has him settling a dispute with a classmate behind the Klee-Coleman bottling plant. The fistfight was recalled as a fast and furious one, and "Notwithstanding the fact that he was bruised and undersized, Louis never raised the distress signal."

For a high school education, one attended city schools. Louis enrolled in the Male High School on January 20, 1871, at the age of fourteen, the only student there, school records indicate, to have attended the German academy. The records then become spotty, giving no indication of Louis's grades or of whether he was graduated.

Louisville then was an attractive city for an immigrant family. Matching the economic opportunity that the Brandeis family had seized was a welcoming of the religious minority. In Europe, Jews were persecuted; in Louisville, they thrived.

There were in the city, when Louis Brandeis was growing up, two Jewish congregations: an Orthodox or traditional group, founded in 1847 with about thirty to, at its high point, sixty members; and a Reform or liberal group, known as Adath Israel. Founded in 1842, Adath Israel built in the late 1860s what a history of the city described as a building "among the most tasteful of the church buildings in this part of the nation." It had about 200 members and a religious school with 250 students. Most of its members were German, and its early records were kept in German.

Adolf's brother, Dr. Samuel Brandeis, was an active member of Adath Israel, but apparently Adolf and Frederika maintained only a casual connection with the congregation. In Europe Frederika's family had been caught up in a Jewish messianic movement known as Shabbateanism, which had developed in the seventeenth century as a reaction to persecution. Frederika's reaction to Shabbateanism was negative. As a young woman, she could not accept the possibility of a Messiah coming, as her parents believed, waiting "hour by hour" because "That the Christian Messiah had not brought salvation to the world became clear to me in spite of my reverence for him."

She came to believe, she later wrote, that "God is the consummation of all virtue, truth and nobility. To strive for these should be our aim wherever life leads us. . . . And this is my justification for bringing up my children without any definite religious belief: I wanted to give them something that neither could be argued away nor would have to be given up as untenable, namely, a pure spirit and the highest ideals as to morals and love." Also her family moved among non-Jews. As a little girl, she had become beguiled by the Christmas festival.

At one point in her youth, Frederika had been introduced by her parents to Reform or liberal Judaism as it was practiced in Prague. She was given home instruction and attended services of a rabbi named Michael Sachs, who is known in Jewish history as a middle-of-the-roader between the German orthodox and liberal wings of Judaism and who went from Prague to Berlin, where he consistently angered both groups.

Frederika Dembitz's experiences as a child in nineteenth-century Europe were not unusual then. Judaism in the seventeenth and eighteenth centuries had been buffeted by prejudice; Jews were fearful, grasped at extremes.

Not all Jews followed that path. Her brother Lewis, when only thirteen and still in Europe, became an Orthodox Jew. When he later moved to the United States and lived in Louisville, he became one of the mainstays of the orthodox congregation in that city and adhered to the traditions regarding meals and daily practices. His book *Jewish Services in the Synagogue and Home* was a distinguished guide for many decades. Frederika considered his orthodoxy "unfortunate."

However tenuous the connection between the Adolf Brandeis family and Judaism, it was never formally severed; the Brandeises did not convert to Christianity. Alfred, Louis's older brother, married a non-Jewish woman and apparently moved away from all formal Jewish religious activities, but as late as 1914 was active as a contributor and member of the executive committee of the Federation of Jewish Charities of Louisville. Adolf and Frederika Brandeis had Jewish burial services when they died and are buried in the Adath Israel cemetery in Louisville.

During and after the Civil War, Adolf Brandeis's grain business prospered, but in the depression of the 1870s its southern clients could not pay their bills. Rather than fret in Louisville through bad times, Adolf closed up his business and took his family touring in Europe. Louis Brandeis attended the Annen-Realschule in Dresden for perhaps a year.

Many years later Louis recalled to Josephine Goldmark why he decided to return to the United States and become a lawyer. "One night coming home late," he said, "and finding I had forgotten my key, I whistled up to awaken my roommate, and for this I was reprimanded by the police. This made me homesick. In Kentucky you could whistle. . . . I wanted to go back to America and I wanted to study law. My uncle, the abolitionist [Lewis Dembitz], was a lawyer, and to me nothing else seemed really worth while." That story has a charm about it, but more likely the romantic view of the United States expressed by his father in 1848 had taken hold of the son—"to make their country bloom . . . to show the despots of the old world what a free people can do." Not yet nineteen, Louis Brandeis had seen a war to end slavery succeed; he had witnessed economic expansion and religious and ethnic tolerance in Louisville. And then he had visited Europe where none of that could have happened. More than a reprimand for whistling brought him back to the United States.

Louis Brandeis entered Harvard Law School in September 1875, a few weeks before his nineteenth birthday. He had no undergraduate college experience, but the Law School, although it preferred students with degrees, would admit others who passed examinations in Blackstone and Latin. The school's program ran two years, and the tuition was $150 for the first year and $100 for the second. The rationale behind lowering the tuition for the second year was the hope that the student—at a time when a person could clerk in a law office to become a lawyer—would not drop out after the first. Because Adolf Brandeis's business had not done well, Louis had to borrow money from his older brother, Alfred, for tuition and also earned money by tutoring, "which fills up both time and pocket."

Brandeis entered the Law School at what for him was an appropriate time; its dean, Christopher Columbus Langdell, was then instituting, against considerable opposition, the case system of instruction. Basically, this meant systematizing the study of law, putting students through a comprehensive process, teaching them law from the principle involved to its application. Brandeis described the process some years after his graduation:

Believing that law is a science and recognizing that the source of our law is the adjudicated cases, Professor Langdell declared that, like other sciences, the law was to be learned only by going to the original sources. . . . No instructor can provide the royal road to knowledge by giving to the student the conclusions deduced from these sources, his chief aim should be to teach the student to think in a legal manner. . . . He should seek to inculcate and develop in legal reasoning the habit of intellectual self-reliance. . . .

The students live in an atmosphere of legal thought. Their interest is at fever heat, and the impressions made by their studies are as deep and lasting as is compatible with the quality of the individual mind.

There was more at Harvard than the classroom instruction. There was a developing tradition. At Harvard in the nineteenth century, Joseph Story, an associate justice of the United States Supreme Court, wrote and had published his *Commentaries on the Constitution.* A Harvard man, James Bradley Thayer, in a twenty-six-page paper called "The Origin and Scope of the American Doctrine of Constitutional Law," influenced American jurisprudence for decades; this was the essay Felix Frankfurter would choose if forced "to name one piece of writing on American Constitutional law." And Oliver Wendell Holmes, Jr., also a Harvard man, produced the book *The Common Law,* which remains a necessity for any serious legal scholar. Harvard then offered to its students the concept of leadership and demanded leadership of the better ones.

Brandeis also learned about money at Harvard. His tutoring business did so well that he paid Alfred the money he had borrowed, and by the end of his second year he sent first $500 and then $250 to his brother to invest for him in bonds—a practice he followed for the remainder of his life, investing wisely and conservatively in strong institutions. "We don't know much about the business [stocks]," he once explained, "and beware people who think they do. Prices of stocks are made. They don't grow; and their fluctuations are not due to natural causes." He believed in treating investments as "a necessary evil, indulging in the operation as rarely as possible." He became a multi-millionaire.

Socially also Harvard was a success for Brandeis. One of his fellow students described Brandeis as "the leader of his class and one of the most brilliant legal minds they have ever had here . . . has a rather foreign look, and is currently believed to have some Jew blood in him, though you would not suppose it from his appearance—tall, well-made, dark, beardless, and with the brightest eyes I ever saw. . . . The Profs. listened to his opinion with the greatest deference, and it is generally correct."

He did remarkably well with his grades. His two-year average stood at 97 and included three marks of 100 and two of 99. When he finished the two-year program in June of 1877, he was five months shy of his twenty-first birthday and almost was denied his law degree because a rule of the school said that students must be at least twenty-one to receive a law degree. A meeting with the university president produced no results and Brandeis, who had been elected class orator by his fellow students, resigned himself to sitting through the graduation ceremony without his diploma. But, at almost exactly the last moment, the morning of graduation, the school's trustees voted to suspend the rules and Brandeis received his degree cum laude. He then stayed on for a third year, doing graduate work.

In Brandeis's third year he was appointed a proctor in Harvard College. James Bradley Thayer, a professor at the Law School, befriended him—"Mr. R. W. Emerson is to be at my house on Tuesday evening and will read a lecture to a few of our friends on 'Education.' If it might interest you to see and hear him, I wish you would come in." Brandeis, the only student present that evening, and although Emerson was "fast decaying," was thrilled at meeting the man whose life, personality, and writings so much embodied the legendary New England virtues. Also pleased at Professor Thayer's attentions, years later Brandeis told the story of that evening to impress upon academics the importance of having contact with students outside of the classroom.

His friendships at the school were not limited to any one group, geographical or social, but one friend in particular was to play an important part in Brandeis's life: his classmate Samuel D. Warren, Jr. Also a top student, Warren was from Boston. At first, after leaving Harvard, Warren worked for the Oliver Wendell Holmes, Jr., law firm, but Warren had ambitions for his own law practice, and his plans included Brandeis as a partner.

Brandeis, at first, was uncertain whether to teach or practice, but leaned toward teaching. "The law as a logical science has very great attractions for me. I see it now again by the almost ridiculous pleasure which the discovery or invention of a legal theory gives me."

Still, Brandeis began his legal career as a practicing attorney in St. Louis, associated with a relative, but St. Louis held him only seven months, from November 1878 to June 1879. After having traveled in Europe as a young man and then having lived three years in Cambridge, the land of Ralph Waldo Emerson and Oliver Wendell Holmes, he did not find St. Louis exciting. His friend Sam Warren joked with him about the move to St. Louis, because, Warren said, Boston was the only city "in which a civilized man can exist much less practice law." And Warren wanted to know from Brandeis: "By the way how is the spring season for buffaloes?"

Warren, then still associated with the Holmes firm, was increasingly restless. Success could be achieved in private practice, he argued, by young lawyers "not afraid of hard work." Also, as he explained in a letter to Brandeis, he was well known through family connections to the Boston business community, and if he opened up an office, "I should get some business to start in from those who know me. . . . Under these circumstances I have been casting my eyes over the market for embryo lawyers, and I don't find any in Boston who fill the bill. . . . I do not like the idea of starting alone."

Brandeis accepted the bait and agreed to join Warren, but there was a problem of money. Warren wanted to advance Brandeis funds for his first year's expenses, but Brandeis was reluctant to accept the offer. Then an opportunity opened, a part-time editorship of a legal journal. Brandeis was anxious to accept it because it would provide him with an income as well as allow him time to practice law; the earlier doubt he had about whether to teach or practice had been resolved. "I wish to become known as a practicing lawyer," he said.

At the last moment the editorship did not materialize, but a clerkship with the Chief Justice of the Supreme Judicial Court of Massachusetts did. This also would allow Brandeis time for private practice, and Brandeis arrived in Boston to open the firm of Warren and Brandeis. Warren's name came first because of the practice of listing the names of the lawyers according to when they were admitted to the Massachusetts bar.

Boston welcomed Louis Brandeis, and for the next twenty-seven years Boston was Louis Dembitz Brandeis's home, the center of his work, the site from which he reached out to affect the United States. Having been clerk to the chief justice of Massachusetts' highest court did not harm him, especially when that justice, Horace Gray, was named to the United States Supreme Court. Brandeis was friendly with Holmes, who had joined Warren and Brandeis to celebrate the opening of their law firm with a mixture of champagne and beer, one beverage representing the two young lawyers' dreams and the other their reality. "Warren and Holmes talked and I lay outstretched on a ship's chair," said Brandeis of that evening.

Holmes remains one of the more intriguing individuals in the history of American law and in the story of both Louis Brandeis and Felix Frankfurter. From one of New England's most respected families, Holmes was a Civil War hero, wounded three times, and was about to give the series of lectures that became *The Common Law*. In 1872 he was appointed to the Massachusetts high court, and then in 1902 to the United States Supreme Court. Brandeis later joined him there, was influenced by him, and influenced him. Holmes was fond of the young lawyer from Louisville. "I have read your article with much pleasure and think it is excellent," was a typical comment of his, along with "Mrs. Holmes as well as I am always glad to see you."

The relationship between Holmes and Frankfurter is easy to understand. Frankfurter was the young man paying court to the older man, flattering him and making no secret of his admiration. But that between Holmes and Brandeis is more difficult to understand. Brandeis did not flatter; rather he constantly challenged the older man's intuition with his own rationality. And Brandeis's austere lifestyle was a marked contrast to the older man's; Holmes enjoyed fine wine, and attending the burlesque house was his favorite form of entertainment. Still the relationship between the two men deepened and became one of the most lasting in American history, stretching over half a century.

Through his first years in Boston, Brandeis, in demand socially, was elected to the right clubs, and a sweet, prosperous, and calm future seemed ahead for him. Financially he also succeeded. In 1894, fifteen years after he had begun practicing in Boston with a part-time job as clerk to a judge to make ends meet, he was worth $125,000, according to a financial statement, primarily in bonds and in interest-bearing notes, with only a few stocks.

But that kind of money was a long way off that July day in 1879 when he and Sam Warren opened their office on the third floor of 60 Devonshire Street. Their rent was $200 a year; often they had to scrape to pay $3 a week for a messenger. As he had claimed, Sam Warren had connections in the Boston business community; the partners' first client was his father's paper manufacturing company. By the end of the second year, business had brightened. "Our fiscal year ends today," wrote Brandeis. "It should be about $3,600 gross earnings which makes $3,000 net profits for the year . . . considerably in excess of last year. The outlook for next year is not good. . . . I don't expect my practice to amount to much for the next fifteen years but I do expect to have a high old time for the twenty-five following."

In the late 1880s Warren had to leave the partnership to take over his father's business, and Brandeis sought other partners. Then the firm moved to larger quarters. By 1904 the office at 220 Devonshire had 3,500 square feet, seven lawyers, six other employees, and one telephone. The firm moved again that year, taking over an entire floor of a new building at 161 Devonshire. Each lawyer had a private office, and there were rooms for secretaries, a library, and conference rooms. The floors were oak and were, according to a history of the firm, scrubbed every night. Firm members argued cases in the state courts, federal courts, and, on at least sixteen occasions, before the United States Supreme Court in the two decades before Brandeis became a member of that Court. "Amounts of money involved in litigation were . . . small," recalled one of the partners. "The question whether a $10,000 shipment was up to sample was large enough to require Brandeis on the one side and Robert W. Morse, one of the leading senior trial lawyers of the day, on the other."

One young lawyer in the firm in those pre-World War I years, Adolf A. Berle, Jr., later recalled the kinds of cases the firm dealt with: "a couple of rate cases . . . and a couple of ordinary tort cases, a good many smaller matters of corporation law. . . . The constitutionality of a couple of acts came into the office; one case I was on the anti-labor side. This had to do with the right to strike against the introduction of a labor-saving device, and as a first year clerk I joined in writing the brief which caused the Massachusetts supreme judicial court to hold that a strike was not justified where its only aim was to prevent the introduction of a labor saving machine"—in this instance, the "machine" was an organ which replaced a union band in a movie theater.

Another associate in the firm recalled that "The expected hours were 8:30 A.M. to 5 P.M., six days a week," adding: "This did not impair the health of any of us." Brandeis's hours were from 8:20 A.M. to 5 P.M., when "he left promptly." Although the law firm eventually had several partners, there was "no partnership agreement in writing. Brandeis increased the percentage of the others from time to time and asked if that was all right. It always was." That last was only accurate after 1896, when two of the associates insisted on promotion to full partnership or they would go elsewhere. Brandeis offered them partnerships.

The firm won many of its cases, more because of thorough preparation than courtroom histrionics. Brandeis and his firm's lawyers prepared their cases, analyzed the issues, and presented their arguments more effectively than did their opponents. And there was another factor to the success. Through the nineteenth century and before, the concept of practicing law meant "hanging out one's shingle." The twentieth century would be the age of the large law firm, with skilled persons assisting each other, drawing on each other's strengths, and shoring up each other's weaknesses. The Brandeis firm was one of the first to develop this approach. "He created a unity in the law partnership then formed which was a tribute to his skill and disposition," recalled one of Brandeis's partners. "It was the firm that did the work as a unit, with the effort to have it done by the individuals best fitted for the particular type of work and with complete freedom from internal rivalry, and without regard for the source of the particular matter except as the client's wishes must be met."

When Brandeis represented a client, no holds were barred. Charles C. Burlingham, a New York lawyer who did considerable work with the Brandeis firm and knew Brandeis personally, reminisced some years later:

Of course, a lawyer's first duty is to his client. But he has a great many clients if he has any success and there are times when he needs favors from other lawyers—an adjournment, for instance, is important to him. . . . But Brandeis always got all he could and never gave any favors to anybody. His justification was that he was representing his client. It's not the way to represent your client, to build up a position where you can get nothing if you need it very much. That's the way we practice law, but that isn't the way he practiced law.

Continued Burlingham: "I think the hatred of him was accentuated very much by the way he practiced law."

Although successful as a practicing attorney, Brandeis never considered himself a "great mouthpiece" for hire but viewed law in its broadest aspects. When he taught a course at the Massachusetts Institute of Technology on business law in the 1890s, he began it by saying that the study of law

is valuable as a part of a liberal education, because the conduct of life is to so large an extent determined by the existing legal institutions, that an understanding of the legal system must give you a clearer view of human affairs in their manifold relations, and must aid you in comprehending the conditions, and institutions by which you are surrounded.

Said Felix Frankfurter: "The attitude Brandeis had when he was at the bar was that a lawyer is a counselor, an adviser. He isn't just a hired man to do the bidding of his clients, but he must exert the independence of his mind and understanding upon the conduct of his client's business."

Said Brandeis: "This is the thing I've always tried to do, I've always tried to be a lawyer with clients, not any man's lawyer."

That attitude was not pervasive throughout the legal profession. John W. Davis, some years Brandeis's junior, a leader of the bar, Democratic presidential nominee in 1924, and a strong contender for a Supreme Court judgeship himself, expressed the more prevalent view: "The lawyer as a lawyer does not build or erect or paint anything. He does not create. All he does is lubricate the wheels of society by implementing the rules of conduct by which the organized life of men must be carried on."

During the closing decades of the nineteenth century, as his law business prospered, Brandeis branched out to other activities. In 1890 he and Sam Warren, his former law partner, collaborated on an article for the *Harvard Law Review* entitled "The Right to Privacy." The article had been provoked by gossip, including newspaper stories, about Warren's personal life. Brandeis and Warren were concerned with the invasion of privacy by the news media, the unwarranted use of photographs and other materials. These were relatively new developments. Was there no redress in the courts?

The article begins: "That the individual shall have full protection in person and property is a principle as old as the common law; but it has been found necessary from time to time to define anew the exact nature and extent of such protection." That line is deceptive. It appears to say that what follows is not unique; actually the article, as one authority— Roscoe Pound—said, did "nothing less than add a chapter to our law." The article then discussed the new evils, the problems, the legal situation, and ended with a call. "Shall the courts thus close the front entrance to the constituted authority, and open wide the back door to idle or prurient curiosity?" To insure that the individual has "full protection in person and property" became one of the driving forces of Brandeis's life and then of Frankfurter's.

Brandeis continued his close association with Harvard, being one of the chief organizers in 1886 of the Harvard Law School Association, a group of graduates working to help the school. Although those graduates in the Boston area always had been generous and helpful, Brandeis wanted to enlist graduates living far from the school. The response was overwhelming. Financial and other support flowed into the Harvard Law School from its graduates living throughout the entire United States. As a result, though not noticed at the time, control of the Law School began to slip away from the Boston area—from the "State Street" establishment—to graduates in other parts of the United States.

Brandeis served on the Board of Overseers and frequently was asked to advise on course content. In 1891 he received an honorary degree from Harvard.

His eligibility as a bachelor continued into his thirties, but not his immunity. On a visit to London in 1887 he wrote to a friend in Boston:

I have seen the English.
Man delights me. Ah!—and women too.
There is danger that Anglophobia will be succeeded by Anglomania.

There had been no lasting relationships, however, until 1890, when he met his second cousin Alice Goldmark. She lived in an era when a woman's aspiration and obligation was to be a wife, and the definition of the word can be taken from her life with Louis Brandeis. But she had talents and passions of her own; she campaigned for social causes, spoke out for political reform, did some writing. Still, her family was more famous for whom its members married than for other accomplishments —she for Louis and her sister Helen for Felix Adler, founder of the New York Society for Ethical Culture. Two other sisters, Pauline and Josephine, became involved with the National Consumers' League and did not marry. Josephine, after assisting Brandeis with the *Muller* brief, then developed the study known as *Fatigue and Efficiency,* which was the first comprehensive attempt to measure those two elements and their interaction.

In Boston, Brandeis's friends welcomed Alice Goldmark. "That you have perceived enough to bring about the engagement . . ." Sam Warren wrote her, "makes me most anxious to know you." He hoped that Alice Goldmark would soon come to Boston so "Mrs. Warren and I may have the pleasure of welcoming you to Boston, and to that important part of our lives which we have in common with Louis."

During the engagement Louis Brandeis was the traditional nervous and anxious fiancé. Almost he could not understand what had happened to him, to have fallen in love with her. "I long for the time when you will be with me always," he wrote. "You have become so large a part of my life that I rattle about sorely when you are absent. Is it not strange? For seventeen years I have stood alone—rarely asking—still less frequently caring, for the advice of others. . . . And now, Alice, all is changed . . . I feel my incompleteness more each day. I feel myself each day growing more into your soul, and I am very happy."

Louis and Alice were married in March 1891. In the early years they were welcomed into Boston society. In later years, when that society turned against her husband, a friend said of Alice, "Never once did she seem to care." There were two daughters, Susan and Elizabeth. When the daughters were growing up, the family "together" time usually was at the breakfast table, where they traded each other's news, shared gossip, enjoyed each other's victories and provided solace for defeats. Summers were spent on Cape Cod; the family sports were canoeing and hunting for nuts.

About this time, in the late 1890s, another aspect of Brandeis's life began to develop. "You know," he once said, "the important thing is that people should be free economically. There are two ways in which you can do that. One is to make millions of dollars; the other is not to spend too much." He had begun practicing the first with his bond investments when he was at Harvard. In the 1890s, with Alice's support, he began practicing the second, living modestly, even frugally.

He once had said that he didn't expect much fun in the first fifteen years from his career as a lawyer but he anticipated a "high old time" in the next twenty-five. That twenty-five-year period was about to begin, and he wanted the economic freedom to enjoy it.

3

Brandeis versus the President

The late 1890s and early 1900s were challenging times for the reformer. With economic expansion had come exploitation. Hours were long, wages low, safety conditions poor. In the 1880s a young member of the New York legislature named Theodore Roosevelt considered himself, and was considered by others, an advocate of *laissez faire,* as expected of a man from a family as socially positioned and wealthy as his. To him, the practice of the cigars manufactured by workers in their homes, paid for on a piece basis, was proper. But then Roosevelt walked through some of those tenement homes where the cigars were made. He saw the poverty, experienced the stench, watched the bent bodies. "Whatever the theories might be," he explained, "as a matter of practical common sense I could not conscientiously vote for the continuance of the conditions which I saw." From an opponent of a bill to end home manufacture of cigars he became its champion. The law was the first in the state to prohibit industrial work at home. The law was later declared invalid by the state's highest court, but Theodore Roosevelt did not forget what he had seen in those tenements.

"The man who wrongly holds that every human right is secondary to his profit," Theodore Roosevelt declared, "must now give way to the advocate of human welfare, who rightly maintains that every man holds his property subject to the general right of the community to regulate its use to whatever degree the public welfare may require it."

Some came to reform through law. In Birmingham, Alabama, in the early years of the twentieth century, the sheriff leased convicts to local industries. When the convicts' jail sentences were up, they weren't always released. The convicts' wages for leased work ranged from dirt cheap to nonexistent, and who would complain? Usually the abused convict was a "Nigra," and who spoke for him? Hugo La Fayette Black, then a young lawyer—and a white man at that—did speak out for a black, an abused convict named Willie Norton. Norton had been kept in jail twenty-two days longer than his sentence. Hugo Black represented him in court and won him a $150 verdict. Not much money, but the courts had shattered a traditional white-supremacy practice; the law had worked for the black man as it had worked for the white man.

Some came to reform from a sense of moral indignation. In 1919 when five Socialists were elected to the New York State Assembly, the Assembly majority refused to seat them. Few understood socialism, but attacking it as a threat to America was a safe tactic. After all, who in a responsible position would defend five Socialists? Charles Evans Hughes was the son of a Baptist minister, a former governor of New York State, a former justice of the United States Supreme Court, and the Republican candidate for President of the United States in 1916. He also was a corporation lawyer, a rich man, a representative of the wealthy and privileged. He defended the Socialists.

"It is absolutely opposed to the fundamental principles of our Government," Hughes declared, "for a majority to undertake to deny representation to a minority through its representatives elected by ballots lawfully cast." Even on economic matters, Hughes was not "safe" for the established order. "Liberty," he said, "implies the absence of arbitrary restraint, not immunity from reasonable regulations as prohibitions imposed in the interest of the community."

Louis Brandeis eased into public service. It was not, at first at least, a deliberate decision. Elizabeth Glendower Evans, a family friend, said the first conscious act was in 1888 when he represented a religious institution attempting to secure funding from the state. Brandeis later, said Mrs. Evans, regretted having represented the church, saying that the discussion of the issues had convinced him he was on the wrong side, "It had shown him that public money should not be spent for any purpose at all except under persons appointed by the Commonwealth."

But that was not the way it was done. Instead, wealthy organizations hired lawyers to appear before government bodies to secure funds and, more important, franchises for their clients. Often an opposing view was not well presented, because its advocates were unable to afford competent legal services. As a result, the legislatures, overwhelmed by legal smooth talk, granted the franchises with little idea of their worth.

Angered, Brandeis volunteered on the side of the public in various franchise fights. He also helped organize the Public Franchise League, which examined the franchise bills introduced in the state legislature. The smooth-talking lawyers were countered by Brandeis.

Once he started that kind of work, Brandeis found more and more public service work. In the 1890s, for example, he became interested in the treatment of the mentally and physically ill. The mentally ill especially in those years were treated almost like animals, locked away, abused, maltreated. Brandeis's arguments for dealing with them as humans with treatable illnesses were in advance of the time and gradually produced the beginnings of reform.

Decades later, Brandeis was quoted as saying that the Homestead steel strike of 1892 was the incident that sent him on the road as the "people's lawyer." Management had determined to destroy the steel workers' union, and twenty-five persons were killed before the confrontation had run its bloody course. Brandeis had been scheduled to give a series of lectures then on the common law, but "After the Homestead riots I saw the law was inadequate and threw the lectures away."

Other factors motivated him. As a Harvard Law School student, he had had the highest grade average in the school's history. As a lawyer, he was at the top in his profession. Financially, he was secure. He needed more. There was too much energy, too much intelligence to continue with the mundane. There was too great a sense of justice. This man's parents had left Europe to find political freedom; his uncle, although from a slave state, had nominated Abraham Lincoln for President in 1860; his family had supported the union. His religion, although he did not practice it, with its demand for social welfare, still had a hold on him.

With each step he took further into public advocacy he became more and more committed to the challenge and the result. His lifestyle came to reflect his determination. He refused to accept clients unless certain of the morality of their cause. He criticized his fellow lawyers for forming "a strong reactionary eddy." He had few amusements and little relaxation beyond the moments with his family. His living style was markedly spare, his body lean, his involvement intense. His zealousness became a fault. "One wondered at times," said a friend once of Brandeis, "whether like some eastern sage the body's grosser part had not been quite burnt away and mere spirit remained."

But Brandeis did not become a Gandhi. He did not live with the poor, nor did he massage the body of the leper. Rather, he became the social engineer, the one who dealt with causes and movements rather than with individuals. As a result, often he became the hero of the causes and the movements if not the idol of the people.

In Boston there was much for him to do. A dispute over the cost of natural gas was insoluble until Brandeis's involvement. The stockholders wanted high dividends, and mill workers and immigrants who made up the bulk of the company's customers wanted lower rates. Under Brandeis's formula, the company could not pay a dividend higher than 7 percent until after reducing the price of gas below 90 cents, and then dividends could be increased by 1 percent for each 5-cent reduction in the price of gas. Within two years, the gas company paid a 9 percent dividend and the price of gas was 80 cents. How did it happen? "The ability to reduce the price of gas and to increase the rate of dividend is mainly dependent upon the ability of the management to increase the consumption of gas," Brandeis explained. "This has been done partly as a result of the lessening of the price and partly as a result of an increase in the efficiency of the service, and also to a considerable extent to the extraordinary courtesy which the present management —unlike most of our public service corporations—has shown to customers."

Brandeis developed an annuity program for workers. Although wealthy himself, Brandeis was aware that the average worker had little to show for his or her years of labor at the end of a career. There was no Social Security then and most workers earned too little to save toward retirement; the only prospect for them seemed to be a human scrap heap. "If we cannot have some system for providing working men with old age annuities at their own expense," he argued, "we are certain to have an irresistible demand for old age pensions fed from general taxation."

Brandeis examined insurance companies' annuity plans, then offered his own. Insurance company administrative costs in 1904 were 37.21 percent while similar expenses for savings banks in Massachusetts were 1.47 percent. There were several reasons for the high costs to the insurance companies. "Financial depravity," Brandeis conceded, although not "an important cause," did exist through watered stock, illegal political contributions, unusually high salaries, and dividends that were excessive when compared to earnings. Other problems, he said, were the high cost of selling the policies and of collecting the weekly premiums. Since such costs did not exist with deposits made to savings banks, why not have savings banks sell retirement plans?

With the help of actuaries, he worked out comparisons between the benefits of a bank plan and those of the insurance companies. He used, as an example, a working man, beginning on his twenty-first birthday, depositing 50 cents a week. The insurance company after twenty years would pay him $165; the savings bank, $746.20. If the money stayed in the program until the working man died, and if the man died at age sixty-one, the insurance company would pay the worker's survivors $820, the savings bank plan, $2,265.90.

The Brandeis plan was proposed in the Massachusetts state legislature and a fifteen-member committee was appointed to study it. At the beginning, only one committee member favored it. Then Brandeis began speaking throughout the state, writing letters and newspaper articles. "Our insurance fight proceeds merrily," he reported to his brother Alfred. "Talk only 3 times this week. Going to Fitchburg Friday. Next week I have 4 performances. Gov. Douglas came out in a strong letter for us this week."

The bill became law, and then Brandeis followed every detail to assure its success, even suggesting how banks should display applications and dispense literature for the plan. The first result was that insurance companies lowered premiums. Although their premiums had not been reduced for twenty years, there was one reduction when the Brandeis bill was first introduced and another two years after passage, for a total reduction of one-fifth. The second result was that the people of Massachusetts flocked to the savings-bank plan. In 1937, after the plan had been in effect for thirty years, there were 150,000 policyholders in the plan with $133 million in insurance. The bank insurance was 25 to 50 percent cheaper than that offered by the insurance companies.

Brandeis's technique of operation in these public-service causes was described by Joseph Eastman, secretary of the Public Franchise League for many years. First, Eastman said, Brandeis rallied around him as many community leaders as he could persuade to join his cause. Next, when Brandeis "waged a battle with those who were financially powerful, he knew he could not win unless he was able to enlist the support of a strong public opinion," said Eastman. And so Louis Brandeis, lawyer, became Louis Brandeis, publicist.

In one month Brandeis wrote at least eighty-five letters seeking support for the insurance program, scheduled for a vote in the state legislature the next month. Each letter was individually dictated and typed —some brief, only one or two lines; others lengthy, running to a page and a half. The letters went to newspapermen, labor-union leaders, friends of politicians, prominent citizens. The letters argued the merits of the Brandeis approach, criticized his opponents, asked for support; they cajoled, fumed, wheedled.

To a union leader: "The Boston Democratic representatives have not expressed themselves definitely on the savings bank insurance and annuity bill. May I trouble you further to write a letter to each of these representatives as per the enclosed list, calling to their attention the importance of voting in favor of the measure?"

To a newspaper editorial writer: "Won't you follow up your powerful editorial of this morning with another calling attention to the annuity feature of our bill?"

To another: "It occurred to me that you might be in a way of getting the movement started among the various Jewish societies and clubs."

In another matter, when a public-interest group caught the board of aldermen in what Brandeis called "petty pilfering," Brandeis said the group should bring information to the public's attention—"you would undoubtedly arrange also with the Press to give it full publicity." He sought publicity as efficiently as he prepared a cross-examination. When he went to Washington on a conservation matter, for example, he asked a knowledgeable friend for names of Washington reporters "friendly to our general insurgency cause."

Brandeis once told an editor friend that American journalism "had to be looked upon as guerrilla warfare—sorties, raids, and sudden opportunities." He was so good at the warfare that the Boston *Post* asked him to take over its editorial columns on a full-time basis. Brandeis declined but in a manner allowing him "to suggest any matter which I think would be of value."

Learning to play the news media well, Brandeis often was criticized as a "headline seeker." But, said Brandeis, "I determined that I would not care and I would not reply to any personal attacks."

Another strength of Brandeis the reformer was his intellectual quickness. Once, when Brandeis was charging a railroad's corporate officers with stealing large amounts of money, the railroadmen's lawyer, Moorfield Storey, launched into a tirade against Brandeis. When Storey finished, Brandeis stood. "Gentlemen," he said, "at an appropriate time I would be happy to answer the charges made against me by Mr. Storey. But my character is not your problem. The only question for you gentlemen to answer is, 'Who stole the ten million dollars!'" In a complicated hearing before the Interstate Commerce Commission, the railroadmen came in with a fat set of statistics to justify a 5 percent rate increase. Brandeis, retained by the Commission, tore apart the railroadmen's case. He showed they had exercised favoritism and bad management, and attempted to pass on to consumers the risks, which should have been assumed by investors. Soon the railroadmen were on the run before Brandeis's relentless cross-examination. How did they know a 5 percent increase was justified? he demanded. One witness finally spluttered, "I know it in the same way you know the things that make you such a clever lawyer." Brandeis responded: "I thank you for the compliment, but whatever knowledge I may have has come from the particular study of specific facts, and so I am seeking to find out from you what the specific facts are upon which you base your judgment in this matter."

Brandeis did collect fees for his regular legal and government work, and they were good fees—$11,500 for the rate case before the Interstate Commerce Commission. But in representing the public interest he declined payment. "Some men buy diamonds and rare works of art," he explained, "others delight in automobiles and yachts. My luxury is to invest my surplus effort, beyond that required for the proper support of my family, to the pleasure of taking up a problem and solving, or helping to solve it, for the people without receiving any compensation. . . . I should lose much of my satisfaction if I were paid in connection with public services of this kind."

This was the era before *pro bono* work by lawyers, and Brandeis's activities often were suspect. A friend associated with Brandeis in numerous public service causes came to his rescue in a newspaper article, arguing:

If a man were to give $50,000 a year for some public cause, and many of our men do give such an amount, or a larger one, that would not create astonishment. If Mr. Brandeis gives, as he does give, his professional services for a cause which he believes he ought to assist in the public interest, the action is yet so uncommon as to lend itself to the rousing of suspicion of his motives, even as all uncommon things may be so used.

The public was more familiar with lawyers like John W. Davis. In the early 1900s he was against monopoly, a defender of the individual, and Solicitor General of the United States. But as the demands of success moved in upon him, his law practice changed. Davis's biographer reports that "the suits against railroads upon which his father had built so much of the practice virtually stopped. Davis' corporate retainers inevitably imposed subtle restraints on his freedom of action." Under those restraints, Davis acquired a taste for haute cuisine, a Fifth Avenue apartment in New York City and a Long Island estate.

Brandeis often was called upon to speak to law school students; the professors and deans hoped that some of his attitude toward public service would turn their students away, even slightly, from the halls of Mammon. One such talk was given in May 1905 before the Harvard Ethical Society, in the Phillips Brooks House. It was part of a series on ethics in the professions, including medicine, literature, and (scheduled) football, and Brandeis's subject was "The Opportunity in the Law."

The talk is interesting for two reasons. The first shows Brandeis's thinking to that time. "You wish to know," he said to his student audience, "whether the legal profession would afford you special opportunities for usefulness to your fellow-men." He conceded that the lawyer was not held in as high repute as he had been previously but insisted "the reason is not lack of opportunity" but rather that the lawyers have become "adjuncts of great corporations and have neglected the obligation to use their powers for the protection of the people. We hear much of the 'corporation lawyer,' and far too little of the 'people's lawyer.' " The great opportunity in the law, he argued, is that "the next generation must witness a continuing and ever-increasing contest between those who have and those who have not. . . . The people are beginning to doubt whether in the long run democracy and absolutism can co-exist in the same community. . . . The people have begun to think; and they show evidences on all sides of a tendency to act." He called upon those students in his audience who were going to be lawyers to become involved in the coming struggle, to help settle it peacefully and with justice. "There is a call," he concluded, "upon the legal profession to do a great work for this country."

The second reason why the talk was so interesting was that a member of the audience was Felix Frankfurter, then finishing up his second year as a Harvard Law School student. Ambitious and idealistic, uncertain of his future course, an admirer of the successful, Felix Frankfurter was ready for a role model, and he found one that day. The two men became friends, co-workers. They were like father and son; the older man was the teacher and the younger man the student.

The Frankfurter story is a familiar one, almost a cliché in American history. Between 1890 and 1920, eighteen million Europeans came to the United States. They were more, in numbers, than all the previous immigrants in the nation's history; greater, in numbers, than any migration the world had ever known. One-third of all the world's Jews, more than three million Italians, one million Germans, Slavs, Slovaks, Croatians, Bulgarians, Hungarians—all came. They crowded into smelly, unsafe ships, scrambled down gangplanks at New York and other port cities, kissed the earth. The new land. Their land.

One of these was Samuel Leopold Frankfurter. He had been born in Pressburg, then part of the Austro-Hungarian Empire, and a center of Jewish life. He had moved to Vienna; the time is not known but certainly after the anti-Jewish riots broke out in Pressburg following the 1848 revolution. He was sometimes talked of as having trained for the rabbinate, but more probably such talk misconstrues that all Jewish young men in Pressburg had formal religious educations. Actually he was a *Handelsagent,* which was not far above a door-to-door salesman.

In Vienna, he and his wife Emma Winter lived at 20 Mohrengasse, in the city's second district, called Leopoldstadt, which was the center of the Jewish ghetto; about half of the city's Jews lived in the second district. Felix Frankfurter was born there on November 15, 1882.

If the Jews in Vienna did not have to fear pogroms, there were restrictions on their lives, economic uncertainties, and an undercurrent of hostility. Samuel Frankfurter, wanting more for himself and his family, began to dream of the America he had heard so much about. As with the Louis Brandeis family, Samuel Frankfurter, the father, came first to scout out the new land for his family, to determine whether a living could be made, and whether Jews would find peace. He arrived on May 5, 1893. For his family in Vienna, without the income earner, the months were difficult. Felix had to live with his uncle, Solomon Frankfurter, then beginning a career as a distinguished scholar.

Once in the United States, Samuel Frankfurter "fell in love with this country," Felix said many years later. As soon as the father could, he sent for his family, and they arrived in 1894. There were Mrs. Frankfurter and five children, including "Felese," as Felix was listed on the passenger list of the S.S. *Marsala.* A sixth child was born in the United States.

The father dropped the Samuel and was known in America as Leopold Frankfurter. He was a retail fur merchant, a person of frail health, "a dreamy and charitable soul" who gave baskets of food to the poor. His son, Paul, described him as "a round peg in a square hole . . . a philosopher whose transactions in goods are clouded with dreams of social justice. He tried to make a living all his life. It was pathetic. He never did."

Leopold hurried to begin the five-year naturalization process, becoming a citizen on June 2, 1898. The children born in Europe became citizens with their father's naturalization. Emma, the mother, quickly learned English. The family lived then at 78 East Fourth Street on the

Lower East Side. This was a rite of passage for the immigrant groups coming to the United States, that they find a niche in the Lower East Side: one for Jews, one for Italians, one for Germans, one for Irish; and later, one for Puerto Ricans. Here each group began the process that could lead either away from the ethnic affiliation to become the assimilated American or, instead, to the world of the hyphenated American. Whichever was chosen, here the immigrants learned English, fought their first battles, dealt with racial and religious slurs. Here they learned of American politics. The "pols" like Al Smith visited them in their stores, talked to them on street corners, at the post–Bar Mitzvah party and at the wake; the message usually the same: if the Jews, the Italians, the Germans, and the others would compromise some of their demands and vote together, they could achieve some of those demands. Combine their vote, that was the trick. Here they tested the traditions of the old world against the demands of the new. Here they began the process of Americanization. And with their learning and their beginning, they—as had the Brandeis family a half-century earlier—brought new energy, new ideas, new effort to the new land.

This is Felix Frankfurter's description of his early education:

It was P.S. No. 25. . . . The important person was . . . my teacher in the first-year class, Miss Hogan by name. In those days boys did not call their teachers by their first names and so I don't know that I ever knew her first name. She was a tender, outwardly fierce and a bit of a martinet, rather peppery Irish dame, who was no longer young—though what a young boy thought old might chronologically merely mean that she was in the late thirties. But she evidently spotted eagerness and teachability in me and saw that the only way for me to learn English was to stop speaking German. Accordingly, she forbade my classmates from a German-speaking neighborhood to speak to me in German, and I seem to have the firm recollection that she threatened any body who did speak to me otherwise than in English with an "uppercut." All my life I have cherished her memory.

He was graduated from P.S. No. 25 on June 29, 1897, and, at the ceremony, gave a recitation on John Adams. After high school, he joined the E. A. Poe Literary Society and presented a paper on "The Dreyfus Case." Then he found Cooper Union, combination meeting hall, reading room, and intellectual stewpot, with doors open to anyone wandering in from the street. "It wasn't merely that it was a warm room and the streets were cold," Frankfurter recalled, "though there were those who found that not an unattractive aspect. But the notion that I could read all the papers of the United States, that there they were and

I had the opportunity to read them, was exciting. It set me afire."

Frankfurter went on to City College, a New York institution that was an important part of the funnel through which the immigrant passed on the way to becoming an American. More European than American collegiate in the early 1900s, City College offered its students the opportunity to live and study in the midst of a thriving, troubled, expanding, sometimes dangerous, exciting city—not separated from it but part of it. The course was prescribed and rigid, and the students did their schoolwork in crowded and distracting conditions, developing the necessary discipline. The five-year program covered half of high school and all of a college course. For relaxation the students drifted to the East Side tea shops and coffee rooms, drinking tea and rum out of tall glasses and talking with all comers until dawn. Frankfurter completed the program with high honors.

"For the most part," said a friend, "he taught himself in his usual way. 'I read a lot,' he has reported, 'a terrible lot.' "

Frankfurter himself stressed the essential point about City College when, many years later, he talked of the College's origins. "This College was ordered to be established by direct vote of the people after full discussion. . . . Higher education was thus made available to those capable of it not as a largesse, not as charity for the poor, but as part of the duties of a democratic government. . . . The cost of higher education for a democratic society was rightly deemed part of the cost of government."

After graduating from City College in 1902, Frankfurter worked for the city's Tenement House Department for a year. First, as a temporary clerk, his annual salary was $1,200; when he was promoted to full clerk, by some bureaucratic legerdemain, his salary was reduced to $1,050. The department "had just got under way," Frankfurter recalled, "and therefore had the freshness and fervor of all such regulatory bodies. I spent a year at the Department and the salary that I earned saw me through three years at the Harvard Law School."

The law, for someone growing up on the Lower East Side, was an avenue to escape the poverty, to achieve respectability and acceptance, to develop one's mind. There were other avenues—medicine for the student interested in science, show business for the individual who could sing or dance, professional sports for the athlete. Frankfurter had no interest in science, could not sing or dance, and was too slight in height and build even to be a bantamweight contender.

As it had been for Louis Brandeis, Harvard Law School was the ideal site for Felix Frankfurter. It had a liberal admissions policy. "The students came from everywhere," Frankfurter recalled. "They were rich and poor. They were sons of obscure workingmen and of cabinet officers. . . . There were always fellows from Oberlin, from Antioch, and from some little Methodist college in the Southwest." Once admitted, the students found the standards strict. A class began with 250 students and ended three years later with only 150. A faculty member compared the process through Harvard Law School to that of crossing the plains in a covered wagon: "The cowards never started out and the weak died on the way."

Much depended upon the student. With a class of several hundred, he could seek obscurity or "was at liberty to jump into the mental scuffle and take part in the discussion. Thus certain keen minds moved to the fore."

When Frankfurter arrived at Harvard, "I was the scaredest kid that you can imagine," awed by his fellow students, "who began to pipe up almost the second day" and impressed by his teachers. "I really had a streak of yellow in me asserting itself from which only fear saved me from saying, 'This is too fast a team for me, and I better go back to New York.' " At midyear he received a B on an optional examination instead of an A, "and I said to myself, 'Maybe this demands more attention than I have been giving it.' " So he worked harder and when, at the end of his first year, his grades came in the mail to his New York home, he recalled, "I remembered how, in a cowardly way—a passing streak of yellow—I dallied with the letter."

Frankfurter stood there holding the envelope until finally, overcoming his cowardice, he opened it. "There were the marks—A in everything. I did not then know that I was first in the class. I was asked to join the Law Review."

Austin W. Scott, later a member of the Law School faculty, entered as a student the fall after Frankfurter was graduated, "and I heard a good deal about you from fellow students who had been in the Law School with you. You began to be a hero to me at that time." Another of his fellow students recalled many years later: "My vivid memory . . . is that the man that stood up most of the time and answered the questions was Felix Frankfurter." Another version, this from a professor to Frankfurter: "You go off like an alarm clock. Don't talk so fast."

Frankfurter particularly treasured his experiences on the *Law Review*. "There was never a problem whether a Jew or a Negro should get on the *Law Review*," he later said. "If they excelled academically, they would just go on automatically." And some years out of Harvard he spoke of his *Law Review* experiences as "the divine feeling of being one of the potentates of the profession . . . for it was our frequent and joyous duty to reverse even [the United States Supreme Court] in an infallible judgment of one hundred and sixty-five words."

And so as he sat in Phillips Brooks House that day in May 1905, listening to Louis Brandeis issue a call for lawyers "to do a great work for this country," Frankfurter's idealism was stirred. This descendant of a "dreamy and charitable soul" saw in Brandeis a "disciplined, highly cultivated mind passionately devoted to the Rule of Law as unfolded in Anglo-American constitutional history, bent on conserving the fruits of civilization and desirous of enhancing them, joined to a compassionate nature that was sensitive to injustices and rejected the notion that whatever is, is right."

The association between Brandeis and Frankfurter beginning that day developed into a unique relationship. Their lives encompassed one-half the history of the United States; one remembered the Civil War, the other joined in the declaration that racial segregation in public schools was unconstitutional a century later. From the early 1900s to the early 1960s, the two of them, either singly or together, were involved in virtually every domestic struggle in the United States: civil liberties, civil rights, and criminal law, as well as economic rights. As lawyers they demanded courts acknowledge and deal with the grievances of the poor as well as the rich. They lobbied in the backrooms of the political houses for laws benefiting the immigrant and the worker. They spoke to the rich and powerful on behalf of those not previously heard.

They became friends and influencers of the powerful, the individuals people listened to. And then from the Supreme Court—Brandeis was an associate justice from 1916 to 1939 and Frankfurter was on that Court from 1939 until 1962—they spoke for the individual in a way few jurists had done before. They often were admired, frequently hated, rarely ignored.

Their story is more than the summation of its specifics. Brandeis, born in America, the child of immigrants, and Frankfurter, who came to the United States as an immigrant; their story is the immigrant story. Brandeis, secure in his American birth, devoted much of his life to assisting the immigrants, identified with them. Frankfurter, always mindful of his foreign birth, became their symbol.

Louis Brandeis, with all of his activities, still had been on the periphery of reform, involved in the kinds of activities that some gentlemen take on in their spare time. If the establishment was jabbed occasionally —gas companies, insurance companies, franchise seekers—there had been no great outbursts against Brandeis. *Muller* v. *Oregon,* for example, was barely reported in the Boston newspapers. And then Brandeis came out against the proposed merger of the transportation facilities in New England. Now he no longer was jabbing.

The New Haven Railroad, controlled by the J. P. Morgan banking house, wanted to buy the other rail lines and means of transportation in New England. Brandeis opposed the move. "The merger question to my mind is this," he said. "Is it for the interest of Massachusetts that all transportation facilities (steam railroad, trolleys and steamboats) within New England and between New England and the South and West, shall be controlled permanently by the New Haven Company?" Approval by the state legislature was needed, and that was Brandeis's battleground. On one day, for example, he sent separately typed letters to fifteen prominent Bostonians; he included a copy of his remarks on the transportation monopoly, and hoped they would "deem it important to aid us in our campaign." The railroad interests, with more money than many of his previous opponents, made Brandeis the target of a highly organized smear campaign. "I seem to be getting a fair share of free advertising in the provinces," he wrote his brother, "to compensate for the damning I am exposed to at home. However you needn't worry. I have not suffered in mind or body, and the only effect upon my estate is to leave me more time to pound the enemy."

The New Haven argued that merger was in the region's best interests because the combined transportation facilities could operate more efficiently than could separate companies. The claim was the kind that Brandeis enjoyed demolishing. Rather than being an efficient railroad operator, the New Haven had, instead, been running its railroad into the ground. Brandeis demonstrated that the railroad's 8 percent dividend had been maintained only because the books had not been kept in 1908 in the same manner as they had been kept in 1907. A total of $1.17 million should have been in the maintenance account but wasn't. There was the matter of "fixed and miscellaneous" charges, which would, so Brandeis demonstrated, exceed the promised earnings by $3 million. Even by juggling the books the railroad was not maintaining its 8 percent rate but actually paid out 6 percent, and managed that, Brandeis said, only because "it is deferring to an extraordinary degree needed repairs so as to keep down current operating expenses."

With his statistics Brandeis also had the experienced publicist's way with words. The merger supporters promise, he said, "to give us better rates between northern and southern New England." A pause, then: "We have heard just that sort of siren song before."

When the merger was voted on in 1908, Brandeis believed he had the votes. He was right that year. "We have beaten them horse, foot and dragoons," he exclaimed. "Merger is dead." On that, however, Brandeis was wrong. It was not dead, only dormant for another year. In 1909 the railroad came back with "all the power of the Republican machine and of the bankers' money." Brandeis reported, "Our situation is pretty desperate and only a miracle can land us safely." There were no miracles, and the merger was authorized and took effect.

In Boston there was an increase in hostility toward Brandeis on the part of the prominent, the business people, the money holders because he had opposed the New Haven railroad merger—he was no longer after only the *nouveau riche,* but after *them.* These Boston Brahmins were either owners or married to owners of New Haven stock. They didn't believe in airing bad news, in publicly reporting juggled figures, in disgracing their friends. A few years after the merger fight, Brandeis would have another struggle with the New Haven. His documentation of mismanagement, stupid and greedy more than illegal, was damning and the railroad failed. Friends turned against him, blaming the railroad's failure not on mismanagement but on Brandeis's demonstration of mismanagement. "Of course," said Herbert B. Ehrmann, a lawyer in Boston during the period, "they would have saved their investments from loss and their reputations from tarnish had they listened to Brandeis. However, it was emotionally easier to stick to the old faith and to denounce as a charlatan the prophet who thundered against their false gods. It is an ancient phenomenon of human behavior."

The proposed New Haven merger was part of a trend, during these early decades of the century, of bigness becoming a goal itself. The United States had grown to its full size—the last of the continental states, Arizona, entered the union in 1913—and industry grew within the nation, Standard Oil and the United States Steel corporations, for example, promising to produce commodities more efficiently and less expensively than did a number of smaller companies.

Brandeis did not accept the goal of bigness. In 1905 he wanted limitations upon the size of insurance companies. Within a few years, he was ready to go along with a size limitation on most companies.

His opposition to bigness was aroused for several reasons. First, he believed that the larger the company, the less—not more—efficient it was. "Standard Oil men," said Brandeis, "with their poor business methods would only have earned a moderate living had they not killed competition and controlled rebates. Without this unfairness in business, officials of the Tobacco Trust would have starved to death." More than incompetence was involved. "When you increase your business to a very great extent," he said, "and the multitude of problems increase with its growth, you will find, in the first place, that the man at the head has a diminishing knowledge of the facts, and, in the second place, a diminishing opportunity for exercising careful judgment upon them."

With the problem of inefficiency was that of separation between the owners and their responsibilities. A wide distribution of stock was, to Brandeis, "absentee landlordism of the worst kind . . . more dangerous, far more dangerous than the absentee landlordism from which Ireland suffered" because it results in "a sense of absolute irresponsibility on the part of the person who holds that stock." But the critical problem of the large corporation, said Brandeis, was "that it makes possible—and in many cases makes inevitable—the exercise of industrial absolutism." This led to an employer becoming "so potent, so well organized, with such concentrated forces and with such extraordinary powers of reserve" that he could endure against strikes. "Under the trusts capital hires men," Brandeis said, "under real cooperation, men hire capital."

Brandeis's comments have about them the sound of the scold, but his feelings were real. Said an associate: Brandeis "believes that the most important natural resource of any country is the people who live in that country. He believes that the creative and constructive possibilities of the mass of the people in this particular country have not yet been realized. He holds that these possibilities are great and that it is the business of democracy to develop them."

In 1913 Brandeis summed up his concerns at a luncheon meeting with Thomas W. Lamont at the University Club in New York City. Lamont was a partner in the J. P. Morgan & Company banking house, one coming under increasing attack by Brandeis for the way it used money. "You astonish me beyond measure," said Lamont. "How in the world did you arrive at the belief that people are afraid of us, or that we have this terrific power?"

By this time the New Haven Railroad had collapsed. "You have no idea, Mr. Lamont," said Brandeis, "and you could have no idea, unless you lived in New England, what anguish has been brought to thousands, almost, by means of this New Haven downfall." Brandeis said he had seen it coming, and had warned the Boston bankers and sought their help in stopping the collapse. But the railroad was financed by J. P. Morgan & Company, and the Boston bankers refused to challenge Morgan. "They said that the New Haven was Mr. Morgan's particular pet, that he resented any interference in its affairs, and that it would be as much as their financial life was worth to try to poke their fingers in. They said that if they did so, they should be cut off J. P. Morgan and Company's list for all future syndicate participation."

Lamont claimed that the Boston bankers' fears were not Morgan's fault. He insisted that the responsibility lay with the men to whom Morgan had trusted the railroad's management.

"I understand, Mr. Lamont," Brandeis replied, "and I accept, at par, without question, whatever you say, but Mr. Morgan was the dominant financial personality in that board, and whether he was responsible by initiation or by acquiescence, the result is equally deplorable."

Thomas Lamont's response had underscored Brandeis's claim that the larger the organization, the more difficult for its leaders to watch over it.

Lamont then challenged Brandeis's charge that large amounts of capital in the bankers' hands endangered the country. "Yes, I do think it is dangerous, highly dangerous," said Brandeis; ". . . it hampers the freedom of the individual." He insisted that "the only way that we are going to work out our problems in this country is to have the individual free, not free to do unlicensed things, but free to work and to trade without the fear of some gigantic power threatening to engulf him every moment, whether that power be a monopoly in oil or in credit."

Lamont ended the luncheon with the claim of improvement. "We have all got to admit that the country has traveled quite fast and quite far in the last ten years," the banker said, "and I think everybody is looking at things through somewhat different glasses."

"Yes," agreed Brandeis, "I think there has been a great awakening, and it has been high time, but I don't think that those things are as far away as you think they are."

One could not then be a critic of industrial giantism without being involved in the question of organized labor. Capital demanded the subjugation of the worker. Labor organized to block that demand. Throughout the century that conflict would be played out against a backdrop of private police forces, picket lines, bloodshed, work stoppages, strikes, scab laborers; for many in the nation it would be an agony.

Brandeis supported labor unions. His friend Elizabeth Glendower

Evans reported that he had first announced his support in the late 1880s, saying that unions were needed to give the worker a position at the bargaining table equal to that of the owner. To bargain equally, Brandeis said, unions needed the right to strike as the "sole effective means of protest." He made that statement when the courts were enjoining a union's right to strike, declaring the strike an "unreasonable" restraint of trade. The law used by the courts was the Sherman Act, originally passed to curb the power of trusts and large corporations; now it was used to protect trusts and corporations from the unions.

Sometimes, however, it was hard to classify Brandeis. When a pro-labor title was attached to him, he turned in another direction. With the right to strike, Brandeis wanted union accountability. Unions should be incorporated, he argued, and then could be sued if they went beyond proper bounds—if a strike, for example, turned violent. For the unions to advance, he insisted, they must renounce violence, the work slow-down, and the closed shop. The last was a device to give the union control over whom the employer hired. Brandeis believed that the unions, with those restraints laid upon them, would fare well before the courts. Once he argued the issue with Samuel Gompers, the labor leader, before the Economic Club of Boston. During the first part of the evening, Brandeis was his usual controlled self. "He made no effort at oratorical effect and assumed a conversational tone and manner, lean-ing for the most part of the time with his left arm on the desk and with his right hand in his trouser pocket," said an account. But when Gompers spoke, and referred to an English case in which, he charged, the court had "mulcted" the union, Brandeis made no effort to hide his anger. "Who is this man," he demanded, pointing to Gompers, "that takes it upon himself to say that a judge or jury returned the decision erroneous upon the fact?" Brandeis, continued the account, "indulged at times in a fine sarcasm, which was phrased with a dignity that rend-ered it all the more biting."

His involvement with unions and trusts led Brandeis, as it always did, to seek solutions. He would often hear that a working man was paid so much an hour or, under contract work, so much a piece. He caught the fallacy. "The important question is not how much a man is paid per day nor how much per piece," Brandeis asserted, "but how much can he earn in a year. He may have high wages, and an opportunity of working only half the year." Or "A man may have six meals one day, and none the next, making an average of three per day, but that is not a good way to live."

Brandeis had been called in to help settle a strike against a shoe manufacturer in New England. The complaint was that the workers were idle ten to fifteen weeks. "This is unnecessary," Brandeis fumed. "It is an outrage that in an intelligent society a great industry should be so managed." From management he heard a refrain of seasonal conditions. But Brandeis knew there was no such thing in the shoe industry. When the plant produced the number of shoes it could sell, it shut down, not opening again until time to manufacture the next group of shoes. With the cooperation of management and labor, Brandeis worked out an arrangement under which both sides agreed to spread out the work to cover the entire year. Brandeis gave credit to the plant owner, saying: "He began to see it as I did. He inclined his thoughts to solve the problem, and it was solved. The disgrace of unemployment in his share of that industry was eliminated."

More had emerged from that conflict in the shoe plant than the spreading out of hours. Often management and labor were so angry with each other, so filled with the fury of their past statements, with shibboleths and slogans, that communication was not possible. Brandeis then was called in as an intermediary. If he could bring the two sides to speak with each other, then perhaps the dispute could be solved to the betterment of both sides. One of his most successful efforts involved the New York garment workers when, in 1910, 100,000 of them struck. This was the sweatshop industry, and resentment had built for years. "Have been here since Thursday morning again trying to settle the garment workers strike . . ." Brandeis wrote his brother. "The outcome is doubtful with probability rather that there will be no settlement because of the Union demand for an all-Union [closed] shop."

The union wanted a closed shop to insure its strength in disputes with management. The owners, insisting they would never yield to that demand, would not meet with the union representatives. Slowly Brandeis inched the two sides together, persuading one to give slightly, then receiving a concession from the other. Once the dialogue began, once the two sides saw each other not as enemies but as groups jointly interested in the success of the industry and the welfare of the workers, the movement toward settlement became irresistible.

The lawyer for the manufacturers told Brandeis, "In the entire history of the industry, so far as I can learn, the acceptance of your proposal marks the first occasion when the manufacturers have dealt, as an organized body, with the Unions, as an organized body, even for the purpose of conference."

For Brandeis, settling the strike was not sufficient. He wanted to solve not only the industry's past problems but its future ones as well. The demand for the closed shop was replaced with an agreement for a "preferential union shop," which assured union membership without the owners' surrendering control over hiring. He established a joint board to arbitrate disputes. Fifteen months after the settlement there were these results: fire protection and sanitary arrangements had been added in 740 shops where they had not previously existed or had been defective; 29 shops "found to be unfit for human beings to work in" had been closed; a sanitary control board had brought about more healthful working conditions in more than 2,000 shops. More than any specific, however, the Brandeis effort had "brought about such an era of good feeling between the employers and the union that, for the first year in the history of the calling locally, there has not been a single strike among the cloak makers of New York."

But Brandeis knew that even more than settling labor disputes was necessary. Once the inefficiency of management, the unwarranted dividend payments, and the bloated hierarchy of industry was altered, there still would not be enough remaining to give the working men and women the benefits they wanted and which Brandeis believed they deserved. "These demands . . ." he explained, "cannot conceivably be met unless the productivity of man is increased." The solution to this problem, he argued, was "scientific management," a popular term at the time, which Brandeis defined as "nothing more than an organized effort, pursued intensively, to eliminate waste." To Brandeis this was more than efficiency experts going through a plant cutting a second from a job here, a minute there. "The fundamental problems are social and industrial," he said. "You cannot eliminate waste unless you secure the cooperation of the worker, and you cannot secure his cooperation unless he is satisfied that there is a fair distribution of profits." To achieve this, "industrial democracy" was needed. This phrase, bandied about for perhaps thirty years, its meaning vague, included such elements as profit sharing between a company and its employees, incentive pay formulas, retirement programs, stock-purchasing plans, and other items to indicate that the employer trusted, respected, and felt affection for the employees. Management balked at industrial democracy.

As Brandeis became more prominent, especially in the Boston area and among public officials, his opinions and support were sought after. "Will you be good enough to give me your judgment upon [the enclosed report] and return it to me at the earliest possible moment, as I desire to lay the matter before Congress very soon?" asked President Theodore Roosevelt in 1907. And as pressures grew on Brandeis, he changed some of his positions. Originally an opponent of women's suffrage, in 1913 he responded to the demands of his wife and other women he had met through his public work and endorsed the vote for women.

With Senator Robert M. La Follette of Wisconsin, Brandeis wanted to keep the Alaskan territory from being exploited by large corporations. He suggested this slogan for the fight:

> Alaska; the Land of Opportunity.
> Develop it by the people, for the people.
> Do not let it be exploited by the Capitalists, for the Capitalists.

Brandeis joined Roscoe Pound of the Harvard Law School and other lawyers to produce a report on criminal law, which asserted that "the demands of industrial and urban communities raise problems which the existing legal system, fashioned to meet the demands of a pioneer and agricultural community of the first half of the nineteenth century, is not well prepared to meet." The study's recommendations sound contemporary: better-trained lawyers, more competent judges, the separation of law enforcement and politics; and "a public examination of accused persons under proper judicial safeguards" to end "third-degree confessions."

Brandeis's political affiliation wavered. In the closing years of the nineteenth century, at least, he was a registered Republican. Not only was this a legacy of his family and growing up in Louisville, but there was the feeling then that the Republican party was the progressive party. In the next half-dozen years or so, however, Brandeis identified more with independent and reform groups and did not hesitate to lend his support to Democrats as well as Republicans, in local elections at least. After 1900 his name was mentioned as a candidate for governor or lieutenant governor. Although he never came close to a nomination, the frequency of these mentions suggest he was aware of them and was not averse to a testing of the political waters.

In 1907 he was approached by a delegation from the Republican City Committee and the Good Government Association, offering to back him for mayor of Boston. He turned them down. He was then involved in fighting the New Haven merger and didn't want to drop out of that fight. He was also aware that he had made enemies. "My course in knocking heads right and left is not exactly such as to create an 'available candidate,' " he acknowledged. In the 1908 presidential election, Brandeis voted for William Howard Taft, the Republican candidate, who, Brandeis believed, "is admirably qualified for the position and doubtless will . . . prove a fine President."

As the "people's lawyer," Louis Brandeis had come to a point where he was known within the Boston and New England community and in Washington. The next event in his public advocacy made him a national figure; assailed a presidency, that of the "admirably qualified" Taft; produced a tumult in Washington; and added another item to the list of reasons for the assault upon him when later Woodrow Wilson appointed him to the Supreme Court. This is what became known as the Ballinger affair.

Washington in the early 1900s was a city of formality. Wives of senators called upon the wives of other senators, but only in proper sequence. Supreme Court justices did not allow their wives to appear at a salon until after certain proprieties had been observed. Evenings were passed over leisurely dinners with men in tuxedos and women in long gowns. On Sunday afternoons, government officials in cutaway coats, striped trousers, and tall hats went from one tea to another, fulfilling social obligations, boring but unavoidable. Underneath the formality and the protocol were the jealousies, hatred, and ambitions that always had marked politics.

After Theodore Roosevelt left the White House in 1909 to make room for his chosen successor, Taft, many of Roosevelt's followers saw Taft—if not in appearance, at least in philosophy—as a replica of the former President. William Howard Taft considered himself a progressive Republican as Roosevelt had been and planned to carry on many of Roosevelt's policies. But Taft was also his own man, especially in conservation matters.

Taft had refused to retain James R. Garfield, a conservationist, as Secretary of the Interior, although he had indicated to Roosevelt that he would. Garfield not only had been in Roosevelt's cabinet but also had been a close friend of the President. In his place Taft appointed Richard A. Ballinger, a lawyer from Seattle, an expert in mining law, and an official in the Interior Department under Garfield, and, more important, a critic of the Roosevelt policies. Ballinger did not appeal to a Roosevelt follower named Gifford Pinchot, who was head of the forestry service within the Agriculture Department. From then on the plot thickened more rapidly than in any Washington potboiler novel, involving more and more prominent figures, the major news media, large corporate powers, the presidency, and, ultimately, Brandeis.

The backbiting between the Pinchot and Ballinger forces began almost with the beginning of the Taft administration. At first it was the usual Washington gossip, becoming louder and louder, meaning less and less. Then Pinchot organized the National Conservation Association to increase support for what Pinchot conceived as the Roosevelt conservation policies. Then from the Ballinger friends came stories that all was not well in the forestry service headed by Pinchot.

At this point a man named Louis Glavis emerged. A land agent in the Interior Department, he sent information about stealing—at least misuse, as he claimed—of public land to the attention of the Secretary of Interior, the Attorney General, and the President. His report was not accepted, and he was fired, by telegram from Interior Secretary Ballinger. Glavis turned his report into a magazine article and then went to see John Bass, the head of Pinchot's conservation group. Bass took Glavis and his story to *Collier's*, a muckraking magazine, headed by Norman Hapgood. "We cleaned out some of the worst senators," Hapgood said. "In the publicity field we led the fight for the Pure Food and Drug Act. We gave the patent medicine business a blow so solid that it has not recovered." To this list he was anxious to add the removal of Richard Ballinger from the Taft cabinet "for giving away our natural resources." He also was a friend of Gifford Pinchot's.

Bass and Glavis "said they had a great many offers for Mr. Glavis' article, some of them at extremely high rates," Hapgood recalled, "but they did not want to have it published in an ordinary journalistic way; that they would like to have us publish it because we were identified with reform in general and conservation in particular, and he wanted me to understand that if we did publish it, it would not be paid for, because he did not want any doubt about it being part of a public principle and not journalism." Hapgood took the article home that night to see if it was "copper-riveted. . . . If it was solid all through, and unmistakably sound." He continued: "I read it very carefully that night and decided it was absolutely accurate and absolutely just, and the next day accepted it."

The article dealt with Alaskan coal claims and its thrust was that the Interior Department, under Richard Ballinger, was giving them away to industry. Publication of the article caused the expected uproar. Congress, especially those members of Congress opposed to the Taft administration, demanded to know the truth of the charges, and there was talk of Ballinger's suing Glavis and *Collier's* for libel and slander. Ballinger called for a joint congressional investigation of his department. At *Collier's* the fear was that an investigation clearing Ballinger would lead to the magazine's being the target of a libel suit.

Hapgood and *Collier's* decided to secure a lawyer to represent Glavis at the Senate inquiry. A meeting was held in the New York law office of Henry L. Stimson. Present were Gifford Pinchot and his brother Amos; Hapgood and Robert Collier, owner of the magazine; Garfield, the former Interior Secretary; and George Wharton Pepper. The Pinchot brothers had had long and distinguished careers as conservationists. Garfield had been a Roosevelt cabinet member. Stimson already was involved in what would be a career of public service lasting almost half a century. Pepper would later become a senator from Pennsylvania. Hapgood and Collier were respected journalistic names.

Hapgood wanted Brandeis to represent Glavis. Eventually it was decided that Pepper, who represented the Pinchot brothers, and Brandeis would handle the Glavis side. Hapgood later recalled that the assumption was that Pepper would take the lead in the Glavis cause, "but it required only a few days to prove to everybody that it was necessary for Mr. Brandeis to lead, since he already knew the facts many times better than any of the rest of us."

For Louis Brandeis, the Ballinger-Glavis episode was another battle in what for him had become a crusade against special interests. Whatever the politics of this situation had been to this moment, for him they disappeared. He explained in a few lines to his brother what was pushing him then, this was the spring of 1910:

There is nothing for us to do but to follow the trail of evil wherever it extends. *Fiat Iustitia.* In the fight against special interest we shall receive no quarter and may as well make up our minds to give none. . . . There is a chance—but a chance merely—that the people will now reverse all history and be able to control. The chance is worth taking, because there is nothing left for the self-respecting man to do. But every attempt to deal mercifully with the special interests *during the fight* simply results in their taking advantage of the merciful.

In the coming congressional hearings Brandeis would show no mercy.

His attacks began in his opening statement. He painted a picture of J. P. Morgan & Company and the Guggenheim interests—"probably the most ambitious, energetic, resourceful combination of capitalists in the world"—conspiring, with Ballinger's connivance, to gain control of the mines in Alaska, and then the fisheries, so that, with control of the railroads, "they would be confirmed in what, to a very great degree, they now have, the control of Alaska." The Interior Department could block the power grab, Brandeis charged, but, rather than blocking it, had aided it.

Only Glavis had stepped forward to stop the special interests, Brandeis said, and for this he was called insubordinate and dismissed. Brandeis, dwelling on the word "insubordination" and the concept it entailed, offered much of his vision of the public servant. "The danger in America," he insisted, "is not insurbordination, but it is of too complacent obedience to the will of superiors." With the power of government expanding, its employees' rolls growing longer, the need was for employees "who will think and act in full recognition of their obligations as part of the governing body." He called upon government employees to have the "virtues of manliness, of truth, of courage, of willingness to risk positions . . . to risk criticism . . . to risk the misunderstandings that so often come when people do the heroic thing."

His call for government employees to rise above the level of clerks and yes-men was a demand, as he put it, not for "the conservation of natural resources merely; it is the conservation of democracy; it is the conservation of manhood."

George Wharton Pepper, Brandeis's co-attorney, was amazed at Brandeis's industry. "Commonly, during the heat of the investigation," Pepper said of Brandeis, "he was at work at four o'clock in the morning in his hotel room, preparing his day's work before the Committee." Since Ballinger had committed no crime, Brandeis's approach was to demonstrate that Ballinger consistently made his decisions regarding the Alaskan coal mines without regard to the public interest. If that was not dishonest, perhaps the public could be convinced that it was at least improper if not immoral. To demonstrate that to the public, Brandeis played for the press. Pinchot agreed with Brandeis on this approach. Pepper did not, believing that Pinchot and Brandeis "were busy trying the case in the newspapers and incidentally making statements for which I often could find no adequate supporting evidence." Pepper retreated more and more from the case. Pinchot and Brandeis always had time to talk with a reporter, to explain a point, to dispute a claim made by the Ballinger forces. They were not the only ones. This was before journalism had pledged itself to objectivity, and newspapers often took positions in their news columns for and against particular issues; many newspapers openly favored Ballinger. The Associated Press then was considered biased in favor of the administration.

John J. Vertrees of Tennessee represented Ballinger. He had been appointed because he was a friend of a friend—of the President himself, according to one account. He was described as "a lawyer of the old school, a fire-eating Southerner, experienced in combats of various sorts." But bombast did not challenge information, and he could not stand before Brandeis's onslaught of facts, figures, and knowledge of the intricacies of the Interior Department.

At one point Vertrees, suddenly jumping to his feet, told the committee chairman, "The gentleman [Brandeis] says what is untrue and what he knows to be untrue."

Brandeis turned toward Vertrees and smiled, waiting.

Again: "The gentleman states an untruth and he states it knowing it to be an untruth."

Still Brandeis refused to respond, refused to indulge in the oral free-for-all that would only distract from his presentation. Vertrees began to sputter and grow red in the face; then Brandeis, his arms folded across his chest, flashing an indulgent smile at his opponent, finally said: "Anything further, Mr. Vertrees?" Vertrees sat down, defeated.

At another point Brandeis told the committee: "Aside from the argument of Mr. Vertrees, which Mr. Pepper has so artistically disposed of, there are some statements of the evidence to which I want to call your attention and which lead me to think that Mr. Vertrees may be in some respects as unfamiliar with the record as he has been proven to be with the principles of conservation."

The hearing lasted from January through May 1910, and they were weary months. Publicly, Brandeis appeared, as a newspaper account said of him, "keen, persistent, tireless, yet quiet . . . ready to meet any attempted evasion from a hostile witness, and [with] a silencing answer for any retort or innuendo by opposing counsel or Senators." The reality, however, was different. He was traveling on weekends between Washington and Boston, and the traveling and the long hours were beginning to show on him. In April his wife, Alice, conceded that "Louis is enjoying the experience," but added, "I think he is getting a bit tired of it now and would be glad to be getting home." On one occasion Brandeis lost his composure and spoke sharply to the committee chairman. "Don't you snap at me like that," said the Senator, hammering his fist on the table. "You may insult the witness, but I want you to understand you must not insult this committee. You can't act in that overbearing way around here."

An associate recalled the moment when Brandeis was about to begin the questioning of an important witness. "I was sitting beside Louis," said the associate, "and for several moments before he rose, he clasped my knee in his hand and held it tightly. He said nothing and there was no other indication of emotion."

Brandeis believed the hearings were going well for his side, against what he conceived as the William Howard Taft side. "They are 'up against it,' " he exclaimed after two months. "W. H. T. can make more mistakes in a week than the rest of them can remedy in a year, if indeed they have any of the curative art."

William Howard Taft was not happy about being President; he had hoped to be Chief Justice. Still, when he assumed office, he determined to handle the job as well as he could and saw the Pinchot attacks against him as an effort to wean the Roosevelt supporters from him. "Theodore may not approve of all I have done," he said, "and I don't expect him to do so, but I shall try not to do anything which he might regard as a challenge. . . . No . . . I am going to give Pinchot as much rope as he wants and I think you will find that he will hang himself."

When Glavis had first brought his charges to Taft's attention the previous August, Taft had been vacationing at Beverly, Massachusetts. On September 6, Ballinger had come to Beverly with a huge mass of material supporting his position. On September 13, seven days later, Taft issued a letter supporting Ballinger. Later the administration issued a summary report by Attorney General Wickersham, dated September 11. The administration's claim was that the President had exonerated Ballinger on September 13 on the basis of the Wickersham document dated September 11.

Brandeis was suspicious. The September 11 document supposedly summarized all the evidence Ballinger had produced for the President on September 6, only five days earlier. If that September 11 report was not legitimate—say it had been written later and then misdated—then chances were that Taft had cleared Ballinger because he had wanted to protect his cabinet member against the charges but without checking the accuracy of the information.

Brandeis's suspicions grew. Too much information had been produced by Ballinger on September 5 to be studied, absorbed, and synthesized into the September 11 report. No one could work that fast. Then there were several references in the report to events that took place after September 11. Finally, Brandeis was brought together with a man named Frederick M. Kerby, who was a Sunday-school teacher, a man with a conscience; he also had been Ballinger's private stenographer, and he had a story to tell Brandeis.

From what Kerby told him and other evidence he gathered, Brandeis believed that the September 11 summary had been prepared much later, was similar to a document prepared by a Ballinger associate, and then had been misdated. The validity of Taft's claim that he had made a careful study of the charges, as embodied in the September 11 report, could be effectively challenged.

Taft and Attorney General Wickersham later acknowledged misdating the September 11 report. Taft claimed that he had read the record and relied on an oral analysis made to him by Wickersham. "I was sorry not to be able to embody this analysis in my opinion, but time did not permit," explained Taft. "I therefore directed him to embody in a written statement such analysis and conclusions as he had given me, file it with the record, and date it prior to the date of my opinion, so as to show that my decision was fortified by his summary of the evidence and his conclusions therefrom." No mention was made of the similarity between Wickersham's report and that prepared by a Ballinger associate.

Wickersham also insisted that he had done nothing wrong in misdating the report. "It remained for the sophistry of a Brandeis to put an immoral construction upon it," he said.

Whatever their intentions, they had misdated a document that had been presented to a committee of the Congress and then attempted to conceal their action, causing widespread belief that the administration had been involved in a cover-up of its Secretary of Interior. "It was the lying that did it," said Brandeis. "If they had brazenly admitted everything, and justified it on the ground that Ballinger was at least doing what he thought best, we should not have had a chance."

Brandeis believed that he had demonstrated in the hearings that Ballinger had consistently decided against the public interest, pulled the law askew to enable the mining interests to ravage the land. This was the source of his anger and of his final charge to the committee. "In view of the unrest in this country," he said, "in view of the widespread feeling that the law is something different for the rich man than for the poor, it is of the utmost importance that men should not trifle with the law; that they should not use it as a tool, or as an excuse, but that they should look upon it as a great standard to be lived up to, and that they should recognize that the law is supreme over man, and in this republic exists for all men alike."

He contrasted Ballinger's actions with Theodore Roosevelt's concept that "law, from now on, should be used for the protection of the people and not against them." Ballinger had presumed the law favored private interests—contrary, Brandeis said, to past practice when "the presumption was in favor of the Government, or in other words, in favor of the people. That . . . is true law; that is law for a true purpose, a law used not as a device or as an excuse to increase the power of the special interests."

Brandeis continued not to rely on a committee verdict but to hope for his victory outside of Washington. Copies of his arguments were mailed out to friends, and Brandeis sent material, including a memorandum about the misdated Wickersham summary, to the news media. The early decades of the twentieth century, the years before radio and television, were the heyday of the magazines. *Collier's* was only one of the muckrakers, and they all liked a good story about the foibles and failures and, if they could prove it occasionally, the misdeeds of public figures. The editors of these magazines saw themselves slashing with their journalistic swords, risking all, with the outcome of the nation at stake. Brandeis played to their egos.

To Finley Peter Dunne of the *American* magazine: "Your interpretation of the Pinchot-Ballinger controversy would aid immensely in securing a proper understanding of it by Americans." To another editor, Brandeis did what he often did, suggested the outlines of an editorial:

Ballinger has ostentatiously proclaimed that his administration was "an administration of law, and not of men." Instead of that it has been "an administration of lawyers, and not of men." . . . Lawyers who . . . have prostituted the law to their purposes. . . . Ballinger is strict in his construction against the people, loose in his construction in favor of the special interests. . . . The readiness to sacrifice Glavis was a readiness to sacrifice the small man to the big.

The committee voted, on a party-line split, to exonerate Ballinger. One Republican who voted for Ballinger was Senator George Sutherland of Utah. Sutherland's friendly biographer conceded that Sutherland never strayed "from the path of party regularity." One of Sutherland's largest supporters in Utah was a newspaper owned by a stockholder in a Guggenheim enterprise. The Guggenheim interests had been after the Alaskan mining claims. Sutherland later served on the United States Supreme Court.

If Brandeis lost in the committee, he won outside of Congress. Ballinger's reputation had been destroyed by Brandeis, aided by the Taft-Wickersham bumbling. Ballinger resigned, and the coal claims granted to the Guggenheim and Morgan interests were canceled.

But Brandeis paid also. A result for him was that his character became then and for many years a matter to be questioned. Theodore Roosevelt, returning from an African safari, determined, on the basis of information fed him, that Brandeis had been a villain in the affair—corrupting Pinchot, luring Ballinger's stenographer (Kerby, the Sunday-school teacher with a conscience) into betraying his employer. "My friend Gifford [Pinchot] was lured from the straight and narrow path by Brandeis," charged Roosevelt. "It may not have been against Brandeis' code, but it was against my code, and against Gifford's." Many thought as Roosevelt did.

On the other side, Brandeis became almost the idol of the progressive forces, sought after to endorse progressive political candidates. And there was another result. At this point the nation's newspapers were organizing their press associations, using the telegraph wires to bring news to the country's front pages. A major story involving a cabinet member, a misdated report, charges of insubordination and of a cover-up made for dramatic reporting and juicy reading. An associate of Brandeis in the hearing said of the Ballinger episode: "It occupied the front pages of the papers during all that time and thus the name of Brandeis became known all over the country. I don't think it would have been likely that he would ever have had the opportunity to influence public affairs, as he did later, if he hadn't been in this particular case and became known as he did become known."

And there was still an additional result. Taft, anxious to heal the breach in the Republican party caused by the fracas and thus assure his own renomination in 1912, appointed along with Ballinger's replacement in Interior a new Secretary of War favorable to the Roosevelt interests. This was Henry L. Stimson. Stimson brought with him to Washington one of his most trusted aides from New York—Felix Frankfurter.

4

Melting Pot

When Frankfurter was graduated from Harvard, he realized he faced problems because of his religion, even though he was the year's outstanding graduate. He confronted the problem head-on. A Wall Street law office, considered one of the best, was his target. Following the mores of the time, the New York office had never hired a Jew and had indicated it would not. Frankfurter approached it for a job. He later explained: "I was a Jew, the essence of which is that you should be a biped and walk on the two legs that man has." Because of his record at Harvard and the recommendations he had received from the faculty members, the firm was interested in him but suggested he Anglicize his name. Frankfurter refused. Still, he was hired.

Private practice, however, did not appeal to Frankfurter. Whether he had yet to complete the transition from the Jewish ghetto of the Lower East Side to the world of Wall Street, whether he quickly came to realize that for him corporate law would be a deadly dull business, or whether his intellect was not challenged, he did not explain but soon wanted to move on.

The opportunity came after only a few months, when Henry Stimson was appointed the United States Attorney in New York. His responsibility was to go after the crooks in the business world, the smart-money men avoiding the law, playing with investments, and repaying themselves with large profits. His method was to hire bright, young, full-time lawyers, rather than rely on his predecessors' practice of using part-time, tired hacks. Frankfurter considered joining Stimson, although it would mean a salary cut. With another young lawyer in the Wall Street office, Elihu Root, Jr., a friend from Harvard, Frankfurter walked through the streets of New York several evenings, weighing the arguments. Said Root later: "We were both quite clear that the path to money lay through the [Wall Street] office and the path to service through the District Attorney's office. Felix chose the generous course."

Frankfurter had sought advice from the Harvard Law School dean, James Barr Ames, who wrote him: "Follow the dominant impulses of your career." Frankfurter accepted that advice and joined the Stimson office; generally he followed that advice through the remainder of his career.

For Frankfurter, Stimson would be part of the forging process along with Brandeis, and then later Oliver Wendell Holmes, Jr. Brandeis, the son of Jewish immigrants, and Stimson, whose American Protestant ancestors had fought in the French and Indian wars, had similar attitudes toward the law and public service. A successful Wall Street lawyer, Stimson devoted much of his time for four decades to public service as a government official. He summed up his role as a lawyer this way: "I came to feel that the American lawyer should regard himself as a potential officer of his government and a defender of its laws and constitution. I felt that if the time should ever come when this tradition had faded out and the members of the bar had become merely the servants of business, the future of our liberties would be gloomy indeed." Brandeis could have written the same sentence.

When Stimson's office moved against business, Frankfurter later said, it was viewed as a revolution. "People spoke of it," he said, "as they might have of the attack on the Bastille."

Although the robber barons pursued by the Stimson office hired the best lawyers money bought, they were no match for the young men Stimson recruited, and the convictions mounted. For Frankfurter the three-year experience was not limited to the courtroom. He remembered that "on many a shivering cold morning I had to get up early to accompany the secret service people who were executing a search warrant to make sure that they kept within the limits of the warrant."

Even then Frankfurter impressed those he met. Learned Hand, one of the most respected of federal judges, remembered him as an "eager, ardent youth . . . who used to come up to my chambers—a very green and timorous judge myself—and overwhelm me with the fertility of his mind and the warmth of his personality."

In 1910 Stimson, with Frankfurter working as an aide, ran for governor of New York, but he was too stiff a person for the political hustings and was defeated. Then, in the aftermath of the Ballinger affair, he went to Washington as Secretary of War.

On July 4, 1911, the *New York Times* reported that "Assistant United States Attorney Felix Frankfurter has been appointed Solicitor to the

Bureau of Insular Affairs, one of the most important posts in the War Department, by Henry L. Stimson, the new Secretary of War. Mr. Frankfurter is the youngest man to hold a corresponding post in the Federal administration in Washington."

A few months later Frankfurter began a diary which he kept intermittently through the years. The first entry, dated October 20, 1911, reads: "I am fortunate enough to meet men of rare spirit, of vaulting vision and fine deeds." Only a few weeks shy of his twenty-ninth birthday, Frankfurter was entering for him a new world. He would not be buried in a Wall Street cubicle as were many of his classmates or lost in the bowels of government bureaucracy. Instead, he would become friendly with the more prominent persons in American life, the men of the law, the men of letters, the men of politics. He traveled in a heady world, and sometimes he had difficulty keeping his equilibrium. One observer has noted of Frankfurter that "there is evidence of that characteristic self-consciousness, of a writer too often concerned about the verdict of history, about self-justification." The observer, Gerald Gunther, the biographer of Learned Hand, continued: "There is also some of what Frankfurter was ready to identify in others as the qualities of a 'Schmeichler'—a flatterer. As Hand once told Frankfurter: 'You are certainly no half-way admirer when you admire.' "

Frankfurter's work was varied. "Just at present am wrestling with the exclusion of Christian Scientists from 'practice' in the Canal Zone and the exclusion of Jews from Russia under our treaty," he wrote in his diary. He made his first appearance before the United States Supreme Court on Monday, November 20, 1911, at thirteen and one-half minutes past noon when he stood up and said: "May it please the Court: In number 408, the People of Porto Rico against Rosay, I beg to submit a consent motion to advance." He said of those twenty-four words that the road behind them had "the pain of ages and the hope of eternity." When the case was later argued, Frankfurter won, and he went on to argue a half dozen cases before the Court, according to his memory. Frankfurter came to know the justices. "Supreme Court Justices should be tall and broad and have a little bit of a bay window," wrote the short, thin Frankfurter.

Frankfurter almost became a Federal district judge, thanks to the Russian Czar. The Czar had offended an American government official because the official was Jewish, and the Democrats in the House then voted to abrogate a treaty with Russia. With Republicans concerned that they were not appearing responsive to the needs and demands of

Jewish voters, President William Howard Taft sought a Jew for a judgeship. Whether Frankfurter actually was offered the position or was informed, instead, that he was being considered is in dispute. In either case, he was not interested. "I told Stimson," he recalled, "that while of course I would take pride if an admirable appointment to the bench turned out to be a Jew, I would have no truck with appointing a man to the bench because he was a Jew. I remember well saying to [Stimson]: 'President Taft is playing with fire in starting that sort of thing.' "

Never naïve, Frankfurter understood the influence of religion on public lives and appointments. He often told this story:

In the early days of the first World War, Fred Keppel, Walter Lippmann and I were assistants to Secretary [of War Newton D.] Baker. There began to come into the Secretary's office letters complaining that the Secretary of War was surrounded by three Jews, Keppel, Lippmann and Frankfurter. Keppel of course was Irish. When this kept up Lippmann asked me one day, "What is a Jew anyhow?" To which I replied, "Walter, I offer you this as a working definition: A Jew is a person whom non-Jews regard as a Jew."

When Frankfurter came to Washington with Stimson, he and some other bachelors rented a house dubbed the "House of Truth." Eustace Percy, a young Englishman then working in Washington, was one of its residents. "That household had a touch of du Maurier's *Quartier Latin*, with law and the erratic politics of the then infant *New Republic* taking the place of art as the focus of its endless talk and even more endless flow of casual guests," he wrote. There were dinner parties and cocktail gatherings, all centering on talk, brilliant, fascinating, and intriguing talk. Walter Lippmann, in those years a government official, also lived in the House of Truth.

For many of those in the house, the experience in Washington was the moving from wide-eyed youth into maturity, the first time they assumed responsibilities that could be described as adult, or, as in Frankfurter's case, the experience was moving upward to a new level of activity. For Eustace Percy, "it was the scene where I began my working life, and of such scenes it is written:

> We've only one virginity to lose
> And where we lost it, there our hearts will be."

A frequent guest at the House of Truth when he was in Washington was Louis Brandeis. "He reminded me sometimes," said Percy, "of the Victorian bishop's comment on a colleague, that he had often heard of the milk of human kindness, but had never before met the cow." Brandeis and Frankfurter had had occasional correspondence since Frankfurter's graduation from law school, usually having something to do with the United States Attorney's office in New York. Now Frankfurter began to assist with legislation that Brandeis was drawing up for the progressives. Brandeis wrote him in 1911, "Please send me . . . as soon as possible your suggestions for amending the Sherman law," in what was a typical request. Frankfurter always answered. The two men traded names back and forth for appointments to various commissions. From this developed a modest friendship. Frankfurter felt sufficiently free with the older man to talk in 1912 about his forthcoming vacation in Wyoming: "It is the first time that I shall see the West, and I am looking forward to it with rational enthusiasm." The next year Brandeis told a friend to discuss water-power questions with Frankfurter. "He is thoroughly with us on conservation, and is so intelligent that I consider him a power for the right." Brandeis recognized in Frankfurter a quality for which Frankfurter became famous in later years, telling a friend that Frankfurter "has a faculty, rarely equalled, of hearing about 'possible opportunities' for men capable of doing good work."

Frankfurter still admired Brandeis, and enjoyed the relationship. "Brandeis has a depth and an intellectual sweep that are tonical," he told a friend in October 1911. "He has Lincoln's fundamental sympathies." Even then, however, Frankfurter recognized some of Brandeis's faults. "I wish he had [Lincoln's] patience, his magnanimity, his humor." But Frankfurter concluded that Brandeis, with his faults, "is a very big man, one of the most penetrating minds I know; I should like to see him Attorney General of the United States."

Another visitor to the House of Truth was Oliver Wendell Holmes, Jr. Holmes enjoyed Frankfurter's companionship. "Most of the time I am solitary and happy in being so—I can't get Frankfurters to talk with every day."

Holmes offered much to the younger person. There was the sheer physical courage of the man wounded three times in the Civil War. There was his audaciousness: Holmes was the one who had yelled at the tall civilian on the battlefield to get his damned fool head down—the civilian was President Abraham Lincoln. There was Holmes's intellectual accomplishment: *The Common Law* continued as an achievement of legal scholarship. There was his loyalty: Holmes stood by his friends. And there was Holmes's independence as a justice of the Supreme Court. "Long afterwards," Holmes once said, "at a dinner at the White House to some labor leaders, I said to one of them who had been spouting about the Judges: What you want is favor—not justice. But when I am on the job I don't care a damn what you want or what [President] Roosevelt wants—and then repeated my remarks to him. You may think that a trifle crude—but I didn't like to say it behind his back and not to his face, and the fact had justified it."

By 1913, after two years in Washington, Frankfurter again had to rethink his career. His mentor, Stimson, was leaving Washington with the defeated Taft administration. Should Frankfurter go into private practice? Years later he told a story many times, and even told it once to W. Averell Harriman, about Harriman's father, E. H. Harriman, the railroad magnate. The elder Harriman was appearing before the Interstate Commerce Commission, flanked by a large contingent of lawyers. "From time to time your father," as Frankfurter told the story to Averell Harriman,

would turn to them for information or verification and I was so struck with the peremptory way in which he would deal with them. It lies in my mind that on several occasions when they would give him some information he would snap back—yes, snap is the word—"Yes, I know that, but, etc." As a result of this treatment by your father of his lawyers and their almost obsequious deference to him, I remember saying to myself, "If that is the way you have to behave toward powerful clients, I never want to be what is called a leader of the bar." And so I have given this experience as the reason why I decided not to become a leader of the bar.

He wrote to a New York friend, Emory Buckner, that he would consider entering private practice with him "if you promise me that I'll never see a client—even if we get one. I don't deny the great disciplinary value of getting and keeping clients—but there are other things I'd rather do."

The year 1913 was a confusing one for him as he pondered his future. His Law School friends, firmly settled in their careers seven years after graduation, chided him on his professional indecision. New Year's greetings from one included the wish that Frankfurter have "a year of complete professional uncertainty as to the future—for this, I know, lies closest to your heart—I hope the year will not be spoiled by any plans more than sixty days in advance." But, as often happened with Frankfurter, outside forces took a hand and his future was determined that year not for sixty days but, rather, for the next quarter of a century.

In June 1913, without Frankfurter's knowledge, a friend of Frankfurter's, Winfred T. Denison, wrote a member of the Harvard Law School faculty about the possibilities of an appointment there for Frankfurter. "You know what I think of him and what everybody thinks of him down here," said Denison, "and you know him yourself. He has made a tremendous impression with the Supreme Court. The Chief Justice and two of the other Justices have spoken to me with great enthusiasm of his work and I understand their views are shared by other members of the court."

Frankfurter, not certain he should go to Harvard, sought advice from Holmes, Brandeis, and Stimson. Holmes offered no objection. Brandeis replied to Frankfurter's concern that he was not qualified: "I would let those who have the responsibilities for selecting you decide your qualifications and not have you decide that." Stimson offered the only serious objection. He believed Frankfurter belonged in "the center of things." Frankfurter granted the point but argued that "geography may not be a dominating determinant, and if it should turn out that way, after an adequate try, would I be too much on the siding—would not New York be available then?" As it turned out, geography would not be a determinant.

There were no immediate openings, but Dean Ezra Thayer began to inquire if an endowment could be raised. Frankfurter, amenable, was asked his reaction to Jacob H. Schiff, a wealthy Jew, being asked to donate because Frankfurter himself was Jewish. Said Frankfurter: "There is no reason why Mr. Schiff should not feel a legitimate pride in a Jew filling a certain position in any sphere of life." But Frankfurter would not agree to Schiff's being asked for money because of Frankfurter's Jewishness, saying: "My whole feeling is only that my personality and my symbolic significance are subordinate to the job that is to be done up there. And, so far as my own feelings go, I should want the donors to be touched with what should and can be done at Cambridge rather than with the indirect significance of the person who does it."

The endowment was unnecessary because there was an unexpected resignation. A Harvard Law School teacher named Bruce Wyman in 1913 had made speeches in the Boston area supporting the New Haven Railroad—this was shortly before its financial collapse. The belief was that he spoke as an independent expert. Actually, however, he was in the New Haven's pay, $833 a month. When the information about the retainer was disclosed, Wyman resigned from the school. "One thinks of the episode with regret and sympathy," said a history of Harvard Law School. The Wyman vacancy meant Frankfurter could be hired.

Negotiations about salary specifics proceeded through much of the summer of 1913. "All discussions of money matters affecting me are constitutionally and by force of habit disagreeable," Frankfurter said, "and apt to make me peevish. I ought to be more sensible about it, but that, just now, is beside the point." Finally the matter was settled, and Felix Frankfurter was appointed January 12, 1914, as Professor of Law, to begin serving September 1, 1914.

When he went to Harvard, he was only across the Charles River from Louis Brandeis in Boston, and the relationship of the two men changed, from role model and admirer to friends. The Brandeis home, often somber, was open to the young, spirited Frankfurter. "I should like you to know," he told Brandeis in 1915, ". . . how much you and your household have entered into the year's satisfaction." In turn, the Brandeises enjoyed his company. "Your son," Brandeis wrote to Emma Frankfurter, Felix's mother, in 1916, "has won so large a place in our hearts and brought so much of joy and interest into our lives." Alice Brandeis called Frankfurter "our sunshine."

In his relationship with Brandeis, Frankfurter enjoyed a friendship with a prominent lawyer, a leading member of the community, a man who led the kind of life that was begging to appeal to Frankfurter. From Frankfurter, Brandeis acquired the viewpoint of the young man, the opinion of another generation—this became a constant in Brandeis's life in later years, seeking to learn from the young.

This, however, did not cement their blossoming friendship into the "half-brother, half-son" relationship it became. For that, Zionism was needed.

From several sources there is a story that in 1897 Brandeis read a newspaper account of the first Zionist Congress in Basel, Switzerland, and remarked to his wife: "There is a cause to which I could give my life." That story has about it the later-imposed justification or explanation of events. More likely, he had always associated himself with Jewish affairs. In 1905 he spoke at a banquet in connection with the 250th anniversary of the coming of the Jews to North America. He spoke the then-accepted litany, that there should be no such thing as "Catholic-Americans" or "Jewish-Americans," that anything indicating "dual loyalty" should be erased from the American conscience.

Two years later when the various Jewish organizations united into the Federation of Jewish Charities of Boston, Brandeis increased his contribution, which had totaled $105 to several charities, to $175 "in recognition of the advantage of not being called upon to pass upon all the requests which would naturally come in from the numerous organizations."

Family life was nonobservant. His daughter Elizabeth recalled it as "definitely agnostic." There was a Christmas tree, she said, but "it had no religious significance whatever."

Although Brandeis was not observant, among non-Jewish Bostonians there was no question of his background. A non-Jewish friend described the situation this way: "Here the homes of Boston's best 'Brahmins' were flung wide open to one of his rare social attractions. At that time the race prejudice against the Jews was not known in this country, and Mr. Brandeis, as American as any in the land, was the last person to feel, 'I am a Jew.' "

A lawyer named William Denman visited Boston in the mid-1890s and, "I enquired of an elderly Boston lawyer concerning the rather youngish looking man, he was then 40, whom I had seen the week before. I learned he was an astonishing fellow. A Jewish lawyer who had broken through the conventional social barriers of Back Bay and Beacon Hill society."

Still, there was a distance from Jewish issues. Charles Burlingham spent summers in the Boston area and visited Brandeis. "He was very handsome," recalled Burlingham. "He had a distinctly Jewish face to my mind. I got acquainted with his mother and father and spent a summer in Peterstown, Massachusetts. He used to come up too and I used to talk with the old man about the Jewish problems and sometimes Louis would be there, and you'd never know he had any interest in it." Burlingham, a non-Jew, considered Brandeis's one great fault was that "He was a Jew but he never took any interest in the Jews." Even in 1912, when Brandeis was already nationally prominent, that he was Jewish was only "sort of whispered" within some Boston Jewish circles.

Although Brandeis's law firm had Jewish clients, his partners were not Jewish and there were many non-Jewish clients. Law firms outside of Boston, if they needed legal representation in that city, called upon Brandeis. This included the New York firms of Charles Evans Hughes and Sullivan and Cromwell as well as that of Charles Burlingham. These were among the most prominent lawyers and law firms of the time.

By all indications Brandeis was living in a community free from anti-Semitism. Generally this was true for much of the United States during the nineteenth century. But there were few Jews in the United States during that century and most were, like the Brandeis family, of

German descent—educated, cultured, thriving business or professional men, persons who fit in well with the mainstream of American life, almost disappearing into it.

Despite this surface appearance, however, there was an undercurrent of ill feeling. In 1891, for example, a man named James A. Healy wrote in his diary of a journey to a beautiful valley "enclosed in mountains" and said: "Eleven years ago I preempted that spot for my possession, when the millennium of earth should come. But unless the purifying fire of the last day is to clear out the Chinese, Jews, and other foreigners who have taken possession of the town, it will have lost all of its charm."

A 1916 book *Marie of the House d'Anters,* written by Michael Early, described a Jew named Steinberg as "Steiny," a villainous man whose nose "hung down over a disgusted mouth."

James Healy was the Catholic Bishop of Boston, and Michael Early was a Jesuit priest and a leader of the Catholic Church in the same city.

Beginning in the late 1890s that undercurrent surfaced more frequently as the Eastern European Jews arrived in the United States in large numbers, and attitudes toward Jews changed, especially in the large cities where Jews congregated.

This surfacing anti-Semitism struck not only at the Eastern European Jew with his side curls, caftan, and broad-brimmed hat, with his Yiddish, kosher ritual, and prayer three times a day, but also at the established American Jew, whether he was Reform, a member of an Ethical Culture Society, or an agnostic, whether he was a merchant or a distinguished lawyer. "By the way," Louis Brandeis wrote Alfred from Detroit, "anti-Semitism seems to have reached its American pinnacle here. New athletic club with 5000 members and no Jew need apply." In Boston the references to Brandeis as an "oriental"—the euphemism then for being Jewish—became more frequent.

Sometimes the anti-Semitism took a nonviolent form—sneers or the closing of doors, as happened at the athletic club in Detroit—sometimes another form. In 1914 in Georgia, Leo Frank was convicted of murder in an unfair trial, his Jewishness being one of the reasons for the anger against him. Brandeis sought help from Roscoe Pound of the Harvard Law School: "It seems to me of great importance that you should, in a public letter, give expression to your opinion on this subject. Your standing among the lawyers of America is such that what you say men will heed, and it is important that this protest should be made by a non-Jew." Pound and others did make statements, but it was of no use;

Leo Frank was killed by a lynch mob, and anti-Semitism became a staple of Georgia politics for many years.

Brandeis's intense involvement with Judaism and Zionism dates from the garment workers' strike in New York in 1910. Most of those union members were Jews; but unlike him, they had little secular education. They could not move in non-Jewish circles with the ease that he did. They did not dress like him. They did not speak like him. Yet he and they were the same: they were all Jews. That athletic club in Detroit closed its doors to both him and them. Jacob de Haas, Brandeis's friend, early biographer, and Zionist confidant, said of Brandeis among the garment workers: "He . . . pondered long and seriously over a new experience. It was his first real contact with Jews."

Meeting de Haas also pushed Brandeis further along the Zionist road. De Haas, a friend of Theodor Herzl, who had founded modern Zionism, was promoting the cause among American Jews. Shortly after Brandeis had settled the garment workers' strike, de Haas visited him in Boston. At the meeting, de Haas brought up the name of Brandeis's uncle, Lewis Dembitz of Louisville—"a noble Jew," de Haas called him. Brandeis was stirred by memories of his uncle; the two men began to talk of Zionism and its goals. "It was [de Haas] who kindled my interest in Zionism," said Brandeis. "He made me realize its importance, and to him, in large measure, I owe what understanding of it I have attained."

Brandeis learned quickly. Soon after the de Haas meeting, a reporter for the *Jewish Advocate* interviewed Brandeis in his Boston office. This was only five years after Brandeis had spoken out against the hyphenated-American concept. His comments in the 1910 interview showed his attitudes had changed. He spoke of "the members of my people" and said that "To be better Americans we must be better Jews, to be better Jews we must become Zionists."

Another factor pushing Brandeis toward Zionism was the plight of the European Jews, especially the Jews in Russia, Poland, and other Eastern European countries after the First World War began. "You cannot possibly conceive of the horrible sufferings of the Jews in Poland and adjacent countries," Brandeis wrote to his brother Alfred. "These changes of control from German to Russian and Polish anti-Semitism are bringing miseries as great as the Jews ever suffered in all their exiles."

The abuse of the Jews called for a response from all American Jews. At a gathering of Jews in Boston, Brandeis on the platform, Dr. Nahum Sokolow reviewed the situation and concluded that only a Jewish state in Palestine could solve the problem of Jewish immigration and Jewish homelessness. When he finished—and it had been an impassioned address—Brandeis jumped up, and without an introduction, came forward and said: "Thank you, Dr. Sokolow, you have brought me back to my people."

In New York, in 1914, the Zionists decided to organize a Provisional Zionist Committee to take charge of all Zionist affairs. Jacob de Haas suggested Brandeis be its chairman, arguing that, of all those considered, only Brandeis was nationally known and respected among American Jews. Other prominent Jews, Jacob Schiff and Henry Morgenthau, for example, were anti-Zionists and never would have accepted the Zionist chairmanship. And a prominent person was needed, one listened to by wealthy Jews in the United States, for, if the European Jews were to be saved, money would be needed, and in large amounts.

Zionism then was a romantic vision: young men and women escaping from the persecution of European monarchies to found a new land, to turn deserts into farms with the help of science, the knowledge of generations; to feed the hungry, to house the poor and the homeless. The more Brandeis learned, the more intrigued he became. "My sympathy with the Zionist movement rests primarily upon the noble idealism which underlies it," he said. And, "Saturday at dinner—talk on 'wild wheat' given by Julius Rosenwald for Aaron Aaronsohn of the Jewish Agricultural Experiment Station in Palestine. Aaronsohn is a Roumanian Jew who at the age of five emigrated to Palestine with his father who is now a farmer there. The talk was the most thrillingly interesting I have ever heard, showing the possibilities of scientific agriculture and utilization of arid or supposedly exhausted land."

In the United States, Zionism, before Brandeis became its leader, was a ragtag movement, without organization, funds, or political knowhow. There had been various "Zionist" groups in the United States since the early 1900s. Generally the membership consisted of Yiddish-speaking people who gave a coin a week, or a month perhaps, or maybe a year. Between 1898 and 1914 there were at least 125 separate Zionist societies in the United States, some never passing their second birthday. Eventually the many small groups combined into the Federation of American Zionists, but the size of this umbrella organization varied from year to year as affiliated organizations for some slight, real or imagined, went off on their own.

The Federation's annual budget never exceeded $5,200. The largest single donation the Federation ever received prior to 1914 was $200.

Members were urged to pay $5 dues for two years; if by some chance the Federation managed to collect the $5 for the first year, it rarely could for the second.

The Federation's headquarters were located in a corner building in New York, one filled with sweatshops. Other Zionist offices and publications were located in catch-as-catch-can sites. Zionist officials, when Brandeis joined them, never took Brandeis to these offices. Explained one: "We were actually ashamed to bring him there."

Brandeis's zealousness, perhaps his greatest fault, was also his greatest virtue. From a tenuous connection with the Jewish religion, strengthened by his experiences in the early years of the twentieth century, fed by the developing anti-Semitism in the United States and by the plight of European Jews, Brandeis became a Zionist, then leader of the American Zionist movement. He did not stop there. Rabbi Stephen S. Wise, a prominent American Jewish leader in the first half of the twentieth century, ranked Brandeis with Chaim Weizmann, Israel's first President, as "the two men who did most to carry on [Theodor] Herzl's inspiration and to give fulfillment to his dream" of a Jewish state in Palestine.

"He seemed to have been waiting to be of service," said one of his fellow Zionist workers. The disparate activities were brought together in one office. Membership rosters were assembled. Brandeis spent days in consultation with the New York committee, brooking no delays. The Provisional Committee was organized within a week and the Emergency Fund was set up in less than a month. To every Zionist worker Brandeis met there was a barrage of questions, with Brandeis taking notes of the answers, producing memoranda for action, follow-up calls, and recommendations. A joke at the time had it that Louis Brandeis "became a Bar Mitzvah at the age of sixty."

Brandeis reached out for the prominent Jews in the United States. A federal judge named Julian Mack joined. Benjamin N. Cardozo, a New York state judge and descendant of a family of sephardic Jews who had been in the United States almost three hundred years, joined. "I have signed the application with some misgiving," he wrote, "for I have confessed to you that I am not yet an enthusiast. But today, the line seems to be forming between those who are for the cause and those who are against it." Others who followed were Eugene Meyer, Mrs. Joseph Fels, Louis Kirstein—the wealthy Jewish philanthropists of the time.

And Felix Frankfurter joined.

Unlike Brandeis's, Frankfurter's separation from his religion had not been great. While the older man would speak of never having had any connection with the formal religion, Frankfurter had grown up in "not an orthodox, but observant Jewish family as a kind of family institution, a kind of emotional habit." He attended services on the high holy days and reported: "Certainly it was not later than my junior year in college, I think, while I was in the midst of a Yom Kippur service that I looked around as pious Jews were beating their breasts with intensity of feeling and anguishing sincerity," and rose and left the synagogue never to return again. He explained that the services had ceased to have an inner meaning for him and that he believed his presence unfair to those for whom the services did have such a meaning.

But he never forgot the warmth of the rituals. He tried to explain his feeling once to the non-Jewish woman he eventually married, saying:

Around the Passover feast there gathered for me, from childhood up, the richest variety of treasures. It's a joyous and pleasantly sad recital, in prayer and anecdote and song of the story of the days of the children of Israel in Egyptian slavery and their triumphant escape. . . .

And so I have loved this Passover feast, and there was an aching loneliness, as of a dog away from its home, comes the first time I was away from its celebration at home, which was my first year at H[arvard] school in 1904. There was great gayety with my father's conducting of the services and lively playfulness and a very sonorous singing voice. And that is gone—irrevocably. . . . On the eve of the feast it is with me deeply.

Frankfurter did not report experiencing anti-Semitism at Harvard. Although the Law School still possessed the tolerant spirit that had characterized it when Brandeis was a student, there was a difference. Where there had been just a few minority members, now they were becoming a noticeable number, and attitudes were changing. Still, if Frankfurter was snubbed socially, he deigned not to report it.

As a lawyer with a Wall Street law firm and then as an assistant United States attorney, he did not possess as much certainty. Professionally there was no question of his status. Socially there was. One of the early Zionists recalled that "Frankfurter we used to meet in the early years in the East Side when he was Assistant District Attorney. . . . And we would meet—usually in a restaurant where a group of Zionists would assemble, but he showed no sympathy with Zionism until in later years." The picture is of a hanger-on, a person who drifts in, then leaves, returns, never quite certain whether he should cross the street and enter the synagogue. "Frankfurter who really was of our group originally though he hadn't been active in these things, and he came in only through Mr. Brandeis becoming active."

Frankfurter joined Zionism with many others then because Brandeis asked for help with the problem of Jewish refugees in Europe. From that slow start, Frankfurter became an active, a zealous worker. His role in those years was as an administrative aide, an assistant to Brandeis.

In contrast to Frankfurter, Brandeis, who was well known, not only was the administrative whirlwind but also the publicist. He spoke around the country: "Had invitations from Rabbis in St. Paul, Minneapolis, and Omaha to occupy their pulpits this Friday. So you see I am making headway in Judaism." And: "Boston is doing well on relief funds and we are getting the Jewish community stirred. . . . Have raised between $60–$70,000 here for one fund or another and expect to bring it up pretty near $100,000 before we stop." Brandeis also gave his own money. When $60,000 was needed, "I am proposing to pledge personally one-tenth of that amount—that is, $6,000 in monthly instalments of $500 each."

His letters went all over the United States; in 1914 and 1915 it was a major activity, sometimes his only one. If a prominent Jew donated, he received a personal thank-you note from Brandeis with an appeal that, in addition to the money, "we need even more the benefit of your judgment on the important questions which arise from time to time, and I hope we may count also on that." What he really was after was for those he approached to then turn around and approach their friends.

He had not forgotten his talent for gaining publicity in newspapers and magazines. "Billy Hard would be a good man to write on Zionism in *Everybody's*, reaching about 750,000 readers." To Ray Stannard Baker: "I am not altogether sure whether there is material for an article, which we could use in the *American Magazine*, but I believe there is."

Brandeis, at this point, was not equating Judaism with Zionism, but he was equating it with the plight of the Eastern European Jews. However, for some Jews there was, with the willingness to assist oppressed Jews in Europe, a concern that, because of Brandeis's involvement with Zionism, their assistance would be understood as supporting Zionism and would raise the specter of divided citizenship. "I can never be made to believe that one can be entirely loyal to two nations," said Jacob Schiff.

The question bothered not only Jews. "Divided loyalty," or being a hyphenated American, concerned many of the newer immigrants to the United States. Brandeis had spoken against it in 1905. The immigrants were still close to their homelands, to their ethnic origins, but the pressures were on them to cut themselves off from their heritages. A four-act play by Israel Zangwill developed this assimilation theme. The play's central character is writing a symphony about the new American, and he says:

America is God's crucible, the great Melting-Pot where all the races of Europe are melting and re-forming! Here you stand, good folk, think I, when I see them at Ellis Island, here you stand in your fifty groups, with your fifty languages and histories, and your fifty blood hatreds and rivalries. But you won't be long like that, brothers, for these are the fires of God you've come to—these are the fires of God. A fig for your feuds and vendetta! Germans and Frenchmen, Irishmen and Englishmen, Jews and Russians—into the Crucible with you all! God is making the American.

. . . the real American has not yet arrived. He is only in the Crucible, I tell you—he will be the fusion of all races, perhaps the coming superman. Ah, what a glorious Finale for my symphony.

The Zangwill play was as popular as *Uncle Tom's Cabin* had been several generations earlier. Called *The Melting Pot,* it described the assimilation process—"the fusion of all races . . . the coming superman" —as the way of the new world as well as God's will.

Many Jews in America believed they were part of this melting pot, this homogenization. They had established a strong position in the new land. This position stemmed from their economic success, their life-styles, their friendships with non-Jews, and it was a position in American life growing more secure every year. When Theodore Roosevelt was President, a Jew was named to the cabinet for the first time. And in 1911 when Roosevelt spoke before a Reform Jewish group, the first cheers interrupting his talk came when he addressed his audience as "fellow-Americans."

A historian of American Judaism, himself a Reform rabbi, has written:

The first way in which some of the leaders of [German-American Jewry] sought to solve the dilemma of living in two worlds was religious adaptation. What we call Reform Judaism today was the product of the effort (which began about the year 1800) to adjust the conceptual foundations and ceremonial forms of the Jewish religion to the secular and religious environment, to give to the Jewish individual a Jewishly approved opportunity to mingle freely with his neighbors (politically, economically, culturally and socially), to develop for the Jew an identity differentiated no longer by an alien nationality but simply by the house of worship he attended, the holy days he celebrated and the theological tenets to which he adhered.

Even this was not sufficient for some. They embraced Christian sects or joined Ethical Culture societies. This included Mrs. Brandeis's brother-in-law, Felix Adler, who founded the New York Society for Ethical

Culture. Walter Lippmann, at Harvard College at the same time Frankfurter was in the Law School, attempted to erase Jewishness from his
life. He had grown up in New York City, a member of a German-Jewish
family. His biographer wrote that for this group "Judaism was not a
matter of pride or a question to be discussed, but an infirmity that could
be rendered innocuous, perhaps unnoticeable, by being ignored." Unlike Brandeis, who looked with sympathy upon his Eastern European
brethren, members of Lippmann's group looked upon them with scorn,
found them an embarrassment, hoped to disassociate themselves from
them.

Brandeis understood these feelings. He dealt with them by saying one
could be a minority member, a hyphenated American, without re-
nouncing or endangering one's Americanism. Through his actions, his
position in American society, and his devotion to the Zionist cause, he
attacked and helped destroy the melting-pot myth that the people from
fifty different lands, of many colors and religious backgrounds, of different mannerisms and with a variety of tongues, would enter the crucible
and emerge—and should emerge—homogenized. No, say the experience and life of Louis Brandeis and also those of Felix Frankfurter. It
is not necessary for Jew to become Gentile, for black to become white,
for the foreign-born to ignore his or her homeland. America is a land
of many, and that is not a weakness to change but a strength to encourage.

Said Frankfurter: "This is the only country without a racially homogeneous population rooted to a particular soil. We represent a confluence
of peoples who derive their bond of union from their common, intrinsic
human qualities."

Said Brandeis: "My approach to Zionism was through Americanism.
The Jewish renaissance in Palestine will enable us to perform our plain
duty to America."

Jewish spirit, Brandeis said, is "essentially modern and essentially
American," continuing: "Not since the destruction of the Temple have
the Jews in spirit and in ideals been, in these respects, so fully in harmony with the noblest aspirations of the country in which they lived."
Then Brandeis argued that because "the Ghetto walls are falling," Jewish life, the spirit and ideals which had contributed so much to Americanism, "cannot be preserved and developed" without the development of a Jewish community in Palestine from which those ideals and
that spirit can radiate.

A Jewish state in Palestine would not require all Jews to live there, nor would it be impossible for a non-Jew to have citizenship there. "The Jewish State, like every other State, ought to admit to citizenship persons of any nationality."

Why should American Jews be interested in a Jewish state, beyond that state's being a center of Jewish spiritual and idealistic development? "Obviously," Brandeis answered, "no individual should be subjected anywhere, by reason of the fact that he is a Jew, to a denial of any common right or opportunity enjoyed by non-Jews. But Jews collectively should likewise enjoy the same right and opportunity to live and develop as do other groups of people." They could not do this, he maintained, without a homeland as other groups had. Mere legal equality—the dispensation by the state of equality—was not sufficient. He argued that no one familiar with Jewish history could doubt that law could be changed. "Many of those in Russia and Roumania who are now the severest sufferers from the Jewish disabilities," Brandeis said, "are the lineal descendants of those who had equality under the law and who had in Spain and in Southern France social equality as well." Those were difficult words to accept and believe in the United States, in the 1910s before the Nazi experience, that government-sanctioned religious freedom and equality might someday be erased.

Only, Brandeis argued, when Jews can live as other groups will their disabilities end. "We can scarcely conceive of an individual German or Frenchman living and developing without some relation to the contemporary German or French life and culture . . . the solution of the Jewish Problem necessarily involves the continued existence of the Jews as Jews."

He acknowledged there would be problems, and to that he answered: "Wer Nichts wagt gewinnt Nichts"—who dares nothing, gains nothing. "It never has been possible for the Jew 'to play safe' or for anyone else indeed 'to play safe,' who has sought advances in conditions." When he wrote that line in 1915, Brandeis had spent almost two decades refusing to play safe and knew what he was speaking about; the social discourtesies and the public criticisms from former acquaintances now were numerous. "But to my mind," he continued, "the thing involving the greatest risk in the world is not to attempt to advance," and then he added in reference to the particular Jewish problem, "and if not Zionism, what is the alternative?"

5

With Woodrow Wilson

Late in 1911, the progressives believed they had an opportunity to capture the White House the next year. No Democrat had been President since 1897, and the Republicans were split between the unpopular Taft in the White House and Theodore Roosevelt, who acted like the candidate he said he was not. A quixotic group, skeptical of trusts, against child labor and sweatshops, and for the farmer and free enterprise, the progressives possessed the idealism but so far had lacked the know-how and numbers to win elections.

They gathered around the candidacy of Robert La Follette, the Republican senator from Wisconsin. They also courted Louis Brandeis because of his reputation as a "people's lawyer" and his role in the Ballinger episode. He joined them, speaking for La Follette and writing letters to his friends, describing the Wisconsin senator as "just the man whom the country needs at this critical time, possessing great courage, indomitable will . . . constructive ability, and that deep sympathy with the working man." Brandeis stayed with La Follette well into the spring of 1912, although after February the candidacy had lost its energy. With Theodore Roosevelt's growing interest in a third-party nomination and Woodrow Wilson's own drive among the Democrats, there was little progressive support remaining for "Fighting Bob" La Follette.

With La Follette out of the running and Theodore Roosevelt angry at Brandeis because of the Ballinger affair, Brandeis supported Wilson, who was nominated by the Democrats in July. A former president of Princeton University and then Governor of New Jersey, Wilson was a southerner who hid his political shrewdness behind the demeanor of a professor above politics.

Brandeis's shift to Wilson may have cost him a seat in the Senate. "There has been more or less talk in the past among the Progressive Republicans of wanting to put me up for the Senate," he said, "but my coming out for Wilson will doubtless dampen what ardor there was." Although he had never met Wilson, Brandeis was impressed with his progressivism, "particularly his discussion of economic problems," and wrote to many of his progressive friends asking them to support Wilson.

One whom Brandeis could not budge was his young friend Felix Frankfurter. "With Wilson nominated . . ." Brandeis wrote him, "it seemed to me that the duty of Progressives was clearly to support Wilson and practically capture the Democratic party."

Frankfurter had come to maturity in the Roosevelt era and could not shake its impact. He believed that "The raucous voices and pugnacities of the Roosevelt days were not merely reflexes of his personality. Rather does Theodore Roosevelt appear to have been a function of his time— the first President to express the need for adjusting our political system to the changes resulting from the practical cessation of pioneer conditions and the increasing concentration of economic power." Also, Roosevelt was the first President Frankfurter had known personally. "What I really want to send you is some indication of what you mean to me, in dealing with the raw stuff of life," he wrote to Roosevelt. Also, Frankfurter found Woodrow Wilson "as a human being decidedly less than appealing."

Because he was still in the War Department with Stimson, Frankfurter did not actively campaign for Roosevelt, although to his friends he made no secret of his feelings, even to the point of issuing one of his few criticisms of Brandeis, who, Frankfurter thought, had given "a very unfair slant to the Progressive position on [the trust] issue."

On one Roosevelt position, however, Frankfurter strongly disagreed; the issue was one that plagued Frankfurter and the nation for years: What to do about the federal judiciary, especially the Supreme Court. Although Brandeis had made his point about the validity of social experience before the courts in the *Muller* v. *Oregon* case, the courts still were the obstacle to advancing social legislation. State laws regulating working conditions continued to fall before the judiciary. "The sacrosanct notion of our judiciary must be hit whenever it can be effectively," Frankfurter wrote in 1911. "There is a growing realization of this on the part of some wise judges but there is a natural tendency of self reverence by the members of an institution." But that attack was a general one; what to do eluded Frankfurter then as it would in later years.

Theodore Roosevelt and his new Bull Moose party believed they knew the answer. In 1910 Roosevelt was speaking of the "purely negative activity of the judiciary" in striking down state laws. Two years later, when he was on the verge of becoming a formal candidate, Roosevelt spoke of limiting the courts as "the highest and wisest kind of conservatism." Soon he spoke of "recall" of judges and of judicial decisions—allowing a popular vote to oust a judge or overrule a court decision. In its platform, the Bull Moose party backed away from those devices, seeking recall only in connection with state court decisions and also asking for wider supervision of the state courts by the federal judiciary. Although avoiding the real issue, the platform statement reflected the public's concern—a concern that would erupt a quarter of a century later in a struggle between the federal judiciary and another Roosevelt.

Frankfurter believed judicial recall too extreme, too violative of the separation of judicial and political power. In August 1912, when the American Bar Association condemned recall, Frankfurter voted for the condemnation "and I should vote for it again." But, as Frankfurter left the meeting, he knew the problem had not been solved. "The conditions of life have changed; the shibboleths remain," he said. What "is reasonably defensible on economic or social grounds, whether or not it accords with our individual notion of economics," he believed, "cannot be offensive on constitutional grounds."

The presidential campaign settled down to a fight between Wilson and Roosevelt, with Taft and the remnants of the Republican party on the sidelines. Wilson needed the support of the La Follette progressives; some came to him. La Follette himself refused to endorse Wilson but did not object to his supporters' campaigning for the New Jersey governor. A major issue was trusts.

"Trusts" was the slogan word in 1912, around which economic arguments revolved, the target of the politicians. The trusts were giant money machines, gobbling up small companies, resources, and individual workers and regurgitating enormous profits for stockholders. Still, the trusts were not the problem but the symbol of the problem. The industrial revolution in the United States after the Civil War had spawned a new economic order. The trusts were at one end of the spectrum; the unemployed and the bankrupt were at the other. Between them were the consumers, often victims of rigged prices and shoddy production techniques. The problem was how to bring those two ends of the spectrum into balance, with fairness to the consumers, and that meant, what role should the government have? The businessmen, those cashing in on the trusts mania, wanted the government out of the marketplace entirely. The progressives and liberals wanted government regulation of basic industries such as power and transportation. Between those two sides were most Americans, and most American politicians, wondering if there was not some middle way between no government involvement and complete government control. Brandeis contributed to fashioning that middle way, establishing the course the United States followed for most of the twentieth century.

Roosevelt hit Wilson hard on the trust issue. "Every big crooked financier is against us and in favor of either Mr. Wilson or Mr. Taft," he said. Wilson did not see himself as destroying the trusts. He understood that the economy had changed. "I dare say," he acknowledged, "we shall never return to the old order of individual competition." But, as he was learning, a politician must not only say what he will not do, he also must say what he will do. For that Wilson turned to Louis Brandeis.

When Wilson was governor, Brandeis's name had been suggested to him occasionally as a lawyer to serve on a state commission or to represent the state in court. Although Brandeis never was called on in those years, the imprint was made on Wilson's mind and Wilson understood and appreciated the significance of Brandeis's endorsement in July. During that summer, Norman Hapgood—friend of Brandeis and now avid Wilson supporter—invited Brandeis to write a series of articles for *Collier's* on trusts. Brandeis wrote not only the articles but also editorials for the magazine. Soon bits and pieces from the Brandeis writings began to appear in Wilson's speeches.

At the end of August, a Wilson aide telegraphed Brandeis, inviting him to Sea Girt, New Jersey, to meet the candidate. "Was very favorably impressed with Wilson," said Brandeis of the meeting. "He is strong, simple, serious, openminded, eager to learn and deliberate." The two men, meeting for a luncheon that stretched out to three hours, produced what became Wilson's "New Freedom." One who had a long talk with Brandeis some years later about that luncheon reported that Brandeis "did not share at all Wilson's idea of individual guilt." Brandeis believed an individual should not have to be a martyr and challenge the system; rather, "The system must be changed." Brandeis continued: "Man's works have outgrown man. Man has remained the same." This was similar to Brandeis's earlier attack on bigness as the enemy. However, at this point in the 1912 Wilson campaign, he changed. The man known then and for years after as the opponent of bigness, the Jeffersonian who preached that individuals should not step beyond their capabilities, the individual who prized smallness in the economy—this man, as he came close to power, knew the trusts could not be destroyed, were too much a part of the American economy to be erased. He would devise a scheme to deal with them rather than destroy them.

Theodore Roosevelt's Bull Moose party called for the regulation of trusts; Brandeis proposed instead government action to insure competition. His ideas were summed up in this statement for Wilson:

The two parties differ fundamentally regarding the economic policy which the country should pursue. The Democratic Party insists that competition can and should be maintained in every branch of private industry; that competition can and should be restored in those branches of industry in which it has been suppressed by the trusts and that, if at any future time monopoly should appear to be desirable in any branch of industry, the monopoly should be a public one —a monopoly owned by the people and not by the capitalists.

Brandeis then would have the government step in with legal action only when an industry became so large as to stifle competition and operate monopolies only when necessary. In contrast, he said, Theodore Roosevelt's party

insists that private monopoly may be desirable in some branches of industry, or at all events, is inevitable; and that existing trusts should not be dismembered or forcibly dislodged from those branches of industry in which they have already acquired a monopoly, but should be made "good" by regulation. In other words, the New Party declares that private monopoly in industry is not necessarily evil, but may do evil; and that legislation should be limited to such laws and regulations as should attempt merely to prevent the doing of evil.

Once Wilson accepted the Brandeis approach, Brandeis did not limit himself. Between October 2 and October 25, he made twenty speeches for Wilson, appearing in New England, Pittsburgh, Detroit, St. Paul, and Omaha to advocate the "New Freedom."

Wilson won the election, probably only because the Republican vote split. He had 6.3 million-votes; Roosevelt and Taft together had 7.5 million. Wilson did not do as well as had William Jennings Bryan, the Democratic candidate who lost in 1896, 1900, and 1908. Clearly he had needed all the support he had received, and every person who had supported him deserved reward. "You were yourself a great part of the victory," Wilson told Brandeis. But Brandeis was not among those rewarded.

Almost from their first meeting, there was speculation that Wilson, if elected, would appoint Brandeis to his cabinet, probably as Attorney General. During the campaign, Brandeis tried to stop such talk, and after Wilson's victory Brandeis was quiet about the matter. Others were not.

Democratic politicians from New England charged that Brandeis never had been a Democrat but was actually a maverick Republican. Others felt that Brandeis was not the man to be Attorney General. Ezra Thayer, who once had worked in Brandeis's office and now was dean of Harvard Law School, believed Brandeis "had grave faults and did not play fair and would hit foul blows,—no idea of sportsmanlike conduct or of Anglo-Saxon idea of fair play."

But it was not the politicians and the Thayers who would destroy Brandeis's chance; it was the money men. Henry Lee Higginson, a Brahmin whom Brandeis had offended, approached Cleveland H. Dodge, a wealthy contributor to the Wilson campaign, and persuaded him to speak to the President-elect. That ended consideration of Brandeis for the attorney generalship.

Norman Hapgood then suggested to Wilson that Brandeis become Secretary of Commerce and Labor (the two departments then were joined). Wilson toyed with the idea for a while but finally decided to bow to the New England powers and not appoint Brandeis to any cabinet position.

There had been a Jew in a President's cabinet before, Oscar S. Straus, Secretary of Commerce and Labor from 1906 to 1909, and there was little public discussion of Brandeis's religion. One commentary, dealing specifically with Brandeis's Jewishness, appeared in *Life,* then a humor magazine. It read:

And in Mr. Brandeis' case the matter is complicated by the fact that he is a Jew. Common, Gentile altruists are hard enough to understand, but that Moses may be a tenant of that unmeasured area in the back of Mr. Brandeis' head makes observers grope all the more. There is no religious prejudice about it. It is not generally known, and we never heard, whether Mr. Brandeis is a Jew in religion. The perplexity is about the Jewish mind when its operations are complicated by altruism; how it works; whether it is constructive or merely combative; whether it is duly tempered with compunctions; whether it duly respects the status quo of a so-called Christian civilization and would use a decent moderation in improving it.

Brandeis may have wanted the appointment; he was, for him, unusually responsive to his supporters. When a Boston friend publicly recommended Brandeis for the appointment in a newspaper interview, Brandeis made a point of thanking him. Felix Frankfurter had denounced the attacks against Brandeis, sending a copy of his statement to Brandeis. "I thank you for yours of the 4th," Brandeis, who rarely conceded emotion, wrote back, "and for the enclosure, which gives me much satisfaction." Still, he reacted stoically. "I am inclined to think that so far as I personally am concerned the dispostion which has been made of the Cabinet matter is best," he told a friend.

Still enamored of Wilson's politics, however, Brandeis did not allow his failure to gain a cabinet post to influence his relationship with the President. Brandeis did not attend the inauguration but was in Washington a few days later to meet with Wilson. "Had a good private talk with the President this evening for an hour," Brandeis wrote to his brother on March 10, less than a week after the inaugural.

Both inside and outside of Washington, Brandeis was viewed as a man who could pull the required political strings. From Wisconsin came an appeal to help a professor get a job drafting a tax bill. Within the cabinet, members suggested to each other that they follow Brandeis's advice, read his memoranda, listen to him for job recommendations. A few weeks into the new administration, Wilson asked Brandeis to become the chairman of the Commission on Industrial Relations. Brandeis turned down the invitation, but made the refusal sufficiently gentle so as not to endanger his relations with the President and recommended several other men.

When Brandeis was not named Attorney General, the post went to James C. McReynolds of Tennessee, a tall, lean man, handsome, with a courtly southern air. For the next twenty-eight years the McReynolds-Brandeis-Frankfurter relationship would be one of the more interesting in American history, as McReynolds sat with both of them on the Supreme Court—they, two of the most prominent of American Jews, and he, as he later showed, an anti-Semite.

McReynolds had been recommended to Wilson, who had never met him, by his aide Colonel Edward M. House. House had not been enthusiastic about Brandeis for the post, saying the Bostonian was "more than a lawyer; he is a publicist." McReynolds had a reputation as a fighter against trusts, House argued, and "His character and legal attainments are of the highest." Brandeis praised the appointment. "McReynolds will make an excellent Attorney General," he said. "You may remember what I said of his work when speaking of the tobacco trust prosecution." As he did to all appointed to the cabinet, Brandeis wrote McReynolds a congratulatory note. "In deciding upon you," wrote Brandeis, "for Attorney General President Wilson has made the wisest possible choice."

In 1913 the two men's correspondence was cordial, and McReynolds frequently sought Brandeis's advice. Once when McReynolds was looking for someone to act as an assistant attorney general on an especially difficult trust case, McReynolds reacted favorably to Brandeis's name. The offer never was made, apparently because the case had to be brought in Kentucky, Brandeis's home state. Brandeis, in turn, looked sympathetically on the plight of the cabinet officer. After a lengthy session with McReynolds, Brandeis wrote his wife that the Attorney General "is very tired and I think must look back longingly to the days of obscurity."

Whatever McReynolds's ability as a government prosecutor of trusts, it did not hold over when he became Attorney General. Why he eventually left the cabinet depends upon who tells the story. According to one Wilson confidant, McReynolds got into an argument over who should control the construction of the new Justice Department building. "The situation grew tense," goes this account, "and the President soon eased it by naming McReynolds as associate justice of the Supreme Court." Some years later the *New York Times* reported that McReynolds was moved from the Justice Department to the Supreme Court because "he refused to make a political grab-bag of the Department." Josephus Daniels, an intimate member of the Wilson Administration, said Wilson appointed McReynolds to the Supreme Court to "get rid of him." On only one point do the explanations coincide; not one suggests that McReynolds was of the caliber and professional attainments to be a Supreme Court justice.

When McReynolds was appointed to the Supreme Court in August 1914, the President appointed Thomas Watt Gregory of Texas as the new Attorney General.

For three years while a lawyer in Boston, Louis Brandeis was an unofficial adviser to Wilson in the White House. Neither a government official nor aspirant for office, he was available to the President and to members of the Wilson administration, frequently involved in strategy and legislative drafting. Wilson respected him as a person and welcomed his ideas on economic policy. In those years, Brandeis established himself as a role model that in subsequent years many followed; Felix Frankfurter learned well from his mentor in these Wilson years and played the same role himself in another President's administration two decades later.

Currency reform was one of the first major problems of the Wilson administration. The United States had been without a central bank for almost eighty years. Without the authority to manage the money supply, Wilson believed, the nation never could bring the economy under control. There were two proposals before him to establish a national banking system, one controlled by bankers and the other by federal officials. The liberal members of his party wanted the system under government control and the conservatives wanted it in the hands of the bankers.

Wilson met with Brandeis on June 11, 1913. Brandeis insisted at that meeting that "power to issue currency should be vested exclusively in Government officials." He argued: "The conflict between the policies of the Administration and the desires of the financiers and of big business, is an irreconcilable one. Concessions to the big business interests must in the end prove futile." Wilson, knowing that for years Brandeis had been critical of bankers and their use—he would say "abuse"—of other people's money, probably already had made up his mind on the issue and was only looking for support or, perhaps, a framework for his arguments. The result was the Federal Reserve Board, made up of government officials rather than bankers, which became one of the significant accomplishments of the Wilson administration.

The second major legislative matter involving Brandeis during the early Wilson years concerned transforming the campaign antitrust rhetoric into reality. Late in 1913, Brandeis sent a long memorandum to Franklin K. Lane, Secretary of the Interior, with his suggestions for legislation. The memorandum, which Lane had requested, repeated basically what Brandeis had told Wilson during the campaign a year earlier, and Wilson incorporated much of it in his message to Congress in January 1914. "You are right about the President's message," a jubilant Brandeis wrote to his brother. "He has paved the way for about all I have asked for and some of the provisions specifically are what I got into his mind at my first interview."

Three proposals evolved. One became the Clayton Antitrust Act, which treated a number of business practices that threatened competition. The second was a proposal by Representative Sam Rayburn of Texas to give the government some control of the issuance of railroad securities. This had been developed with Brandeis's assistance but failed of passage and remained on the sidelines for twenty years until, with the help of Felix Frankfurter, a version of it became law.

The third proposal, to establish the Federal Trade Commission, was a provision in the Clayton Act legislation but attracted attention on its own merits. As first presented to Congress by Attorney General McReynolds, the commission was only an investigative body, with powers to recommend but not to act. Liberal members of Congress, with Brandeis's support, added a long list of proscribed activities. There was concern, however. George Rublee, who had worked with Brandeis on the Ballinger affair and had been brought to Washington by him to work on developing the Commission, explained the problem. "These definitions," he said, "expressed in abstract language with numerous qualifications, appear not only to be obscure, but also to be susceptible of interpretation in a manner that would interfere with legitimate business operations. Moreover, they left open a wide field for the exercise of ingenuity in devising other practices destructive of competition." It would be a lawyer's bill, one that the legal profession would spend a great deal of time learning to circumvent. Rublee suggested to the House leaders that the specifics be eliminated from the bill and the "unfair competition" phrase, which had a specific meaning in antitrust law, be inserted, to allow the law to be interpreted according to legal precedents that had been building up. When the House leaders would not go along, "I then decided to make one more effort in behalf of our idea by going to President Wilson and discussing it directly with him," said Rublee.

Rublee, Representative Raymond B. Stevens, Democrat of New Hampshire, a congressman who also agreed with this approach, and Brandeis, who only learned of the proposed change overruling his own approach the day of the meeting, met with the President at the White House. "We had our appointment for half an hour but actually the interview lasted considerably beyond the time allotted to us," Rublee recalled. "We'd arranged that Stevens, as Congressman, who'd made the appointment should make the opening statement to the President. He should say why we'd come and so forth. Then I was to make the main statement exploring the matter, why it was a good thing and why we thought it should be done."

He remembered that "it was a beautiful late May or June day. It was such a beautiful summer day that the meeting was outdoors in the garden on the south side of the White House. I remember the President was beautifully dressed—white linen—and looked very well."

Rublee spoke after Stevens. "When I finished speaking," said Rublee, "to my great surprise, Brandeis entered the fray with enthusiasm and backed me up strongly. The President was curious about what we had to say from the beginning. It wasn't merely a perfunctory interest. Of course, the fact that Brandeis was there made him think that there was something serious afoot."

Wilson accepted the change. "I remember that on the way out," said Rublee, "Brandeis took my arm and said, 'That's the most remarkable interview that I've ever been present at. I've never seen anything like this before.'" Brandeis was so enthusiastic about the change that, at Wilson's request, he hurried to Capitol Hill to secure the agreement of two senators. Ultimately the Federal Trade Commission was organized to counter monopolistic business practices along the lines recommended by Rublee that day.

In November 1915, Louis Brandeis became fifty-nine years old. His appearance had not changed much from his earlier years. His face was thin, tanned from canoeing and riding in his carriage, his eyes absorbing, the great shock of blue-gray hair thrusting out from his head. His dress had a casual air about it. Even when he appeared before a Congressional committee, he rarely bothered with the frock-coat-and-striped-trousers uniform. At one hearing he appeared in a tweed suit and a shirt with a soft collar. When he cross-examined, he was likely to slouch slightly and thrust his hands deep into his pockets. A newspaper article of the time described him as "a man of an engaging smile and quiet manner."

He continued his abstemious life. The furniture in his house on Otis Place was even more bedraggled than it had been when Josephine Goldmark and Florence Kelley had visited him late in 1907 to discuss the *Muller* v. *Oregon* case. His enjoyments were reading and entertaining small groups of friends in his house. He did not, and never did, own an automobile.

Brandeis enjoyed being with his family; Sunday picnics were a mainstay for him, his wife, and their two daughters. He watched his diet, exercised moderately, spent time out of doors, and found moments to relax. "I am in excellent shape," he wrote to his brother. "Everybody seems to say: 'Was der lebt noch?' But with a man who would rather fight than eat, the surprise is unwarranted."

A sense of humor still seemed lacking. Edward F. McClennen, his law partner at this time, later denied that, saying that when preoccupied with a legal problem, Brandeis allowed nothing to interfere with his concentration. "Away from the stress of this, if his mind was free, he was one of the quickest to perceive a humorous situation and to present things in a humorous way." McClennen told of the time Brandeis "could hardly repress his mirth until the interview was over, where the client told him what a successful year the client had had and started to relate the story by saying that his wife had died in April."

Brandeis's secretary of twenty-three years, Alice Grady, said that she had never seen him lose his temper. She described him as "a tireless worker. He rises early, and works late. He hates to leave work undone. He never goes to theatres, and cares nothing for games. He used to say, 'If there is going to be anything doing, I want to be doing it, not watching somebody else do it.' "

McClennen once described Brandeis as a "Puritan," but then hastily backed away, saying that Brandeis had "neither belief nor complacency in the eternal damnation of those who disagreed with him." Actually Brandeis was imbued with a sense of modern religion, that one should act in a righteous manner but not for the prospect of reward. "He got his joy, his happiness," said McClennen, "out of the performance itself."

Once when discussing proposals to limit the number of hours of workers, the point was made that he and the other lawyers in his firm worked much longer hours, and Brandeis replied: "You must remember that we are practicing a profession which gives us, without more, a full enjoyment of life. These men are engaged largely in a monotonous pursuit that must be relieved by time for enjoyment outside."

He was also generous with his money. Norman Hapgood had left *Collier's* for *Harper's Weekly,* and Brandeis seemed determined to make a financial success of that publication single-handedly. He bought subscriptions to the magazine for New England libraries, paying $822, and persuaded others to pay for subscriptions for libraries in other parts of the United States. When he received a check for an article he had written, Brandeis returned it, explaining, "I don't want to be paid for anything I do for Harper's until after it has reached the state of earning dividends on common stock." He sent Hapgood lists of possible subscribers, and became excited when he learned that sales of the magazine at one Boston newsstand had jumped from fifteen copies a week to two hundred. For some years Brandeis also had been assisting financially various individuals involved in public works, and he broadened his support at this stage of his life.

Brandeis continued willing to lend his name to causes. When he received a detailed report that a union radical named Joe Hillstrom had been unjustly convicted in a Utah murder trial, he did not hesitate to write George Sutherland, Republican Senator from that state, to ask him to intercede. There was no intercession by Sutherland or others, and Joe Hillstrom, after he was executed, became a legend in union folklore as Joe Hill.

In Boston he lived the social life he apparently enjoyed. If the Brahmins had turned against him, he still belonged to several clubs, had friends important to him. The hovering anti-Semitism in Boston was not allowed by Brandeis to intrude into the small house on Otis Place or the office on the top floor of the building on Devonshire Street. There occasionally were problems. He recommended a friend and Harvard graduate, Henry Hurwitz, for the Harvard Club. When Hurwitz was turned down, Brandeis wrote him, "You are evidently a victim of my enemies." There also was difficulty in 1915 with his joining the Cosmos Club in Washington. The appeal of the club was its dining and residential facilities, important for a person who spent much time in Washington.

When the admissions committee delayed acting on the application, Felix Frankfurter, already a member, sent a letter from Boston expressing amazement. "It would seem that there are very few men in this country who should be more eagerly welcomed than Mr. Brandeis by a club whose aim of membership is men 'who are distinguished in a learned profession or in public service,' " wrote Frankfurter. He called Brandeis "an inventor of ideas propelled by a great moral force." Frankfurter knew the cause of the delay. "I am quite aware," he continued in the letter, "that in the process [Brandeis] has offended and alienated good men and true. That is quite inevitable in the case of a man who feels as passionately, who sees stupidity and wrong as profoundly, and believes as uncompromisingly as does Mr. Brandeis."

The admissions committee wrote Frankfurter that the application had been delayed because of charges against Brandeis of unprofessional conduct, making irresponsible statements, unethical conduct in his collection of fees, and of being blacklisted by most Boston clubs. Frankfurter refuted each of the charges. He also asked Dean Ezra Thayer of the Harvard Law School to write a letter of endorsement. Thayer, overcoming his 1913 fear that Brandeis lacked the "Anglo-Saxon idea of fair play," wrote a letter which, perhaps more than any other document of the time, described Brandeis at a point in his life when many individuals consider their professional activities coming to a close.

Thayer had known Brandeis for twenty years, since he had entered the older man's office as a student. Thayer stayed in the Brandeis office for eight years, rising to be a partner in the firm, before joining another Boston firm. At Harvard, Thayer continued to have contact with Brandeis, who was a member of the Visiting Committee to the Law School and who continued as an active and interested alumnus. Thayer said that he had met everyone in the bar and in the Boston community "least favorably disposed toward Mr. Brandeis" and "I can fairly claim to qualify as a pretty competent and pretty disinterested expert upon him." The letter to the Cosmos Club, dated March 3, 1915, continued:

It would be a grave mistake for the Club to exclude Mr. Brandeis—the sort of action which would reflect on the Club and not on him. . . . Socially Mr. Brandeis is in every way desirable. His accomplishments and attractions together with his club membership in Boston make it plain beyond question that a vote against him must be based not upon social considerations but upon a condemnation of his moral character. A club can hardly be justified in passing such a judgement unless it has satisfied itself that the facts warrant it. I feel confident that this is not so here. Mr. Brandeis, of course, has his defects. Foremost among them are the defects (joined with the merits) of the advocate. He is an eager and strenuous partisan, throwing himself utterly into his side of a case, and increasingly unable to do justice to the other side. Furthermore he is a severe and not always a fair fighter. The natural result of these qualities in a man of his ability is to leave great soreness in his adversaries after the complaint is over. If you go to the bottom of the different complaints of him you will, I think, always find that it is this upon which it rests. It is *his adversary* only who has reason to complain. Stories suggesting disloyalty or unfairness toward his associates or clients are baseless; indeed the trouble is just the other way. His notions of loyalty to a client are extravagant, and this is one of the things from which the adversary suffers. When this is said the end is reached of the legitimate criticism of Mr. Brandeis. To set against them are merits of various kinds, including, among others, genuine public spirit and a high sense of duty. If the sort of facts which I have mentioned were made the basis of exclusion from club membership, and the test were consistently applied, the result so far as the bar is concerned might be startling. I think you will agree that considering the weakness of human nature in a contentious profession there are many lawyers in good odor of whom the things I have said above, and more, would be true. The peculiarity of Mr. Brandeis' case lies in his ability, and in the financial and political standing of the people whom he has hurt. The Ballinger case makes a good illustration.

On March 15, 1915, Louis Brandeis was elected a member of the Cosmos Club.

He was by this time virtually in the "elder statesman" category. In 1915 he was invited to deliver the Fourth of July oration at Faneuil Hall in Boston. This was a major city celebration and previous speakers had included Harrison Gray Otis, John Quincy Adams, Lemuel Shaw, Oliver Wendell Holmes, Henry Cabot Lodge, and Edward Everett Hale.

Brandeis, the child of immigrants and friend of immigrants, spoke of how the United States always had admitted the homeless—"We had faith that thereby we would best serve ourselves and mankind. This faith has been justified." Together the immigrant and the native-born

American had come into harmony on their ideals and aspirations. What were these ideals? Brandeis then spoke of the development of the individual for his good and the community's good. This meant, he said, "we become necessarily our brother's keepers." He spoke of making education available to all and said that people must be free, but "men are not free if dependent industrially upon the arbitrary will of another," he insisted. "Some curb must be placed upon capitalistic combination."

He also talked, this man who had developed for the working people of Massachusetts a form of private social insurance, about the need for each individual to have "some degree of financial independence" for the later years of his life.

Brandeis then spoke of how in Europe the struggles had been against the concept of aristocracy, of the superman. America, he said, had rejected that concept to believe "that each race had something of peculiar value which it can contribute to the attainment of those high ideals for which it is striving. America has believed that we must not only give to the immigrant the best that we have, but must preserve for America the good that is in the immigrant and develop in him the best of which he is capable." No more melting pot. "America has believed that in differentiation, not in uniformity," said Brandeis, "lies the path of progress. It acted on this belief; it has advanced human happiness, and it has prospered."

At the beginning of 1916, Brandeis was invited to speak on "The Living Law" before the Chicago Bar Association. He talked there of law developing in response to demands, needs, and understandings. He spoke at great length about his own role in developing the concept of reasonableness before the courts. Brandeis reviewed the travels of the lawyer from generalist to specialist and said that could not be reversed but must be dealt with by broader education—"Study of economics and sociology and politics which embody the facts and present the problems of today." And he closed with a story that revealed much about how Louis Dembitz Brandeis viewed the law.

The story was of a man named Bogigish, "a native of the ancient city of Ragusa off the coast of Dalmatia,—a deep student of law, who," said Brandeis, "after gaining some distinction at the University of Vienna, and in France, became Professor at the University of Odessa. When Montenegro was admitted to the family of nations, its Prince concluded that, like other civilized countries, it must have a code of law." Brandeis told how, because Bogigish's fame had reached Montenegro, the Prince arranged for Bogigish to come to Montenegro and undertake the task of preparing a legal code. "But instead of utilizing his great knowledge of laws to draft a code," said Brandeis, "he proceeded to Montenegro, and for two years literally made his home with the people—studying everywhere their customs, their practices, their needs, their beliefs, their points of view. Then he embodied in law the life which the Montenegrins lived. They respected that law; because it expressed the will of the people."

The Thayer letter with its homage to Brandeis had showed the man's position in the community. Brandeis's Fourth of July oration had underscored his own devotion to American democracy, his belief in the obligations of citizens to other citizens, and the place of the minority member in American society. And with the talk on "The Living Law" he had made clear his alignment with Oliver Wendell Holmes's insistence that the life of the law is experience and not logic.

This was Brandeis at a point which for others would be near the end of their professional lives, a time when one begins to relax, to reminisce, to putter; a time to watch life wind down. But for Louis Brandeis it was the beginning of another, even more controversial career than he had previously known. On January 28, 1916, President Woodrow Wilson nominated Louis Dembitz Brandeis, son of immigrants, minority member, scourge of the rich, successful lawyer, to the United States Supreme Court.

6

Mr. Justice Brandeis

Louis Brandeis was in Washington late in January to attend a dinner at the home of Treasury Secretary McAdoo and to file papers at the Supreme Court in connection with two cases. Associate Justice Joseph R. Lamar of the Supreme Court had died earlier in the month but no names were on the gossip circuit to replace him. "It is fairly certain today," commented one of the associate justices to a friend, "that neither the President nor the Attorney General has reached anything approximating a definite conclusion upon the subject." Brandeis did nothing to seek the position. Asked years later if he ever anticipated going on the Supreme Court, Brandeis replied: "I never thought about it—I never worked *for* anything. I merely went ahead with what I had to do."

Attorney General Gregory recommended him to Wilson. The President probably did not require much persuasion. He had relied on Brandeis, trusted his judgment, accepted him as a progressive, and perhaps felt some guilt about his failure to appoint Brandeis to the cabinet three years earlier.

Whatever Wilson's motivations, he did not spell them out after the nomination. He told a senator that the nomination was "the wisest that could possibly have been made, and I feel that few things have arisen more important to the country or to the party than the matter of his confirmation." But that was almost in passing. Comments he made later that year, however, give a clue to his reasons. "The day of cold thinking, of fine-spun constitutional argument, is gone, thank God," he said late in 1916. "We do not now discuss so much what the Constitution of the United States is as what the constitution of human nature is. . . . The Constitution, like the Sabbath, was made for man and not man for the Constitution. I have known of some judges who did not perceive that. . . . But judges of that sort have now gently to be led to a back seat.

... And men must be put forward whose whole comprehension is that law is subservient to life and not life to law."

Brandeis learned of the appointment a few days before the announcement but said nothing until the public statement was made, then wrote his brother Alfred in Louisville: "I am not entirely sure that I am to be congratulated, but I am glad the President wanted to make the appointment and I am convinced, all things considered, that I ought to accept."

Alice Brandeis wrote Alfred a few days later: "I had some misgivings for Louis has been such a 'free man' all these years but as you suggested —his days of 'knight erranting' must have, in the nature of things, been over before long." She talked then about the opportunity for service and acknowledged that charges of politics would be made, but the President himself told Louis that "he wanted him on the Court because of his high respect for and confidence in him."

"The great excitement in the newspapers is amusing is it not?" she continued. "We never expected that! I tell Louis if he is going to retire, he is certainly doing it with a burst of fire works!"

Confirmation by the Senate, she said, would "no doubt" come through. A few days later Brandeis made a quick trip from Boston to Washington to confer with Attorney General Gregory about confirmation possibilities and telegraphed Alice: "Weather miserable. Gregory seems confident." This was, however, before the opposition had organized.

Appointment to the Supreme Court, barring impeachment, is for life or until the appointee retires. It is a means for a President to impose his philosophy on the nation for a period longer than he actually serves in the White House. If that did not upset Wilson's opponents, there was Brandeis's record as the people's attorney over the years. Opposition developed rapidly.

"How they howl! Let 'em," said Felix Frankfurter in Boston of the opponents. Frankfurter appointed himself defender of Brandeis's record and character. During the next several months he wrote letters to newspapers and magazine articles, and asked his friends to support the Brandeis nomination.

The day after the appointment, Saturday, January 29, 1916, the *New York Times* predicted a struggle to confirm Brandeis but called that a compliment, saying that "Judges of little distinction and no very marked qualities often miss the honor of a contest over their nomination." Louis Brandeis then was to be highly complimented. The squabbles previously over appointing him to the cabinet or his admission to the Cosmos Club became merely that—squabbles, modest previews of the struggle over his confirmation. Involved in this four-month fracas were political power, the power of the press, of America's money men, of the legal profession. Arrayed against Brandeis were some of America's most influential. Perhaps no nominee, before or since, has been subjected to as searching an examination as he was, the target of such baseless charges and innuendoes.

Traditionally, when a President sends a nomination to the Senate, he first clears the name with the two senators from the nominee's state—minimally, he informs the senators of his intention. Wilson did neither. Henry Cabot Lodge and John W. Weeks, both Republicans, had strong connections to the Boston Brahmin establishment opposed to Brandeis. Wilson was not so much defying them as ignoring them. "If Mr. Wilson has a sense of humor left," said a newspaperman, "it must be working overtime today. When Brandeis' nomination came in yesterday, the Senate simply gasped. Today some of the Senators are coming up for air and trying to take stock."

In the pre–Civil War years a Jew named Judah Benjamin had been considered for a Supreme Court appointment, but he had requested the nomination not be made. Brandeis then was the first Jew formally nominated to be a justice. Attorney General Gregory advised against public Jewish support. His strategy was to have Brandeis's name go forward as the Democratic party nominee to insure a favorable vote in the Senate, where the Democrats held 56 of the 96 seats. This meant, he explained, the vociferous progressive element in the party should "figure as little as possible." Any public activity by Jews, he said, is "not likely to help with the Bourbon Democrats. They know what this support means in coming elections, without having it called to their attention." Frankfurter agreed to separate the Brandeis nomination from the religious issue, writing to a Jewish friend: "It is terribly important that no Jews should make the slightest peep about the race issue. You know as well as I do that the Jew in Brandeis has nothing to do (I except negligible isolated individuals) with the grounds of opposition." He said that many prominent Jews were as opposed to the Brandeis nomination as were prominent Bostonians "and for about the same reasons."

Brandeis publicly took the same low-keyed approach. When a Boston Jewish lawyer wanted to organize his fellow Jews in a show of support, Brandeis cautioned against the move. As the fight dragged on and mass meetings in support of Brandeis were planned, he opposed them and asked Rabbi Stephen Wise for help in canceling a New York meeting. Privately, however, he had a different approach, sending Norman Hapgood a list of Jews who could be influential.

William Howard Taft, still smarting from Brandeis's role in the Ballinger affair, was upset over the appointment. "I venture to think that the leading Jews of New York, Boston, Chicago, St. Louis, Cincinnati and other cities," he said, "who are not bound up in emotional uplifting, and who do not now tend to socialism, are as much troubled over his appointment and as indignant as any of us can be."

To his friends, Taft grumbled that Brandeis had deliberately used his Jewishness to gain a presidential appointment. According to Taft's scenario, Brandeis, stung by being passed over for a cabinet position in 1913, sought to become a "representative Jew" by embracing Zionism so that Wilson's Jewish supporters would press the President to give him an appointment. Taft saw no sincerity in Brandeis's Zionism. Since 1913, he thundered, Brandeis "has been a hat-wearing Jew . . . preaching a return to Zion and Jerusalem" and "has metaphorically been re-circumcized."

This charge, that Brandeis manipulated American Jewry in hopes of gaining a presidential appointment, continues to follow Brandeis's memory. A 1971 account, using language almost identical to Taft's, charges that beginning shortly after Wilson's 1913 inaugural, Brandeis "was working to establish himself as a representative Jew" by becoming more active in Zionism and "was building up his power in the [Boston] community by donating sums of money to various Jewish organizations." Brandeis, of course, had been publicly advocating Zionism and proclaiming his Judaism since 1910 and had been donating to Jewish charities for years earlier than that. Never naïve politically, Brandeis must have understood that one did not become a "representative" Jew then by advocating Zionism—most of America's prominent Jews were strong anti-Zionists, especially those close to Wilson, such as Henry Morgenthau. No documentation ever has been found suggesting any of these Jews recommended the Brandeis court appointment to Wilson. Also, although not visible to William Howard Taft in 1916, Brandeis's commitment to Zionism continued virtually to the day he died; it was not a political ploy.

American Jews were concerned about the Brandeis appointment at first, but not for the reasons Taft suggested. Aware of the rise of anti-Semitism, fueled by the attacks, pogroms, and other anti-Semitic outbursts in Europe, they wondered how America would respond to a prominent Jew's being nominated to an important government position. Eventually, however, American Jews, their pride showing, lined up behind the appointment. The prominent, wealthy Jews, influential in the Democratic party, who had in the past several years been angered by Brandeis's Zionist involvement, also came around to support Brandeis after the appointment had been made.

Jacob Schiff praised the appointment publicly and also privately to Attorney General Gregory. In addition, Schiff asked Henry Morgenthau to "take some prominent position in the campaign as such Jews as could add lustre to the reputation of the Jews should do all they can in that direction." Morgenthau also supported the nomination.

Nathan Straus, another prominent Jew, persuaded Arthur Brisbane, a journalist, to write an editorial for the New York *Evening Journal* supporting Brandeis. Straus then wrote Brandeis a personal note advising him not to be upset by the opposition for "you will be most admired through the enemies you have made."

Another charge raised was that Wilson had appointed Brandeis in hopes of gaining the Jewish vote. As governor of New Jersey, Wilson had appointed a Jew to the state supreme court, the first time that had been done, and so had experienced the controversy surrounding such an appointment. The Brandeis opponents believed that, in appointing a Jew, Wilson had played to the politicians' fears of being labeled anti-Semitic if they opposed Brandeis. The *New York Times* made that point in reverse, saying that "the appointment might appeal to advocates of religious tolerance." Gus J. Karger, a Washington newspaperman and Taft confidant as well as informant, reported to the ex-President that the Senate opponents were "not courageous enough to come out in the open, when the coming-out might be provocative of the charges of anti-Semitism."

Henry Cabot Lodge, the Massachusetts Republican senator, granted neither Wilson nor Brandeis any positive qualities. "For the first time in our history a man has been nominated to the Supreme Court with a view to attracting to the President a group of voters on racial grounds," Lodge said, continuing to a friend: "If it were not that Brandeis is a Jew, and a German Jew, he would never have been appointed and he would not have a baker's dozen of votes in the Senate."

If Wilson did gain support because of Brandeis's being Jewish, he also lost some. A. Lawrence Lowell, president of Harvard University, was accused of opposing the appointment because of Brandeis's religion; Lowell denied anti-Semitism. Although few commented on Brandeis's religion publicly, they were not so reluctant privately. One Boston Democratic party politician lamented that "a slimy fellow of this kind by his smoothness and intrigue, together with his Jewish instinct, can almost land in the cabinet, and probably on the bench of the Supreme Court." Edward McClennen, Brandeis's law partner, intimately involved in the Washington hearings that spring, later placed anti-Semitism at the top of the list of the reasons for the opposition to Brandeis, particularly among southern Democrats.

Lodge's references to Brandeis's German origins underscored another speculation: that Wilson had made the nomination to curry political favor with German-Americans. But that issue also, like the religious issue, cut both ways. The United States then was watching the First World War in Europe, and anger was turning toward the Germans in Europe and then—in the way that prejudice runs—toward German-Americans. "The heat and prejudice here against Brandeis and any kind of 'pro-Germanism' . . ." wrote Frankfurter from Boston, "is almost unbelievable."

Contrary to the speculations, Wilson supporters saw the appointment not as luring ethnic votes but instead the votes of progressives. The figures from the 1912 election told a story of more persons voting Republican than Democratic, of progressive Republicans supporting Theodore Roosevelt; to win in 1916, Wilson needed those progressive votes. The President was aware of the progressives' affection for Brandeis, and actually only made the appointment after Robert La Follette of Wisconsin, a leading progressive, assured him of his personal support for the nomination. A member of La Follette's family, after the appointment had been announced publicly, wrote Brandeis that the appointment "is going to draw us nearer to the administration than anything the President could have done; not merely because you are such a dear personal friend of us all, but because we can't but feel that the President has come over to our side."

The reaction was similar from Wilson supporters around the nation. "You may say to the President," a Democrat in Colorado wrote to a White House aide," that the appointment of Brandeis has had a greater effect upon the Progressives here than anything else." Amos Pinchot, with a long progressive record, wrote Norman Hapgood that, "although I don't think the appointment was political, Brandeis will pull a strong oar for Wilson in Wis, Minn, S & N Dakota and other Roosevelt strongholds."

Other progressives supported the appointment. Walter Lippmann, then editing *The New Republic,* told Brandeis that "all of us here look upon the fight as the most important one now taking place in the country."*

On February 5, *The New Republic* ran an editorial, unsigned but written by Felix Frankfurter, reviewing Brandeis's accomplishments, praising him for his judicial qualities and for seeking "to make the great reconciliation between order and justice." Acknowledging that Brandeis had made enemies—even then the protests over the appointment were being heard—the Frankfurter editorial responded: "The Law has not been a game to [Brandeis]; the issues he has dealt with have been great moral questions. He has often fought with great severity. He has rarely lost." Said the Frankfurter editorial:

It is true he has a passion for justice and a passion for democracy, but justice and democracy enlist a common fealty. It is by his insistence on translating these beliefs into life, by his fruitful intellectual inventiveness in devising the means for such translation, that Mr. Brandeis is distinguished.

Frankfurter wrote editorials, letters, and articles in those weeks endorsing his friend, in his hurry scrawling many by hand. Frankfurter's handwriting, being what it was, gave Brandeis a new name when one typesetter read the hastily written Lovis Dembitz Brandeis as Louis David Brandeis. "I plead guilty to the Brandeis article," said Frankfurter, "and have been in penance ever since over 'David.' My friends think it will reform my handwriting." It, of course, did not.

On the morning of Wednesday, February 9, 1916, a subcommittee of the Committee on the Judiciary of the United States Senate met to consider the nomination of Louis D. Brandeis to be a justice of the United States Supreme Court. The chairman was William E. Chilton of West Virginia. He and the four other subcommittee members would hear testimony, receive communications, judge the criticism against Brandeis and the praise in his behalf, then issue a report to the full Judiciary Committee. The full committee would then make a recommendation to the Senate, which is charged by the Constitution to advise

*What impact the Brandeis appointment had on the 1916 election in November, if any, can be disputed. Against a single candidate, Wilson increased his popular vote margin by almost three million votes; but the Republican candidate, Charles Evans Hughes, tallied more votes than any previous Republican presidential nominee. Wilson won with only a twenty-three-vote electoral college margin. He gained Colorado, North Dakota, California, and the State of Washington, which had gone against him in 1912. Those four states gave him thirty-one electoral college votes. On the other side, New York State had gone heavily for Wilson in 1912 but turned against him in 1916, although even then with many Jewish voters, to support Hughes, a native New Yorker.

and consent to such nominations. A majority of the senators present and voting would have to vote in Brandeis's behalf before he could be addressed as "Mr. Justice."

The Senate did not fulfill its responsibilities casually. Brandeis's was the ninety-eighth nomination to the Supreme Court. Of the ninety-seven nominations before his, only sixty-six—about two-thirds—actually had resulted in the individuals' becoming justices.

The chamber was crowded that day with senators and witnesses, newsmen, and friends and enemies of Brandeis. Not present, however, was the nominee himself. Tradition dictated then—and that tradition lasted until Felix Frankfurter was nominated twenty-three years later—that Supreme Court nominees did not appear at their confirmation hearings.

The hearings dragged on. Then additional weeks passed while the subcommittee reports were prepared; the final vote did not come until the end of May. During that time, every criticism of Brandeis ever made was dragged out at the hearings. The strong were attacking Brandeis. Their intention was to do what he had done to Ballinger, to cast sufficient shadow over his reputation to provide a reason for doubtful senators to vote against him. A member of the Senate, perhaps pro-business, anti-Semitic, or anti-German, could not voice those reasons to vote against Brandeis, but the member could vote "nay" if an "unethical" or "improper" charge could be attached to Brandeis.

At first Brandeis joked about the opposition. "What a commotion the President has created!" he wrote to one friend, and to another: "What a rumpus the President has started up! And all over a peace loving individual." Brandeis realized that the hearings involved not only his confirmation as a Supreme Court justice but also his personal reputation. After spending one-third of his life as a "knight errant" in public causes, he did not intend to be branded a charlatan. Edward McClennen recalled that "Brandeis did not relish the appointment." But if Brandeis had concerns whether he should have accepted the appointment when first offered, "the opposition," he said, "has removed my doubts." His feelings had become, "Go it husband, go it bear."

Brandeis was not a novice. He knew about publicity and influencing public opinion. He also had many friends, among whom were some of the most brilliant and respected of the nation's lawyers. He was in a battle, but it was one of the strong against the strong.

When Senator Chilton, the chairman, suggested to Norman Hapgood that letters from prominent lawyers supporting Brandeis would help, they were quick in coming. On February 1, Brandeis sent Hapgood a list of thirty-seven people who had sent congratulatory letters to him and "who could be applied to." The list included Roscoe Pound, about to be appointed dean of Harvard Law School; faculty members from Harvard; a dozen state and federal judges; a state attorney general, and the president of the Chicago Bar Association.

That was only the beginning. From a friend of Brandeis's in Los Angeles: "I succeeded yesterday in getting a large number of telegrams sent to Senator Works, as well as to about a dozen other senators." When a Pittsburgh lawyer wanted to push for an organized endorsement, Brandeis suggested that would not be wise but added, "Of course there is no objection to anything that individual lawyers may see fit to do in opposing or favoring the nomination." To another correspondent Brandeis hinted that "many men who think as you do have written letters" to the Senate subcommittee.

There were hundreds of letters from Massachusetts to Senator Chilton praising the appointment—from clergymen, lawyers, teachers, citizens who had fought by Brandeis's side for better and more efficient government in Boston. Dean Pound of the Harvard Law School wrote Chilton "that Mr. Brandeis is in very truth a great lawyer."

On the other side, the letter-writing campaign was equally organized. Henry Lee Higginson, a leader of the Boston business and social community, once had welcomed a young Louis Brandeis to Boston. But as Brandeis had taken stands against the interests of the Boston establishment, Higginson had turned against him. Opposed to a possible cabinet appointment for Brandeis three years earlier, Higginson was shocked at the new development, writing Senator Henry Cabot Lodge that Brandeis "has not the judicial quality. It would be well to investigate sundry questions about him." Lodge agreed and suggested that "The apparent indifference of the Bar is undoubtedly making a good deal of impression here. . . . If they should protest I should think he might not be confirmed."

And so began a movement to have a long list of prominent Boston lawyers file a formal protest against the appointment. The Brandeis forces were ready for the attack. Brandeis's lieutenants in the fight, serving unofficially, were two of his law partners, Edward McClennen, who moved to Washington for the hearings, and George R. Nutter, operating out of Boston. McClennen suggested checking the political affiliation of the protest signers: "I imagine most of them are Republicans." In Boston, Nutter planned a counter protest, but rather than having all the signatures on one letter, the plan was to have "each written in the writer's own way." He explained: "We have made a list of members of the Bar, and are having them interviewed by several trusty volunteers, with the idea of having each one of them write a letter to Chilton."

The Harvard Law School faculty endorsed the nomination, to the regret of William Howard Taft. He lamented that he always had considered Harvard the best law school in the world, because the faculty had viewed advanced progressive ideas with sanity and common sense. "Frankfurter has evidently been hypnotized by Brandeis," said Taft, "and has legged around to get signatures."

Taft organized a protest of six former presidents of the American Bar Association and himself. "It is better to hit hard and say what we exactly think," he said, "even if we don't get the signature of all the Bar Association Presidents." Taft believed the statement "will certainly have a good effect with the lawyers of the country, and the lawyers after all have a good deal of influence."

Brandeis had another reaction. "I think Taft's injecting himself into this controversy is a fact which, if properly used," he said, "will compensate somewhat for the annoyances of the last six weeks; and, if properly used, I think may be of great political importance." Brandeis's plan was to have some publications resurrect the facts of the Ballinger case when Taft, while President, agreed to the misdating of a document submitted to a Senate committee. Walter Lippmann at *The New Republic* quickly responded when Frankfurter, at Brandeis's request, broached the idea to him. *The New Republic* then ran an editorial, beginning: "One would have supposed that ex-President Taft was the last man qualified to express a judgment on Mr. Louis Brandeis. For if Mr. Taft will search his memory he will remember that it was Mr. Brandeis who caught him in what is perhaps the most discreditable episode in which a President of the United States had been involved."

From the beginning the hearings had about them the atmosphere of a trial. The subcommittee allowed the Brandeis opponents to be represented at the hearings by Austen G. Fox, a Boston lawyer, whom Felix Frankfurter called "a pompous, stuffed-shirt fellow with a great deal of atmosphere about him, top hat, moustache, fine voice, a kind of professional Harvard manner."

With Fox appearing for the opponents, Brandeis's friends suggested that George W. Anderson, also a prominent Boston lawyer, United States Attorney, and a Brandeis supporter, appear formally as his advocate. McClennen opposed the idea. No one was to appear for Brandeis. "It is important," he said, "to keep the spectacle of a trial or contested hearing away." Instead, Anderson agreed "to act for the subcommittee in seeing . . . that the truth may be developed."

The strategy of the opponents was to place into the record all the critical stories about Brandeis as a lawyer. McClennen's role was to provide the Democrats on the subcommittee with information answering such charges.

Brandeis's public stance was one of not being involved in the Senate hearings. Actually, he devoted considerable time to the hearings and, in effect, masterminded his side's presentation. Although bowing to the tradition that nominees do not appear, staying in Boston, and allowing McClennen to act for him, Brandeis was sending McClennen information and directives; these challenged claims made by opponents, suggested courses of action. On many days there would be three, four, or five messages from Brandeis in Boston to McClennen in Washington. Nothing escaped Brandeis. When a Massachusetts newspaper quoted an insurance publication saying insurance companies cannot permit Brandeis on "the Supreme Court bench if they can prevent it," Brandeis sent it to Frankfurter, pointing out that among the public opponents of his nomination were several insurance company officials. Frankfurter passed the letter on to Lippmann at *The New Republic.*

The hearings reviewed the thirty-five-year record of Louis Brandeis as a lawyer. Some of the charges quickly fell. He was criticized for accepting a "secret" retainer from *Collier's* during the Ballinger hearings; *Collier's* had reported in its own columns at the time that it was paying Brandeis. Another time in the hearings Brandeis was criticized for not accepting a fee. Brandeis had declined a fee in a public-interest cause, then estimated his law firm had lost about $25,000 because he had donated his services. He then paid his law firm the $25,000 from his own pocket—an action "bound to bring him under suspicion," said one unfriendly senator.

He was criticized for not arguing for lower railroad rates when he was counsel to the Interstate Commerce Commission in an inquiry. His defense was that he was appearing as an impartial counsel, employed by the Commission, and that his recommendations were applauded at the time. Brandeis once had represented the liquor industry and also E. H. Harriman, and was criticized for both clients.

Brandeis's role in the collapse of the New Haven Railroad had not been forgotten. Clarence W. Barron, publisher of the *Wall Street Jour-*

nal, had described the Brandeis appointment as "an insult to New England and the business interests of the country." But, when Barron testified before the subcommittee, he conceded, "I have been no witness of these events." The facts in controversial cases in which Brandeis had been involved were publicized to make Brandeis appear culpable. Lawyers who had been bested by Brandeis in the courtroom spoke against him. Moorfield Storey, a Boston lawyer, for example, advised the subcommittee to discount the support Brandeis was receiving from the Harvard Law School faculty. "Mr. Pound, one of the professors," said Storey of the newly appointed dean, "came here only a few years ago from one of the Dakotas, I think. Mr. Frankfurter is a young man who came from New York. I think they are not familiar with the reputation which prevails among the practicing lawyers of Boston."

Sometimes this tactic backfired. Waddill Catchings, a lawyer from New York, subpoenaed by Austen Fox, told of coming from New York to the Brandeis law firm in 1907 to seek its aid in a case. Then Catchings took Fox off balance. Catchings told of meeting with George Nutter, the Brandeis law partner, and of Nutter's saying that "the firm could not accept such a retainer unless Mr. Brandeis was convinced of the justness of our position; that he would not care to have his firm associated in a matter of such nature without personally passing on the merits of the contest." Catchings continued that he met with Brandeis for an hour or two, "and I may say that the hardest interview I had during the whole campaign was with Mr. Brandeis in convincing him of the justness of our cause." Catchings added: "I had occasion to retain other lawyers and no one ever raised that question."

Some charges raised against Brandeis disappeared slowly. One involved the family of Samuel Warren, Brandeis's old friend from Harvard days and former law partner. When Sam Warren's father had died and Warren had left the law firm to manage the family business, Brandeis was retained to deal with the legal matters. Four heirs were involved, and Brandeis handled the legal matters for many years without complaint. Later, one of the heirs challenged the way the business was being operated and Brandeis's role. No wrongdoing on Brandeis's part was demonstrated.

In another instance, Brandeis was charged with representing two parties in a dispute. Brandeis, however, was described by one of the other lawyers involved as demonstrating "a larger and broader duty to all the interests involved." Brandeis, in other words, had believed himself counsel for the situation rather than for any party. The lawyer,

Sherman L. Whipple, criticized Brandeis for that stance but told the subcommittee that he did not believe Brandeis "culpable" and did support the Brandeis Supreme Court appointment.

The most serious criticism emerging during the subcommittee's review of Brandeis's thirty-five-year career involved charges that he double-dealt with the shoe industry, first representing one side in a dispute and then the other. Prior to 1906 he had been lawyer for manufacturers of shoemaking equipment. In 1910 he represented the shoemakers in a legal dispute with those manufacturers. A lawyer is not required, once he represents a client, always to represent that client. The sticking point came for Brandeis in whether, when he opposed the manufacturers in 1910, he was acting in the same matter in which he had represented them four years earlier. If he were acting in the same matter, then he could be accused of a conflict of interest because his advocacy would be strengthened by the information he had gained while representing the manufacturers. John P. Frank, who did an exhaustive study of Brandeis's legal ethics as revealed by the confirmation hearings, concluded that Brandeis's ethics could not be faulted but conceded that in the shoe manufacturers' matter, "the episode is marginal, and reasonable attorneys can certainly differ about it."

Outwardly during the hearings, Brandeis in Boston kept cool, giving no indication he was perturbed by the challenge to his reputation in Washington. Jacob de Haas, his Zionist associate, recalled, at the time of the hearings, visiting Brandeis to learn "the latest news from Washington" to find Brandeis reading the *Jewish Encyclopedia*. "He turned to me: 'DeHaas, why have the Galician Jews always been poor?' " And the news from Washington was forgotten as the two men discussed Galician Jews for the next hour.

But the coolness was a facade; as the hearings dragged on, Brandeis became increasingly nervous and thin-skinned. He wrote to a close friend, for example, that "Austen Fox and Clarence Barron are the modern substitutes for the bravos of the renaissance period, and the assassins of other days." To another: "By the way, it is interesting to see these lawyers holler about my position as to Shoe Machinery after Wickersham's attitude in the New Haven matters—first prosecuting as attorney general and then defending." And when Felix Frankfurter suggested to him that the discussion over one of the cases before the subcommittee was complicated, Brandeis snapped: "It really is not complicated and it is only by making it appear so that there can be made to appear even the excuse of criticism." Brandeis wrote McClennen that "Delays are not only unwise but perilous."

For his wife, Alice, who had been with him in so many fights, who had shared his glories and stood with him against the slurs, the months dragged also. She wrote to a friend from Cape Cod, where the Brandeises had gone for a few days of escape: "We are all out here for the weekend, in the quiet and open and the girls have gone for a walk with their father. I have a heavenly sense of peace and calm. The beauty and loveliness of life seem so real, so possible, and then think of the world we have made!"

As often happens with a controversial appointment, not all of the opposition was visible. Senators came to Attorney General Gregory with reports that Brandeis "did not believe in a written constitution" or he had said that Supreme Court justices "should not be restrained from responding to a demand of the people by a constitutional restriction." Brandeis quickly sent denials, asking if the charges could be traced to their sources.

Another colorful charge floating around during 1916 was that Woodrow Wilson had appointed Brandeis to the Supreme Court as a payoff for Brandeis's quieting a woman who had believed the then-widowed President intended to marry her. This story had, and continued in subsequent years to have, all the embellishments of illicit relations and a $75,000 hush payment. "No decent person should have been guilty of circulating this vile slander," said Brandeis when a minister reported hearing it from a Boston lawyer. "For a lawyer to do so is unpardonable," said Brandeis.

After a month had gone by, McClennen reported to George Nutter: "Things look well. The general impression seems to be that a vigorous and mean attempt has been made to discredit L. D. B. and that it has been a miserable failure." After the hearings had closed, when there was talk of reopening them, the Brandeis forces were not frightened. "I am inclined to think that from the standpoint of tactics," said George Nutter, "this request for a re-opening may prove a boomerang in our favor. None of the matters will turn out to be important, and the animus behind it all will appear even more clearly."

At times McClennen, who sat through all the sessions, even enjoyed them. Once, when the anti-Brandeis forces tripped over a point, McClennen compared Austen Fox to looking like "after a shampoo before the hair is fully dry." But he also conceded to Nutter that the subcommittee and full committee probably would divide close to party lines.

For the Republicans, whatever their liberal or conservative inclinations, there were reasons to vote against Brandeis, other than his merits. They believed Wilson would be defeated in the November elections. If he was and the Supreme Court seat was still vacant, then a Republican President could fill the seat with a loyal party follower. For some individual Republicans there were particular problems. William E. Borah, Republican senator from Idaho and member of the Judiciary Committee, was considered a progressive and was expected to go along with the Brandeis appointment. However, the lumber interests in his state opposed Brandeis because of his support for conservation, and they wanted Borah to vote "nay."

Borah's vote became significant when the subcommittee reported on April 3 for the Brandeis confirmation by a party-line 3-2 vote. The way McClennen sized up the coming full-committee vote, Borah's vote would be needed to counter a defecting Democrat, John K. Shields of Tennessee. Otherwise, the eighteen-member committee, ten Democrats and eight Republicans, "would presumably stand nine-to-nine." A full-committee split, rather than an outright endorsement, would give wavering senators an excuse to vote against the nomination.

With the subcommittee's work finished and its report passed on to the full committee, the Brandeis nomination, despite McClennen's optimism, could have gone either way, especially if the full committee produced a tie vote. For many it was difficult to challenge statements by former presidents of the American Bar Association or the president of Harvard University, all of whom had opposed Brandeis. For others, it was difficult to vote against Brandeis and appear to support the trusts and railroadmen.

Frankfurter understood that the outcome would be influenced by the attitude of distinguished lawyers both in and outside the Senate, men who could be appealed to on the basis of the issues and not on petty concerns. He wrote to Senator Chilton, the subcommittee chairman in Brandeis's favor. He asked George Rublee, Brandeis's former associate from the Ballinger and Federal Trade Commission fights, to urge Attorney General Gregory to make a public statement. He wrote to former Senator Elihu Root of New York, father of his Harvard Law School classmate: "Two men have influenced most my standards in professional and public matters, one is Henry L. Stimson, the other is Louis D. Brandeis." He continued to Root that, in the nomination dispute, "Mr. Brandeis and the injustice to him are quite immaterial. Like all individuals he is only of passing importance. But there is involved the prestige of the Supreme Court, the whole position of our Federal Judiciary in the minds of the people." He closed the letter:

A very dangerous force is loosened when ground is afforded for the thinking of the laity that one who has fought with great effectiveness and disinterested devotion for causes that have disturbed conventional comforts and interests should thereby disqualify himself for service on the Supreme Court—a Court watchful of the interests of the entire country as defined by the Constitution which embodies no partisan economic theories however old or however long accepted by uncritical custom.

Root would not go along with Frankfurter, writing that Brandeis "seems to draw distinctions . . . to justify himself in conduct which I do not think in accordance with the standards of honor which always have and always ought to govern the great court for which he has been nominated." For many years Brandeis had pursued his causes relentlessly, and he was paying for it.

Another person whom Frankfurter approached for support was Henry Stimson, the man who was always "Mr. Stimson" to him and whose standards of personal integrity, selfless service to his country, and fair play always guided Frankfurter's own career. Frankfurter tried to explain Brandeis to Stimson. "Law practice presents to [Brandeis] entirely moral issues and he fights accordingly. Add to that, he usually wins," said Frankfurter. In 1910, Stimson had been on the periphery of the Ballinger case and had complimented Brandeis on his handling of it. Also, Stimson's own career had gone toward public service, as had Brandeis's. Still, his loyalties were with the Elihu Roots and William Howard Tafts, and the endorsement never came in 1916.

The Brandeis fight brought Frankfurter more attention at Harvard. One night he was the guest, with several others, of Charles Townsend Copeland of Harvard's English Department. "Copey" was one of the respected traditions at the school, revered by his students and admired by his fellow teachers. That particular night Frankfurter was arguing the merits of the Brandeis appointment, as he did most evenings, when "Copey" told him: "I am sure that we shall not only see Brandeis a Justice of the Supreme Court," and here Copeland turned to Frankfurter, "but that the day will come when you will sit there by his side."

One who could not speak publicly in the dispute because of his own position on the Court but who greatly cared was Oliver Wendell Holmes, Jr. He could not understand the furor. He said of Brandeis: "He always left on me the impression of a good man when he called, and I never have fully fathomed the reasons for the strong prejudice against him shown by other good men." That comment, that Brandeis always had left on Holmes "the impression of a good man" is one that Holmes repeated to his friends on many occasions. Frankfurter recalled years later that "of no other man have I ever heard Holmes express himself in ethical terms."

Throughout the February and March hearings, the Brandeis forces would not publicly lobby for the appointment, although the private lobbying continued as extensive on the Brandeis side as on that of his opponents. One Brandeis friend in the administration informed a Brandeis partisan that he and a friend "were doing all in our power to mould public opinion and I only wanted to know what more to do in order to do it."

The reluctance to move publicly began to crack in April after the subcommittee report became available. The two Republican senators concluded:

We regard it as a great misfortune and a distinct lowering of the standards heretofore maintained in making appointments to this high office that one should be selected for the place whose reputation for honesty and integrity amongst his associates at the bar has been proved to be bad, which reputation has been justified by his own source of conduct. We cannot conscientiously give our consent to the confirmation of such an appointment.

The Democrats responded:

It will not do to oppose the nomination of a man like Mr. Brandeis and then, after a complete investigation, admitting that the charges are not supported, ask that the nomination be rejected because of the charges rather than of their truth. This would be an injustice to the nominee and to the court, and we would be out of line with that sense of justice which pervades all classes of people. Having failed in the charges and admitting the eminent ability of the appointee, it would be the manly thing to concede the evident error in making the charges and ask for a confirmation.

One of the Democrats, Thomas J. Walsh, offered a separate defense of Brandeis: "The real crime of which this man is guilty is that he has exposed the iniquities of men in high places in our financial system. He has not stood in awe of the majesty of wealth. . . . He has been an iconoclast. He has written about and expressed views on 'social justice.' . . . They all contemplate that a man's a man and not a machine."

The rebuttal by the Democrats was not sufficient to erase the shadow cast by the charges made during the weeks of hearings, the publicity given to the prominent opponents of Brandeis, and the innuendoes and slurs passed around in whispers about Brandeis. George Nutter wrote an account, which appeared in the New York *World,* and the columns of *The New Republic* were open to the Brandeis forces. However, when a Boston newspaper printed a pro-Brandeis letter, the newspaper owner berated the editor. Ray Stannard Baker, a journalist, attempted to do an account friendly to Brandeis for the *New York Times,* but the newspaper rejected it. "This gives us a fair measure of the degree of pressure being exercised," wrote Brandeis to Baker, "for there must be few occasions when the columns of the Times would not be open to communication from you."

But there were other routes. Frankfurter had two thousand copies of the majority report sent to Boston for distribution. He believed the policy of "lying low giving clear field for misrepresentation by the other side is all wrong." He told Walter Lippmann of *The New Republic* that he and his friends were all set "with positive presentation of case through channels of Press, Labor and Bar if authority be given to go ahead." The go ahead would come shortly.

The major asset for the Brandeis forces was Woodrow Wilson. Controlling patronage, Wilson still could be re-elected to the White House in November no matter how bleak that prospect looked in the spring. But his silence since making the appointment had led to talk that he did not care whether Brandeis was confirmed or not. From California came a report that the "Brandeis confirmation may fail because of insufficient interest of President," and the report added: "I am convinced that failure of confirmation will lose Wilson many thousand votes in California alone." Norman Hapgood, a Brandeis partisan, warned his friends in the Wilson administration that Democrats were watching to determine if Wilson could hold the party together on the issue.

Wilson waited three months before acting. A skillful politician, Wilson understood that one does not expend one's political energy uselessly or at the wrong time, but hoards it and strikes only when action will be effective. "There was a conference I am told with the President today," McClennen reported to Brandeis on May 2. "He is as earnest as ever and it is to be hoped that something may result, in the way of ending the delay. I have nothing definite."

Two days later McClennen reported that the word in Washington was that Wilson was "ready to go to the mat" for the appointment. After writing the letter, McClennen realized that Brandeis, so removed from daily distractions and entertainments, might not have understood the "go to the mat" phrase and added, "It is favorable even if not a Supreme Court term."

The arrangement worked out at the White House was that Charles A. Culberson of Texas, the Democratic chairman of the full Judiciary Committee, would write Wilson a letter asking him to explain why he had appointed Brandeis. That letter was sent May 5.

Wilson's response is a typed, five-page, double-spaced letter also dated May 5. Closely resembling a memorandum prepared in Boston by friends of Brandeis, it defended both Brandeis the man and Brandeis the lawyer. The President called the appointment of Supreme Court justices "probably" his most important duty, "and I need hardly tell you that I named Mr. Brandeis as a member of that great tribunal only because I knew him to be singularly qualified by learning, by gifts and by character for the position."

The President said that the charges against Brandeis "threw a great deal more light upon the character and motives of those with whom they originated than upon the qualifications of Mr. Brandeis." He had examined the charges three years earlier when he had considered Brandeis for the cabinet and found they "proceeded for the most part from those who hated Mr. Brandeis because he had refused to be serviceable to them in the promotion of their own selfish interests." The President spoke of Brandeis's "extraordinary ability as a lawyer," "his fairness and love of justice," and of "his impartial, impersonal, orderly and constructive mind, his rare analytical powers, his deep human sympathy."

The Wilson letter not only was an endorsement of Louis Brandeis but —by its enthusiasm, its length, its rejection of the charges against Brandeis—was also a party document. Wilson was the leader of the Democratic party. He wanted Brandeis. The Democrats must follow him. That was the letter's message.

The letter was kept confidential for several days, to allow the committee to examine it first, and then made public on May 8. The full committee met on May 9, then adjourned for a few days without setting a time for voting, some members still unsure of which way they wanted to go.

George Nutter, working in Boston for the Brandeis nomination and agreeing with Frankfurter about the need for publicity, considered sending a copy of the Wilson letter to every lawyer in the country, but wanted to be certain that the mailing would not be attributed to the Brandeis firm, that nothing challenged the picture that "L. D. B. and his firm are doing nothing in the publicity line to forward his candidacy."

The details were worked out to shield the firm, and the law firm gave the signal to begin a widespread publicity campaign. Some ten thousand packets of pro-Brandeis information were sent out to members of the American Bar Association throughout the country. The message was not subtle: Brandeis was worthy of appointment to the Supreme Court and lawyers should urge their senators to support his nomination.

The Senate subcommittee reopened the hearings briefly to hear additional attacks on Brandeis, but these were largely ignored, especially after the subcommittee received a letter dated May 17, 1916, from Cambridge, Massachusetts. The letter was signed by Charles W. Eliot, who had preceded A. Lawrence Lowell as president of Harvard University. Now retired, Eliot was one of the most respected men in the nation. To reject Brandeis, Eliot said, "would be a grave misfortune for the whole legal profession, the court, all American business, and the country."

Moorfield Storey, during the hearings, had discounted the support for Brandeis from Roscoe Pound, dean of the Harvard Law School, and from Frankfurter, saying they had come to Boston only in recent years and were not familiar with Brandeis's reputation. The same charge could not be made of Eliot.

In the full committee, three Democratic votes were crucial: John Shields of Tennessee, Hoke Smith of Georgia, and Lee S. Overman of North Carolina. Their conservatism had pushed them toward opposing Brandeis, but as the spring months wore on the factor that was believed turning them definitely against Brandeis was anti-Semitism. The Leo Frank case had demonstrated the potency of that force among their constituents.

Shields had served on the Tennessee supreme court before his Senate election. The Brandeis forces, through friends in Nashville, organized a petition among lawyers there to support Brandeis and also worked through the local newspaper. But the factor that tipped Shields into the pro-Brandeis camp was a Washington event. He met with Wilson at the White House, where it was pointed out that Shields would become the senior senator from Tennessee after the November election, and if Wilson was reelected, Shields would have the chance to control patronage in his state. Did he want that chance? Shields voted for Brandeis.

On May 18, Henry Morgenthau, a confidant of the President and a Democratic party financier, met for three hours with Hoke Smith in Smith's Senate office. "I feel that I made an impression upon him and that he will vote for Brandeis," Morgenthau told the President. There was considerable personal ill-feeling at the time by Smith toward the President, and Morgenthau advised Wilson to "send for him *after* Brandeis has been confirmed" to discuss public matters and "give him back his 'self-respect' about which he is much concerned."

Morgenthau's account of the meeting was written at the time but made public five years later. Hoke Smith then acknowledged a meeting having taken place but denied that the Brandeis matter was discussed. The subject of the 1916 meeting, said Smith in 1921, was a speaking engagement Morgenthau had in Georgia, and Smith said—in an apparent reference to Morgenthau's being Jewish—he, Smith, had discussed "the dangerous state of public feeling in Atlanta, due to the case of Leo Frank." As for his vote to support Brandeis, Smith said, "Certain charges had been made against him; these I examined carefully and satisfied myself that Mr. Justice Brandeis had acted in each of them from a high conception of duty. This being true, I did not hesitate to support his confirmation."

Overman of North Carolina consistently described the appointment as a mistake and spoke against it in the Senate cloakroom. Wilson took care of him. The President was traveling by train with Overman to Charlotte for a public celebration. On the way the train stopped at Salisbury, North Carolina. This was Overman's home town, and he wanted the President to come out on the train's rear platform with him and speak to his townspeople, to show how he ranked with the President of the United States. Wilson was reluctant, saying he preferred not to make any speeches from the rear of trains. Overman became desperate: "If I cannot induce the President to speak in my home town, the people there will be disappointed and blame me." Finally, the President consented. In his brief talk, Wilson castigated his Republican critics, praised Overman highly, and did not mention the Brandeis nomination. He made such an impression, produced so much warmth from the audience, that Overman became frightened about opposing the President on such a major issue as the Brandeis nomination.

After the talk, as Wilson settled into his seat, he turned to an aide and said: "What do you think now? Did I pull it off all right? Do you think Overman's vote is cinched?"

The vote in the full committee was a straight party line, ten Democrats for the appointment and eight Republicans against. The political division was another asset for Brandeis in the upcoming Senate vote, making the issue more and more a party-line affair. That was the strategy Attorney General Gregory had mapped out in the beginning. Now they would know if it worked.

On Thursday, June 1, 1916, the Senate—acting under a unanimous-consent agreement—voted, without discussion, on the nomination of Louis Dembitz Brandeis to be a member of the United States Supreme Court. The vote was scheduled for five o'clock in the afternoon to bring "the said nomination to a final conclusion." Chilton, the chairman of the subcommittee, asked that the vote be recorded, and the clerk began to call the roll.

Mr. Ashurst.

Whatever else the members of Congress do—the backroom deals, the patronage promises, the public-works-projects trading—they cannot dodge the record vote.

Mr. Bankhead.

At this point, they must be recorded one way or another. No delays are allowed. Even if a member is absent, he is expected to announce his inclination, so that, if he is not formally counted, he is at least judged.

Mr. Beckham.

Here the senators become part of history, the deciders of the events that shape the United States, enhance or harm it.

Mr. Borah.

For whatever the senator has promised his constituents before this point, now he no longer promises; rather, he must justify.

Mr. Brady.

Religious bias, fear of retaliation at the polls, and financial ambitions now compete with decency, courage, and selflessness.

Mr. Brandegee.

To this moment of vote, everything is preparation. The vote is fact.

Mr. Broussard.

In this Senate chamber others had been the subject of controversial confirmation fights, wars had been declared, Presidents attacked, secession vowed. Given the controversy over the Brandeis nomination and given what the senators could not see—the twenty-three years of service he would have on the Supreme Court—this vote also was one of those times when the Senate was an arena of history.

The names droned on.

There were ninety-six names to be called, two for each of the forty-eight states then in the union. Some had to be called twice, because the senator did not hear or was not in the chamber. Some because the senator wanted to delay his vote, to see how his fellow senators were voting, to know how much his vote was needed by the two sides. At five-thirty the results were announced. of the ninety-six senators, sixty-seven were present and voting.

Three telegrams from Edward McClennen to Louis Brandeis tell the story of that vote.

The first: "Voted to vote without debate five o'clock, June first. Twenty-five minimum majority predicted."

The second: "Confirmed forty-seven to twenty."

The third: "Mr. Justice Brandeis, Supreme Court, Washington, D.C., My congratulations to the Supreme Court and to the United States."

The vote was on party lines. The strategy of making the nomination a party issue had worked. Of the forty-seven "yea" votes, all were Democrats except for Robert La Follette and George Norris. Miles Poindexter of Washington, who then preferred being called Progressive rather than Republican, also supported Brandeis. Henry Cabot Lodge, Republican of Massachusetts, voted "nay" and Weeks, the other Massachusetts Republican, was absent but was paired against the nominee. Senator Borah, the progressive Republican from Idaho, also was paired against Brandeis.

The congratulatory messages poured in. "Welcome," said Holmes. "Greetings and what greetings," said Frankfurter. One telegram was not enough for Frankfurter. The second read: "And now, that it is dear Justice Brandeis—'O, the difference to me!' Effort finds new zest, and hope new activity, all one's powers a deeper source of strength." Frankfurter's exultation was without limits. He wrote Mrs. Brandeis that her husband's going on the Supreme Court began "a new era for the profession, the Court, American business and the nation." Frankfurter believed he had gained much himself from his involvement in the experience. "It has brought experiences such as fashion manhood if the stuff is there."

Brandeis himself continued to show the outward calm that he had maintained throughout the fight. "Needless to say, there is a great sense of relief throughout the office," said his Boston secretary. "Mr. Brandeis himself is just as sweet and undisturbed as he has remained during all the strain of the past four months." He resigned his memberships in the Boston City Club, the Exchange Club, the Social Law Library, and the Union Board Club in preparation for moving permanently to Washington.

His partnership in the law firm was ended, and his name was taken off the door. He received his share of the firm's profits through June 1, which amounted to $12,795, after various expenses were settled, including his paying $441.21 to the firm to reimburse it for expenses "in connection with meeting the opposition to the nomination."

At this point in his life, Brandeis was a wealthy man, and he was concerned about possible conflicts of interest on the Court. Although public officials then were not required to report, or to discuss, their personal financial matters with anyone, he informed Chief Justice Edward Douglass White: "It has been my custom since I began the practice of law to invest my surplus income wholly in what were believed to be absolutely safe investments intended to be permanent and yielding a low rate of return." He had done this, he said, to avoid having financial considerations interfere with his work or to be distracted by concerns over his investments while working. His investments largely had been left to others, he explained, and he did not believe they constituted a conflict of interest. White assured Brandeis there was no need to juggle his financial interests because of his role on the Court.

William Howard Taft considered the confirmation vote as abhorrent as was the nomination. He was to call the coming presidential election "the most critical one during my career" because, if Wilson was re-elected, he probably would be able to appoint four more justices to the Supreme Court. "He has disgraced the Supreme Court already by putting Brandeis on it," said Taft, "and he is seeking to break down the guarantees of the Constitution by selecting men who are radical in their views, who have no idea of preserving the rights of property or maintaining the protection of the Constitution, which has enabled us to live and be strong."

Felix Frankfurter, naturally, viewed the arrival of Louis Brandeis on the Supreme Court differently. "In law also men make a difference," he would write later. "There is no inevitability in history except as men make it." He believed that Brandeis was a man to make history. Later Frankfurter wrote of him that "probably no other man has come to the Court with his mind dyed, as it were, in the very issues which became his chief judicial concern . . . the solution of those social and economic problems of American society with which he was preoccupied for nearly a generation before his judicial career."

Louis Dembitz Brandeis was sworn in as an associate justice of the Supreme Court on June 5, 1916. The ceremony was in the same chamber where years earlier he had appeared, in a borrowed frock coat, to defend a railroad against the taxing powers of a county. In this Old Senate Chamber also, in 1908, he had, in the case of *Muller* v. *Oregon*, established with his "Brandeis brief" the concept of reasonableness as part of law. Today the chamber was so crowded that people stood in the aisles.

Dressed in a new judicial robe, Brandeis stood and raised his right hand to take the judicial oath, promising to "administer justice with respect to persons, and do equal right to the poor and to the rich," and "faithfully and impartially discharge and perform all the duties incumbent" as an associate justice "according to the best of my abilities and understanding, agreeably to the Constitution and Laws of the United States."

He closed: "So help me God."

Whatever can be said about Louis Brandeis's career to this point, whatever could be said about his future—whether Taft was right in his prediction or Frankfurter was correct in his later appraisal—at this moment with the taking of that oath by the child of immigrants, by the Jew, by the knight errant, none could deny that the outsider was now the insider.

BOOK
TWO

The One Above the Clouds

7

On the Court

"Have just come from the opening day of Court . . . many motions presented. We heard our first case. An important one tomorrow . . . the amount of work piled up is stupendous," wrote Louis Brandeis to his daughter Susan on October 9, 1916, the opening day of his first term as an associate justice of the Supreme Court.

At the beginning, Brandeis worked seven days a week, morning and evening. It "went hard with me," he told Felix Frankfurter. Accustomed to establishing his own work schedule, shaping the demands upon him to fit his strengths, Brandeis no longer determined what cases he did or did not deal with, what causes he did or did not support. He approached his new job with his customary thoroughness. Almost from the time of his confirmation the previous June, he had begun the study of all previous Supreme Court decisions. And, although as an advocate before the Supreme Court he had been intimate with its procedures, politics, and personalities, he came to believe that, as Frankfurter later reported, "No one can have the right kind of feel regarding the distinctive jurisdictional and procedural problems touching the Court's business in less than three or four terms of actual service on the Court."

Still, in that first year he thrived. "Had 1½ hours with the C.J., half on his, half on my cases," Brandeis wrote his wife. "He has a cold & was quite doleful. I have 4 opinions in printers hands & feel over the peak of the load. Two more in process & then a raft of others to peruse."

The judicial term for the Supreme Court is similar to the academic year, beginning in the fall and ending with the coming of summer. During his first term on the Court, Brandeis was not assigned any controversial opinions that would split the Court. Rather, he was allowed to learn his way through the judicial corridors, to develop a working relationship with his Court brethren. Brandeis, however, being who and what he was, quickly demonstrated in his decisions and dissents his independence and his scholarship. More, he demonstrated the value of the coming to the Supreme Court of the outsider, the one whose concern had been not with profits and business expansion but with the incomes, the illnesses, and the tragedies of the worker.

The first decision issued by the Court under Brandeis's name was *Van Dyke* v. *Geary,* argued March 23, 1917, and decided May 7, 1917. Built around the specific issue of control over an Arizona water source, the case asked how far a governmental unit could go in regulating a public utility, one of the controversial issues during the next several decades.

When the Arizona Corporation Commission asserted authority over rates charged by a privately owned water source, the owners sued the commission, charging its property had been taken unconstitutionally when the commission forced it to lower prices, citing Section 1 of the Fourteenth Amendment denying government the right to deprive a person of "life, liberty, or property, without due process of law." This was the amendment ratified after the Civil War to assure equal protection of the laws to all persons but used by industry to protect itself from governmental supervision.

The blunt question was: could the State of Arizona, through its Corporation Commission regulate the water company's prices?

Brandeis said it could. The first point he dealt with was whether the state law was "reasonable" or not. Brandeis, as a judge, responded as he had as a lawyer arguing *Muller* v. *Oregon.* Since the Arizona legislature had written the law and the state court had upheld it, "this legislative construction . . . ought not to be set aside by this court," he said.

The second point was whether the water system was a private business or a public utility. Brandeis was guided by the public need—"the character and extent of the use" make the company public although privately owned, "and since the service is a public one the rates are subject to regulation."

The owners had charged that the rates allowed were unfair, that what was attractive for the consumer was confiscatory for the owners. Brandeis replied that it was not possible for the Supreme Court in Washington to judge the rates allowed by the Arizona Corporation Commission. Here he followed precedent, asserting that the Supreme Court in Washington was not to impose its wisdom for that of the local government at the scene but was only to determine if the local government, or its agency, had acted in an appropriate, lawful, and reasonable way. To Brandeis this was the essence of conservatism.

Only one justice dissented: James McReynolds, who offered no explanation. Almost two decades later, when the Supreme Court was in the midst of its greatest constitutional challenge, McReynolds would insist on the right of the Court to judge the wisdom of an act, not only its constitutionality.

Brandeis's second decision of the 1916 term, *Sutton* v. *New Jersey*, also was characterized by his brand of judicial conservatism, stressing reasonableness and not affronting precedent. A New Jersey statute required streetcar companies to carry police officers free of charge when on duty but not in uniform. The street railways challenged the law, again under the Fourteenth Amendment, claiming they were denied their property, the lost fares. Brandeis upheld the state law, saying that a result could be increased protection both to the public and the company. "We cannot say that the requirement . . . is an arbitrary or unreasonable exercise." he wrote. Brandeis also pointed out that the Supreme Court in the past required "street-using corporations" to assume burdens more severe than carrying policemen without charge. He spoke for a seven-member majority, Justices McKenna and Pitney dissenting.

Brandeis wrote six other decisions that term having to do with business law. One involved a surety company's refusal to pay off on a loss of goods and a dispute before a lower court, but, said Brandeis, in ordering that the amount be paid, "Technical rules . . . never have been applied in proceedings under this statute."

Nor was Brandeis controlled in his decisions by the bias he had exhibited against large corporations before joining the Court. In another case the issue was whether an individual stockholder could sue for damages in the place of a corporation when the corporation declined to do so. Brandeis said no because the corporation's decision not to sue "has the approval of all the stockholders except the plaintiffs."

More than in Brandeis's decisions, clues to his concept of his role as an associate justice that year were in his dissents. When the Supreme Court had first convened after the nation's founding, the justices tended to give their decisions *seriatim,* one after the other. The Supreme Court then was not so much an institution as a group of men going off in different directions, giving little guidance either to the nation's citizens or to its courts. This changed after John Marshall became Chief Justice in 1801. Influenced by practices in England and in his native Virginia, he realized the Court would have more prestige, and become a more powerful institution, if it spoke its majority decision with a single voice.

But dissents were not eliminated and continued to play a controversial role in Supreme Court decisions. An American Bar Association *Journal* article in the 1920s suggested that dissents not be allowed in decisions dealing with constitutional issues. Pierce Butler, who joined the Court about then, spoke of the dissenters' "vanity." On the other side, Benjamin Cardozo, then a New York State judge and later a Supreme Court justice, said dissents allow their authors to feel "a good deal better." Charles Evans Hughes, in the years between his being an associate justice and Chief Justice, called the dissent "an appeal to the brooding spirit of the law, to the intelligence of a future day." He also asserted that merely formal unanimity is not desirable because justices "are not there simply to decide cases, but to decide them as they think they should be decided."

Brandeis would become known in the 1920s for his dissents. Often out of rhythm with a majority of the Court, Brandeis spoke to the law's "brooding spirit" and to a future day's "intelligence." If not in his lifetime, then in that of Frankfurter's, his dissents often became the nucleus of majority opinions.

Despite his philosophical differences with his fellow justices, however, and the reputation for dissent he gained, he was not frivolous and often withheld a dissent. "I have concluded that dissent would only aggravate the harm. Hence I shall not dissent," he told Holmes about one opinion. There, of course, were personal matters involved. Brandeis once wanted to dissent on a Holmes opinion but "I was rushed with other work and so would have had to hold up Holmes . . . and to hold him from firing off is like sending an executioner after him."

Brandeis's law clerk that first year, Calvert Magruder, said later that he did not know why Brandeis in one instance had written a dissent and then had not released it, but "I can understand the reluctance of a newly elected member of the Court to file a dissent in such a case when he had dissents on more important cases in the offing." Frankfurter believed that Brandeis often withheld a dissent "in order not to expose the mischief to which the [majority] decision could be put."

Brandeis's technique of dissent owed much to that of Holmes: "One can say what one thinks without having to blunt the edges and cut off the corners to suit someone else."

Because the dissent suggests a challenge to the Court itself, Brandeis began his career as a dissenter almost with an apology. "I dissent from the opinion of the court," he began his first dissent, "and the importance of the question involved induces me to state the reason." The case dealt with employer's liability, an issue occupying the American economy for decades.

The case involved a New Yorker named Winfield who, while working for the railroad, had lost an eye in an accident not caused by negligence but "out of one of the ordinary risks of the work." He sought and received compensation under the New York State workmen's compensation law. The railroad appealed. The case went first to the state courts, which decided in Winfield's favor. The railroads then went to the United States Supreme Court, which reversed the state action and the state courts. Winfield was not entitled to any compensation.

Willis Van Devanter, fifty-seven, wrote the majority opinion. He had been a lawyer and judge on the western frontier and was a stranger to the complexities of the new industrial society. Van Devanter argued that a federal workmen's compensation law, dealing with negligence only, had preempted the state law. "No State is at liberty thus to interfere with the operation of a law of Congress," he declared.

The Van Devanter decision required seven pages; the Brandeis dissent, sixteen. Six justices joined Van Devanter; only one joined Brandeis.

Brandeis's technique was to present both sides of an argument, not to shy away from a challenge but to revel in it, and then to demolish the opposing side. "Actually he decides the case in the face of opposition," wrote one of his law clerks, "whereas many a man decides his case as if there was no opposition worth mentioning."

And so with this dissent, Brandeis began by accepting the majority's position that Congress has the power to preempt state laws, but then he argued never mind that Congress could, the real question, in this instance, is, did it?

The federal act had been passed not to secure uniformity, as Van Devanter implied, but because "the number of accidents to railroad employees had become appalling. In the year 1905–6 the number killed while on duty was 3,807, and the number injured 55,524." He then argued that the federal law, passed as emergency legislation, was compatible with state laws and did not preempt them. As proof of that, he pointed out that, when the federal law was passed in 1908, no state had a workmen's compensation program. At the time of the decision, nine years later, thirty-seven did. These laws were jeopardized by the Court's decision, and Brandeis said that was a matter for regret because "society, as well as the individual employee and his dependents, must look for adequate protection. Society needs such a protection as much as the individual, because ultimately society must bear the burden, financial and otherwise, of the heavy losses which accidents entail."

The second dissent Brandeis wrote that year also dealt with the responsibility of society. Washington State prohibited employment agencies from collecting fees from job applicants; fees could be collected only from employers. The law had been enacted because the state's labor bureau found the agencies were exploiting the workers. The workers were employed only for short-time work but paid a fee to the agency for each job, and often found themselves owing the agency a substantial amount of money.

The case was *Adams* v. *Tanner* and the majority decision was by McReynolds, who ruled the employment agencies could collect fees from the workers. Acknowledging that abuses might exist, McReynolds said regulation was the proper response rather than "destruction of one's right to follow a distinctly useful calling in an upright way."

Brandeis began this dissent, twenty pages long compared to the five-page decision by McReynolds, as he had his first dissent, almost with an apology—it "is a matter of such seriousness that I state the reasons for my dissent from the opinion of the court." He argued that the state law was a reasonable exercise of its police powers, pointing out that the agencies had been found to steal the applicants' money, entice them into prostitution, misrepresent working conditions, and charge exorbitant fees. Regulation had been tried—this apparently placed in the dissent to respond to McReynolds's suggested solution—but without success. "There gradually developed a conviction that the evils of private agencies were inherent and ineradicable, so long as they were permitted to charge fees to the workers seeking employment," wrote Brandeis. He also pointed out that the state had its own employment office, which charged prospective employees only four cents for job assistance compared to the one and two dollars charged by private agencies.

That 1916–17 term, Brandeis joined in five other dissents; in four of them he was with Holmes. "Now I am sketching possible dissents in various directions," said Holmes to a friend, "sometimes with, sometimes against my brother B. It is a fine sport." In the coming years, the two men were to enjoy the sport perhaps more than any two men who had yet sat on the Court.

Once he became part of the Supreme Court's rhythm, Brandeis enjoyed being a justice. He was able to research a decision thoroughly, write it, then watch the consternation his opinions produced.

He believed the process of judging to be "the almost intrinsic correlation of a thousand imponderables." A close associate from those early years, Benjamin V. Cohen, recalled Brandeis saying: "Sometimes, when you are dealing with a question, a question whether you should move one way or another, after making the decision, if I think I'm fifty-one percent right and the other view is only forty-nine percent, if I feel strongly, I will push my decision." Other persons tell the same story about Brandeis, sometimes varying the percentage. The point stays the same.

Brandeis had a messenger supplied by the Court and a clerk-secretary. This "clerk-secretary" was an innovation. Each justice was allowed funds for a stenographer, but both Holmes and Brandeis, following a precedent established by Justice Horace Gray, dropped the stenographers and used Harvard Law School graduates—chosen for them by Frankfurter—for a year. Holmes and Brandeis, said Dean Acheson, who was Brandeis's third clerk, "believed that these young men, fresh from the intellectual stimulation of the law school, brought them constant refreshment and challenge, perhaps more useful in their work than the usual office aides."

As for the dictation and typing that a stenographer would handle, they dispensed with such services. Holmes and Brandeis answered their own mail by pen—those letters, that is, that they did not throw away.

The Court Brandeis joined in 1916 had changed since 1908 when he argued *Muller* v. *Oregon.* Chief Justice Fuller had died in 1910, and President Taft named Associate Justice Edward White to be Chief Justice. In Supreme Court folklore, Oliver Wendell Holmes once said of Chief Justice White: "His opinions remind me of seeing a man on the brink of a roaring chasm. Then you look away for a moment and when you look back he is on the other side." Holmes was still on the Court. Fifty years earlier on the Civil War battlefields, he and White had faced each other—Holmes wearing the blue uniform of the Union soldier and White the gray of the Confederacy. Now they were colleagues.

Holmes, of course, welcomed Brandeis, their friendship going back many years. It had been Brandeis who, when Harvard needed funds to endow a teaching chair for Holmes, found a wealthy graduate with $90,000 to donate.

Joseph McKenna, the child of immigrants who then had voted for legislation restricting other immigrants, and William R. Day, friendly to business interests, also remained on the Court.

Of the new members, Willis Van Devanter had been appointed in

1911 to replace White as associate justice. Born in 1859, Van Devanter, a Republican politician from Wyoming, served until 1937 and was respected for his technical expertise. Brandeis called him a "master of formulas that decided cases without creating precedents." When John Marshall Harlan died in 1911, he was replaced by Mahlon Pitney, a New Jersey lawyer and judge. Born in 1858, Pitney served on the Supreme Court from 1912 to 1922. He was William Howard Taft's last Court appointment and an example of what Taft meant by justices being a bulwark against radicalism. Dean Acheson considered him as representative of "the highest general average that one can hope for on the bench."

David Brewer, who had written *Muller* v. *Oregon* in 1908, died in 1910 and was replaced by Charles Evans Hughes. When Hughes, in turn, resigned, about the same time Brandeis was sworn in, to become the 1916 Republican candidate for President, Woodrow Wilson appointed John Hessin Clarke to replace him.

Rufus Peckham had died, replaced by Horace H. Lurton, who served only four years before dying at age seventy; Wilson replaced him with Attorney General James McReynolds. Born in 1862, McReynolds served on the Court from 1914 to 1941. His animosity toward Brandeis increased during their years on the Court together.

Because the Court met in the Old Senate Chamber in the Capitol building, there was no office space for the justices, so they worked at home, circulating their opinion drafts by messenger, and were denied the day-to-day intimacy of other collegial bodies. Still, many of the relationships were marked by warmth. "Grandfather Brandeis does mighty well!!" wrote Chief Justice White, who was eleven years Brandeis's senior, on the draft of a Brandeis opinion. White often walked with Brandeis to the Court, and Brandeis shared some of White's tribulations. "The Chief was up most of last night with a sick dog, which left for the Vet. Hospital at 5 AM," wrote Brandeis to his wife explaining a delay in the Supreme Court's business, continuing: "Thus are great affairs of men dependent upon beasts."

The nine men—Chief Justice White, and associate justices Holmes, McKenna, Day, Van Devanter, Pitney, McReynolds, Brandeis, and Clarke—made up what Brandeis called, with a forward gesture of his right hand, "our Court."

That amiability outside the Court, however, hid the conflict inside, the deliberate intellectual combat. The Supreme Court was designed as the Agincourt of the mind. Of the nine justices on the Supreme

Court, five can make up a majority, decide whether a President is wrong or right, whether a state legislature acts properly, whether a criminal goes free because his or her constitutional rights were violated, whether a union is legally constituted. Every problem that traumatizes the nation can—and most probably will—come before the Supreme Court.

Appointed for life or for good behavior, the justices virtually cannot be ousted. Their salaries cannot be reduced. Their decisions have rarely been challenged successfully.

The Supreme Court Louis Brandeis had joined was established formally by Article III, Section I of the United States Constitution: "The judicial power of the United States, shall be vested in one supreme Court." Its origins go further back. In 1701, the English Parliament had guaranteed British judges lifetime tenure. The colonists wanted the same for their own judges, to be certain that laws would be interpreted by judges free from coercion.

Those Americans understood the authority of an independent judiciary. Its greatest power had been enunciated in the early 1600s by Sir Edward Coke: "And it appears in our books, that in many cases, the common law will controul acts of parliament, and sometimes adjudge them to be utterly void, for when an act of parliament is against common right and reason, or repugnant, or impossible to be performed, the common law will controul it, and adjudge such act to be void." The practice of overruling acts of the legislature and then of the Crown itself grew in the colonies. In the 1730s the Superior Court of Judicature of Massachusetts Bay refused to enforce an order of the King because "they have no authority by any law of this province, or usage of this Court to order such an execution." In numerous other instances also local courts struck down acts of the King, of the Parliament, and also of the colonial governments themselves.

England, not wanting to lose authority over the colonies, resented that judicial independence. In the Declaration of Independence in 1776 the Americans, no longer colonists but revolutionaries, charged George III with making "Judges dependent on his Will alone, for the tenure of their offices, and the amount and payment of their salaries."

In 1787 in Philadelphia, the authors of the federal Constitution, familiar with judicial history, intended the federal court system to be independent. Several times there were proposals to have the Supreme Court members also serve on a presidential advisory council or be required to join with the President in vetoing laws enacted by Congress. In each instance the proposal was defeated because the judges will have "a sufficient check against encroachments on their own department by their exposition of the laws" and because "the judicial ought not to join in the negative of a law, because the Judges will have the expounding of those laws when they come before them; and they will no doubt stop the operation of such as shall appear repugnant to the constitution."

In the various state conventions called to consider ratification of the Constitution, the same point—the powers of the judiciary to "stop" unconstitutional laws—was made. In the Connecticut convention, Oliver Ellsworth, later a Chief Justice of the United States, argued: "If the general legislature should at any time overleap their limits, the judicial power is a constitutional check. If the United States go beyond their powers, if they make a law which the Constitution does not authorize, it is void; and the judicial power, the national judges, who to secure their impartiality, are to be independent, will declare it to be void." At the Virginia convention, John Marshall argued: "To what quarter will you look for protection from an infringement on the Constitution, if you will not give the power to the judiciary: There is no other body that can afford such protection."

The Federalist Papers, written by Alexander Hamilton, John Jay, and James Madison to explain the proposed Constitution to the colonists, stressed the same point. "The courts were designed to be an intermediate body between the people and the legislature in order, among other things," said the *Papers,* "to keep the latter within the limits assigned to their authority."

Armed with such power, John Marshall, Chief Justice from 1801 to 1835, stretched the Court's boundaries to their outer limits. And the history of the Supreme Court became, as did the histories of the Presidency and the Congress, a history of the United States. The attack on the national bank, the ousting of the American Indians from their homeland, the refusal to confront slavery, the income tax, the separate but equal doctrine—all came before the justices of the Supreme Court. At times the Court showed weakness, retreating, for example, when President Grant packed the Court in retaliation for the Court's having declared the Legal Tender Act unconstitutional. But the power always was there, waiting for justices strong enough to use it.

The justices knew they used law to deal with politics. "The provisions of the Constitution are not mathematical formulas having their essence in their form," said Holmes. "They are organic living institutions." After

William Howard Taft became Chief Justice in 1921, he spoke in public about the application of constitutional principles "as they are written. ... They may not be remoulded by lawmakers or judges," but in private he spoke differently. When a new member joined the Court in 1922, Taft told him: "A Supreme Court judge must needs keep abreast of the actual situation in the country so as to understand all the phases of important issues which arise, with a view to the proper application of the Constitution, which is a political instrument in a way, to new conditions."

For the Court to survive, it treads carefully. James Bradley Thayer of the Harvard Law School, in the 1890s, had laid out an approach that influenced Holmes, Brandeis, and Frankfurter. Known by the phrase "judicial restraint," his formula allowed the legislatures to make their own choices, free from judicial intrusion, unless the legislators "have not merely made a mistake, but have made a very clear one—so clear that it is not open to rational question." He warned that "Under no system can the power of courts go far to save a people from ruin; our chief protection lies elsewhere."

In a democracy, he insisted, the people must rely on themselves and the power they wield in elections. Brandeis, as an advocate before the Supreme Court, had stressed that point. If the state legislatures had acted reasonably when regulating working conditions, then the Court had no business to call such regulation unconstitutional. The wisdom of the act is not the Court's business.

In the Court, this arena of intellectual combat, Brandeis represented three traditions. One was an extension of Holmes's argument that the life of the law is experience rather than logic. This was consistent with Brandeis's Jewish background. Brandeis has been compared to the Pharisees living at the time of Jesus and attempting to fit the law of the Hebrew Bible into the needs of the life around them. This melding of life and law is also part of the Talmudic way of life for Jews; their rabbis commented on the Bible, not only to elucidate the genius in its pages but to help people live within its moral boundaries. The rabbis could have written as Holmes did: "The felt necessities of the time, the prevalent moral and political theories, intuitions of public policy, avowed or unconscious, even the prejudices which judges share with their fellowmen, have a good deal more to do than the syllogism in determining the rules by which men should be governed."

Second, Brandeis operated within the rigid frontier American tradition, which spoke of self-reliance, local government, and camaraderie among neighbors. In law, this tradition had been expressed in James Bradley Thayer's essay calling for judicial restraint—allow people to control their own lives unless their actions abridge constitutional guarantees. It was a theme for self-government.

Third, Brandeis spoke from the Supreme Court bench as a moralist. The law to him was not a routine but a route to solving problems with fairness to both sides. And his decisions and dissents must be read not only as answers to legal questions but as devices to alert the public to a particular problem and to suggest a means for solving it. For some he was the equivalent of an Old Testament prophet warning of dire consequences; to others, he was a scold. At times he undoubtedly was both. But rarely was his impact not felt.

He was aware, and this reflected his days as a manipulator of publicity, that his audience was not only the participants in the particular case but those outside the courtroom. Dean Acheson, one of his first law clerks, explained: "The purpose was education and persuasion."

Sometimes he was too obvious. Harold Laski, after Brandeis had been on the Court less than two years, wrote Holmes that "if you could hint to Brandeis that judicial opinions aren't to be written in the form of a brief it would be a great relief to the world." Holmes agreed, replying that on at least one occasion he had told Brandeis that "I thought he was letting partisanship disturb his judicial attitude." Eventually Holmes came to accept Brandeis's practice of amassing documentation for his opinions and then inserting it in footnotes. The practice, said Holmes, "certainly enables him to put in a lot of facts that no one but he could accumulate and which overawe me, even if I doubt the form."

Calvert Magruder, Brandeis's first law clerk, said: "There were two striking things about him that first term on the bench. Doubts had been expressed as to how this embattled and controversial crusader for public causes could adjust himself to the calmer role of a judge," he said. "So far as I could observe, there was no adjustment problem at all. The transition seemed an easy and natural one for him." Magruder explained that, as a lawyer, Brandeis "had learned to detach himself from the narrow interests of his clients, to probe into the larger issues from the point of view of the public interest, and thus to seek a long-range settlement of the particular controversy along statesmanlike lines."

The second "striking" fact about Brandeis, said Magruder, was "the suddenness with which the whirlwinds of controversy that had howled about his head died down and subsided once he took his oath of office. That phenomenon is to be ascribed to the Justice's shrewdness and tact." By "tact," Magruder said he meant that Brandeis withdrew from all non-Court activities, except for Zionism, "and was content after 1916, with that sole exception, to limit his public expression to austere and magisterial pronouncements in his judicial opinions."

Brandeis withdrew from the numerous causes he had defended in previous years and seemed above the battles of ordinary men. Eventually he would be thought of almost as an institution, the radical of earlier years replaced by the judicial philosopher who, said one journalist, "sits above the clouds and looks tolerantly upon the follies of the world."

8

In World War I

Since the National Consumers' League's success in the 1908 *Muller* v. *Oregon* case, a number of states had passed laws regulating working conditions. In 1911 alone, twelve states enacted or strengthened laws dealing with women's working conditions; but for each new law enacted, so it seemed, there was a legal challenge.

Brandeis had continued as the League's counsel and was involved with three cases when nominated to the Court, all of them from Oregon, where *Muller* had originated; two dealt with a minimum-wage law, *Stettler* v. *O'Hara* and *Simpson* v. *O'Hara,* and one dealt with a ten-hour workday law for men, *Bunting* v. *Oregon.* After joining the Court, Brandeis withdrew as the League's counsel and recommended that Frankfurter at Harvard replace him. The League agreed.

Frankfurter was excited at the prospect. Each case promised a breakthrough. The *Bunting* case, dealing with a limit on working hours for men, offered a new challenge. "With women you could talk about maternity, motherhood, the next generation, and so on," recalled Frankfurter. "Well, you couldn't talk about maternity in the case of men workers."

Frankfurter accepted the League's invitation under the same conditions as had Brandeis: he would not be paid—"The public issues at stake foreclose the thought of any such private interest"—and he would be invited by the state to appear as counsel.

Because the cases had previously been argued before the Supreme Court by Brandeis, Oregon asked that oral arguments be dispensed with, and that the Supreme Court decide the cases on the basis of submitted briefs. The National Consumers' League officials remembered the New York case *People* v. *William* had been lost after oral arguments had been dispensed with, and appealed to Frankfurter: ". . . can we do anything?"

Frankfurter immediately wired the Oregon attorney general, and asked him to reconsider: "Since there are now two members on court, Day and Clarke, who did not hear original argument, I think it is very detrimental to the important public interest at stake not to argue the case orally." Frankfurter's concern was more than the presence of the two justices. Because the Court had heard arguments on the cases previously without reaching a decision, obviously questions remained. Frankfurter wanted to answer those in the direct manner oral argument allowed.

But the Oregon attorney general thought Frankfurter had another reason. In presenting the cases through the courts, he said, "I have always done so with the single purpose of the results to be achieved and not notoriety in presenting the same." Also, he was irritated because the case was going out of his hands: "I am convinced that the efficient handling of any action or suit at law, can be in charge of but one commander."

Frankfurter was not finished.

On October 28, 1916, he wired Chief Justice White: "A matter of great delicacy and urgency takes me to Washington in an endeavor to see you if possible." He came the next Saturday morning to the Chief Justice's home on New Hampshire Avenue. White had known Frankfurter well when Frankfurter was with the War Department and had liked him. A former Louisiana senator, White was interested in the number of southern students at Harvard Law School—Frankfurter had the figures; and White wanted to talk about how the Civil War had ruined the South—Frankfurter had the sympathy.

Then, finally, the Chief Justice hunched his big frame forward and said: "Well, son, tell me what brings you here. Tell me what's on your mind." As Frankfurter stared back at White, a Roman Catholic, there came over him what he later described as "one of these special interventions, divine interventions." He replied: "Mr. Chief Justice, I am not at all sure that I have a right to be here. I am not at all clear that I should put to you the matter that I'm about to put to you, but I come to you as though in the confessional."

As Frankfurter later described it: "Well, that was a master stroke. I felt at once as though the whole church was enfolding me. He came nearer, more intimately, he said, 'Tell me. Just speak freely.' "

Frankfurter explained the situation, and White suggested the Court would require the oral argument. "Now, I'm supposin'," Frankfurter recalled the Chief Justice's saying, "I'm just supposin'. I'm just one out of nine, but supposin' the court were to take that position, would that meet the situation?"

Frankfurter replied that would meet the situation admirably.

The cases were reargued January 18 and 19, 1917, with Brandeis disqualifying himself. Justice McReynolds gave Frankfurter a difficult time, and Frankfurter described the arguments as "trench warfare." A reporter's account at that moment is appropriate as a description of Frankfurter through most of his life.

"Anyone who looked in at the Supreme Court chamber a few weeks ago, while the two cases involving the constitutionality of the Oregon labor laws were undergoing reargument," began the article, "saw that august tribunal intently listening to the plea of a small, dark, smooth-faced lawyer, mostly head, eyes, and glasses, who looked as if he might have stepped out of the sophomore classroom of a neighboring college." The writer said that Frankfurter's "mode of address indicated that he had merely exchanged one group of pupils for another. He lectured the court quietly, but with a due sense of its indebtedness to him for setting it right where it had been wrong, and giving it positive opinions where uncertainty had been clouding its mental vision." Frankfurter, at Harvard only two years, had already developed the characteristic most noted about his demeanor. Whether addressing his students in Langdell Hall or standing before nine Supreme Court justices, or, later, sitting on the Supreme Court bench and confronting lawyers, he was always the professor lecturing to students.

The article noted that Frankfurter "is a Hebrew by blood" and concluded, "His racial heritage is stamped on his face, and his idealism also —a combination of such frequency, by the way, that we of these later days have ceased to wonder at it."

The Court decided the cases as Frankfurter had anticipated. The *Bunting* case, establishing a maximum number of hours for men, was upheld. On the minimum-wage laws, the Court split evenly. The result was that the lower-court decision, upholding the minimum-wage laws, was allowed to stand. Because the Supreme Court did not settle the point, however, the constitutionality of minimum wages would remain an issue for two more decades.

The three cases together established that an hours law could be enacted for male workers as well as female and that minimum-wage laws were still viable in those states that had them. When *Muller* v. *Oregon* was argued, the attorneys for Muller had said: "The question involved is far-reaching. If such legislation may be sustained and justified merely because the employee is a woman, and if such employment in a healthy vocation may be limited and restricted in her case, there is no limit beyond which the legislative power may not go." They had been right.

Arguing those cases before the Supreme Court had been only one of Felix Frankfurter's activities. Pint-sized—five feet six inches tall—and peppery, he darted across the Harvard Yard and through Washington and New York as if he had more things to do, students to see, problems to solve, letters to write, in the next ten minutes than others had in a month.

During the next several years and through the 1920s his friendship with Brandeis became closer, and he strengthened his relationship with Associate Justice Oliver Wendell Holmes. But with that, Frankfurter also emerged as a prominent person himself, recognized for his attainments, listened to for the soundness of his advice, and respected for the independence of his views.

Henry Stimson remained a friend. "I have never known a person with a more excessive feeling of loyalty than Felix," said Stimson about this time. Another friend was Morris Cohen, Frankfurter's roommate at Harvard, who had yet to attain the fame that would come to him as one of America's foremost philosophers. At Harvard there were new friends like Harold J. Laski, the English economist and Socialist who taught briefly there.

Frankfurter became part of the Boston community. The "Cooper Union" of Boston's South End in those years was the Temple Ohabei Shalom. On Sunday nights there would be a speaker and the residents of the South End—immigrants, the poor, the lonely; some undoubtedly in need of a place to be warm—came to listen, to question, and to heckle. Frankfurter spoke there twice. Herbert B. Ehrmann introduced Frankfurter both times and then, when the talk was done, funneled the questions to him.

"After he had discussed the public interest in many current industrial matters," Ehrmann said, "he was asked the inevitable question: 'Professor Frankfurter, since you believe these things, why aren't you a Socialist?' " Ehrmann said that Frankfurter replied immediately:

"Because I cannot compress life into a formula." He then spent some time discussing the complexity of modern life, pointing out that difficulties in different industries required distinct remedies—some public ownership, some governmental control, some free competition, some various incentives, and so on.

For me at least, Felix in eight words had banished "isms" forever. He had also compressed his own philosophy into a phrase.

Frankfurter thrived as a teacher at Harvard. "Precedents, not underlying philosophic principles, form our legal habit of thought," he argued with Morris Cohen. "It is the case system, which is the empiric, scientific method, that gave us the necessary data and method, first, for a historic, and then for a sociological basis of law." Frankfurter believed law was the necessary element to deal with the "almost magical industrial growth" since the Civil War. "The concentration of life and activities in cities has scattered working ganglia throughout the nation," he wrote in 1915. "These changes in the physical, economic and social aspects of life, all this new vast mass of facts, are necessarily so much raw material for the law." With that he showed that he had learned much from Louis Brandeis, a concern for the world and a determination to use the law to deal with that concern. Next Frankfurter showed he also had learned much from Holmes. "The finished product should be the legal means for accommodating the various interests of life," said Frankfurter, "for law is not outside of life; it is part of it."

Frankfurter believed that "the difficulty is not primarily with the individuals who administer the law, but with the accepted ideas consciously or unconsciously expressed by law." However, he argued, those ideas were beginning to change, and "If the Bar and bench will require of law schools their needed share in the development of the law, the law schools will be compelled to meet the need. Therefore the profession should demand law schools fit for this work—the work not merely of training practitioners but of helping to develop the law, of participating in a great state service." So teaching for Frankfurter became an adventure, a means of changing the law to meet the demands of a modern age. He would hit his stride in the 1920s; the war and Zionism led him in other directions for several years. But he never lost that image of himself, his classroom, and his school as participants in a service to society.

In 1914 Frankfurter became involved with *The New Republic,* then a new liberal magazine that truly intended to solve all the world's problems in a relatively short time. Frankfurter was trustee, kibitzer, sometime writer, and constant critic. Lippmann was the editor, progressivism—if not Socialism—was the battle cry, and Theodore Roosevelt was the original hero. It was great fun. There were lengthy lunches marked by intelligent conversation, brilliant repartee, and an interchange of ideas, some of which appeared in the magazine's columns.

Even then Frankfurter was the catalyst bringing together the brilliant and famous. At a dinner given by the magazine for Brandeis and some prominent lawyers, so the story was repeated, "One after-dinner speaker rose and said, 'I wonder how many present have met each other through Felix?' Sixteen out of the twenty-four raised their hands."

Frankfurter stayed with the magazine through the 1920s, often writing for it or suggesting approaches for its columns. Frequently he was a conduit for his friends; when they thought the magazine should comment on a point, they mentioned it to Frankfurter, confident that if he agreed with them the comment would appear in *The New Republic.* If the magazine never achieved the hoped-for impact, it did become over the years a respected liberal journal—one often watched for its intelligence, perception, good writing, and the constant precariousness of its financial condition.

Like Brandeis, Frankfurter did not pay much attention to party labels, although he understood how persons like Charles Evans Hughes, the Republican's presidential candidate in 1916, and Henry Stimson were "born to their [Republican] association. Their fathers or their uncles, for one thing, fought in the Civil War, and that tradition is a perfectly terrific force in binding them to the Party." He had leaned toward the Republican party, but in 1912 had gone with Roosevelt's Bull Moose party because "big business dominated [Republican Party] councils," making it "simply a class and not a national party."

After the 1912 election, under Henry Stimson's influence, Frankfurter wrote, "My hopes were for the Republican Party as a national instrument," and in 1916 he first favored Hughes over Wilson. "I like Mr. Hughes," he explained. "I do not like Mr. Wilson . . . his unctuous goodness, his rhetoric, a certain quality of Jesuitry." Frankfurter's dislike of Wilson remained a constant. The few times he said something positive about Wilson, he quickly added a negative.

Still, Frankfurter voted for Wilson in November because of Wilson's domestic program and his promise to commit the United States to "a League to Enforce Peace." Said Frankfurter: "No more radical step has ever been taken by an American statesman." In contrast, Hughes had not produced any viable alternatives, said Frankfurter. Also, although he did not mention it, Frankfurter probably supported Wilson because of his appointment of Brandeis to the Supreme Court. Although in the future Frankfurter did not consider himself tied irrevocably to either political party—in 1924, as he had in 1912, he supported a third party—still, with his 1916 vote for a Democrat, he edged toward an alignment with the Democrats. Later, he would become one of the party's movers, thinkers, and, for a while, one of its powers.

In April 1917 the United States entered the First World War. "I can't get Father to admit any regret over our entrance into the war," Brandeis's daughter Elizabeth confided to a friend. "He calls it highly desirable, and thinks the world more hopeful than any time since 1848 with more basis of permanent gain now than then." But what of deaths and destruction? "I don't think he's hard hearted," the daughter continued, "he merely sees things on such a broad plane—in terms of nationalities rather than individuals. I wish I could!"

The war destroyed Brandeis's resolve to refrain, except for his Zionist work, from extrajudicial activities. Actually, for a justice to take on an outside, public activity not conflicting with his court work was not unusual, and Brandeis had come close to doing so after joining the Court in 1916. President Wilson asked him then to accept a position on a commission dealing with a dispute between the United States and Mexico. Brandeis accepted on condition that Chief Justice White did not object. But White did object, saying the Court was too overloaded with work to lose one of its members, even briefly. Then over breakfast at the City Club in New York, Frankfurter advised Brandeis not to begin his court career by what would be a lengthy absence. Brandeis then turned down the appointment.

With war the city of Washington changed. The American soldier needed a long line of supplies and support stretching from the American land to the European trenches, and young men sped from government office to government office, requisitioning, planning, ordering. Many could not handle the intense pace or the bureaucratic demands. To them Brandeis became a resource. He knew almost everyone of importance in Washington, had a supportive word for anyone in trouble, advice, ideas, and the experience to assist.

Eugene Meyer's job was to find the metals needed to fight the war, but the bureaucrats' promises made to him were not kept, as they were not to most people in wartime Washington. "Eugene's nerves went from bad to worse," his wife, Agnes, reported. "He has not sufficient of the politician in him to let these things slide off his back. He took it as hard as he does everything else." She talked to Brandeis, who helped calm her husband down. "He knows the political game infinitely better," said Mrs. Meyer of Brandeis, "and best of all he has Eugene's welfare at heart."

Some of Brandeis's efforts, as the years passed, were exaggerated. Herbert Hoover, the nation's food administrator, was having difficulty moving his food-control bill through the Senate and occasionally discussed his problems over dinner with Brandeis, who was a close friend. Hoover's particular problem was Senator James A. Reed, Democrat of Missouri. Later it was reported: "It was Brandeis who advised him [Hoover] in June 1917 how to secure enactment of the Lever Food Control bill." That report then grew to another published report that Brandeis had "helped either draft or administer" the act and, when its constitutionality came before the Court, did not disqualify himself "as the circumstances seemed to require. Instead, he simply refused to sign the court's opinion and concurred only in its result." Actually, Brandeis's advice and help were a suggestion that Hoover meet personally with Reed to discuss their differences. Whether Hoover ever attempted to follow that advice, he never gained Reed's support and years later referred to the senator, in connection with the food-control bill, as one "expert in the practice of malice beyond the average." In 1921 the act did come before the Supreme Court and the Court ruled the act unconstitutional. Brandeis joined a concurrence by Mahlon Pitney, saying the act's technical defects were sufficient to destroy it without going to its constitutionality.

Brandeis's advice was rarely imposed but given when sought. Late in 1917, for example, President Wilson pondered whether Treasury Secretary William McAdoo should be made railroad czar to assure that supplies, raw materials, and troops were delivered at the proper time. Although McAdoo seemed a proper appointment, Wilson hesitated. McAdoo was not only his Secretary of the Treasury but also his son-in-law, and Wilson "resented the crown-prince talk." Time was short; this was Christmas 1917 and the federal government was to assume control of the railroads January 1, 1918.

Joseph P. Tumulty, then Wilson's secretary, telephoned Robert W. Woolley, an Interstate Commerce Commission member and Brandeis friend. Tumulty wanted Woolley to go with him to see Brandeis; together the two men would ask Brandeis to use his influence to persuade Wilson to appoint McAdoo.

With Brandeis's experience as counsel to the Interstate Commerce Commission investigating railroads and with his personal knowledge of McAdoo, he was responsive. Still, Brandeis understood the restraints of his office. "He said he could not go to the White House on any such mission," Woolley reported.

Tumulty then asked: "What if the President were to ask you to come?"

"That would be a command, and I should obey."

The next afternoon, Sunday, at five o'clock, Wilson arrived at the Brandeis apartment. "He deemed it not to be proper to ask a Justice of the Supreme Court to come to the White House on a matter which necessarily had political aspects," said Woolley.

Wilson and Brandeis talked nearly an hour. The White House announced McAdoo's appointment the next morning.

Wilson often sought help from Brandeis. Finding himself in charge of a war effort but without the manpower to staff it, the President turned to the individual who had been so helpful in the campaign and in his first administration. Brandeis helped many government officials find the men they needed for their suddenly widening bureaucracies. He had introduced Hoover, who had been involved in Belgian war relief work, to administration figures. Joseph B. Eastman, whom Brandeis had first met when he was involved with the Public Franchise League in Boston, was appointed to the Interstate Commerce Commission by Wilson on Brandeis's suggestion.

Problem with obtaining munitions? Why didn't the administration ask Brandeis, said Felix Frankfurter, then scurrying around Washington; he argued that Brandeis, with his experience as a corporation lawyer and investigator, understood management structure.

Frankfurter believed so strongly in Brandeis's ability as a wartime manager that he suggested, unsuccessfully, that Brandeis leave the Supreme Court to become "a director general of labor." In a memorandum signed by him and another official, Frankfurter said:

We are not unmindful of the important part the Supreme Court must play in the process of healthy readjustments after the war, nor of the need of an atmosphere of non-partisanship if that part is to be wisely exercised. But if it is a world of "illusions," it is also a world of relativity—of balancing speculative fears against the exigent dangers of a pressing crisis.

When Brandeis refused to consider leaving the Supreme Court, Frankfurter pleaded with him, saying, "I'm sorry but absolutely no one else can do it." But Brandeis was adamant; he would not leave the Court.

In dealing with the war effort, Brandeis's technique was the same as it had been as a practicing lawyer, becoming "counsel for the situation."

He recommended a munitions czar in the War Department, although the czar concept was contrary to his basic belief against giving too much power to one person. But in this instance a "czar" was what the situation demanded. Solve the problem; win the war; put aside the bias against bigness.

In contrast to Brandeis's role as a counselor, Frankfurter's involvement in the war effort was intense. Early in 1917, as the threat of American involvement in the war grew, Frankfurter considered his options. He talked with Holmes about joining the army. Holmes, the Civil War veteran, understood Frankfurter's emotions, but he also understood that more than combat soldiers were needed in a war effort and that Frankfurter had too many talents needed on the home front. Also, he had personal concerns for his young friend. "I only rejoice," he said, "that if you have to serve it is not likely to be in the field."

Because of his experience under Stimson a few years earlier, Frankfurter was a candidate for the rapidly expanding War Department. He already knew Newton D. Baker, the Secretary of War, and had not hesitated to send off advice to him: "I learned confidentially that woolen and textile industries of Massachusetts confronted with heavy domestic war orders are planning wholesale letting down of the bars as to hours, Sunday work and night work for women. Necessity seems urgent for the adoption of a resolution by the Council of Defense. . . . Time is of essence."

By the summer of 1917 he was in Washington full time, operating as an assistant secretary of war. Harold Laski reported to Holmes that President Wilson was in charge of foreign policy and "Felix seems to sponsor the rest of the government. To my certain knowledge he directs the War Department. . . . I saw that he has almost annexed the Shipping Board; there are similar rumours about the Department of Justice." As busy as he was, Frankfurter remained, said Laski, "light and debonair, purposive and a skillful administrator." Frankfurter's move to Washington became official when A. Lawrence Lowell, the Harvard president, granted Frankfurter a leave of absence at the request of Secretary of War Baker.

Almost immediately Frankfurter was involved with attempts to bring labor peace to the United States. American industry had more orders than it could fill. To expand, it needed more workers, as many as it could find. And the workers realized their opportunity. Now, they insisted, recognize our unions, pay decent wages, install safe working conditions, stop exploiting women and children workers. Now, they argued, understand that an employee is a human being worthy of and demanding respect. Now, they shouted, meet with us across the table to talk about hours and night work and salaries. Now, the workers exalted, it is our turn.

The strikes, threatening the war effort, spread across the nation. Frankfurter's headquarters were in Washington but his base of operations was the country. To this point, Frankfurter had operated in an atmosphere above the economic battle. Like Louis Brandeis, his model, he had been a social engineer, dealing with causes and movements. Frankfurter had operated primarily in the courtroom and classroom. What he felt, he felt intellectually, not emotionally. His reactions were cerebral, not from the gut. The First World War changed that for him. He traveled, met the union members in their sites, talked—not only to the lawyers and the professional representatives, but also to those actually involved. He studied their faces, heard their complaints, felt their passions. He was never again the same.

Frankfurter had written in a 1915 article that labor and management "interests are conflicting, not identical; there is, however, a need of composing or adjusting these different interests." The way to do this, he said, then, "is according to the theory of Anglo-Saxon law, a balanced representation of those interests." The World War gave him the opportunity to put those beliefs into action as secretary and counsel to the President's Mediation Commission, formally headed by Secretary of Labor William B. Wilson.

The Commission's first challenge was a copper strike in Arizona. Four copper districts in that state produced 28 percent of the nation's copper output, and the strike there cost the United States 100 million pounds of copper. Labor was scarce, and the workers were doing better than they had in the past in terms of wages and working conditions. In addition, the IWW—the Industrial Workers of the World, "Wobblies" —was agitating for union members but not making much headway. Still, the workers knew they were in an emergency situation; once the war ended, they would again be abused, wages would again decrease, safety rules would be ignored, job security forgotten.

Frankfurter met with both sides, often separately because the business representatives refused to meet with the union leaders. Let others fight the Hun in France, the owners' representatives seemed to say; we fight the union men here. One night in October 1917, after a long day of meeting with both sides, thrashing out arguments, going back to each side again, hearing new arguments, Frankfurter sat in his room in the

Dominion Hotel in Globe, Arizona, and wrote of his troubles to Louis Brandeis.

"You said it all," Frankfurter wrote in his letter. "Autocracy and anarchy sums it up, not the less so because the managers here are very decent and hardly conscious of the autocratic powers they are wielding, and anarchy even tho there has been a surprising lack of violence and disorder." Frankfurter said the "basic" trouble was a "lack of government in the industry, so that men lack security in their employment, and the management is unprotected against wanton or unwarranted strikes."

Frankfurter ran over the list of grievances; all were soluble. "In a word," he said, "the issue is not material but spiritual." To management, the workers and their union leaders were the enemy; one pulls from them all the work possible, pays them the least possible, stands over their shoulder to measure their effort, brings in hired guns to make certain they don't cause trouble. To the worker, the owner was stripping him of his dignity as a human being, destroying his ability to earn a living for his family, denying his intelligence, attempting to reduce him to a near-animalistic state.

Felix Frankfurter brought them together. The immigrant Jew who never had worked in a mine, never been an employer, who had never walked a picket line or had to fill in a profit sheet—he did it. As he had told Brandeis, the problems were spiritual rather than material, and he hammered at that point in his meetings with both sides and in his formal reports—"the human problems of the industry."

He respected each person he met, whether that person was a miner or an owner; he did not ridicule the foreign-born union organizer who spoke broken English or scoff at the manager with an absentee owner pressuring him for more profits. He did not tolerate management blaming the labor troubles on the IWW or the union leaders claiming that management didn't care. The solution he brought about was a structure offering workers steady employment and the company a strike-free atmosphere. He insisted that each side acknowledge the other's problems and respond to them.

While negotiating an end to the copper strike, Frankfurter became involved in the Bisbee deportations. "Bisbee," like "Mooney" and later "Sacco-Vanzetti" were points marking Felix Frankfurter's path. More than 1,100 miners had been run out of Bisbee, Arizona, by vigilantes under the pretext of attempting to stop union violence. The miners were left stranded in the desert for two days until the federal government rescued them. To management, "Bisbee" meant an owner's right to defend himself against union violence. To the workers, "Bisbee" meant an owner's use of violence against peaceful workers. The Mediation Commission—that is, Frankfurter—investigated.

The Commission branded the deportations as outside the law, castigated the local authorities, and made clear that the government would not stand by while working men and women were abused. Times had changed, said the Commission, and the way of strike-breaking "detectives" and vigilantes was ending.

Frankfurter came under personal criticism for his role in the Bisbee investigation. It was the beginning for him of a series of attacks because of the other Bisbees he would find in the future. The attacks did not stop him. "Keep at it," he advised Will Scarlett, an Episcopal minister, who was attacked also for siding with Frankfurter in the Bisbee case. "Expect misunderstandings," Frankfurter continued, "attacks, and worst of all disappointments in those you have hitherto regarded as your friends. That is part of the essential cost of doing what you are trying to do."

One attack especially hurt. This came from Theodore Roosevelt. The leader of the Bisbee vigilantes was Jack Greenway, a Roosevelt Rough Rider in the Spanish-American War. Roosevelt could not accept that Greenway, who had stormed San Juan Hill with him, could have done something illegal or immoral; Frankfurter must be wrong.

Theodore Roosevelt had continued to be a Frankfurter hero, from his presidency, through his Bull Moose days, to his jingoist war announcements in 1917. Although stung by Roosevelt's criticism, Frankfurter believed that disputes between friends could be solved by facts. Frankfurter had been abroad when the Bisbee vigilantes had attacked the miners, he wrote in a long letter to Roosevelt, but he had studied all the material with "conscientious purpose to ascertain the facts." He conceded that Greenway, Roosevelt's friend, might have been propelled by patriotic purposes, but, said Frankfurter, "it is not a law of necessity that whatever Jack Greenway does is right."

Roosevelt was not moved, especially because of another case in which Frankfurter was involved. In 1916 a parade, organized by businessmen to support the Allies, was held in San Francisco. Threatened violence materialized. A bomb exploded, killing nineteen persons and injuring forty. Thomas J. Mooney and several others were arrested and charged with the crime. Mooney was a labor agitator who had been arrested previously in a dynamiting case, but not convicted. He was convicted in the parade bombing, however, and sentenced to die. His case, like the Bisbee deportations, became a cause célèbre. To American industrialists, Tom Mooney was a dangerous labor agitator who, like most of his fellows, would not hesitate to use violence for his ends, or care how many persons he killed. To union members, Mooney was an innocent victim, convicted by what was close to a lynch mob because he fought for the working man and not because he was guilty of any crime. Mooney, in fact, had been convicted on the basis of perjured evidence.

Frankfurter and the Mediation Commission had been directed by President Wilson to investigate the Mooney case because of the resulting labor unrest. When Frankfurter arrived in San Francisco and learned of the perjured evidence, he reported back that, if there was no retrial, President Wilson should urge the governor of California to seek a retrial. The Commission's report, written by Frankfurter, did not speak to Mooney's guilt or innocence, but only to the fairness of the proceeding.

The district attorney who had prosecuted the case, Charles M. Fickert, attacked Frankfurter's report as an attempt to buy labor peace. After Fickert received a telegram of support from Theodore Roosevelt, Frankfurter attempted to convince Roosevelt that the issue was "in no wise one between patriotism and anarchy and is not conceived to be such here by people whom the colonel would be the first to regard as leaders in the war." Roosevelt replied that Frankfurter had taken "on behalf of the administration an attitude which seems to me to be fundamentally that of Trotsky and other Bolsheviki leaders in Russia."

Frankfurter has been accused of playing up to the prominent people he admired; he did. He had written Theodore Roosevelt flattering letters over the years, as he had written such letters to Henry Stimson and to Louis Brandeis, and as he would write to Franklin D. Roosevelt. But Frankfurter's desire to associate with the important and significant had limits. In the Bisbee and Mooney cases, he believed he had been acting in the cause of justice. No matter how many friends it cost him, he would always believe that. The relationship between him and Theodore Roosevelt ended.

The Mediation Commission continued its travels, demonstrating that sincere conciliation efforts could soothe unrest and bring labor peace. In the California oil fields, according to the Commission report, "as in the copper districts, machinery of enforcement was essential. . . . The men thus secured betterment in hours and conditions of employment and the means of redress for future grievances." In Chicago, a strike in the meat-packing industry threatened the continued meat supply to

America's allies. Arbitration machinery was established. Secretary of War Baker, when the conflict was settled, notified President Wilson that Frankfurter's results were "fine beyond anything believed possible." And so it went. The Mediation Commission, with Frankfurter managing it, was like a traveling road show, offering arbitration and conciliation, intelligence and respect to audiences that previously had seen only anger and violence.

There was much to learn. The lumber industry in the Pacific Northwest was seething. In a letter to Brandeis, Frankfurter called it "ugly —no other word describes it. . . . All the elements of bitterness and strife are smouldering beneath the surface." The IWW moved in. Certainly leftist, believed to be Communist, the IWW was struggling with the American Federation of Labor to represent the worker. Management, instead of cooperating with the more respectable AFL, opposed all union representation, pushing the worker toward the IWW. "The I.W.W. is filling the vacuum created by the operators . . ." reported Frankfurter. "The hold of the I.W.W. is riveted instead of weakened by unimaginative opposition on the part of employers to the correction of real grievances."

At the end of the Mediation Commission's work, Frankfurter wrote a report, signed by all the members, which drew some general truths from the group's experience. The causes of the unrest, he said, "have long been familiar and long uncorrected. War has only served to intensify the old derangement." The problems were that "American industry lacks a healthy basis of relationship between management and men," that "Force becomes too readily an outlet" to solve disputes because of the lack of arbitration processes, that both sides become the victims of their rhetoric, and efforts to repress labor unions "turn radical labor leaders into martyrs and thus increase their following." Frankfurter acknowledged that "sinister influences and extremist doctrine may have availed themselves of these conditions," but he insisted, "they certainly have not created them."

He concluded: "Too often there is a glaring inconsistency between our democratic purpose in this war abroad and the autocratic conduct of some of those guiding industry at home."

Frankfurter's next Washington job was as executive director of the War Labor Policies Board, its purpose to impose uniform hour, wages, and working conditions on government contractors. It was, in reality, a spokesman for organized labor. His responsibility was to meet with union and employer councils and work out agreements for industrial peace. Their talks focused on the eight-hour day, overtime pay, work-men's compensation, life insurance for the worker, almost all the issues that would occupy industry and labor for the next forty years.

Women in the war effort were one issue that plagued Frankfurter. He had had too much experience watching women like Josephine Gold-mark and Florence Kelley to discount the effectiveness of women. But he, and Franklin D. Roosevelt, who was the Navy's representative on the Board, were from a generation of males reluctant to see the genteel female in the hurly-burly of the workplace, especially some workplaces. Mary Anderson, working in Washington for the Women in Industry Service, would not tolerate such chauvinism. "We had a good many tussles with the board on matters of policy," she said. "I think the most serious one occurred when the board wanted us to set up a list of industries in which women should be employed. We felt we could not do that because, if they were really needed, women could work almost anywhere, provided the working conditions were satisfactory."

She and another woman met with Frankfurter. "It was a warm spring day and we met in the park near the Washington monument," she said. "Mary van Kleeck and I sat on a bench and Mr. Frankfurter sat on the grass at our feet while we had a hot discussion, trying to make him come over to our point of view."

At one point Frankfurter insisted that, if the women did not produce a list of "safe" occupations for females, he would ask another agency to do it. "But we stuck to our guns," said Miss Anderson, "and in the end we won out with the decision that instead of offering a list of occupa-tions in which women should be substituted for men, we would promul-gate standards with the statement that in any occupation in which these standards were upheld increased employment of women would be desirable."

On July 12, 1918, the War Labor Policies Board formally called for women to take over some defense jobs but said that "women should not be employed to replace men in occupations or places of employment clearly unfit for women owing to physical or moral conditions, as for instance in bar rooms and saloons, in pool rooms, in or about mines, smelters and quarries, on furnace work in glass works . . ." Women under twenty-one should not be employed, the Board said, "in the public messenger service, in street car, elevated and subway transporta-tions service, as elevator operators, as bellboys in hotels and clubs . . ."

Frankfurter had one encounter that, as much as any single incident can, symbolized the confrontation between the old and the new and outlined the economic conflicts the United States would face for decades. This was his meeting September 20, 1918, with Elbert Henry Gary, chairman of the board of directors of the United States Steel Corporation.

Gary's family, like so many Americans in the middle of the nineteenth century, had migrated from the New England states to the Midwest in search of greater opportunity. Elbert, born in 1846, learned to work on the farm; he worked hard and, although assisted by his family's financial success, Elbert Gary called himself a "self-made" man. He eventually became a lawyer and then board member of railroads and industries. His work in developing the Federal Steel Company attracted the attention of J. P. Morgan, who was putting together the United States Steel Corporation. Morgan brought Gary in to run U.S. Steel, then the largest industrial corporation in the world's history.

The picture of Gary's attitude toward labor is not clear. A friendly biographer described him as a "grand seigneur" to labor, continuing: "He . . . did more to improve the lot of the American worker with his hands than any individual of our time, probably more than has been accomplished by all the labor unions together." Gary was credited with sacrificing dividends to maintain workers' salaries. On the other side, United States Steel did not end the seven-day work week until 1910 and then only after public criticism. It was U.S. Steel and Gary personally that Brandeis had attacked over the years for paying employees substandard wages and using an optional pension plan to keep employees out of the unions: if they joined the union, they lost their pensions. Gary was not concerned about a shortage of workers willing to work cheaply; the purpose of immigration laws was to supply those workers. "The number allowed to come here should be equal to the necessities of our industries," he said.

Frankfurter decided to take on Elbert Gary.

The issue was the eight-hour day. Frankfurter, through the War Labor Policies Board, hoped to impose the eight-hour day on all government contractors; in the steel industry the men worked a twelve-hour day. For Frankfurter the eight-hour day was not merely a union or working man's goal. Two years earlier he had written, "The crucial fact of modern industry is its failure to use the creative qualities of men, its deadening monotony and its excessive fatigue." The result, Frankfurter said, is "stunted citizenship." But with extra time "for the cultivation of amenities of civilized life," the people would be capable of "disciplined democracy." He continued: "In a word, leisure has a real social value, and there is every moral and political reason to seek its increase." Frankfurter also said that shorter hours raised efficiency and provoked inventiveness, "all kinds of savings."

To Elbert Gary, the eight-hour day was "a fraudulent wage-maker," a device sought by the employee to earn extra pay. The steel worker, Gary argued, wished to work twelve hours but agitated for eight hours to receive time and a half for hours nine through twelve. As Frankfurter's pro-eight-hour beliefs were the product of years of social concern, Gary's advocacy of the twelve-hour day was a direct result of his years as a youth working long hours on a farm or in a law office.

Charles Schwab, who had headed two steel companies and now worked for the government, suggested to Frankfurter that he meet with Gary. The time seemed appropriate to force the eight-hour day on U.S. Steel and, through the American Iron and Steel Institute, which Gary controlled, on the remainder of the industry. Steel was needed, plants closed for years were reopening, and industry was reaping large profits. In 1917, Gary had been reluctant to go along with price agreements, fearing they meant reduced profits in a soaring market. He was, of course, against government interference with business, except to purchase supplies from it. "The natural law of supply and demand should not be interfered with by the Government or by any administrator of the laws excepting in cases involving turpitude," he said. (After the war, however, he encouraged price agreements, with government blessing, to assure profits in a declining market.)

On July 9, Frankfurter invited Gary to a meeting in Washington. Gary replied July 19, suggesting Frankfurter come to his office in New York. Frankfurter, acting as a government official, declined. On July 25, Frankfurter repeated his invitation. This was wartime. Was industry bossing government, or was government bossing industry?

Frankfurter won.

The War Labor Policies Board issued a directive for government contractors demanding the eight-hour day. So on September 17 a telegram went from Frankfurter to Gary: "In view of the definite government policy with regard to the eight hour day, it is important for me to learn from your committee its views with regard to this policy and the steel industry. I understand your committee will be in Washington this week, and I shall be glad to arrange a conference to learn your views at a time mutually convenient."

There was no answer. Two days later another telegram went from

Frankfurter to Gary. It closed with a reference to working out problems "with the benefit of the suggestions and knowledge and experience of all those at interest." The suggestion was implicit: Either come to the meeting or we will impose the eight-hour day whether you like it or not.

They met in Washington the next day.

They were an odd pair, Frankfurter and Gary. Gary was twice Frankfurter's age. Both were careful, neat dressers. Frankfurter never seemed slowed by, or to notice, being only five feet six inches tall. Gary claimed to be two inches taller than that, but, conceded a friend, "I suspect the measurement was taken in rather high-heeled shoes." Frankfurter was a professor, with virtually no money. Gary was not a thinker or a teacher but a doer, and his equals were people with funds sufficient to buy Frankfurter if not his school. Gary's family had deep roots in American soil; he believed he understood what made America great. Frankfurter's roots in America stretched back less than three decades; he believed he understood what made America great.

The meeting began with Frankfurter discussing the progress of the eight-hour day throughout industry—where the government was the actual employer, where government contractors voluntarily adopted it, and where the War Labor Policies Board or other government agencies had extended it by fiat. Frankfurter then said it was necessary for the government to develop an overall policy. Before doing so, the Board wished to have "the benefit of the experience and judgment of the great basic industry of the country, namely, the steel industry, on the question of what should be done."

Gary requested a definition of the eight-hour day. To him, it continued to mean that the workers worked twelve hours but earned more money per hour for the last four hours than they did for the first eight.

Frankfurter answered that he was talking about "eight hours as a standard of work and that overtime pay provisions should act as a break to working long hours."

Gary became angry. The eight-hour day was a "sham" and "a method of obtaining a wage increase under false pretenses." Any employee, he said, who wanted a wage increase "would receive a favorable hearing, and in all probability, a generous decision."

They went back and forth on whether the government had or had not decided on a policy. Introducing the eight-hour day, said Gary, would be a calamitous interference with war production. Frankfurter snapped back that many industries disagreed with that.

Frankfurter later recalled that Gary at one point said to him: "Professor Frankfurter, you work more than eight hours every day."

"That happens to be so," replied Frankfurter.

"I work more than eight hours every day. You and I work more than eight hours every day. Why shouldn't these men in the factories?"

Brandeis had once responded to a similar question. Frankfurter's answer was much like that response. "Ah," he said, "Judge Gary, but think what interesting jobs you and I have."

On September 25, five days after the confrontation, Frankfurter telegraphed the Secretary of Labor: "You will be glad to hear Judge Gary announces that the Steel Corporation is going on the basic eight hour day effective October 1st."

That was optimistic. The war soon was over, and whatever agreement Gary had made, or Frankfurter believed Gary had made, quickly faded. There would be a lengthy strike and much anguish before labor peace and the eight-hour day came to the steel mills.

But the meeting between the two men involved more than the steel workers. Much at that session, unique then, was common in a few years. There was the professor lecturing the businessman, the capitalist bridling as the government told him how to operate, and, finally, there were the workers, their livelihoods, the whole ambiance of their lives dependent upon how well the government spoke for them.

In succeeding years Frankfurter would reflect on what he had learned during the First World War, as would his associate on the War Labor Policies Board, Franklin D. Roosevelt. "What American business needs is a substitution of law and order for the present status between anarchy and violence, by which it is governed." Frankfurter wrote. "Not until we realize that a copper camp is a community, and that a factory makes the same demand upon its people as a civil government or institution . . . not until the management realizes that the labor movement is essentially not a belly movement, but a movement for the assertion of personality, and the workman recognizes that industry is a complicated organism, shall we see the light." As for political extremism in labor unions, said Frankfurter, "American industry must be organized in a way to prevent exploitation of labor. The workers will not keep silent under that. Given the proper opportunity, however, labor can be stabilized and organized in the same manner as we have stabilized and organized the political life of the country."

During the war the United States had become the world's largest employer. Working with labor and industry, the government had set standards for wages, hours, working conditions, and had established methods for dealing with employees' grievances. "All these things received thought and attention and were studied in a scientific way," said Frankfurter, but with the end of the war, "there arises the impending danger of things going back to their former state." Frankfurter said the "United States today has an opportunity to grow industrially such as has never before been given to any nation. There is an ever-increasing demand for goods, and an ever-increasing market for them. We can meet that demand and fill those markets only on the one condition that there is a different spirit in industry. The hostility and resentment and enmity . . . must by a more scientific process of education grow into one of mutual understanding."

When the war ended, Felix Frankfurter and Louis Brandeis had reason to be proud of their contribution. Frankfurter had helped bring labor peace to the United States and to mobilize the working man. Brandeis had done much to smooth the bureaucratic way in Washington. There was one more thing Brandeis did. On November 11, 1918, the day the war ended, he wrote to Woodrow Wilson, not as to a President but as to a friend, to say that "Throughout the war I have refrained from burdening you with communications. Today, I venture to send you some lines from Euripides." The selection sent begins with the line: "O Strength of God, slow are thou and still, Yet failest never!" and ends with

> What else is Wisdom? What of man's endeavour
>   or God's high grace so lovely and so great?
> To stand from fear set free, to breathe and wait;
> To hold a hand uplifted over Hate;
> And shall not loveliness be loved for ever?

Felix Frankfurter resigned as head of the War Labor Polices Board on February 8, 1919. He intended to return to Harvard; this was the second academic year he had been on leave. But the academic year did not begin until the fall, and he had to confront one more adventure before returning to Cambridge. This would bring him together with Brandeis again; it was the time they worked most closely. The trip was to Paris. The cause was Zionism.

9

The Balfour Declaration

In the first half of 1916 when Brandeis was involved with his Supreme Court nomination fight, his second activity was Zionism. During those months, he continued his fund-raising efforts to assist Jewish settlement in Palestine and his efforts to organize more Zionist chapters in the United States.

He also became a participant in a major controversy. The assimilated German-American Jews had donated funds to assist beleaguered Jews in Europe and Palestine while continuing their own personal anti-Zionism. Since they also controlled the American Jewish Committee, which appeared to speak for American Jewry, the widespread impression was that American Jews were anti-Zionist.

This angered not only Zionists like Brandeis but also the Eastern European Jewish immigrants, who saw themselves squeezed out of any leadership position in the American-Jewish community. Talk of organizing a new group began to circulate. "On the East Side of New York," wrote one participant, "in cloudy, stuffy rooms, tortured by wordy reiterated debates, with all factions represented in proportions wildly unreal, a provisional committee met week after week to talk about an American Jewish Congress. They knew what kind of a Congress it was to be. It was to be a permanent body, based on democratic elections, free and untrammeled."

The American Jewish Committee responded to the unrest by calling its own "conference." In July of 1915, Brandeis, representing the Provisional Executive Committee for General Zionist Affairs, had met with American Jewish Committee leaders with hopes of broadening that conference into a congress. Frankfurter, then a member of the American Jewish Committee and of Brandeis's Provisional Executive Committee, was also present. Nothing came of the meeting; the German-American Jews in charge of the American Jewish Committee were not willing to surrender any of their power to the Zionists and Eastern European Jews. They could not surmount the fear that a congress would suggest, as Jacob Schiff had said, "that we are Jews first, and Americans second."

At a January 1916 meeting in Chicago, however, the various factions did agree to elect delegates to a national congress. Brandeis was largely responsible for the development, and his position as a leader both in fact and in name of the American Zionists could not be challenged—or so it seemed.

He was set up for what can be described only as a political massacre.

After Brandeis's confirmation and swearing-in as an Associate Justice, he decided he could be both a Supreme Court justice and leader of American Zionism. But the powers at the American Jewish Committee wanted him out. With his new position and prestige, he would be considered the leader of the American Jewish community, whether it was a committee or a congress, and what he could be expected to say would be in favor of Zionism.

A meeting had been scheduled for July 16 at the Astor Hotel in New York, sponsored by the American Jewish Committee. Brandeis was invited to the meeting not as a delegate but as an "honored" guest to make a statement about the problems of Jews in Eastern Europe. When Brandeis finished, he planned to leave, but he was asked to remain. As he sat there, Committee leaders rose and attacked him. They charged him with using his position as an associate justice of the Supreme Court to force a pro-Zionist view on the Jewish community. The attacks were not genteel and were repeated in the *New York Times,* then owned by anti-Zionist Jews.

Brandeis believed his service as a public leader of American Zionism had been ended by the meeting, and he resigned all his posts. Still, there was also a sense of victory. "There is at least this compensation," he said. "My enforced withdrawal did not come until after the triumph of the Congress movement has been assured, and the desired unity of the Jews of America has been made possible."

At the Astor Hotel meeting there also had been a statement about financial needs. With his resignation, Brandeis enclosed a check for $250 "toward current expenses."

Frankfurter had resigned from the American Jewish Committee earlier because he believed that "Jews in America must think their own thoughts, make their collective personal sacrifice, express their own will, choose their own leaders, if the Jews in America are ever to reach self-respect."

The struggle for leadership of the American Jewish community, between the German-American Committee and the Eastern-European-dominated Congress, continued for years, as did the tug-of-war between the Zionists and the non-Zionists. Brandeis's and Frankfurter's involvement in Zionist and Jewish affairs also continued; the two men continued as powers in and shapers of the movement.

Henrietta Szold, active those years in the American Jewish movement, offered a picture of Louis Brandeis as the leader of the Zionist movement in fact if not in name. "After he had left Boston and moved to Washington—that is, the Zionist office remained in New York—he kept daily tally of all statistics, incidents, activities, conversations, of everything that transpired in the offices," he said. "From these detailed accounts he was able to deduce the line of action to be followed and to inform us of it in brief."

Since 1910 Brandeis had made Zionism his cause. He had devoted his time, his energy, and much of his money to it. His standing as a community leader had been involved. For his work he had been attacked by Jew and non-Jew; his motives had been questioned by ex-President Taft. Then in December 1917 an event seemed to make it all worthwhile: British troops liberated Jerusalem from Turkish control, making way for the Zionist dream of a Jewish homeland.

Frankfurter, in Seattle at the time for the War Labor Policies Board, wrote Brandeis: "And Jerusalem is finally fallen—the great beginning of the realization of the great dream." Brandeis believed the same. "The work for Zionism has seemed to me, on the whole," he said, "the most worthwhile of all I have attempted; and it is a great satisfaction to see the world gradually acquiescing in its realization."

The Palestine liberated by the British was, according to the official British description, "a country exhausted by war. The population had been depleted; the people of the towns were in severe distress; much cultivated land was left untilled; the stocks of cattle and horses had fallen to a low ebb; the woodlands, always scanty, had almost disappeared; orange groves had been ruined by lack of irrigation; commerce had long been at a standstill."

Brandeis had realized this and believed the challenge before the Jews in and outside of Palestine was an economic one, to renovate the land. The political struggle, he believed, was ended because of the British government's issuance, a few weeks before Jerusalem's liberation, of the Balfour Declaration calling for a Jewish homeland in Palestine. That was one of the worst miscalculations he had ever made. Rather than at an end, the political struggle was at a beginning.

The Balfour of the declaration was Arthur Balfour, a leader of the English Conservative party, a former Prime Minister, and Foreign Secretary in 1917. Not Jewish himself, Balfour had long been interested in the problem of the Jewish dispersal. His family members remembered "in childhood imbibing from him the idea that Christian religion and civilisation owes to Judaism an immeasurable debt, shamefully ill repaid." In 1905, when Balfour was campaigning for Parliament in Manchester, he met Chaim Weizmann, a Russian émigré, scientist, and ardent Zionist. A few years earlier the British had offered the Jews a homeland in Africa, and Balfour could not understand why they had turned down Africa to wait for Palestine. Weizmann answered: "Mr. Balfour, if you were offered Paris instead of London, would you take it?"

Balfour replied: "But London is our own!"

Said Weizmann: "Jerusalem was our own when London was a marsh."

In 1916, Balfour, then first Lord of the Admiralty, and Weizmann met again. England was at war, and Weizmann the chemist, working for the British Admiralty, had developed a process important to the war effort. At the end of one meeting, Balfour, recalling their 1905 encounter, said: "You know, Dr. Weizmann, if the Allies win the war you may get your Jerusalem."

Balfour explained his motives once to the House of Lords:

Surely it is in order that we may send a message to every land where the Jewish race has been scattered, a message that will tell them that Christendom is not oblivious of their faith, is not unmindful of the service they have rendered to the great religions of the world, and most of all to the religion that the majority of Your Lordships' house profess, and that we desire to the best of our ability to give them that opportunity of developing, in peace and quietness under British rule, those great gifts which hitherto they have been compelled to bring to fruition in countries that know not their language and belong not to their race? That is the ideal which I desire to see accomplished.

Before the First World War, Palestine, home to both Arab and Jew, was part of the Ottoman Empire, controlled by Turkey for centuries. In the war, Turkey joined the Central Powers against England. If the Central Powers, headed by Germany, were defeated, and with them Turkey, land in the Middle East would be available as spoils to the victors. The Zionists hoped that, in this postwar carving-up, the Jews would have a chance for Palestine.

Frankfurter once defined Zionism as "essentially a psychological force—the passionate longing by Jews for a home of their own." At this particular moment in history it must be a political force also. The Zionists, building on moral sentiments such as Balfour's, had to persuade the British government that a Jewish homeland in Palestine was advantageous to the British.

This Chaim Weizmann attempted to do. Before he was done, Brandeis and Frankfurter would be involved. For Brandeis this new involvement ultimately led him to confront, as he never had before, his role as a minority member in American society. Was he a Jew? Did being Jewish automatically mean being a Zionist? Was he an American? Was he a Jewish-American? Does the melting pot claim the individual? Or is the United States the land of the hyphenated American?

The British did not require much persuasion about the advantages to them of a Jewish homeland in Palestine under a British protectorate. They were warm to the proposal for two reasons, in addition to Christian morality. One reason was the traditional British commercial and empire interests in the Middle East. Palestine always had been a crossroads for land-based travel and commerce—to this was added the importance of the Suez Canal in neighboring Egypt—and if Palestine became a British protectorate, England would become the dominant power in the Middle East.

The second reason involved the course of the war. England in 1916 and early 1917 needed American support for its war effort, if not America to join in the fighting. But England was concerned that the United States might be kept out of the war because Jewish sentiment in the United States favored the German side. Even after the United States entered the war in April 1917, the British feared that the American war effort would be hampered by lack of Jewish support. To Eastern European Jews in the United States, Germans were fighting Russians, who had for centuries led pogroms against Jews in Eastern Europe. For German Jews in the United States, there remained ties to the ancestral homeland. These feelings could be countered, the British believed, by the promise of a Jewish homeland. By offering a new home for the displaced and oppressed in the wake of the First World War, the Balfour Declaration would appeal to all American Jews, whatever their origins, whether they were Zionists or non-Zionists.*

*In subsequent years it has been reported that the English need for American-Jewish support was not one of the motivations for the Balfour Declaration but was invented later, in the 1930s and 1940s. However, Winston Churchill, speaking in a House of Commons debate on Palestine on July 4, 1922, said: "Pledges and promises were made during the War, and they were made not only on the merits, though I think the merits are considerable. They were made because it was considered they would be of value to us in our

So, to increase the American war efforts against the Germans and in the interests of a growing empire in the postwar world, and because of Christian morality, the British began to look favorably on a Jewish homeland in Palestine under a British mandate. Balfour told Weizmann to meet with David Lloyd George, then Prime Minister. "You may tell the Prime Minister," said Balfour to Weizmann, "that I wanted you to see him."

But this was in 1917 and first the British had to deal with the secret 1916 Sykes-Picot agreement, in which they and the French had agreed to carve up the land known as Palestine. Only after the French, if hesitantly, accepted the Jewish-homeland concept and then the Pope endorsed the idea did the British begin the process aimed at transforming Palestine into the land of the Jews.

The deal, as it was worked out, was that the British would grant the homeland if the Jews would accept, even request, that there be a British protectorate. The protectorate approach assured the presence of the British to watch over their empire interests. To wrap it up, to reassure the continued-nervous French, a declaration of support from President Wilson was needed.

Brandeis was the go-between.

The approach was through Brandeis because there were few other persons with Zionist sentiments who had connections to the White House. The usual avenues were closed. The State Department had so little interest in the area at the time, for example, that most of its Middle East information came from an oil company official there sending occasional letters. Even if there had been accurate, unbiased information, the State Department might not have responded; its officials were not then—and were not for many years—responsive to concerns of American Jews.

In April 1917, Weizmann informed Brandeis: "Unless the [American] Jews give expression to their heartfelt desire that Great Britain should protect a Jewish Palestine and should keep it in trust for the Jews in naturally safeguarding the interests of other nationalities like the Arabs, Great Britain would find it difficult to oppose the demands of the French for the internationalisation of Palestine."

About this time Arthur Balfour himself visited the United States. "I

---

struggle to win the War. It was considered that the support which the Jews could give us all over the world, and particularly in the United States, and also in Russia, would be a definite palpable advantage."

met Balfour at the reception last evening," said Brandeis. "As soon as he heard my name his face brightened up and he said: 'I have heard much of you and I want to have a talk with you.'" That same day Brandeis and Frankfurter talked for two hours with British embassy officials about the possibilities of a Jewish state in Palestine. "Those here are still timid of their allies . . . are afraid of the word State at present, loving 'liberty & equality of opportunity.' But 'Homeland in Palestine' sits well," wrote Brandeis.

In a meeting with President Wilson on Sunday, May 6, Brandeis explained to the President the thrust of Zionism, the Jews' interest in Palestine, the British willingness to go along with a Jewish homeland there, and concerns about French reluctance.

Wilson replied that he sympathized with the Zionist movement and supported the concept of a Jewish homeland in Palestine. At the moment, however, he was concerned about the French attitude and also about the Turks, who, although joined with the Central Powers, were not at war with the United States. Wilson promised to make a statement later supporting the homeland concept. He even offered to have Brandeis draft the statement for him.

The next day Brandeis told Balfour that there could be no American involvement in a Palestine protectorate, but that eventually a statement of support would be forthcoming.

At this point in the politics of the Balfour Declaration there was an interruption, another development, frightening a number of people, threatening—some thought—the issuance of a homeland declaration, and over which suspicions linger.

Henry Morgenthau, the wealthy non-Zionist Jew, was a close friend of Wilson's and a large financial supporter. As a reward, he had been named ambassador to Turkey, returning to the United States at the beginning of 1916. The next year he approached the President with a plan. He had heard that Turkey was disenchanted with Germany and might welcome friendly overtures from the Allies. He suggested that he, Morgenthau, return to Turkey and try to detach it from the German powers, and, it was hoped, end the war sooner. That is one version. Another is that he suggested that he be sent to Turkey merely to scout around. Whichever the facts, he received the President's permission to go; Wilson had no reason to refuse.

Brandeis learned of the projected trip and, fearing Morgenthau might promise the Turks they could keep their empire, including Palestine, if they dropped out of the war, wanted a committed Zionist to go with Morgenthau. According to one account, Morgenthau himself suggested Felix Frankfurter as the one to go with him. More likely, however, Frankfurter's name was suggested by Brandeis. Frankfurter sent Brandeis a note that "[Secretary of War] Baker said O.K. and will work out some errand for the War Dept. The Colonel [apparently Wilson's aide Colonel House] sent word that he wanted to see me. The thing went through." Whatever the origin of Frankfurter's involvement, Morgenthau's correspondence at the time shows Morgenthau welcomed Frankfurter.

The trip was explained with the statement that the Americans would visit the Middle East to investigate the Jews' plight there. No mention was made about Turkey in the public announcement.

When the British Foreign Office heard of the trip, it feared the result would be Turkey's dropping out of the war and keeping its empire intact. This was the same fear the Zionists had, for a different reason. Where the Zionists were alarmed about losing a Jewish homeland in Palestine, the British were concerned about losing postwar control of trade interests in the Middle East. They had not been fighting a World War for three years to give up that possible booty. The British documents are firm on that point, saying that "a policy of expelling the Turks from Europe at the probable price of leaving them in control of, with suzerainty over, Syria, Palestine and Mesopotamia is not one for our support."

In England, Weizmann, learning of the Morgenthau mission from a Brandeis letter, approached the British Foreign Office. In his view, officials were treating the mission as of little importance, except to repeat that "there is still a danger that these negotiations may be carried out on the basis of an integral Turkey." Weizmann understood that to mean no homeland for the Jews in Palestine. He bluntly put to the Foreign Office a question about the future of Palestine and was told that "it is axiomatic that no arrangement with Turkey can be arrived at unless Armenia, Syria, and Arabia are detached."

Weizmann became the British delegate to the Morgenthau mission. For the British, he was an ideal choice—he was as interested in the dismemberment of Turkey's empire as were the British.

The delegates rendezvoused at Gibraltar on July 4 and 5. "It was midsummer, and very hot," Weizmann recalled. "We had been given one of the casements in the Rock for our sessions, and the windows were kept open." The only language that all the participants could speak was German, "and the Tommies on guard marched up and down outside, no doubt convinced that we were a pack of spies who had been lured into a trap."

At the meeting, the Turkish situation was reviewed and the Americans conceded that "we have no definite plan to propose for penetrating into the Turkish situation, much less any program of terms of dealing with the Turks."

Weizmann presented the British position: "the separation from Turkey of territory containing subject races." Weizmann also raised the possibility of American troops joining in the Middle East campaigns, to which the Americans "deemed it appropriate to recall that America is not now at war with Turkey." Weizmann's point there seemed to be that America should not attempt to change Britain's policy regarding the Turkish lands if it was not willing to put up its own men. The delegates were at an impasse. Morgenthau had no course for them to follow. The British did not appreciate American interference.

At Gibraltar the decision was made to cancel the mission. It never reached the Middle East or Turkey.*

In fall 1917 the British cabinet continued to consider issuing what became known as the Balfour Declaration, and the problems continued. In England, influential Jews, like their German-American counterparts, feared that a Jewish homeland would cast their loyalty to England in doubt. The French, and also the Italians, were skittish. Because strong American support for the homeland would bring the situation to a conclusion, the British Zionists again turned to Brandeis.

On September 18, Weizmann wired Brandeis that American support in some form was needed. With the message was a text of the proposed declaration.

Jacob De Haas, who had fought alongside Brandeis in many Zionist battles, described him as a negotiator:

If Brandeis knows chess he has never alluded to it, and has never employed its tactics. He never thinks in the accepted terms of diplomacy. He is too precise, concise and definite for its circumlocutions and its circumambulations. If, to use a chess term, he never indulged in a "surprise opening" it was not because he

*A 1949 article—W. Yale, "Morgenthau's Special Meeting"—has Weizmann twisting the British government to the Zionist purpose rather than Weizmann being used by the British government to achieve a goal both the Zionists and the British wanted. Yale had been an oil company official in the Middle East during the First World War. The sole basis for his frequently cited article is a purported conversation with Weizmann in 1920 which "so astonished me that I can almost recall word for word what he said" in 1949. Because all the documentation argues against this interpretation, I am not willing to accept Yale's twenty-nine-year-old memory of the Weizmann conversation.

avoided all forms of fencing and came directly to the point. In every discussion with Brandeis there existed the presupposition that both sides knew why they met.

Brandeis, as de Haas had said, never a chess player, understood immediately what he had to do. On September 23 he and Rabbi Stephen Wise met with Colonel House, the President's adviser. House reported later: "The views outlined [by Brandeis and Wise] were practically identical with the suggestion I cabled [the British ambassador] after discussing the matter with the President at Magnolia. I dictated a cable for them to send Weitzman [sic]." The next day Brandeis telegraphed Weizmann: "From talks I have had with President and from expressions of opinion given to closest advisers I feel I can answer you that he is [in] entire sympathy with declaration quoted in yours of nineteenth as approved by foreign office and the prime minister. I of course heartily agree."

Since Wilson still could not originate a public statement because the United States and Turkey were not at war, Colonel House and Brandeis suggested that the British have the French and Italian governments ask the United States about Wilson's attitude toward the declaration. Brandeis telegraphed Weizmann to that effect. But the French and Italian governments were not picking up the bait.

In England the opposition, especially from assimilationist Jews, increased. "Our Jewish opponents have not been idle," Weizmann wrote to Brandeis. Again there was a plea for Wilson to accept the declaration "without reservation."

All involved knew the stakes: the splitting of the Ottoman Empire, the beginning of a new state, the relationship between the United States and Turkey, the relationship between Jew and Arab, the political reactions of Jews in the United States, England, and around the world. It was not a small game, and individuals were nervous, felt harassed, had other obligations, were not certain they were making the right decisions.

On October 9, Weizmann telegraphed Brandeis: "It is essential to have not only President's approval of text but his recommendation to grant this declaration without delay." Again Brandeis produced. He wired Weizmann: "Your cable tenth received. President has sent London message of approval, but believes public declaration by him would be injudicious." Wilson, however, did agree that at a later time he would respond to a request from American Jewry for a formal endorsement of the declaration; he kept that promise the next year.

The Declaration, as finally issued on November 2, 1917, was a collective decision made by the British cabinet, representing that nation's government, after months of deliberation and debate. Neither a secret treaty nor an individual statement, it was the promise of a nation. It reads:

His Majesty's Government view with favor the establishment in Palestine of a national home for the Jewish people, and will use their best endeavours to facilitate the achievement of this object, it being clearly understood that nothing shall be done which may prejudice the civil and religious rights of existing non-Jewish communities in Palestine, or the rights and political status enjoyed by Jews in any other country.

"Joyous congratulations," Brandeis wired Weizmann when the declaration was issued. Then, after Jerusalem was liberated by the British in December, there was nothing to stop the Zionist dream from fulfillment—or so it seemed. A few weeks later, Brandeis met with Sir Cecil Spring-Rice, the British ambassador to the United States, and told him that he regarded Zionism not from the point of view of territory but of idealism. "He thought," reported Sir Cecil, "that it served as a rallying point to the Jewish race, especially on its idealistic side." At about the same time, in a letter to Jacob de Haas, Brandeis showed another facet of his thinking. "The sailing direction for our workers now should be: 'Let no Jew escape,'" wrote Brandeis. "Every one ought to have put to him the proposition: 'Will you help or won't you?' The question is no longer: Do you believe in Zionism? It is at the door and every Jew must say whether he will shirk."

That was the rallying cry: political Zionism had achieved its purpose; now the task was to turn to the land. The one dream, or so it was thought, would be replaced by another. A dream of healthy men and women, with sun-browned skins, hoes in their hands and songs on their lips, turning the desert of Palestine into a garden. A dream of Jew and Arab living together in peace. A dream of Jews from Eastern Europe, beaten by the whip of anti-Semitism for centuries, now free to work and study. A dream of a resurgence of Judaism; its teaching and morality becoming one of the great forces in the world. A dream once as America had been: a new land, a promised land, a land of milk and honey.

The dream was farther away than anyone realized in 1917.

What had been promised by the Balfour Declaration first had to be affirmed by the Peace Conference in Paris in the spring of 1919. Brandeis could not himself go to Paris with the Supreme Court in session, but he was watching over what was happening. "William C. Bullitt of the State Department—a very good friend of Felix Frankfurter and a good friend and co-worker of mine—will accompany the President," Brandeis assured Jacob de Haas. Brandeis was certain that Frankfurter would "make clear to him our position on Zionist matters. [Rabbi Stephen] Wise can secure his aid, whenever proper." The Zionists were also to remember that other "good" friends of the Zionists in the American delegation were Walter Lippmann and Lewis L. Strauss, who had worked with Herbert Hoover in developing war relief programs.

The Peace Conference was to cap the "war to end war." Lincoln Steffens wrote in a famous line that the people of Europe watched Woodrow Wilson arrive as if "sailing on a cloud through the air to save the Old World." The reality was less as deals replaced idealism. Felix Frankfurter had left the government by this time and was in Paris representing American Zionism. "My months at the Paris Peace Conference in 1919," he recalled later, "were probably the saddest of my life. The progressive disillusionment of the high hopes which Wilson's noble talk had engendered was not unlike the feelings that death of near ones brings."

Frankfurter's immediate responsibility was Palestine. He said that he had come to the conference "not under any retainer by anybody, but went to Paris solely because of my devotion to Zionism." That was undoubtedly true, but he also was and acted as a representative of Louis Brandeis.

He arrived in Paris on Friday, February 28, 1919. The problem for the American Zionists there was the Arabs. The conflict did not involve land, although it would be fought in terms of land, but, rather, the introduction of a democratic society into the midst of an Arab feudal society, the mixing of the modern era and the middle ages without a transition period.

The Arab leader in Paris as a spokesman for the Arab peoples was Prince Feisal. His job was to see that the British kept their promises of independence for the Arabs made in exchange for the Arabs' having resisted the Turks. That Arab-British agreement had been worked out in 1915 by Sir Henry McMahon and Sherif Hussein, Prince Feisal's father. Because that agreement did not include the Palestine territory, the Jews believed the Arabs would support the Zionist dream. Chaim Weizmann and Feisal had already met and dealt together as friends.

Against this background, Felix Frankfurter—three days after his arrival in Paris—met with Prince Feisal. T. E. Lawrence—the legendary

Lawrence of Arabia—acted as interpreter. Frankfurter described Lawrence as a "young English don of singular charm, intrepid military exploits and commanding power."

Frankfurter found Feisal gracious and responsive. They first discussed the Zionist attitude toward the aspirations of both Arab and Jew in Palestine, Feisal agreeing with Frankfurter. The two ratified their agreement in an exchange of letters; Frankfurter and Lawrence had worked up the two drafts. Feisal signed the Arab letter.

In their exchange of letters, the two men spoke of the Jews and Arabs being "cousins in race" and each expressed sympathy and support for the other's nationalist ambitions. They acknowledged difficulties, "For it is no easy task to rebuild two great civilisations that have been suffering oppression and misrule for centuries." But they agreed, as Frankfurter concluded his letter, "The Arabs and Jews are neighbors in territory; we cannot but live side by side as friends."

The meeting with Prince Feisal impressed Frankfurter deeply. "The Arab question," he wrote to Brandeis, "has ceased to exist as a difficulty to the realisation of our programme before the Peace Conference." He realized that problem continued in Palestine and "is a challenge to the wisdom, the sympathetic understanding and the generosity of Jewish statesmanship." He described Feisal as "a genuine friend," and continued: "At all events, at the least, we must deal with him on the basis that we are his genuine friends and the friends of his people. I do not think the Arab question is out of the way; I do not even say that it is easy of solution; I do insist however that it can be solved by cooperative effort."

The letter to Brandeis had been typed, and as Frankfurter read it over he wrote with pen in the margin by the above paragraph that the face of Feisal "makes you think of the face of Jesus."

Even with the Feisal letter, which was widely publicized, the fate of the Zionists' hope for Palestine was precarious at the Paris Peace Conference. Woodrow Wilson, by this time, had publicly supported the Balfour Declaration, but the rumor circulated that he, under the pressure of solving other world problems, was willing to let the promise to the Jews go by. On May 8, Frankfurter wrote him to plead for America's renewed interest in a Jewish homeland. When Wilson replied a few days later in a perfunctory manner, Frankfurter was upset and told Wilson so. "Your note . . . has occasioned almost despair." Wilson, knowing Frankfurter was present in Paris as a representative of Zionism, responded on May 16, 1919:

I have your letter of May 14th. I never dreamed that it was necessary to give you any renewed assurance of my adhesion to the Balfour declaration, and so far I have found no one who is seriously opposing the purpose which it embodies. I was very much taken by surprise that you should deem anything I wrote you discouraging. I see no ground for discouragement and every reason to hope that satisfactory guarantees can be secured.

Frankfurter, with Wilson's approval, publicized the contents of the Wilson message and telegraphed them to Brandeis in the United States.

Frankfurter and the other Zionists in Paris were particularly concerned about Palestine because of recent news about the fate of Jews in Eastern Europe. Similar stories had reached them since the beginning of the war, but the new accounts were beyond anything previously received. A letter from Warsaw so upset Frankfurter that he sent it to Wilson so the President could understand the Zionists' concern. It read:

I don't know what you people are doing in Paris, but I know what you ought to be doing. There are more than a million Jews in the New Poland being starved, and persecuted to death . . . [who] are slowly also rotting to death. Here in Warsaw there is filth and rags and disease and starvation. . . .

The filth and poverty are indescribable. Further out in the country, the Jews not only starve, but they also have to suffer directly from the terrific persecution with which the new republic tries to solve the race problem. . . . A thousand Jews were murdered in Vilna when the Poles took it. In Lida the death toll was in proportion and so all through the country that the Poles are taking back from the Bolsheviks. . . .

All the Yiddish papers print from eye-witnesses. In the small villages in the Northeast, the people have absolutely nothing to eat. The bread sold at so many marks a pound in Vilna consists of straw, dung, and dirt. . . . The poor Jews in the little villages, who are not allowed to go out of the village bounds to get food, have gotten down to eating grass. . . . This sounds funny, unless it has happened to you when it is damn serious.

The whole race is being rooted out. . . .

Allow me to impress upon you, that if something is not done of a radical nature to relieve the situation, there will be no Jews left to go to Palestine.

Frankfurter later made a trip to Poland: "A packed week . . . brief and inadequate but enough to make me feel I know the essentials of the situation . . . distressing . . . because of the squalid misery I saw."

The United States and other nations at Paris did endorse the Balfour Declaration, but a decision was made to send an exploratory commission to Palestine to determine the land's ability to absorb new immigrants. Zionists were suspicious of the plan, believing any such commission would not be supportive of Jewish aims. The Zionists' counter plan was to send a prominent Jew to Palestine at the same time. There was talk that the Jew would be Frankfurter, but he realized that if the Jew was to be an American—and because of the status of the United States at the Peace Conference, it should be—the person should be someone more prominent, Louis Brandeis.

Brandeis agreed to make the trip to Palestine during the Court's summer recess, under Zionist auspices, only after being assured by Frankfurter that British authorities approved of the trip and would cooperate with him. The problem was, as Frankfurter reported, "the alleged hostility of the British administration" in Palestine. This was a military administration and, despite England's authorizing and supporting the Balfour Declaration, the British military had no use for Zionists. Partly this was due to anti-Semitism; British military officers traditionally were products of the upper economic groups in that country, which had even a stronger anti-Semitic tradition than did comparable groups in the United States. Partly it was the military man's disdain for politicians. And partly it was an ambition to create a Pan-Arab union stretching through the Middle East. Also it may have been due to the British officers' simply not wanting to be bothered with an influx of thousands of new immigrants. Why did they need more immigrants, grumbled one British officer, when they already had so many unemployed?

Brandeis went to Palestine by way of England and France. Frankfurter met him at Southampton, and in London they conferred with Chaim Weizmann. This was the first meeting between Brandeis and Weizmann, and Brandeis brought away from it no hint of the discord that would develop between them and that would affect the future of Zionism. "Weizmann is neither as great nor as objectionable as he was painted," Brandeis wrote after the meeting, "but he is very much of [a] man and *much* bigger than most of his fellows." Brandeis was in Paris two days later—"to the Champs Elysee—the Boulevard—and the Seine. A new world for me of beauty."

That same day he and Frankfurter met with Balfour and Lord Eustace Percy, who had lived a few years earlier in the House of Truth in Washington and now was with the British Foreign Service, to talk about Palestine.

Balfour discussed the immediate problems—particularly the pressure from Eastern European Jews to escape persecution and emigrate to Palestine. The situation was complicated, said Balfour, "by the extraordinary phenomenon that Jews now are not only participating in revolutionary movements but are actually, to a large degree, leaders in such movements."

This was the old argument that because one Jew is a revolutionary all Jews are revolutionaries. Brandeis would have none of it. He said he had come to Zionism not as a revolutionary but "wholly as an American." He argued for three conditions essential to the Zionist program: "Palestine should be the Jewish homeland and not merely that there be a Jewish homeland in Palestine"; second, "there must be economic elbow room for a Jewish Palestine"—enough land and facilities for economic development and "not merely a small garden within Palestine"; and third, there must be public ownership of the land and its natural resources. These conditions stemmed from the position taken by American Zionists in 1918. Meeting in Pittsburgh, they had called for political and civil equality in Palestine "irrespective of race, sex, or faith of all the inhabitants of the land," and for public ownership "of the land, of all natural resources and of all public utilities." This was unadulterated Brandeis, the same approach he had taken for the Alaskan territory a few years earlier.

Balfour accepted the three conditions. Although England faced political and diplomatic problems because of Palestine, he agreed not to make any final decisions on boundary or economic matters until Brandeis returned. Frankfurter, who kept notes of the meeting, wrote at the end: "No statesman could have been more sympathetic than Mr. Balfour was with the underlying philosophy and aims of Zionism as they were stated by Mr. Justice Brandeis, nor more eager that the necessary conditions should be secured at the hands of the Peace Conference and of Great Britain to assure the realisation of the Zionist programme."

Brandeis felt the same way, saying: "My interview with Balfour [was] very delightful and satisfactory."

July 1, 1919, Brandeis arrived in Cairo. A twenty-three-piece Zionist military band greeted him with "Hatikva"—The Hope—the Zionist anthem, "a stirring and politically encouraging" reception, he called it.

He traveled throughout Palestine in a Ford automobile, studying town and rural life, the land's physical resources and possibilities for future development. "I know now why all the world wanted this land and why all the peoples loved it," Brandeis concluded.

After his month's visit, despite the intransigence of the British military and the hostility of local Arabs, Brandeis's view of Palestine's future was still romantic. "What I have seen and heard strengthen greatly my conviction that Palestine can and must become the Jewish Homeland as promised in the Balfour Declaration," he wrote. "On the whole I think Zionist affairs about the most hopeful of all the world's problems."

Back in London, reporting to the Zionists' "Greater Actions Committee," Brandeis said malaria was the immediate problem and recommended that immigration be discouraged until it was eradicated, and that Zionist funds go directly to that task. Within this committee developed the first signs of Brandeis's eventual split with Weizmann. Weizmann, with his roots in Eastern Europe and his frequent contacts with the Eastern European Jews, understood the emotionalism they felt toward Palestine and believed any future policy must acknowledge and accept that emotion, which meant accepting the effusiveness of the East Europeans. There seemed no role or understanding of that effusiveness in the economic strategy of Brandeis.

Brandeis had been asked to preside at an Actions Committee session when it was to vote on the makeup of the Jewish Agency—the shadow government in Palestine. Weizmann wanted the Agency made up of the Zionists plus other Jewish organizations, including the Jewish Minority Councils in Eastern Europe. Brandeis opposed extensive eastern European representation, believing it would result in a boisterous and inefficient governing body. When the resolution was before the Committee, the vote was four to four; but de Haas was out of the room. "Where is de Haas?" Brandeis asked, then demanded: "Get de Haas!" De Haas was "got" and voted correctly. The meeting ended in an uproar, but Brandeis's formula—to include only Zionist groups among the organizational membership of the Jewish Agency—was included in the ultimate League of Nations mandate to Britain for Palestine. Weizmann was furious.

Brandeis received assurances from the British that they would urge their military leaders in Palestine to accept the Balfour Declaration as part of British policy. Working out boundary details had been postponed for a year, but Brandeis could feel confident, he thought, about the future of the homeland he had done so much to create. When he returned to the United States, one of his Jewish acquaintances talked with him about the trip and said "his big frame vibrated with enthusiasm—but also with the thought of difficulties ahead for the land of promise and problems." In Washington, Oliver Wendell Holmes found Brandeis "transfigured by his experience."

The boundary problem was dealt with in the next months. The French, finally aware of what was happening in the Middle East, demanded part of the Ottoman Empire and talked of splitting Palestine in half, and denying water sources in the North to the British mandate section in the South. Brandeis, arguing that the new Jewish land would not be economically viable without water, again intervened.

The time was now February 1920 and President Woodrow Wilson was ailing, a victim of a stroke suffered after he had returned to the United States. Although ill, Wilson contacted his Secretary of State, Robert Lansing. Lansing had no interest in Zionism, the Balfour Declaration, or any promises made about them. But he was forced to act when he received the following letter from Wilson: "I enclose an impressive letter which I have just received from Mr. Justice Brandeis and which I beg that you will read. I agree with its conclusions and beg that you will instruct Mr. Wallace at Paris to use every means that is proper to impress this view upon the French and English authorities." He concluded: "All the great powers are committed to the Balfour Declaration, and I agree with Mr. Justice Brandeis regarding it as a solemn promise which we can in no circumstances afford to break or alter."

Leaving nothing to chance, Brandeis checked with Lansing to make certain that the President's orders were transmitted to Paris; when that was done, Brandeis told Frankfurter: "The President responded handsomely to our request."

Brandeis and Frankfurter both missed something at that moment. Being men of the law, schooled in it, teachers of it, and practitioners of it, they believed that, when responsible leaders and nations agreed to perform certain actions, the agreements would be fulfilled. British Palestine did—because of the intercession of Wilson, spurred on by Brandeis—retain much of the natural borders the Zionists had wanted for it. But it had been a near-miss. To smooth over a difficulty, the British had been willing to retreat on their promise. That this set a pattern was not understood in 1920.

Beginning in 1916 and 1917, the American Zionists had heard troubling remarks about Weizmann. Scrupulous himself, Weizmann countenanced slipshod work by the Eastern European Jews. Brandeis and Frankfurter at first stood by Weizmann. "I have heard much about [Weizmann]," said Brandeis in 1916, "and my friends here consider him absolutely trustworthy." Brandeis said the next year, "We must, to the utmost of our ability, support Weizmann and not permit his heavy task to be increased by any desertion in the ranks."

But this ignored that Weizmann's constituency was a group of volatile people with romantic notions about Palestine and a tendency to ignore detail. Brandeis and the Zionist groups he headed were dreamers but hard-headed ones who followed the trail of each detail.

The growing dispute between Brandeis and Weizmann, between the one's relentless efficiency and the other's understanding of the emotional needs of his constituency, came to a head in the summer of 1920. And with the resolution of that dispute also would come a definitive answer to the question plaguing Louis Brandeis for the decade he had been espousing Zionism: Can a Jew in the United States be a loyal American while working for a homeland for Jews in Palestine? For years, to the chagrin of the Henry Morgenthaus and Jacob Schiffs, he had insisted the answer was "yes." Now, in 1920, Brandeis had the opportunity to prove it.

A world Zionist conference met in London in 1920; to it came the Zionists from Eastern Europe who for a quarter of a century had attended these meetings, spoken for hours about their dreams, rhapsodized over late-night coffee, vented the frustrations they had known in their shtetls, where, between begging for coins to finance the trip, they had dodged the anti-Semites' attacks. For them these conferences were an emotional explosion, a release for the tension that had built up over the previous years. Chaim Weizmann understood that; Louis Brandeis did not.

Trailed by his supporters—Jacob de Haas, Julian Mack, and Felix Frankfurter—Brandeis led the American Zionist delegation to the London conference. Because of his stature as an American Supreme Court justice, his relationship with Woodrow Wilson, and his work with the Balfour Declaration and with the Palestine boundaries a few months earlier, he was a revered figure. It was assumed he would be elected chairman of the London meeting, as he was. It also was believed he would be asked to become head of the world Zionist movement.

On the boat going to London, Jacob de Haas and other delegates urged Brandeis to accept the position as the world leader of Zionism. Felix Frankfurter spoke against the move; the step, he said, would force Brandeis to give up his seat on the Supreme Court. Frankfurter argued that "it was Brandeis' duty to the American liberal cause as the only Jew who held the illustrious position on the Supreme Court to stay at his present post." Brandeis did not respond to either side.

Julius Simon, one of the American delegates, believed it was Brandeis's destiny to become the world Zionist leader. As soon as Simon arrived in London, he went to Chaim Weizmann, the only challenger of Brandeis for the position.

"Chaim," Simon said, "you have rendered an immortal service to the cause of Zionism. Now I ask you to crown your work by offering leadership to Brandeis."

Simon did not report Weizmann's reply, if any, but he did report Frankfurter's comment when he heard the story: "You could not have said anything worse." Frankfurter understood the egos involved, if Simon did not.

The Americans did not associate with Weizmann's East European followers, preferring a London society they were more at home with. "Felix and Brandeis, I needn't add, are great people here," Harold Laski reported to Holmes. "Chancellors, Judges, Astors all vie for their entertainment. And I believe they like it—Brandeis unbends delightfully. Felix, in his whirlwind ways, sees everyone and everything."

The World Zionist Congress opened with a few brief remarks by Brandeis, instead of the spellbinding oration the delegates had anticipated. That was their first disappointment. Their second was in what he had to say. The political struggle was over, Brandeis declared. The Balfour Declaration had been included in the British mandate. The boundary problems were settled. And the British had appointed Herbert Samuel, a Jew believed friendly to the homeland concept, as High Commissioner for Palestine. The new problem, Brandeis asserted, was a technical one: how to make the land work. Emotionalism was done; the time for technical expertise was at hand.

This shattered the Zionists; emotionalism was their forte. More than that, they understood something Brandeis did not and could not. Anti-Semitism was not a way of his life; what little he had experienced did not detract from his accomplishments and the personal acceptance he had won. But for them anti-Semitism was the reality of life. They had never worried about being denied admission to a riding club or boating club. They had no concerns about Jewish quotas at colleges or about being able to find an apartment in the city. Such worries would have been luxuries. Their worries were of the confiscatory taxes on the Jews' crops and the twenty-five-year military service requirement for their sons. Their worries were of being spit at on the street, of their wives being raped. Those were the fears they lived with day by day, why they barricaded the doors and windows of their homes at night. They knew they were dealing with a movement that was hundreds of years old, a movement that became part of people almost from the moment they were born. They knew that hate that deep, that violent, that uncompromising would not be erased by a mandate or a treaty agreement. They knew decades were required, perhaps centuries. They knew it in their heads, in their bodies, and in their hearts. They knew. Brandeis did not.

At the conference, Lord Reading, the Lord Chief Justice of England

and a Jew, proposed that Zionism and the future of Palestine be controlled by a seven-man committee, divided between three Americans and three English, three Zionists and three non-Zionists, and Brandeis as the seventh, in effect the leader with the swing vote. The responsibilities would be full time. Here it was: Would Brandeis surrender his Americanism to devote himself entirely to his Jewishness?

Brandeis met with the American delegation on the afternoon of July 14, 1920. Although he was not in the habit of speaking personally of himself or his life, Brandeis opened by saying he intended to be frank with the delegates, and acknowledged that he had been concerned for some time with the possibility of assuming a leading part in world Zionist affairs. He said the question had been before him since his trip to Palestine the previous year. "I have become more and more convinced that, treated purely as a question of Zionism," he said, "it would be a mistake for me to resign from the Bench with a view to taking up definitely and exclusively this work."

There were several reasons. First, he pointed up the importance to the Jewish homeland in Palestine of Jews living outside Palestine, especially the ability of American Jews to contribute money to the new land. But there was a more important reason. He explained:

I felt that owing to the accident of my position in America, not only the fact that I was on the Bench—the highest Bench of the world—but the fact that I represented, independently of being on the Bench, in a certain sense the Liberals, Progressives, that hope in American life, I feel and have felt that if I retired from the Bench, you would have on the one hand, a convention developed by the overt act of my resignation, that all we have been saying is not true —that a man cannot be a Zionist and a good citizen of his country because there was Brandeis, who was supposed to be one of the most American of Americans, who left his court and his country at the time that many will believe to be, its greatest need.

He had said that he had come to Zionism as an American; now he reiterated that view. More also was involved. The melting pot had not claimed him; he did not deny his Jewishness. Nor did he give up his Americanism. He insisted, as he had claimed before, that there was a role in the United States for the ethnic. Other nations might discourage diversity; the United States thrived on it.

Brandeis did believe he could be an honorary president of the Zionist movement, a role similar to one he had played with American Zionism—"and in that way advise; and, during the period of my vacation, I see no reason why I should not, as I have during the last two years, give more than occasional advice in the conduct of our affairs."

But even that did not happen. Weizmann's support for Brandeis moved back and forth. Then there were troubles with Zionist finances. Thievery was not the problem, but funds moved from one account to another in order to cover losses, deficits, needs, unexplained expenses. Brandeis, always meticulous with money, was appalled at the way the Zionists played this particular game. He did not understand that there probably was not an accountant among them.

Brandeis controlled the Hadassah funds from the United States and had allowed them to be channeled through the Zionist organization for Hadassah purposes in Palestine. "I have decided in the future," he announced, "not to remit the funds of Hadassah through the Zionist Commission or the Zionist Executive. They will be sent directly to the Hadassah headquarters in Jerusalem."

"Are you doing this in order to punish us?" asked one delegate.

"That is an improper remark," snapped Brandeis.

Frankfurter sidled over to the delegate and whispered: "Withdraw what you said," but the delegate did not.

Louis Brandeis returned to the United States and retained his seat on the Supreme Court. Chaim Weizmann remained with the Zionist movement and became the first President of Israel.

Those two men continued as friends, but only for a brief period. The next year, in 1921, Brandeis's followers left the American Zionist movement in a split with Weizmann's American supporters. The differences in approach, as well as the ego conflict, could not be reconciled. Brandeis said the split was inevitable, "resulting from differences in standards. The Easterners—like many Russian Jews in this country—don't know what honesty is and we simply won't entrust our money to them. Weizmann does know what honesty is—but weakly yields to his numerous Russian associates. Hence the split."

Although formally separated from Zionism, Brandeis did not, could not, disassociate himself from the land of Palestine and its promise for his fellow Jews. His biographer, Alpheus Thomas Mason, reported that Brandeis donated more than $600,000 during his lifetime to Jewish charities and Zionist programs. A law clerk from the 1920s recalled Brandeis's spending an occasional Sunday morning with Frankfurter, Julian Mack, Robert Szold, and Jacob de Haas, "and the chief subject was how he should channel his funds to Palestine."

He had not forgotten the malaria he had seen in Palestine during his 1919 trip. In 1923 the *New York Times* reported:

The banks and waters of the Jordan . . . have been drained and freed of their malaria-breeding places through the gift of Louis D. Brandeis. . . .

Dr. Rubinow . . . spoke of the anti-malaria campaign . . . which was made possible by the gift of $25,000 from Supreme Court Justice Brandeis. "In the Midgal region alone," he said, "there were extensive swamp areas, overgrown streams, bad irrigation systems, an Arab village and a floating tent population. In the Kinneret region there were swamps and breeding places along the Jordan. We systematically examined all of the inhabitants and treated all chronic cases, removed stagnant water near houses, repaired canals and undertook a thorough cleansing. This work is progressing—that of ridding the Holy Land of the malarial taint and making every district safe.

Until his death, Brandeis's correspondence frequently dealt with Palestine, Zionism, and problems of the new land. In addition to giving his own funds, he encouraged others to give theirs. This Brandeis letter, to a Zionist official in 1923, was typical: "I understand that Israel N. Thurman has retired from the laundry business, having sold out for a 'fortune.' I suggest that you send for him and put up strongly to him his duty to himself and to the cause."

He had come to his Jewishness late in his life and then had never surrendered his status as a Jew, or as an American; he refused to be enveloped by the melting pot; he worked for the promised land. His life defines the hyphenated American.

10

Holmes and Brandeis Dissenting

In the years following the First World War, Washington, still a small city, had an unhurried atmosphere, a graciousness. One sauntered down the broad Connecticut Avenue sidewalks, swam in the Potomac River, and rode the streetcar to Glen Echo for a Sunday hike. "The tension is relaxed," said Brandeis after the armistice, "and the evidence of return to the easy-going are developing on all sides."

Having many of the attributes of the southern town, Washington also had its share of anti-Semitism, and apartments that accepted Jews in 1916 and 1917 were few. Brandeis finally found a place on Connecticut Avenue, in a new building called Stoneleigh Court, where the manager, David Edgar Stephan, had been raised a Lutheran, was married to a Presbyterian, and attended the Foundry Methodist Church; he said that the building would be "honored" to have Justice Brandeis and his family as tenants. Years later Stephan's son, Albert E. Stephan, went to Harvard Law School with an endorsement from Louis Brandeis. While at Harvard, Albert Stephan came under the eye of Felix Frankfurter, who kept track of him for many years.

That the Brandeises were Jewish was never forgotten in Washington. When Lord Reading, the English jurist, visited Washington in 1919, a hostess remarked that Reading and "Brandeis are very interesting examples of what the environment can do—even to a Jew."

The Brandeises kept a horse, and in pleasant weather, with "the Stoneleigh so dreary," Brandeis went riding in a runabout carriage, then returned "to clear my desk again and take another nibble at the law." This continued into the 1920s, when automobile traffic became too heavy even for as skillful a horseman as Brandeis. The family often went canoeing, Brandeis's favorite sport, on the Potomac. As always, the father exhausted the family. "I am very sleepy after a Sunday in the open," lamented Elizabeth Brandeis, "5½ hours paddling on the river with my father."

The city was far away from the agonies of another America. In the Senate and House of Representatives, as in the White House, there was little concern with the unemployed and the hungry. This was the roaring 1920s; money was to be made by stock-market gambling, pyramiding companies, latching on to a "good thing." Get on board! That was the cry. Don't cause trouble! Who was or was not invited to last night's embassy party was a more important question than unemployment compensation, union organization, civil liberties.

This social life had its "problems." At dinner parties who should sit on the hostess's right: the Speaker of the House of Representatives or the Chief Justice of the United States? No one could answer such a question, except one State Department underling, who suggested inviting the two dignitaries to different parties.

At one dinner party in the home of Eugene and Agnes Meyer, the Brandeises were not seated near the hostess. Mrs. Brandeis, a few days later, complained to Mrs. Meyer. "The whole question of precedence is taken very seriously," lamented Mrs. Meyer, "and Mrs. B. declared that some Justices would leave the table if not properly placed. She is a very fine woman but I cannot warm up to her."

But the Brandeises did not last long on the Washington dinner-party circuit. "Louis' friends do not seem to wash enough," confided Mrs. Meyer. "And the Brandeis atmosphere is awfully wrong—no spontaneity, no freedom."

The frugal life Louis and Alice Brandeis had led in Boston, the careful husbanding of financial resources to have more to give away, became more pronounced in Washington. James M. Landis, one of Brandeis's clerks in the mid-1920s, recalled, "All the time I knew him, he was very much of an ascetic. I'm told that prior to that time, he did go out and enjoy himself and so on. But I never recall him once going out to dinner, or to lunch, for that matter."

Another clerk, Henry J. Friendly, said, "The bed he slept in looked like a camp bed, and the furniture showed distinct signs of wear. It was unattractive." That was the way the Brandeises had lived on Otis Street in Boston. Why buy new furniture? Why buy stylish clothes?

"Some industrial researchers should determine and make clear to consumers how much of the high costs of some necessities, e.g., clothing and shoes, is due to mere change of styles," Brandeis once suggested to

Frankfurter, calling these changes "wasteful" and saying it was "an important factor in irregularity of employment, since it prevents production of articles otherwise staple."

Brandeis opposed passive entertainments, such as movies, already three decades old in the 1920s, and radio, just becoming popular. He never owned an automobile, hiring one if necessary. His dislike of automobiles stemmed not only from their chasing his horse and runabout off the Washington streets but also from his belief that funds going to highway construction should have gone to education. He also objected to installment buying. "Nothing down. Pay as you ride," a slogan of the time, aroused his moral indignation.

Brandeis continued his summer vacations with his family on Cape Cod, canoeing, reading, or—dressed in old tweeds and a baggy sweater—hiking across the moors. These periods were his only known times of relaxation.

There never was time for frivolity. Harlan Fiske Stone, who served on the Supreme Court with him for fourteen years, recalled after Brandeis's death, "I never realized how serious Brandeis always was. There is little that I can recall of him in the lighter vein."

Brandeis's zealousness often was criticized. When Brandeis once lamented that a politician friend was taking time out from politics to earn money, a mutual acquaintance commented: "I do not think Brandeis has any appreciation of the situation of a man fifty-five years old, in debt, with a large and needy family, some of them infants entitled to support and assurance for the future. Brandeis was rich before he was forty, and never needed any money anyway."

Oliver Wendell Holmes, once when praising Brandeis, provided one of the better estimates of him: "I'm not sure that he wouldn't burn me at a low fire if it were in the interest of some very possibly disinterested aim."

With the criticisms, however, all understood Brandeis's selflessness. Even this could be too much at times. In 1942, Robert H. Jackson, then an associate justice of the Supreme Court, attended a service at the Court intended to eulogize Brandeis. After listening to the speeches of praise, he conceded, "I fear I had gotten into the state of mind of my daughter who once said to her Sunday School teacher at about Easter, 'Can't we study something else a while—I'm tired of this Jesus Christ story.'"

As the years passed in Washington and Brandeis became more accustomed to his judicial work, he seemed—if still austere in his personal lifestyle—"infinitely more mellow and human and fond of people," according to Dean Acheson, who graduated from Brandeis law clerk to Brandeis friend. "It may be, of course," continued Acheson, "that I have just gotten to know him better. . . . But he seems somehow different to me. He is a person to whom one gets most ungodly attached, isn't he?"

The entertainment form practiced by Supreme Court justices then was weekly teas. The Brandeises followed that practice but shaped it to their own style. "All that you'd get would be a cup of tea and a sort of ginger snap. That's all you ever got there," said Landis of the Brandeis's teas. But no one ever came for the refreshments; they came for the company—union leaders, journalists, government officials, Zionists, priests, the rich and famous, the poor and obscure, Republicans and Democrats, liberals and conservatives, characterized by their intelligence and their accomplishment.

Brandeis moved among them, asking questions, learning from them, offering advice. Landis recalled that, when a stranger came to these teas, "Within three minutes of talking with the Justice, they would be expressing their innermost desires—what they thought about this life, what they cared for in this life, and so on. He spent a good deal of his time listening to and advising people with regard to, not personal problems in the sense of marital problems or anything of that nature, but problems with regard to ideals that they should pursue, what careers they should pursue." One guest found himself talking to Brandeis about small community life in Palestine, something about which the guest knew nothing. "Some days later," the guest remembered, "I found in my morning's mail a set of pamphlets on Palestine, all rolled in a plain envelope with no identification beyond the familiar strong, straight handwriting of L. D. B."

The early 1920s were the years of the Harding administration scandals—Teapot Dome, "The little green house on K Street," mistresses, Attorney General Daugherty's shenanigans—the panoply of shady politics. Brandeis was not immune to the gossip. Acheson, by now a practicing lawyer in Washington, visited Brandeis; Mrs. Brandeis, ill for part of this time, was attended by nurses, and the justice was alone in the evenings. Acheson recalled that "Being lonely, [Brandeis] would send word that, if convenient, he would welcome an evening call on him in the office. There, with no work to stand between us, and all alone, he would say conspiratorially, 'Dean, what is the latest dirt?' "

Those Republican scandals had been uncovered, to a great extent, by the investigations of Senator Burton K. Wheeler, Democrat of Montana and a Brandeis friend. The Republican administration responded by indicting Wheeler on a fake bribery charge. Brandeis was upset at the development because Wheeler "has been terribly hard hit." At Harvard, Frankfurter was angered by the legal profession's silence. The Wheeler indictment eventually was dropped, but not before Frankfurter exercised his sharp tongue against his Wall Street lawyer friends. "What bothers me most about the attitude of lawyers like yourself," he wrote a Wall Street acquaintance, "is how little you seem to care about these Washington disclosures, and how casually you have taken it all . . . not one lawyer of importance . . . has said anything in public since the stench of Daugherty has befouled the air."

Mrs. Brandeis's illness, to which Acheson had referred, apparently was emotional. "I am told that [she] is still broken down in nerves and hysterical," said Oliver Wendell Holmes to a friend; Brandeis appeared "tired."

Although she had her causes, her interests, and her activities, Alice Goldmark Brandeis, for most of her life, was known only as Louis Brandeis's wife. In 1924 she did become involved in the presidential campaign, publicly accusing American capitalists of attempting to gain control of Latin America. One newspaper account said that government officials criticized her statement as "particularly unfit and hurtful to the United States."

Her husband made no public comment about her activities, but it was after the campaign that she became ill. By the end of the next year, however, she seemed to have recovered and Brandeis himself, again according to Holmes, was "well and cheerful."

In the 1920s, as in the earlier decades, Brandeis continued the role of Old Testament prophet. "Refuse to accept as inevitable any evil in business—e.g., irregularity of employment. Refuse to tolerate any immoral practice—e.g., espionage," he preached. Do not look for remedies in any "isms," do not rely on legislation. "Remedial institutions are apt to fall under the control of the enemy and to become instruments of oppression." Work within existing institutions, "proceed from the individual to the general . . . progress is necessarily slow . . . that always and everywhere the intellectual, moral and spiritual development of those concerned will remain an essential—and the main—factor in real betterment." He continued to argue for individual development; better living conditions were valuable "mainly" to increase opportunities for development. He talked about individual responsibility and the difficulties of democracy—"It substitutes self-restraint for external restraint" and "is more difficult to maintain ru1n to achieve."

He was a moralist in an immoral time. He spoke of self-restraint in the flapper age. He called for ending business excesses when Wall Street was ripping every nickel possible from the economy. He exalted the individual when Fascism, the scourge of individualism, was on the rise in Europe and showed signs of sprouting in the United States.

Almost an anachronism, a spirit out of joint with his time, he took himself seriously. To his credit, if he became a scourge, he did not become a joke.

He continued his penchant for detail. One Thanksgiving, when Dean Acheson was a guest at the Brandeises, he was tempted to debate Brandeis on the French contributions to civilization at the end of the eighteenth century but decided against it because Acheson knew that Brandeis "would floor me by quoting their export statistics for the same years."

With his family—his wife and daughters, brother and other relatives —Brandeis's affection overflowed. He wrote hundreds of letters over the years to his wife and to his daughters, Susan and Elizabeth; they were warm letters, showing concern for feelings and interest in the smallest detail of family life. He was proud of his children. Susan was a lawyer practicing in New York and argued before the United States Supreme Court.* Elizabeth received her doctor of philosophy degree from the University of Wisconsin. "There is much enthusiasm at Madison about her thesis," boasted the father.

Brandeis, conscious of how wealth had destroyed children in other families, determined to teach his children to handle money. When they were young, he and they entered into a contractual arrangement; he paid each daughter five cents a week and they polished his shoes, understanding that "there are no catchwords in this contract." In later years he gave each daughter $10,000 in bonds so they would have a base for charitable giving. "As you know," the father explained, "mother and I have, for many years, given a large part of our income to public causes in which we took an active part; thus rendering our own work more effective. We think you and Susan may wish to do the like."

As his children grew up, he continued to be generous with them.

*The case, *Margolin* v. *United States*, 269 U.S. 93, was argued October 5, 1925, and on November 16, 1925, Susan Brandeis's side lost in an 8–0 decision written by Justice McReynolds. Brandeis did not participate in the case. It is occasionally reported that this was the first time that a woman had argued a case before the Supreme Court. Actually, women lawyers had been admitted to the Supreme Court bar and had been appearing before the Court since the 1880s.

"You do not say how much money you and Susan need—So I send you another, as heretofore, check for $1,000," he wrote to his son-in-law Jack Gilbert.

In 1926, Louis Brandeis became seventy. "You turn the third corner tomorrow," Holmes wrote to him. "You have done big things with high motives—have swept over great hedges and across wide ditches, always with the same courage, the same keen eye, the same steady hand. As you take the home stretch the onlookers begin to realize how you have ridden and what you have achieved. I am glad that I am still here to say: Nobly done." In honor of Brandeis's birthday, his friends donated $50,000 to the Harvard Law School Endowment Fund for research fellowships bearing his name.

The Court, "our Court," Brandeis still called it, changed. Chief Justice White, after a year's illness, died in 1921. The man named by President Warren G. Harding to replace him was former President William Howard Taft, the Taft of the Ballinger affair and leader of the opposition to Brandeis's nomination.

Since the Brandeis confirmation fight, they had met only once. It was in 1918 and Brandeis was walking toward his apartment house early in the afternoon when, coming toward him, was Taft. There was no mistaking either man: Taft still rotund, Brandeis still of the Lincolnesque face. The two hesitated, eyed each other warily, then Taft spoke: "Isn't this Justice Brandeis? I don't think we have ever met."

Brandeis responded by saying they had met once, years before, at Harvard. "He at once began to talk about my views on regularity of employment," said Brandeis. "After a moment I asked him to come in with me." The two men spent a half hour together in the Brandeis apartment, talking about labor and war problems. "Was most confidential," said Brandeis, "at one point [he] put his hand on my knee." Brandeis congratulated Taft on his war service; Taft then was serving with the War Labor Board. "We parted with his saying in effect—He hoped we would meet often."

Taft had begun campaigning for the Chief Justice's seat almost as soon as White had become ill; the former President saw himself as a bulwark against radicalism, especially the kind promoted by Brandeis. Although the two men often opposed each other, Taft came to like Brandeis. "He thinks much of the court and is anxious to have it consistent and strong, and he pulls his weight in the boat," said Taft of his former nemesis.

At the decade's end, Taft, aged and ailing, spoke more critically of Brandeis for his "progressive" inclinations. And because Brandeis, Holmes, and Harlan Fiske Stone were on the Court advancing their liberal ideas, Taft himself hesitated to resign in the late 1920s, despite failing health, because "I must stay on the court in order to prevent the Bolsheviki from getting control."

Brandeis's views of Taft were mixed. Before the ex-President was nominated, Dean Acheson speculated that Taft would be President Harding's choice. "Impossible!" snorted Brandeis. After the appointment, however, "any suggestion of frivolity or criticism was out-of-bounds," Acheson reported.

Years later Frankfurter recalled Brandeis's speaking of Taft positively —"a man who is so good as Chief Justice in his function of presiding officer." In the early 1920s, Brandeis was more critical of Taft in discussions with Frankfurter. He had taken to speaking openly with Frankfurter about the Court; it seemed that if he did so with Frankfurter, then being quiet with others was possible.

In those sessions, Brandeis spoke of Taft as looking like "a benevolent, good-natured, distillery drummer. . . . He is a first-rate second-rate mind," and has "all the defects but also the advantages of the aristocratic order that has done well by him."

The Holmes-Brandeis friendship that had begun forty years earlier continued. Although Holmes was in his eighties during the 1920s, there was no diminution of either his spirit or his capacity for work. One of Frankfurter's favorite stories of the "Magnificent Yankee" revolved around a balmy spring day in Washington. Holmes's law clerk suggested that he and the justice take a walk; Holmes refused, explaining he had to read a decision sent to him by one of the justices. The clerk insisted, and Holmes was about to give in when a second decision to be read arrived. The clerk persisted and Holmes, relenting, put on his hat and coat. He made it to the front door when still a third decision arrived. "It's no use, my lad," said the justice. "I have to go back. The goddam fecundity of my brethren will kill me yet."

Brandeis was always loading down Holmes with data. "I hate facts," said Holmes, preferring ideas. "He bullies me a little," said Holmes of "young Brandeis," who was fifteen years his junior.

In 1922, after Holmes had been on the Supreme Court for twenty years, Brandeis sent him a note: "Still the dash of a D'Artagnan." A few years later, when there were rumors of Holmes's retiring, Brandeis told him: "You have no right to retire. You are now the most useful man on the bench." For the next few years, as Holmes moved into his nineties, Brandeis continued the loyal friend, walking with him, visiting him, caring for his needs, protecting him from criticism.*

With McReynolds, Brandeis developed a modus vivendi; they did not deal with each other except by commenting on one another's decisions. McReynolds during the 1920s and 1930s was the headache of all the justices: he was lazy and did not do his share of the work, and his decisions usually were collected quotations from a submitted brief or a lower-court decision.

Willis Van Devanter, who had joined the Court six years before Brandeis, became one of his good friends, although their backgrounds and philosophies were different. Through the years Van Devanter developed a writing problem; the physical act of using pen or pencil on paper was difficult for him, and so he did not carry as much of a load as did the other justices. Brandeis realized that Van Devanter's great strength was not in his legal analyses but in his political skills; he often won the needed fifth vote with his politicking. "In the middle ages," said Brandeis, "Van Devanter would have been the best of Cardinals. He is indefatigable, on good terms with everybody, ready to help everybody, knows exactly what he wants and clouds over difficulties by fine phrases and deft language."

John Hessin Clarke, appointed to the Court a few days after Brandeis's swearing-in, had been close to him both socially and philosophically, but Clarke resigned in 1922 because he came to believe a justice lived "a dog's life." He also had grown apart from Brandeis. The two men, said Clarke, "were agreeing less and less frequently in the decision of cases involving what we call, for want of a better designation, liberal principles." He blamed this on Brandeis's not joining with him. Brandeis, amused, quoted the line "If I were an artist, I would paint only pretty girls and interesting women."

Clarke's replacement was George Sutherland, sixty, a former senator from Utah. A conservative, Sutherland had opposed Brandeis's nomination to the Court. He was a party man, had voted the wishes of the cliques and financial interests that controlled his state's Senate, which, in turn, elected United States senators. In 1916, a few months after the

*In the 1920s Brandeis was not a frequent guest in the Holmes house, and it is sometimes reported that this was because Mrs. Holmes was anti-Semitic. In earlier years both Brandeis and Frankfurter had been welcomed in the Holmes house and been treated with warmth by husband and wife. But in the 1920s Mrs. Holmes was elderly and ill, and those factors undoubtedly were responsible for her curtailed social life. She died in 1929 at the age of eighty-eight.

Brandeis confirmation, he was not renominated for the Senate; the Seventeenth Amendment, ratified in 1913, had moved the choice of senators from the state legislature to the electorate at large. Sutherland stayed in Washington practicing law and served a term as president of the American Bar Association. He retained close ties to the Republican hierarchy and was a friend of Ohio Senator Warren G. Harding. When Harding became President, Sutherland was his first nominee as associate justice. Sutherland remained on the Court until 1938.

Justice William Day resigned in 1922 and was succeeded by Pierce Butler. In his late fifties when appointed, Butler had been a corporation lawyer primarily in his native Minnesota. Considered a reactionary, Butler had used his position as Regent of the University of Minnesota to take revenge on professors with whom he disagreed or who he believed had slighted him. Butler served on the Court until 1939.

Mahlon Pitney also resigned in 1922, replaced by Edward Terry Sanford of Tennessee, who served only until 1930. A federal district judge with a competent record, Sanford was nominated because President Harding believed appointing a southerner to the Court would be wise politically.

The fifth Republican appointee to the Supreme Court in the 1920s was Harlan Fiske Stone, who replaced James McKenna. In his early fifties then, Stone served for twenty-one years, until 1946. With Taft, Sutherland, Butler, and Sanford, the Republican leadership had been careful to urge the appointment of proven conservatives as a "bulwark" against progressivism, and they were not disappointed. The Republicans believed Stone would join this group. He had the right credentials—dean of Columbia law school, a successful New York law practice, counsel for J. P. Morgan, Attorney General in the Coolidge administration, and he had been President Coolidge's classmate at Amherst. But the Republicans had overlooked something about Stone. The son of a farmer and as much a self-made man as any of that generation who claimed the title, he had not allowed that to skew his perspective, and he never forgot that others needed help. Nor did he forget that law was universal; individuals could not choose which laws to obey and which to ignore. On the Supreme Court, Stone often joined Holmes and Brandeis—to the chagrin of his fellow Republicans.

Brandeis thrived on the oral arguments before the Court, the lawyers for the two sides, arguing their points before the nine justices, jousting with precedents and points of constitutional law. Brandeis rarely read the briefs submitted in the cases in advance of the argument, preferring that the sparks of his mind be struck by a good lawyer.

After a week of oral arguments, the justices met in conference to discuss the cases and assign the proposed opinions. The conferences were held on Saturdays, beginning at noon and often lasting until the early evening. "We've had some interesting times," Brandeis said to Frankfurter of those sessions, "but the atmosphere is very friendly. When we differ, we agree to differ, without any ill feeling."

Sometimes the pressure hit them. "Often wrong decisions due to haste and fatigue at end of term—Saturday *night* at Chief's," Brandeis reported to Frankfurter once. The decision making went like a ticking clock. At one seven-hour Saturday conference, Holmes said, "we disposed of 60 certioraris as well as seven argued and submitted cases and outside matters." Holmes called the conference "our regular Saturday afternoon jaw . . . where, without discredit to my brethren, I expect to be bored."

To these conferences the justices brought their own special expertise. Brandeis and Pierce Butler led in discussions of cases having to do with railroads and rate making. Van Devanter was looked to in cases dealing with land law and Indians. McReynolds made admiralty law his specialty.

Usually the conference did not change any justice's inclinations, no matter how persuasive the arguments behind the closed doors. "Van Devanter wouldn't change, nor Clarke," said Brandeis. "Day couldn't be persuaded by anybody but himself. He does change his own views; he is a fighter, a regular game cock."

In the conference, the Chief Justice traditionally begins the discussion of a case, and the other justices speak in descending order of seniority. In voting, the process is reversed, with the most junior justice voting first and the Chief Justice last. A vote cast in conference is not final; a justice can change his mind, either moved by the written opinion or dissent of other justices, by further study, or merely by whim.

After a conference vote, if the Chief Justice is in the majority, he either assigns the opinion to an associate justice or writes it himself. If he is not in the majority, the senior associate justice in the majority fills that role. The senior member among the minority, be he the Chief Justice or an associate justice, determines who will write the dissent. Each member is free to write a concurrence or dissent.

"The statement that genius is the capacity for taking infinite pains might have originated in speaking of the justice," said Acheson about

Brandeis's approach to opinion writing. A Brandeis decision went through many drafts; he scrawled out the opinion with pen, sent it to the printer to be set in type, and then revised the galleys. He would do that four, five, sometimes twenty times, a revision often being a complete rewrite.

Because Brandeis put his decisions through so many revisions, using the Supreme Court printer as a typewriter, he offered to pay the costs of his revisions. "It would not, in the least, embarrass me to pay," he told Chief Justice Taft. But Taft would not allow it: "I think we would make a great mistake if we allowed the fear of expense to interfere with the necessary procedure in making our opinions what we wish them to be. . . . It is a legitimate and necessary expenditure in the discharge of our duty."

Brandeis's research was voluminous, material coming from federal and state agencies, the then Legislative Reference Service at the Library of Congress, history books, law journals—anything or anyone to illuminate the subject.

His statement of the case, in addition to being detailed, was always scrupulously accurate. This made his conclusions more difficult to rebut. Along with detail and accuracy, there was his desire to educate, growing stronger the longer he was on the Court. Before he released an opinion, he asked: "What can we do to make it more instructive?"

Over the years, he became known as a stylist, his opinions worth reading for their literary quality. The reader found his data and organization impressive, his prose lean, his analysis persuasive, and the results —if not always convincing—difficult to ignore.

The work was exhausting. Brandeis went to bed early, rose early, and was at his desk before his law clerk arrived. At work, his energy was unflagging. Occasionally he stretched out on his couch, pulled an old steamer rug over him, and fell asleep. Ten or fifteen minutes later, he woke up completely refreshed and returned to his desk.

Brandeis believed the lengthy process of developing decisions, no matter how laborious, was an important part of being a justice. "The court has no establishment," he once said.

Even the law clerks Frankfurter supplied from Harvard were rarely involved in the decision-making process. Once Brandeis drafted the first version of a decision, the clerk then checked all citations, sometimes wrote footnotes, and, on occasion, suggested including additional material. After the mid-1920s, when the justices reviewed petitions for writs of certiorari to determine which cases they would hear, Brandeis used the clerks to check the writs for defects, but once Brandeis had decided to grant the petition, to allow the case to be heard, he was not interested in challenges from a clerk. With a petition denied, however, he would listen to a clerk's plea and sometimes change his mind.

When Brandeis anticipated a case involving a major point of law, he had the clerk research the question. "Herewith is some good law, some new law, and doubtless some bad law," said a memorandum on a case by one of his clerks. "The part of the memo headed Fifth is, of course," said the clerk, "based on prayer only."

With the clerks a personal relationship developed; if not father-son, it was the benign elder watching out for the younger man. To all, he offered advice about careers, usually trying to persuade them to stay away from practice in New York, Boston, or other large cities—advice, if anyone had given to Brandeis when he was a beginning lawyer, he had not heeded.

The clerk attended the Brandeis teas. "You'd have to act as a kind of bouncer to see that people were steered in to see him," said one. Once a week or so, the clerk was invited to dinner or to stop by the apartment after dinner.

With the warmth of the justice-clerk relationship, however, Brandeis was a stern taskmaster. Acheson told a story of spending "the hours, the days with the digests" to find "the nuggets in the pan, shining up from the work sheet like good deeds in a naughty world"—that is, two footnotes. Acheson went to Court expecting Brandeis to read a decision with Acheson's two footnotes, but the decision was not read. "It was as though the Queen Mary lay dead and silent when the bridge rang for 'Engines!'" Acheson realized an error had been made. Who was responsible? Brandeis? Poindexter, the Brandeis messenger, whose experience included working for Brandeis's predecessor? Or Acheson himself? Had he erred with the footnotes? "The answer," said Acheson, "was not in doubt." At the confrontation, Brandeis "looked at me for far too long a time—so it seemed—and said: 'Dean, your function is to correct my errors, not to introduce errors of your own.'"

Once a decision was written, it was circulated to the other justices for comment. The author might then revise the decision to suit those comments, rather than have a justice withdraw support. "I have a little case," said Holmes once to Frankfurter, "whether it will go or not I don't know. As originally written it had a tiny pair of testicles—but the scruples of my brethren have caused their removal and it sings in a very soft voice now." In one case, McReynolds wrote an opinion that Brandeis believed would "bother us in the future." McReynolds made some changes, but Brandeis still was not satisfied. Taft then wrote the draft that became the Court's decision. Brandeis supported it.

When circulating opinions, some of the justices held them up until the end of the week so that other justices would not have time to review them carefully before the final votes were taken at the Saturday conference. Brandeis refused to do that, insisting that his opinions arrive with sufficient time for study.

McReynolds's comments on a Brandeis decision generally were surly —"I suppose it will be but I like it not." Sometimes, however, even McReynolds had to acknowledge the power of a Brandeis decision—"I voted the other way, but if you get a majority I shall not say anything."

Taft was impressed with Brandeis's ability to handle decisions involving complicated business and tax matters. "It relieves me greatly to get rid of such a case satisfactorily," said Taft in one instance, and in another: "I am glad I don't have to consider and decide such a case as this every year. Once a year would be more than I can stand."

Brandeis seemed more effective with his circulated written opinions than the Saturday conference discussions. Frequently on the circulated opinions there would be comments such as, from Pierce Butler: "I think you make a strong argument for the result and it is likely you are right. As you know I inclined the other way. I am content and concur"; from James McKenna; "This leaves me no excuse not to be right so I say Yes"; and from Sanford: "While I voted to reverse with some doubt, the doubt has been removed by your clear and strong presentation of the case— and I unreservedly *concur.*"

Brandeis, in the 1920s, had tenuous personal connections with two cases before the Court. One, *Hamilton* v. *Kentucky Distilleries Company,* concerned the liquor industry in Kentucky, Brandeis's home state. Although Louis Brandeis was not involved in the industry, his brother Alfred, still in Louisville, was, through his grain company, and Louis had friends in Kentucky.

The sale of liquor had been restricted during wartime. When that restriction ended, the Eighteenth Amendment prohibiting the sale of all liquor took effect. This meant the liquor companies were stuck with liquor they could not sell for drinking purposes. They argued before the Supreme Court that the government should compensate them for the liquor. "Whiskey is property," they said, "and when taken for public use is entitled to the protection of the Fifth Amendment."

The decision was one of those instances when the brethren moved toward unanimity in order to avoid controversy and because no one was quite certain how best to resolve the issue. At first the decision was 5 to 4, with a majority for the liquor industry, but with Brandeis against the industry. The Chief Justice, then White, was with Brandeis, but Holmes was siding with the liquor industry. White lobbied Holmes, and then asked Brandeis to write the decision against the liquor industry "because he thought I could get Holmes more easily," said Brandeis—which explained why Brandeis, the son of Kentucky, wrote the decision so adversely affecting that state. Holmes came along, reluctantly. "Undoubtedly his impatience with prohibition explains this," said Brandeis. When Pitney quarreled with Brandeis's draft, Brandeis said, " 'Let Pitney go over my opinion' and Pitney worked hard for a few days and we agreed." The final opinion, representing the haggling and compromise, eventually brought in the other Court members.

The decision was not welcomed in Kentucky, or in other parts of the country where prohibition was unpopular. "I heard that in the New York movies they hissed the Justice for ten minutes after the Prohibition case," Dean Acheson, then Brandeis's law clerk, wrote to Felix Frankfurter. "However, if there ever was a man who didn't give a damn whether he is approved, applauded, hissed, or cursed, it is the Judge."

The second case in which Brandeis had a tenuous personal connection, *Myers* v. *United States,* decided in 1926, involved Woodrow Wilson. As President, Wilson had fired a postmaster without either officially informing the Senate or seeking its consent. This appeared to violate an 1876 Tenure of Office law which said that postmasters were appointed for four years or until removed by the President with the advice and consent of the Senate. The postmaster sued for back pay. As with most cases before the Supreme Court, the issue involved more than the surface dispute—in this instance, the back pay for the postmaster. The separation of powers was a major issue. Could a President fire a member of the executive branch if and when he wished? Could Congress limit that power? And, if so, what other presidential powers could it limit?

William Howard Taft headed the Court at this time. More important to him than Wilson's having defeated him in the 1912 election was the threat to the presidency. He was determined to uphold the presidential power to fire anyone in the executive branch. Taft hoped for a unanimous Court in this case, but Brandeis in conference said he intended to dissent, and Holmes along with McReynolds, the other justice appointed to the Court by Wilson, indicated they planned to join him.

Brandeis had several concerns. First was his affection for Woodrow

Wilson. After Wilson had left the White House as a sick man, Brandeis had sent him copies of his decisions, short notes, flowers at Christmas and other holidays. This affection had led Brandeis into committing one of his few judicial "indiscretions." Wilson, living in political isolation in a house on S Street in northwest Washington, dreaming of a return to national politics, enlisted the help of a few friends in the drafting of a political statement. The sick, dying man hoped the statement would electrify the Democratic party's 1924 nominating convention and perhaps lead to Wilson's again being nominated for the presidency—or at least restore Wilsonian idealism as the party's philosophy. Brandeis had worked on the project, dubbed "the document." It dragged on through 1921 and 1922 before fading out. Brandeis's involvement with "the document" became known years after Wilson's death in 1924, and Brandeis has been criticized for violating judicial propriety by involving himself in a "political" matter.

Despite this affection for his friend and concern for his memory, Brandeis did not believe that Wilson had the right to dismiss officials without the Senate's consent. To do so would allow the civil service system to move from under the Senate's control and widen its own power. Also, Brandeis anticipated legislation by Congress to cut back the President's power if the Court upheld Wilson.

Taft met with the other justices at his home to shape the majority decision. Taft eventually spent more than a year on the opinion and was proud of his achievement; he did not understand Brandeis's dissenting. "McReynolds and Brandeis belong to a class of people that have no loyalty to the court and sacrifice almost everything to the gratification of their own publicity," Taft complained privately when he realized the two associate justices intended to dissent.

James Landis was Brandeis's clerk then and worked on the Brandeis dissent, going through every page of the Senate journals from the time of the Tenure of Office Act's passage in 1876 to determine what the practice had been. When the research was done, it was an exhaustive account of a President's power both to appoint and fire a person—"as thorough a piece of historical research as you would find in the Supreme Court reports anywhere," boasted Landis.

Holmes, McReynolds, and Brandeis filed separate dissents. Brandeis, in voting against Wilson, said Congress had "exercised continuously some measure of control by legislation." He saw the separation of powers as not making each branch "completely autonomous" but leaving each "in some measure, dependent upon the others."

During the twenty-three years after Brandeis heard his first case as a justice in October 1916, he spoke from the Bench on issues of concern to him, speaking as he had before he joined the Court, for the individual, and for the power of the state to assist and protect the individual. Usually he was on the losing side.

Child labor was one such issue. In the early 1900s children, some as young as ten, worked long days and six- and seven-day weeks. New England and the Middle Atlantic states argued that child labor was necessary because the mills and factories in the South used child labor, paid children less than adults, and underbid the North. Where North Carolina had 5,000 cotton-mill operatives under fourteen years of age, Massachusetts had 199 and New York only 51. But the pressures were hard to resist. In Massachusetts an adult male averaged $410 a year as a cotton-mill operator in 1904; a woman earned $340; and a child under sixteen, $233. That $233 figure was the highest among the New England states. In North Carolina the comparable figures were $256, $194, and $130 for the child laborer. Across the country the story was the same for factory workers. In the cities an adult male earned $566 a year; a woman doing the same job earned $307, and a child, $186. For industry the statistics meant one thing: hire more children.

There had been sporadic efforts in the states to outlaw or reduce child labor, but they were generally unsuccessful. In North Carolina, for example, when the state legislature considered a bill raising the age limit for cotton-mill operators to fourteen, prohibiting night work for women and children as well as shortening the work week from sixty-six to sixty hours, the cotton-mill lobby defeated it. "I think children, especially boys ten years of age, should be allowed to work in mills," explained the mill owners' spokesman. Such work is "the savior of the people, religiously, educationally, and . . . physically."

Senator Albert J. Beveridge of Indiana in the early 1900s proposed legislation to outlaw "brutal and horrible" child labor. He argued that action, under Article I, Section 8 of the Constitution, giving the federal government authority over interstate commerce, was needed rather than action by the separate states because—and this became the rationale for federal regulatory action in the future—"If one State passes good laws and enforces them, and another State does not, then the businessmen in the former State are at a . . . disadvantage."

An opponent in Congress was Representative John W. Davis of West Virginia. He believed the proposal violated states rights, but he argued from another position in 1907: "If Congress can prohibit the transportation of the product of child labor, it can also prohibit the transportation of goods manufactured by 'scab' labor . . . and thus close the door of the factory to every workman who does not have a union card."

In Boston in 1907, Brandeis opposed child labor but accepted that using the Constitution's interstate commerce clause to prohibit it was undesirable; his alternative was a well-publicized federal investigation to bring "the present conditions before the public."

By 1916, despite child-labor conditions' being well publicized, the exploitation continued. Congress then prohibited the *transportation* across state lines of goods manufactured with child labor, considered a national matter, bypassing the question of the *manufacture* of such goods, considered a local matter.

Quickly challenged, the child-labor law came before the Supreme Court on April 15 and 16, 1918. Representing the government, upholding the constitutionality of the law, was the same John W. Davis who had opposed the concept ten years earlier. Then he had been a representative from a state with industry relying heavily on child labor; now he was Solicitor General of the United States. His arguments for the law were a reprise of those Senator Beveridge had used a decade earlier, and which Davis had then opposed.

Davis told the Supreme Court that Congress had a right to regulate commerce, that there was a long history of its having done so. "It cannot be denied," he said, "that a change in public opinion regarding child labor has occurred like that in relation to lottery tickets. Neither the ticket nor the labor are inherently bad. But the facts of life have disclosed undesirable evils in the use of both."

Again, almost echoing Beveridge's 1907 argument, Davis said that working children had more accidents, were more likely to die of tuberculosis and to have stunted intellectual and physical growth. He referred to child labor as "child slavery" and equated its evils with prostitution and alcoholism. Still using the Beveridge arguments, Davis said that the state laws varied so much that the result was "unfair competition in trade among the States."

As Davis relied on arguments others had used a decade earlier, his opponents used themes he himself had expressed then. If child-labor is abhorrent, they argued also that

It is abhorrent to many people that manufacturing processes should be carried on by underpaid hands; therefore Congress may prescribe a minimum wage scale and forbid the produce of a factory in interstate commerce unless such minimum rates are paid. It is abhorrent to many people that negroes should not have the same industrial opportunities that whites enjoy; therefore Congress may provide that no factory which refuses to employ negroes, side by side with whites, may ship its goods in interstate commerce.

That argument paralleled the one made against Brandeis when he had argued for the legitimacy of working-hours legislation in *Muller* v. *Oregon*. If industry can be regulated in one area, it can be regulated in all areas. *Muller* v. *Oregon* had been the point of the attack; the other wage-hours legislation, which first Brandeis and then Frankfurter had argued before the Court, had been the follow-up assault. This child-labor case—*Hammer* v. *Dagenhart*—was a more blunt attack. It was revolution by litigation.

In a 5–4 decision, the Supreme Court struck down the federal law prohibiting child labor. The ten- and twelve-year-olds would continue working the twelve-hour days and the six-day weeks. The majority said that Congress could only regulate commerce when the manufactured goods themselves were harmful.

The dissent, by Holmes, was co-signed by McKenna, Brandeis, and Clarke. Although Brandeis did not file separate comments, his joining in the dissent showed his willingness to accept federal legislation, something he had not been willing to do a decade earlier.

First, Holmes dealt with the constitutional issue. The interstate commerce clause gives Congress the right to regulate commerce. "Regulation means the prohibition of something," he wrote, "and when interstate commerce is the matter to be regulated I cannot doubt that the regulation may prohibit any part of such commerce that Congress sees fit to forbid."

Then he went on to the moral issue, the point motivating the law:

... if there is any matter upon which civilized countries have agreed—far more unanimously than they have with regard to intoxicants and some other matters over which this country is now emotionally aroused—it is the evil of premature and excessive child labor. I should have thought that if we were to introduce our moral conceptions . . . this was preeminently a case for upholding the exercise of all its powers by the United States.

Federal regulation of child labor again came before the Court in 1922 when a second federal law sought to tax goods manufactured with child labor, an approach developed to circumvent the majority decision in *Hammer* v. *Dagenhart*. As much as some of the justices disliked child labor, they agreed that the new law extended taxing powers beyond what were then allowed limits. This law was also struck down, Brandeis writing the decision. The right of the federal government to regulate child labor was not upheld by the Supreme Court until 1941. Brandeis was not a member of the Supreme Court then; Felix Frankfurter was.

In 1922, Brandeis and Holmes had one of their rare splits, over the extent of a state's police power. Since 1878, the Pennsylvania Coal Company had had an agreement with a family to mine coal beneath the surface of the family's property. The family claimed a 1921 state law abrogated the contract by restricting mining beneath the surface.

The issue had long been before the Court, beginning before *Muller* v. *Oregon:* How far can a state regulate?

Said the company: "The theoretical right to remove the coal without disturbing the surface is, as a practical matter, no more available than was Shylock's right to his pound of flesh."

Said the state: "The protection of the life, health and safety of the public in the anthracite mining communities is the primary purpose of the act. Its interference with property rights is merely incidental."

Although Holmes usually sided with the state's power to regulate, this time he wrote the majority decision for the company. "The question," he said, "is whether the police power can be stretched so far." There must be limits, he said, and concluded that the law worked advantageously to those who had surface mining rights.

Brandeis, dissenting, wrote: "If the public safety is imperiled, surely neither grant, nor contract, can prevail against the exercise of police power." Pointing out that the law in question had been written by the state Legislature and upheld in that state's court system, "it is for a State to say how its public policy shall be enforced," said Brandeis, not the federal government.

The question arose again the next year in a Nebraska case involving a law prescribing minimum and maximum sizes of bread loaves, *Burns Baking Company* v. *Bryan.* The law had been enacted because bakers were substituting smaller for larger loaves. As in the Pennsylvania coal case, the state's judicial system had upheld the state law.

The Supreme Court's majority decision, written by Pierce Butler, favored the bakers: "A State may not, under the guise of protecting the public, arbitrarily interfere with private business or prohibit lawful occupations or impose unreasonable and unnecessary restrictions on them."

Originally there had been four dissents, by Sutherland, Sanford, Brandeis, and Holmes. "But Van Devanter 'got busy,' in his personal way, talking and laboring with members of the Court," explained Brandeis, finally persuading Sutherland and Sanford to suppress their dissents.

Only Holmes and Brandeis dissented then, Brandeis writing for himself and Holmes. Where Butler's majority decision was seven pages long, Brandeis's dissent was seventeen pages. Where Butler parroted the arguments made by the baking-industry attorneys, Brandeis compiled data about such laws from other states, demonstrating their success and their necessity. "Much evidence referred to by me is not in the record," Brandeis wrote. "Nor could it have been included. It is the history of the experience gained under similar legislation. . . . Of such events in our history, whether occurring before or after the enactment of the statute or of the entry of the judgement, the Court should acquire knowledge, and must, in my opinion, take judicial notice, whenever required to perform the delicate judicial task here involved."

Brandeis defended the insertion of this material because "Knowledge is essential to understanding; and understanding should precede the judging. Sometimes, if we would guide by the light of reason, we must let our minds be bold. But, in this case, we have merely to acquaint ourselves with the art of breadmaking."

Again, as he had in the Pennsylvania case, Brandeis argued for a conservative approach by the Court. The Court's proper role, he said, was not to judge the wisdom of the state's action. To do so, as he argued the majority had done, "is . . . an exercise of the powers of a super-legislature—not the performance of the constitutional function of judicial review."

If anyone had missed the point, Felix Frankfurter in an unsigned editorial in *The New Republic* said: "Let any disinterested student of constitutional law read the [*Burns* majority] decision . . . and deny that we have never had a more irresponsible period in the history of that court."

With labor-union cases, Brandeis was even more the dissenter. As an associate justice he asserted that labor needed equality at the bargaining table with management, not only to settle specific issues such as wages and hours, working conditions and fringe benefits, but to deal with the entire range of employee problems and potential employee contributions. Instead of the negotiation Brandeis advocated, however, management, supported by a majority of the Supreme Court, sought confrontation with labor.

Following the First World War, Brandeis believed that "The struggle for [labor] rights is over. They are now recognized as much as anything ever is in a world where you cannot expect unanimity." As with Zionism, Brandeis was too much the optimist—what he perceived was not the reality others created. Shortly after he had predicted that the struggle for labor rights was over, Brandeis was responding to violence and repression. He told Acheson that he was not discouraged but "simply deeply humiliated and filled with a sense of sin that we with the greatest possibilities of any people should waste ourselves on these age-old methods of oppression."

His hostess at a 1922 dinner party reported, "Brandeis talked . . . like a defeated man about the labor movement. He said that a big corporation like the steel company was a state within the state and that the worker is quite powerless to combat it. He sees organized labor beaten at every turn."

His concern was not that the United States would retreat. "We cannot go backward," he said, but that the techniques used against unions would radicalize union leadership. "We shall pay dearly," he warned.

The specific issues before the Supreme Court in the 1920s were, for the union: the rights to organize, to picket, and to wage a secondary boycott—without such powers the union could not operate; and for management: the rights to sue and to enjoin unions—with such powers management could block a union's organizing efforts.

The union's right to organize was the pivotal point in the case involving the Hitchman Coal and Coke Company. The company's attitude was blunt: If you want a job here, you don't belong to the union. When the United Mine Workers attempted to organize the company, Hitchman secured an injunction halting the union activities. Those 1907 events came before the Court early in 1916, were reargued later that year after Brandeis joined the Court, and decided late in 1917.

The company won. "The same liberty which enables men to form unions . . ." wrote Mahlon Pitney for the majority, "entitled other men to remain independent of the union and other employers to agree with them to employ no man who owes any allegiance or obligation to the union." Pitney was the man appointed to the Supreme Court in 1912 by President Taft to assure a Court membership against such forces as unions. Taft had chosen wisely. Pitney's decisions were not bred so much in the law as they were in his biases. At a Saturday-afternoon conference during a labor case discussion, he remarked that there was "no such thing as peaceful picketing."

Brandeis caught the point the Pitney decision had avoided, saying: ". . . it is coercion also to threaten not to give one employment unless the applicant will consent to a closed nonunion shop."

Holmes and Clarke joined with Brandeis in this dissent, leaving the decision against the unions 6 to 3. It was only the beginning.

Picketing was the issue in *Truax* v. *Corrigan*. This case had begun in Arizona, but its implications, as with the other labor cases, were national. In the town of Bisbee, a union struck the English Kitchen restaurant. The union members picketed within five feet of the restaurant, carried signs, shouted, and otherwise caused a commotion near the restaurant entrance. The restaurant's business dropped 75 percent, and its owners sought to enjoin the union from picketing and harassment. Because Arizona law did not permit an injunction in a labor dispute, the restaurant owners took their case to the Supreme Court. If they lost, unions representing workers at a work site would be free to picket and go through the other motions of striking unions. If the owners won, then any employer would be able to go into a court and obtain an injunction preventing a union from picketing or taking other measures near the work site.

When this case had been first argued, with White still Chief Justice, the tentative vote was 6–3 to strike down the Arizona law, that is, to allow an employer to obtain an injunction against a striking union. The three dissenters were the usual ones: Brandeis, Holmes, and Clarke. When White died, there still would have been a majority against the Arizona law except for an unusual development. Justice Pitney, who had written three decisions against unions, was swayed by Brandeis.

Brandeis wrote his dissent before the majority decision had been completed. Although assigned to write the majority opinion, Pitney, after reading Brandeis's dissent, switched. "I can find no grounds for declaring that the State's action is so arbitrary and devoid of reasonable basis that it can be called a deprivation of liberty or property without due process of law," Pitney said. If the state wishes to outlaw labor injunctions, let it.

With Pitney's switch and White's death, the Court was divided 4–4. This was Taft's first major case; he believed in moving cases and was anxious to begin with this one. Knowing it was controversial, he wanted to establish his reputation immediately as one willing to take on controversy. He urged Pitney to return to the fold, but Pitney refused, and the final vote—to allow the injunctions against labor unions—was 5–4, with Taft writing the majority opinion.

If the picketers, instead of being union members, had been other restaurant owners, said Taft, "an injunction would necessarily have issued." For that reason, citing the Fourteenth Amendment's prohibition against a state's denying equal protection of the laws, Taft ruled that the Arizona law prohibiting labor injunctions was unconstitutional.

There were three separate dissents: one by Holmes, arguing that Arizona had the right to prohibit labor injunctions: "Legislation may begin when an evil begins"; the one by Pitney, with Clarke concurring; and one by Brandeis. He saw the issue as part of the "struggle of contending forces," and what is permissible is "determined in part by decisions of the courts, in part by acts of the legislatures. The rules governing the contest necessarily change from time to time."

He advised the majority to remember that "Nearly all legislation involves a weighing of public needs as against private desires; and likewise a weighing of relative social values." The labor injunction, Brandeis insisted, endowed "property with active, militant power which would make it dominant over men."

The labor injunction became an anti-union weapon. While some judges attempted to define what was and was not permissible under an injunction, generally the injunction was used to stop all union activity, peaceful or not, whether harmful to the business or not. Injunctions also often resulted in sweeping arrests of union members.

Brandeis's criticisms of the injunctions inside the Supreme Court were repeated by Felix Frankfurter outside. Writing in *The New Republic,* after *Truax* v. *Corrigan,* Frankfurter castigated the injunction as a device to solve industrial conflicts. "It does not work," said the Harvard professor. "It neither mines coal, nor moves trains, nor makes clothing." With that failure, the injunction has "cut off labor from confidence in the rule of law and of the courts as its impartial organs." Brandeis had said much the same thing in his discussions with Dean Acheson when he had warned that techniques against unions would radicalize union leadership. "Mounting embitterment in masses of men and women has generated the growing conviction that the powers of the government are perverted by, and in aid of, the employers, and that the courts are the instruments of this partisan policy," wrote Frankfurter. If the rhetoric was powerful, the concern was revolution.

In 1928, Frankfurter assisted George W. Norris, chairman of the Senate Judiciary Committee, in preparing an anti-injunction bill; but nothing happened to it. In 1932, Frankfurter, assisted by Nathan Greene, wrote a tirade against the injunction. The two men charged that labor injunctions have "restrained conduct that is clearly permissible, like furnishing strike benefits, singing songs, and maintaining tent colonies." But restrictions on the use of injunctions did not come for many years.

In another labor dispute—involving whether a union could be sued —Brandeis's position was not understood; he was with the majority in what apparently was an attack on the labor movement. In that case, *United Mine Workers* v. *Coronado Coal Company*, however, he demonstrated that he was, when necessary, a skillful politician on the Court, giving one point to gain two.

The case began as part of the war by the mine owners against the United Mine Workers. Management had locked out union members, hired scabs, armed guards, and then waited for the violence to begin; they did not wait long. This was the Arkansas hills; and if it was not the western frontier, here was the line between urban and rural, between the lawful and the unlawful. This was the place where experience had convinced the union members there were no more peaceful solutions, the place where insults were responded to with the rifle.

As a result of the violence, the mine owners sued the union for damages, and lower courts ruled in the owners' favor. They declared that the national union should pay more than $700,000 in damages. If the decision held up before the Supreme Court, the United Mine Workers probably would be destroyed financially.

The union was represented before the Supreme Court by Charles Evans Hughes, and the company by John W. Davis.

The case presented three questions to the Supreme Court: Could a union, then unincorporated, be sued? Could the national union be held responsible for the activities of its local? and, Could the union be charged under the Sherman Antitrust Law with a conspiracy to restrain interstate commerce?

The unions believed a negative answer to all three questions necessary for their survival.

Brandeis always had believed that unions should be suable, arguing the point years earlier with Samuel Gompers, the labor leader. For a union to be suable would force it to behave more responsibly, Brandeis argued, as well as elevate its status in law.

He also knew that to assess more than $700,000 against the national union and to bring the union under the Sherman Act, as Chief Justice Taft wanted to do, would be a double blow that the union could not endure.

This case also was a holdover from the time when White had been Chief Justice. "I determined to have the thing decided and gotten out of the way," Taft told his brother Horace. He also hoped, with significant and controversial cases, that he could have a unanimous court. So he was particularly disturbed when Brandeis announced he would dissent. Given the past history of Brandeis dissents in labor cases, Brandeis would have either two or three justices with him.

Against this background, as Taft was writing the majority opinion, he received a note from Brandeis: "I hesitate to [make] the following suggestions. Please feel entirely free to discard any or all of them." The next day Taft, grasping at the possibility of unanimity, accepted all the suggestions. The result was a decision allowing unions to be sued but not holding the national union liable for the acts of its local—it did not have to pay the $700,000—and not bringing the union under the antitrust law. Taft had his unanimous court.

Brandeis was pleased with the decision, content to have brought Taft around on the final two points. He told Frankfurter that the conservatives "will take from Taft [but] wouldn't from us. If good enough for Taft, good enough for us—they say, and a natural sentiment." On August 16, 1922, a Frankfurter article in *The New Republic* praised the decision.

There was another point about Taft and this decision. He had come to the Supreme Court as the representative and spokesman for the economic establishment, as the advocate of free enterprise, unhindered. But even for Taft there were limits. During the First World War, as chairman of the National War Labor Board, he had conducted hearings on labor conditions. "Why I had no idea," he said at the conclusion. "How can people live on such wages?" And so now, although he could not submerge his anti-union feeling, he also could not allow the moment to go by without acknowledging how the company's actions had upset him. In his decision, he criticized the "hugger-mugger of . . . numerous corporations." When the case went back to the lower courts for reargument, John W. Davis, the counsel for the company, objected to "hugger-mugger" and asked for a substitute. Taft's suggested replacement was "evade his obligations by a manipulation of his numerous companies." "Hugger-mugger" stayed.

Secondary boycotting was the issue in two cases. The first was *Duplex Printing Company* v. *Deering*. The company was one of four specialized companies in the United States; three were organized but Duplex was not. By ignoring minimum wage, the eight-hour day, and other union standards, Duplex undersold the other three companies. The union, not wanting the three unionized companies penalized, sought to organize Duplex. When this failed, the union then tried a secondary boycott—other unionized companies should not purchase from Duplex until Duplex was organized.

The specific legal issue before the Supreme Court was whether the boycott was a traditional labor-capital issue or a violation of antitrust laws, as outlined in the Clayton Act, the law written partly by Brandeis as an attack against trusts.

Again the majority decision was by Pitney and the dissenters were Brandeis, Holmes, and Clarke. Brandeis conceded the majority's claim that the union had injured the company, "not maliciously, but in self-defense." He argued that those with a common interest in the outcome had a right to act together. As for using the Clayton Act against the union, Brandeis said that Congress's intention had been the opposite, to make relations between employer and employee competitive, and to declare "that organized competition was not harmful and that it justified injuries necessarily inflicted in its course."

Acknowledging that conditions as developed in industry "may be such that those engaged in it cannot continue their struggle without danger to the community," he insisted that "it is not for judges to determine whether such conditions exist, nor is it their function to set the limits of permissible contest and to declare the duties which the new situation demands. This is the function of the legislature which, while limiting individual and group rights of aggression and defense, may substitute processes of justice for more primitive methods of trial by combat."

The second Supreme Court case in the 1920s dealing with the secondary boycott, the Court's last major labor case of the decade, was *Bedford Cut Stone Company et al.* v. *Journeymen Stone Cutters' Association of North America et al.* The case was argued in 1927; for the previous six years the company had closed its doors to members of the stone cutters union. The union had some 150 locals, and each member of the local was also a member of the general union. The union called for a secondary boycott, ordering its members not to work on any stone made and shipped by the Bedford company with nonunion labor.

There was little question how the Supreme Court would decide; its membership had not changed significantly since it had ruled against secondary boycotts in *Duplex*. The *Bedford* opinion was written by George Sutherland. While a Senator from Utah in 1914, he had said a secondary boycott by a union was "an evil thing." For Sutherland an evil thing in 1914 continued an evil thing in 1927. Because the boycott's intention was to restrain interstate commerce, said Sutherland, an injunction is allowed if there is a probability of harm to the company, "and this clearly appears." He concluded: "Where the means adopted are unlawful, the innocent general character of the organizations adopting them or the lawfulness of the ultimate end sought to be attained, cannot serve as a justification."

Justices Sanford and Harlan Fiske Stone concurred in separate opinions. Brandeis, joined by Holmes, dissented.

At this point, in 1927, Brandeis had been on the Supreme Court for eleven years; he had passed his own seventieth birthday the previous year. He had, before he joined the Court, and since then, argued for the rights of union members, not only as a matter of law and of human decency, but as a matter of national unity. The confrontation tactics he had witnessed between management and labor had produced strife and promised more strife. This dissent then became his plea, his cry for an end to the strife, an end to the confrontation.

Brandeis began by repeating what he had been saying most of his adult life in matters dealing with federal jurisdiction, that the test was reasonableness. "What is reasonable must be determined and the application of principles by the common law," he argued and then insisted that the secondary boycott imposed by the union was "in my opinion, a reasonable one."

Then again he stressed the unevenness of power between the company and the union. Management, he said, does not consist of "weak employers opposed by a mighty union. They have large financial resources. Together, they ship 70 per cent of all the cut stone in the country. . . . They had combined in a local employers' organization."

In contrast, said Brandeis, each of the union locals is weak. "The average number of members in a local union is only 33. The locals are widely scattered throughout the country. . . . It is only through combining the 5,000 organized stone cutters in a national union, and developing loyalty to it, that the individual stonecutter anywhere can protect his own job."

Brandeis closed his dissent with a simple statement appealing to rationality and to fairness. "If, on the undisputed facts of this case, refusal to work can be enjoined," he began his last paragraph, "Congress created by the Sherman Law and the Clayton Act an instrument for imposing restraints upon labor which remind of involuntary servitude." He pointed out that the Sherman law permitted one corporation to control 50 percent of the steel industry and another corporation to control practically the entire shoe-machinery industry of the country.

Brandeis continued: "It would, indeed, be strange if Congress by the same act willed to deny to members of a small craft of workingmen the right to cooperate in simply refraining from work, when that course was the only means of self-protection against a combination of militant and powerful employers." He concluded: "I cannot believe that Congress did so."

At the same time in the 1920s that labor-management relations were going through challenges in the Supreme Court, the United States was beginning to reexamine its criminal laws. For the Supreme Court, the principal area of concern was the extent of powers allowed to police officers. The question had been dealt with prior to the First World War in a case known as *Weeks* v. *United States.* From it stemmed the rule upon which many of the writings from the Bench by Brandeis and Frankfurter hinged—the "exclusionary rule." That 1914 case involved a man, Fremont Weeks, arrested without a warrant at Union Station in Kansas City, Missouri. While he was held, other police officers went to his house, entered and searched it. The local police, accompanied by a United States marshal, later returned to the Weeks' house and took other papers. When those papers were used as evidence against the man in the trial, he was convicted. Although there had been time to secure a search warrant, none had been sought. Weeks said his rights had been violated because of that failure to obtain a warrant and sought to have his papers returned to him.

The Supreme Court agreed with Fremont Weeks that his rights had been violated and upset his conviction. However, since the amendments to the Constitution did not then in all cases protect individuals in conflict with local government, the decision restricted only the action of the United States marshal and not the actions of the local police officers. Specifically, the decision excluded evidence unlawfully obtained; generally, the decision announced that federal law officials would be held to a standard of conduct which the justices found in the Constitution.

The exclusionary-rule statement, that evidence gained in violation of the Constitution cannot be used by federal law officers, seems simple and direct. But the history of the litigation surrounding the rule is a story of intricacies so complicated and bewildering as to be not only Jesuitical but also Talmudical.

The 1920s cases were characterized by the Supreme Court's narrowing of the exclusionary rule—allowing federal police officers more leeway. In *Bureau* v. *McDowell*, in 1921, there was no disagreement that the government wished to use unlawfully seized evidence. The problem was that the government had not unlawfully seized it; that had been done by an unknown person who then turned it over to the federal government. Must it still be excluded? No, said the Supreme Court in a 7–2 decision: "In the present case the record clearly shows that no official of the Federal Government had anything to do with the wrongful seizure of the petitioner's property, or any knowledge thereof until several months after the property had been taken from him."

Yes, said Brandeis in a dissent joined by Holmes. If the papers were still in the thief's possession, he argued, the Court would order them returned. "At the foundation of our civil liberty lies the principle which denies to the government officials an exceptional position before the law and which subjects them to the same rules of conduct that are commands to the citizens. . . . Respect for law will not be advanced by resort, in its enforcement, to means which shock the common man's sense of decency and fair play."

Brandeis was attempting to draw the line tighter against illegally gained evidence, to hold law-enforcement officers to a stricter standard than they had previously followed. The necessity for stricter standards was demonstrated by the next major criminal-law case to come before the Court, *Ziang Sung Wan* v. *United States*. It revolved around a murder in the District of Columbia; because the district was a federal enclave, the practices of its police were reviewable by the federal courts.

The facts in this case were so extreme, demonstrated such an outlandish flouting of fairness that the Court's opinion, written by Brandeis, was unanimous. The case, coming to the Court in 1924, involved the murder of three Chinese in the District of Columbia in 1919. Acting on a tip, District of Columbia police went to New York City and apprehended Ziang Sung Wan on February 1, 1919. When they entered his room, he was in bed, sick. Police searched his room without a search warrant although there had been time to obtain one.

Picked up on February 1, Ziang was not formally arrested until February 9. During that time he was held by District of Columbia police in a secluded room and questioned for five or six hours at a time. On the eighth day, Ziang, still sick, was taken to the scene of the crime. Kept there for ten hours, he was led through the building while police fed him the facts of the case as they knew them. The police questioned him in relays; he was not allowed to rest.

Not until the tenth, eleventh, and twelfth days after his apprehension did he initial pages of the police report. This material was used against him at his trial, as a confession, and at issue before the Supreme Court was whether it should be allowed.

On the thirteenth day, according to the Brandeis decision, Ziang was visited by a doctor who found him "lying in a bunk in the cell, very weak, very much exhausted, very much emaciated; he complained of abdominal pain, which was rather intense . . . he vomited if he attempted to take food . . . it was difficult or impossible for his bowels to move unless they were assisted by an enema." The doctor concluded that Ziang was suffering from spastic colitis and had been ill for weeks. The doctors testified that he "would not know what he was signing" and would have initialed the reports "to have the torture stopped."

Brandeis concluded his decision: "The alleged oral statements and the written confession should have been excluded."

"Yes sirree," said Holmes when he read the Brandeis decision. "I suppose you are right not to show disgust or wrath. I don't know whether I could have held it in."

In 1928 there were two cases dealing with the conduct of federal law officers. The first was *Casey* v. *United States.* Casey was a Seattle lawyer who defended prisoners addicted to narcotics. Police believed he distributed morphine to prisoners in jail, for money, by giving the prisoners towels soaked in a morphine solution. Guards at the prison set him up, had an informant ask Casey to bring in the morphine. When he did, Casey was arrested. The case was spicy. Not only were there stool pigeons, one named Cicero, and payoffs involved, but there was a recording of the incriminating confession, money supplied by federal officers for the purchase of drugs, and a woman friend of one of the prisoners who testified she saw an "oriental" person in Casey's office earlier in the day. "Oriental" was the *bête noire* of the West Coast in the 1920s, the one around whom fancy cloaked much evil, criminality, and lust.

The Court's majority decision upholding the conviction was written by Holmes, who usually did not accept such behavior. "We do not feel at liberty to accept the suggestion that the Government induced the crime," he said. "Casey according to the story was in no way induced to commit the crime beyond the simple request of Cicero to which he seems to have acceded without hesitation and as a matter of course."

There were four dissents, including one by Brandeis. He refused to consider the basis of the conviction, "for, in my opinion, the prosecution must fail because officers of the Government instigated the commission of the alleged crime." Said Brandeis: "The Government may set decoys to entrap criminals. But it may not provoke or create a crime and then punish the criminal, its creature."

Brandeis closed with what he perceived as the essence of the problem: "This prosecution should be stopped, not because some right of Casey's has been denied, but in order to protect the Government. To protect it from the illegal conduct of its officers. To preserve the purity of the courts."

This case was the kind which usually brought Holmes and Brandeis together. "I have much sympathy with my Brother Brandeis' feeling about this case," Holmes conceded to the other members of the Court, but "I am not persuaded that the conduct of the officials was different from or worse than ordering a drink of a suspected bootlegger."

Two months later, however, in *Olmstead* v. *United States,* Brandeis and Holmes were on the same side again. Olmstead, in those Prohibition days, operating out of Seattle, Washington, sold $2 million worth of liquor smuggled in from Canada. His headquarters were in an office building and orders for the liquor were taken over the telephone. Federal law officers tapped his telephone for a period of months. They made notes of the conversations heard on the taps, then retyped their notes; they revised the typed pages, then retyped them, and then went through the process again. This third version, 775 pages, was used to convict Olmstead.

Olmstead charged that his constitutional rights were violated. Specifically, he said the tapping of his telephone violated the Fourth Amendment right of people "to be secure in their persons, houses, papers, and effects, against unreasonable searches and seizures," and the Fifth Amendment right not to be "compelled in any criminal case to be a witness against himself"—using his own words, from the telephone conversations, against him.

There were complications. A Washington State law forbade interfering with or delaying a telephone message, so the federal law officers may have violated a local law when tapping Olmstead's telephone. Also, when the Fourth and Fifth amendments were written, 150 years earlier, devices such as telephones and wiretaps were unknown. Did the

Founding Fathers intend that the Constitution be interpreted in an expansionary way or did the Constitution apply only to the world of the 1780s?

In Brandeis's office, research began early in the Court term. Brandeis particularly was interested in the state laws having to do with wiretapping and sent his law clerk, Henry Friendly, to the Library of Congress to do the research. Friendly labored several weeks at the library and produced a report showing the laws of the forty-eight states falling into three groups: those banning wiretapping, those allowing it, and those in various stages between. A few days before the argument, to Friendly's chagrin, telephone companies filed an *amicus curiae* brief with identical information.

The telephone companies—Pacific Telephone and Telegraph, American Telephone and Telegraph, and others—unanimously supported Olmstead. "It will be observed that whenever a telephone line is tapped the privacy of the persons at both ends of the line is invaded, and all conversations between them upon whatever subjects, however proper, confidential and privileged they may be, are overheard." And then said the telephone companies: "It is better that a few criminals escape than that the privacies of life of all the people be exposed to the agents of the government, who will act at their own discretion, the honest and the dishonest, unauthorized and unrestrained by the courts."

The Court's 5–4 decision, written by William Howard Taft, upheld Olmstead's conviction. The decision said the Fourth Amendment prohibition against unlawful search and seizures did not extend to wiretapping telephone conversations. And, since the wiretapping had not violated the Fourth Amendment, the Fifth Amendment prohibition against self-incrimination could not be invoked.

Taft, in his decision, also anticipated a Holmes dissent. "Some of our number," he wrote, objected to the use of the wiretapping evidence because it apparently was in violation of a Washington State statute. "The common law rule is that the admissibility of evidence is not affected by the illegality of the means by which it was obtained," said Taft.

Holmes did dissent, saying that wiretapping was unlawful and society must choose between apprehending criminals and the government's becoming involved in a crime. His next sentence, one of the most famous in constitutional law, closely resembles the line in the telephone companies' *amicus curiae* brief: "We have to choose, and for my part

I think it a less evil that some criminals should escape than that the government should play an ignoble part."

Taft was furious at Holmes's dissent. "The truth is," Taft grumbled privately, "Holmes voted the other way till Brandeis got after him and induced him to change on the ground that a state law in Washington forbade wiretapping." Taft was correct. "I should not have printed what I wrote," confided Holmes to a friend, "however, if [Brandeis] had not asked me to."

Brandeis believed that, as in the Casey case, federal law officers should not violate the law, in this instance the Washington State law forbidding interference with a telephone message. But his law clerk, Henry Friendly, pushed him also to oppose inclusion of the wiretap evidence because of the Fourth Amendment's prohibition against unreasonable searches and seizures. Brandeis did so, and that section of his dissent is among his most eloquent writings.

"The makers of our Constitution undertook to secure conditions favorable to the pursuit of happiness," he wrote. "They recognized the significance of man's spiritual nature, of his feelings and of his intellect. They knew that only a part of the pain, pleasure and satisfactions of life are to be found in material things." Then he homed in on his target. "They sought to protect Americans in their beliefs, their thoughts, their emotions and their sensations. They conferred, as against the Government, the right to be let alone—the most comprehensive of rights and the right most valued by civilized men." Almost four decades earlier, Brandeis, then a young lawyer in Boston, had joined with his friend Sam Warren to write "The Right to Privacy," which had, according to Roscoe Pound, added a new area to law. In that article, Brandeis and Warren had sought to protect the privacy of the famous and rich from the press. Now Brandeis wished to assure the privacy of the poor, the oppressed, and those branded criminal. "To protect that right," he said, "every unjustifiable intrusion of the Government upon the privacy of the individual, whatever the means employed, must be deemed a violation of the Fourth Amendment." And once so deemed, "evidence in a criminal proceeding of facts ascertained by such intrusion must be deemed a violation" of the Fifth Amendment against self-incrimination.

That the purpose of the wiretap was law enforcement, said Brandeis, was immaterial. "Men born to freedom are naturally alert to repel invasion of their liberty by evil-minded rulers. The greatest dangers to liberty lurk in insidious encroachment by men of zeal, well-meaning but without understanding."

Then he turned to the violation of the state law. "To prove its case," he said, "the Government was obliged to lay bare the crimes committed by its officers on its behalf. A federal court should not permit such a prosecution to continue."

In his concluding paragraph, Brandeis framed the argument that ever after has been used in support of the exclusionary rule and against the lowering of standards of law enforcement:

Decency, security and liberty alike demand that government officials shall be subjected to the same rules of conduct that are commands to the citizen. In a government of laws, existence of the government will be imperiled if it fails to observe the law scrupulously. Our Government is the potent, the omnipresent teacher. For good or for ill, it teaches the whole people by its example. Crime is contagious. If the Government becomes a lawbreaker, it breeds contempt for law; it invites every man to become a law unto himself; it invites anarchy. To declare that in the administration of the criminal law the end justifies the means —to declare that the Government may commit crimes in order to secure the conviction of a private criminal—would bring terrible retribution. Against that pernicious doctrine this court should resolutely set its face.

Among the justices, the decision and the dissents left a bitterness. Chief Justice Taft was angry at the press comments his majority decision had received, believing they had been stirred by the Brandeis and Holmes dissents. "You may have seen the severe criticism of our judgment in the wire tapping case," he wrote to Sutherland, "but I think the more that the case is read and understood, the less effective will be the eloquence and denunciation of Brandeis and Holmes."

For Brandeis there also was bitterness. He told Felix Frankfurter that he hoped "some reviewer of the wire tapping decision will discern that in favor of property the Constitution is liberally construed—in favor of liberty, strictly."

The state regulatory, labor, and criminal cases before the Supreme Court were easily understood; they meant more or less power to the unions, to the government agencies; more or less restrictions on federal law officers. Perhaps as significant to the American citizenry, but more complicated, were the cases involving the rate of return allowed utilities. While the issue was profits, the problem was how much the consumer paid, and the dispute showed how business operated and thought in that decade.

In many of the cases, the fight was over the "reproduction rate concept." Utilities, in exchange for the right of monopoly, agreed to limit profits to rates set by public commissions. Since profit rates were a

Adolf and Frederika (Dembitz) Brandeis were typical of the immigrants to the United States in the middle of the nineteenth century. They wanted to escape, as Adolf said, "the despots of the old world" and come to a country where "even the hard work . . . is a kind of patriotism." The children are Amy, Alfred, and Fanny (left to right). Louis had not been born when this photograph was taken. *University of Louisville Archives*

After growing up in Louisville, Louis Brandeis attended Harvard Law School and became a successful lawyer in Boston. He became the "people's advocate," taking on unpopular causes, often without pay. Although originally a Republican, he supported Woodrow Wilson in the 1912 presidential election and was one of the architects of Wilson's "New Freedom." *University of Louisville Archives*

The Brandeis appointment to the Supreme Court in 1916 shocked the business community and led to a four-month fight over his confirmation. The caption for this contemporary cartoon has the conservatives lamenting: "Oh, what an associate for such a pure and innocent girl! And we have tried to bring her up so carefully, too!" *Library of Congress*

THAT BRANDEIS APPOINTMENT

CHORUS OF GRIEF-STRICKEN CONSERVATIVES: Oh, what an associate for such a pure and innocent girl! And we have tried to bring her up so carefully, too!

Twenty-three years later, when Brandeis retired from the Supreme Court, the nation's attitude had changed. He had become respected, loved, and admired. On the Court, Brandeis had been an advocate of judicial restraint in the 1920s and then, in the 1930s, a supporter of Franklin D. Roosevelt's New Deal legislation. *U.S. Supreme Court*

The Court that Brandeis joined was known for its defense of business. The members are, left to right, in the back row: Brandeis, Pitney, McReynolds, Clarke; and in the front row: Day, McKenna, Chief Justice White, Holmes, and Van Devanter. Holmes and Brandeis had been friends for many years and remained so. Van Devanter and Brandeis, although they differed philosophically, became friends. McReynolds, an anti-Semite, rarely spoke to Brandeis and never stood next to him when the Court's annual photograph was taken. *Library of Congress*

This is the last formal photograph taken of the Court before Brandeis retired in 1939. The members are, left to right, in the back row: Cardozo, Stone, Roberts, Black; and in the front row: Sutherland, McReynolds, Chief Justice Hughes, Brandeis, and Butler. When Brandeis retired from the Court, McReynolds did not join with the other justices in signing the customary letter of good wishes. *Library of Congress*

Edward Douglass White

William Howard Taft

Charles Evans Hughes

A constant of Brandeis's life from 1910 until his death in 1941 was his devotion to Zionism. He led the American movement, influenced President Wilson to support the Balfour Declaration, and donated large amounts of money to the cause. In the caption to this newspaper photograph, Brandeis is quoted as saying: "The Jews of America must lead in the struggle for liberation and opportunity for all Jews." The man on the right is Julian Hawthorne. *U.S. Supreme Court*

During Brandeis's years on the Supreme Court, his friendship with Felix Frankfurter grew. Brandeis thought of the Harvard professor as "half brother, half son" and offered him encouragement and moral support. Beginning in the mid-1920s, when Frankfurter's wife became ill, Brandeis gave Frankfurter an annual allowance so that Frankfurter would be able to meet his wife's medical expenses without having to give up his public-service work, for which he always had declined payment. *Franklin D. Roosevelt Library*

"Holmes and Brandeis dissenting" was a frequently used phrase on the Supreme Court in the 1920s. The two men spoke out for the right of states to experiment economically and for the civil liberties of individuals. Friends from their Boston days, they continued close during the sixteen years they served on the Supreme Court together, Brandeis constantly concerned about and caring for the older man.
U.S. Supreme Court

In 1937, President Roosevelt, angered by what he perceived as a conservative political Court blocking his New Deal legislation, sought to enlarge its membership or "pack" it with liberals. Brandeis and Chief Justice Hughes, two wily politicians, worked behind the scenes to defeat him. *U.S. Supreme Court*

AN EXTRAORDINARY SESSION OF THE SUPREME COURT WILL BE HELD ON THE EVENING OF MARCH 9.

Alice Goldmark Brandeis lived in an era when a woman's aspiration and obligation was to be a wife, and the definition of the word can be taken from her life with Louis Brandeis. But she had talents and passions of her own: she campaigned for social causes, spoke out for political reform, and did some writing. This apparently was not always sufficient. In 1924, a year before this photograph was taken, Holmes described her as "still broken down in nerves and hysterical."
Library of Congress

Austere in his personal life, ruthless in his determination to achieve his goals, Brandeis also was loving and devoted to his family. He and Mrs. Brandeis are with their grandchildren at their summer home on Cape Cod. *Franklin D. Roosevelt Library*

Associate Justice Louis Dembitz Brandeis of the United States Supreme Court.
U.S. Supreme Court

Felix Frankfurter, on the right, was approximately 30 years old when this photograph was taken. An immigrant, a Harvard Law School graduate, he had chosen public-service work rather than high-paying private practice. In the following years his insistence on fair judicial procedures in the Bisbee, Mooney, and Sacco-Vanzetti cases made him one of the most notorious persons in the United States.
U.S. Supreme Court

Almost fifty when this photograph was taken, Frankfurter was nearing the end of a quarter century as a teacher at the Harvard Law School, where he had worked "to cross-fertilize between the laboratory of thinking and its application to life." He also had come close to power as an advisor to President Roosevelt, and when FDR's New Deal was described as the "Jew Deal," the speakers were referring to Frankfurter and Brandeis.
Franklin D. Roosevelt Library

Marion A. Denman, who became Felix Frankfurter's wife, as a student at Smith College. She told him once that "someday living will be a lot easier than it is now for you and me. I hope at least some of the unhappy moods that attack me now won't strike me then so frequently." There were problems in the marriage, but she always made him sing, in Harold Laski's phrase, "an unceasing song." *U.S. Supreme Court*

Henry L. Stimson in 1910. He, along with Louis Brandeis and Oliver Wendell Holmes, Jr., was a career influence on Frankfurter. The three men were his role models and from them he learned of commitment to public service. *Library of Congress*

FELIX
FRANKFURTER
APPOINTED TO
SUPREME COURT
BY
PRESIDENT
ROOSEVELT

PUBLIC
OPINION

Franklin Roosevelt had been concerned about appointing Frankfurter to the Supreme Court because Frankfurter had not been a practicing lawyer for many years, because he had supported unpopular causes, such as Sacco-Vanzetti, and also because Frankfurter was a Jew. But the appointment, when it came in 1939, caused almost universal acclamation. The Senate hearing was a triumph for Frankfurter, shown here reaching for his hat at its conclusion, and he was confirmed unanimously. Frankfurter himself believed that Roosevelt's appointment of a Jew to the Supreme Court, at the time of Nazism's rise in Europe, "was the historic significance of the appointment."
Franklin D. Roosevelt Library

The Supreme Court in 1939, just after Frankfurter joined it. The members are, left to right, in the back row: Frankfurter, Black, Reed, Douglas; and in the front row: Stone, McReynolds, Chief Justice Hughes, Butler, and Roberts. Douglas had replaced Brandeis shortly after Frankfurter joined the Court. Frankfurter had been a critic of Hughes but became an admirer when both men were on the Court together. Frankfurter and Black became philosophical opponents, and Black—the "Alabama hillbilly" who had been a Ku Klux Klan member—eventually bested the Harvard Law School professor.
Library of Congress

The Supreme Court in 1961, Frankfurter's last term. The members are, left to right, in the back row: Stewart, Harlan, Brennan, White; and in the front row: Douglas, Black, Chief Justice Warren, Frankfurter, and Clark. The Warren Court had ordered public schools desegregated and an end to malapportioned legislatures, and had challenged the Presidency and the Congress on internal security matters. *U.S. Supreme Court*

Chief Justice Harlan Fiske Stone

After Chief Justice Hughes, the Supreme Court was headed by Chief Justices Harlan Fiske Stone, Fred Vinson, and Earl Warren while Frankfurter was a member. Stone and Frankfurter had been friends before Stone became Chief Justice, but Frankfurter came to resent Stone's methods of leadership. Frankfurter had never been an admirer of Vinson's, and when Warren was appointed Chief Justice, Frankfurter predicted that "after a good many years ... life promises to be extremely agreeable." That was not to be. Warren became the leader of the "liberal" bloc on the Court, and the arguments between him and Frankfurter eventually became public.

Chief Justice Fred Vinson

Chief Justice Earl Warren, with Felix Frankfurter

Marion Frankfurter, early 1940s. Never happy as a professor's wife, she liked Washington even less than she had Cambridge. She refused to be interviewed by the press and declined to play the etiquette and protocol games then expected of the wives of Washington personages. The newspapers were kind to her—"Quietly aloof, her intellectual interests detach her from things mundane," said one. Her illnesses came more frequently, and she became more of a recluse than she had been in Cambridge. The Frankfurter law clerks, knowing the closeness of husband and wife, always spoke well of her. "Her attendance at a dinner was regarded as a great treat," said one, "and everyone appreciated it, knowing that her health was bad."
Franklin D. Roosevelt Library and the Supreme Court

Two areas of controversy for Frankfurter while he was on the Supreme Court were his dispute with Hugo Black and his support of Alger Hiss. Black and Frankfurter, despite their philosophical disagreements, became personal friends. This was not true of William Douglas and Frankfurter: Frankfurter respected Black but not Douglas. After Hiss had been accused of being a Communist spy, Frankfurter and Reed appeared as character witnesses at his perjury trial. Reed had to be subpoenaed, but Frankfurter, who had brought Hiss into the government in the early New Deal days, appeared voluntarily. Chief Justice Harlan Fiske Stone is depicted to the left of Black in the cartoon above. *U.S. Supreme Court*

percentage of costs, higher costs meant greater dollar profits and higher charges to the consumer. At that point, the cases became an accountant's game, with utilities attempting to show costs high, warranting higher dollar profits, and the public commissions attempting to show costs low, warranting lower profits.

A major chip in this game was the cost of a utilities' plant: the more it had cost, the higher must be the earnings. The traditional way of measuring cost was to begin with the actual dollar cost of the plant, subtract from that cost the salvage value at the end of the plant's useful life, and then divide the remaining sum by the number of years the plant was expected to operate. The result was the cost for each year, or depreciation. This figure represented the annual cost of the plant against which profits should be measured.

In the 1920s, however, the utilities and the railroads pushed another approach: reproduction cost. How this would work was shown in one of the first of these cases before the Court, *Southwestern Bell Telephone Company* v. *Public Service Commission of Missouri.*

The Commission had ordered the telephone company's rates reduced and its action was upheld by local and state courts. The Supreme Court, however, ruled for the telephone company in a decision by McReynolds. He said the actual plant cost had been $22.8 million but that the company should be allowed to base its earnings on the cost of reproducing the plant (minus certain items), or $31.3 million.

Brandeis, with Holmes concurring, also reversed the lower courts, allowing higher rates, because, he said, the Public Service Commission had not permitted the telephone company a reasonable profit. In previous years, he had objected to the Court's second-guessing local decisions on what constituted reasonable rates of return. But here Brandeis was the politician. Since his position was lost anyhow, nothing was gained by attacking the profit. But his concurrence gained power as he agreed to the higher rates but attacked the company's accounting procedures.

The McReynolds opinion for the Court is eight pages long; the Brandeis concurrence, twenty-two. McReynolds repeated the telephone-company arguments; Brandeis mustered economics, history, and legal precedents.

He asserted that the Constitution allowed a company to earn a profit on money invested (the usual depreciation method of accounting) but not on the buildings themselves (the reproduction-rate method). He conceded that a quarter century earlier the Supreme Court had allowed the reproduction-rate approach but insisted "that the rule there enunciated is delusive. . . . It has failed to afford adequate protection either to capital or to the public."

His argument was an appeal for business to adopt orderly procedures. It was, in effect, a restyling of his Brandeis brief. Using the reproduction rate, Brandeis argued, "sets the laborious and baffling task of finding the present value of the utility," baffling because utilities are not commonly bought and sold. He then pointed out that the reproduction rate can cut both ways. The utilities now wanted to use it because it meant bigger profits, but in a recession, Brandeis argued, the value of the plants would drop and the reproduction-rate approach would mean lower profits for the utilities. He then included a long footnote, number 16, running almost two pages, showing the fluctuation in prices during America's history, especially after wars, and said: "The experience [after World War I] may be similar."

He then closed with his most telling point. If the purpose, he said, was to ascertain reproduction cost, the proper inquiry should not be the cost to reproduce the building, "but what it would cost to establish a plant which could render that service . . . at what cost could an equally efficient substitute be then produced." He closed: "The utilities seem to claim that the constitutional protection against confiscation guarantees them a return both upon unearned increment and upon the cost of property rendered valueless by obsolescence."

During the remainder of the 1920s, Brandeis hammered at the issue in other decisions. Sometimes he allowed the utility or railroad a price increase, saying it had not earned a proper return, but always challenging the reproduction-rate approach. Often Holmes was with him— "Count me in—I admire without having the time to master this fudge but generally I am with it"—but sometimes not. Once Brandeis was joined by Harlan Fiske Stone. In that case, *McCardle et al.* v. *Indianapolis Water Company*, they said finding the reproduction rate "would be impossible of accomplishment without the aid of Aladdin's lamp."

Brandeis worked hard on these cases. In one, for example, *St. Louis, O'Fallon Railway* v. *United States*, he collected twenty-five folders of background material. He then produced a thirty-two-page memorandum that in essence said the Interstate Commerce Commission was not required to use the reproduction-rate method in figuring costs. The memorandum eventually grew into a forty-seven-page dissent. In this case, as with many others, Brandeis traveled far from the official record for information needed to support his points.

The Brandeis method, using the standard-depreciation accounting method rather than the reproduction-rate method, has come to be the accepted technique. Many businesses used it then, and in later years it became a staple of the income-tax rules for businesses. American business then, however, could not agree that he was right. Two decades earlier, when Brandeis lambasted the management of the New Haven railroad, he had been correct; business had not listened to him, and the railroad failed. Again business, captivated by the prospect of making an extra dollar's profit in the coming year, could not accept his argument of depreciation over reproduction rate. Prudent management was not the 1920s' god; the quick buck was.

11

The Jew at Harvard

What Louis Brandeis was attempting to do on the Supreme Court—to mix the mustiness of precedent with experience—Felix Frankfurter hoped to do at Harvard Law School. "We have got to cross-fertilize between the laboratory of thinking and its application to life," he told Dean Roscoe Pound. "I resent more and more shallow dichotomy between 'theory and practice.' " That was his ambition, to bring the theory and the practice together, to transfer the law from the school to life.

But Frankfurter had changed in the two years he had been away. When he had left in the spring of 1917, he was a promising professor with government experience called to assist the war effort. When he returned in the fall of 1919, he was all that—plus the author of the Mooney and Bisbee reports.

He still was the Jew. Oliver Wendell Holmes commented at the time: "There is also a prejudice against Frankfurter: I think partly because he . . . is a Jew." From Harold Laski, then a visiting professor at Harvard, Holmes heard that Frankfurter was regarded by some "as a dangerous person" and that there was a "real effort in Boston to make Felix's position here untenable." Laski had a few names of the responsible persons, and he had heard that the origin of the attack was anti-Semitism.

Frankfurter did have tenure and the support of Dean Pound, but even Pound was under attack. "The Pound forces in the school are generally having a difficult time. There are three appointments to be made and where Pound wants—and can get—real scholars they want to force on him typical State Street lawyers whose success is doubtful." Pound would "stick by his guns" and had the faculty behind him, Laski believed, "but the animus against him (a relic of the Brandeis affair) is apparent at every stage."

The situation was more serious then even Laski believed. Pound considered resigning. He turned to Brandeis, still a power at the Law School, for advice, and perhaps also for political support. The two men, Brandeis and Pound, met for four hours in New York in June 1919.

"I am sure the sympathy helped him," wrote Brandeis to his wife, "and I think I hit upon advice which fits the occasion and which he will follow. This is clear: Old Boston is unregenerate and I am not sorry to have escaped a struggle there that would have been as nasty as it is unending. F. F. is evidently considered by the elect as 'dangerous' as I was." Brandeis added: "And it looks as if some whom F. considered his friends are as unrelenting as were some who were called mine."

In the year following Frankfurter's return to Harvard in September 1919, the school became a battleground. In October, Dean Pound wrote Brandeis that Laski was then the center of controversy and Frankfurter was next. Pound said that Frankfurter and Julian Mack "are too guileless. They don't appreciate the Puritan conscience that enabled these people to stick a knife into those with whom they maintain cordial relations with a serene consciousness that they are doing goodwill." Pound described A. Lawrence Lowell, president of the University, as the one behind the attacks against Frankfurter.

The attack on Frankfurter, in preparation for months, came in the spring of 1920. Several endowed professorships were to be filled; he was a leading candidate for one. If, however, Frankfurter did not receive the appointment, his enemies hoped his embarrassment would cause him to leave Harvard.

Frankfurter was, Pound reported, overly cheerful, and so were his friends. On April 20, 1920, for example, Brandeis, after communicating with Harold Laski, reported to his wife that Frankfurter's situation was strong and that "he will be firmly seated."

But that same day, Julian Mack—a Zionist friend of both Brandeis and Frankfurter as well as a member of the Harvard Board of Overseers— reported to Pound that Frankfurter was being denied the endowed Byrne professorship. The Frankfurter nomination to the Byrne Professorship of Administrative Law, along with nominations for three other endowed professorships, had been made by the Law School faculty to the Harvard Corporation, which, in effect, meant to A. Lawrence Lowell. He—in the name of the Corporation—recommended the other three individuals, but not Frankfurter, to the Board of Overseers for appointment. Without this recommendation, the Overseers could not act. "This," thundered Roscoe Pound to Brandeis, "is a monstrous outrage."

At Pound's request, Brandeis informed Holmes of the situation. "Let me know if there is anything that I can do," Holmes replied. "I shall keep quiet unless I hear from you as you say the matter is confidential." Frankfurter regretted that the older man had been bothered. "There is absolutely no occasion for concern," he told Holmes. "I'm here as long as I want to stay—and whether I have a named or nameless chair doesn't matter."

In May the appointments of the other three men to endowed professorships were announced. "The result is to make the passing over of FF conspicuous," Pound reported to Brandeis, "and everyone is talking about it." Pound was on the attack, badgering Lowell, members of the Corporation, writing numerous letters to friends and supporters of the Law School for help. The help came.

In the past, the Law School had generally been governed as Boston's State Street wanted. But the "establishment" was changing. When Brandeis was a young lawyer in Boston, he helped form the Harvard Law School Association to bring financial and other support to the school from graduates across the United States, rather than only from Boston. That strengthened the school but weakened the Boston base. The immigrants who had come to the United States in the century's early years had saved their nickels and dimes and sent their children to Harvard. There were Jews, Italians, blacks—not many perhaps but enough to change the center of gravity among the alumni. Harvard was the United States in miniature; it was a different world with new rules, with new people asserting themselves, exerting influence, making demands—the State Street establishment was losing control.

On June 12, 1920, Julian Mack reported to Roscoe Pound that the Harvard Corporation had approved the appointment of Frankfurter as Byrne professor.

State Street had lost this battle. But there would be others, and it did not give up easily.

In the 1910–20 decade Frankfurter was in his thirties. A short but handsome man, he knew everyone, was widely liked. But he had not married. He was not immune. A friend of those days, Emory Buckner, described the bachelor Frankfurter as "not infrequently on the prowl." Once a mutual friend asked Buckner: "What did Felix do in those early days? Run around with pretty girls?" Buckner recalled, "I told him you were never interested in any girl that I knew of—but I did not tell him it was the sex as a whole."

There had been romances, even one engagement to a Jewish woman in New York. But that relationship ended; the excitement Frankfurter craved was not the life she wanted.

In 1916, Harold Laski told Holmes that Frankfurter "badly needs some kind of settling influence. He is always nervously restless, dashing here and there in a kind of creative fertility that drives me to despair. I don't find him able to sit down solidly to a single thing." A couple of years later, Agnes Meyer, a leader of Washington social life, told Frankfurter after a party that "I could marry him but nobody else I knew. Also that he would not marry as he could not hold down all he expected in the lady."

Frankfurter had, in fact, met the woman he loved. She was Marion A. Denman, born in 1890; she was five feet seven inches, taller than Frankfurter, beautiful, with red hair and hazel eyes. She had graduated from Smith College in 1912 as a Phi Beta Kappa. She also was restless.

There was not much for attractive, intelligent, educated women to do in the early decades of the twentieth century, except marry. They could become secretaries at girls' finishing schools, which Marion did for a time. Social work was "respectable," and she did that also. But mostly, and this was true before she married Frankfurter and more true after the marriage, she searched for some fulfilling purpose for Marion Denman.

She was not Jewish but the daughter of a Protestant minister whose family had been in the United States for generations.

Frankfurter had met her in Washington in 1913 and their early relationship was not such as to spark rumors; their romance was over tea and poetry readings. For Marion, Frankfurter was the key to a new world. "You are a kid you know," she told him once. "You like to play so. You know I was brought up in a dour Presbyterian family that didn't know how to play and didn't dare play anyhow,—that's the influence of the Christian church, along with morals and purity—and a lot of other boring things (I *think* this is so, anyhow)—*and* it's such fun to be in a family that's irresponsible (that's you) and likes to laugh a lot and gets fun out of things."

She was honest with him. "I've got the mind of a child—not being wealthy, nor being tubercular, nor being away from home and friends." And "someday living will be a lot easier than it is now for you and me. I hope at least some of the unhappy moods that attack me now won't strike me then so frequently."

There also was the capability for happiness: "I wish you could see me tonight. I'm not bronzed or beautiful like Ernesta, but I have been walking through pine woods and ambling over rocks all day, beside water that was as blue as mystery and under a sky as clear as diamonds. My face was wind-blown and sun-kissed all day—and looks it."

In return, Frankfurter was effusive. His letters constantly told her of his affection and of his need for her: "I wonder if you have sources that tell you how persistently I miss you. I do", "I'm just happy Dearest— and I like to tell you so!"

By 1916, his friends began to suspect that something was happening. Brandeis met Marion Denman that year; so did Holmes, who quickly checked with Harold Laski, saying his interest was piqued by Mrs. Holmes. Laski replied: "Please tell Mrs. Holmes that her perceptions *in re* Marion Denman really seem to have their usual acuteness. We shall see."

In the First World War, Marion Denman sailed for England to survey Englishwomen's war organizations. The night before her departure, she and Felix became engaged while riding around Central Park in a hansom cab. Some things Felix Frankfurter did right.

After the war, there was another separation, with Frankfurter at the peace conference. There were dozens of letters, some lengthy with detailed descriptions of what was happening at the conference; some scrawled notes—"Why should I not tell you, Marion, that at times I hide myself by myself and am particularly wretched—for want of you."

Finally in 1919, with Frankfurter at Harvard, the engagement was announced. His friends were pleased. "Felix is safe," said Laski. The Brandeises sent a congratulatory note. Holmes, enraptured by Marion Denman's beauty, compared her to a portrait by Luini and ever after referred to her as "Luina."

The wedding was set for December 20, 1919, in New York. Frankfurter had asked Emory Buckner to check on the details; Frankfurter had hoped that Holmes or Learned Hand, a federal judge, could marry them. But the only judge who could officiate at a New York wedding was a state judge. The details became confused, as only Frankfurter could confuse them, and Buckner wrote him in exasperation: "Have you forgotten that you are to get married on or about December 20th?"

Frankfurter replied: "Thank you for the reminder, but that's one appointment even I shall keep. After the Federal Courts—Holmes and L. Hand—failed us, we rather lost interest in the performance that the state courts insist upon. But it will be done as the Law says it should. [Benjamin N.] Cardozo will say the few and final words."

They returned to Harvard the next month, after their honeymoon. "Felix and Marion are back and like two cooing doves," Laski reported to Holmes. "To see their anxiety for each other's proper protection against the snow etc. is charming. The boy is very happy. The girl is still rather reticent and shy so that I can't expound her much, but she makes him sing an unceasing song and I therefore add my tribute."

Felix and Marion Frankfurter continued married until his death forty-six years later. There were problems. For her, "the unhappy moods that attack me" magnified as she was caught up in the whirl of his life. From shy, retiring minister's daughter to wife of an active man always under attack or attacking, to partner in a marriage to a Jew during decades when the word was hurled as an insult—these were not easy transitions, and Marion did not always make them well. She increasingly became ill, some of her plagues real and some imagined. During the 1930s she and Felix spent much time apart, he at Harvard or in Washington and she visiting relatives in California or Florida. Beginning in the 1940s her illnesses became such that she was confined to her home and then to her room. He never stopped loving her. The attraction was intellectual, spiritual, emotional, and also physical. "Sweetheart—I'd kill you to pieces were you here, to tell you in overflowing measure my love for you," and "Good morning Sweetheart ... how do you like 'separate bedrooms!?!?! I DONT—at least not in the same city!! Fixi" are typical of his letters to her. He needed to be near her, to see her, to touch her. There was always, in Laski's phrase, that "unceasing song" he sang because of Marion Denman.

At Harvard, Frankfurter taught until 1939. "Graduate work," he once wrote, "implies a personal relation between two students, one of whom is a professor." His purpose in that personal relationship was to impart his understanding of how law and life intersect. He had told Roscoe Pound that "We have got to cross-fertilize between the laboratory of thinking and its application to life." The Harvard Law School classroom was the site of this cross-fertilization.

He taught administrative law, which dealt with the legal control exercised by law-administering agencies other than courts and the control exercised by courts over those agencies. "The control of banking, insurance, public utilities, finance, industry, the professions, health and morals, in sum, the manifold response of government to the forces and needs of modern society," he wrote, "is building up a body of laws not written by legislatures, and of adjudications not made by courts and not subject to their revision." It would be bureaucracy versus industry, commissions against the banks, detail in conflict with detail. That would be modern life, and in that life of complications and confusion, sophistication and skulduggery, there was a place for the lawyer to guide and to insist on fairness.

"Frankfurter took us through the most illuminating paths of discussion," recalled one student, "down the whole history of the unacknowledged development of administrative law as a distinct legislative and judicial power. Nothing that was said sticks in my mind. There are no episodes or no vivid pictures except such things as Felix perching on the back of a chair or running around the table and sitting on the other end. He is a very restless, inquisitive, and excitable man with a mind that could excite anybody working with him."

"We were not learning law; that was not our business," said another student. "We were gaining some measure of understanding of law that both reflected and shaped a nation's growth." Erwin N. Griswold, a student of Frankfurter's and later Harvard Law School dean, said Frankfurter taught courses in public utilities, administrative law, and federal jurisdiction, but "all of these . . . were essentially courses in Frankfurter—or perhaps more accurately, in being stimulated by Frankfurter."

In the classroom, Frankfurter and the students discussed a case line by line, precedent by precedent, implication by implication. The students learned not only the law but the people who had pressured for the law, written it, and judged it. Frankfurter constantly spoke from his own experience. In the 1930s, when the Supreme Court dealt with the Tom Mooney case, Frankfurter "bounced" into his federal jurisdiction seminar and began questioning a student about the case. When it was apparent the student, Joseph L. Rauh, Jr., was uninformed—"I started faking about having to understand the reaction of the California courts to the war fever and went on with an inane sociological filibuster"— Frankfurter responded with "a roar of disbelief audible as far as the Boston Common" and continued with a detailed history of the case, including—emphasizing—his own involvement.

If the classroom discussion was free and easy, it also was demanding. "Let [a student] arise and say something that reveals sloppy thinking," said one account, "and a small, keen man, who may just come up to his shoulders, has cut him off in the middle of a sentence. 'You didn't mean to say that.' "

Not everyone appreciated Frankfurter the teacher. Some preferred the more structured approach to learning; others found his courses too demanding. Some believed that Frankfurter played favorites—"the bright boys, the end-men of his minstrel shows, revered him. He made much of them, not only in class but out . . . he got adulation in return." Frankfurter did have his favorites, but he was after more than adulation.

The point came up once in a conversation in 1930 with Charles E. Wyzanski, Jr., who had been one of his students. Frankfurter mulled over the conversation during the night and then in a note to Wyzanski spoke of what he believed the teacher's role should be:

In the course of our talk yesterday, you made one remark which deserves comment. You were good enough to say that I "underestimated" the impression or the influence which I leave on students. I know you were wholly sincere in saying that, and, of course, I appreciate it because everyone likes to have his life work tell—and mine happens to be the education of youth. But I should be very sorry indeed if you thought that I am interested in having students take the color of my views or that I thought influencing the views of students is the function of a teacher. I believe no such things. For a teacher to inculcate in a student his own views is, on the whole, apt to be a disservice, for it usually means that he is a persuasive dogmatist.

Frankfurter was fond of many of his students, helpful to them, and concerned about their careers. Some became part of his family while at Harvard; for those having financial difficulties, Frankfurter often found someone to finance a scholarship. Whatever his "influence" on them, among the hundreds of students who went through his classes in a quarter century there are law-school deans, judges, Wall Street lawyers, small-town lawyers, politicians of both major parties, Frankfurter admirers and Frankfurter critics. More than that, however, there are lawyers who understand how law and life intersect.

Frankfurter used graduate students to assist him with his writings. But Frankfurter gave more of himself to the students than did most academics. "He was a time-consuming man to work with," James M. Landis recalled. "He could spend two or three hours just talking around the subject before he either got down to the point of going over a memorandum that you had written or dictating anything on it himself. But it was a pleasant conversation and I certainly never resented it." In 1925, the *Harvard Law Review* published "The Business of the Supreme Court of the United States," written by Frankfurter with Landis's assistance. By that time Landis had gone from being Harvard student to becoming Brandeis law clerk, and for that reason, said Frankfurter, "it was deemed imprudent for his name to appear on the article." But Frankfurter wrote to his fellow faculty members to inform them of Landis's contribution: "The profession at large will know of Landis' share in this work when these articles eventually appear in book form, but I would like my colleagues to know the fact now."

Landis once helped Frankfurter with an article for *The New Republic,* for which the two men were offered a total of $150, twice as much as the magazine then paid. Frankfurter, aware of the magazine's financial status, suggested it pay only $75, its normal fee, all of it to Landis, "and leave me out of it."

Frankfurter continued his personal relationship with his students after they were graduated. And so to Charles Wyzanski in 1933: "You may have heard me express a favorite foolish notion of mine that it is good for a lawyer to lose his first case. . . . I know you assimilate experience, and I know how wisely you will assimilate this." Several years later when Wyzanski argued his first case before the Supreme Court, Frankfurter was quick with a note to say "how deeply I rejoiced to hear, authoritatively, of the high qualities of your maiden argument."

Life in Cambridge was pleasant. Cut off from Boston by the Charles River, the Harvard faculty cultivated the town-gown separation. Cambridge, then without a movie theater or a five-and-ten-cent store, was a city from another time. The pace was slow, the entertainment genteel, and the discussion fiery as the academics went at each other, each knowing he must win if the world, university, political party—or whatever—was to survive. Arthur M. Schlesinger, Sr., recalled:

National and international events, state and University happenings, all ran the gantlet of the talk. Felix, but five feet five, more than compensated for his height with his exuberant spirits and vigor of expression. Generally the spark plug of the proceedings, he saucily interjected challenging comments for the evident purpose of provoking controversy. Then, he was a debater rather than a clarifier of issues, often gesticulating to underscore his points.

Frankfurter conceded his language sometimes became extreme and often loud but insisted that was "merely the manifestation of eagerness or, if you will, intensity." He insisted: "If I am not a Socrates, neither am I just a slugger."

He and Marion settled on Brattle Street, the famous "Tory Row" of Cambridge, which dated back to pre-Revolutionary days, its old mansions with wide lawns leftovers from a time of wealth and elegance. There in a cottage back from the road the Frankfurters became a center of the local social life, entertaining students and faculty members at teas and dinners; he dominated the scene as he stood before the fireplace, ready to take on all comers in oratorical combat.

Frankfurter's mother, Emma, now a widow, lived in Cambridge, as did his two sisters, Ella and Estelle. If there was occasional friction between Marion, with her New England, Protestant background, and Frankfurter's mother and sisters, with their Lower East Side, Jewish immigrant background, it was generally smoothed out quickly. Felix became the center of his family, the confidant of his mother and sisters —the more so for his sisters after his mother died in 1928. The affection never ceased to flow, and eventually the family's hesitancy toward Marion abated.

Harvard then for Felix and Marion Frankfurter had all the potential for an idyllic life. Surrounded by friends and family, sheltered from the outside world, respected as a teacher, Frankfurter in the early 1920s stood at the beginning of a challenging career promising personal and professional success. But he was who he was, and Harvard was what it was. The gulf between them, revealed by the dispute over his receiving the endowed chair, still existed.

In 1919 there had been a policemen's strike in Boston and Harold Laski had sided with the strikers. In its issue of January 16, 1920, the Harvard *Lampoon* criticized Laski, calling him "scum," satirizing him in an anti-Semitic cartoon, and said: "In the parlance of the ghetto, He would 'shake a mean stiletto.' "

Holmes was shocked. "It is disgusting that so serious a scholar and thinker as [Laski] is should be subject to the trampling of swine."

Frankfurter and Brandeis also were disturbed. The rudeness and religious bias exhibited by the *Lampoon* staff was not unique, not that much different from what others said in private or when Frankfurter or Brandeis were not present. Harvard was changing; as more Jews came to the school, anti-Semitism increased, reflecting a changing America. When there had been few Jews in the nation, there had been little anti-Semitism; now that the numbers had increased, so had the anti-Semitism.

The dispute over the Jews began at Harvard in the early 1920s, spread to New York, continued through the 1930s at other schools; it never ended.

Harvard had first hired a Jew for its faculty in the 1700s but only after he had converted to Christianity in "an impressive public ceremony in the college hall." In the late 1800s, Harvard, guided by its liberal president Charles Eliot, hired a Jew to teach medieval history. The teacher had been turned down by a number of universities, apparently because of anti-Semitism, and was about to enter his father's clothing business. As students, Jews had been at the school at least since the beginning of the nineteenth century, when Catholics and Jews were excused from attending classes on their holy days.

The Jewish student population at Harvard had grown from 7 percent at the beginning of the century to 21 percent in the early 1920s. The authorized biography of A. Lawrence Lowell, then president of the University, reported: "A considerable group of Harvard men, including representatives of the Governing Boards, the Faculties, the graduates and the undergraduates, looked on this increase with grave concern. Lowell was one of them." The concern was that a continued increase in Jewish students meant Harvard losing "its character as a democratic, national university, drawing from all classes of the community and promoting a sympathetic understanding among them." Lowell wanted to restrict the number of Jews entering Harvard, to establish a religious quota.

He argued that the quota would be better for the Jews. "If every college in the country would take a limited proportion of Jews, I suspect we should go a long way toward eliminating race feelings among the students," he explained.

Many years later, in 1979, Henry Rosovsky, dean of the Faculty of Arts and Sciences at Harvard, and himself a Jew, spoke to the issue:

Lowell had also watched America change through successive waves of immigration, and he realized that an admission system based exclusively on academic merit would, in a short time, change the character of the institution. That was the real issue: the ancient character of the College versus the claims of newcomers; the rights and privileges of Old Boston—founders and supporters of Harvard—versus new ethnic groups; the continuance of a school in which gentlemen from New England had a reserved seat versus the goal of a national university. Jews were the special cutting edge of a confrontation that is still with us today; the reaction to Italians or the Irish might have been similar.

America had welcomed immigrants because they provided cheap labor, groomed the horses and brushed the clothes. Now the immigrants' children were growing up, and they wanted into the mainstream of American society. The pressure to resist them, conceded Charles Eliot, retired Harvard president, came "from New York lawyers and businessmen who are really concerned with the recent rise of the Jews in business circles, social clubs, and the professions of the law."

What Rosovsky called "Old Boston"—and a like contingent existed in every city—had not anticipated that "recent rise of the Jews."

Harvard appointed a thirteen-member committee to examine the issue and make recommendations. For political reasons, several of the members had to be Jews; three were.

Julian Mack suggested to Lowell that Frankfurter be one of the Jewish members. The response came quickly: "I do not myself feel . . . that Professor Frankfurter has the quality of solid judgment that would make him a good member of the committee." This was followed by an exchange of letters, almost of a name-calling level, between Lowell and Frankfurter. Frankfurter was not appointed to the committee.

The committee worked for almost a year, and the subject brought out the worst in many. Walter Lippmann had been born Jewish, been stung by the anti-Semitism he had experienced, especially at Harvard, and blamed not the anti-Semites but his fellow Jews. He told a member of Lowell's committee, his biographer reported, that he was prepared to accept a 15 percent quota for Jewish students. "I do not regard Jews as innocent victims. They hand on unconsciously and uncritically from one generation to another many distressing personal and social habits, which were selected by a bitter history and intensified by a pharisaical theology." Frankfurter and Lippmann had been friends for many years; Frankfurter had helped Lippmann enter government service in the First World War, which led to Lippmann's being at the Paris peace conference with Wilson. On this issue, however, they eventually dissolved their friendship.

A prominent Jewish alumnus of Harvard, Albert I. Stix of St. Louis, wrote Lowell asking if the proposed quota would have any impact on his son's chances for admission to Harvard. Lowell replied: "There is, most unfortunately, a rapidly growing anti-Semitic feeling in this country, causing—and no doubt in part caused by—a strong race feeling on the part of the Jews themselves. In many cities of the country Gentile clubs are excluding Jews altogether, who are forming separate clubs of their own." It was here that Lowell suggested that all schools across the nation accept some Jews. But Lowell had ignored the point of Stix's letter, something Stix pointed out in a second letter: "Is there any possibility that my son will not be able to enter Harvard, or any other man's son for that matter, who, were he not a Jew, would be able to enter?"

Lowell replied that the "strong candidates, the good scholars, the promising men, will of course always be admitted." This did not satisfy

Stix. Did the reply mean "there is a possibility of a discrimination against these men who cannot be so classified—a discrimination which would admit the other kind of men, if they are not Jews and would exclude them if they are Jews"? The correspondence between Lowell and Stix, and Lowell and other Jewish alumni, dragged on, Lowell not understanding, or not acknowledging, that Jews were asking to be considered on the same terms as the other students.

At times the fight became dirty. Rumors circulated that a dormitory housing many Jews was "a house of assignation" and that Jews were responsible for campus crimes, such as stealing books from the library and money from student associations.

The committee of thirteen filed its report in April of 1923 and called for Harvard to maintain its "traditional policy of freedom from discrimination on grounds of race and religion." Despite the report, during the remainder of Lowell's tenure as University president, the percentage of Jewish students at Harvard declined, reversing the trend up to 1922. The percentage did not again rise until after the Second World War.

A Jewish quota for Harvard students had been the first problem; the next was a Jewish quota for Law School faculty members. Nathan Ross Margold was an immigrant like Frankfurter and, like Frankfurter, had grown up in New York and gone on to City College, and—still following the Frankfurter path—had a brilliant record at Harvard Law School. In 1926, Frankfurter recommended him to Dean Pound for a faculty position. "Of course, Margold is a Jew," said Frankfurter in his letter to Pound. "It would not embarass me in the slightest to have it discussed in the open, but if others would feel more comfortable, I can, of course, absent myself."

Margold received a temporary appointment for a year and then was recommended to Lowell by the Law School faculty for a further appointment. The routine was that Lowell, receiving such a recommendation, passed it on to the Harvard Corporation to make the formal appointment. This time Lowell declined to pass the faculty's recommendation; Margold would not be appointed. Lowell did not explain his decision.

On February 21, 1928, the Harvard Law School faculty met to discuss Margold's rejection. Dean Pound said Lowell's action meant there was no other course but to find another nominee. Many of the twenty-two faculty members present talked of revolt—some because their recommendation had been spurned and others because they believed in Margold as a teacher. Frankfurter and another faculty member engaged in a meandering debate on whether any other school at Harvard had the right to recommend faculty appointments.

Some members were willing to give in to Lowell to keep the peace. The day grew long and tempers short when Calvert Magruder demanded to know whether Lowell's action "implied a policy of not having any more Jews on the faculty." Roscoe Pound jumped back in the fray, saying he could get Henry Friendly appointed to the faculty "tomorrow if Friendly were ready to come." Finally, the faculty decided, by a 13-8 vote with one abstention, to take no action.

Margold went on to become a New Deal official and an active fighter and strategist for the civil-rights movement. Pound's reference to Friendly, also a Jew, indicates that opposition to Margold may have been based on Margold's admittedly abrasive personality and that the anti-Semitism was imagined. Friendly, years later, recalled being approached to teach at Harvard at this time. He was not interested in the position, however, and did not pursue the offer. But two years after the Margold fracas, the Harvard Law School faculty unanimously recommended another person to Dean Pound to pass on to Lowell for appointment to the faculty. "Pound opposed," reported one faculty member, "offering all kinds of excuses, although every source had praised the man highly. Pound 'said something also about not wanting to go to Lowell with another Jew.'"

Harvard was not unique; open anti-Semitism was becoming part of American life. Morris Cohen, Frankfurter's former Harvard roommate, had difficulty receiving an appointment as a philosophy professor; when it finally came, he went on to a distinguished career. In other law schools the situation was much as at Harvard. "I have been concerned to learn," Roscoe Pound wrote to Frankfurter "that two law faculties in A grade universities unanimously recommended Isaacs for appointment and in each one the Trustees turned him down on the sole ground that he was a Jew." Brandeis was particularly interested in having one of his law clerks enter teaching and talked to Frankfurter about recommending the man to the Yale Law School, saying "that the right man there would find no opposition on the score of anti-Semitism."

Another example of the attitude toward Jews came, in a roundabout fashion, when Emory Buckner, Frankfurter's friend in New York, recommended a member of his firm to the Yale Law School. Buckner explained that the candidate "is fifty per cent Jewish but has his father's name and is, of course, somewhat Jewish in appearance. He is completely, utterly, one hundred per cent devoid of every known quality which we in New York mean when we call a man 'Jewy.' " Buckner continued: "To be more specific, he is modest, extremely well mannered, intensely loyal, has no personal mirrors, sinks himself completely in the cause or the institution which he is serving."

The Jewish situation in law firms was similar to that in law schools. Harvard Law School graduates, especially the top-scoring ones, were prime candidates for the major firms; not, however, if they were Jews. "I assume that you have all the Jews that the traffic can bear," said Frankfurter in a letter to one firm, "but you're letting a rare thing go by in Birnbaum." There were many letters like that—"If your office does not bar Jewish juniors." Until individuals are hired on their merits, find a job for one Jew here, place another Jew there. Don't overload any one firm, don't push anti-Semitism too far. Move slowly. That was the strategy.

Even with his teaching, his struggle against anti-Semitism at Harvard, and with his pleasant life in Cambridge, Felix Frankfurter still was not satisfied. He was too energetic, too spirited. The role model of Louis Brandeis as the "people's lawyer" was too much before him. In the 1920s he began a career of professor–active citizen. He involved himself in labor disputes, crime studies, politics, continued writing for *The New Republic,* strengthened his relationship with Brandeis. He didn't stop. He couldn't.

In the 1920 presidential elections, Frankfurter voted neither for Warren G. Harding, the Republican, nor for James M. Cox, the Democrat, considering both "lacking too much in understanding and courage." He believed that both parties needed "the jolt of protest that would come from voting for neither."

He was not quiet about his decision. "Why is it so terrible to stick out your neck?" he once asked. As a professor, he believed he was obligated to speak out. "I do not conceive scholarship to imply servility and an acquiescence in wrong and corruption. Such acquiescence is complicity . . . we are *professors,* and that means to profess those qualities which lie at the very foundation of independent truth-seeking."

Not aligned with any party, he wanted to apply the lessons of government involvement learned in the First World War, to transform government into a mechanism for bringing America's bounty to more of her people. He argued, for example, that a child-labor law "withdrawing children from the mine and shop is not enough unless provision is made to put the children into schools."

Harold Laski once described a conversation he had with some Frankfurter acquaintances. He was showing them around London and attempted to explain Frankfurter to them.

"Why is he a democrat, Mr. Laski?" one asked about Frankfurter.

"Because he is an aristocrat with an infinite sense of pity."

"Why does he not want to make money?"

"Because most people who have it are vulgar," answered Laski.

"Why doesn't he collect books or pictures?" they asked.

"Because," concluded Laski, "he collects people."

His "infinite sense of pity" was expressed in a 1924 editorial in *The New Republic*. Frankfurter said the "most significant characteristic of our social-economic life" was a "great inequality of property." Of the 6.7 million tax returns filed in 1922, 6.2 million showed incomes below $5,000 while 4,000 listed incomes over $100,000; 1,860, over $150,000; 537, over $300,000; 228, above $500,000; and 67 showed incomes over one million dollars a year. "Beneath these quiet figures lie the most pulsating problems of American society," wrote Frankfurter.

That editorial was written as part of Frankfurter's support of third-party candidate Robert La Follette in 1924. Calvin Coolidge was the Republican candidate; and John W. Davis, the Democratic candidate. Frankfurter wrote many private letters to influential friends. "Let's stop being 'practical' for a season!" he demanded, urging them to support La Follette. Frankfurter did not believe Coolidge had the ability for the presidency, and he doubted Davis's morality. In many of his letters he described Davis's "crass materialism" as a negative example for Harvard students.

In supporting a third-party candidate, Frankfurter was influenced by his wife. Although shy and retiring, Marion had strong opinions about public affairs. Also, Frankfurter was influenced by Brandeis. "Marion is dead right about J. W. Davis—in every word she says," Brandeis wrote to Frankfurter. "J. W. D.'s acts & omissions during the last 3 years have been thoroughly in harmony with the judgment which she expresses."

La Follette, in his campaign, attacked the Supreme Court. Charging that the Court had gone too far in overturning acts of Congress, especially minimum-wage and child-labor laws, he advocated a two-pronged attack on the Court: allowing Congress to veto judicial decisions and limiting federal judges to ten-year terms. Frankfurter had first entered public life when Theodore Roosevelt was criticizing the Court; he himself had criticized the Court in *The New Republic* and other media. Now there were the La Follette attacks. Although not endorsing

La Follette's specific attacks, Frankfurter, with Brandeis's encouragement, did criticize the Supreme Court in *The New Republic* for "slaughtering . . . social legislation on the altar of the dogma of 'liberty of contract.'"

In 1928, Al Smith was the Democratic presidential candidate. Years earlier, as a Tammany politician, Smith had tramped through the streets of New York—listening to the Catholics, the Jews, the Italians; the immigrants and the poor—and fashioned political programs designed to bring them safe working conditions, livable incomes, and economic security. He became governor of New York and then the first Catholic nominated for the presidency by a major political party.

Frankfurter endorsed Smith in *The New Republic,* saying: "Our politics will regain its rightful function as the pursuit of those ideals and traditions which have always blended a country of diverse races and religions into a single people." Smith was defeated. The 1920s were good times, a soaring stock market, a relaxation of personal living codes; a time when Prohibition was more fun than legal drinking. The nation was not yet ready to vote Republicans out of the White House.

Even dabbling in politics was not enough for Frankfurter. Beginning in 1920, he began a series of additional outside activities that eventually led to his being one of the most notorious men in the United States.

During the First World War, Frankfurter had worked occasionally with Sidney Hillman, head of the Amalgamated Clothing Workers Union. In 1920, Hillman came to Frankfurter for help. His union had tried to organize a clothing manufacturer in Rochester. The company replied by obtaining an injunction to bar union picketing and disband the union. Frankfurter agreed to work on the case, which would be argued in Rochester. It was his first encounter with the labor injunction. A condition of working with Hillman, which Frankfurter insisted on, was that he not be paid. "I regarded this as the kind of thing a scholar in the law should do," he explained, "provided he does it disinterestedly and has no stake, certainly no money stake, in the outcome."

The results were mixed. Picketing was barred, but the existence of the union was maintained. Not too long after, Hillman's union succeeded in organizing the industry. Frankfurter was satisfied with the outcome.

Frankfurter's next project was the Cleveland Crime Survey. On May 9, 1920, in Cleveland, gunmen shot and killed a man; the crime caused a commotion because a municipal court judge was implicated. The people of Cleveland were angered by the incident, and the Cleveland

Foundation, backed by the bar association and civic organizations, funded a study of crime in the city. Dean Roscoe Pound and Frankfurter were asked to head the study.

The study was innovative. It involved experts—lawyers, social workers, psychologists, psychiatrists, and criminologists; it brought modern science to the study of crime. Its 1922 publication, *Criminal Justice in Cleveland,* demonstrated how politics and law enforcement were intertwined.

A third point about the Cleveland Crime Survey was Frankfurter's refusal to accept any payment for such public-service work. Raymond Moley, director of the Cleveland Foundation, offered him $2,000. Frankfurter, although short of cash, turned it down, suggesting that Moley send it along to Harvard as a donation. Moley would not accept this suggestion "as the relations of the committee in this survey were wholly with you rather than with the University . . . [and] it would be best to make payment to you." Frankfurter again refused, explaining that he considered the work for the Foundation part of his obligation as a law professor. Even A. Lawrence Lowell thought Frankfurter wrong not to accept payment "for outside work properly done." But Frankfurter was adamant; he did not accept compensation for outside work.

"Felix has always had this strange antipathy toward money," his wife once said. "He's always trying to think of some reason not to take a fee, or an honorarium, or a payment. He feels victorious when he avoids money." The Frankfurters never owned a house, and his friends do not remember his ever speaking of stocks and bonds. Frankfurter, in his later years, enjoyed telling the story of being a young immigrant in the United States and saying to his mother: "Mutter, don't worry, I shall never commit vealth."

Frankfurter's next major outside activity resulted in his appearing before the United States Supreme Court, for the first time since 1917. This also would be his last appearance before the Court as an advocate. When Frankfurter in 1917 had taken the three Oregon cases over from Brandeis, the minimum-wage issue, in *Stettler* v. *O'Hara,* had not been settled by the Court. In a 4-4 decision (with Brandeis abstaining), the Court let the state wage law stand while at the same time not making a definitive ruling on its constitutionality.

Between 1917 and 1923, the minimum wage was upheld by state courts, with the National Consumers' League involving itself in most of the cases. As part of this pattern, Congress enacted a minimum-wage law for the District of Columbia, and it came before the Supreme Court in 1923 in the case known as *Adkins* v. *Children's Hospital.*

The National Consumers' League rallied behind the District law and asked Frankfurter to argue the case. The minimum wage was first upheld and then struck down by the lower courts. "It is beyond belief what courts don't know," commented Frankfurter after losing in a District of Columbia court. "I do not mean their views but their ignorance of facts and events, even in the field of law."

Determined to educate them, he appealed to the United States Supreme Court and for his arguments produced a new Brandeis brief. Mary W. Dewson, who had succeeded Josephine Goldmark as research secretary for the League, solicited material from states with minimum-wage laws for the brief.

At the offices of the Consumers' League, the excitement recalled the days in 1907 when in a few weeks Josephine Goldmark and her friends had pulled together the material for the *Muller* brief. "We are in the last agonies of sending to the printer today the last pages of copy for a brief of 1,000 pages. . . ." Florence Kelley wrote a friend. "You know what the last day for the printer means! We have two special proof readers, two extra stenographers and Merry Hell in general! Mary Dewson has taken the veil and cannot be spoken to until February 5th. . . . Even Felix up in Cambridge is jumping high jumps twice daily."

Frankfurter's arguments were consistent with the arguments of James Bradley Thayer and Louis Brandeis that the Court should not be a super-legislature, that the congressional law establishing the minimum wage must be respected "unless transgression of the Constitution is shown beyond a rational doubt."

His "Brandeis brief" consisted of more than a thousand pages of data about the operation of minimum-wage laws in Europe and in several of the American states. His opponents challenged the approach: "If this act is constitutional it is unnecessary to show that there is any public sentiment in favor of it; if it is unconstitutional it cannot be sustained no matter how many people desire it."

On previous occasions when the Court considered a law dealing with working conditions, the opposition pointed out that the law, if upheld, had wider ramifications than its own specifics. This case was no exception. "Of course," argued the opponents, "it is obvious that once the power to fix wages is conceded, the power follows to make the bargain between employer and employees in all cases."

The Supreme Court Felix Frankfurter argued before in 1923 was not the Supreme Court that Louis Brandeis had educated in 1908. In a 5–3 decision, it struck down the District of Columbia's minimum-wage law. Brandeis did not participate because his daughter Elizabeth was secretary to the District's minimum-wage board, which was involved in the case.

The decision is credited to George Sutherland, but Willis Van Devanter also had worked on it, modifying some of Sutherland's extreme statements and positions. The decision said, "In principle, there can be no difference between the case of selling labor and the case of selling goods." A law establishing a minimum wage is "clearly the product of a naked, arbitrary exercise of power." As for the material in the Frankfurter brief, the majority found it "interesting but only mildly persuasive."

Holmes dissented. The opposition had claimed the law violated the Fourteenth Amendment's provision for liberty of contract by forbidding large organizations to bargain on wages with each individual employee. "Pretty much all law," said Holmes, "consists in forbidding men to do some things that they want to do."

That point was picked up by the other two dissenters, Sanford and Chief Justice Taft. Single employees were not on a par, they argued, with powerful employers "and in their necessitous circumstances are prone to accept pretty much anything that is offered."

The decision's effect was to eliminate the legal basis for the minimum wage in all states, not only in the District of Columbia, as well as for other legislation dealing with working conditions. Florence Kelley, after having fought for more than forty years to better working conditions, did not wish to accept defeat.

Adkins was handed down April 9, 1923. On April 19, the National Consumers' League held a conference in New York City. Frankfurter spoke after Mrs. Kelley. The problem, he explained, was not party politics, sectionalism, or who was President. "This issue is far deeper," he said, "it has a great deal to do with facts." What needed to be changed, he said, "has something to do with the education of these men [on the Supreme Court] and nothing else, and we are here to see what we are going to do about it."

Jesse C. Adkins, chairman of the District of Columbia's minimum-wage board, commented: "There are really three difficulties that we see —no money, unsympathetic lawyers as well as judges." The ideas suggested, mostly by Frankfurter, were accepted—to continue arguing the need for minimum-wage legislation through the state legislatures and through publicity.

But the feeling of many was summed up by a Florence Kelley comment to Frankfurter a few days later. "As to my impatience with further tinkering with legislation," she said, "what have I done but tinker for forty-one years?"

There was talk of attempting to restrict the Supreme Court's power, mostly by requiring seven votes to call federal or state legislation unconstitutional. John Hessin Clarke, the retired justice, wanted the Court to do this voluntarily. Mrs. Kelley wanted a constitutional amendment. The *Adkins* decision was one of those that led La Follette to attack the Court in his 1924 campaign, and Frankfurter to join in the criticism in *The New Republic*. Realistically, however, all knew that the Court would not change and would not be changed as long as its present membership stayed the same.

Fifteen years earlier, Louis Brandeis had won an important victory for the progressive forces in the United States when he had convinced one of the three branches of the government that the Constitution did not prohibit legislation protecting those in need of protection. Now, his protégé and friend, follower and successor had lost a similar case before that same branch of government.

During the 1920s the relationship between Brandeis and Frankfurter drew closer. To Brandeis, Frankfurter perhaps had become the son he never had. To Frankfurter, Brandeis was a role model guiding him to the life that Frankfurter would himself like to lead.

Both Brandeis and Frankfurter had been nurtured by James Bradley Thayer and Oliver Wendell Holmes, Jr.'s philosophy of judicial restraint. Both men believed in Zionism, were progressives. If not philosophical and legal twins, they were trusted colleagues and devoted friends.

In later years, it was alleged that Brandeis, by using Frankfurter, exerted an extraordinary influence on *The New Republic* and the *Harvard Law Review*. The charge, however, misunderstands the nature of the two publications. The magazine's progressivism had sprung, in part, from Brandeis's early writings and his Court decisions; it could not be true to itself unless its positions paralleled those of Brandeis. The same was true with the *Law Review*. Erwin Griswold, an editor of the *Law Review* in the 1920s, was asked about the Brandeis influence. "I don't think it had to be," he said. "The whole atti-

tude of the school was supportive of the Holmes-Brandeis outlook."
He cited the faculty members who supported that approach—Zechariah Chafee, Austin Scott, and Thomas Reed Powell, as well as
Frankfurter. "The student body would have voted nine-to-one in
favor of [the Brandeis] position," said Griswold. "That was the Harvard Law School line."

Although Brandeis lived an austere life, he understood that others did
not wish to live that lifestyle themselves, nor did he believe they should.
For years he had been concerned about Frankfurter's finances, knowing that Frankfurter had no outside income. In November 1916, when
Frankfurter was assisting Brandeis with Zionist activities, Brandeis sent
him a $250 check for expenses "for travelling, telephoning and similar
expenses in public matters undertaken at my request." When Frankfurter refused the check, Brandeis replied that he and Mrs. Brandeis
"are clearly of opinion that you ought to take the check . . . this is
nothing different than your taking travelling and incidental expenses
from the Consumers League or the New Republic—which I trust you
do." In May 1917, Brandeis sent Frankfurter a check for $1,000.

The expense money then stopped. In 1920, when Frankfurter was
going to the World Zionist Congress as part of the Brandeis party,
Brandeis told Zionist officials that he would pay Frankfurter's expenses
if the Zionist organization would not. "Of course, he must not be permitted to pay his own," said Brandeis.

In the early 1920s, as Frankfurter's outside public activities became
more numerous and he continued to refuse outside payment, his friends
became concerned about the precarious state of his finances. Julian
Mack and another Frankfurter friend, Mary Fels, considered helping
Frankfurter financially, but Mack first discussed the situation with Brandeis. Brandeis insisted on helping Frankfurter himself—"Of course,
anything that I can do for Felix, which is best for him and for the causes
he so generously serves, I am more than glad to do." Brandeis was
concerned about "what it is best to do. You know my apprehensions of
'easier ways' and the removal of financial limitations; also my belief in
the saving grace of what many call drudgery." But Brandeis offered to
give Frankfurter $1,000 "this year to pay expenses incident to his public
work." That was in January 1922; the next year, also in January, Brandeis sent Frankfurter a second $1,000 for "defraying your disburse-
ments on public affairs."

In 1925, Marion Frankfurter's "unhappy moods" necessitated psychi-
atric care, which Frankfurter could not afford. His salary as a Harvard

professor never exceeded $12,000. Frankfurter then had to choose between giving up his public activities and devoting his time to high-paying Wall Street legal work or seeking help from Brandeis. He chose to seek help from Brandeis.

Brandeis's attitude toward money, rarely understood, aroused suspicion in his lifetime and since. He believed money was, first, to assure his own economic freedom and the security of his family, and, then, to give away. Alpheus Thomas Mason, Brandeis's biographer, reported that Brandeis, from 1890 to 1939, donated $1,500,000 to charities, friends, and relatives. That figure may be an underestimate; so much money flowed from the Brandeis fortune that keeping track of every gift or donation was difficult. The donations were made before income-tax laws made charitable giving so attractive a device for the rich to avoid taxes.

For Brandeis the practice had begun in Boston. When the groups with which he was involved needed funds, he usually provided the needed amount out of his own pocket. Sometimes he suggested that people who owed him money donate the amount to a charity rather than pay him back. In 1916, for example, when a man started to repay Brandeis a $1,000 loan, Brandeis told him: "I prefer that you should do it as your direct contribution to the Zionist cause rather than by reimbursing me for the advance which I made in December last." That same year a group of American Jews, in honor of Brandeis's sixtieth birthday, put together a sum of $8,000 for his use. These were primarily poor Jews; the average donation was one dollar each. Brandeis directed the money be used for the benefit of Hebrew University, then being planned in Jerusalem.

He gave to Jewish and Zionist groups, and supported family members for years. Many of his relatives in the Louisville area, like his brother Alfred, did well financially, but others did not. Alfred had been helping some of them, but Louis told him: "I think you had better let me take care (through you) of any amounts which may be required for the relatives hereafter—be they Brandeis, Dembitz or Wehle. . . . You must remember that you have four daughters and I only two." Brandeis gave more than half a million dollars to relatives and friends, more than half of it during the depression years.

Brandeis gave funds to the Harvard Law School, many of the donations marked "anonymous." He took on the financial development of the University of Louisville as his personal project. "It is a task befitting the Adolf Brandeis family," he said, "which for nearly three-quarters of a century has stood in Louisville for culture, and, at least in Uncle Lewis [N. Dembitz], for learning."

As with the gifts to Harvard, those to the University of Louisville were marked by anonymity. To his niece Fannie Brandeis, he wrote: " 'The Fine Arts Library of the University of Louisville' seems to us admirable for the book plate. Do not let the Louis D. Brandeis name creep in there or in the Museum. . . . We want to stimulate action, and to this end it is important that others have the memorials." In 1936 he turned down the University's request to name its law school after him.

So in 1925, when Frankfurter turned to him for financial assistance, Brandeis did not hesitate. Actually, since 1921, Frankfurter had been included in the Brandeis will, a bequest to allow him "the more freely to devote time to the public service." Brandeis responded to Frankfurter in 1925: "I am glad you wrote me about the personal needs. . . . Your public service must not be abridged. Marion knows that Alice and I look upon you as half brother, half son."

An account was opened for Frankfurter in October 1925 in the Brotherhood of Locomotive Engineers National Bank of Boston. Brandeis had placed his own personal account there when the bank opened in 1924; in 1927 the bank became the Engineers National Bank of Boston. Frankfurter signed the identification cards for the account on October 7, 1925, and sent them to E. Louise Malloch, Brandeis's Boston secretary. Each year, from that point on, $3,500 was deposited into the account. The two men rarely discussed the arrangement, and it continued when they were in agreement on public matters and when they disagreed, ending when Frankfurter was nominated to the Court in 1939.

That type of financial assistance was not unusual when professors' salaries were low, consultants' fees were nonexistent, and foundation grants were sparse. Generally such aid was not discussed publicly; it was not considered a subject for discussion by gentlemen and ladies. Frankfurter, however, was not secretive about it. One of his students from the late 1920s recalled that "Frankfurter told our 'Federal Jurisdiction Seminar' when he was chatting about the problems of living on a professor's salary that he received an annual stipend from Brandeis." Toward the end of the year, the student met with Frankfurter to discuss his financial problems; he needed $500 to see him through to graduation. "He told me in substance 'You know that I would like to lend it to you personally, but I don't have enough money. I have told you before of the annual stipend I receive from Brandeis.' " Frankfurter was able to arrange a loan from another source for the student.

Brandeis also discussed his assistance to Frankfurter on a few occasions, without there being any suggestion of secrecy. Even into the 1940s the Brandeis assistance was general knowledge. John P. Frank, who received his law degree from the University of Wisconsin and then became a law clerk to Associate Justice Hugo L. Black in 1942, recalled that "this was common change . . . that Brandeis had backed Frankfurter financially during the pre-Court period."

Because of this act of kindness by the older man to the one he considered "half brother, half son," Frankfurter, from 1925 to 1939, was free from financial worries. He was able to dash to Washington on the overnight train when necessary, place the long-distance telephone call, send the lengthy telegram—without worrying about costs. He was free to be active, to travel the road toward the fame—or notoriety—that waited for him.*

*B. A. Murphy, in *Brandeis-Frankfurter Connection,* 1982, stated (1) that the annual assistance began in 1916 and was for political purposes—"in one of the most unique relationships in the Court's history, Brandeis enlisted Frankfurter, then a professor at Harvard Law School, as his paid political lobbyist and lieutenant" (p. 10); (2) that the arrangement was "secret" (p. 11) and "covert" (p. 44); and (3) that the money was paid, beginning in fall 1916, into a special fund in the "Engineers National Bank in Boston" (p. 41).

As shown above, however, the financial assistance was because of Marion Frankfurter's need for medical care and not for political purposes, was not secret, did not become an annual event until 1925, and there was no Engineers National Bank in Boston prior to 1927.

12

Sacco and Vanzetti

And here let me state a fact—and it cannot be repeated too often: The working class who fight the battles, the working class who make the sacrifices, the working class who shed the blood, the working class who furnish the corpses, the working class have never yet had a voice in making peace. It is the ruling class that does both. They declare war; they make peace.

The place is Canton, Ohio. The time is Sunday afternoon, June 16, 1918 —the height of America's involvement in the First World War.

If war is right, let it be declared by the people—you, who have lives to lose; you certainly ought to have the right to declare war, if you consider a war necessary.

The speaker is Eugene V. Debs, long-time labor leader—"agitator," some call him—and Socialist.

He was only one of many to protest the prevailing war fever, speaking to union members, to those outside the mainstream of American society. Some spoke in English like Debs; others used Yiddish, Italian, Lithuanian—whatever they believed their audience understood. They were Socialists, Communists, anarchists, and Wobblies; some represented philosophies no one understood or recognized. Others were clergymen astounded by war's tragedy.

They believed they were exercising their American right of free speech. The country did not agree with them. Fighting the war was national policy. The enemy could not be defeated if people like Debs were allowed to undermine the war effort.

Civil liberties, including the freedom to speak and print one's thoughts, had not been a federal concern since the Alien and Sedition Laws of John Adams's administration in the late 1790s. But during the First World War, Congress, angered and concerned by the antiwar movement, passed the Espionage Act. Before that law had run its course, 1,956 persons faced prosecution and 877 were convicted, most for talking as Debs had talked.

That was the beginning. A frightened America did not understand the strange ideologies, refused to countenance attacks on wealth, was adamant against any challenge to the war fought "to make the world safe for democracy." America began a campaign of terror against the "Reds," the "Pinkos," those outside the standard mold.

In January 1919, the Supreme Court heard a constitutional challenge to the Espionage Act, *Schenck* v. *United States,* involving a man, Schenck, who had distributed Socialist party material—"A conscript is little better than a convict. . . . Are you one who is opposed to war, and were you misled by the venal capitalist newspapers or intimidated or deceived by gang politicians?" The government charged the purpose of the material was to encourage violation of the draft law and arrested Schenck under the Espionage Act. The lawyers for Schenck replied that a person is not free to criticize the government when "twenty years in prison stares him in the face if he makes a mistake and says too much."

Two months later, in March 1919, less than a half year after the war had ended, the Supreme Court unanimously upheld the constitutionality of the Espionage Act. Oliver Wendell Holmes wrote the Schenck decision: "The character of every act depends upon the circumstances in which it is done. . . . The most stringent protection of free speech would not protect a man in falsely shouting fire in a theatre and causing a panic." The standard Holmes laid out is "whether the words used are used in such circumstances and are of such a nature as to create a clear and present danger that will bring about the substantive evils that Congress has a right to prevent."

A few days after the "clear and present danger" standard was applied against Schenck, Holmes also used it against Debs, who had been convicted for his remarks in Ohio; again Holmes spoke for a unanimous court. To Holmes there was no doubt of Debs's guilt although conceding privately that "there was a lot of jaw about free speech." Holmes considered himself more prone to support free speech than the other justices, "and I daresay it was partly on that account that the C.J. assigned the case to me."

Brandeis, although agreeing with Holmes on *Schenck* and *Debs,* was not happy about the outcome. "I had not then thought the issue of freedom of speech out—I thought at the subject, not through it," he explained to Frankfurter. In retrospect, he would have preferred reaching the same result, not by creating the "clear and present danger" standard but by the war power.

"The scope of espionage legislation would be confined to war," he said. "But in peace the protection against restrictions of freedom of speech would be unabated. You might as well recognize that during a war . . ."

"All bets are off," said Frankfurter.

"Yes," said Brandeis, "all bets are off. But we would have a clear line to go on. I didn't know enough in the early cases to put it on that ground. Of course you must also remember that when Holmes writes, he doesn't give a fellow a chance—he shoots so quickly."

In the next case growing out of the Espionage Act, *Abrams* v. *the United States,* Holmes and Brandeis, prodded by their friends and associates off the Court, began to think through the subject, not at it. As a result, the clear and present danger standard was transformed from a weapon suppressing free speech to one defending it. In *Abrams,* five men had been charged with violating the Espionage Act by distributing antiwar circulars. The Court in a 7-2 decision written by John Clarke upheld the convictions. Holmes, joined by Brandeis, dissented.

Holmes expected criticism at the Saturday conference "and perhaps be persuaded to shut up." He was right; the justices did try to persuade him to silence, but he did not give in. Three of his fellow justices then visited Mrs. Holmes to ask her to use her influence with her husband. That failed also.

In the Holmes dissent, he and Brandeis framed the arguments used again and again in subversive cases. An individual has the right to criticize, attack, lambaste the American government; that is what free speech is about. Congress can establish a limit on expression only to counter an "immediate evil or an interest to bring it about" and not to counter some vague future possibility. Relying on truth, Holmes argued, "is the theory of our Constitution. It is an experiment, as all life is an experiment."

With that decision, Holmes and Brandeis were off and running, beginning a series of dissents outlining the right of the dissenter, the meaning of free speech, the promise of the Constitution.

Schaefer v. *United States* came down four months after *Abrams.* The defendants were officers in a German-language association and published newspapers during the war which, according to the government, printed "false reports and statements . . . or otherwise violated the Espionage Act." Said the Supreme Court majority: "Free speech is not an absolute right, and when it or any right becomes wrong by excess is somewhat elusive of definition." The majority decision, written by

James McKenna, found little elusive in this instance; convictions of three of the defendants were upheld.

This time Brandeis wrote the dissent. He described the clear and present danger standard as a "rule of reason," and to apply it correctly, the "exercise of good judgment" is needed. For that, he said, "calmness is, in times of deep feeling and on subjects which excite passion, as essential as fearlessness and honesty." He continued that the German-language publications were not such as to violate the Espionage Act and no jury "acting in calmness" would reasonably say that they did. He concluded:

The constitutional right of free speech has been declared to be the same in peace and in war. In peace, too, many men may differ widely as to what loyalty to our country demands; and an intolerant majority, swayed by passion or by fear, may be prone in the future, as it has often been in the past, to stamp as disloyal opinion with which it disagrees. Convictions such as these, besides abridging freedom of speech, threaten freedom of thought and of belief.

Holmes joined him. John Clarke filed a separate dissent.

In the next internal security case, *Pierce v. United States,* four men had been convicted for distributing a pamphlet, "The Price We Pay," written by an Episcopal clergyman, charging: "Our entry into [the First World War] was determined by the certainty that if the Allies do not win, J. P. Morgan's loans to the allies will be repudiated, and those American investors who bit on his promises would be hooked." The government claimed the charge was false and, to prove it, cited President Wilson's April 2, 1917, message to Congress asking for a war declaration. For his dissent, Brandeis found congressmen making the same charge about the Morgan loans in the *Congressional Record.*

Speaking against the Court opinion written by Mahlon Pitney, Brandeis conceded that the Episcopal clergyman's pamphlet contained "lurid and perhaps exaggerated pictures of the horrors of war . . . [which] appear to us shallow and grossly unfair." But, Brandeis closed:

The fundamental right of free men to strive for better conditions through new legislation and new institutions will not be preserved, if efforts to secure it by argument to fellow citizens may be construed as criminal incitements to disobey the existing law—merely, because the argument presented seems to those exercising judicial power to be unfair in its portrayal of existing evils, mistaken in its assumptions, unsound in reasoning or intemperate in language. No objections more serious than these can . . . reasonably be made to the arguments presented in "The Price We Pay."

When Holmes read the draft of the Brandeis dissent, he wrote, "Please count me in heartily," and the decision came down 7-2.

In the 1920 case *Gilbert* v. *Minnesota,* Brandeis continued the argument that "In frank expression of conflicting opinions lies the greatest promise of wisdom in governmental actions; and in suppression lies ordinarily the greatest peril." Brandeis remained on the losing side; even Holmes did not join him.

Gilbert raised points that previous cases had not, and Brandeis took special care with his dissent. An early draft went to Harvard to be researched for "any flaw in the reasoning" by Frankfurter and Zechariah Chafee, who was developing a reputation for expertise in the field of civil liberties.

Involved this time was not a federal but a state law. Brandeis believed a state had the right to enact legislation it thought proper, but not if the legislation abridged fundamental freedoms: "The state law . . . affects rights, privileges and immunities of one who is a citizen of the United States; and it deprives him of an important part of his liberty. These are rights which are guaranteed protected by the Federal Constitution, and they are invaded by the statute in question."

In contrast to Brandeis's argument that rights were protected by the Constitution, the understanding had been—until at least passage of the Fourteenth Amendment, with its statement that "No State shall make or enforce any law which shall abridge the privileges or immunities of citizens of the United States"—that the freedoms detailed in the Bill of Rights, including that of free speech, were protected only from federal, not state or local, incursion. This stemmed from an 1833 case, *Barron* v. *Baltimore,* when the Supreme Court, headed by John Marshall, ruled that the Bill of Rights "contains no expression indicating an intention to apply them to state governments. This court cannot so apply them."

When Brandeis planned to challenge that, proposing to say, "The right to speak freely concerning the functions of the Federal Government is a privilege of immunity of every citizen of the United States which, even before the adoption of the Fourteenth Amendment, a State was powerless to curtail," Dean Acheson, Brandeis's law clerk then, questioned the challenge. Brandeis acquiesced, writing, instead, that he did not consider whether the Fourteenth Amendment had been violated because he believed the state statute invalid for other reasons.

Gilbert was the first case in the states resulting from war hysteria. Next the Supreme Court dealt with laws in Nebraska and Iowa prohibiting the teaching of German in public schools. Both states had large

German populations, and the laws' intent was to attack their ethnic consciousness. Too much even for the conservatives on the Supreme Court, these laws were ruled unconstitutional in a decision written by James McReynolds. "Mere knowledge of the German language cannot reasonably be regarded as harmful," he wrote. "Heretofore it has been commonly looked upon as helpful and desirable." Brandeis joined him.

Holmes, joined by Sutherland, dissented. His dissent is interesting because it could have been written by Brandeis. If the states wish to experiment by restricting German, he said, in a clear echo of the Brandeis argument at other times, "I am unable to say that the Constitution of the United States prevents the experiment being tried."

At Harvard, Frankfurter agreed with the Holmes dissent, believing it consistent with James Bradley Thayer's argument against the Supreme Court's becoming a super legislature. To argue otherwise, he said, is to accept that "the Supreme Court of the United States is the revisory legislative body."

Brandeis was splitting somewhat from his friends' judicial philosophy. Still opposed to the Supreme Court's considering the "wisdom" of legislation, Brandeis did believe, however—and the belief strengthened as more civil-liberties cases came to the Supreme Court—that the Constitution prohibited state infringement of individual rights. The decision by McReynolds to protect the rights of teachers to teach and students to learn also, Brandeis believed, protected civil liberties.

This split was understood by his opponents on the Court, as they showed in the next civil-liberties case, *Gitlow* v. *New York*. Involved was the constitutionality of a New York State law punishing speech advocating overthrow of the government. The majority opinion, written by Sanford and upholding the New York law, sounds borrowed from previous Brandeis writings: "We cannot hold that the present statute is an arbitrary or unreasonable exercise of the police power of the State." Brandeis and Holmes dissented, considering the state's action both arbitrary and unreasonable. Holmes wrote the dissent: ". . . it is manifest that there was no present danger of an attempt to overthrow the government. . . . It is said that this manifesto was more than a theory, that it was an incitement. Every idea is an incitement."

Holmes was less formal in his comments to his friends. "The last day of Court I let out a page of slack on the right of an ass to drool upon proletarian dictatorship but I was alone with Brandeis. Free speech means to most people, you may say anything that I don't think shocking."

In *Whitney* v. *California*, Brandeis went along with the majority upholding the conviction of a Communist, but with reservations. *Whitney* involved "criminal syndicalism," meeting together—Communists, in this instance—to plan for the eventual overthrow of the existing order. California law prohibited such meetings. Originally, Brandeis intended to dissent on the basis that the "clear-and-present danger" standard had not been met, that the supposed overthrow was too far removed from the meeting. Statements "however reprehensible morally," he said in an early draft, "are not ordinarily a justification for denying free speech; because where the element of incitement is lacking the danger is remote."

In this early draft, he also included a remark on his fellow justices' propensity to defend business interests but not individual liberties. "Statutes imposing absolute prohibition," he wrote, "as distinguished from regulation, have been repeatedly held invalid in cases involving the liberty to engage in business. The power and duty of the Court is no less where the liberty involved is that of free speech and assembly."

When the time came for decision, however, there were several changes. Originally, the California case and another from Michigan were considered together. Then the Michigan case was dropped, and the California case was narrowed, not to the clear-and-present-danger standard but to whether Fourteenth Amendment rights had been violated. Because Brandeis did not feel rights under that amendment had been violated, he did not dissent. But his separate concurrence is virtually a dissent, criticizing the majority for its attack on free assembly and free speech.

But a point had been made, as illustrated by a case decided the same day as *Whitney* v. *California.* This was *Fiske* v. *Kansas,* also a criminal-syndicalism issue. Prior to this case, Holmes and Brandeis had used the clear-and-present-danger standard as an argument against a witch hunt —the government could not move against people simply because it disliked what they were saying—and had consistently been on the losing side. This time, however, after almost eight years of dissents, Holmes and Brandeis were in the mainstream.

Although the phrase "clear and present danger" was not used in the unanimous decision written by Sanford, the point was clear; the Holmes-Brandeis arguments had been heard. Sanford wrote that the defendant, a Wobblie, was convicted "without any charge of evidence that the organization in which he secured members advocated any crime, violence or other unlawful acts or methods as a means of effecting industrial or political changes in revolution."

There always has been an argument over the "clear-and-present-danger" standard as used by Holmes and Brandeis. Gerald Gunther of the Stanford Law School, some years later, commented that the standard "required factfinders to guess about the risks created by the challenged speech." Zechariah Chafee believed the test eventually reversed many convictions "and no doubt it staved off many prosecutions again." In either case, it applied a standard at a time when the tendency was to attack on the basis of belief.

How anxious the nation was to attack the individualist, the critic, the loner was illustrated by the last significant civil liberties case to come before the Supreme Court in the 1920s. Rosika Schwimmer was, when she applied for naturalization, forty-nine years old, an atheist and a pacifist.

The naturalization process included the question, usually asked of men but not of women, whether they would take up arms for the United States. Rosika Schwimmer said she would not do so, but added that if ever women were compelled to take up arms, "I would recognize the right of the Government to deal with me as it is dealing with its male citizens who for conscientious reasons refuse to take up arms." That she was willing to suffer the consequences of law was not sufficient, especially to the Women's Auxiliary of the American Legion, which had demanded the question of taking up arms be put to her.

When she was denied citizenship by naturalization, she appealed her case to the Supreme Court. She lost, 6-3. The majority decision, by Pierce Butler, acknowledged that naturalized and native-born citizens are alike before the law, but said aliens "have no natural right to become citizens, but only that which is by statute conferred upon them." That she was an older woman was not a factor, said Butler, claiming that the influence of conscientious objectors "is apt to be more detrimental than their mere refusal to bear arms."

Associate Justice Sanford dissented, supporting a lower court decision upholding Rosika Schwimmer. Holmes dissented, joined by Brandeis. Holmes was angered, saying the question of whether she would or would not fight was irrelevant because of her age and sex and she "would not be allowed to bear arms if she wanted to."

Now eighty-eight years old, the descendant of Boston Brahmins, war hero, almost fifty years a public servant, Oliver Wendell Holmes, Jr. took the occasion to lecture his brethren and, with them, his fellow countrymen and women, those who would prohibit the distribution of leaflets, who would force women in their late forties to answer questions so they could be prosecuted for their answers.

"Surely," he said, "it cannot show lack of attachment to the principle of the Constitution that she thinks that it can be improved. I suppose that most intelligent people think that it might be." He spoke of Rosika Schwimmer's horror of war, and Holmes sympathized with her. "Most people who have known it," he said of war, "regard it with horror, as a last resort, and even if not yet ready for cosmopolitan efforts, would welcome any practicable combinations that would increase the power on the side of peace."

And then he made his major point, the point of all those who had fought for civil liberties in the 1920s, and beyond. "Some of her answers might excite popular prejudice," he said, "but if there is any principle of the Constitution that more imperatively calls for attachment than any other it is the principle of free thought—not free thought for those who agree with us but freedom for the thought that we hate."

Holmes and Brandeis had failed in the 1920s. The individual's civil liberties had fallen before the prejudice of government. But with their dissents, their words, Holmes and Brandeis had appealed to America's conscience, to that "brooding spirit" Charles Evans Hughes had spoken of, and they had left a legacy, one that others would pick up in later years.

The Supreme Court was only one arena of battle for the civil-liberties cause in the 1920s; among the others were academe and the state courts. These were Felix Frankfurter's arenas of battle. Like Brandeis, he would fail. But also like Brandeis, he would leave a legacy.

Given his inclinations and his experiences with the Bisbee and Mooney cases, Felix Frankfurter could not avoid involvement in the civil-liberties movement. He joined the national committee of the newly formed American Civil Liberties Union in 1920, along with Roger Baldwin, Jane Addams, and, among others, William Z. Foster, then a union official and later a Communist party leader.

Frankfurter joined with Zechariah Chafee in signing (along with Roscoe Pound and Francis B. Sayre, Woodrow Wilson's son-in-law) an amnesty petition for the individuals in the *Abrams* case. And then he joined with Chafee as *amici curiae* in a Boston case known as *Colyer v. Skeffington*. This case stemmed from the "Red raids" of 1919.

A. Mitchell Palmer, Woodrow Wilson's third Attorney General, fumbled with a technique that later politicians practiced in a more sophisticated fashion—the exploitation of public fears for political profit. Warning of the "Red menace," Palmer ordered the Justice Department's Bureau of Investigation to round up thousands of persons, citizen and alien. They were detained in jail, maltreated, forced to sign statements they could not understand. Supposedly the purpose of these "Red raids" was to find Communists, agitators, people who would destroy America. In actuality, the search was by Palmer for votes for the 1920 Democratic nominating convention.

Colyer v. *Skeffington* was a setup. To head off a threatened deportation action before a judge friendly to the Palmer side, the anti-Palmer forces looked for a test case to produce a decision against Palmer. They wanted the right judge to hear the case, the appropriate lawyers to be involved, and evidence placed in the record to embarrass Palmer. "Could you take up the matter with Mr. Chafee and Mr. Frankfurter, who are reported to be interested, and see what can be done to get this case speedily before the court?" a Labor Department official asked a Chafee friend.

The case involved an English couple, "people of a high type, intelligent, [who] do not advocate and have not advocated violence, much less attempted to use it,—but they are bona fide members of the Communist Party." The judge was George W. Anderson, respected Boston lawyer, liberal, friend of Brandeis. And the lawyers appearing as *amici curiae* were Frankfurter and Chafee.

They had themselves a time, embarrassing the government lawyers, demonstrating that rules had been changed specifically to deny aliens constitutional rights, that minimum legal standards had not been adhered to. Judge Anderson ruled that the Colyers' rights had been denied.

After the case had been argued but before Anderson's decision, Frankfurter and Chafee joined with other prominent American lawyers in signing a "Report upon the Illegal Practices of the United States Department of Justice," a listing of the denial of civil liberties in the "Red raids."

Attorney General Palmer attacked the report's signers: "We find several of them appearing as counsel for Communist and Communist Labor party members at deportation hearings. I have difficulty in reconciling their attitude with that of men who have sworn to uphold the Constitution of the United States."

That was all Frankfurter and Chafee needed. The day they read that statement in the newspaper, they wired Palmer ready for battle. "The writ of habeas corpus is guaranteed by the Constitution of the United States," they said. "May we respectfully ask you, the official head of the bar of the United States, to state since when it has become otherwise than ethically proper and professionally right for members of the bar to invoke the writ of habeas corpus in cases in which, according to the opinion of responsible lawyers, arrests, detentions, searches and seizures were resorted to in violation of Constitution and statutory requirements." The telegrams careered back and forth and were publicized, making the dispute almost a personal duel between Palmer on one side and Frankfurter and Chafee on the other.

The demagogue's hold on the public's attention is not long, as A. Mitchell Palmer learned at the 1920 Democratic national convention. He was not nominated for the presidency, and he began his slide into obscurity. But the rhetoric of Chafee and Frankfurter lived on; their enemies were not done with them.

Austen Fox, who had challenged the Brandeis Supreme Court nomination in 1916, decided in 1921 to take on Chafee and his friends. A member of the Harvard Board of Overseers, Fox submitted a statement to the Board, signed by himself and twenty others, criticizing Chafee for an article he had written on the *Abrams* case, claiming it was so inaccurate as to be unworthy of a scholar. Frankfurter, Pound, and others on the Law School faculty also came under criticism for their support of civil liberties.

Chafee was a mild-mannered man whose family was impeccably New England Yankee; he had not been involved in extremist causes before this fight and would not be again for many years. As a lawyer, scholar, and teacher, he had commented on something in which he believed. Now he was under attack.

Chafee and his friends felt at bay, surrounded by the powers that controlled the school. At Frankfurter's request, Brandeis wrote Chafee a note: "Word comes of the attack upon you for desiring to be free. You did a man's job. The persecution will make it more productive. By such follies is liberty made to grow, for the love of it is reawakened. Of course there are growing pains; but with the throes comes also the joys of the struggle and of creation."

What became known as "The Trial at the Harvard Club" took place at the Harvard Club of Boston on a "sizzling hot" Sunday, May 22, 1921. A committee of fourteen was to hear the charges but only eleven attended, including judges and practicing lawyers. No transcript of the proceedings was kept but there is general agreement that two moments of the "trial" transcended the time and the place and the heat of the day.

The first was the defense of Chafee by A. Lawrence Lowell, president of Harvard University. Lowell had sided with Austen Fox against Brandeis five years earlier; his conservatism always was taken for granted. But now outside forces were encroaching on his domain, the arena of academic freedom. Frankfurter recalled Lowell's telling the committee he would resign "if any of these people are fired, or anything is done to them." And Chafee later quoted Lowell as saying to the eleven "judges" that "The teaching at Harvard could not be controlled from Wall Street." Lowell himself did not recall the day as so dramatic. "I had not intended to conduct the case," but, he said, apparently referring to Pound and Frankfurter, "some members of the Law School were so excited that I had to do what would naturally have fallen to them."

The second moment was a statement by Chafee himself. After a calm presentation of his position in the Abrams article—in what Felix Frankfurter called one of the most impressive statements he had ever heard —Chafee said:

Gentlemen, I had no sympathy with the political and economic doctrines of these prisoners. I can hardly imagine any persons with whom I should get along worse than with Abrams and his associates. My sympathies and all my associations are with the men who save, who manage and produce. But I want my side to fight fair. And I regard the Abrams trial as a distinctly unfair piece of fighting.

With the defense by Lowell and Chafee's impassioned defense of himself, the charges against the members of the Law School faculty faded. Late the night of the meeting, Lowell telephoned Chafee to report that the committee had unanimously reported that no action be taken. When Chafee thanked him, Lowell replied: "Don't thank me. I had to protect my front." Chafee later collected his articles on free speech in a book and dedicated it to Lowell in appreciation of his defense that Sunday.

For Frankfurter, the Palmer raids, the Chafee trial, even the Bisbee and Mooney incidents, were all prelude to what became his major civil-liberties activity in the 1920s. Sacco-Vanzetti was a case, a cause, a passion, a heartbreak; it defined the term "liberal"—one was either on one side or the other; its ending with the execution of the two Italian anarchists in 1927 did not quiet the controversy. More than half a century later people still argue about the case, still hate because of the case, still cry because of Sacco-Vanzetti.

Nicola Sacco and Bartolomeo Vanzetti were charged with robbing and killing a paymaster on April 15, 1920 in South Braintree, Massachusetts. Sacco was a shoe factory employee, and Vanzetti, a fish peddler; both were Communists, draft dodgers, and deeply involved in radical causes. A year after the crime, Sacco and Vanzetti, in a trial before Judge Webster Thayer at Dedham, were convicted of killing the paymaster and sentenced to death. The case was appealed to the Supreme Judicial Court of Massachusetts, which decided in 1926 that there was no basis for reversal of the convictions. The two men would die. The case was then appealed to the Supreme Judicial Court a second time.

Popular feeling against the two convicted men was high. The brutality of the crime, Sacco and Vanzetti's politics, the fact that they were immigrants who had lived in the United States but had not become citizens, all combined to produce a vendetta against them. During the years of the trials and appeals, a suspicion developed among more thoughtful persons in the Boston area that the two men had been convicted in an unfair trial, and that the unfairness would not have existed if Sacco and Vanzetti were not who they were and did not believe as they did.

However deep the movement against civil liberties in the United States during the 1920s, there were many—lawyers, teachers, writers; clergymen and agnostics; rich and poor; foreign-born and those from old-line families—who did not forget that the Constitution had made its promises to all, to the Communist and draft dodger as well as to the Democrat and Republican and to the veteran. They determined those promises be kept in this case.

No one living in the Boston area during the years of the crime, the arrests, the trial, and the appeals, was immune from the case; most had strong opinions. In late 1923, Frankfurter wrote his friend Learned Hand, "I am not as confident as in the old district attorney days that 'the ghost of the innocent men convicted is an unreal dream.' The case of the politicos—Sacco-Vanzetti up here, etc.—tends to give me a different perspective about procedural safeguards."

Frankfurter then continued with the argument he made in the coming years: "The worst of it is that protection for the accused does the least good where it is most needed—namely where the passion of the community is aroused, and convictions come not from the evidence but from the atmosphere."

Still, it was not his fight, and Sacco and Vanzetti had—for their appeals if not for their trial—prominent members of the Boston bar, William G. Thompson and Herbert B. Ehrmann. But as the months and years passed, the pugnacious law professor interested in protecting procedural safeguards became enveloped in the widening circle of procedural abuse.

Frankfurter's involvement often was misunderstood. Gardner Jackson, who participated in the fight with him, reflected that Frankfurter was "an intellectual type. I've never felt in my long relationship with him that he's essentially motivated by emotions for other people." Frankfurter, copying his Brandeis model, did attempt to deal with causes and movements rather than individuals, but unlike Brandeis, Frankfurter was not always able to keep his passions within himself—as would be demonstrated by the Sacco-Vanzetti case.

Joseph P. Lash, who edited the Frankfurter diaries, said that Frankfurter's involvement with Sacco-Vanzetti, although earning "him a reputation for liberalism, even radicalism, can be seen to have had little to do with approval of the doctrines they espoused." For lawyers, however, "liberalism" never has meant espousing the causes of clients but rather assuring the clients their constitutional rights. This was Frankfurter's approach. If privately the apparent injustice burned him, publicly he spoke to the law. He believed that if he made speeches about injustice, he was only another speechmaker; if he picketed, he was only another picketer. But if he, the legal scholar, spoke to the law, if he demonstrated the law had not been exercised fairly, then he moved the Sacco-Vanzetti debate to a different level. That is what he did. Because of the involvement of Felix Frankfurter, any discussion of Sacco-Vanzetti cannot avoid the question of whether the law was followed.

Thompson, who handled the appeal, had asserted that the ballistics evidence, supposedly establishing Sacco and Vanzetti's guns as the murder weapons, was flawed. Frankfurter, intrigued by Thompson's thesis that the district attorney and the ballistics expert had collaborated to deliberately mislead the jury, began to study the trial records. Then in 1926, Herbert Croly of *The New Republic* asked him either to write something about the case or find someone who would. The result was an article without byline but written by Sylvester G. Gates, a Commonwealth Fellow from London associated with Frankfurter at Harvard.

The deeper Frankfurter delved, the more of the trial transcript he read, the more he found himself pulled into the dispute. He attended the hearing before the Supreme Judicial Court of Massachusetts when Thompson argued the second appeal—"the art of advocacy infused by a deep moral passion at its highest" is how he described Thompson's argument. By this time, Frankfurter was convinced. "The poor Judge

[Thayer] is himself the victim of forces and of emotional and intellectual limitation he has not a glimmer of," said Frankfurter. "I am very pessimistic of the outcome. I cannot believe that the Governor will ever allow them to be hung, but I fear they will not get a new trial, confident as I am that a new trial would acquit them."

Frankfurter's belief that a new trial would acquit Sacco and Vanzetti was based on new evidence. However, a quirk of Massachusetts law—a "blind spot," according to one authority—was that the appeals court did not review the evidence but only the procedure to determine whether the trial judge, Thayer, had made an error of law. John M. Maguire, a professor at the Harvard Law School and an authority on Massachusetts criminal procedure, explained: "The evidence presented in connection with the motions for a new trial has been passed upon in the colloquial sense only by Judge Thayer and not by the Supreme Judicial Court. As you know, many people in the community gravely doubt Judge Thayer's capacity to take an impartial judicial attitude with respect to this evidence." That meant there would not be a new trial.

To this point, Frankfurter had not publicly involved himself in the cause but began to consider writing an article, from his scholar's seat.

The New Republic was an outlet for Frankfurter, but he had concerns about publishing a signed Sacco-Vanzetti article there. Most of its readers already believed in the two men's innocence. In Boston, however, was the *Atlantic Monthly*, a venerable and staid publication edited by Ellery Sedgwick; "stuffy," some called it.

Stuffy, perhaps; but the magazine had a tradition of involvement in public issues going back decades—publishing Jacob Riis and Jane Addams's critiques of urban slums and Booker T. Washington on the black American. Sedgwick, hearing that Frankfurter was considering doing an article, wrote to him and suggested the *Atlantic* as an outlet. Sedgwick edited the article, "blue-penciled myself passages which I thought unfortunate, and very much regret that in the performance of a long and rather troublesome job I made the serious mistake of leaving in one or two strongly prejudicial remarks."

Frankfurter's article appeared in the magazine's March 1927 issue and then was published as a book by Little, Brown as *The Case of Sacco and Vanzetti*. It became the *J'Accuse* of the case.

My aim is to give in brief compass an accurate résumé of the facts of the case from its earliest stages to its present posture.

Until this point, America could ignore the case; it was an argument in Boston between some radicals and the law with a few members of the Boston bar, undoubtedly well-meaning but probably misguided, defending two Italian men—"wops," most Americans called them.

Sacco and Vanzetti spoke very broken English, and their testimony shows how often they misunderstood the questions put to them. A court interpreter was used, but his conduct raised such doubts that the defendants brought their own interpreter to check his questions and answers.

Until this point, America could believe in the fairness of the judicial system which had dealt with Sacco and Vanzetti, believe that, if the men were innocent, they would be freed.

In modern times Judge Thayer's opinion stands unmatched, happily, for discrepancies between what the record discloses and what the opinion conveys. His 25,000-word document cannot accurately be described otherwise than as a farrago of misquotations, misrepresentations, suppressions, and mutilations.

Until this point, America could believe that, while occasional excesses in the name of law and order occurred, never would a state's judicial system, its law-enforcement agencies, and its respected community combine over a period of years to destroy two men barely able to speak English.

After publication of Frankfurter's article and book, such things were easier to believe.

Working from the trial record, Frankfurter charged that the judge and prosecuting attorney had appealed to the jurors' prejudice, that the eyewitness testimony did not hold up, that the prosecuting attorney and ballistics expert had conspired to mislead the jury. He cited the record, used actual quotes, and explained the legal machinations in a way easily understood. "What *is* unparalleled," he said, "is that such an abuse should have succeeded in a Massachusetts court."

Frankfurter became one of the most popular and most hated men in America.

"Your flaming zeal for truth and justice is exhilarating and contagious," Benjamin Cardozo wrote him from New York. And William O. Douglas recalled that "Frankfurter's book on the case . . . had been our bible. Clark and Hutchins at Yale, and I at Columbia, had promoted its cause." A lawyer friend in Philadelphia told Frankfurter that "your name will be ranked with Voltaire."

On the other side, the most serious onslaught came from John Henry Wigmore, dean of the Northwestern University law school. He wrote two articles for Boston newspapers, accusing Frankfurter of error. There is a story that A. Lawrence Lowell said: "Wigmore was a fool! Wigmore was a fool to enter into controversy with Frankfurter. He should have known that Frankfurter would be accurate." Whether that story is true, Wigmore was foolish to challenge Frankfurter. In response to each article, Frankfurter—with the help of Sylvester Gates—answered Wigmore in a rival newspaper point by point. Erwin Griswold, then a second-year law student, recalled: "I can remember how my roommates and I used to walk to Harvard Square every afternoon to get the early edition of the *Transcript* with the latest instalment—the somewhat heavy-handed work of Wigmore attacking the 'plausible pundit,' and the scintillating, rapier thrusts, with an instinct for the jugular, which characterized Frankfurter's replies."

Some were not moved by evidence. A Harvard Law School alumnus, writing in the student newspaper, doubted that Frankfurter would have involved himself "had the condemned men not been members of an anarchistic organization." Others attacked Frankfurter through his Harvard relationship, withholding contributions unless Frankfurter was punished for his writing.

Frankfurter had anticipated this. He recalled years later that he knew there were those who believed "a more important interest than whether these two Italians had had a fair trial was not to cast doubt on the reliability of Massachusetts justice. Such views were held by men of importance in the affairs of Harvard." Because of this, Frankfurter tried to keep the Law School out of the fracas. Dean Roscoe Pound was unaware of the article until it appeared in print, "nor did I take into confidence even my closest friends on the faculty," said Frankfurter. To assure accuracy, he did ask Professor Maguire, the expert on Massachusetts criminal procedure, to check his references. He also had been assisted by Sylvester Gates, the Englishman.

One criticism made against Frankfurter was the article's timing; it appeared while the second appeal was pending. Sedgwick, the *Atlantic* editor, answered, "I fully realized that the case was under review of our highest state tribunal, but this case had been in the courts for six years and if a responsible magazine is estopped from speaking until the last pronouncement is made, then the press is obviously impotent."

But a Harvard Law School professor is held to different standards than the press. Had Frankfurter violated legal ethics with his article? He insisted that he had not. Publication actually was delayed until after the court had taken the case. When publication was finally scheduled, no one could know if the article would appear before or after the court handed down its decision. Also—and this especially angered Frankfurter—when the second appeal was pending, the Worcester County Bar Association formally expressed confidence in Judge Thayer, one of its members, in connection with his handling of the Sacco-Vanzetti case. Thayer's conduct of the trial was an issue before the court. Frankfurter did not believe he should be condemned while the Worcester Bar Association's action was condoned.

But his was not the most effective answer to the timing charge. That came from A. Lawrence Lowell. "Of course I do not share Professor Frankfurter's views in the Sacco-Vanzetti case," said Lowell. "But he was entitled to have these views, nor was he required to wait to express them until after the men were dead."

There were personal attacks against Frankfurter: that he was in the pay of the Sacco-Vanzetti Defense Committee, that he was one of its members and therefore biased, that, in some way, he had a personal stake in the outcome. At every opportunity, Frankfurter explained that he had no connection with the Defense Committee, that he had received $250 from the *Atlantic* for the article and given one-half of that to Sylvester Gates, and had spent considerably more than the $125 remaining "in connection with the case, solely on my own account, for such expenses as long distance telephones, telegrams, traveling, books, newspapers, postage, stenographic work, etc., etc." Royalties from the book version of the article were donated to the Defense Committee. "I was neither instigated by anyone to write my book nor did I represent anyone but myself in writing it," he insisted. "I have held no brief at any time for the defense."

On April 5, 1927, the second Sacco-Vanzetti appeal was denied. On April 9, a Saturday, in the Dedham Court House, Judge Webster Thayer sentenced the two men to death. "If it had not been for these thing," Nicola Sacco said in the courtroom that day, "I might have live out my life talking at street corners to scorning men. I might have die, unmarked, unknown, a failure. Now we are not a failure. This is our career and our triumph. Never in our full life could we hope to do such work for tolerance, for joostice, for man's onderstanding of man as now we do by accident. Our words—our lives—our pains—nothing! The taking of our lives—lives of a good shoemaker and a poor fish-peddler—all! That last moment belongs to us—that agony is our triumph."

Frankfurter was present. "Those two so-called ignorant Italians," he said of the courtroom session, "managed to make all of us who heard them realize that the true concern which their cases raise is for society and not for them."

Frankfurter said, "For the present, the Sacco-Vanzetti case has taken rather exclusive possession of me." A friend recalled: "A group of us got together and asked Frankfurter to go over the case for us. His wife was there, and she said, 'Oh, don't do it. He will get so wound up over this, he just won't sleep.' "

The case also had taken possession of Marion Frankfurter. The faculty wife served tea to students at five o'clock and sympathy when the occasion warranted. This never had been sufficient for her. But the Sacco-Vanzetti case had touched her, as it did many like her—people brought up in religious families and taught to believe in the fairness of the American system.

"I did not go to Dedham that day," she wrote Vanzetti. "I did not think I could bear to be there." But Felix had described the scene, she said, "and I was lifted up and sustained when he told me about it. Ever since then the pain and bitterness of spirit I felt that such things could be, have been relieved, because I said to myself: 'If these men can have such composure, such dignity and beauty of spirit, then I must strive for calm.' "

The sentencing to death was not the end. A petition for clemency was addressed to Governor Fuller. Frankfurter and others contacted their prominent and influential friends: "I think a personal letter from you to the Governor, speaking as one human being to another, is the way in which you would reach his understanding, might really help." The governor responded by appointing a three-member advisory committee, including A. Lawrence Lowell, to recommend whether the sentence should be carried out.

The other two members were Robert Grant, a retired judge of probate for Suffolk County, and S. W. Stratton, president of the Massachusetts Institute of Technology. Although there was no chairman, the committee became known as the "Lowell committee" because Lowell sat between the other two men at the hearings and was the most aggressive questioner.

From the beginning of the committee's deliberations, strung out over ten days, its objectivity was questioned. Stories floated around of Lowell's bias, of his having said in private that the two Italians were guilty and that the Massachusetts judicial system could not be at fault. Gardner Jackson believed there might have been a different outcome if Frankfurter had not been involved. "I am satisfied that the intensity of

Lowell's animosity to Felix was a very large factor in what happened to his mind in the face of the evidence," said Jackson, "since Felix had become the chief intellectual protagonist of the two Italians."

Reports that the three committee members agreed on the guilt of Sacco and Vanzetti before they began the hearings drifted out to Thompson and Ehrmann, then handling the Sacco and Vanzetti side. "Convinced that we were captive actors in a tragic farce," recalled Ehrmann, the two lawyers determined not to cooperate with the committee. One night they met for dinner at the Harvard Club in Boston with Frankfurter and Julian Mack. Frankfurter argued that Lowell "was not entirely hopeless" and that a withdrawal might spark talk that the two lawyers were no longer convinced of their clients' innocence. "And so," continued Ehrmann, "we were persuaded to continue with the hearings, despite our strong sense of preordained hopelessness."

Lowell had been reluctant to serve on the committee, well aware there was no way to avoid making enemies. "I never undertook anything with greater repugnance than this job," he later wrote. "It was, of course, a thankless one."

Frankfurter's article and book had at least caused Lowell to wonder about the fairness of the trial, "but when I came to read all the stenographic report of evidence in the case I found it quite a different matter from what I had supposed." He also interviewed ten of the twelve Sacco-Vanzetti jurors. His ultimate impression was that "the whole matter had been grossly misrepresented to the public." He and the other two committee members stated to the governor that the original trial had been conducted fairly, that subsequent evidence introduced after the trial did not warrant a new trial, and that they were convinced that Sacco and Vanzetti were guilty of murder.

The governor accepted their report on August 3, 1927. The execution would be carried out on August 23.

Twenty days.

William Thompson, who had been leading the defense efforts, was exhausted; a new leader was needed. Frankfurter approached Arthur D. Hill, one of the most prominent Boston lawyers. If Hill accepted, Frankfurter told him, there would be no fee. Hill did not hesitate. He mused that if the president of the city's largest bank had asked him to defend his wife for $50,000, he would accept. Then: "I do not see how I can decline a similar effort on behalf of Sacco and Vanzetti simply because they are poor devils against whom the feeling of the community is strong and they have no money with which to hire me. I won't particularly enjoy the proceedings that will follow but I don't see how I can possibly refuse to make the effort."

Frankfurter tried for an appeal to the governor. He sought signatures from prominent New York lawyers, told people to check with Walter Lippmann, then editor of the New York *World*, for names to solicit. He was constantly on the telephone, calling this one for help, beseeching that one for a signature, warning another that "Extremists from New York have come on here to capture this thing . . . they are absolutely desperate."

He went to the *New York Times*, to the *World*, to his friends in New York. Always he talked as if there were a chance, if only each person acted. Once from New York, exhausted, he telephoned Marion.

"I'm afraid that you won't save the men from the chair," she told him.

"Oh, I don't know. Why do you say that?" he answered.

"I don't see how you can," Marion said. "In the first place you haven't the time."

"Arthur Hill certainly did awfully well," he told her, "and I feel that there is a ray of light and I am also hopeful."

Privately, Frankfurter knew better. "Those men will die," he acknowledged, "and the civilized world will be horrified."

Frankfurter's efforts, in those last few days, although prodigious, had been private. Then he was asked to join in the signing of a public statement to the governor. He refused. Gardner Jackson was astonished. "This is quite serious," he said. "It startles me terribly not to have you say something." Frankfurter did not explain, except to say: "There are things I cannot tell you. It would do nothing but hurt the case." That was Sunday, August 14.

The pressure on Frankfurter continued, and two days later his explanation finally exploded from him. "I am as much on trial in this case as these two men, and that is why I have deemed it absolutely fatal to inject my personality before the public." If he signed any public statements, he argued, "it will be Frankfurter versus Lowell or Lowell versus Frankfurter." He had never been in "so personal a community," and his name would set off Governor Fuller and the others whose sympathy they were after.

His reluctance was not from personal fear. "It so happens," he said, "that I am just as free as a bird, absolutely . . . nothing would please my wife more than if I quit the Law School and went to New York to practice law. I could earn a living at the bar—I have nothing to fear— I am not tied up socially." No, he stressed again, his reluctance was based on his knowledge of how the Massachusetts powers regarded him: ". . . as a 'hardheaded lawyer'; they regard me as an 'official damned radical Jew' who has meddled with this case."

Thirty-three years earlier twelve-year-old Felese Frankfurter had arrived in New York aboard the S. S. *Marsala* after the lengthy journey from Vienna. He had traveled much in those thirty-three years—to public school, to City College, to Harvard, to dine at the White House, to advise at the peace conference. His closest friends were judges and Wall Street lawyers. Every so often, however, Felix Frankfurter knew those thirty-three years did not count; they were erased—the honors, the accomplishments, the intelligence—and he was no longer the scholar and the citizen, the civilized and honorable man, but only the "damned radical Jew."

Even he did not realize how correct he was. The State of Massachusetts was at that time tapping his telephone. The tap began on August 1, 1927, three weeks before the Sacco-Vanzetti executions, and continued until October 3, more than a month after the executions, on an order of Arthur K. Reading, attorney general of the state of Massachusetts, to General Alfred F. Foote, commissioner of public safety. In addition to Frankfurter's attempts to build up public pressure on behalf of Sacco and Vanzetti, the state wiretappers heard Marion make appointments with her hairdresser and arrange to have the gas turned on in their Cambridge house at the end of summer.

Nothing moved the state; if Massachusetts had its way, the two men would be executed as scheduled. On August 10, the Sacco-Vanzetti lawyers began a series of appeals to the United States Supreme Court. The Court was not then in session, and the lawyers hoped one of the justices might issue an order delaying the executions until the full court could hear argument on the case in the fall.

"What are the chances with Judge Holmes and Brandeis?" Frankfurter was asked.

"It is speculative," he answered, "and I would not express any opinion." Frankfurter was being kind then; he knew there was no chance. As the relationship between the federal government and the state was then understood, the Supreme Court had no power to interfere with the Sacco-Vanzetti case.

Holmes was the first to tell them. "Stirred I guess by Felix," said Holmes, "Arthur Hill has come into the case and last week appeared here with other lawyers and reporters tagging on to try for a habeas corpus from me. . . . I said that I had no authority to take the prisoners out of the custody of a State court having jurisdiction over the persons and dealing with a crime under State law." He had done that once before in a case involving a black in the South, but there a mob surrounded the courthouse and "made the trial a mere form." He grumbled, "If justice was what the world is after, this case is not half so bad as those that are more or less familiar in the South. But this world cares more for red than for black." That night a relative of Holmes came by and, appreciating the emotions unleashed on all sides by the case, offered to spend the night "against the chance of some violence being attempted." Holmes declined the offer.

Frankfurter understood Holmes's position, commenting many years later, "The views a man may have as a citizen are not necessarily views that as a judge he can translate into constitutional law. Thus, Mr. Justice Holmes wrote me very appreciatively about my little book on the Sacco and Vanzetti case. But as a Justice of the Supreme Court he could not stay the execution of Sacco and Vanzetti."

When Holmes turned them down, the lawyers turned to Brandeis. Frankfurter was even less optimistic about him than he had been about Holmes. Still, he told the Sacco-Vanzetti forces they could locate Brandeis in Chatham and gave them the telephone number—Chatham 330.

Arthur Hill, now the chief counsel for Sacco and Vanzetti, was even less optimistic than was Frankfurter. "I speak without knowledge of it," said Hill, "but [Brandeis] may feel himself disqualified from sitting for reasons which you can divine."

For Louis Brandeis, the pressures were strong. Nicola Sacco and Bartolomeo Vanzetti were two of the people he had dedicated his own life to helping, not because they were Communists or anarchists but because they were in difficulty with the law and appeared to be victims of prejudice because of their ethnic background and political beliefs. Brandeis had preached that there was a place in the United States for the individual who maintained his ethnic background, who spoke out for what he believed. To many, the Sacco-Vanzetti case denied that.

Brandeis had followed the case for years. In 1925, when the Sacco-Vanzetti Defense Fund announced that costs then already had reached almost $300,000, Brandeis commented to Frankfurter that the figure was "a terrible indictment of our criminal justice [system]." The case was mentioned occasionally in their correspondence, and Brandeis encouraged Frankfurter's efforts, describing his Sacco-Vanzetti book as "an event of importance with bench and bar; perhaps a turning point." When on April 5 the state Supreme Judicial Court refused an appeal for a new trial, Brandeis thought the action "damns [the court] pretty effectually; but it will help the holy cause."

He encouraged Frankfurter to work through the committee appointed by Governor Fuller, writing, "Lowell can't be altogether unfriendly." In June 1927, when Governor Fuller denied clemency, Brandeis praised Frankfurter for having played a "noble" part. Also, Brandeis offered to assume the costs of some of Frankfurter's efforts; this was in addition to the allowance of $3,500 a year Brandeis had been giving to Frankfurter since Marion became ill in 1925.

Still, the same restriction working on Holmes as a judge applied to Brandeis. A judge is guided by legal tradition; he does not create law, however appealing such a creation might be at the moment. For Brandeis, however, there were, in addition, personal considerations. Brandeis, through his family and friends, was intimately involved in the Sacco-Vanzetti case. The Brandeis's closest family friend was Elizabeth Glendower Evans. Years before, when her husband had died, Brandeis had taken her under his protection and his care. She continued close to the Brandeis family; Elizabeth Brandeis was named after her and both Elizabeth and Susan Brandeis called her "Auntie Bee." She eventually blossomed into an active participant in social causes, and became one of the stalwarts of the Sacco-Vanzetti defense committee.

In 1921, when Sacco and Vanzetti had been convicted, Mrs. Evans was staying in the Brandeis summer home when the Brandeises were away. She had as guests the wife and children of Nicola Sacco. A question exists whether the Brandeises were aware of the Sacco family's staying at their house and whether they approved of it; but there is no question that the Saccos stayed in the Brandeis house for a period of time. In addition, Mrs. Brandeis had long been interested in the case as had the Brandeis's second daughter, Susan, a lawyer. Although the family involvement was not formal, their interest was not secret.

Also, Frankfurter was so well known as a friend of Brandeis that his appearance before Brandeis on behalf of the appeal might have been considered prejudicial. However, he was not averse to advising Arthur Hill on the correct strategy to use with Brandeis. "Don't worry about Hill," said Frankfurter to Gardner Jackson. "Hill is professionally all right, Gardner, and I talked with him and there's no trouble about that." Still, Frankfurter, knowing the interest of the Brandeis family and friends in the case and understanding that Brandeis's view of judicial limitation was similar to that of Holmes, anticipated that Brandeis would not hear the arguments for an appeal.

Brandeis met the party early Sunday morning. Arthur Hill tried to explain their side, but Brandeis, almost seventy-one years of age, standing on the front porch of his house, was implacable. "He was very emphatic," said a witness. "Said he couldn't possibly do anything definite about it." Hill then announced to the press that Brandeis had stated that "because of his personal relations to some of the people who had been interested in the case, he felt that he must decline to act on any matter connected with it." The *New York Times* reported the reasons for the Brandeis refusal:

Mrs. Brandeis, it is understood, has befriended Mrs. Rose Sacco. Her daughter, Susan, has been interested in the case and Professor Felix Frankfurter of Harvard University, who wrote a book on the case, is a close friend of Judge Brandeis. Mrs. Margaret [sic] Glendower Evans, a Boston society woman who has been an active defense sympathizer from the beginning, is an occasional house guest of the Brandeis family.

In addition to being turned down by Holmes and Brandeis, the Sacco-Vanzetti Defense Committee was turned down by Associate Justice Harlan Fiske Stone and by United States District Court Judge George W. Anderson; this is the Judge Anderson who had decided against A. Mitchell Palmer in the *Colyer* case.

As the time of the execution neared, Frankfurter came under increased personal criticism, and he was becoming increasingly thin-skinned.

"It is a most awful situation," said Gardner Jackson, "where your legal system will not insure moral demands; that is what leads to revolution."

"Now don't talk to me about that," Frankfurter exploded, "because I have had to listen to my wife all day. I can shut you up but not her. All day long I have had to listen to it. I have tried to explain the situation but not defend it. She just won't take it in."

He told Jackson: "I can tell you to shut up, but not her."

Nicola Sacco and Bartolomeo Vanzetti were executed on August 23. When she heard the news, Marion Frankfurter collapsed. Felix Frankfurter did not speak.

Learned Hand saw Frankfurter the next day. "He was like a madman," said Hand. "He was really beside himself. I wouldn't have thought of trying to talk with him." When a Boston lawyer suggested to Frankfurter that "the whole matter is settled," Frankfurter replied: "Executions do not 'settle' truth."

There were, and continue to be, a variety of reactions to the Sacco-

Vanzetti case and Frankfurter's involvement in it. At Harvard, when alumni believed Frankfurter's activities improper and threatened to cut off their donations to the Law School's endowment campaign, Dean Pound and President Lowell did not flinch before these attacks. Frankfurter never appreciated the pressures they were under and did not acknowledge the support they had given him. Of Pound: "What he did or didn't in connection with Sacco and Vanzetti, and one or two morally similar instances, made our relation different—I ceased to be his friend." Of Lowell: "When people ask me, 'Do you plan to resign?' I say to them, 'Why should I? Let Mr. Lowell resign.'"

Frankfurter never lost his belief that "The two men were innocent —as innocent as you and I—of the murders for which they were executed." He did more than speak of their innocence. Through two friends, Bernard Flexner and Emory Buckner, a committee was formed to print the entire record of the case; its 1928 publication in five volumes and a supplement has become the basic document for all subsequent studies of the case.

Marion, with Gardner Jackson, edited the letters of Sacco and Vanzetti, published by Viking Press. When a newspaper insinuated they had manufactured the letters, Marion and Jackson sued for libel; they won.

The case and Frankfurter's involvement continue a matter of controversy. In 1961 further ballistics tests "corroborated" the earlier tests and "confirmed much other evidence indicating that Sacco was guilty and that Vanzetti had knowledge of his guilt." Such statements, never having been subjected to the cross-examination of a lawyer in a courtroom, belong in the speculative category. Occasionally the accuracy of Frankfurter's book is challenged, but such challenges consistently are rebutted.

For Felix Frankfurter, the Sacco-Vanzetti case was "the generator of the most painful episode in the joint lives of Marion and myself, giving searing pain which we vividly recall to this day"—the comment came thirty-six years after the execution—"and which is now assuaged only by virtue of our justifiable satisfaction for our share, both joint and separate, in our participation in this awful tragedy."

In Massachusetts several years after the execution, there was another reaction, specifically involving Frankfurter. The emotions, hostilities, and angers caused by the Sacco-Vanzetti case still smouldered in the state. Most of those feelings were directed at Frankfurter; Thompson and Ehrmann had done a lawyer's job in defending the two men but

Frankfurter had challenged the integrity of the state's judicial system. "Thompson and I decided to do something about it," Ehrmann recalled.

The state's new governor was Joseph B. Ely, a lawyer and one who had believed Sacco and Vanzetti innocent. "He was also an admirer of Felix from a distance," said Ehrmann. "We decided that an effective answer to the slanders was for Ely to put Felix in the Supreme Judicial Court of Massachusetts. We brought them together at our home for a number of dinners and very enjoyable evenings." The campaign had begun in 1931, and Thompson said he had talked with Frankfurter many times about his intentions, and "while he has never said to any of us that he would accept the position, he has never told us that he would not accept it."

In January 1932, when a vacancy occurred on the Massachusetts court, Holmes, who had once sat on that court, wrote Governor Ely recommending Frankfurter. Other prominent persons also were solicited to approach Ely about Frankfurter. Ehrmann and Thompson made no secret of why they wanted Frankfurter appointed. If Frankfurter was nominated and confirmed, then they could argue that the state no longer considered him an outcast, that his position—and that of the other supporters of Sacco and Vanzetti—had been accepted.

In June 1932, without first consulting Frankfurter, Governor Ely nominated him to the state court. In reporting the action, the *New York Times* described Frankfurter as Sacco and Vanzetti's "champion."

"I think the appointment is admirable," said Holmes. "In the matter of learning, understanding of affairs, and passion for justice, Professor Frankfurter is much more than ordinarily qualified."

There were many other similar letters and statements. Frankfurter, except for his World War I service, had been teaching almost twenty years and had many friends and admirers. Many believed as did Ehrmann and Thompson that a state judicial appointment would vindicate the Sacco-Vanzetti defense.

Frankfurter declined the appointment. This angered many people, especially Thompson, who believed Frankfurter should have previously indicated his unwillingness to serve. Frankfurter explained, "You know me well enough to know that I just cannot make decisions in the abstract or chase butterflies." Most of his friends had advised him to accept, except Brandeis, who believed Frankfurter could be of greater service without the formal ties of a state judgeship.

Frankfurter said he wanted to continue teaching. Certainly this was true. But probably he was uninterested in the work of a state court, "ninety-five percent of the businesses of which concerns the conventional grind of private litigation." Nor was he interested in retreating from public affairs; for Frankfurter, this was not the time to step back. Governor Ely's offer had been made public at about the same time that the Democrats in Chicago had nominated the man likely to be the next President, Franklin Delano Roosevelt. What Roosevelt would do in the coming years was, at that point, unknown; that he would do something definitely was known.

Frankfurter and Roosevelt were friends, and Frankfurter did not wish to deny himself the excitement of involvement.

BOOK THREE

The Most Influential
Single Individual

13

The New Deal

Of the nation's twelve largest cities, none had gone Democratic in the 1920 presidential election, two went Democratic in the 1924 election, five in the 1928 election; and all twelve went Democratic in the 1932 election. Those twelve cities were located in ten states, and the Democratic margins in those cities gave Franklin Roosevelt the electoral votes in nine of those states.

Those cities had been moving into the Democratic column because of the religious and racial minority members, immigrants, and first-generation Americans who lived there. Since the time of Theodore Roosevelt's Square Deal and Woodrow Wilson's New Freedom, liberalism and progressivism had been shunted aside in the search for and hallowing of the corporate dollar, and the minority and new Americans realized in the 1920s that they were being left behind, that the corporate profit did not trickle down to them.

Then the depression of 1929 ended their decade of concern and introduced a new decade of despair. The figures stagger; unemployment soared from 1.5 million in 1929 to 12 million in 1932, the wholesale price index plummeted from 95.3 to 64.8 in those three years, and the gross national product fell from $104.4 billion to $74.2 billion, on a per capita basis dropping from $857 to $590.

Using any statistic, America was shattered, on the ropes. More than in the statistics, the despair was written on the faces of hungry children and of homeless teenagers roaming the country, in the streets of the "Hooverville" tent towns and in soup-kitchen lines. In Washington, government seemed incapable of acting. Most Americans then became convinced of what the minority and new Americans had realized: it was time for a change. Franklin Roosevelt swept to victory with three popular votes for every two of Herbert Hoover's and eight electoral college votes for every one of Hoover's.

Franklin Roosevelt's New Deal, so much a part of Frankfurter's and Brandeis's lives in the 1930s, began as a slogan, was sometimes described as a philosophy or political approach, but, actually, was another attempt to accomplish what Brandeis wanted to do from the bench and Frankfurter wanted to do in the classroom—bring together the law and the living, government and people. The 1920s had been the decade of the businessman and the soaring stock market. The 1930s was the decade of the planner, the professor, the expert. There were theories: nationwide planning, managed economies, public works, returning people to the farm. If the theories worked, fine; if they didn't, devise something else. Legislative proposals, dormant for years, suddenly were revitalized. That was the New Deal's glory, that it so much stressed experimentation. That was also its problem; with so many of its followers wedded to particular theories, special approaches, those followers often ranked the New Deal's failure not by whether it fell short of its goals but by how far it strayed from their own theories and approaches.

When Roosevelt was nominated for the presidency by the Democratic party in 1932, he and Felix Frankfurter had known each other for almost twenty-five years. They had first met when Frankfurter was a prosecutor working for Henry Stimson and Roosevelt was practicing law in New York. The friendship resumed during World War I when both were members of the War Labor Policies Board. They saw each other socially then; although Frankfurter, with his ethnic background, was not a regular member of the Roosevelt social circle, Roosevelt's developing egalitarianism increasingly brought him into contact with persons outside that circle.

When FDR was elected governor of New York, he called on the Harvard professor for ideas for modernizing New York State's judicial system. Even in 1928, Roosevelt was coming to enjoy what Frank Freidel has described as Frankfurter's ability to provide "instant laudatory reassurance." During the 1928 campaign, for example, when Frankfurter had written Roosevelt praising him for his "pure-mindedness and real public zeal," he added: "As a Jew I am particularly happy that your nomination prevented the New York contest from degenerating into an unworthy competition for the 'Jewish vote.' "

Because of the depression of 1929, the next Democratic presidential candidate obviously had a chance to win, and Roosevelt, as the governor of the most populous state, was a prime contender. From Harvard, Frankfurter watched with interest and sometimes with misgivings as Roosevelt shifted with the vagaries of politics. "Tell Frank Roosevelt in language that he cannot misunderstand," he wrote a mutual friend in 1931, "that once again courageous response to the public need also happens to be the surest road to the White House."

When the campaign year opened, Frankfurter claimed Al Smith for his first choice but did not expect Smith's nomination, or, if he were nominated, his election, saying that the prejudices against the Catholic Smith "are still very powerful."

When FDR was nominated in July, he telephoned Frankfurter long distance to congratulate him on his appointment to the Supreme Judicial Court in Massachusetts. This was the appointment by Governor Ely; although not accepting the appointment, Frankfurter had agreed not to speak publicly about it for several days. "Felix," said FDR, ". . . I haven't been able to tell you how happy I am that you got your big chance. I wish it were the Supreme Court of the United States—that's where you belong."

During the campaign Frankfurter was involved in strategy and speechwriting for Roosevelt but only in a peripheral way when compared to the Brain Trusters—Raymond Moley, Rexford Tuxwell, Adolf A. Berle, Jr., and others. But Frankfurter was valuable for other reasons. Al Smith, angry at being denied his party's nomination, had refused to surrender his votes at the convention to Roosevelt, blocking a unanimous nomination. During the campaign, Smith, who commanded a large following in the urban East and among the nation's Catholics, refused to speak out for Roosevelt. Months passed with Smith adamant. Finally, Bernard Baruch, the Wall Street speculator; Herbert Bayard Swope, a newspaper editor and Baruch publicist; and Frankfurter took Smith to lunch and implored him to endorse Roosevelt. "We all had a turn at it," Baruch recalled, "and Felix gave him a particularly stirring speech. Smith listened silently, and I could see the conflicting emotions rising within him as his face flushed red and the perspiration stood out. When Frankfurter finished, Smith surrendered. 'Well, you're right,' he admitted, 'and that's that.' "

There was another reason why Roosevelt wanted Frankfurter on his side. Roosevelt was aware of the popular movement toward the Democratic party, as evidenced in the presidential campaigns of the 1920s. The Democrats had been a minority party since the 1890s, generally considered conservative, and Roosevelt knew he had to change that image. He had to go after the Smith voters and capture more. He had to unite the farmer and city dweller, factory worker and professor, southern Bourbon and Tammany Hall official, Gentile and Jew, Catholic and Protestant. The war had been between the outsider and the insider, the new immigrant and the established order. Franklin Roosevelt wanted to appeal to them all, to bring them together.

Frankfurter was an important part of this plan. A Jew, an immigrant, a teacher, a liberal who had risked his reputation in the Sacco and Vanzetti case, Frankfurter had an important constituency—not in the number of votes but in the influence he had among others.

Frankfurter has been described as a "Schmeichler," in Gerald Gunther's phrase, one who worked his way into the councils of the mighty by saying the right word at the right time. That he was. But Roosevelt was the same. He wooed Frankfurter as he wooed others to build his constituency. As FDR responded to Frankfurter's praise, Frankfurter responded to—and assisted—the man who most likely would be the next President. It was *Schmeichler* meeting *Schmeichler*.

Frankfurter entered the campaign publicly toward the end, in a radio address, entitled "Why I am for Governor Roosevelt." The talk anticipated the thrust of the New Deal.

To realize the new economic order, to understand its new problems, to devise ways of dealing with these new problems and not persist in the old ways of obsolete society—that is the essence of modern statesmanship . . . to prevent these terrible ups and downs in business. . . . More effective participation by labor and agriculture in the nation's councils are needed; more sustained and wider diffusion of the purchasing power on the part of the great masses . . . better housing, more health, higher levels of education, better and wider use of leisure.

Frankfurter's speech was actually a sketch of the progressivism of the previous thirty years, the litany of the Theodore Roosevelt and Woodrow Wilson liberal. It underscored the belief of the poor, the minority member, and the new American that what they had perceived in the Democratic party in the 1920s' elections could indeed be realized with Roosevelt in the 1932 election.

Between Roosevelt's election in November 1932 and his inaugural in March 1933, Frankfurter strengthened his position as friend and adviser. He cautioned Roosevelt against making a trip abroad before the inauguration, advised there was nothing wrong with FDR's vacationing on a rich man's yacht, and generally made himself helpful and pleasant. He and Marion began then what became a ritual for many years, visiting the Roosevelts during the Christmas season. Marquis W. Childs, a Washington reporter during the New Deal, said Roosevelt liked Frankfurter for his "play of wit and humor." Roosevelt, said Childs, "didn't like politicians. He found them very dull."

During the pre-inaugural period, Frankfurter was involved in bringing together the President-elect and Henry Stimson, Frankfurter's old boss and, in 1932, Secretary of State in Herbert Hoover's outgoing administration. The specific problem was international war debts and Hoover's hope of cajoling FDR into endorsing the Republican solution. Behind this, however, was the hostility of Hoover toward FDR; beaten, disgraced, wallowing in self-pity, Hoover was not offering a gracious or easy transition. The American government was not continuing. It was stopping, then starting again.

Frankfurter believed that Stimson with his "integrity and disinterestedness" could transcend that hostility. There was no Democratic endorsement of the Republican war debts position, but the meeting was a sign that the transition would not be totally without grace.

Also, during this pre-inaugural period Frankfurter brought together Franklin Roosevelt and Louis Brandeis. More was involved than the President's only responding to a Frankfurter request. Now seventy-six, with sixteen years on the Supreme Court, Brandeis was the acknowledged philosophical father of the liberal movement. If not everyone accepted his specific ideas, many who called themselves liberal or progressive accepted his philosophy of change and experimentation. He had expressed that philosophy earlier in 1932, in a major dissent, calling for government, both state and national, "to remould through experimentation, our economic practices and institutions to meet changing social and economic needs." If the dissent was not a charter, it was a slogan. The Brain Trusters were interested, and they interested Roosevelt in Brandeis.

Brandeis had watched FDR as governor and admired him. After the 1932 nomination, Brandeis told a niece that "Aunt Alice and I think Franklin Roosevelt is much underrated by the liberals." Brandeis, who believed a person's worth could be determined by his enemies, added: "The opposition of the vested interests who have opposed [Roosevelt] indicate that they fear him."

As the 1932 election campaign neared its end, and Roosevelt was confident of winning, he asked Frankfurter to arrange a meeting with Brandeis. After some starts and stops, it took place late in November 1932 at the Mayflower Hotel in Washington. "Yesterday had 15–20 minute satisfactory interview with F.D.R. at which he did most of the talking," Brandeis reported to Frankfurter. Roosevelt, Brandeis continued, "seems well versed about fundamental facts of the situation—Declared his administration must be liberal and that [he] expected to lose part of his conservative supporters—I told him 'I hope so.'—That he must realign . . . part of the forces in each party." They spoke about Roosevelt's hope to move millions of people from the city to small farms. The talk for Brandeis was "encouraging. [F.D.R.] has learned much."

Roosevelt had said what Brandeis wanted to hear; that was the Rooseveltian tactic: make few promises, don't bind yourself to any particular approach, keep your options open.

Frankfurter frequently sent off messages to Roosevelt and his aides praising Brandeis's ability, mentioning favorable reactions by Brandeis to Roosevelt statements and policies. Roosevelt did meet with Brandeis on several occasions after his inaugural and reported to Frankfurter after one: "I had a most satisfactory talk with Justice Brandeis before he left. He has and is 'a great soul.' " Brandeis found the early New Deal stimulating: ". . . life in Washington now is stirring, intellectually far more so than I have ever known it. There is much noble thinking and high endeavor; sometimes impatience."

The atmosphere was not always so cordial.

Almost from the time of Roosevelt's election, there was speculation that Frankfurter would be offered a post in the new administration. At first, the talk centered around his being either Attorney General or Solicitor General. When Roosevelt chose Senator Thomas J. Walsh of Montana for Attorney General, the speculation about Frankfurter was limited to the Solicitor General position. But the Solicitor General is in the Justice Department, under the Attorney General, and Walsh did not want Frankfurter, explaining that he opposed "somebody in there who will lose cases in the grand manner." When Walsh died unexpectedly before the inaugural, Homer S. Cummings became Attorney General, and he did not object to Frankfurter.

The incumbent was Thomas D. Thacher, who years earlier had been a tenant in the House of Truth with Frankfurter. "I hear you are to succeed me in this office," he wrote Frankfurter. Frankfurter replied that he had not yet been offered the job and hoped Thacher would not discuss the matter because "The President of the United States is entitled to follow his own ways, and the least any of us can do is not to embarrass his own procedure in carrying out his various tasks by any kind of talk." Raymond Moley, a Roosevelt aide, reported talking to Frankfurter several times about the position.

Still, Frankfurter said that when the offer came it "took me completely off my feet." On March 8, Oliver Wendell Holmes's ninety-second birthday, Frankfurter was having lunch with Holmes, unaware that the President expected him at the White House. When the message finally reached him, Frankfurter told Holmes of the confusion. "Usually," said Holmes, "the White House has the right of way, but it's rather amusing to put the President's nose out of joint."

Frankfurter then joked with Holmes about, in those Prohibition days, the two of them having had sauterne and champagne for lunch. Frankfurter recalled that Holmes looked at him with simulated sternness and said: "Young fellow, I don't want you to misunderstand things: I do not deal with bootleggers but I am open to corruption."

When Frankfurter arrived at the White House late in the afternoon, Roosevelt offered him the Solicitor Generalship. Frankfurter turned it down.

He explained that the job demanded sixteen hours a day, and "It is my genuine conviction . . . that I can do much more to be of use to you by staying in Cambridge than by becoming Solicitor General." Frankfurter had accepted a visiting professorship at Oxford University for the academic year beginning in the fall and did not want to lose that opportunity. Perhaps, also, there was a third reason. Felix Frankfurter was an independent person. He valued his independence and was not ready to give it up.

Roosevelt did not dispute Frankfurter's arguments, but he added another point. "You ought to be on the Supreme Court," he said, "and I want you there." Then Roosevelt listed the problems with putting Frankfurter on the Court: Frankfurter taught law rather than practiced it and had never held judicial office—the only person appointed to the Supreme Court from a professor's chair had been William Howard Taft, but he had had previous experience of interest, having been a judge and President of the United States. Frankfurter had been involved in the Sacco-Vanzetti case. And, third, Frankfurter recalled FDR saying, "this time with a grave countenance, 'your race.' " FDR argued that a period as Solicitor General would eliminate those three problems. There was another side to the "race" problem. Roosevelt had no Jews among his initial cabinet appointments—Henry Morgenthau, Jr., as Secretary of the Treasury came later—and perhaps believed having a representative of that politically muscular group in a prominent position advisable.

Frankfurter discussed the matter with Brandeis, who said Frankfurter's accepting the Solicitor Generalship would be "absurd." Holmes agreed. But Frankfurter's old friend Benjamin Cardozo, a justice of the Supreme Court in 1933, did not. He wanted Frankfurter to accept "not merely because of the arguments that the Court would have from you, but because of the importance of just having you down here these days." Cardozo complained that there were few in Washington capable of thinking on "socio-economic matters" except Brandeis and Frankfurter.

Roosevelt's reported reaction to Frankfurter's refusal of the post was "Felix is a stubborn pig!"

Despite that refusal, Frankfurter was perceived as someone whose closeness and influence with the President continued. The next month, for example, Frankfurter was enlisted to help promote a bureaucrat named J. Edgar Hoover from political appointee to lifetime public servant. Hoover had been named to head the Bureau of Investigation (later called the Federal Bureau of Investigation) in the 1920s by Harlan Fiske Stone, then Attorney General. The Bureau, before that appointment, had been a political mess, but Hoover, with Stone's backing, had operated it free from politics, if also with a flair for publicity and ability to avoid rough challenges to law enforcement.

Hoover was a Republican appointee and Stone, a Supreme Court Justice in 1933, was concerned that, if Hoover was replaced by a Democrat, politics would reenter the Bureau. He wrote Frankfurter: "This, of course, is the kind of matter in which I cannot be active, but I know that you appreciate the dangers which attend an organized police force and how quickly such a force may be degraded if it gets into the hands of the politicians or the usual type of professional policemen."

Over the years, Stone had sent Frankfurter his decisions, waited eagerly for the Harvard professor's comments, and suggested articles for Frankfurter to write. With this background, Frankfurter quickly caught the hint in Stone's letter and gave it directly to Roosevelt. At the White House, Hoover's future was caught in a patronage scuffle; several of FDR's advisers believed a Democrat should head the Bureau of Investigation and take advantage of a number of the job openings that would be created there. But a number of others joined Frankfurter in endorsing Hoover, especially Raymond Moley, and after some months Hoover was named to stay as head of the Bureau; he kept the job for the next thirty years.

During the 1920s, Frankfurter often had lent a helping hand in drafting legislation, and as the Roosevelt administration cranked up, Frankfurter moved within its power circles, offering help, comment, and ideas. He wanted a managed economy, along the lines suggested by the English economist John Maynard Keynes—although this was contrary to the Brandeis philosophy so much a part of his thinking through earlier years. Frankfurter wanted so many things that Adolf A. Berle, Jr., an FDR aide, threw up his hands in despair. "Typically, F. F. comes in at the last minute with many ideas, some very good, none of which could be got into legislative shape in less than a year or got by this Congress," said Berle, "and would like nothing unless he can have everything he wants; but will take no responsibility for getting anything done."

Frankfurter's first major involvement with New Deal legislation was the Securities Act of 1933, his role then establishing the framework for his later activities. One result of the 1929 crash had been a series of investigations, exposés, and shocks demonstrating that Wall Street had manipulated the investing public. Stocks had been touted and sold without regard to their value. If the public had been so gullible as to believe in the integrity of its institutions, the institutions, in turn, had been venal in taking advantage of that trust. Roosevelt, wise enough to refrain from speculation, as governor had described stocks as "a package too often sold only because of the bright colors on the wrapper."

What easterners like Roosevelt had learned in the late 1920s, westerners like Sam Rayburn of Texas had known for years. Before the First World War, Rayburn, with the help of Louis Brandeis, had guided a railroad securities act through the House of Representatives. But it had died in the Senate. Its purpose was to limit speculation and prevent unfair practices by guaranteeing that information about stocks was available to the public.

In 1933, with a President from the East as alarmed about the stock market as he was, Rayburn was confident that this time there was no question that, if properly drawn, a bill would pass Congress; the more responsible Wall Street executives were behind it. The catch was "properly drawn." That meant it had to be agreed on by most parties and be enforceable. That is where Frankfurter came in.

Given the public's disenchantment with Wall Street, the administration probably could have obtained from Congress a stringent bill, which would have pushed the government into the business of examining the soundness of securities issued. Roosevelt and Rayburn sought instead legislation guaranteeing full publicity and information. Armed with knowledge, the buying public could decide for itself.

The first draft of the securities bill went far beyond the informational aspect and would have had the government judge the securities' quality. For that reason, plus the faulty writing of the draft bill, Rayburn had

asked Raymond Moley to find someone to help write a new bill, someone "who knows his stuff." Moley telephoned Frankfurter.

Frankfurter brought in Thomas G. Corcoran, Benjamin V. Cohen,
and James M. Landis, recently appointed Professor of Legislation at
Harvard Law School. "I can recall well the morning of that request,"
Landis wrote some years later. It was a Thursday in early April and
Landis's next classes were scheduled for the following Monday. When
Frankfurter argued that the job required only that weekend, "We con-
sequently left on the night train for Washington."

They worked around the clock to fashion a bill using an English
legislative model. Frankfurter spent little time with them because, said
Landis, of "his preoccupation with other political matters." On Monday
morning they appeared before Rayburn's committee to explain their
new draft; Frankfurter was the spokesman. "He had the copy of the bill
that we had given him the night before, but whether he had read it,
and, if so, how carefully, none of us knew," said Landis.

There was no need for worry. "It was a brilliant performance," said
Landis of Frankfurter's appearance before the committee. "Questions
of detail were referred by him to Cohen and to me, but he handled the
main structure of the bill magnificently."

At Rayburn's request, Frankfurter asked the bill drafters to continue
in Washington. That night Frankfurter returned to Cambridge and
Cohen and Landis stayed on, Landis recalled, "for what I believed
would be only another few days. It became almost two months." Corcoran, already active in Washington, worked with them on nights and
weekends.

During those two months Landis and Cohen lived on the Carlton
Hotel's seventh floor. Above them was J. P. Morgan, Jr., king of Wall
Street, one of those who would be most affected by the Cohen and
Landis bill. "We frequently met in the elevator in the morning or in the
evening," said Landis. "We naturally recognized him, but we passed
unnoticed, happy that our burrowing into the structure of that empire
had no noticeable reverberations above."

Rayburn, chairman of the House Committee on Interstate and Foreign Commerce, was pleased by the bill's progress. "I believe we are
going to be able to get out a good workable bill," he wrote Frankfurter
in Cambridge.

When the House passed the bill, it went to a House-Senate conference committee chaired by Rayburn, who persuaded the group to drop
a Senate version and to adopt the basic House version. Frankfurter then

telegraphed Roosevelt to agree to the Rayburn version: "You may have noticed comment in House debate as to great care with which Rayburn bill was drawn to effectuate your purposes."

Frankfurter's contribution had been bringing together the legislative drafting team of Corcoran, Cohen, and Landis and then urging the President to accept the finished bill. In purpose and scope, the bill was what Franklin Roosevelt and Sam Rayburn wanted. Frankfurter and his friends had done an effective job, but as skilled technicians not creators. That multiplied several times was Frankfurter's role in the New Deal.

Frankfurter did provide another service to the New Deal. He brought the "happy hotdogs" to Washington, the young men to staff the new agencies quickly being created in Washington. The New Deal meant not only the changing of parties in power but the expansion of government. That required bringing to Washington a number of bright, aggressive, and loyal persons to staff the government. The jobs paid adequately—for the depression. That they paid at all, for some, made the salaries excellent. They offered opportunity for achievement and had a romantic lure: involvement in governing the nation. As every administration learns, people seeking jobs are plentiful; people with ability less so. This was particularly true in 1933. When the New Dealers looked to the Democratic party to recruit the party faithful for the new bureaucracy, they found a group, largely, of older, tired, conservative party hacks. The New Deal needed better.

That Frankfurter supplied many of these new young people is not surprising. "Felix Frankfurter had been recommending promising lawyers to Presidents and Justices for many years," recalled Raymond Moley. "Quite naturally, it became routine not only for me but for a number of others to talk with him about men." Many of those Frankfurter had recommended in previous years worked in Wall Street law firms and in Washington during the Hoover administration. "Drop me a line about some really promising youngish men, preferably not from New York or New England, who have come to your notice in the past few years and who might be availed of down here," was a typical request Frankfurter received in those Republican years. He was not the only Harvard Law School professor recommending individuals. Erwin Griswold first came to Washington in the Hoover administration at the recommendation of Professor Austin Scott.

Also, prior to his election, Roosevelt had anticipated recruitment difficulties and used Frankfurter to check out promising persons. "Do you know anything about Mr. Jerome N. Frank?" FDR asked in 1930.

"I am shooting these questions to you merely to line up your opinion on various individuals in connection with the general problem."

There is a dispute over Frankfurter's role in staffing the New Deal. According to one account:

I don't know that there was any particular discussion about bringing new men into the Department of Agriculture. We had one thing after another that needed to be done and we obviously needed a different kind of people than were there to do it so we looked for them. We got many suggestions, of course, from Frankfurter, particularly about lawyers.

And another account:

Felix Frankfurter didn't come into this at all. We never heard of him in Agriculture. He was never much heard of around Washington—that was mostly a fancy. He told me one day at a time when the newspapers were full about his influencing the President that he hadn't seen or communicated with the President at that time for fifteen months.

They came. There was Nathan Ross Margold, who became solicitor for the Interior Department after Harold L. Ickes, the Interior Secretary, spoke with Frankfurter and Brandeis. Margold then asked Frankfurter to help find new people: "You know the type of men I want. I need only add that it is important that most of them be from the western and southwestern United States."

There was Alger Hiss—thin, handsome Harvard Law School graduate, clerk to Justice Holmes; the epitome in appearance and background of the eastern establishment. "He is first rate in every way," said Frankfurter. When Hiss delayed going to Washington—"I had fairly recently come to work for my firm [in New York] and felt a little guilty about pulling out"—Frankfurter wired him, as Hiss recalled, "On basis national emergency, you must accept Jerome Frank's offer." Hiss came.

There was Thomas Corcoran—"Tommy the Cork": energetic, charming, ebullient, almost as brilliant as he was reputed to be; "a person of entire dependability," said Frankfurter to the White House. "I commend him to you warmly." Corcoran and Ben Cohen became the White House's chief errand boys during the 1930s.

There was Charles E. Wyzanski, Jr., also from Harvard Law School. When Senate confirmation of Wyzanski as solicitor for the Labor Department was delayed, Frankfurter telegraphed Corcoran "to get his friends in the Senate behind Mr. Wyzanski."

Those Frankfurter recommended were Jews, Catholics, and Protestants. Some were fresh from law school and others had corporate law backgrounds. They were teachers like James Landis and former teachers like Nathan Margold. They were liberal and conservative, Republican and Democrat. In later years, some, like Corcoran, went on to become wealthy. Others, like Erwin Griswold, who stayed with the Democratic administration on Frankfurter's intercession, crisscrossed between public and academic life.

They were not the only young people marching to the New Deal drummer in the 1930s. Many were graduates of other law schools; Abe Fortas from Yale and William O. Douglas from Columbia are examples. These young people came to a city still southern, "sleepy," its people uncertain of their ability to manage a large nation. They lived in narrow Federalist houses in Georgetown, talked loudly, joked, probably drank too much, partied a great deal, and consumed work voraciously. They created a style: *Here is a problem. What's the solution? No solution! Cut it out. We can handle that. I met somebody at a party the other night who was talking about that very thing. Wait a minute, I'll remember his name.*

The pace was frantic. The solutions often extreme. Some of the newcomers, losing their perspective, drifted off into aimless "isms." Most stayed on course. Eventually the work lost its glamour and became routine. They aged, these young people, gained weight, lost hair, became lost themselves in the gray buildings that housed their agencies. For a few years, however, they had been involved in a noble experiment. The New Deal had been their crusade. If they never found the Holy Grail, at least they had tried. It was a time they could not forget.

Joseph L. Rauh, Jr., reminisced some years later, after a career as a Roosevelt administration official and then as a Washington lawyer defending labor unions, civil liberties, and many government employees against security-risk charges in the McCarthy era. "I would likely be an overstuffed corporate lawyer in my hometown of Cincinnati," said Rauh, "muttering about forced busing and all that damn government regulation of business if a teacher affectionately known as FF hadn't sent me to Washington as one of the Happy Hot Dogs back in the 1930s."

Frankfurter was attacked, in 1933 and in later years, for bringing these people into government, for "masterminding" the New Deal. His critics ignored that he had not checked the politics or religion of those he had recommended, ignored that Washington was desperate for talent, ignored that no one had to use anyone Frankfurter recommended.

Archibald Macleish, a Frankfurter friend, government official, and literary personality, once spoke to that point:

Anyone who seriously wonders why so many of Mr. Frankfurter's students went to Washington when the world fell apart in the thirties and forties has only to consider what teaching of [FF's] kind would mean to a young mind. It was not, as some of Mr. Frankfurter's critics supposed, because he had used the Law School to propagate New Deal philosophy—whatever that may have been. It was because he had used the Law School, as the greatest teachers in the School have always used it, to examine the relation between the law and the living.

14

The German Jews

Felix Frankfurter had an appointment as Eastman Professor at Oxford University from fall 1933 to summer 1934, and the period for him was an interlude, a time to refresh himself intellectually and spiritually. More than a respite, however, the trip offered him the opportunity for a quick visit, his first, to Palestine and brought him closer to the scourge that would so challenge the American, native-born and immigrant, outsider and insider—Adolf Hitler. He believed the trip would "send me back more passionate for what the United States means to me" and joked that the trip was part of "the controlled experiment of proving that the United States can run without F. F."

Frankfurter had loved England since his first visits during and after World War I. Its traditions of law, tolerance, and public service added up, for him, to a successful society. He missed much—the social stratification, the restriction on educational opportunity, the poverty, the militancy of the British unions; these did not exist for him. As he was loyal to his friends, Frankfurter was, as he entered his fifties, loyal to his biases. When the appointment had come, "I felt," he said, "about the first time in my life that there was a Santa Claus."

In his previous visits to England, Frankfurter had not had time to savor the charm of the English countryside and the gentility of the English people. This trip he and Marion, from two-thirty in the afternoon until teatime, "sniff at the new sounds, and sights and smells, for there is the smell of centuries about this place." He found the English "very imaginative in their hospitality."

He gave several lectures and conducted a seminar. "I trounce along in my cap and gown . . . and eat my dinners 'in Hall' and drink my series of tonics and spirits."

"What was truly remarkable was how quickly he made friends," recalled an English acquaintance, "not only with the great of Oxford like the revered Gilbert Murray, but also, by his sure instinct, with men far junior . . . who were destined years afterward to have a profound influence in the circles of humanism."

Between semesters he and Marion spent ten days in London. They had borrowed an apartment overlooking St. James's Park, "two doors from Haldane's old house, and next door to the house in which Palmerston was born." They went to restaurants, the theatre, art galleries, parties. "London does something to me that no other city does—there seems to be so much more vitality, such incessant and boundless streaming of life, with the sudden unexpected retreats of peace," said Frankfurter. Marion summed it up better, telling him that for the first time since the war he had "a complete loaf for ten days."

A high point was a discussion, more a debate, on the American Constitution between Frankfurter, George Bernard Shaw, the Socialist and playwright, and Sir William Beveridge, former head of the London School of Economics. Frankfurter spoke of how the New Deal had to be devised within the restraints of the American Constitution. Beveridge commented on the difficulties of that process, and Shaw leaped on that to launch a criticism of the American Constitution, calling for its elimination. As Shaw continued, Frankfurter whispered to a friend: "The Lord hath delivered him into my hands."

Frankfurter's response is not recorded, but Harold Laski, who was present, described it as "a triumph," continuing: "It's not everybody who can make an audience feel that, e.g., poor Bernard Shaw is, of course, very bright and brilliant as a rule, but that this is one of his off-days."

For many years, Frankfurter enjoyed telling of his encounter with Shaw. "I can't report it honestly without seeming immodest," he said, "but I must tell you that I made mincemeat of him."

In his first Oxford lecture, October 10, 1933, Frankfurter spoke of Nazi Germany. "In England, happily," he said, "the most precious conquest of civilization—the free pursuit of reason—is still taken for granted," and it had been possible "to assume that this condition of civilized life had become the settled habit at least of the Western World." But in Germany the Nazi government already was moving against the universities. "The land that was once the proud home of academic freedom," said Frankfurter, "and, indeed, gave it its honorable technical name, has made outcasts of its citizens of distinguished learning for no other reason than the accident of birth, or for the possession of beliefs to which they were led by reflection and scholarship." In Germany, Frankfurter said, academic freedom had become a "mischievous toy and a menace to the new revolution."

Frankfurter became a one-man, unofficial intelligence agency. Government officials, journalists, friends, Jews and non-Jews, stopped by to see him at Oxford, and Frankfurter sent his friend in the White House telegrams and letters, copies of editorials and articles about the Jews' plight in Germany.

Frankfurter soon understood more clearly than many the situation of the German Jews. "There is no doubt that the Jew in Germany is doomed," wrote Frankfurter in the spring of 1934, a time when few wished to accept that statement. "The home of Goethe and Schiller and Lessing has in the completest possible fashion rejected those conceptions of reason and science and a common humanity which were until last year deemed the most precious achievements of civilization."

Frankfurter commented: "Palestine is undoubtedly the most promising place for settlement by the German Jews."

Although Frankfurter, with Brandeis, had withdrawn from his public Zionist activities in the early 1920s, he had never ceased being a Zionist. Much had happened to the Zionist dream and the British promise of a Jewish homeland in Palestine since the time of Woodrow Wilson, the Balfour Declaration, and the Paris Peace Conference; most of it unfortunate for the Jews. The homeland had not materialized. Its promised boundaries had shrunk as the British bought off Arab dissenters with land. The prospects for peace had diminished as the British had given up attempting to quell the violence, blaming it on whichever side was politically weakest at the moment. England had promised the Jews a homeland in Palestine for three reasons: Christian morality, a desire to control the Middle East, and the need to bring the United States into the First World War. With the second and third reasons accomplished, the first was, if not forgotten, ignored.

Frankfurter wrote to Julian Mack for Zionist funds to finance an airplane trip to Palestine. Mack then asked Brandeis to underwrite the costs. "I assume Felix goes to Palestine in the Zionist interest (Had not heard of the project)," Brandeis responded. He told Mack to forward the funds and promised to send a check "when I know the exact amount." Brandeis continued: "I am surprised Felix is short of cash. Of course, he has spent much cabling, telegraphing and the like—but I have for years made him an allowance of $3,500 for public purposes."

Because of his activities during and immediately after the First World War, Frankfurter deserved to be called a father of the Jewish development in Palestine. So his arrival there was almost a time of the wanderer returning home. "Pesach in Jerusalem, who would have thought it," he wrote his sister Ella.

To another he described Palestine as "a most exciting land—its beauty is magical and the achievements of the Jewish renaisance almost incredible." In a few days he was meeting people, asking questions, trying to understand. Once when visiting an Arab sheik, while sipping coffee, Frankfurter admired a woven place mat on the wall. The sheik, following Arab custom, immediately insisted the embarrassed Frank- furters accept the place mat as a gift. Outside, Marion smiled at her husband and said, "Felix, you admired the wrong place mat."

Frankfurter was in Palestine long enough to rhapsodize about "the reclamation of what was desolate and infertile and squalid [which] make a combination of the glories of the past and the triumphs and hopes of the present quite unique."

His fascination with Palestine had been Brandeis's and also that of many Jews who visit the land of their religion's birth. Whatever their own status in life, in whatever nation they are citizens, those few square miles on the Mediterranean Sea intrigue them. Here men and women turned from the gods of hate and destruction to a God of love, justice, and peace, from a life of licentiousness and the power of physical strength to one of discipline and law. Here began the civilization of the intellect and the personal relationship. If this civilized level of life did not become an attainment of the modern world, at least it became a goal. This was the Biblical Jews' contribution, the definition of that goal. And now thousands of years later they were making a new contribution: the desert bloomed again, the land fed the hungry, provided a home. "I suspect there is no place in the world at present," said Frankfurter, "where there is a comparable happiness from the achievement of build- ing a worthy civilization."

For Marion Frankfurter the year away was less of an idyll. At Oxford, Frankfurter was so busy that "in order that Marion and I may see each other, she has asked me—to use her own words—'like other people, for an appointment.' " She had her dinner invitations and her own friend- ships—a lifestyle much like the Harvard years, constantly being the faculty wife, being known and accepted for the one she had married and not for herself.

Often ill since the mid-1920s, in England she developed new health problems. During the summer she had pains in her hip; they reap- peared during the ocean crossing, and again at Oxford. The Frankfurt- ers' English physician contacted her American doctor, who said that

Marion Frankfurter "represents the highly organized, thoroughbred type who might easily win the Derby, but would be more bothered by one fly on her back than a cart horse would be by a hundred."

Commented one of her physicians: "I found it always important to remember with her that emotion and apprehension and desire played perhaps a very considerable part in her symptoms." And another: "I have had a long talk with her and her husband, and can, I think, appreciate the great strain they have both been through in anticipation of their visit to Oxford, and I am surprised on the whole that she had stood that strain without more disablement, especially in view of the history of previous breakdowns."

Perhaps because of the ten days they spent in London, away from the academic setting, Marion not being seen only as her husband's adjunct, the ailment, an abcess on her hip, faded and an operation was not needed. "It was all very queer," commented her husband.

Her health problems would be a constant in the relationship between Felix and Marion Frankfurter. Eventually they became *the* constant in their relationship.

The year abroad, actually ten months, came to an end in June 1934. Harold Laski wrote to Brandeis that Frankfurter not only had done a superb job but had a restful time and gained "refreshment and new courage." He added a line: "If I judge aright that these next months are decisive for F.D.R.'s choice of objective, Felix will be far more influential now that if he had been consistently in the midst of such cloud-hidden matters."

While Frankfurter had been away, the New Deal had changed, not in its goals but in the relationships of the power structure. During the campaign, after the election, and during the first few months of the Roosevelt administration, there had been a camaraderie. All were in it together, experimenting, working, expounding ideas.

Roosevelt was readily available in those early days. "He could listen when he wanted to, and he had the knack of making the person doing the talking feel important," Bernard Baruch recalled. "He concentrated on his visitor, and he seldom disagreed. While listening, the President had a habit of smiling and nodding his head. The uninitiated naturally took this to mean that the President was in full agreement with what they were saying." He was not, of course. But those who came away believing the President was sympathetic toward their particular programs did not understand when the plans were jettisoned a few weeks later.

Rejected, they tried to reargue their cases with the President; but as the New Deal grew, more people sought access to the President and he had less time to hear their arguments, calm their angers, soothe their egos. The disappointed did not understand what was happening; they looked for enemies, those thwarting their plans.

Roosevelt realized he was losing advisors whose loyalty was to a philosophy and not to him. Frankfurter was not one of those, however. He had turned down an appointment in the administration. He had brought his friend Brandeis together with FDR but had not stalked out in anger when Roosevelt did not follow Brandeis's advice. Frankfurter recommended certain approaches, gave advice; if this was not accepted, he shrugged it off. He believed in Franklin Roosevelt and his overall goals rather than the popular recovery theories of the time. "I am by temperament not an ideologue," he said, "but a stark empiricist." He was the kind of person Roosevelt needed.

Perhaps for that reason, although thousands of miles away, Frankfurter was attacked as one of the New Deal powers. "One objective of the general attack is a drive on so-called radicals," Tommy Corcoran reported to him, ". . . and has become particularly virulent against you." Frankfurter, his time up in England, hurried home.

In Washington controversy centered around the Supreme Court. The first change in the Court's makeup since the 1920s had been the replacement by President Hoover early in 1930 of the ailing Chief Justice Taft with Charles Evans Hughes. Hughes's return to the Court surprised some people, Brandeis among them. But, if surprised, Brandeis also was pleased; he and Hughes were old friends.

Felix Frankfurter, at Harvard then, had hoped that Associate Justice Harlan Fiske Stone would be named Chief Justice and was unhappy when the position went to Hughes. Since Hughes's defeat for the presidency in 1916, he had moved back and forth between successful corporate practice and government service, and also had spoken for liberal causes. But this was not sufficient for Frankfurter, who considered Hughes a bad example to law school students. "Hughes ought to be free from the need of making money," Frankfurter grumbled in 1929, "and ought to serve as an example to younger men by not taking every case in which there is a big retainer." In opposing the Hughes appointment the next year, Frankfurter realized he was disagreeing with Brandeis, "which makes me doubly unhappy."

The next change was the replacement of Edward Sanford by Owen J. Roberts, also in 1930. President Hoover had first nominated John J.

Parker, a federal judge from West Virginia, but the Senate had refused to confirm him. Roberts was confirmed easily. He was a Republican from Philadelphia, so Republican senators accepted him; he also had uncovered much wrongdoing by Republicans in his investigation of the Teapot Dome scandal in the 1920s, so the Democrats were for him.

The third change was the retirement of Holmes. For seventy years, approximately one-half of the nation's history, Holmes had been soldier, scholar, teacher, lawyer, and judge, state and federal. On January 11, 1932, Chief Justice Hughes met with "the Magnificent Yankee" to suggest he resign. "This was for me a highly disagreeable duty," said Hughes, "but Justice Holmes received my suggestion . . . without the slightest indication of his resentment or opposition." Hughes had first discussed the situation with Brandeis, who agreed that his elderly friend —Holmes was nearing the end of his ninety-first year—had reached the point where he no longer could keep up with the Court's work. After Hughes had left with Holmes's resignation complete, Brandeis visited with the man who had been his friend for half a century, since that time they had drunk beer and champagne together to celebrate the opening of the Warren-Brandeis law office.

Because the day Holmes resigned was a Sunday and Holmes had a decision to announce the next day, the resignation was dated January 12, after Holmes gave his last decision from the bench.

Benjamin Nathan Cardozo, a New York Court of Appeals judge, was the candidate of the scholarly legal community to replace Holmes. Through the years his decisions and his extrajudicial writings had outlined the judge's work, the freedom he had and the limitations. But there were problems with Cardozo. One was that he was from New York, and the Court already had two New Yorkers, Hughes and Stone; the second was that he was a Jew, and the Court already had Brandeis.

Cardozo and Frankfurter were friends of many years; Cardozo had officiated at Frankfurter's marriage. As far back as 1916, Frankfurter had spoken of Cardozo's being appointed to the Supreme Court but assumed he would not be because Brandeis had just been named. "I wish [Cardozo] were a Roman Catholic or an Irishman or something irrelevantly relevant to the appointment," Frankfurter lamented at the time.

When the Holmes seat opened in 1932, Frankfurter's letters and meetings with his old friend Henry Stimson, then Hoover's Secretary of State, and with Associate Justice Stone, a Hoover confidant, contributed to their taking Cardozo's case before the President. However, the appointment probably would have gone to Cardozo without Frankfurter's involvement. Two years earlier, in a conversation with Brandeis, Hoover had spoken favorably about the possibility of appointing Cardozo, and both Stimson and Stone had been willing to recommend Cardozo without Frankfurter's urging.

Because both Brandeis and Cardozo were classified as "liberals" and undoubtedly because both were Jewish, the expectation was that they would become close on the Court. That was not to be. The two men had a cooperative relationship, and they often voted the same way, but there was no conviviality. Cardozo, a bachelor who lived with grace and taste, could not reconcile himself to the austerity of the Brandeis lifestyle or with the restlessness of the Brandeis thinking process. Frankfurter spoke of the two men's differences in temperament and in "propulsive energy."

With the Cardozo appointment in 1932, the Supreme Court was cast for the New Deal era. There were three liberals: Brandeis, Stone, and Cardozo; and four conservatives: Pierce Butler, James McReynolds, George Sutherland, and Willis Van Devanter—the "four horsemen" they were called. There were two justices moving between the liberal and conservative camps: Roberts, the Republican who had prosecuted Republicans and had ambitions perhaps beyond the Court itself; and Chief Justice Hughes, whose political skills were an important attribute during the 1930s for a court keyed to both law and politics, and also with Republican credentials going back decades.

The "four horsemen" assisted occasionally by either Roberts or Hughes produced a majority to block Roosevelt's progressivism. In the resulting turmoil, Brandeis, in the last decade of his life, was involved perhaps as he never before had been, as was Frankfurter.

15

Powers Behind the Presidential Throne

"The secret of the Administration's tenacity, ingenuity and boldness depends to a great extent on four men . . . two of whom happen to be Jews and two professors," according to a popular 1934 book, *The New Dealers*. Brandeis and Frankfurter were the Jews referred to by the author.

Newspaper accounts agreed. "The Frankfurter influence at Washington," said one, "is a masterpiece of remote control." Another: "The voluntary codes reflect Brandeis's deep concern for industrial cooperation." And: Brandeis is the person of "some deeper and more mature mind" on whom Roosevelt relied. Finally, in a magazine: Frankfurter "is the most influential single individual in the United States."

Dorothy Thompson, a columnist in the 1930s, told Frankfurter: "At present you are, as you must be aware, the *bête noire* of the reactionaries." And Grenville Clark, a New York lawyer, friend to Roosevelt and Frankfurter, wrote the President: "I like many things you are doing and spend a fair amount of my time saying so. Also I spend considerable time sticking up for Felix, as to whom many people, otherwise fairly sane, have a real neurosis."

None of the principals took the talk too seriously. At the White House, Brandeis was referred to as "Isaiah," and Felix and Marion Frankfurter joked about Felix's closeness to the President. In 1936 Marion was visiting relatives in California and Felix was at the White House. She wrote him: "Mother tells me that if I mail this letter addressed to the White House, everybody in town will know it—and then what? Say I, will the Ku Klux come and get us tonight? What the hell, it's no disgrace to be at the White House. But maybe I won't send it that way."

That characterization of the two men continued in history books; Brandeis and Frankfurter wrestling with New Dealers—usually Rexford G. Tuxwell, Raymond Moley, and Adolf Berle—for Franklin Roosevelt's legislative soul.

That "power-behind-the-throne" interpretation of history suggests that the New Deal was the inspired invention of a relatively small elite group, which manipulated the government to adopt liberal measures, and that Roosevelt's legislative recommendations were a result of what he heard from the last person standing behind him. This interpretation ignores that most legislation results from years of trial-and-error, a demonstration of need, and the efforts and interplay of countless people. New Deal legislation was no different. The drive for securities legislation, for example, had origins going back at least twenty years and took its immediate motivation from the 1929 stock-market collapse.

Another example is the National Industrial Recovery Act, NIRA, signed into law in June 1933. It also had multiple origins. Its system of developing codes—allowing industry to manipulate prices in exchange for certain benefits to the employee and the consumer—went back to World War I's War Labor Policies Board, with both Roosevelt and Frankfurter as members. Another origin was the nation's businessmen themselves; a number thought along those lines prior to FDR's election. Perhaps the act's major impetus was its promise of quickly bolstering the economy and benefiting the owner and the worker at the same time.

A third example is the Tennessee Valley Authority. Proposals for reclaiming the Tennessee River Valley, to restore the land, provide cheap electric power, and provide inexpensive fertilizer for farmers had been bruited about extensively in the 1920s. Roosevelt's genius was to bring these ideas together in one program that could pass Congress; although he was the ultimate authority for the contents of the legislation, neither he, nor anyone on his staff, had originated the proposals.

Another point ignored by the power-behind-the-throne interpretation is that Roosevelt "needed people, too," as James MacGregor Burns wrote, "and he reached out for them." He pulled from a Tugwell and a Frankfurter, a Moley and a Brandeis, and anyone else around at the time. The power was in the throne itself.

Why then do Brandeis and Frankfurter have the reputations they do? They were active in the New Deal, especially Frankfurter, but so were others. They were influential, and at times persuasive. But dozens of people wandered through the White House in the 1930s, a friend of someone or one with an introduction from somebody—influential and persuasive.

There are two reasons for the prominence of Brandeis and Frankfurter. First, they were visible. When Roosevelt entered the White House in 1933, Brandeis already was a historical figure, a crusader for social causes in the century's earlier years, the controversial Wilson appointee to the Supreme Court, the author of decisions and dissents that made Wall Street shudder, the writer of articles, pamphlets, and books criticizing bankers and trusts. All this made Brandeis an easy target. When Hugh S. Johnson spoke on the radio about his troubled leadership of a New Deal agency and said, "During this whole tense experience, I have been in constant touch with that old counselor, Judge Louis Brandeis," Brandeis's name was quickly recognized.

Frankfurter was equally well known. In the 1930s he was remembered for his role in the Bisbee, Mooney, and Sacco-Vanzetti cases, known for his writings in *The New Republic* and other publications, and considered one of the nation's most prominent law professors. When William Randolph Hearst, the newspaper publisher, spoke of the "Frankfurter radicals" in the New Deal, all knew to whom he referred.

The second reason is that they were Jews. The United States had been through an anti-Semitic binge in the 1920s and was entering a new one in the 1930s. The religious bigotry, and with it a racial and ethnic bias, had come out of the country-club closet.

Henry Ford, the automobile industrialist, had spent millions of dollars disseminating the theory of a secret society of Jews attempting to dominate the world, "the Elders of Zion." Whatever A. Lawrence Lowell's motives for wanting a religious quota at Harvard, the device had caught on at other colleges for reasons of blatant anti-Semitism. Industries did not hire Jews. Home owners signed restrictive covenants agreeing not to sell to them. Rabblerousers like Father Charles E. Coughlin turned anti-Semitism into a political tactic. The New Deal became the "Jew Deal." and Brandeis and Frankfurter—influential in Washington, friends of the prominent, believed to have FDR's ear—became the prime targets of the haters.

Brandeis did not condescend to the situation. Frankfurter, never possessing the self-assurance of the older man, was candid about his concerns. When his friend Archibald MacLeish wrote an article about the New Dealers, Frankfurter wrote to him: "When I see you, I want to put to you the implications of generalizations like yours in these days when ritual murder tales and the Protocols of the Elders of Zion are again gaining considerable currency, indeed are receiving more credulity than at any other time in recent history. It seems to me you throw adjectives about Jews around with too ready a belief in the basis of racial generalizations." When a rabbi wrote Frankfurter that many of the attacks against him were "beginning to assume an anti-Jewish tinge," Frankfurter replied that "my ideas and work . . . will have to speak for themselves."

But if Louis Brandeis and Felix Frankfurter were not the powers-behind-the-throne they have been reported to be, if they were not the wrestlers struggling for FDR's legislative soul, what was their influence? What did they accomplish?

In the 1930s, Brandeis lived on California Street in northwest Washington, where he had moved in 1926, continuing the austere style he had made so much the way of his life. The furniture was rarely replaced. Art objects did not exist. Clothing was utilitarian but not stylish. He steadfastly refused to buy an automobile. "I cannot recall a single beautiful or distinctive object in the apartment," said Marquis Childs, the newspaper reporter. And Brandeis continued to give away his money. In 1934, 1935, and 1936, he gave more than $100,000 to Jewish charities and Zionist activities, $20,000 to educational institutions, and $25,000 to relatives and friends.

Despite the austere lifestyle, an invitation to a Brandeis tea or dinner was still sought after. "I would say that he was the least seclusive of the justices," reported Marquis Childs. In those gatherings he was thought of as influencing the young people in Washington, moving among them, finding out what they were doing, his success in disseminating his philosophy equal to his success in persuading them to his ways. And many young persons came to bask in the glow of being near the venerable Brandeis. William Douglas, then working with the Securities and Exchange Commission, has written of how, before he had come to Washington, he had been influenced by Brandeis's writings and of how, while in Washington, he enjoyed being in the Brandeis presence.

But the influence was reciprocal. Brandeis learned from these young people. Contrary to what Marquis Chiles reported, Brandeis lived a secluded life in the 1930s. He did not watch movies or go to the theatre; he rarely accepted invitations to go out—even turning down social events at the White House. Charles Burlingham, an acquaintance for many years, commented of Brandeis: "I could almost call myself intimate with him but I don't know if there was anybody who could be intimate with him except his own family. He was very much alone in the world."

But Brandeis thrived on new people and their ideas, ways of doing things, and their varied viewpoints. He shared with them his knowledge, experience, and moral perspective, but he received much in exchange. "He kept up in the world, and the reason he was so young mentally when he was in his eighties, was that he kept replacing his friendships and acquaintances, you might say," reported one law clerk.

In the early days of the New Deal, the tendency was to accept bigness in industry and government. This was the direct opposite of the Brandeis philosophy. To him the ideal world continued as close as the United States could come in the twentieth century to the Jeffersonian vision of the small farmer and mechanic of the early nineteenth. Even then, as Brandeis was described as fathering the New Deal, he was concerned by its direction. The discerning understood this. Max Lerner wrote in 1935 that, although Brandeis was "most often mentioned" as "the philosopher behind the New Deal. . . . He is still in opposition."

At times Brandeis grumbled to his friends. He vowed to Jerome Frank that he would vote against New Deal proposals on the Court. In 1935, after doing just that, Brandeis, "visibly excited and deeply agitated," met with Tommy Corcoran and Ben Cohen. "You must see that Felix understands the situation and explains it to the President," Brandeis said. "You must also explain it to the men Felix brought into the Government. . . . The President has been living in a fool's paradise."

But at other times Brandeis could be rhapsodic. He had plans "to make men free," explaining that "The Government is to impose limitations in order to achieve that object." He envisioned cutting deeply into the nation's banking system to restructure society.

Brandeis urged specific legislation in two areas. One traced back to his interest years earlier in regularity of employment; he had been impressed then with how an employer, by planning, could guarantee a full year's work. Why not extend that philosophy during the depression through unemployment compensation?

In 1932, Wisconsin had enacted the first unemployment-compensation measure; it placed the onus for unemployment upon the individual company. The company's payment to an unemployment fund was based on its history of unemployment: more unemployment, more money paid into the fund; less unemployment, less money paid into the fund. That same year, 1932, a six-state commission on unemployment insurance (organized the previous year by Governor Franklin Roosevelt of New York) endorsed the Wisconsin plan. A United States Senate Committee was also enthusiastic, and the Democratic party endorsed unemployment compensation in its national platform. In 1933, unemployment-compensation bills passed at least one house in each of seven states, but none was enacted, for two reasons: because of disagreement about details and because of the argument following this kind of legislation through the years—if one state passed such a law, adding costs to doing business in that state, it would lose business to those states that did not have such a law.

Brandeis favored the Wisconsin plan. Not only did it place responsibility on the employer, where he believed it belonged, but the plan's chief advocates were his daughter Elizabeth and her husband, Paul Raushenbush, both economists in Wisconsin. The difficulty with the plan, however, was the presumption that unemployment was the individual employer's responsibility. Others, watching the depression widen, believed unemployment was caused by economic and political factors beyond any single employer's control.

In 1932, Senator Robert F. Wagner of New York had proposed allowing a company to deduct its payment under a state unemployment-benefits law from its federal income tax. That concept had not generated much interest because it seemed to add apples and oranges, crediting one kind of state tax, the unemployment tax, against another kind of federal tax, the income tax.

In the summer of 1933, Paul and Elizabeth Raushenbush, while vacationing with Brandeis at Cape Cod, were discussing the problem when the justice reminded them that the Supreme Court already had permitted an apples and apples approach. The Court, in a 1927 decision, *Florida* v. *Mellon,* had allowed the crediting of state inheritance taxes against federal inheritance taxes. This encouraged states to enact inheritance taxes. The analogy was obvious: Let the federal government enact a national unemployment tax on employers but give credit to funds paid by those employers to a state unemployment tax. The result would be to encourage states to pass unemployment-tax programs.

Brandeis agreed with that approach. Although it gave more authority to the federal government than he would have liked, he saw the alternative as having no bill or one giving the federal government total control. He discussed it with his friends, including A. Lincoln Filene, a Boston businessman who had been associated with him in reform activities thirty years earlier. In late December 1933, Filene explained the approach to a number of government officials at a meeting in Filene's daughter's Washington apartment.

Brandeis was not at that meeting, but he made no secret of his interest. He sent information about the plan to government officials and discussed it with as many people as possible, including President Roosevelt. In June 1934, the two men met for an hour and fifteen minutes at the White House. Before the President was a plan giving the federal government total control. Roosevelt was not enthusiastic about it, but he kept his thoughts to himself. "Isaiah did not like the scheme in the Skipper's mind . . ." Tommy Corcoran reported. "The Skipper gave the impression that there was nothing as yet cut and dried about the scheme and that it was all in the making."

Brandeis had not played a decisive role. As enacted, the unemployment-compensation program did not place responsibility for unemployment upon the individual employer, as he had hoped, but rather established a system of statewide reserves to which all employers contributed regardless of their unemployment record. The program was not one of the total federal control, although indirectly through the tax-abatement scheme the federal government absorbed the cost and exercised some influence over the state program. Paul Freund, close to Brandeis then, described his reaction to the final bill as "disappointed."

The second area of particular concern to Brandeis and one with which he has become associated was public works. Early in 1933 he suggested a massive public-works project, including reforestation and control of water sources. Brandeis argued that the plan would directly result in two million people going to work immediately and another million or two indirectly, "and would turn many a wheel now idle." The costs would be met, according to Brandeis, by closing tax loopholes and by an inheritance tax.

Brandeis outlined the proposal in a letter to Frankfurter, hoping Frankfurter would bring it to the attention of the White House. Frankfurter spoke of it to Moley, and then badgered Moley to meet with Brandeis. "I do recall clearly the discussion I had with the old Justice," said Moley, "and some painful recollection of the very hard chair on which I squirmed while Brandeis presented his views."

Even then, early in the New Deal, a "palace-intrigue" atmosphere was developing within the Roosevelt circle. For many people, working with Roosevelt was their chance for power, their opportunity to influence the nation's course, their time to earn a listing in the history books. They became suspicious, then jealous, of anyone seeking the President's time and energy.

Moley had disliked Frankfurter since the early 1920s, when Frankfurter was involved in the Cleveland crime study for the Cleveland Foundation, headed by Moley. The more Frankfurter approached

Moley in 1933 with ideas and requests, the more Moley's dislike increased.

In his meeting with Brandeis, Moley did not respond to the public-works proposal, but privately he called the Brandeis-Frankfurter plan (he regarded the two men as one) "vague and impractical." He continued: "For anyone, perhaps with the exception of people who had spent their lives reading legal abstractions, could see that public works of such magnitude could not possibly be useful in meeting an emergency. Their views of financing such works by plugging loopholes in the tax law and by waiting for the super-rich to die, despite the distinction of their source, were frivolous to the point of absurdity."

The New Deal did adopt the public-works approach but again Brandeis had not been decisive. Many had recommended it and Roosevelt had been considering it as a make-work process for those for whom unemployment compensation had run out. Funding did not come from specified sources, as Brandeis had recommended, but from general revenue.

These activities of Brandeis were extrajudicial. Through the years, as these activities have been reported or talked about, a question continues to nag: With this kind of activity, did Brandeis act in a manner improper for a Supreme Court justice?

When the Constitution was written, several proposals were made to have Supreme Court justices assume extrajudicial activities; all were defeated. At the same time, however, nothing was included in the Constitution prohibiting such activities. One analysis has suggested that "many of the framers expected judges to make off-the-court contributions to the government, and furthermore that they viewed such a prospect favorably," believing that the judges "had a wisdom which should not be limited to adjudication." Although the intention of the Constitution's authors may be in dispute, the actions of the justices have not been. Since the nation's beginning, they have been involved in extrajudicial activities.

There are two kinds of extrajudicial activities, public and private. Examples of the public are the personal political campaigning of John McLean, an associate justice in the 1800s, and Salmon P. Chase, Chief Justice after the Civil War; both had sought a presidential nomination. Justice Joseph P. Bradley served on the Electoral Commission of 1877 to resolve the question of who had been elected President in 1876. Brandeis's Zionist activities are another example. More recent examples are Justice Robert H. Jackson's acting as chief prosecutor at the

Nuremberg war crimes trials after World War II, Chief Justice Earl Warren's chairing the commission investigating the assassination of President Kennedy, and Justice William O. Douglas's lobbying to protect the environment. Because those activities were public, the nation's citizens had the opportunity to determine whether they violated judicial propriety, to criticize the justices if necessary, and perhaps to consider whether legislative curbs on such activities were necessary. Brandeis's Zionist activities, well reported at the time, never produced any criticism of him for taking on that activity as an outside endeavor.

Private activities are, however, another matter. Because they are not generally known, even though not prohibited, the nation's citizens cannot make a judgment about them. These private activities also have a lengthy tradition. John Jay, the first Chief Justice, advised President George Washington. The contents of the Dred Scott decision were leaked to the White House by Supreme Court justices. Oliver Wendell Holmes discussed his decisions at White House dinners and advised Presidents on appointments. In 1918, Justice Willis Van Devanter redrafted a bill in detail for an assistant attorney general and told him: "If I thought there was any impropriety in this note I would not write it, but I will prefer that you regard it as personal to you."

William Howard Taft did not permit his position as Chief Justice to deter him from involvement in the Harding and Coolidge administrations. He advised President Harding on messages to Congress and was one of those helping to extricate the Republicans from the Teapot Dome scandals. He tried to persuade Calvin Coolidge to run for reelection and opposed the nomination of Herbert Hoover. When the Chief Justice wrote in detail of his activities to Horace Taft, his brother, Horace responded: "It seems to me that you and the president are a good deal closer than most Presidents and Chief Justices." Harlan Fiske Stone, who served on the Court as an associate justice from the 1920s through the New Deal era, planted articles in news media, one at least sharply criticizing a fellow justice; lobbied for presidential appointments; was an advisor to President Hoover as a member of his "medicine ball" cabinet; and dropped hints on legislative constitutionality in cocktail-party tidbits. Chief Justice Charles Evans Hughes advised the Republican congressional leadership in the early 1930s.

If Brandeis was not sitting above the clouds and looking tolerantly upon the follies of the world, as the journalists claimed, he was never involved in Washington politics with the detail of Van Devanter or with the frequency of Taft or Stone, although he did retain strong opinions about contemporary politics. In 1924, when Robert La Follette asked him to join his third-party ticket as the vice-presidential candidate, Brandeis refused, although tempted. "If I had several watertight compartment lives," he wrote his brother, "I should have liked to be in it. The enemies are vulnerable and the time ripe."

In June 1916, after Hughes resigned from the Court to run for President, Brandeis, a justice only two weeks then, urged Thomas Gregory on President Wilson as a replacement. Wilson did not accept the recommendation. Such recommendations were not unusual. Harlan Fiske Stone was appointed to the Court after Chief Justice Taft told President Coolidge that Stone "was the strongest man that he could secure in New York that was entitled to the place."

Perhaps the most extreme example of sitting justices' involving themselves in judicial appointments is Van Devanter's and Taft's efforts to fill a vacancy in 1922. The two justices wanted John W. Davis but feared he would turn down the nomination. Justice Van Devanter wrote Davis, then practicing law in New York, that if Davis wanted the nomination, Chief Justice Taft "at an appropriate time and in an appropriate way" would inform the President. Davis turned Van Devanter down because he did not wish to give up the economic rewards of a successful private practice. Van Devanter and Taft then determined that the nomination should go to Pierce Butler of Minnesota, whose conservatism they admired.

Van Devanter wrote his friends in Minnesota, asking them to begin a letter-writing campaign in support of Butler: "If the president of your State University and some others in like station are disposed to commend Mr. Butler, it probably would be helpful for them to do so . . . not as if there were a campaign in his behalf, but rather along the lines of voluntary suggestions and commendations by thoughtful persons interested in the maintenance of high standards." Butler was a Catholic, and Chief Justice Taft suggested that he have the archbishop of the diocese write to the President, "and the sooner they are sent, the better." He also detailed to Butler the members of the Senate Judiciary Committee, who should be "properly primed," and Taft promised to "attend to" one of the senators himself.

So there were no rules to define whether Brandeis's extrajudicial activities were improper, only traditions which he did not push beyond accepted bounds. He has been described as one of the most extrajudicially active judges in the Court's history, but against the activities of his brethren—those preceding him, contemporaneous with him, and following him—that description becomes an exaggeration.

Also, more to the point, his extrajudicial activities, his comments to associates like Corcoran, Cohen, and Frankfurter, and his supposed "influence" on the young New Dealers at teas and dinners in his apartment were *ad hoc*. Brandeis was an associate justice of the Supreme Court, and his influence and power with the New Deal must be measured by how he fulfilled that responsibility.

The New Dealers anticipated much from Brandeis. As they developed their programs and jockeyed for "palace-guard" positions after Roosevelt's election, they found strength in Brandeis's dissent early in the year in *New State Ice Co.* v. *Liebmann*, when he spoke about the needs for states "and the Nation" to remold economic practices. An Oklahoma statute required ice-plant operators to be licensed. A licensed company was spending $500,000 to build a new plant when a second company, unlicensed, moved in, and claimed—citing the due-process clause of the Fourteenth Amendment—that its economic rights were denied if the state said it couldn't operate.

In a 6-2 decision, the Supreme Court upheld the second company, denying Oklahoma the right to license ice plants. The majority decision, written by George Sutherland, conceded that businesses were subject to regulation, but said the question was "whether the business is so charged with a public use as to justify the particular restriction."

Brandeis's dissent, joined by Harlan Fiske Stone, partly repeated the "reasonableness" argument he had been advancing for years—if the Oklahoma legislature wanted to regulate manufacture of ice because of the state's climate, that was the state's business. Stone joined him for this reason. "While I doubt the wisdom and efficacy of much attempted regulation of business," he told a friend, "I think those are questions to be determined by the legislature and not by the Supreme Court."

Brandeis went beyond that point, however. First, in the midst of a depression and with the nation's economy disintegrating, he considered adding a warning. "We may not forget," said Brandeis in an early version of his dissent, "that if States are denied the power to prevent the harmful entry of a few individuals into a business, government ownership may close it altogether to private enterprise." Brandeis dropped that in the final version, apparently not willing to raise the threat of state ownership. But he did include his support for government's power to remold economic practices. "I cannot believe that the framers of the Fourteenth Amendment, or the States which ratified it," he said, "intended to deprive us of the power to correct the evils of technological unemployment and excess of productive capacity which have attended progress in the useful arts."

He closed with the warning: "If we would guide by the light of reason, we must let our minds be bold." He had used that same phrase in an earlier decision, then more as a joke. Now he was serious, and the New Dealers believed he would support them in their boldness.

But those intrigued by Brandeis's boldness forgot his bias against bigness. They shouldn't have; in addition to preaching against bigness in private, he also had done so from the bench. Since 1840, Pennsylvania taxed corporations more heavily than individuals in similar businesses. The Supreme Court in 1928 declared the Pennsylvania statute unconstitutional, ruling that a corporation is entitled to the same legal protection as are individuals—that it could not be taxed more heavily. Brandeis and Holmes dissented, Brandeis upholding a state's right to enact a tax structure advantageous to the individual entrepreneur.

Brandeis's passion to defend the small businessman against the large corporation was stated more strongly in 1933, in *Liggett Co. v. Lee.* Florida had imposed an "anti-chain-store" tax to protect independent merchants from chain-store competition. The more stores a chain had, the more warehouses and other installations, the more county lines crossed, the higher the chain's taxes. The state courts had upheld the law.

The Supreme Court reversed, in a 6-3 decision by Owen Roberts, calling the state law "unreasonable and arbitrary." The nation was then in the depths of the depression, and Brandeis could not resist the opportunity to speak in his dissent on more than the law. After saying the law was within the state's powers, his reasonableness argument again, he branched out. Quoting from the liberal bible of the early 1930s, *The Modern Corporation and Private Property* by Adolf A. Berle, Jr., and Gardiner C. Means, Brandeis recited the litany of evils perpetrated by large corporations—their powers to administer prices and influence employment, their concentration of wealth and of productive energies. "There is widespread belief," Brandeis said, "that the existing unemployment is the result, in large part, of the gross inequality in the distribution of wealth and income which giant corporations have fostered." America's true prosperity, he argued, "came not from big business, but through the courage, the energy and resourcefulness of small men." If the citizens of Florida accept those premises and therefore wish to subject corporate chains to discriminatory license fees, he concluded, "To that extent, the citizens of each State are still masters of their destiny."

A couple of weeks before the decisions came down, Brandeis sent his dissent to Roberts, author of the majority decision. Roberts replied that he agreed with much that Brandeis said. "The only difficulty I find," he continued, "is in agreeing that these matters are involved in this particular case."

Cardozo filed a separate dissent, saying simply that he believed that taxes against chains were allowable, and therefore found it unnecessary to consider the views presented by Brandeis because "They present considerations that were not laid before us by counsel."

Stone joined with Cardozo and told Frankfurter that he believed Brandeis's dissent "a very powerful presentation. . . . My failure to join in it was not due to any necessary disagreement with it, but because I was anxious to get before the profession the point made by Justice Cardozo." He used stronger language to Brandeis, however: "I think you are too much an advocate of this particular legislation."

A year later, in March 1934, the Court in a 5-4 vote accepted the reasonableness argument Brandeis had been presenting for so many years. The Court had previously said that states could not regulate the size of bread loaves or license the manufacture of ice. Now, in *Nebbia* v. *New York,* the Court said that New York could establish a minimum price for milk to protect the farmer.

During that year the depression had worsened and the nation was more responsive to promised results from government regulation. Against that background, Owen Roberts wrote the majority decision saying, "A State is free to adopt whatever economic policy may reasonably be deemed to promote public welfare." That was the position he had denied in the *Liggett* case.

The minority decision in *Nebbia* was written by James McReynolds and joined in by Willis Van Devanter, George Sutherland, and Pierce Butler—"the four horsemen" who made up the Court's conservative bloc. In attacking the New York law, McReynolds set the stage for the battle that would erupt in 1937 between Franklin Roosevelt and the Supreme Court.

"But plainly, I think," McReynolds wrote, "the Court must have regard to the wisdom of the enactment."

Quickly he modified what he had said: "At least, we must inquire concerning its purpose and decide whether the means proposed have reasonable relation to something within legislative power—whether the end is legitimate, and the means appropriate."

Still, his reference to "wisdom" revealed "the four horsemen's" flirting with being a superlegislature, something which previously had been the responsibility of elected representatives.

For years Brandeis had argued against the Supreme Court's becoming a super legislature and for the Court to limit its role to determining the reasonableness of legislation, and for this he had been called "liberal." He, of course, had been the conservative insisting the Court stay within its proper bounds, adhere firmly to its purpose. The McReynolds dissent had made that point apparent. The fight the President would resolve was in the open.

As broad as were the divisions within the Court, there were issues on which it was united. Some early New Deal measures had been drawn sloppily or without regard to constitutionality. The excitement of the early New Deal days, perhaps the arrogance of the bill drafters, and the submissiveness of Congress had combined to produce legislation that could not stand scrutiny. One such bill was the National Industrial Recovery Act and another was the Frazier-Lemke Act. Both were ruled unconstitutional by the Supreme Court on May 27, 1935—"Black Monday," the New Dealers called that day—with the nine justices unanimous against the measures.

Brandeis wrote the Frazier-Lemke decision. Enacted as an emergency measure to help those farmers who had lost their property in bankruptcy proceedings, the measure had popular support. It seemed to be for the poor farmer and against the greedy banker. The farmers had been caught by depression forces for which they were not responsible; the banks were anxious to gobble up the land.

Prior to the act's passage in June 1934, when a debtor declared bankruptcy, he surrendered his property to his creditors and then was relieved of his debts. Frazier-Lemke changed that. A debtor declared bankruptcy and was freed of his debts, but retained his mortgaged property rather than surrendering it to the mortgage holder.

The act had been written to deal with an extreme situation, but its extreme solution disrupted the traditional mortgage structure in the United States. "The right of the mortgagee to insist upon full payment before giving up his security has been deemed of the essence of a mortgage," said Brandeis in his decision. The Fifth Amendment to the Constitution prohibited the taking of property—the bank's interest in the mortgage, in this case—without just compensation. If, Brandeis continued, the public necessity required so protecting farmers, the burden should be placed not upon banks but upon the public through the government's power of eminent domain.

Because Frazier-Lemke was a New Deal measure, the Supreme Court's unanimous decision appeared as an attack on the New Deal itself, especially when the Court, on the same day, dealt with the National Industrial Recovery Act.

This act established the National Recovery Administration, and the NRA appeared to be the key to the New Deal's economic recovery program with its "codes of fair competition," allowing industry to bypass antitrust laws and establish minimum prices for products in exchange for accepting government-imposed conditions benefiting the worker and the consumer. Industries adhering to the codes flew the "Blue Eagle" symbol.

There seemed much in favor of the program; one company would not take advantage of the surplus labor situation and hire workers cheaply and then undercut the competition. But there were problems. The "codes" were a hodgepodge, impossible either to comprehend or administer.

The case before the Court, *Schechter Corp.* v. *United States,* involved the poultry industry. FDR had approved a code for that industry on April 13, 1934, fixing hours at forty a week and the minimum wage at fifty cents an hour, prohibiting the employment of those under sixteen, authorizing collective bargaining, and gearing the minimum number of employees to a weekly sales volume. Opponents claimed the act was vague: "Congress has set up no intelligible policies to govern the President, no standards to guide and restrict his action, and no procedures for making determinations in conformity with due process of law." They said the law was confused: "The Recovery Act authorizes the President to re-delegate the almost illimitable powers conferred on him by the Act to various commissions, bureaus, officers, and other agencies. The result is that these various bodies and functionaries have the power to make the laws of the United States. It is common knowledge that it is impossible for an ordinary citizen to know what these laws are."

This act, and its history from enactment until the Supreme Court struck it down, offers an example of how both Frankfurter and Brandeis were pulled to the front of the New Deal and became targets for its opponents.

The charge that the legislation was vague and confusing was accurate. William Douglas, then an ardent New Dealer, conceded years later that "any court that has ever sat would hold unanimously that the NIRA was an unconstitutional delegation of legislative power." In 1935 no one was more aware of that than Felix Frankfurter. He had had nothing to do with the bill's drafting or with its administration, but he had watched its progress and realized the future was not bright. When Frankfurter learned that the administration planned to push *Schechter* before the Supreme Court as a test, he anticipated that the Supreme Court would decide against the government, and he telephoned Tommy Corcoran to urge the President to delay going to the Supreme Court. The original act would expire soon, and Frankfurter wanted new legislation written correcting the faults of the first NRA rather than allowing it to be destroyed entirely in the Court case.

Corcoran wired Frankfurter's advice in a "Rush-Confidential for the President" telegram to FDR, who was traveling. Either because the telegram arrived late or because the advice was ignored, the government proceeded with *Schechter.*

After the Court ruled against the NRA, its backers looked for a scapegoat. They found Frankfurter. The story was "leaked" to Arthur Krock, columnist for the *New York Times,* that Frankfurter, in a Machiavellian ploy, had urged the President to bring *Schechter* as a test, deliberately to insure the NRA's demise. Frankfurter's actions had been just the opposite. The Krock story made Frankfurter enemies among the New Dealers. Krock, years later, conceded having written the story without checking with Frankfurter for comment.

The sniping at Frankfurter came from behind the scenes: the slipping of stories to friendly newspaper writers, the nasty comments. In contrast, Brandeis was a public target.

The National Recovery Administration was run by Hugh S. Johnson. Bernard Baruch, who had previously employed Johnson, called him "a good number-three man, maybe a number-two man, but he's not a number-one man. He's dangerous and unstable. He gets nervous . . . tell the President to be careful. Hugh needs a firm hand."

With Johnson running the NRA, the agency immediately ran into criticism and problems. In the midst of this controversy, Johnson gave his 1934 speech in which he spoke of being "in constant touch with that old counselor, Judge Louis Brandeis."

Although NRA was an attempt at the large-scale organization Brandeis abhorred, the implication of Johnson's statement, that Brandeis was intimately involved in the NRA's development, was accepted. Said the New York *Herald Tribune:* "... the fact seems beyond question that the point has been passed at which such assertions can be calmly ignored and anonymously denied." A newspaper reporter called the sentence of Johnson's "most illuminating" and continued in his column: "From the time the New Deal program, in all its glory and grandeur, was first revealed, there had been a certain mystery as to its inception, inspiration and directing intelligence."

Brandeis, adhering to a practice of many years, declined to comment publicly. "The Herald Tribune's editorial of today and an attempt to disqualify me are not agreeable to contemplate," he said privately, "but the incident must be regarded as a casualty—like that of being run into by a drunken autoist, or shot by a lunatic." Brandeis felt so strongly that nothing should be said that a public apology by Johnson was not released. In June of the next year, Johnson did send a personal apology to Brandeis, and Brandeis responded, "It was good of you to write me."

Johnson and Brandeis had talked, prior to the Johnson speech, a total of five times. All the discussions had been brief and general, and did not include NRA's constitutionality.

Brandeis reported the details of those meetings to Frankfurter, to Harlan Fiske Stone, and to Chief Justice Charles Evans Hughes. The last two, both Republicans, sympathized with Brandeis's situation. "I can only admire Justice Brandeis' patience and serenity under such provocation," said Stone. When the Court planned to rule against the NRA in the spring of 1935, Chief Justice Hughes offered to let Brandeis write the opinion. Although appreciating the Chief Justice's action, Brandeis deferred to Hughes, who wanted to write the decision himself.

There was a third decision that "Black Monday" in May 1935 which, when combined with NRA and Frazier-Lemke, truly made that decision day one to upset Roosevelt. This third case involved the firing by Roosevelt of a Federal Trade Commissioner. In 1926 the Supreme Court in *Myers* had said that Woodrow Wilson acted properly in dismissing an appointed official without first clearing the action with the Senate. In 1935, the Court said that Franklin Roosevelt could not do the same thing.

Brandeis had voted against the President on all three cases, but his votes did not represent animus against the New Deal. His vote in the third case was consistent with his 1926 vote in *Myers;* he voted against Roosevelt's unrestricted power as he had voted against that of Wilson, his personal friend and benefactor. With the NIRA and the Frazier-Lemke acts, the unanimous decisions reflected how badly drawn the bills were. Earlier that year Brandeis had voted against the administration in the "Hot Oil" case; Congress had given the President power to regulate the amount of oil shipped between states. The bill's purpose was to limit production, to save the industry from destroying itself by overproduction. But that legislation also had difficulties and the vote was 8-1, only Cardozo supporting the President.

But those cases were the exceptions; whenever he could be, Brandeis was with the New Deal. Among the first major New Deal tests were the four decisions in the gold-clause cases. The United States had devalued the dollar—reduced the amount of gold backing each dollar—to keep pace with other nations which had devalued. But many contracts had gold clauses specifying that payments be made in gold or its equivalent. The holder of a railroad bond, for example, said his bond promised he would be paid $22.50 in gold. After the dollar was devalued, the bondholder claimed he should receive $38.10 in paper money to receive the equivalent of $22.50 in gold. That was one of the cases argued before the Supreme Court. If the bondholder won, debtors would have to repay nearly twice as much in paper dollars as they had borrowed. Congress had dealt with this by declaring the gold clauses null and void. The Supreme Court upheld the congressional action by a 5-4 vote; Brandeis supplied the fifth vote.

Brandeis also supported the Railroad Retirement Act. This 1934 law created a compulsory retirement program for railroad employees, with all railroads contributing toward it. The Supreme Court the next year, 5-4, ruled it unconstitutional. "A pension plan thus imposed," said the majority decision written by Owen Roberts, "is in no proper sense a regulation of the activity of interstate transportation. It is an attempt for social ends." That five-man majority opinion not only outlawed the railroad pension but seemed to preclude any nationwide social security program then being discussed. Brandeis was with the four dissenters.

He supported the Agricultural Adjustment Act of 1933, allowing the government to prop up farm income through tax measures. Owen Roberts again wrote the majority opinion, knocking down the New Deal act, saying that the tax imposed by the act was incidental to the regulation of agricultural production. The dissent, in which Brandeis joined, was written by Stone, who wanted to uphold the government's powers to deal with economic problems. "The power to tax and spend," said the dissent, "includes the power to relieve a nationwide economic maladjustment by conditional gifts of money." In joining with the recommendation for broad federal powers, Brandeis demonstrated his opposition to bigness was not total.

Brandeis also voted with the majority to uphold the power of the Tennessee Valley Authority and supported a New York minimum-wage law. This case, *Morehead* v. *Tipaldo,* continued the struggle begun in 1908 when Brandeis had first argued a maximum-hours law for Oregon women working in laundries. He had then defended an Oregon minimum-wage law before the Supreme Court. Felix Frankfurter had defended that minimum-wage law before the Court the second time it was argued, winning an indecisive 4-4 vote, and in 1923 Frankfurter had lost the *Adkins* case, involving a minimum-wage law in the District of Columbia. The New York law, drafted by Frankfurter and Ben Cohen, was ruled unconstitutional by the Supreme Court in a 5-4 vote in June 1936; Brandeis was with the four dissenters.

Despite his fears of big business and big government and despite his private fumings, Brandeis was a supporter of the New Deal as an associate justice.

Frankfurter, a private citizen, had a different role. His economic philosophies would allow the federal government to play a larger role than would those of Brandeis. "In our day," Frankfurter wrote, "no government, whatever its party livery, can avoid responsibility for insuring minimum economic security," and "various forms of collaborative enterprise, including the largest club to which we all belong, namely the government, must step in."

Prior to Roosevelt's inaugural, Frankfurter developed a series of legislative proposals for the railroads, amounting to virtual federal control. "The point is," insisted Frankfurter, "that such legislation should be put through when it can be; and if there is any time for doing it, now is the time."

In 1932, Frankfurter reiterated a policy he had developed during World War I as a member of the War Labor Policies Board—"that the United States was as free as any other purchaser of commodities to exact certain decent social and economic standards in the manufacture of the commodities it was buying. . . . Just as you and I are free not to patronize sweat shops and to buy from people who observe healthy social standards." Frances Perkins, the Secretary of Labor, picked up that affirmative-action concept from Frankfurter and incorporated it into a public-contracts bill to guide labor conditions for government contractors. She also called upon Frankfurter, as well as a number of other lawyers, for ideas on a general wages and hours law. In the past the Supreme Court had refused to allow such legislation for the manufacture of goods. A New Deal law was drafted, on the recommendation of Frankfurter and others, to include goods "produced" for interstate commerce.

Whatever Frankfurter's activities, as a friend of Roosevelt, as a gadabout in Washington, he was associated, to quote Adolf A. Berle, with "ultra free markets and return to small-scale production." Raymond Moley said there was "no doubt" that Frankfurter opposed the AAA and the NRA, that he and "his young disciples in Washington" were avowed enemies of bigness in business and looked upon the Supreme Court's invalidating the NRA "with no little satisfaction." The Berle-Moley clique wanted it both ways with Frankfurter. In the same account where he reported Frankfurter's devotion to smallness, Moley also reported that in discussions of holding-company legislation, Frankfurter brought Roosevelt to a more pro-business attitude, in favor of the large holding companies, than the President originally had. "It was suggestive of the President's attitude," said Moley, "that he twitted Felix that day by calling him 'John W. Davis.'"

Frankfurter moved easily through the Washington bureaucracy, soothing egos and solving problems. Harold Ickes, the Interior Secretary, was having trouble with a White House aide—"When I got back to the office I was feeling pretty down in the mouth so I called Dr. Frankfurter and asked him if he would come over."

Frankfurter spent much time in Washington, especially on weekends, during school vacations, and in the summer. Arthur Schlesinger, Sr., described him as "a sort of minister without portfolio," who did not speak about his activities to his Harvard colleagues. Or, as one of his 1930s students recalled: "When Felix did not show up for a class, we said, 'I wonder what he's telling the President today.'"

What Frankfurter was "telling" the President was names of persons to staff federal agencies and legislative approaches to problems, and he was offering drafts for presidential speeches. But he was one of many doing the same. What James MacGregor Burns said about FDR's advisers in 1932 was also true for the remainder of the 1930s: "not one of them dominated the channels of access to Roosevelt's mind." Frankfurter, for example, worked on the 1935 gold-clause message and another message on tax revision the same year. In both instances, the final message included enough Frankfurter to warrant the statement that he had been involved with its preparation but was changed enough from the Frankfurter recommendations, both in wording and intent, to demonstrate that Roosevelt received contributions from more than one person.

Brandeis and Frankfurter sometimes are credited with masterminding the "second hundred days" in 1935, when Congress gave the White House the Wagner Labor Act, Social Security, a holding company bill, a tax act, and other legislation—more sweeping in its impact on the United States than that of the first hundred days in 1933. Some of this legislation was consistent with what Brandeis and Frankfurter had advocated for years. The Wagner Act, for example, gave unions the right to bargain collectively. Still, this 1935 legislation, like that in 1933, reflects many factors and influences—the necessities of the time, a liberal Congress, the hardening of conservative positions, the intention to overleap a far-left movement, and the failure of other programs. This legislation was the culmination of the progressive movement, which had begun decades earlier; the Brandeis-Frankfurter contribution stemmed more from their involvement in that movement over the years rather than from their political activities in the 1930s.

Frankfurter was closer personally to the President than many others. Partly this was due to his energy, certainly his loyalty to Roosevelt the man and his devotion to Roosevelt the cause. He was one of a small number, probably less than a handful outside of the Roosevelt family, who addressed the President in private as "Frank" or "Franklin" instead of "Mr. President." He used that intimacy to write encouraging, warm letters to the President—"I would add four hours to your day." To his prominent acquaintances, Frankfurter wrote glowing letters telling of his visits with the President. "He has grown up with his job and assimilated his experience . . . with most people optimism is either an evasion or an opiate, with F.D.R. it is an energy."

There was time in the mid-1930s for humor. The President's secretary "certified" once (and the President "attested") "To Whom It May Concern, But more especially Mrs. Frankfurter" that her husband had appeared for his White House appointment five minutes early "strange as it may seem" and "Since this is the first time in history he has ever been anywhere near on time, we feel it should be made a matter of record." Marion replied: "I always knew that if he felt enough respect or enough fear, said Felix Frankfurter could get anywhere on time."

Frankfurter and Brandeis continued their friendship. Actually it was more than friendship. Brandeis extended security to Frankfurter when the difficulties sometimes became too much. "It's the storm that makes the sailor," said Brandeis once to the one he had described as "half son, half brother."

In exchange, Frankfurter kept Brandeis abreast of the White House gossip. "Tax matters are really moving & *Here* is a real determination on part of F.D. . . . the boys (Ben & Tom) are a legion," and Roosevelt "seems keenly aware of intention of Big Business & Finance" are typical of remarks in the letters Frankfurter wrote to Brandeis in those New Deal years. Some were designed to appeal to the ego of the aged Brandeis—"I hope you'll tell me what to tell F.D.R. when I see him about 'business revival.'" Generally, the letters contained little substance and were such as are sent to the outsider.

Then, in 1937, suddenly Frankfurter and Brandeis, New Deal insider and outsider, were confronted with what has been called "a constitutional crisis," appropriately so.

16

Pack the Supreme Court

A few minutes before noon on Friday, February 5, 1937, Tommy Corcoran hustled over to the Supreme Court building. He caught up with Brandeis in the robing room, and the two men edged out to the hallway between the robing room and the Court chamber, talking softly as the other justices filed by. Corcoran, speaking with FDR's permission, gave Brandeis notice of a judicial reorganization bill which, at that moment, FDR was announcing to the press. This was no ordinary piece of legislation; shortly it would be the talk, as well as the concern, of the nation. Corcoran knew this; he knew too that members of the liberal community would be incensed by the apparent attack on "Isaiah," and he had sought Roosevelt's permission to inform Brandeis personally so the justice would not have to learn of the plan from the press.

The older man listened attentively to Corcoran's explanation. When Corcoran finished, Brandeis told him to thank the President. Then "Isaiah" said he opposed the President's plan and that the President was making a mistake, a serious one.

Roosevelt's plan was to enlarge or "pack" the Supreme Court. Of the nine Supreme Court justices, six were more than seventy years old; for each member who declined to retire at seventy Roosevelt proposed that a co-justice be appointed to the Court to sit with the elderly justice. If FDR's proposal became law, he would have six appointments to the Court, and the Court membership would immediately rise to fifteen. If a justice over seventy retired, Roosevelt could still replace him, and the Court membership would rise to fourteen. If all justices over seventy retired, Roosevelt would have his six appointments but the Court would remain at nine members. Whatever the justices did, if Congress enacted the law, Roosevelt could appoint men who, it was assumed, would find his New Deal measures more compatible with the Constitution than did those then on the Court.

Congress received the presidential message on Capitol Hill at noon, shortly after Corcoran and Brandeis had met. Setting the number of justices on the Supreme Court is its job, and Congress had permitted that number to fluctuate through the nation's history. The most recent example had been a half century earlier when Congress responded to President Ulysses S. Grant's attempt to construct a Court that would declare the Legal Tender Act constitutional by increasing the Court from eight to nine members. As with Grant's effort, most changes in the Court's size had been for political reasons, but Roosevelt's attack was the most severe in the nation's history.

This morning, Friday, February 5, Roosevelt believed he was fulfilling a mandate with his plan to "reorganize" the judiciary. Since coming to power in 1933 in the midst of a depression, by bits and pieces, legislative and administrative acts, he had slowly put the economy together. Congress cooperated, rubber-stamping, almost, his legislative requests. But the Supreme Court had blocked him—the decision against the Railroad Retirement Act, with its implied threat against any social security system, the Hot Oil case, Frazier-Lemke, the NIRA, the Agricultural Adjustment Act, the New York minimum wage—these and others had fallen before the Supreme Court.

In the 140 years from 1790 to 1930 the Supreme Court had overruled sixty acts of Congress, but once the New Deal came to power, the pace increased. In FDR's first term, the Court declared twelve acts unconstitutional, five in one year. Each time the Court ruled against the New Deal, FDR's determination to find some method to act against the Court, to strike at its power, became stronger. As early as 1935, Roosevelt's animosity toward the Court was transformed into a desire to find a way to act against it. Justice Department aides then scurried around, looking through history books and legal precedents to discover some means of moving against the Court.

Also, and this Roosevelt found personally disturbing, he had not had the opportunity to make one appointment to the Court during his entire first term. Charles Evans Hughes, in the 1920s before he became Chief Justice, had written of the reluctance of aged justices to retire, saying: "They seem to be tenacious of the appearance of adequacy." Roosevelt believed they were being tenacious at the expense of himself and of his New Deal.

He believed he understood the reason why: Politics.

To Roosevelt, the Supreme Court was as much a political institution as were the presidency and the Congress. During the 1932 campaign, he had argued: "After March 4, 1929, the Republican Party was in complete control of all branches of the federal government—the Executive, the Senate, the House of Representatives, and I might add for good measure, the Supreme Court as well." The charge was not far from wrong. In addition to William Howard Taft, the Chief Justice in the 1920s and former Republican President, who was an intimate adviser to Republican Presidents in the 1920s, Charles Evans Hughes, Chief Justice in the 1930s, had not only resigned once from the Supreme Court to become the Republican presidential candidate but also, at least during the early days of the New Deal, advised Republican congressional leaders on how to thwart the Roosevelt program.

Supreme Court justices were often chosen for their political influence and economic interests, to advocate a particular philosophy while on the Court. If that didn't make them political, Roosevelt believed, what did?

At the White House, Supreme Court decisions were read as a scorecard, either for or against the President: "Three favorable and two unfavorable," said a 1936 memorandum from Attorney General Cummings to the President.

During 1936 the Supreme Court occupied more and more of Roosevelt's time. "How do you feel about going up against the Supreme Court?" he asked Cummings. "It is like a golf match, Mr. President," answered Cummings. "Four down and five to play."

Cummings developed what became the Court-packing plan. While researching a book on the federal administration of justice, he came across a bill proposed twenty-two years earlier by Woodrow Wilson's Attorney General, calling for the co-judge approach for federal judges not retiring at seventy. That plan did not include Supreme Court justices, but if the approach was wise policy for justices below the Supreme Court level, it also was wise policy for justices on the Supreme Court. The plan was all the more palatable because Wilson's Attorney General, the one who had originated the plan, was James McReynolds, at this point a seventy-four-year-old associate justice of the Supreme Court.

In November 1936, Roosevelt, in seeking a second term, had made the Supreme Court an issue, perhaps the major issue of the campaign. His overwhelming reelection commanded him to action.

Cummings met with the President the day after Christmas 1936 to discuss his plan to enlarge the Court. "As I read this memorandum," said Cummings of the President's reaction to his proposal, "he expressed approval of almost every sentence. He also was intrigued by the plan itself and began to talk of ways to put it into effect."

Although Louis Brandeis and Felix Frankfurter were now considered at the height of their New Deal power, neither man had been consulted. Roosevelt was interested in talking with people who would assist him, not with those who would attempt to dissuade him. He understood the veneration that Brandeis and Frankfurter felt for the Supreme Court and moved warily with them.

Brandeis had turned eighty the previous November, a few days after Roosevelt's election. Although a friend of the New Deal on the Court, he was then its oldest member and appeared to be the prime target of Roosevelt's plan.

Publicly, Brandeis maintained silence about the plan. The *New York Times* wired him that if he chose to make any public comment the *Times* would "esteem it a privilege to publish anything you may choose to send us," but he did not answer the newspaper. Privately, his attitude was obvious. On Saturday, February 6, the day after the plan was announced, Brandeis wrote Frankfurter one of his customary short notes: each sentence numbered, each to the point, asking one question, replying to another; as always, no idle talk. The first sentence was about a mutual acquaintance, the final sentence about another matter, but the middle sentences read:

Whom did F. D. rely on for his judiciary message to the hill?
Has he consulted you on his matters of late?
It looks as if he were inviting some pretty radical splits in the Democratic party and Allies.

Brandeis's law clerk that year, Willard Hurst, remembered that the justice did not speak at length about the plan. "The most specific thing I recall," said Hurst, "is [Brandeis] observing that the bill showed, as a defect in FDR, the President's tendency to be 'smart,' in the Yankee-deprecatory sense of the term."

In subsequent years, Brandeis's friends have argued over whether he was hurt by the President's attack on age. Arthur Schlesinger, Sr., then a friend of Brandeis, recalled that the justice, at the time of the Court-packing plan, "expressed the view that the conservative mentality is a product of genes rather than of years, that in fact age, with its accompaniment of financial security, tends to emancipate judges from the economic pressures and illiberal predilections which may have conditioned their previous thinking." That comment was as much as Brandeis's dignity allowed him.

More than the personal affront, Brandeis was concerned about the affront to the Supreme Court. This was the institution he referred to as "our Court" with a forward thrust of the hand. Within its councils, he was a tenacious foe; outside, he allowed no attack upon the Court or its members. "Brandeis valued [the Court's] independence of decision even more than rightness of decision," said one New Dealer.

Brandeis's days as a politician went back more than thirty years to the time when Franklin Roosevelt was still a college student. He was, as Roosevelt would learn, a wily foe.

Felix Frankfurter, at Harvard, had been tipped off about the plan. On January 15, Roosevelt wrote him a lengthy letter, adding at the end: "Very confidentially, I may give you an awful shock in about two weeks. Even if you do not agree, suspend final judgment and I will tell you the story."

After the plan's unveiling, a student in Frankfurter's federal-jurisdiction seminar asked: "What about it, Professor?" Frankfurter dodged an answer. "Well," he said, "I think you gentlemen have somewhat more to know about the Supreme Court than you know now before we can discuss the Court plan." The plan was not discussed again in class.

For Frankfurter, Court packing presented a dilemma. On one side was Brandeis, who, with Stimson and Holmes, had most influenced him. And attacked with Brandeis was the institution of the Supreme Court. Frankfurter understood, as well as did the justices, the need for the Court to retain its independence.

On the other side was Frankfurter's knowledge that the dispute between the President and the Court was neither new nor one-sided. From the time Frankfurter had entered public life, Presidents and presidential candidates had been critical of the Supreme Court for usurping powers, for going to the "wisdom" of legislation, in James McReynolds's phrase, rather than to its constitutionality. Theodore Roosevelt, an early Frankfurter hero, had attacked the courts, as had Robert La Follette, whom Frankfurter had supported in his 1924 independent party presidential bid. The American Bar Association had criticized the Supreme Court in the 1920s and so, indeed, had Frankfurter himself.

In 1922 he had criticized the Court majority for being "conscious moulders of policy instead of impersonal vehicles of revealed truth." Two years later, he argued that although "In all governments there must be organs for finality of decision . . . distinctions must be taken as to the power of the Supreme Court, and the wisdom of the grant of power, in the different classes of cases over which the Court has jurisdiction."

Frankfurter did not support judicial recall and congressional overriding of a judicial veto, the remedies offered in those years although he had supported their advocate, La Follette, for the presidency. But those recommendations, he argued, deal with "real grievances and with a tendency on the part of our courts . . . which, if unchecked, may have very serious consequences."

In 1935, after "Black Monday," Frankfurter suggested Roosevelt wait until the Court ruled against even more New Deal measures, *"Then* propose a Constitutional amendment giving the national Government adequate power to cope with national economic and industrial problems. That will give you an overwhelming issue of a *positive* character arising at psychological time for the '36 campaign." In 1936, Frankfurter frequently criticized the Court in his discussions with Roosevelt, with other New Dealers, and with Associate Justice Harlan Fiske Stone but was less critical to Brandeis, realizing Brandeis's sensitivity to criticism of the Court.

In addition to believing the Supreme Court had overstepped proper limits with New Deal measures, Frankfurter also idolized Roosevelt. So he was caught between those two motivations on one side and his veneration for Brandeis and for the independence of the Supreme Court as an institution on the other.

Two days after Roosevelt unveiled his Court-packing plan, Frankfurter wrote him a carefully phrased letter. If Frankfurter was dismayed because he had not been informed in advance of the plan, he gave no indication. The first paragraph of his letter reiterated his previous criticism of the Supreme Court. The second paragraph was Frankfurter's reaction to the plan:

And so it was clear that some major operation was necessary. Any major action to the body politic, no less than to the body physical, involves some shock. But I have, as you know, deep faith in your instinct to make the wise choice—the choice that will carry intact the motley aggregation that constitutes the progressive army toward the goal of present-day needs, and that will, at the same time, maintain all that is good in the traditional democratic process.

Roosevelt caught Frankfurter's hesitancy, his endorsement of the President but reluctance to speak positively of the specific plan. "I am awfully glad . . . to know that although shocked you have survived; but most important of all that you understood the causes and motives,"

Roosevelt replied. He then explained why he had not chosen the amendment process, which Frankfurter had recommended two years earlier. Said Roosevelt: "If I were in private practice and without a conscience, I would gladly undertake for a drawing account of fifteen to twenty million dollars (easy enough to raise) to guarantee that an amendment would not be ratified prior to the 1940 elections." He said the nation could not wait until 1940 for effective social and economic legislation.

At the President's request, Frankfurter provided Roosevelt with a memorandum criticizing the Supreme Court for "disregarding all judicial restraint" for the President to use as background material for speeches, but that memorandum carefully avoided any reference to the bill's specifics. In private letters to Stone, Frankfurter continued his criticism of the Court, but again without reference to the plan. His correspondence with Brandeis at this time dropped off; as if by mutual understanding, they agreed not to discuss the issue.

With all of his criticisms of the Supreme Court, Frankfurter had long opposed manipulating its size. In the early 1920s, when there was such talk within the American Bar Association, Oliver Wendell Holmes told Frankfurter that enlarging the Court would be "the worst of mistakes." Taft, then Chief Justice, spelled out the reasons against such a move. "I hope nothing will be done to give us a town meeting . . ." he said. "Consider the danger of setting a precedent to a demagogue Democratic administration." FDR in his Court-packing plan, had countered the "town-meeting" concept by suggesting a fifteen-member Court could sit in smaller units.

In 1934, Frankfurter, in what he intended as a definitive article on the Supreme Court, wrote in the *Encyclopaedia of the Social Sciences:* "There is no magic in the number nine, but there are limits to effective judicial action. . . . Experience is conclusive that to enlarge the size of the Supreme Court would be self-defeating." The next year, 1935, there was a rumor that Frankfurter had discussed enlarging the Court with Roosevelt. Frankfurter said the rumor was "wholly without foundation . . . at no time have I believed in, nor have I ever advocated, publicly or privately an increase in the members of the Supreme Court."

After the President's plan was announced, Frankfurter was pressured to speak out on the plan; he declined either to criticize or defend it. When requested to support a group of lawyers endorsing the plan, his response had little connection with the request: "Lawyers, above all other citizens, should not yield to passion and violent utterance."

His friends who opposed the President's plan wanted Frankfurter to restate his opposition to manipulating the Court's size, but he refused, falling back on the explanation that education and discussion were values emerging from the dispute. "If we get enough of that—if we get enough real education—the enduring interest of the country will be safeguarded and promoted," he said.

Numerous letters went from his Law School office to his friends, Charles Burlingham, Grenville Clark, and others, all skirting the issue but failing to make a statement either for or against the President's plan. Clark replied: "I am not satisfied, to be frank. The only real point is that, as one of the few people in the country who is known to have considered the problem of the Supreme Court and the Constitution for years past," Clark wrote Frankfurter, "it is really up to you to let the public, or those of them who are interested in your views, know what you think of this plan."

For Frankfurter the year 1937 was almost too much. As the New Deal had progressed through the 1930s, its critics had continued to single him out for attack, much of it *ad nominem*. The Court plan had placed him on a tightrope between Brandeis and Roosevelt. The first was his friend and the second was his idol, and he had loyalties to both men. He himself was ill, with a testy back pain that put him in bed for weeks. Marion, more and more escaping the Cambridge faculty wife's drudgery, was in California with relatives. And the letters continued to come in. Why didn't he speak up? When would he speak? How could he not speak?

"Why don't I speak out publicly . . ." Frankfurter wrote on March 6 to Grenville Clark, one of his oldest and best friends. "Fundamentally, because through circumstances in the making of which I have had no share, I have become a myth, a symbol and promoter not of reason but of passion. I am the symbol of the Jew, the 'red,' the 'alien.' " Anti-Semitism had continued its hold on the United States. From quotas at universities it had progressed to beatings of Jews on the streets. Desecrations of synagogues were common. If the violence was extreme, it was nurtured by the sneers, bad jokes, and offensiveness of the educated, the prominent, the successful, the established. Frankfurter continued:

In that murky and passionate atmosphere anything that I say becomes enveloped. I would be heard and interpreted by what you call the average man —the reader of the Hearst newspapers, the Chicago Tribune, the American Legion, the D.A.R.s, the chambers of commerce, I am sorry to say the "leading members of the bar" all over the place, the readers of Time, the Saturday Evening Post, etc., etc., etc.—not as the man who by virtue of his long years of service in the government and his special attention to problems of constitutional law and the work of the Court spoke with the authority of scholarship, but as the Jew, the "red," and the "alien." Instead of bringing light and calm and reason, what I would be compelled to say about the work of the Court—and it is the only subject in this debate on which I can speak with a scholar's authority—would only fan the flames of ignorance, of misrepresentation, and of passion.

Frankfurter never wavered in his refusal to discuss publicly the Court-packing plan. Twenty-five years later when an author of a doctoral dissertation requested comment on the plan, Frankfurter scrawled at the bottom of the request: "Reasons at the time for abstention, no less for today."

However, if doubts existed about Frankfurter's public stance, there were none about his private attitude. He opposed the plan and said so to his friends. "Frankfurter never went along with the President on that," said James Landis, ". . . He had no use for it at all." And Robert H. Jackson, an assistant attorney general then, close to both Roosevelt and Frankfurter, said: "Frankfurter had not been friendly to the Court plan. He had not appeared against it, but he wouldn't appear for it."

Frank Buxton, a Boston newspaper editor and friend of Frankfurter's at the time, recalled "there was no doubt of the displeasure" the President's plan caused for Frankfurter.

In his chats with me, [said Buxton] he spoke angrily against the proposed change. He advised me to oppose it editorially. He did not write any editorials himself on the subject for the Boston *Herald,* but he telephoned to me many times, suggesting arguments against. In private, he condemned it to his Law School associates. He said that many of his friends had urged him to come out publicly in criticism against the packing, but he refused. He told them that even if he objected to the scheme recommended by the President, he could not decently head the opposition. He felt that many of the opponents of the proposal were against it because "they were against almost anything suggested by the President."

Frankfurter has been accused of keeping quiet for fear that, if he publicly criticized the plan, Roosevelt never would appoint him to the Supreme Court. Buxton believed there was another reason: "The truth seems to be that Felix's heart and his head were in conflict," he said. "He thought that, in this instance at least, a friend should bear his friend's infirmities. To jeopardize his close relationship with a man whom he loved and who loved him, to break with him on a matter regarding which first class minds held completely opposite convictions did not seem proper to him."

Frankfurter was not the kind of person to criticize his friends publicly. "Some foolish folk (enemies of yours) are doing their damndest to make me attack the court so as to start a new line of attack against your proposal," he told Roosevelt. "They miss their guess. I shan't help them to divert the issue from the misbehavior of the Court. There are various ways of fighting a fight!" Some weeks later, Governor Herbert H. Lehman of New York unexpectedly announced his opposition. FDR grumbled that Lehman, a liberal and almost an FDR protégé, was taking "pot shots at us from the rear." Frankfurter was equally incensed. "Some things just aren't done," he said, "they violate the decencies of human relations and offend the good taste and decorum of friendship." Those comments objecting to Lehman's action probably explain Frankfurter's inaction.

Whatever Frankfurter's motives, the fate of the court plan would not be determined by him or the President. The Supreme Court made the decision. Here Brandeis was active.

In 1935 the Supreme Court had moved into its own building, after a century and a half of being shunted from building to building and room to room. The new structure, Grecian in design, ornate in execution, was across a small park from the Capitol. The chamber measured ninety-one by eighty-two feet, its walls supported by twenty-four marble columns. The building had been the brainchild of Chief Justice William Howard Taft a decade earlier, and it rivaled the White House and the Capitol in its splendor. The building caused many stories, most told by the justices themselves. Each justice had a three-room suite, and when Mrs. Brandeis saw her husband's, she supposedly remarked, "They showed me the shower bath and the running ice water—two things my husband never uses!" Brandeis rarely was in his chambers in the new building, preferring his study at home. And when Holmes, while on the Court, viewed the plans for the building, he remarked— so a story at the time went—that "the abandonment of a common men's room meant that off the bench he would no longer see his brothers at all." Harlan Fiske Stone thought, so a friend reported, that the nine black-robed justices would look in the building like nine black beetles in the temple of Karnak. Stone supposedly suggested that when the justices moved to the new building the Chief Justice lead them in a parade to the new building "on a properly caparisoned elephant."

After the jokes, however, the new building stood as a strength, a fortress of justice, the citadel of a powerful adversary.

Although Roosevelt's motives in attacking the Court were heavily political, he had argued in his message that new justices were necessary because the Court was falling behind in its workload. The justices were reluctant to speak to this point publicly, as they were reluctant to speak about the bill at all. One of the chief Senate opponents, Burton K. Wheeler of Montana, a Democrat and one-time Roosevelt supporter, believed the justices' silence confused the public into assuming some justices supported the President. With two other senators, he invited Chief Justice Hughes to appear before the Senate Judiciary Committee to answer the President's charges. Hughes was amenable, but he wanted another justice—preferably Brandeis because of his status with the liberal community—to appear with him. Brandeis believed an appearance demeaning, and nothing came of the plan.

Hughes recalled offering to give the senators a letter defending the Court against the President's attack, but either the offer was not as definite as Hughes remembered or the senators did not appreciate the offer's significance. Wheeler considered the approach to Hughes a failure. This was Friday, March 18.

Brandeis did not permit the effort to fail.

In the mid-1920s Brandeis had remained loyal to Wheeler when the Republicans retaliated against him for his Teapot Dome investigation, and the Brandeis and Wheeler families had been friends for years.

On Saturday, March 19, Mrs. Brandeis crossed from Washington to Alexandria, in Virginia, to see Burton Wheeler's new grandchild. After chatting with Wheeler's daughter, Mrs. Brandeis suddenly said: "You tell your father I'm for him." After Mrs. Brandeis left, Wheeler's daughter called the senator and reported the conversation to him. "I'm going to call up Brandeis," Wheeler announced. "He may throw me out, but I'm going to try it."

Brandeis did not throw him out. The two men met that Saturday in Brandeis's study. Wheeler argued that a statement signed at least by Hughes and Brandeis defending the Court against FDR's attack carried more weight than denunciations from senators. Brandeis responded: "You call the Chief Justice. He'll give you a letter."

Wheeler hesitated. A leading opponent of the Hughes appointment in 1930, Wheeler was reluctant to approach Hughes alone. Brandeis insisted, saying, "I'll call him up." So Burton Wheeler stood by as Brandeis dialed and then handed him the telephone when Hughes came on the line. Hughes was friendly and invited Wheeler to his home.

The letter was prepared the next day, Sunday, and signed by Hughes, Brandeis, and Willis Van Devanter. Hughes did not ask the other six justices either to read or to sign the letter although they lived within a five-minute walk of his home. In the letter Hughes insisted the Court's workload was up to date, and then the letter challenged one possibility raised in Roosevelt's original proposal, that a fifteen-member court could sit in units. This part of the letter was, in effect, an advisory opinion, which previously the Court had refrained from giving.

When Wheeler picked up the letter from Hughes that afternoon, the Chief Justice handed it to him and said: "The baby is born." The next morning Wheeler appeared before the Senate Judiciary Committee. Its chairman, Henry F. Ashurst of Arizona, catching the smug look on Wheeler's face, remarked to another Democrat: "I don't know what he's going to spring, but it'll blow us out of the water."

The Hughes letter not only attacked the President's plan, but Hughes's statement "I am confident that [the letter] is in accord with the views of the justices" gave the impression that all nine agreed to it when six were not even aware of it. Wheeler encouraged this interpretation, saying later that "the members of the Supreme Court . . . are unanimous with reference to the letter of the Chief Justice."

Frankfurter believed the letter "indefensible on several scores": to claim that there was not sufficient time to consult the other justices was "disingenuous" and to give an advisory opinion "grossly violated the settled practice of the Court."

But his opinion was a minority one. After the letter was made public, Vice President John Nance Garner telephoned Franklin Roosevelt, then at Warm Springs, Georgia, and said: "We're licked."

The Supreme Court still was not done.

When Felix Frankfurter and Ben Cohen had written the New York minimum-wage law, they had based it on the need "to meet the minimum cost of living necessary for health." This, it was hoped, would distinguish the New York law from the District of Columbia law—based on workers' general needs—which the Supreme Court had struck down in 1923 in *Adkins* v. *Children's Hospital*.

This New York law came before the Supreme Court in *Morehead* v. *New York ex rel. Tipaldo*. Theoretically, at least, the Court could deal with it without having to reconsider *Adkins*—that was how Frankfurter and Cohen had written it. In conference, however, when the justices discussed whether to hear the case, Associate Justice Roberts did not accept that argument, saying he believed there was no reason to hear the New York case "unless the Court was prepared to re-examine and overrule the Adkins case." His comment was passed over, however, because there were already the required four votes to hear the case.

That conference had been early in 1936 when Roosevelt was being criticized for his policies and the Court was being praised for blocking him, the criticism and praise being so loud that many, especially in Washington, considered them more widespread than they were. There also was another factor. That spring of 1936, with the Republicans considering different candidates for their party's presidential nomination that year, the suggestion that Owen Roberts be drafted from the Court as Hughes had been drafted twenty years earlier was mentioned frequently. Until this time, Roberts's philosophy as an associate justice appeared to seesaw between liberal and conservative. As his name was mentioned more frequently for the presidency, his decisions became more conservative, in line with the philosophy of the Republican party.

Years later Roberts conceded that "ill-advised but enthusiastic friends of mine urged me to let my name go up as a candidate for President while I was on the Court."

Against this background he voted in the *Morehead* minimum-wage case, and in that 5-4 vote against the minimum wage, Roberts provided the crucial fifth vote. The decision, written by Pierce Butler, held the New York law similar to the one in *Adkins*. With Butler and Roberts were George Sutherland, who had written the original *Adkins* decision, McReynolds, and Van Devanter.

Chief Justices Hughes wrote the dissent, joined by Brandeis, Stone, and Cardozo. The dissent sounds as if Brandeis were its father: "I can find nothing in the Federal Constitution which denies to the State the power to protect women from being exploited by overreaching employers through the refusal of a fair wage."

Morehead in June 1936 was a factor turning Roosevelt and the nation against the Court.

After that decision, Alf Landon became the Republican presidential candidate and the Supreme Court became a major issue in the campaign; by October that Roosevelt would be a big winner was apparent. On October 10, 1936, the justices met in conference to deal with another state minimum-wage law case; this time the 1923 decision was specifically challenged. Given the 1923 decision and the *Morehead* decision only four months earlier supporting it, reasonable expectation was that the Court would not hear the new case. It did. One of those agreeing to hear it was Roberts. He acknowledged the surprise, recalling that a fellow justice nudged his neighbor: "What is the matter with Roberts?"

The case, *West Coast Hotel Co.* v. *Parrish,* was argued December 16 and 17, 1936. The nine justices took their preliminary vote at the next conference, December 19. This was still before the unveiling of the President's Court-packing plan but after the President's unprecedented victory. Eight members of the Court divided as expected: against the minimum wage were Sutherland, Butler, McReynolds, and Van Devanter; for it were Hughes, Brandeis, Cardozo, and Stone. The key vote then was Roberts, who had voted against the minimum wage in June when presidential politics still was a possibility for him.

Now in December, when that possibility no longer existed, "I voted for affirmance"—a change that a young New Dealer named Abe Fortas called "the switch in time that serves nine." Roberts denied his switch was motivated by politics, insisting it was caused only by the direct challenge to *Adkins.*

Announcement of the decision was delayed, because of Harlan Fiske Stone's illness, until March 29, 1937, almost two months after the President's plan was announced. Hughes delivered the opinion upholding the minimum wage. He explained that the change had been caused by the different attitude toward the 1923 *Adkins* case. Robert Jackson, then assistant attorney general, was sitting at the government's table in the Supreme Court chamber that day and considered the explanation for the switch a joke. "This doctrine that the Court would apply bad constitutional law to a case unless the lawyers asked it specifically to correct itself was a bit of face-saving for the Court," he said.

Whatever its motivation, the Supreme Court had switched from being anti-New Deal to being pro-New Deal. It stopped Roosevelt's attack by joining his army.

The decision had another repercussion. For almost twenty-five years, Brandeis and Frankfurter had been fighting to establish a minimum wage. Brandeis had argued the issue before the Court prior to becoming an associate justice. Frankfurter had picked it up and reargued it. Then, in 1923, Frankfurter had argued the minimum wage before the Supreme Court a second time, then had written the New York law which the Supreme Court in June 1936 had disallowed. Now, the Supreme Court had said that the minimum wage was one protection that states could provide within their borders. Brandeis and Frankfurter had won.

The day of the decision, Brandeis wrote to Frankfurter: "Overruling Adkins Case must give you some satisfaction."

Frankfurter thanked him for the note, "but, unhappily," continued Frankfurter, "it is one of life's bitter-sweets and the bitter far outweighs the sweet." He expressed pleasure that the Court had gone along with the minimum wage, "what must have seemed axiomatic to you in 1914." Still, the decision day when the minimum wage had been upheld was "one of the few, real black days in my life." For Frankfurter, "Something precious—a deep old devotion—died within me to a considerable extent, namely, my confidence in the integrity of the Court's process." He was angered by much, he said, but "Above all, Roberts' reversal . . . a shameless, political response to the present row."

As the Court continued to hold New Deal measures constitutional, Frankfurter became bitter at what he construed as its politicalization. On April 12, 1937, after the Court upheld the National Labor Relations Act, Frankfurter telegraphed the President: "After today I feel like finding some honest profession to enter."

Within the Court itself, the domination of politics was accepted. Justice Cardozo, recalled a law clerk, "took particular delight in reporting the details whenever the Chief Justice or Justice Roberts, under the pressure of President Roosevelt's Court-packing plan, would reverse themselves." Once, when the Court overruled a case not one year old, Cardozo only commented that it was "quite an achievement." Frankfurter, at Harvard, found no humor. "The lawyer who won these cases," he said, "is the lawyer who never argued them, Franklin D. Roosevelt."

The justices, especially Brandeis, after attacking the President's plan with the Hughes letter and the "switch in time," were still not finished. A reason none of the justices had retired, it was assumed, was that Conress could cut their retirement pay—Congress actually had done that with Holmes—and, except for Brandeis and Hughes, none of the justices was financially independent. On March 1, 1937, however, Roosevelt signed legislation insuring that retirement income for Supreme Court justices could not be decreased. Still, there were no retirements.

Pressure was on several of the justices to retire and then denounce the President. Brandeis, because he was the eldest justice and because he had the support of the liberal community, was a constant target. Republicans inquired through their Washington friends, sounding out the possibilities. Not only Republicans wanted him to resign. Dean Acheson, a former law clerk, a New Dealer (for a short time), and in 1937 a Washington lawyer, also believed Brandeis should resign. "I do not think that further service will add to his already great reputation," said Acheson.

But Brandeis would not retire. Before him was the example of his friend Holmes, who had stayed on the Court into his nineties, his work not slipping until the end. For many years Brandeis had believed the elderly should not be discarded. "We ought to have provision for presidents and members of [the] Court to sit, say in [the] Senate, without vote." Also, seemingly as the President's chief target, Brandeis could not give in; that was not his style. He was again meeting with Frankfurter when the law professor was in Washington. "No," reported Frankfurter late in May, "L. D. B., in confidence, will not resign!"

But Brandeis was not the only justice eligible for retirement under the March 1 law. Willis Van Devanter had long considered retirement because of his physical incapacities, but his politics had kept him on in the face of the Roosevelt New Deal and his friends, such as Brandeis, had asked him to stay because of his contributions in conference. But on May 18, 1937, the time had come for Van Devanter. The choosing of that day was not an accident. Brandeis had known that Van Devanter probably would retire shortly and, using a willing newsman as a courier, tipped off Burton Wheeler. Wheeler than approached William Borah, the Republican senator, who opposed the Court-packing plan and was a good friend of Van Devanter's. Borah persuaded Van Devanter that his resignation should come at a time when it would have the most effect on the President's plan.

Van Devanter's resignation arrived at the White House at 9:45 on the morning of May 18; it then was public. At 10 o'clock, fifteen minutes later, the eighteen members of the Senate Judiciary Committee filed into their committee room to vote on Roosevelt's Court bill. William Borah, a committee member, made certain each senator knew of Van Devanter's resignation; another reason to support the President's bill had disappeared. The closed-door committee session began with six votes, each designed to give the President some part of his packing bill. Each of the six votes went against the President. Then the committee voted on a report to the full Senate. The report attacked the President for "a needless, futile, and utterly dangerous abandonment of constitutional principle" and called the packing plan "a measure which should be so emphatically rejected that its parallel will never again be presented to the free representatives of the free people of America." That report was adopted by the committee, 10-8, with seven Democrats voting against the President.

Later that day a newsman asked the President for his reaction, and he replied: "I have no news on that subject today."

If the President faced an ignominious defeat, Frankfurter provided him with the text to claim a victory: "The Supreme Court reversed itself. But the Supreme Court reversed itself only after it had become the duty of the President to protest the want of cooperation between the judicial and legislative branches of Government and to insist that what was needed was not a change in the Constitution but a proper interpretation of our fundamental law." The President used that argument as the basis for his not continuing his efforts to enlarge the Court. The measure finally voted by Congress had little relation to the original bill. The size of the Supreme Court was not altered.

There were many after-effects of the effort to enlarge the Supreme Court. Roosevelt, who had come to his second term with an overwhelming mandate, never regained his momentum in domestic affairs. Senator Joseph T. Robinson of Arkansas, the Senate Democratic leader, had been expected to receive the first opening on the Court in exchange for supporting the Court-packing plan in the Senate, but he died, apparently from the stress of the Court fight, and the Van Devanter seat went to Hugo La Fayette Black, a Democratic senator from Alabama. Black had been a New Deal stalwart but faced reelection troubles. Roosevelt appointed him to reward him, provide him with a job, and assure confirmation from a Senate angered at the White House because of the Robinson death—the Senate rarely turns down one of its own. Black, a former Ku Klux Klan member and at the time apparently lacking the competence to be a Supreme Court justice, developed into one of the most powerful judicial philosophers in the nation's history. His constant adversary on the Supreme Court was to be Felix Frankfurter.

Another effect was the split among the New Dealers. To those who had revered Franklin Roosevelt, anyone opposing him on such a major issue was an enemy. Tommy Corcoran, who had sat at Brandeis's feet for many years—he was to be described later as Brandeis's "man" in the White House—did not visit Brandeis after the Court plan's defeat and vowed never to do so. Ben Cohen visited Brandeis in October and reported Brandeis's "deep disappointment that Tom was not with me. He mentioned Tom several times. . . . He hoped that he would come soon." Harold Ickes, who had been an admirer of Brandeis at the beginning of the New Deal, also turned against him. "Brandeis has been rather insistent in invitations to me," said Ickes, "but I have felt embarrassed about going." For these men, the Brandeis involvement in the Hughes letter to Wheeler was treasonous.

The Supreme Court itself did not make its annual fall visits to the President for two years. There was no announcement of a policy change. Chief Justice Hughes simply refrained from requesting an appointment. By the fall of 1939 the breach had been healed, and the Court again made its annual visit. Roosevelt, acknowledging being bested by an even more skilled politician than he was, greeted Chief Justice Hughes with enthusiasm and "they were in intimate conversation something like forty minutes."

Brandeis and Frankfurter resumed their friendship; the interruption during the Court fight had not represented hostility but an awareness by both that friendship sometimes requires discretion. Whatever Brandeis's feelings about Roosevelt, he kept them to himself and had no difficulty continuing to deal with the President.

Brandeis also continued as a friend on the Court of progressive legislation. Late in 1938, Ben Cohen reported to the President that "your talk with Isaiah seems to have had unexpected repercussions upon our jurisprudence. . . . Isaiah surprised all of us by his vigorous and zealous defense of the government's position. He scarcely permitted a single sentence in Wood's argument to go unchallenged."

Frankfurter, by maintaining his silence on the packing plan, had maintained his relationship with the President. There were two other results for him. One was the gossip, constantly following his career, that he had paid with his silence for the seat on the Supreme Court that came to him in 1939. The second result was a reticence that would mark his years as a justice. He said of the Supreme Court in the 1930s, "Its ghosts will walk for many a day." Those ghosts haunted him.

17

Against Adolf Hitler

On May 11, 1933, at the Biltmore Hotel in New York, Felix Frankfurter received an award from the National Institute of Immigrant Welfare. In accepting it, Frankfurter spoke of the "gratitude . . . [of] millions of our people, born, like myself, under other skies, for the privilege that this country has bestowed in allowing them to partake of its fellowship."

A few months shy of his fifty-first birthday, Frankfurter was the example of the successful American immigrant: professor in America's most prestigious law school, distinguished government servant, friend and adviser to Presidents. His life demonstrated that the United States constantly nourished itself on the influx of new peoples.

But Frankfurter did more than express gratitude. Always the professor, he used this occasion to lecture, not only his audience in the hotel but also the America outside its walls. In those remarks he developed a theme constantly emerging in his later talks and writings, that the United States was a nation of immigrants, its history, "the story of the most significant racial admixture in history."

Three months earlier, on January 30, 1933, Adolf Hitler had come to power in Germany, proclaiming the superiority and "purity" of one race. Hitler opposed all minorities, but especially the Jews, and he moved against them quickly. There were denunciations, police turning their backs on street beatings, and Boycott Day—non-Jews were not to buy from Jews.

"Of the 56 signers of the Declaration of Independence," Frankfurter said that day in May, "18 were of non-English stock. When the Continental Congress chose John Adams, Franklin and Jefferson as a committee to devise the national emblem, they recommended a seal containing the national emblem of England, Scotland, Ireland, France, Germany, and Holland as representing 'the countries from which these States have been peopled.'"

Frankfurter's view of the United States was romantic. "If one faith can be said to unite a great people," he said, "surely the ideal that holds us together beyond any other is our belief in the moral worth of the common man, whatever his race or religion. In this faith America was founded, to this faith have her poets and seers and statesmen and the unknown millions, generation after generation, devoted their lives."

The 1930s was a time of testing for that romantic vision. Adolf Hitler was not only a man, a ruler, and a dictator, but also an event. His passionate hatred of Jews spilled beyond the bounds of his own country into other nations. He made war against the Jews, his intention not to conquer them but to annihilate them. He became a challenge for the world, for the United States, and for that "one faith" that Felix Frankfurter spoke of that day.

Brandeis saw the danger early. In his late seventies when Hitler came to power, of German parentage, having traveled in Germany as a young man, Brandeis knew. "I guess the Jews of Germany had better make up their minds to move on—all of them," Brandeis said to Frankfurter in 1933. ". . . life there can never be safe." To Rabbi Stephen Wise, he said: "No Jew must live in Germany."

Although he had dropped formal ties with Zionism, Brandeis had retained his interest in Palestine. His home had been a stopover for anyone from Palestine with information on how the land was developing. There were letters to him dealing with events in Palestine, the progress of kibbutzim, the raising of funds, and Zionist politics. During the 1930s, he donated more than $300,000 to Zionist and Jewish activities, usually with the advice of Frankfurter, Julian Mack, and other Zionist associates.

However, the American Zionist organization had deteriorated in the 1920s, and several of its leaders had realized that the return of Brandeis was needed if the movement was to survive. Brandeis was willing to work in the background but unwilling again to be identified publicly as an American Zionist leader. Brandeis, said one of the Zionist leaders, "seems not to understand that the moral impact of his personality is of so great an importance at this juncture that without it, i.e., without the personality, a more orderly administration and more sensible Palestine-work will remain a ghost."

Negotiations had begun, people working through friends of friends, until finally Brandeis agreed to speak at a Zionist rally in November 1929. He would not again become the formal leader but would show that he was cooperating with the new leaders. Frankfurter opposed the appearance because he believed it would involve Brandeis in public controversy and would result in demands for appearances by Brandeis for other causes. Brandeis wrote his friend a long answer saying that the deteriorating situation required action by him, the scheduled meeting would be neither taxing nor controversial, and "abstinence at this time on my part would naturally be interpreted as loss of faith."

In 1929 the preeminent fact of life in Palestine for the Jews was Arab attacks. Brandeis spoke to the November Zionist meeting of the Arab "massacre of helpless old people and peaceful religious students, a terrible thing to have happened in any part of the world." He again endorsed the Balfour Declaration, saying that a Jewish Palestine was advantageous for British as well as Jewish interests. "For when the Jew is there in numbers," Brandeis said, "there will be no anti-Semitism. There will be Jewish joy as well as Jewish sorrow."

The Brandeis theme was picked up later by Frankfurter in an article for the prestigious *Foreign Affairs.* He traced the history of the Balfour Declaration from the British promise through the League of Nations and said that "thereby the establishment of a Jewish national home became an international obligation." But the British had begun their rush away from the promise of the Balfour Declaration in 1922 when Winston Churchill cut off the Trans-Jordan area from the Palestine territory and gave it to a Hashemite tribe chased out of Saudi Arabia. After that, the British were not even subtle. Whatever the British government had said in 1917, in the late 1920s the opposite was true. Acknowledging the problem of the Arabs in Palestine, Frankfurter insisted: "If the Jewish homeland cannot be built without making the fellaheen's lot worse rather than better, it ought not to be built." He argued that the Jews have not been the Arabs' problem. "That is precisely the untruth by which a small body of economically powerful Arabs are exploiting the religious feeling of Arab masses whom they themselves oppress."

A dozen years earlier Frankfurter had met at the Paris Peace Conference with Prince Feisal and Lawrence of Arabia, and their letters had held out hope for Jew and Arab to work and live together. In his *Foreign Affairs* article, Frankfurter repeated the call for a Palestine where "Arab cannot dominate Jew, nor Jew Arab" and said that only "in a fellowship of reciprocal rights and reciprocal duties can be realized the distinctive values to civilization of Jew and Arab." This could happen, argued Frankfurter, when Britain—"and more particularly its Administration in Palestine—abandons the negative role of umpire and assumes the creative tasks of the Mandate."

Brandeis and Frankfurter relied in England on Harold Laski to intercede with the British government. Laski, although Jewish, was not a Zionist. If Brandeis and Frankfurter were not his good friends, he grumbled, "I think I would have told them long ago to go to hell and see what they could accomplish without my intervention. I can't run daily to the Foreign Secretary because Brandeis has doubts about a semi-colon." He believed that "at some point in a negotiation one has to assume that the cabinet really means what it says." Brandeis had believed the British cabinet when it approved the Balfour Declaration in 1917. By the early 1930s he knew better.

On the afternoon of June 18, 1930, Brandeis left Chatham on Cape Cod and checked into a downtown Boston hotel. Staying at the same hotel, his presence unannounced, was Sir Ronald Lindsay, the British ambassador to the United States. As previously arranged, Brandeis left a note for Sir Ronald inviting him to come to his room. The next morning at 9:20, Sir Ronald knocked on Brandeis's door; Brandeis opened it, ushered Sir Ronald in, and "without a word of preliminaries," the two men began to discuss Palestine and British responsibility. Brandeis did most of the talking; Sir Ronald making notes, asking an occasional question.

The history of the British involvement was traced, the cause of the current unrest examined, Brandeis stating that "there would be no doubt on anybody's part that the Arabs were the aggressors." Then Brandeis made two points. First, he expressed the fear of American Jews that the British were reneging on their commitment. If so, he said, "our plan for cooperation between the United States and Great Britain in the long future would be most seriously menaced." This was, Brandeis said, because of the influence of Jews in American politics, an influence "due in part to the fact that they form so large a part of the population of New York State; in part due to their political activity and in part to their own ability, education and character." What Brandeis was saying was that, because of New York's having then the largest number of electoral votes in a presidential election, Jews had an impact on the selection of an American President disproportionate to their actual numbers in the United States. The danger to British-American future cooperation was "dwelt upon considerably," recalled Brandeis. Sir Ronald said he recognized the danger.

Brandeis's second point underscored the difficulties Jews faced in

Palestine: the dangers to life and property. Brandeis told Sir Ronald "that it was wholly contrary to any conception of civil rights with which I was familiar, through study of the Anglo-Saxon institutions and the American experience, that when a government found itself unable to afford protection, citizens should not be permitted to protect themselves." The English did not protect the Jews, nor allow the Jews to arm themselves against the Arab threat. Brandeis said: "It was the old, weak, defenseless Jews in Safed and Hebron who were the chief victims of the massacres; and in the colonies where there were the new Jews, able to protect themselves, there were few casualties."

At twenty minutes before noon, Sir Ronald rose to leave. The two men had been together for two hours and forty minutes. "Then your position," he said, "is that the course of conduct of the local administration conduced to disturbances of 1929 and that the course of conduct since has been inconsistent with the obligations of the mandate?"

Brandeis said the statement was correct, and again warned about the future of American-British relations. Sir Ronald knew nothing of the Palestine situation, conceded having no background in the area, and had never visited the land. He told Brandeis: "No other country could do as well as Great Britain."

Brandeis responded: "I agree entirely with you, but to prevent the agitation, it is essential that American Jews should not believe that Great Britain's action as mandatory is influenced by fear of political considerations."

A long series of negotiations began with the British government to allow more Jews to enter Palestine. Consistently Britain refused, bending only when pressured, usually by the American government, which, in turn, was influenced by prominent American Jews such as Brandeis and Frankfurter. This was true even after the danger to the Jews in Europe was apparent. It was bloc politics.

After Hitler came to power, the struggle to increase Jewish immigration into Palestine changed. Before that event, the struggle had been to fulfill the dream of a national homeland. After that event, it was a desperate passion to save a people.

Never politically naïve, Brandeis understood what he, Frankfurter, and other Jews must do if the United States was to help the German Jews. Cordell Hull, Roosevelt's Secretary of State and a former Democratic national chairman, understood the political ramifications. In 1933, early in the New Deal, Raymond Moley, then an assistant secretary of state, suggested that Hull meet with Brandeis. Moley had been badgered into making the suggestion by Frankfurter. Hull agreed.

Brandeis's law clerk, Paul Freund, took the call from Moley, and there was a dance of words. Moley said the Secretary would come at the justice's convenience. "No," said an annoyed Brandeis, "the Secretary wishes to see me, and I will be happy to receive him at his convenience." Brandeis was observing the judicial proprieties; a justice responds to requests from the executive branch but does not initiate them.

The two men met in Brandeis's study in the California Street apartment house, Hull arriving promptly at six o'clock in the evening. He told Brandeis that the United States had been assisting the Jews, "but all in private." Brandeis did not accept this, saying to Hull, "I felt more ashamed of my country than pained by Jewish suffering." European nations, Brandeis continued, had publicly protested the Nazi actions against the Jews, and "how unlike [America's] present attitude to our nobler past."

Hull responded that the American action was private on the advice of the American consul in Germany. Brandeis countered with three suggestions to Hull: (1) that FDR should publicly criticize the Nazis for their treatment of Jews, the kind of statement "which [Woodrow Wilson] would have made"; (2) that immigration curbs be relaxed in favor of refugees; and (3) that Americans treat Hjalmar Schacht, president of the German Reichsbank and Hitler's representative to a Washington meeting, with disdain.

The Brandeis-Hull session lasted a little more than an hour; Hull left at 7:05 and had impressed Brandeis. "He has a beautiful face," said the justice of Hull. The law clerk, Paul Freund, recalled that after the meeting Brandeis said he also had requested a boycott of German goods by the United States.

Whether Hull made a commitment to Brandeis for any of the Brandeis requests is not known, but probably not; Hull was too smooth a politician for commitments.

There were several reasons for the State Department's reluctance to act. At that time Germany and areas in the United States were trading partners. American labor unions worried about the impact of German refugees in an already labor-surplus country. There was the argument that actions within another nation's borders, no matter how uncivilized, were that nation's business and no other's. Those pressures were stronger than pressures American Jews could exert despite Brandeis's threat to Sir Ronald Lindsay in 1930. And the State Department itself was, in the words of Harold Ickes, "a conglomeration of ambitious men consisting mainly of careerists who, because they are career men, feel no obligation to follow Administration policy. I believe that, in substance, it is undemocratic in its outlook and is shot through with fascism."

In addition to engineering the Hull-Brandeis meeting, Frankfurter, at Brandeis's suggestion, petitioned the President.

With Franklin Roosevelt, Frankfurter had not sought to advance his own personal interests, and one time even refrained from asking the President for help in saving a relative who was a Nazi victim. Was assisting the German Jews a violation of this rule? Frankfurter, at least in the spring of 1933, was not certain. "For once in my life," he said, "I wish that for a brief period I were not a Jew. Then I would not have even the appearance of being sectarian in writing as I have written."

Frankfurter had received a telegram from Rabbi Wise, saying that a protest movement, including possible congressional action, was building against the Nazis. Frankfurter sent the telegram to the President with the suggestion that action by him would assist the protest movement in Congress. Frankfurter also discussed the situation with Roosevelt privately.

Franklin Roosevelt had his priorities. In the spring of 1933 they were launching the New Deal, tackling the depression, and correcting the international currency problems; the German Jews were toward the bottom of his list. In what was probably the first demonstration by Roosevelt as President that he used Frankfurter for his purposes as he used his other aides, rather than being used by him, he passed on the Frankfurter message to Secretary of State Hull, who answered politely but did not offer assistance. Frankfurter then wrote directly to Hull: "To give public expression of our readiness to facilitate admission of refugees who are the victims of a brutal official policy is merely to assert the unbroken and honorable tradition of this country for over a century. To withhold such public action out of deference to the sensibilities of the Hitler regime is in effect to give support to the baleful aspects of Hitlerism."

Hull did not respond, being "so preoccupied" with a monetary conference. An assistant offered assurances that Germany was aware of America's concerns.

Roosevelt did raise the question of Nazi mistreatment of Jews in a private talk with Hjalmar Schacht, but Schacht treated the conversation as a casual one in his report to his government. The United States did not relax its refugee quota; Secretary of Labor Frances Perkins had attempted to bring in more Jewish refugees but was blocked by Hull's State Department. Nor was there any boycott of German goods. Brandeis blamed the inaction not on Cordell Hull but on "career officers in the State Department, who cautioned against ruffling Hitler's feelings."

As opposition to Hitler's actions against the Jews diminished, the virulence of his moves increased.

Brandeis and Frankfurter were more successful with people outside of government. One of Adolf Hitler's first moves had been the ousting of Jews from teaching positions in German universities. Frankfurter helped organize "The University in Exile" to employ some of the ousted Jews. Lending their names in support of the "University" were such prominent non-Jewish Americans as Oliver Wendell Holmes, Herbert Bayard Swope, Robert M. Hutchins, John Dewey, and George A. Plimpton. A directory of the ousted scholars was printed and circulated among American universities. The directory included seventeen hundred names.

Frankfurter began a frenzied round of meetings, telephone calls, and letters to influential friends. "Can't you get the 'leaders' to do anything?" he demanded of one. "Is the legal profession really going to remain silent?" The Harvard law professor was particularly incensed at the reluctance of American lawyers to speak out as the evidence of Nazi barbarities mounted.

Frankfurter, the man of law, could not understand this reluctance. "There are times for finesse and there are times for simple directness," he argued to Charles Burlingham, the New York lawyer. "The German situation calls for simple directness and not for finesse."

There was movement: a protest by lawyers, one signed by academics, another by churchmen. But the movement was glacial. America in the 1930s was preoccupied with its own problems, frightened a little of its foreign-born population, still smarting from its "red" scare, sometimes admiring of Hitler, seeing Jews as outsiders. As late as 1940, a best-selling book, *The Wave of the Future,* suggested that the Nazi cruelties were merely aberrational excesses of a new movement, the vanguard of a better world to come.

Frankfurter never believed that. In 1920, when he had attended the Zionist conference in London, he also had visited Germany for a few days. "I happened to have been in Berlin at the very time when one of the most significant minds now alive, Einstein, and one of the gentlest human beings I have ever encountered was made the subject of the most brutal and vulgar attacks," he said, "for no other reason than that he was a Jew." That memory stayed with him. Still, even Frankfurter was shocked at the mounting atrocities under Hitler. "That things should be happening," he said, "that are happening in 1933 in the land of Goethe, Schiller, Lessing, Kant and Beethoven requires a complete re-orientation of one's sense of reality as well as one's historical sense."

Frankfurter and Brandeis were in frequent contact with James G. McDonald of the Foreign Policy Association, who was eventually placed in charge of refugees for the League of Nations. Brandeis opposed the appointment of McDonald because he was an American and "no American ought to be selected—unless . . . America should adopt a policy of generous admission and emphatic denunciation of German policy of discrimination." Frankfurter also was not happy with the McDonald appointment, telling McDonald that he too much played the diplomat "rather than relying on homespun and courageous truth-telling."

These were still the days before Nazi Germany was to offer the Jews and non-Jews a new understanding of the word "genocide," and no one was certain how to respond to events in Germany. A friend of Frankfurter's, Dr. Alfred E. Cohn, revealed some of the frustrations of American Jews in a letter to McDonald early in 1934. Cohn was working with Frankfurter to assist Jewish scholars exiled from Germany, and McDonald approached him about raising large sums of money from American Jews. Said Cohn:

The general description of your plans also leaves me with questions. You want tens of millions of dollars. There is no harm in assuming you can collect the money. But what is to be secured with it? You will no doubt reeducate, retrain, rehabilitate a certain number of people and settle them somewhere. But to what end? Will any of these procedures do more than solve temporarily our age long problems? Are the Jews to go on paying, as they have for centuries, for the privilege of a hazardous existence. Has there not been enough of this? . . . Has not the time come to say frankly, if we're to go on, there must be a settlement, different perhaps in different places, but one in which decency and dignity enter, for Gentiles as well as for Jews? The main responsibility lies after all with the majority.

Cohn's concerns, like the fears expressed by Brandeis and Frankfurter, had their impact on McDonald. In 1935 he stopped playing at diplomacy, resigned from his League of Nations post with some "courageous truth-telling." Reporting that Germany's domestic policies were threatening hundreds of thousands of human beings, McDonald said, "the considerations of diplomatic correctness must take second place to the considerations of simple humanity." He would be "unworthy" if he did not demand that the nations of the world "move to abate the already existing and still threatening tragedies."

As the 1930s stretched out, rather than avert the tragedies, the nations of the world contributed toward them. Frankfurter's particular concern was the universities in those nations, especially Harvard.

Ever since the problem of hiring Jewish faculty members had emerged in the late 1920s at the Harvard Law School, Frankfurter had been skeptical of its dean, Roscoe Pound. In 1934 he believed his skepticism confirmed. Pound, after traveling in Germany that summer, had told the press that there was no military presence in Germany, no tension, and Hitler was saving central Europe from "agitators." As for the persecution of Jews, Pound said it was not happening, except for some actions against a few Polish Jews who recently had come to Germany. The remarks, widely printed because of Pound's position, added to Hitler's stature. Frankfurter, reading them shortly after returning from his year in England, was appalled.

He was settling in for the new semester on Friday, September 7, arranging things in his office, when Pound, without knocking, entered. "I heard your voice and so came in to say hello. What a joy it is to hear your voice again; I missed you so," said Pound. They talked for a few moments, then Pound continued: "Next Friday I think there will be a ceremony at the School here, at which I want you especially to be present."

Several days later, Frankfurter received a message from Dean Pound's secretary:

Miss McCarthy said the ceremony about which the Dean spoke to you will be on Monday the 17th at noon in the lobby, with luncheon for the German Consul afterward.

Frankfurter sat down and drafted this note to Pound:

Of course I cannot attend any function in honor of a representative of a government which Mr. Justice Holmes has accurately characterized as "a challenge to civilization." And it would be cowardly for me to suppress my sense of humiliation that, while other leading law schools have offered hospitality to distinguished juristic victims of German oppression, my beloved Law School, the centre of Anglo-American law, should even by indirection confer special distinction upon an official representative of enthroned lawlessness.

Frankfurter decided, because the school was involved, to discuss the matter with the president of Harvard, James Bryant Conant. From

Conant he learned that Pound was to receive an honorary degree from the University of Berlin, to be presented by the German ambassador to the United States, not consul. Conant said that he did not believe he could tell Pound to decline the degree "consistent with academic freedom of speech. Nor did I see how I could deny the request of the Ambassador to present the degree to Pound in the Law School."

If he were not university president, Conant said, he "would write the kind of letter you are proposing to send to Pound." Conant added: "And since we are talking about Pound, we might as well recognize the fact his is a pathological case."

Frankfurter admitted that "I abstained from pointing out to Conant that to exercise a veto power on Pound's personal right to accept the degree from Germany is one thing; to allow Langdell Hall to be turned into a Nazi holiday quite another," but he did not attend the Pound presentation.

If Harvard gave in to Nazism on that point, as Frankfurter believed, it resisted a few weeks later. Earlier that year Ernst Hanfstaengl, a sometime Harvard student and in 1934 an aide to Adolf Hitler, had written Conant proposing a "Dr. Hanfstaengl Scholarship," worth $1,000, for traveling in Germany. At the Harvard Corporation meeting a few weeks following the Pound affair, the scholarship was rejected. "We are unwilling to accept a gift from one who has been so closely associated with the leadership of a political party which has inflicted damage on the universities of Germany through measures which have struck at principles we believe to be fundamental to universities throughout the world," said the Conant statement.

Frankfurter wrote Conant that his statement was "a heartening and noble reaffirmation of the very basis of modern western civilization."

The Harvard situation seesawed. Pound over the next several years made anti-Jewish remarks. Publicly, Frankfurter kept his relations with Pound civil, but privately he made no secret of his dislike and disrespect for the man. There were other incidents.

The glow from Harvard's refusal of the Hanfstaengl offer did not last two years. In 1936 the University of Heidelberg in Germany was having an anniversary celebration and invited the major universities of the world to send representatives. Oxford and Cambridge universities in England declined their invitations because faculty members at Heidelberg had been abused. Harvard accepted. "What was done in the Hanfstaengl matter gave wide encouragement to the enduring principles which underlie the western conception of a university, and was therefore greeted with corresponding resentment in Germany," Frankfurter wrote to his friends who were members of the governing Harvard Corporation. "The Heidelberg acceptance furnishes the wrong symbol for American institutions," he continued.

Shortly after Frankfurter finished writing that letter, he received a list of recent dismissals from German universities. On the list were six persons dismissed from Heidelberg. "All of them, so I am credibly informed, are academic notabilities," said Frankfurter in a postscript. Such dismissals "are surely sufficient to deny Heidelberg's claim to be a university rather than a political agency."

Frankfurter, a believer in Oliver Wendell Holmes's "We live by symbols," understood that when universities countenance racism or embrace those who advocate racism, others will follow. This was spelled out in letters between Frankfurter and Henry Sloane Coffin, president of Union Theological Seminary, early in 1936, concerning a bequest left to Yale University.

A man named Charles Howard Warren had left his estate to Yale for scholarships and, according to the will, "as a memorial to the Anglo-Saxon race to which the United States owes its culture, I direct that such beneficiaries shall be confined to those boys who shall be adjudged to best exemplify such qualifications, ideals and traditions, and who shall be the sons of white Christian parents of Anglo-Saxon, Scandinavian, or Teutonic descent, both of whom were citizens of the United States and were born in America."

That was too much for Frankfurter. He hoped, he said publicly, that Yale would not allow itself to be "bought for Nazism" by the Warren bequest. Coffin, a member of the Yale corporation, which had accepted the bequest, heard the charge, was "outraged" by it, and responded to Frankfurter. For Yale to accept the money, he argued, did not involve Nazism because Nazism discriminates *"against* a certain racial group" and not in favor of one group.

The Frankfurter response says much of what was of concern to Frankfurter and to other American Jews. For Yale to place its "moral imprimatur" both on the suggestion that the United States owes its culture "to the Anglo-Saxon race," as the Warren bequest said, and on an ethnic consideration was to support "these dark forces" advocating racial and religious discrimination. Although Yale was not throwing stones through windows and painting swastikas on synagogues, its action, Frankfurter was saying, encouraged the less sophisticated to do just that.

As he often did, Frankfurter sent the exchange of letters to his friends. Harlan Fiske Stone, with whom he had become close in the previous half-dozen years, agreed with Frankfurter. "I think the fatal defect in [Coffin's] argument is that he overlooks the fact that the gift was not made to promote religion. Its obvious purpose is to further good citizenship and leadership in the community, but . . . makes the smug assumption that only white, Anglo-Saxons, Scandinavians or Teutons can possess the qualifications. Germany today affords a fine example of the logical conclusion from such assumptions."

Not all agreed. Samuel Eliot Morison, the Harvard historian, said he could understand Yale's attitude. "We Yankees whose fathers reclaimed this country from the wilderness are being hustled and shoved from every side," he grumbled, "politically, mainly by the Irish; economically, by the Jews. Let us at least save *some* places at mother Yale for *our* boys!"

In 1939, a "Committee of Eight" at Harvard, including Frankfurter and Arthur Schlesinger, Sr., produced a report covering, in part, religious bias in American universities. It said:

It is a common opinion that Jews, regardless of their qualifications, have found it increasingly difficult to obtain academic posts in America.

. . . Anti-Semitic feeling has operated within the universities themselves, in the form of prejudice which is difficult to prove and never officially proclaimed.

. . . Discrimination may exist in some [Harvard] departments. . . . Those who raised the issue seem in agreement, to use the words of one of them, that "racial prejudice is so thoroughly ingrained and taken for granted that no one takes much notice of it except in particularly flagrant cases."

The Committee is informed . . . that certain members of the faculty object to the appointment of Jews to the tutorial staff in the belief that they are unacceptable to undergraduates.

Not all American Jews reacted as did Frankfurter and Brandeis. In 1933, Walter Lippmann was an influential columnist, syndicated by the New York *Herald Tribune*. While others denounced Nazi attacks on Jews, Lippmann in one of his columns described Hitler as "the authentic voice of a genuinely civilized people" and blamed Jews in Germany for the Nazi attacks on them. This was consistent with his attitude a decade earlier when Harvard considered a quota system—blame the minority for being discriminated against. Frankfurter could not stomach it. Although Lippmann had been his friend for many years, Frankfurter dropped him.

In 1936, Frankfurter heard that Lippmann was talking about the incident and wrote him, explaining that the cause was the 1933 column —"something inside of me snapped." Lippmann retaliated with a column suggesting that university professors should not involve themselves with politicians. At the time, Frankfurter was the most prominent professor involved with politicians, and all knew of whom Lippmann was writing.

Except for his 1933 columns, Lippmann did not write again about the European Jewish situation until 1938. Even then he did not refer to the persecution of Jews in the columns but suggested that, because Europe was overcrowded, "surplus" Jews be shipped to Africa.

To all of the motives for Frankfurter to be concerned for the fate of European Jews, in 1938 there was another motive added. Frankfurter's uncle, Solomon Frankfurter, lived in Vienna. Before coming to the United States, Frankfurter had lived with his uncle for two years "and the bond between us became deep." The last time Frankfurter had seen his uncle was in 1920, but he had followed his uncle's career with admiration.

In 1938, Solomon Friedrich Frankfurter represented the Jewish scholar who had successfully managed to thrive in both the religious and secular world. He had been director of the University of Vienna Library, and in the 1930s was a member of the Austrian Federal Board for Cultural Questions. He also had written extensively in the fields of archeology, education, and biography. In the area of Jewish scholarship, he had been a consultant on Jewish community questions to the Austrian Ministry of Culture and Education, president of the Society for the Collection and Investigation of Jewish Historic Monuments, and director of the Vienna Jewish Museum, and had written extensively on Jewish subjects. On Sunday, March 12, 1938, at eight o'clock in the morning, Nazi storm troopers broke into his house, pulled him from his bed, and, without giving him time to find an overcoat, took him off to jail. His cell was cold, lacked a stove, and Solomon Frankfurter had only a thin jacket and trousers, a shirt without collar, and shoes without laces. Solomon Frankfurter was eighty-two— the oldest person in the crowded cell; his cellmates heard him cry but not complain.

At night two of his cellmates slept with him, warming his body with theirs. "We put a clean handkerchief under his head," recalled one.

"Though the storm troopers repeatedly threatened with bayonets any one who should dare to speak," the prisoner recalled, "we had a whispering conversation from which I learned that the Professor had relatives in the United States. But he didn't tell me who they were."

Solomon Frankfurter's friends in Vienna, however, did know that his nephew was Felix Frankfurter of the Harvard Law School and friend of President Roosevelt. They managed to contact Frankfurter at Harvard ten days after his uncle had been arrested.

In this kind of emergency, Felix Frankfurter was as close to the President of the United States as he was to the telephone. However, Frankfurter did not believe he should impose on that friendship for a personal matter, no matter how extreme the emergency. Instead, he called upon a friend in England with contacts within the German government, Nancy Astor, doyenne of the Cliveden set, the group seemingly willing to accept Hitler as a bulwark against Russian Communism. Frankfurter had first met her, and visited her home, Cliveden, during the First World War. He had met her again in 1920 and in the 1930s. In recent years the friendship had cooled because of her apparent sympathy with Nazism, including its anti-Semitism. Frankfurter did not hesitate. He cabled her, asking her to use her "good offices with German authorities."

"Am taking drastic steps," she wired back.

As soon as she heard from Frankfurter, Nancy Astor spoke to the German ambassador in London "and gave him, in no uncertain terms, our views on arresting aged scholars." Three days later she spoke with the ambassador again, vowing to go to Vienna herself unless Solomon Frankfurter was released. As a result of her intercession, Solomon Frankfurter was released on March 28. "The Ambassador tells me," Nancy Astor wrote to Felix Frankfurter, "that he was only imprisoned a few days as a result of some unguarded remark." Three years later, when Solomon Frankfurter was eighty-five and about to leave for the United States, he died in Vienna of natural causes.

As a result of her help with Solomon Frankfurter, Nancy Astor and Felix Frankfurter began a correspondence about the "Cliveden set." Speaking of the need for "candor among old friends," Frankfurter said, "I ought not to withhold from you the disquietude with which the attitude of yourself and your friends toward the Nazi regime has filled so many of us here." For Frankfurter the problem was the same as with the Harvard participation in the University of Heidelberg's anniversary celebration and Yale accepting a bequest for Anglo-Saxons only. Nancy Astor and her friends might not be throwing stones and painting swastikas but their actions encouraged the less educated and less sophisticated to do so.

She replied: "There is not one word of truth in all this propaganda. It started in a Communist sheet."

Said Frankfurter: "I hate war as much as you do, and I am not suggesting an offensive policy by Great Britain against the present German regime. But to avoid war surely does not require that your moral weight should be cast on the side of ruthless tyranny. The fate of my uncle is symbolic of the philosophy and the practice of Nazism. Here is an old gentleman of eighty-two treated like the worst criminal, when his only crime was that he had devoted a long life to scholarship and the things of the spirit."

As for Nancy Astor's defense against the charge that she was anti-Semitic, Frankfurter told her that "you must not be too surprised if you are widely misunderstood. . . . When you make the kind of statements that you made . . . earlier in the year, about the control of advertisements in the American Press by Jews, and offer that as an explanation of what is the instinctive, traditional liberalism of American opinion against Hitler's brutality and cruelty . . ."

The Frankfurter-Nancy Astor dialogue changed no minds. Frankfurter knew that the Cliveden attitude—Hitler had stopped Bolshevism, the atrocity stories were exaggerated—was becoming pervasive, both in the United States and especially in England. His friend Harold Laski had become more of a Zionist over the years as the Nazi attacks against the Jews mounted and the British attitude opposing Jewish immigration to Palestine hardened, and had been keeping Frankfurter and Brandeis aware of the details of the British actions.

Laski's messages were consistent. The British government was giving up its promise made in the Balfour Declaration, retreating from its commitment to the Jews, unless the Americans "somehow" stirred up London.

Frankfurter, in the fall of 1938, reminisced with a friend about his love affair with England, going back to the first time he had visited it during World War I. "London felt like home to me—in a strange unaccountable way it was much more indigenous than Vienna would have been or New York was." He recalled once arriving at Waterloo Station and crossing Westminster Bridge with an English friend, and, as the towers of the Parliament appeared, the friend "said to me very quietly, 'Take off your hat in reverence to the mother of parliaments.' "

British behavior in Palestine, Frankfurter said, reminded him of Napoleon's line "This is worse than a crime; it's a blunder."

He telephoned Franklin Roosevelt.

In 1933 Frankfurter had been hesitant about approaching his friend in the White House about the Jewish situation; he had done it then but only in a roundabout manner. He did not ask the President to help save his uncle. Now the situation had reached a point demanding directness: Would the United States pressure England in the Palestine matter?

The President suggested Frankfurter draft a message for British Prime Minister Neville Chamberlain in the President's name. This was done, and Ben Cohen dictated the text to Missy LeHand, the President's secretary, the next day. It called for the opening up of Palestine to Jewish immigration, as promised in the Balfour Declaration, not only because of the Nazi persecutions but because "Palestine is a significant symbol of hope to Jewry."

Roosevelt was willing to help the Jews, but—his conversation with Frankfurter had made clear—he was not well informed about Palestine. His State Department did not serve him well in that area. As a result, on October 14, 1938, Brandeis went to the White House to discuss the Palestine question with the President. A month shy of his eighty-second birthday, Brandeis's appearances outside the Supreme Court now were so infrequent that his very presence at the White House caused a page-one story in the *New York Times*: ". . . The White House announced only the purposes of the discussion and the fact that the justice had come there at the request of the President."

Brandeis found the talk encouraging. The President, he told Frankfurter, appreciated Palestine's significance, "the need of keeping it whole and of making it Jewish." Roosevelt had been unaware, and was "tremendously interested" to learn, that the Arab population in Palestine had doubled between World War I and 1938 because the land under the Jews had become more productive for them than the neighboring Arab lands. Roosevelt also made specific inquiries about the availability of land for the Arabs in the neighboring Arab nations.

In late September, Prime Minister Chamberlain had met in Munich with Hitler and then returned to London to announce that peace had been secured "for our time." Astonished at how easily the Western nations capitulated, Adolf Hitler felt free to take his next step—in the words of the American military attaché in Berlin, "the liquidation of that non-German element within the German people, which in his eyes, stood in the way of the realization of the concept of National Socialism on a racial basis."

On the night of November 9, 1938, shortly after the end of the

Munich conference, thousands of Germans, with the open support of their government, went on a rampage against the German Jews. The figures are approximate: two hundred synagogues destroyed; eight thousand Jewish-owned shops destroyed, looted, or badly damaged; about three dozen Jews killed; thousands arrested. Many of the abused Jews traced their ancestry in Germany back hundreds of years and had fought for Germany in the First World War. Even with all that had happened to that date, the world was stunned. Newspapers around the world reported the events in blaring headlines and with photographs of burning synagogues. The time became known as Krystallnacht, the night of the broken glass.

In the United States, the State Department prepared a three-sentence statement for the President to issue. It read: "The news of the past few days from Germany has shocked public opinion in the United States. Such news from any part of the world would inevitably produce a similar reaction among the American people. With a view to gaining a firsthand picture of the situation in Germany I asked the Secretary of State to order our Ambassador in Berlin to come home for report and consultation."

As Franklin Roosevelt stared at the three-sentence statement, bland as the diplomat's language and unemotional as the diplomat's posture, weak as diplomacy had consistently been on this issue, the politician slipped away from the man who was President, leaving instead the Christian gentleman who had been educated by churchmen and who had taken his oath on the Bible, his hand touching these words: "Though I speak with the tongues of men and of angels, and have not charity, I am become as sounding brass, or a tinkling cymbal . . . and though I have all faith, so that I could remove mountains, and have not charity, I am nothing"—this man added a fourth sentence to the State Department draft: "I myself could scarcely believe that such things could occur in a twentieth century civilization."

A few days later Brandeis met again with the President at Roosevelt's request. The American minister to Germany had been recalled, and Roosevelt reported that he had met with the British ambassador to encourage a meeting between the British government and Arab leaders. "The British should explain to them that they, the Arabs, had within their control large territories ample to sustain their people. Palestine and Transjordan constituted only a small portion, probably not over five percent of their territories," reads the report of the meeting. When the ambassador spoke of Arab opposition to Jewish immigration, Roosevelt belittled it and said it was "due largely to British indecision and conflicting policy."

Then Brandeis and Roosevelt spoke about financial aid for settling Jewish families in Palestine. Roosevelt talked of a plan to settle 100,000 families at $3,000 a family. He thought one-third of the money would come from the American government, one-third from the British and French governments, and one-third from private subscription.

About to leave on a ten-day vacation, the President said that, if there was anything Brandeis believed he could do, the justice should communicate with him and, if necessary, he would return to Washington on short notice.

There was one other step Franklin Roosevelt took, this less than two months after Krystallnacht. With the world still trembling from the German onslaught against one of its minority peoples, Roosevelt announced that in the United States racial and religious background did not matter. In a world where the status of the Jew was precarious, raising question of the Jew's ability to survive, Franklin Roosevelt appointed a Jew—a person well known for his active involvement in Jewish and Zionist affairs—to one of the highest positions in American government. At a time when Nazi Germany was lashing out at minorities, calling them "outsiders," Franklin Roosevelt announced that the outsider, the Jew and the immigrant also, were insiders in America. Whatever his intentions and reasons, Franklin Roosevelt's naming of a Jew as an associate justice of the United States Supreme Court in January 1939 was a proclamation to the world that the United States, acting through its elected leader, would not go the way of Nazi Germany. Less then two months after the newspapers of the world had proclaimed that in Germany the Jews' houses of worship were destroyed, those same newspapers announced that in the United States Felix Frankfurter had been appointed to the Supreme Court.

18

Mr. Justice Frankfurter

In December 1937, Benjamin Nathan Cardozo became ill. The belief at first was that he would return to the Supreme Court, but by summer, when his illness worsened, the expectation was that his replacement on the Court would have to be named. This would be Roosevelt's third Supreme Court appointment. In the one year since the Court-packing fight, he had named Hugo Black to replace Willis Van Devanter and Stanley F. Reed to replace George Sutherland. After a cabinet meeting July 6, Roosevelt and Attorney General Homer Cummings discussed the need to appoint a progressive "in view of the narrow liberal majority." Because the Court then was filled with easterners and southerners, they spoke of appointing someone from the West. Three days later, on July 9, 1938, Cardozo died.

Although not an economic or progressive crusader, Cardozo also had understood, as had Holmes and Brandeis, the law as an expansionary device to deal with the present rather than to enshrine the past. And so among the liberal community he was mourned.

An editorial in the Boston *Herald* on Monday, July 11, lamented the nation's loss of "one of its great men." The editorial not only praised Cardozo's career in law but also saw him as "a vindication of our basic American traditions." Describing him as "a direct descendant of those who were made outcasts at the time of the inquisition," the editorial continued: "How incomprehensible it must be to Herr Hitler to read of the mourning of the whole American people without regard to race, color, creed or political affiliation over the death of Cardozo the Jew." Felix Frankfurter had written the editorial.

On Monday, October 3, the first day of the 1938 term, Chief Justice Hughes opened the session with an expression of sorrow at Cardozo's death. On Monday, December 19, formal memorial services were held in the Court chamber for Cardozo. Both events are traditional when a Supreme Court justice, retired or sitting, dies. Associate Justice James McReynolds attended neither event.

In appointing a replacement for Cardozo, Roosevelt could seek advice from others and he could use whatever criteria he chose, but the ultimate decision was his. George Washington, the nation's first President, and John Adams, its second, used party affiliation as a criterion, appointing in their administrations fourteen men to the Supreme Court from their own Federalist party. The next four Presidents—Thomas Jefferson, James Madison, James Monroe, and John Quincy Adams—also named only members of their party. William Howard Taft, a Republican, however, when he was President a century later, named three Democrats to the Supreme Court.

Another criterion is prior judicial experience. Until 1938, of the 77 men who had served on the Supreme Court, eight had previously sat on the federal bench, thirty-one on non-federal benches, and seven on both—a total of forty-six with prior judicial experience. Those forty-six include John Marshall, the nation's fourth chief justice and the one conceded to be its greatest; his entire judicial experience before being named Chief Justice in 1801 was three years on a Richmond court that met once a month and generally dealt with small personal debt cases. Hugo Black had less than two years' experience on the non-federal bench before his appointment. While there are others with seemingly insignificant experience on the bench, the forty-six also include Holmes and Cardozo, both of whom had gained judicial fame on state courts before coming to Washington.

Geography and religion sometimes are criteria. Roosevelt and Cummings felt the demand by the West for representation on the Supreme Court. They also heard from America's Catholic community. With one Catholic on the Court, Pierce Butler, the administration was told that American Catholicism deserved a second seat.

But the factor that may be most controlling in the selection of a Supreme Court justice is the nominees' politics. Theodore Roosevelt, when he was President, spelled this out. "In the ordinary and low sense which we attach to the words 'partisan' and 'politician,'" he wrote, "a judge of the Supreme Court should be neither. But in the higher sense, in the proper sense, he is not in my judgment fitted for the position unless he is a party man, a constructive statesman . . . and . . . [keeps] . . . in mind also his relations with his fellow statesmen who in other branches of the government are striving in cooperation with him to advance the ends of government." Such motivations had led Woodrow Wilson to nominate Brandeis.

With Cardozo's death, the President recalled his wish stated five years earlier to place Frankfurter on the Supreme Court. There were several reasons. Frankfurter on the Court could be expected to be a New Deal liberal. Roosevelt liked to reward loyalty; Frankfurter had been his aide through the New Deal rather than a partisan of any philosophy, had kept quiet during the Court-packing fight, had been reliable. And there was a third factor. For almost half of the Court's existence, this particular chair had been considered "the scholar's seat." Its second occupant, from 1811 to 1845, was Joseph Story, whose role as a Harvard Law School teacher after he became a justice and his written commentaries on the Constitution had first staked out that designation. Its seventh occupant, from 1902 to 1932, was Oliver Wendell Holmes, author of *The Common Law.* Cardozo, the eighth occupant, had continued the scholarly tradition.

Robert H. Jackson, an assistant attorney general and friend of Roosevelt's, pointed out that neither Black nor Reed, the President's first two appointments, was known for his scholarship. But Frankfurter, insisted Jackson to the President, because of his years at Harvard, his familiarity with the Court's inner workings, and his writings about the Court, "from the day he went on the Court . . . would be able to hold his own with the most experienced men on the Court."

Roosevelt understood that Presidents often are remembered for the quality of their judicial appointments. So, when Attorney General Cummings came to him with the name of a lackluster westerner, Roosevelt responded that "the country would not be very much stirred by that appointment." Cummings replied: "No, the country would not be much stirred by that appointment but it would be greatly satisfied by it." Cummings said he sympathized with the President's desire to find someone both colorful and safe, "but it has been my experience that it is a rare thing to find a man who is both colorful and safe, and that most of the colorful people get into trouble at one time or another."

There were factors against Frankfurter, the same ones Franklin Roosevelt had pointed out to him five years earlier when Frankfurter had declined the Solicitor General's post. Frankfurter had not argued a case before the Supreme Court, or, actually, in any court since the *Adkins* case in 1923. With the exception of William Howard Taft, who had had prior judicial experience as well as having been President, no one ever before had gone to the Court from a teaching position. In addition, there was Frankfurter's reputation as a radical, going back to his involvement with Bisbee and Mooney during World War I and Sacco-Vanzetti in the 1920s, the animosity toward him because of his New Deal involvement, and geography. Finally, he was a Jew.

The impact each of those problems would have on his possible appointment was unknown, but the Jewish question was the most difficult to gauge. William Allen White, the Emporia, Kansas, newspaper publisher, friend and admirer of Roosevelt and Frankfurter, noted for having a "feel" for the American mood, had considered writing a letter to Roosevelt urging Frankfurter's appointment; White, a canny liberal Republican, had been helpful with both the Brandeis and Cardozo appointments. But he hesitated about writing FDR, as he explained to a friend:

Will not his appointment to succeed Cardozo give the Jew baiters a chance to say that the Jews have preempted a seat in the Court? Also the big rich reactionaries, both Jew and Gentile, have made Felix Frankfurter their head devil. The rich Gentiles are glad to fan the racial question. Would not their instinctive and entirely proper dislike for Frankfurter leave them free to encourage, more or less secretly, anti-Semitic propaganda?

Prominent American Jews feared a Frankfurter appointment would increase anti-Semitism in the United States. According to an often-told piece of New Deal gossip, a group of those Jews approached Roosevelt and asked him not to replace Cardozo with a Jew.

Against those factors, however, there was considerable support for Frankfurter.

Even the western opposition cracked. Tommy Corcoran met during the summer with George W. Norris of Nebraska. A Republican, a liberal, former chairman of the Senate Judiciary Committee, which receives Court nominations first, and an old friend of Frankfurter's, Norris was the first from the western United States to call for Frankfurter's appointment. Corcoran wrote a draft for a letter from Norris to the President endorsing Frankfurter, but before that draft reached the Norris summer home at Waupaca, Wisconsin, Norris already had written his own letter and released it to the press, saying that Frankfurter, more than any other, "fully and truly represents the philosophy of government of Justice Oliver Wendell Holmes and his successor, Justice Cardozo."

Corcoran and Ben Cohen called their friends, asking them to contact the President or someone who could reach the President. Stories and editorials appeared in the newspapers, as if by accident. "The movement to put Professor Frankfurter on the high bench is quite spontaneous," went one account. Even David Lawrence, dean of conservative columnists, endorsed the Frankfurter appointment. Conceding "the very mention of the name is like waving a red flag at the conservatives," Lawrence argued that "at least [Frankfurter] has a high respect for the tradition of the Supreme Court and its background."

Another boost came in September when a cross-section of the nation's 175,000 lawyers endorsed Frankfurter for the appointment in a poll. Frankfurter received 27 percent of the lawyers' vote. The next highest percentages were five points each for Learned Hand and John W. Davis. Although the lawyers were for Frankfurter, they were not for the New Deal. Of those polled, 38 percent supported Roosevelt and 62 percent opposed him.

Still Roosevelt dallied. In September he talked with Attorney General Cummings for the first time in several weeks. Cummings mentioned the Cardozo vacancy; he had his own favorite candidate, not Frankfurter. Roosevelt replied that he still did not have a choice. Cummings suggested some names, but the President rejected them.

The Court reconvened in October of 1938, but Roosevelt continued to delay making an appointment. A nominee could not be confirmed until Congress convened in January 1939, and Roosevelt saw no reason to close out his options until then.

Frankfurter did not initiate any discussion of the Court seat with the President. In October, he and Marion visited the President and Mrs. Roosevelt at their Hyde Park home for a weekend. The press immediately speculated that the Court appointment would be discussed, but the President suggested the newsmen restrain their speculation, explaining that the Frankfurters customarily made a fall visit to the Roosevelts at Hyde Park.

The speculation was correct, however. The Court opening was discussed.

The Frankfurters arrived Friday afternoon. That night, after dinner, Marion said to Felix, "Something's the matter with the President—he seems so constrained and he isn't spontaneous, isn't natural—something . . ."

"Probably some affair of state," Frankfurter responded.

The "affair of state" was the Court vacancy. The next day Roosevelt pulled Frankfurter aside and said: "Of course, you ought to be on the

Supreme Court of the United States, but I've got to appoint a fellow west of the Mississippi—I promised the party leaders he'd be a Westerner the next time."

The two men then spent several hours discussing candidates from the West. Frankfurter promised to check records and lower-court decisions, and prepare a memorandum on some of the candidates. The memorandum was sent to Roosevelt on November 17, two days after the *New York Times* had speculated Frankfurter's name was "still in the foreground." At the end of the month Cummings sent Roosevelt data on three possible appointees—their ages and religious affiliations. Frankfurter was not one of the three, nor had a prominent Catholic emerged as a prime candidate.

After Krystallnacht, Roosevelt wrestled even more with the problem of Frankfurter's Jewishness. A few days before Christmas, in a conversation with Cummings, the President said that if Brandeis retired "the matter would be simplified, so far as Frankfurter was concerned." Cummings replied: "I always have assumed that when Brandeis retired, Frankfurter would get his place." Appointing Frankfurter before Brandeis retired meant two justices from Massachusetts as well as two Jews on the Court.

Brandeis had turned eighty-two in November, and a movement began to persuade him to resign. "One thought that since Brandeis was not going to be on the Court long and one didn't know at that time Roosevelt was going to have two more terms," recalled Ben Cohen, "there was the feeling on the part of a great number of people that Brandeis might at that time in light of his great interest in many things, that he would not be handicapped in the things he would do and the things he would be asked, if he were free from the Court." Said Cohen: "It was a delicate thing."

A friendly newspaper column reported that "Justice Brandeis's decision may be influenced by the fact that if he resigns, his old friend and disciple, Felix Frankfurter, is all but certain to be appointed in his place."

At the end of the year, Ickes recommended Frankfurter to Roosevelt. The President acknowledged Frankfurter's value and said he would be appointed when Brandeis resigned. "But will Brandeis resign?" asked Ickes. Roosevelt said he believed Brandeis would resign in time to allow Roosevelt to name his replacement. Ickes said he hoped so. "If you appoint Frankfurter," Ickes continued, "his ability and learning are such that he will dominate the Supreme Court for fifteen or twenty years to come. The result will be that, probably after you are dead, it will still be your Supreme Court." Roosevelt did not reply.

Congress returned to Washington the first week of January; Roosevelt had to decide on the Cardozo replacement then. No western candidate had emerged with an overall lead, although at least two, one a federal judge and the other a senator, were widely discussed. Brandeis had not resigned, despite the hints. There was no explanation, but for Brandeis to have resigned under such pressure would have been contrary to his lifestyle.

Frankfurter's friends stepped up their pressure on the President. Pressuring Franklin Roosevelt was always a delicate procedure. "He has a real streak of stubbornness and he does not like to have anyone try to force his hand," said Harold Ickes. But Roosevelt listened to the comments about Frankfurter.

Harry Hopkins, a presidential aide, urged Frankfurter's appointment, telling Roosevelt to consider the appointment the last one he would make. Frank Murphy, who had replaced Homer Cummings as Attorney General, endorsed Frankfurter after Corcoran and Hopkins spoke with him. Associate Justice Harlan Fiske Stone told Roosevelt that the Court needed Frankfurter.

On Wednesday, January 4, the President held a cabinet meeting but did not mention the pending appointment. Harold Ickes commented to Harry Hopkins he was confident the President would name Frankfurter. Hopkins was uncertain, feeling the pressure still coming from the West.

That night at 192 Brattle Street in Cambridge, Felix and Marion Frankfurter were having a guest for dinner. It was seven o'clock, and Marion said to him: "As usual you're late—do hurry." As usual, she was right. He was still in his underwear.

The telephone rang.

"Hello, and how are you?" said the voice of the President of the United States when Frankfurter picked up the receiver.

"You know," the President continued, "I told you I couldn't possibly appoint you to the Supreme Court."

"Oh, yes, I remember that."

"But I mean it. I mean it."

The President was known for his jokes, and Frankfurter wondered what the point of this one was. Less than two weeks before, he and the President had talked about other nominees for the Supreme Court.

"But everywhere I'd turn," continued the President, "to people that matter, whose judgment I care about, they said, you are the only person fit to succeed Holmes and Cardozo and unless you give me an insurmountable reason, your name will go in tomorrow."

Frankfurter finished dressing, then went down to dinner. The guest had already arrived, and Frankfurter had promised the President not to mention the appointment until after it was publicly announced the next day. This particular guest dined with the Frankfurters whenever he came to Cambridge. His usual arrival time at the house was seven and he invariably left at ten o'clock. "For some reason or other he stayed till midnight that night," recalled Frankfurter, "and I didn't say a word, of course; and there I had to sit knowing the course of your whole life had been turned into totally different channels—from seven to 12—and as soon as the door was closed, I said, 'Well, Marion,' then I told her this thing. . . . Very funny."

The appointment was announced when Congress convened at noon on Thursday, January 5. About two o'clock that afternoon Harold Ickes, Frank Murphy, Robert Jackson, Tommy Corcoran, Missy LeHand, and several others gathered in Ickes's office and split two magnums of champagne to celebrate. Later that day, Missy LeHand wandered back to the White House and told the President about the party. "I suspect that this was a little bunch of conspirators," said Roosevelt, adding, "and I think, too, that if I had decided against them they would have accepted my decision cheerfully and loyally."

Harold Laski, in England, wrote Roosevelt congratulating him on making the appointment, and the President replied: "I think Felix's nomination has pleased me more than anybody else in the whole country."

With Felix Frankfurter, many people were appointed to the Supreme Court on Thursday, January 5, 1939—his parents testing the new land, tugging their children behind them; Miss Hogan, his P.S. 25 teacher, vowing an "uppercut" to any student not speaking English to the young immigrant; the faculty members of City College of New York and Harvard Law School, teaching with equal zealousness the poor and the foreign-born and the wealthy and native-born; the people of New York City, the Jews, the Italians, the whites, the blacks, the Protestants, the Catholics, all demanding of their neighbors but giving also; Theodore Roosevelt and Louis Brandeis; Oliver Wendell Holmes and Henry Stimson—teaching the younger man by their examples of decency and selflessness; finally, there was Franklin Roosevelt, the scion of the establishment fighting for the "forgotten man," challenging fear, promising and generally delivering a New Deal. From all these people, Felix Frankfurter had taken. But there was something of himself also. He had the immigrant's desire for liberty, the demand he not be bullied as Solomon Frankfurter had been bullied in Vienna; and from this had come a passionate patriotism. It was Frankfurter the patriot who had attempted to place himself between what he had perceived as state oppression and Bisbee, Mooney, and Sacco and Vanzetti; who had spoken out against racial quotas at Harvard; struggled before the courts and congressional committees for legislation benefiting the poor, the weak, and the uneducated. Felix Frankfurter, that January 5, was a mixture of American values absorbed from friends, teachers, mentors, and neighbors as well as values of the recent immigrant, the one who brings fresh passion to the land.

Of the many congratulatory messages Frankfurter received, one was especially important to him. "F. D.'s action is grand—for several reasons. Hope you will join us soon." It was signed "L. D. B."

Other justices, liberals, old friends, all joined in the outpouring of well wishing. There was one message recalling many battles: "I suppose I might not agree with all the decisions you will render, I know that you will be no man's tool, but stand squarely upon your own legal principles." It was from A. Lawrence Lowell, now retired as president of Harvard. He had confronted Frankfurter many times—the Brandeis confirmation, religious quotas at Harvard, Sacco-Vanzetti. But Lowell meant what he had said to Frankfurter, telling others that he considered the appointment "first rate" and that Frankfurter "is not going to be a mere tool." The insider was formally acknowledging the presence and success of the outsider.

Across the nation, reaction was equally positive. Newspaper editorials were virtually unanimous in their praise. The controversy that had swirled around Frankfurter for decades, the names he had been called, the charges hurled against him, all disappeared that week as the United States accepted him as legal scholar, fighter for individual rights, friend of Presidents, patriot. The popularity of the appointment was without question.

Still, the Jewishness of Felix Frankfurter was not ignored. One letter came from Father John A. Ryan, who had been with Frankfurter and other progressives since the early 1920s, fighting for reform legislation. He told Frankfurter he was pleased at the appointment for several reasons, one being "the fact that you are a Jew, and that your appointment will, I think, go far to offset or moderate the attitude of enmity toward your people which is so deplorable in more than one country today."

Frank Buxton, Frankfurter's newspaper friend, considered the appointment "another little caveat to Hitler. [Roosevelt] has magnificently defied the misguided persons who think that the way to fight anti-Semitism and anti-social forces is to turn tail and run for the cyclone cellar."

Frankfurter himself said his being Jewish was a factor both in the appointment and in its acceptance. Reminiscing years later, he said, ". . . in the context of world affairs in 1939, with all the brutal, barbaric behavior of Germany and generally the infection that was caused thereby elsewhere in the spread of anti-Semitism, and not least in this country, for the President of the United States to appoint a Jew to the Supreme Court had such significance for me to make it impossible to have said 'no.' "

From his friends abroad, Frankfurter heard that European newspapers headlined: "Roosevelt Appoints Jew to Supreme Court." Said Frankfurter, "I think that was the historic significance of the appointment."

Since the Brandeis confirmation fight, there had been only one Senate rejection of a Supreme Court nominee, that in 1930 of John J. Parker, the Senate responding to opposition by organized labor and the NAACP. In retrospect, there is agreement that Parker's opponents erred; he was neither anti-union nor racist and probably, if confirmed, would have been a liberal justice.

The Senate subcommittee hearing the Frankfurter nomination was headed by Matthew M. Neely of West Virginia; he set a preliminary session for Saturday, January 7, and hoped for a favorable report to the full committee within a few days.

There had been minor exceptions to the practice of nominees' not appearing at their confirmation hearings; at least two nominees had submitted autobiographical statements and Harlan Fiske Stone, at his 1925 confirmation hearing, had made a brief appearance. The practice had continued for the nominee to ask a lawyer, usually a friend, to provide information at the hearings, as Brandeis had done with Edward McClennen. Frankfurter asked Dean Acheson to attend the hearing for him. Tall, groomed and tailored to the image of a British diplomat, the son of a New England minister, often the legal representative of corporations, Acheson appeared the opposite of the short immigrant Jew with a radical reputation.

Acheson took the same attitude toward the hearing that McClennen had taken with the Brandeis hearing—it was not an adversary proceeding, and Acheson did not seek the right to cross-examine. If the "anti-Semites and witch hunters of the Palmer days" appeared, said Acheson, "fools and bigots would show themselves up, and friends on the Committee, with help where necessary, could correct downright falsehood," Acheson saw his job, instead, "to aid [Frankfurter's] unanimous confirmation."

Although there had been no opposition expressed to the Frankfurter appointment, the bigots did appear at the confirmation hearing. Of the three days of hearings before the Neely subcommittee, "Two," said Acheson, "were given over to the oddest collection of people I have ever seen . . . fanatical and some were very definitely mental cases. One poor old fellow informed the Committee that this country was founded on five principles—Christianity, Masonry, checks and balances, the Trinity, and God. This is the kind of thing we listened to for two days, interspersed with vicious misrepresentation of Felix's views and undisguised anti-Semitism."

That had not happened with Brandeis. Whatever individuals' personal motivations were, however extreme their biases, there had been no anti-Semitism expressed at his confirmation hearings. At the Frankfurter hearing, none of the anti-Semites was considered responsible, but the difference was that in less than a quarter of a century the bigots had come out of hiding. The members of the Senate subcommittee would not give even a nod of acceptance to any of the bigotry. A reaction by Senator Norris typified the subcommittee's attitude. When one witness read into the record a telegram saying, "Why not an American from Revolution times instead of a Jew from Austria," Norris commented: "An American from Revolution times would be too old."

The subcommittee members decided that, despite past practices, Frankfurter should testify before them. This was not explained, but probably stemmed from Frankfurter's notoriety and a new senatorial urge to exercise more control over nominations. Acheson agreed, on three conditions: (1) that the committee formally request Frankfurter's appearance, (2) that he not be asked how he would decide questions coming to the Court, and (3) that he not be asked about Roosevelt's Court-packing plan "since he had meticulously refrained from expressing any views" on the 1937 plan.

Felix Frankfurter was fifty-six years old when he appeared before the Senate Judiciary subcommittee. He was handsome, his hair had grayed but receded only slightly, his face was barely lined; he was neatly and formally tailored in a dark double-breasted suit, and wore a pince-nez. "He gives an impression of adequate physical energy," said a journalist friend, "but not of the athletic type of hardiness." The friend continued: "His fires are inner, and they do not blaze out all the time." This Thursday morning, January 12, the fires blazed.

The hearing was in the Senate Caucus Room, so crowded that the Capitol police had to clear a path for Frankfurter and Acheson to the witness table. Some of the subcommittee members were obviously friendly—Norris of Nebraska, for example, the first western senator to endorse Frankfurter; others not so friendly—Senator Patrick A. McCarran of Nevada feared Frankfurter was the kind of dangerous radical from whom McCarran should save the nation.

The subcommittee members went down the list—Bisbee, the Palmer raids, the American Civil Liberties Union, and others—and the hearing became almost a history of liberal causes for the previous three decades. The questioning, generally friendly, allowed Frankfurter to explain his role. "He did a superb job," said Acheson of Frankfurter, "was vigorous, dignified, and did not try to be adroit, and made an excellent impression."

McCarran was not friendly. He held up a book, entitled *Communism*, written by Frankfurter's friend Harold Laski. The senator and the professor sparred for a few moments. Then said the senator: "If it advocates the doctrine of Marxism, would you agree with it?"

Frankfurter's answer wrapped up the hearing. "Senator," he said, "I do not believe you have ever taken an oath to support the Constitution of the United States with fewer reservations than I have or would now, nor do I believe you are more attached to the theories and practices of Americanism than I am. I rest my answer on that statement."

The audience had been with Frankfurter from the beginning. Now it burst out into applause and cheers. After the hearing, the senators lined up to shake his hand.

There was a luncheon with Henry F. Ashurst of Arizona, the chairman of the full Judiciary Committee, then Frankfurter and Acheson made an unscheduled stop at the White House. For forty minutes Frankfurter regaled the President with an account of the hearing, the President enjoying every moment. The day had been Felix Frankfurter's triumph, and he and his friends relished it.

The morning of January 17, Republican senators caucused to decide if there should be any organized opposition. Given the reaction to

Frankfurter's appearance before the subcommittee, the Republicans concluded that the better part of valor was silence. Later that day Frankfurter's nomination was called up on the Senate floor, and only a voice vote was sought. No senator voted "nay."

He was at Harvard, with a class in Langdell Hall. As was his practice, when the class began, he pushed a student to the head of the classroom, then Frankfurter took a seat in the third row. "I don't think I came in that morning aware that I was going to be put in the podium," the student, Seymour J. Rubin, recalled. "He did that sort of thing. Whether he put the student in the podium or not, you would find that you were, in effect, conducting the class . . . he would conduct a dialogue with you."

Frankfurter had been holding such dialogues with his students since joining the Law School faculty in 1914, telling them something of the life of the law, attempting to instill in them certain virtues of service and selflessness, and—through the example of his life outside the classroom—speaking of personal courage. From his classrooms had come teachers, judges, government servants, defenders of the poor; he had not been the only influence on their lives, perhaps not the greatest, but all who had gone through his classes had been touched and influenced by him, and some, perhaps, ennobled by him.

In the middle of the class, another professor, Thomas Reed Powell, entered the classroom and handed Frankfurter a note. Frankfurter read it, smiled, but did not say anything. At the end of the class, however, he stood and spoke to the students. The note informed him of the Senate's unanimous confirmation. "Pardon me, gentlemen," he began. "This is the last time I shall speak to you in this classroom. I should like you to know that it is not an easy thing for me to go to Washington."

A pause. Then Frankfurter continued. "While there, I shall think of you often. I wish you well in June and a very full life thereafter."

In that manner Felix Frankfurter's quarter-of-a-century career as a teacher of the young came to an end.

The next two weeks were a triumphant processional for Felix Frankfurter. When he and Marion took the train to Washington, the Boston newsmen and photographers joined the Frankfurter friends to wish the couple well and to record the event. The expectation of all was summed up by the porter who carried their luggage, Warren Williams. "That fellow," said Williams of Frankfurter, "is sure going places when he gets on that bench."

Franklin Roosevelt had invited Frankfurter and Marion to the White

House judicial dinner, but Frankfurter, citing "a fastidious regard for hallowed precedents," declined, explaining that until he was sworn in he was a justice-designate and no justice-designate ever had attended such a dinner. Franklin Roosevelt pulled rank and the Frankfurters attended the dinner—actually they were the President's house guests that week.

The Supreme Court reconvened on Monday, January 30, and Frankfurter was sworn in that day, wearing a judicial robe presented to him by his former colleagues at Harvard. A Supreme Court justice takes two oaths, a constitutional oath administered in private by the Chief Justice and a judicial oath administered by the Court clerk in open courtroom. For that ceremony the Supreme Court chamber housed one of its largest crowds, as Frankfurter's former co-workers, students, and friends pushed in to see this moment in Frankfurter's career. When the oath taking was done, Frankfurter took his chair on the judicial side of the bench, reached over to shake the hand of Justice Hugo Black, and began his career as a Supreme Court justice, a career that would extend twenty-three years, nearly as long as his tenure at Harvard.

Later that day, in his office, Felix Frankfurter wrote his first letter as a Supreme Court justice; it went to the man who had appointed him, Franklin Roosevelt.

Felix Frankfurter was the seventy-eighth person to serve on the United States Supreme Court, the sixth born outside the United States. The first three were James Wilson of Scotland, James Iredell of England, and William Paterson of Ireland; all born before the formation of the United States. The fourth was David Brewer, born in Turkey of American missionary parents; and the fifth was George Sutherland, born in England. Frankfurter was the first foreign-born justice to come from a background in which English was not the native tongue, the first to come from a non-Anglo-Saxon heritage, the first to come from central Europe.

He was too much a historian, too much a romantic, too much a patriot not to relish the moment and to understand its significance. "Dear Frank," he began his letter to the President. "In the mysterious ways of Fate, the Dutchess County American and the Viennese American have for decades pursued the same directions of devotion to our beloved country."

The day was Franklin Roosevelt's fifty-seventh birthday. "And now," continued Frankfurter, "on your blessed birthday I am given the opportunity for service to the Nation which, in any circumstances would be owing, but which I would rather have had at your hands than at those of any other President barring Lincoln."

He closed: "This is my first writing as an Associate Justice and it brings you my affectionate good wishes."

In November of 1938, a few weeks before Felix Frankfurter was appointed to the Supreme Court, when Louis Brandeis had turned eighty-two, newspaper stories extolled his keenness of mind but also hinted at a weakening of his physical strength, which had become noticeable: he walked slowly, at his teas he no longer stood to greet guests but sat waiting for them to come to him, and there were not as many opinions and dissents as there had been in past years.

On January 7, two days after Frankfurter's appointment, Brandeis attended the regular Saturday-afternoon conference with the other justices but left early. He had not been feeling well. On Monday, January 9, he did not sit when the Court convened, and a public announcement was made of his illness. A case of flu, it was called.

During the remainder of January, he continued ill and did not appear in court to see Frankfurter sworn in as an associate justice; Frankfurter had visited him the previous afternoon. The next Monday, Brandeis returned to the Court and sat that week. Friday, February 10, Justice Stone passed Frankfurter a note, inviting him to a caucus of the "liberal" justices in Brandeis's chambers that evening. Present were Brandeis, Stone, Roberts, and Frankfurter; the meeting was a practice held over from the mid-1930s, when the liberals started meeting before the Saturday conference to counter a similar tactic by the conservatives. Neither at the meeting, the regular Saturday conference the next day, nor when the Court convened for its regular session on Monday, did Brandeis say or do anything to suggest he was considering retirement.

But that afternoon, Monday, February 13, he wrote a letter to the President of the United States: "Pursuant to the Act of March 1, 1937, I retire this day from regular active service on the bench."

The letters poured in, from Brandeis's relatives, friends, long-time associates, all praising his public service and wishing him well. His fellow members of the Supreme Court signed the customary letter of regret at his resignation, all except James McReynolds.

Brandeis wrote his relatives, and asked Frankfurter to write to many of their mutual friends, explaining that he was retiring "not because of ill health or impaired judgment, but solely because of age and the reduced capacity." One of the most important letters going out in those weeks was from Mrs. Brandeis to the widow of President Wilson; Mrs. Wilson still lived in Washington. Mrs. Brandeis said her husband was now well but had slowed "and so it seemed wisest to withdraw." She added: "I shall always remember that it was Mr. Wilson's vision and courage which made my husband's great career possible."

Twenty-three years earlier, when Wilson had appointed Brandeis, the United States had been shocked. Newspaper editorials had fumed against the appointment; senators had spoken against it; businessmen had shuddered. Now the tone was different. The warmth of the editorials and public comments of 1939 were summed up in Franklin Roosevelt's letter to him, accepting the retirement: "The country has needed you through all these years, and I hope you will realize, as all your old friends do, how unanimous the nation has been in its gratitude to you."

William O. Douglas, a lawyer who headed the Securities and Exchange Commission, was named to succeed Brandeis. The choice especially pleased Brandeis. Douglas was a Brandeis disciple, intellectually sitting at Brandeis's feet, admiring his passion for liberty, his wrath against bankers who used other people's money, his belief in individualism.

Brandeis in the months after his retirement was not as healthy as his friends said, but that summer he went to his beloved Cape Cod, and the short walks, the sound of the surf, the books, all conspired to restore his health. "Brandeis has had an extraordinary comeback," Frankfurter reported that fall. "Not in years have I enjoyed talk with him as extensively as I did the other day."

Politics continued to intrigue Brandeis, and during the 1940 campaign he wrote letters to Frankfurter extolling Roosevelt and Roosevelt's third-term campaign. In 1941, when he was eighty-four, he administered the oath of office to Dean Acheson, his former law clerk, who had been named Assistant Secretary of State for Economic Affairs. Acheson was a connecting link between Brandeis and Frankfurter, having come into Brandeis's service on Frankfurter's recommendation, then becoming first Brandeis's good friend and then Frankfurter's; Frankfurter and Marion were present at the swearing-in, in the Brandeis apartment.

What strength Brandeis had remaining in those last years he conserved for helping the European Jews. Since Adolf Hitler's coming to power, Brandeis had badgered the American government to help the European Jews. In January 1939, even when ill, he sent messages to Acheson asking him to use his influence against economic concessions to Germany. After his retirement the letters still flowed, usually to President Roosevelt, asking him to intercede with the British, who were blocking Jewish migration to Palestine. Brandeis realized that the fewer Jews going to Palestine, the more caught by the Nazis.

Roosevelt responded. At Brandeis's urging, he had been able to persuade the British to delay announcing the White Paper restricting Jewish immigration into Palestine, but that was all. Brandeis shuddered for the fate of the Jews. "He saw his people facing new and horrible ordeals under the Nazis," said William Douglas, who was with Brandeis the day Hitler invaded Poland. "He paced his apartment, old and bowed, his hands behind his back, whispering, "Will England fight?' " The flow of letters to the President continued. The meetings with Zionists went on. The demands. The pleadings.

On the evening of Tuesday, September 30, 1941, as Louis Brandeis neared the end of his eighty-fifth year, he was visited for more than an hour by Felix Frankfurter. "In that hour his mind was as lucid and as trenchant and as stimulating as I had ever known it," recalled Frankfurter. They talked primarily of national politics, and Brandeis continued his praise of Franklin Roosevelt, comparing him to Jefferson.

That being the end of the month, Brandeis also had done his routine housekeeping chores, signing and sending out the checks due; one was for his $5 dues to the Washington chapter of the Zionist Organization of America. The next morning, he and Alice, his wife for half a century, were taken for a drive in Rock Creek Park. They sat there in the car for an hour or so, and Alice Brandeis read to her husband. They returned to the apartment. Early in the afternoon, without any sign of pain or suffering, Brandeis lost consciousness. He never recovered.

Brandeis died in his California Street apartment at 7:15 the evening of Sunday, October 5. With him were his wife and two daughters, Elizabeth Raushenbush, a faculty member of the University of Wisconsin, and Susan Gilbert, a judge in New York City. "I should not mourn," Elizabeth Raushenbush told a friend. "Father was quite ready to go. He felt that he had lived to the full and others must now carry on the work he had attempted."

The next day a small group gathered for a memorial service in the apartment. Dean Acheson spoke for the law clerks "in this moment of farewell to the Justice." He talked of the pleasure and the assistance they had received from Brandeis, the influence he had upon them. Then, speaking of the clerks, Acheson said: "We are the generation which has lived during and between two wars. We have lived in the desert years of the human spirit. We have lived in the barren years of disillusionment—years when the cry was 'What is truth?' "

With Brandeis during these years, said Acheson, they had seen "that evil never could be good; that falsehood was not truth, not even if all the ingenuity of science reiterated it in waves that encircled the earth."

Then Felix Frankfurter spoke. "Two dominant sources of our culture are Hebraism and Hellenism," he began. "They express the intellectual and moral impulses of man. Not often have these two streams of Western civilization been so happily fused as they were in the great man whom we are bidding farewell." Frankfurter spoke of the moral law being a goad to Brandeis. "That was his Hebraic gift. It gave him ceaseless striving for perfection; it also gave him inner harmony." Frankfurter closed with John Bunyan's story of the death of Mr. Valiant-for-Truth from *Pilgrim's Progress:*

When he understood it, he called for his friends, and told them of it. Then said he, "I am going to my fathers, and tho' with great difficulty I am not hither yet now do I not repent me of all the Trouble I have been at to arrive where I am.

"My sword I give to him that shall succeed me in my pilgrimage, and my courage and skill to him that can get it. My marks and scars I carry with me, to be a witness for me that I have fought his battles who now will be my rewarder."

When the day that he must go hence was come, many accompanied him to the river-side, into which as he went he said, Death, where is thy Sting? And as he went down deeper, he said, Grave, where is thy Victory? So he passed over, and all the Trumpets sounded for him on the other side.

BOOK
FOUR

A Sentinel on Watch

19

In World War II

This is an old Supreme Court story: Justice Holmes, once during oral arguments, curious about the legal maneuverings that had brought a case before the bench, asked a nervous lawyer, "How did you get here?" Replied the flustered lawyer: "By the Santa Fe Railroad."

Felix Frankfurter told a similar story of his first day on the bench, January 30, 1939. The case being argued involved a direct appeal from an action by a federal district court. "I was puzzled to know why the case was here," Frankfurter recalled—that is, what jurisdiction the Supreme Court had over a case which had not gone through the Court of Appeals route. He leaned over to ask Justice Black, sitting next to him, but Black could not offer any help. Frankfurter suggested that Black ask the lawyer, arguing before them, about jurisdiction. "For one reason or another he was not willing to do so," said Frankfurter. "I then struggled with my soul to consider the great problem of when a new justice could ask a question from the bench. . . . I summoned my daring." The question Frankfurter asked was "Why are you here?" The lawyer's answer was "Because the Court assigned me as counsel in this case." From that moment on, Frankfurter framed his questions more carefully.

His first written opinion was handed down February 27, 1939, less than a month after he joined the Court. As usual with a first opinion by a new justice, it was unanimous. A Florida statute, upheld by its highest court, imposed an inspection requirement and fee on all cement imported from out of state. There was no inspection or fee for cement originating in Florida. The law was a device by the state to assist its own cement manufacturers, and the Supreme Court found that the law violated the constitutional prohibitions against states' imposing trade barriers among themselves. "It can never be pleasant to invalidate the enactment of a state," said the Frankfurter opinion, "particularly when it bears the imprimatur of constitutionality by the highest court of the state. But it would not be easy to imagine a statute more clearly designed than the present to circumvent what the Commerce clause forbids."

(That same day, however, Frankfurter joined in an opinion by Owen Roberts that dealt with Pennsylvania's attempt to regulate the milk industry, and although the justices found that "The United States could not exist as a nation" if each state discriminated against milk coming from another state, Roberts then said the regulation should be allowed because it represented only a small imposition. For Frankfurter, there were no absolutes.)

Also, on February 27, Frankfurter was responsible for a second unanimous decision, concerning whether a government corporation could be sued. The lower federal courts said that it could not; the Frankfurter decision concluded the opposite. Taking a Brandeisian tone, Frankfurter said: "Congress may, of course, endow a government corporation with the government's immunity. But always the question is: has it done so?" In the eleven-page decision, Frankfurter held it had not done so.

Two weeks later he released his first concurrence. The question was which of four states should tax an estate. Frankfurter agreed with the findings of a special master that Massachusetts of the four states could tax the estate, but objected to the special-master approach, saying the issue first should have gone to the state courts. "It is not to be assumed that the state courts will make findings dictated solely by fiscal advantages to their states," said Frankfurter. "The contrary assumption must be made."

Frankfurter wrote several concurrences that year. When the Court upheld a state's right to tax federal employees, Frankfurter said that the plea for tax immunity apparently was based on a phrase of Chief Justice John Marshall that "the power to tax involves the power to destroy." The Court should not rely on "merely what has been judicially said about the Constitution," Frankfurter said, continuing, "The ultimate touchstone of constitutionality is the Constitution."

Another time, in a decision by Stanley Reed, the Court upheld the right of a state regulatory commission to set utility rates. Years earlier the Court had not allowed Oklahoma to regulate the manufacture of ice; Brandeis had dissented then. Now, state regulation was accepted, and Frankfurter was with the majority. He concurred in this decision, again using language Brandeis could have written: "The only relevant function of law in dealing with the intersection of government and enterprise is to secure observance of those procedural safeguards in the exercise of legislative powers which are the historic foundations of due process."

That year there were two cases involving maltreatment of blacks in the South. In one, a unanimous decision by Hugo Black, the Supreme Court voided the indictment of a black on a murder charge because of the practice of excluding blacks from juries. In the second case, Frankfurter writing the decision, the Court overturned an Oklahoma law which, although never mentioning race, disenfranchised blacks. To Frankfurter there was no question that the disenfranchisement violated the Fifteenth Amendment—"The right of citizens of the United States to vote shall not be denied or abridged by the United States or by any State on account of race, color, or previous condition of servitude."

Frankfurter's other decisions that year indicated much about the future for him. The *New York Times* commented, somewhat in awe, about his scholarship, reporting that in one of his concurrences "Fifteen pertinent prior decisions of the Supreme Court are cited in the three page opinion." Also, there was about him, in his decisions, statements from the bench, and in the conference, still the air of the professor, mistaking the lawyers and his fellow justices for pupils. Chief Justice Hughes sometimes in conference jokingly referred to him as "Professor Frankfurter." Once Frankfurter replied: "You could not give me a title that I esteem more."

There also was, as there had been in the Brandeis writings, a respect for the states. Like Brandeis, Frankfurter was willing to allow the states reasonable leeway in economic matters. Since Brandeis had left the Court so soon after Frankfurter joined, Frankfurter's early decisions increased the expectation that the religion of judicial restraint, enunciated by James Bradley Thayer a half-century earlier and carried on by Brandeis, would continue. The Pope had changed but not the Papacy.

The early 1940s were whirlwind years for Felix Frankfurter, and he never seemed to catch up. He was operating from a new environment and with new friends. A wartime government was coming into operation and commanding the largest military effort the world had ever seen, and he—armed with boundless energy and experience from the First World War—could not stay out of the activity. In these years also, his relationships changed. That with Franklin Roosevelt fluctuated and that with the American liberal community, to which he had been a hero for many years, began moving in a new direction, one that Frankfurter himself often had difficulty understanding.

In the 1920s and 1930s, Brandeis was called "liberal" for his advocacy of judicial restraint because the right of government to experiment economically free from judicial interference was the "liberal" creed then. In the 1940s and 1950s, however, "liberal" meant the opposite. As government moved to restrict areas of personal freedom, the "liberal" position became one of limiting government. Frankfurter, staying with judicial restraint, became the liberals' target rather than their hero.

There was another change. Brandeis had been in the philosophical minority; he never could dominate the Court. But, with the coming of the Roosevelt-appointed justices, New Deal liberalism seemed the new philosophical theme of the Court, and the question—if not the expectation—was whether Frankfurter would dominate the Court.

The Supreme Court, inside, is a political institution. With five votes needed for a majority, the success of one person hinges on his ability to persuade four others to his opinion. This may require flattery, threats, surrenders, power plays, knowledge, iron will (sometimes bent), and all the other qualities necessary for political success. Such, however, were not Felix Frankfurter's strengths. He was argumentative, often imperious. Hugo Black's son wrote, "There was something about FF's manner and speech that tended to make you believe that all your good, chivalric, higher aspirations required agreement with his beliefs."

Throughout much of his life Frankfurter had been a loner. Bisbee, Mooney, and Sacco-Vanzetti are examples of his being against the mainstream. Others are his arguing against quotas at Harvard and speaking out against anti-Semitism in the 1930s. His frequent feuding with Roscoe Pound at Harvard and his disputes with A. Lawrence Lowell showed an irreverence for authority.

His relationship with Franklin Roosevelt was an exception. Frankfurter worked within the White House circle, earning Roosevelt's respect and gratitude. But even there Frankfurter was not a team player. He associated well in the 1930s with people like Corcoran and Cohen, who owed him their Washington jobs; but almost from the beginning he made enemies of other members of the White House circle who viewed him as a rival for power.

Frankfurter did not have the personal qualities necessary for leadership of the Court, for building a consensus, for persuading four other justices to join him. His leadership, if any, would emerge from the enunciation of his judicial philosophy only.

Two weeks after taking his seat, Frankfurter described being an associate justice as "unreal" and later that first year compared being on the Court to "being in prison." Those, however, were the remarks he was expected to make. He enjoyed himself in Washington, beginning a new career at age fifty-six, a career that was the top of the legal profession, and having a new arena in which to operate. Before, he had lived in the academic setting of Cambridge. Now he was a permanent resident of the nation's capital city.

Frankfurter had known the Supreme Court justices previously and had good working relations with them; even McReynolds spoke to him on occasion. Although Frankfurter had criticized Charles Evans Hughes in the 1920s for taking cases that paid high fees, on the Court he was soon won over by Hughes. Partly it was the manner in which Hughes conducted the conference. His opening statement of a case was brief and to the point; he avoided pointless debates with other justices and made certain votes were taken promptly when all had finished speaking. Partly it was Hughes's courtesy. Frankfurter often told of attending his first Supreme Court conference and wearing his old, comfortable alpaca "working" jacket—always acceptable at Harvard faculty meetings. To his embarrassment, the other justices wore full suits. When the conference broke for lunch, Frankfurter changed into his suit jacket. But, when the conference resumed, Chief Justice Hughes had switched his suit jacket for an alpaca coat.

"I have known or know about all the leading men of my time both here and in England enough to justify me in forming a judgment," said Frankfurter. "There isn't the slightest doubt that C. E. H. is among the very few really sizable figures of my lifetime."

Off the Court, Frankfurter also enjoyed himself. In addition to relating well to his mentors, such as Brandeis, Stimson, and Holmes, to his students and his clerks, Frankfurter had numerous and varied friendships—with fellow justices Robert Jackson and Hugo Black, with theatre personalities Garson Kanin and Ruth Gordon, with the raconteur Alexander Woollcott, with statesmen such as Dean Acheson and Jean Monnet, with journalists and writers, and on and on; the list is endless. He was even more the social gadabout in Washington than he had been in Cambridge. Archibald MacLeish, who knew him well, described him as "a simon-pure, unmitigated intellectual with a limitless relish for living in a human world."

The key word is "intellectual," Frankfurter did not suffer fools. "Wherever Frankfurter is, there is no boredom," said a 1940 account.

"As soon as he bounces in—he never walks, he bounces—the talk and laughter begin, and they never let up." His diary was filled with mentions of luncheon at this friend's house, cocktails at another's, dinner at the home of a third, all names of the prominent in Washington then. But it was not their prominence that attracted Frankfurter as much as it was their intelligence. He loved talk, witty, intriguing, significant. "Felix Frankfurter was as lively as ever," said one of his dinner-party hosts. "He can do enough talking for three or four persons."

He never tired. One of his law clerks recalled a dinner "and at two o'clock in the morning, most of us wanted to go home, but we had to take him home. He was ready to go on."

Frankfurter was a physical person. "He loves the touch of people," said MacLeish. "He stands near them when he talks. He catches men he questions by the arm, holding them above the elbow with a gripping hand. He turns the talk of two or three at one end of a self-conscious dinner into a drama of the whole table in which self-consciousness is lost. He moves quickly and precisely from one place to another in a crowded room and suddenly the room is drawn together."

Frankfurter was not a Brandeis clone in his personal life. Not for him boiled-chicken dinners and teas with ginger snaps. In Washington, Frankfurter lived the life of the man of taste. The meals served at his house were marked by fine food and gracious service, good wines as well as scintillating conversation. If he was not a politician on the Court, he was a charmer on the social scene, one who added to every event he attended, intriguing because he was believed to have his hand in all political doings, the one who knew everyone who knew everyone. He was spoken of with affection by his friends, with derision by his enemies, and usually with humor by those in between.

The Gridiron Club, a Washington newspaper reporters' institution, at its annual dinners pokes fun at the city's powerful. In an early 1940s skit, the Frankfurter character used words like "primigravida" and "hecatontarchy." Then the Frankfurter character used the telephone to give direct orders to various cabinet members and fellow justices. The skit ends with Frankfurter going off to rewrite the Ten Commandments. Frankfurter's response to the skit is not recorded, but he probably joined in the laughter. He loved good conversation, good humor. He loved life.

If he never tired, Marion did. She disliked Washington even more than she had disliked Cambridge. The Washington newspapers were kind to her—"Quietly aloof, her intellectual interests detach her from things mundane," said one. She refused to be interviewed by the press, declined to play the protocol games then expected of the wives of Washington personages, continued to dislike her role as the wife of a prominent man. There were no "intellectual interests" then for Washington wives, and she became even more of a recluse than she had been in Cambridge. Her illnesses came more frequently. Less than a month after Frankfurter joined the Court, he had to rush her to the hospital. "The Doctor thought that was the wisest way of taking care of her," Frankfurter explained, "in view of the difficulties in maintaining an even temperature in our house." Marion had an operation in 1944 and that summer was consumed with her convalescence. The Frankfurter law clerks, knowing the closeness of husband and wife, always spoke well of her. "Her attendance at a dinner was regarded as a great treat," said one clerk from the early 1940s, "and everyone appreciated it, knowing that her health was bad."

At the beginning of his years in Washington, Frankfurter's relationship with Franklin Roosevelt continued close. He sent FDR encouraging notes to massage the presidential ego as he had throughout the 1930s. One letter from Marion suggests something of their closeness. It was written to the President late in December 1939, after Frankfurter had been on the Court one year, and reads:

Felix and I are going away tomorrow to be gone over Christmas, but before we go I have an irresistible impulse to say something. It is that I shall be very sad when the time comes, whenever that is (laughter and applause) when you leave the White House. I don't want to see anybody else there, ever, though I shall try to be polite in years to come. . . . I don't know why I think of all this now.

Roosevelt continued to seek Frankfurter's advice at the beginning of Frankfurter's tenure in Washington. In 1940, when the President considered running for a third term, he spoke with Frankfurter, knowing that his friend would endorse the idea. In June 1941 when Chief Justice Hughes decided to retire, Roosevelt discussed his successor with Frankfurter. Previously, Frankfurter had expressed to Harold Ickes the hope that Robert Jackson would receive the post. But when the President and Frankfurter met at a private White House luncheon to discuss the vacancy, Roosevelt indicated that he was leaning toward appointing Harlan Fiske Stone, whom Hughes had recommended. Frankfurter supported Stone, not only because Stone was the senior associate justice on the Court but also because he was a Republican and with a war looming "the country should feel that you are a national, the Nation's President, and not a partisan President." Stone did become Chief Justice, and Jackson, then Attorney General, was named associate justice.

In a meeting with Jackson, Roosevelt indicated that if Stone left the Chief Justice position while Roosevelt was still President, he would appoint Jackson to the post.

In September 1941, Roosevelt, depressed by his mother's recent death, asked Frankfurter to come to the White House to discuss plans for a Roosevelt memorial "because," said FDR to his friend, "you are much more likely to be here longer than I shall be." Roosevelt's thought was for a simple stone slab in the middle of the green plot in front of the National Archives building in Washington. "I shall indeed remember," Frankfurter replied, "and you deeply honor me in putting this wish in the keeping of my memory."*

In 1940 and 1941, as the United States prepared for war, Frankfurter increased his extrajudicial activities. He recommended individuals for jobs in the expanding wartime bureaucracy. Along with associate justices Murphy, Douglas, and Jackson—like him, FDR's personal friends—Frankfurter was often at the White House, helping to draft speeches, offering advice. In 1940 he was involved in having his old mentor Henry Stimson appointed Secretary of War; Frankfurter was inclined toward Harold Ickes for the post but Grenville Clark, a Harvard classmate, persuaded him that Stimson, a Republican, would better prepare the nation for the anticipated war. Frankfurter also was involved in bringing Robert P. Patterson, a judge of the Circuit Court of Appeals, into the War Department as Assistant Secretary.†

When Roosevelt sent Harry Hopkins to England in 1941 to see Prime Minister Winston Churchill, Frankfurter informed the Australian min-

*Frankfurter fulfilled this obligation; the stone memorial, as simple as Franklin D. Roosevelt wished it, stands today.

†The Frankfurter-Stimson-Patterson involvement is a well-known and frequently told story. A new twist was added in 1982 by B. A. Murphy, *Brandeis-Frankfurter Connection*, who reported that Patterson, at the time of his appointment, "within the previous year . . . [had been] in the throes of what appeared to be a complete nervous breakdown," and that Judges Learned Hand and Augustus Hand, who served with Patterson on the Circuit Court, found the "situation . . . so grave" that they suggested he resign "immediately" from the court. Frankfurter, according to this account, although aware of Patterson's condition, approved his appointment to the War Department (p. 200). That account, based upon reminiscences of persons on the periphery of events attempting to recall incidents of many years past, appears to be inaccurate. The Patterson family denies that the late Robert P. Patterson ever had an emotional disorder. Keith E. Eiler, who has been preparing a biography of Patterson for some years, has found no evidence suggesting that Patterson had any such problem. Gerald Gunther, who is writing a biography of Learned Hand, has found no evidence that Hand had any of the concerns reported in the 1982 account. When Patterson became assistant secretary, Hand, in fact, wrote him, July 11, 1940, that "The more I think of what you are going to do, the better I approve it." In the same letter, Hand regretted Patterson's leaving the court. "It is hard on me personally," he said, "but I have the feeling that doesn't much matter, or anything else either."

ister to the United States of the closeness of FDR and Hopkins and advised, as the surest way of guaranteeing the success of the Hopkins-Churchill session, Churchill's beginning with laudatory remarks about Roosevelt. The Australian minister, Richard G. Casey, telegraphed a summary of Frankfurter's remarks to a friend in London and received this reply: "I saw the Prime Minister last night and conveyed your point. He is most grateful and will certainly act on it." More and more, Frankfurter saw himself in the role that Brandeis had filled during World War I, as an administration advisor.

Whatever extrajudicial roles Supreme Court justices fill, assisting with drafting legislation that might come before the Court always had been considered improper. Early in 1941, however, Frankfurter responded to Henry Morgenthau, Jr., and Ben Cohen's request for assistance in redrafting the Lend-Lease legislation. The bill would allow the United States to arm the Allies without worrying about how the Allies would pay for the materials. Frankfurter's help, which was major, enhanced the proposal's chances of withstanding a constitutional challenge.

When Frankfurter's work on the Lend-Lease bill became known after the Morgenthau diaries were published in the 1950s, Frankfurter was criticized. In another context, Brandeis and Frankfurter had once agreed that in wartime "all bets are off," and Frankfurter had followed that course with the Lend-Lease program. (The legislation's constitutionality never was challenged; if it had been, Frankfurter, of course, could have refrained from participating in the case.)

A legend has grown up about Frankfurter during the prewar and war years, of a man running the United States government. Joseph P. Lash, editor of the published Frankfurter diaries, commented about Frankfurter in the war years that "never had Frankfurter's 'unimaginable gift of wiggling in wherever he wants to' been exercised more vigorously than during the war." A newspaper columnnist wrote: ". . . it is a fact that second only to the President himself, Justice Felix Frankfurter has more to do with guiding our destinies of war than anyone in Washington."

There is some evidence to support those assertions. Frankfurter's diaries for those years offer a glimpse of his involvement in the war effort. Bureaucratic disputes were solved. The problem of controlling civilian supplies was dealt with. If Frankfurter did not have the official authority in the war administration, he had the authority of experience, knowledge, and a wide acquaintanceship among people in Washington in power.

Whatever assistance he gave, he came to believe that it was separated from politics, that assisting the war effort was neither a Democratic nor a Republican task. This belief became stronger as the war years progressed. In 1943, perhaps at the height of Frankfurter's involvement, he was writing in his diary of "how shocked and outraged I was—the very notion of thinking about men after they were on this Court in terms of New Deal or Old Deal." He spoke of a judge as having taken "the veil." Again in 1943, when a Democratic governor asked him to help with obtaining a fourth-term nomination for Roosevelt, Frankfurter said no, forgetting his 1940 activities and explaining, "I have an austere and even sacerdotal view of the position of a judge on this Court." That same year he was concerned about William Douglas, his fellow associate justice, making a try for the presidency in 1944, and making the Court "a jumping-off place for politics."

Sometimes accepting Frankfurter's separation was difficult. Joseph Rauh, a former Frankfurter law clerk and later Frankfurter friend, reviewed the Frankfurter diaries when they were published and commented, "It will seem strange to many that he could tell Justice Murphy in the morning that 'this Court has no excuse for being unless it's a monastery' and advise Bob Sherwood and Archie MacLeish at dinner that evening how to resolve the conflict between the OSS and the OWI and who should have authority over 'political warfare as between the civil and military authorities.' "

Frankfurter denied being a behind-the-scenes power. "I thought the myth of me would be buried once I got on the Bench," he wrote to a friend, "but the poor scribblers are evidently hard put for something to write so they revive the old stuff." To another he wrote: "Despite those veracious sources of history—the columnists—I do not run this government."

The evidence suggests that the truth lies between the two versions. Frankfurter is often pictured as a constant advisor to Stimson during those years. Stimson kept detailed diaries, listing his meetings, appointments, dinner and luncheon engagements, subjects discussed, his likes and dislikes, and his personal feelings. Frankfurter, during Stimson's five-year tenure as Secretary of War, appears in those diaries only a half-dozen times, and two of those entries have to do with persuading a former Stimson associate to return to work for Stimson.

Also, during the war, Franklin Roosevelt, drained of energy, had less time for friends, and the meetings between him and Frankfurter were less frequent. From January to June 1943, Frankfurter's diary entries are detailed and personal enough to include all sessions with the President, but list only three meetings with him, each a formal session with others present.

Also, as a wartime President, Roosevelt had new people surrounding him, more conservative in relationship to the war than Frankfurter; or if not more conservative, more discreet. To Frankfurter the problem was Nazi Germany. To the White House, prior to Pearl Harbor, the problem was persuading a nation, generally isolationist, to face up to the possibility of war. Frankfurter, for example, had produced a draft for one of FDR's most famous fireside chats, the one in which he called for the United States to become the "arsenal of democracy." But Roosevelt used little of Frankfurter's draft; it was too strong.

In 1941, FDR asked Frankfurter for a memorandum on the decisions of a federal judge whom the President was considering for a Supreme Court appointment. Frankfurter responded with a ten-page analysis of the man's opinions. He sent the memorandum on to Missy LeHand at the White House and in an attached note asked to meet with the President to discuss "two or three matters of real importance." Missy LeHand called Frankfurter's secretary and said that the President was "jammed" that week but perhaps would be available the next. This was to the man who had been a frequent guest at the White House and who had dropped in to see the President almost at will. Shortly after that, Frankfurter waged a campaign to have his friend Learned Hand appointed to the Supreme Court. Hand did not receive the appointment, for several reasons, one of them apparently being FDR's negative reaction to Frankfurter's pushing so strongly,

Frankfurter's wartime efforts changed in the storytelling. In 1940 he was agitated by Allied losses in Europe, was concerned about the advance of Nazism, feared for the fate of England under siege, and worried that the United States was not fully alert to the problem. Frankfurter talked about his concerns loudly. Those concerns, *circa* June 1940, have been reported three ways.

At the time, Harold Ickes wrote in his diary:

Felix cannot talk about the war without becoming highly emotional. . . . Earlier during the dinner, Felix had talked and talked and talked, and then when he was reached in regular order about 10:30, he started in all over again repetitiously and emotionally. . . . He wanted the President and other members of the Administration to start out as evangelists to arouse the people to the peril that confronts us. . . . Felix was still going strong at 10 minutes to 11:00, and I quietly took my departure. These resounding talkfests by the intellectuals tire me.

They spend so much time in useless speculation and in expounding the obvious. I know that Felix was not anywhere near wound up and Archie MacLeish was next and the last on the list.

Here is how Frankfurter, also *circa* June 1940, was described in an article as prepared for *Fortune* magazine five years later:

Felix Frankfurter appears to be the man above all others in the Presidential group who grasped where the real decision lay. The man of law knew Europe. In England, which he visited often before the war, he had many talks and exchanged many letters with Winston Churchill, who proclaimed the mortal danger.* He saw a good deal of the President after being appointed to the bench early in 1939; he helped innumerable refugees to find sanctuary here; his fears ran deep.

The Fall of France shook Frankfurter to the core. To his home in Georgetown, one sweltering night in June, he summoned his favorite intellectuals, most of whom he had placed in the government. . . . There ensued an episode which will surely figure prominently in more than one book of memoirs. The Justice spoke eloquently and passionately; the war was all that mattered; the country must be rearmed; the internal strife must come to an end; reform must be abandoned, the opposition appeased, and the industrialists who control the means of production and alone knew how to manage them would have to be brought into the government. In other words, the New Deal was to go on ice. That was the choice Frankfurter put before the President's most influential advisers on the left. He said the same things to the President, and some of those present took the words as a lecture from the White House.

The third version of Frankfurter, *circa* 1940, is in the article as published, unsigned, in the March 1945 issue of *Fortune*. It had been sanitized, at least, by Harry Hopkins, and the references to Frankfurter saying "the same things to the President" and delivering "a lecture from the White House" had been deleted.

During the war years, Frankfurter's major involvement was with atomic energy. The United States was developing the atomic bomb in the Manattan Project. Although the project was "top secret," a number of people in Washington, beyond those expected to know about the project and including Frankfurter, had heard rumors. Actually, that the United States and Germany were both working on such a bomb was widely suspected.

Frankfurter was concerned, as were many, with the future prospects for atomic energy: peaceful usage under international control or a deadly arms race? In 1943 Niels Bohr, the Danish physicist, an old friend of Frankfurter's, and a war refugee, came to the United States.

*The various collections of Frankfurter correspondence contain less than a half-dozen letters between him and Churchill, all indicating the two men barely knew each other.

He had been deeply involved in atomic research, was troubled about its future, and sought Frankfurter's help in persuading FDR and Winston Churchill to accept international control.

Frankfurter did succeed in persuading Roosevelt to meet with Bohr, and the president's promise was given to discuss the matter with Churchill. Frankfurter believed he had accomplished more than he had. Despite his promise, Roosevelt was skeptical, as was Churchill, of sharing atomic secrets in the postwar world to avoid an arms race, and Bohr's proposal was rejected.

When Roosevelt and Frankfurter had first discussed atomic energy and Bohr's concerns, the President had professed ignorance of what Frankfurter was talking about. He later told his aides he was concerned about how Frankfurter "happened to know anything about the subject whatever."

Not everyone in his administration was as concerned as the President. Stimson wrote in his diary: "Felix Frankfurter pleaded for an interview at ten-thirty and came in and spent half an hour to tell me about the great Dane, Professor Bohr, most of which I knew already. However, he, Bohr, is a fine old fellow and I am willing to give some time to ease his worries."

Frankfurter had become an outlet for the pent-up concerns of a number of physicists involved in the atomic project; influenced by his reputation as a power-behind-the-throne, they had approached him in hopes he could persuade Washington officialdom to the dangers of the postwar atomic age.

Fearing a critical security leak, Leslie R. Groves, director of the Manhattan project to develop the atomic bomb, approached Frankfurter and asked his cooperation. Years later he wrote to Frankfurter this estimate of Frankfurter's response:

I have never forgotten your help in maintenance of security on the atomic bomb project. I wish sometimes that the part you played could be put on paper in detail, not necessarily for publication but for the students at our various war colleges as well as others interested in the conduct of affairs in higher government circles. It would furnish an excellent example of how Americans in their official positions can by their discretion greatly assist in the best interests of the United States.

With the change in Washington from a peacetime capital to a wartime city, with the added pressures on the President, there was also a change in the New Dealers themselves; many no longer were characterized by the wide-eyed, energetic, idealists of a decade earlier. For

Frankfurter, the one who most personified this change was Tommy Corcoran, who had left the administration.

Frankfurter discussed Corcoran early in 1941 with Harold Ickes, and Ickes recorded: "I think Felix is also troubled that Tom is earning sums of money lobbying contracts through for his clients. This is really a fact and I regret it exceedingly myself. When [Mrs. Ickes] saw Marion Frankfurter recently, Marion was more outspoken on the subject of Tom than Felix was. She has never really liked Tom and she likes him even less these days."

The final break between the two men came in the summer of 1941. Corcoran wanted to be Solicitor General, and lined up endorsements from Speaker of the House Sam Rayburn, Mayor Ed Kelly of Chicago, and several other prominent Democratic politicians and administration figures. Then he turned to the Supreme Court. In June, associate justices Reed and Douglas wrote FDR formally endorsing Corcoran for Solicitor General. In August, Associate Justice Byrnes sent a similar letter. In September, when Associate Justice Black also sent a letter, all the FDR-appointed justices had endorsed Corcoran for Solicitor General—except Frankfurter.

Frankfurter was reluctant to endorse Corcoran. He believed the appointment would cause hostility to FDR on Capitol Hill because of Corcoran's high-handed manner demanding votes there when he was a White House emissary and also because of the publicity Corcoran had received in the previous months for his lobbying. There may have been another reason. Frankfurter placed great store in loyalty; that was why he had not spoken out against the Court-packing plan. Corcoran was not only using administration contacts to earn large sums of money as a lobbyist but also was noisy about it, embarrassing FDR. Frankfurter told Bill Douglas that he opposed the appointment because he would "never want a fixer . . . as Solicitor General."

There is a Washington story that Corcoran confronted Frankfurter and demanded his endorsement. Frankfurter refused. Corcoran then said: "I put you in that chair, and now I want you to produce." Given the nature of the two men, the story could be true. Frankfurter did not endorse Corcoran, and the two men did not speak again.

Frankfurter still had critics in Washington, hangovers from early New Deal days, and they continued their carping about him. Adolf A. Berle in his diary accused Frankfurter of attempting to ease Cordell Hull out as Secretary of State; of being a chief influence on White House speeches (with Associate Justice Douglas), although conceding that Sam

Rosenman, Robert Sherwood, and Harry Hopkins were the actual speechwriters; of encouraging the British point of view in the war effort.

On this last point, in October 1940 Berle referred to Frankfurter as a member of "the Jewish group." "It is horrible," he continued, "to see one phase of the Nazi propaganda justifying itself a little. The Jewish group, wherever you find it, is not only pro-English, but will sacrifice American interests to English interests—often without knowing it." That "a Jewish group" existed, influencing American policy in some improper way, was a constant bugaboo in those years. In June 1941, Representative John E. Rankin of Mississippi charged that "Wall Street bankers and international Jews are dragging the country into the war." Because of Rankin's history of racism, not much attention was paid to him.* Three months later, however, Charles A. Lindbergh, still basking in the glow of his heroic, nonstop, solo New York–Paris flight fourteen years earlier, charged in a major speech that "The three most important groups who have been pressing this country toward war are the British, the Jewish and the Roosevelt administration." Lindbergh was speaking under the auspices of the America First organization, the major isolationist group of the time. His speech so shocked the nation that it destroyed the America First group and perhaps also the isolationist movement.

Despite the rejection of such attitudes by the majority of Americans, many American Jews were cautious in their public pronouncements. "They were sensitive to their visibility as Jews and vulnerable to the malice of the anti-Semites who charged that they were a government within a government," wrote Lucy S. Dawidowicz, a Holocaust historian, continuing: "All through the Roosevelt years, Baruch, Frankfurter and Morgenthau were vilified, not necessarily because of the policies they advocated, but because they were Jews. Understandably, they tried to keep their Jewishness out of their public lives. 'I don't feel that I should push myself into Jewish matters when the skipper [Roosevelt] does not ask my advice,' Ben Cohen once wrote [Rabbi Stephen] Wise."

That was not true of Frankfurter. He remembered his origins, had not become part of the melting pot, acknowledged his relationship to

---

*Berle, Rankin, and other Americans making similar charges were not alone. In Europe, Nazi propaganda posters blamed the war on Frankfurter, Treasury Secretary Morgenthau, Bernard Baruch, Rabbi Stephen Wise, New York Governor Herbert Lehman, and New York Mayor Fiorello LaGuardia, one of whose parents was Jewish. (See *Trial of the Major War Criminals Before the International Military Tribunal*, Nuremberg, Germany, 1947, v. 7, p. 19.)

other Jews who had not shared his success or security. That had been Brandeis's way during the First World War when he politicked for the Balfour Declaration, and it was Frankfurter's during the Second World War. Rather than being part of "a government within a government," running bureaucracies or manipulating people, Frankfurter was a frantic seeker of assistance. He besieged his friends, officials, and even the President to help the Jews endangered by the Nazis in Europe. He was unsuccessful. During the war years, Roosevelt became more and more insulated, having direct contact with fewer and fewer persons, shunting aside more and more problems to conserve his time and energy for what he perceived as the ultimate issue—military victory. The plight of minority peoples, although sometimes given lip service, was one of those issues put aside at the White House. Even the President's old friend Herbert Pell, then American representative to the War Crimes Commission in London, did not have access to the President.

Frankfurter and his entreaties met the same results. In 1942, for example, he tried to bring Franklin Roosevelt together with David Ben-Gurion, then a Palestinian leader. "The President asks me to tell you," wrote Gracy Tully, the President's secretary, "that he is very sorry he cannot see Mr. David Ben-Gurion. He also asks me to tell you, that quite frankly, in the present situation in Egypt, Palestine, Syria and Arabia, he feels that the less said by everybody of all creeds, the better."*

Frankfurter wrote friends encouraging them to speak out against anti-Semitism, objecting to references to Jews subject to misunderstanding, attempting to explain the role of the Jew in modern society. Jewish leaders like Ben-Gurion and Chaim Weizmann were his guests. He continued his efforts to find jobs for Jews who had been discriminated against. In the 1944 presidential campaign, the Republicans made much of Roosevelt's involvement with the labor leader Sidney Hillman. Said Frankfurter in his letters: "The use that had been made of Sidney Hillman's Lithuanian birth—which is a cowardly way of saying that he is a Jew—is one of the saddest things in my life. Only one thing is sadder—the way those who themselves would not indulge in

---

*Roosevelt had not forgotten his promises to Louis Brandeis in the late 1930s to help the Jews in Palestine, and, as the war pressures eased, sought to fulfill them. In 1945 during his trip to Yalta, Roosevelt met with King Ibn Saud of Saudi Arabia in hopes of bringing the Arab-Jewish problem to an end. "Oh, yes," said the President of that meeting, "I had an exceedingly pleasant meeting with Ibn Saud and we agreed about everything until I mentioned Palestine. That was the end of the pleasant conversation."

such poisoning of the American atmosphere are silently allowing others to do so."

Nazi atrocities against Jews had turned into sporadic killings in 1939. Late in 1941 and early in 1942, however, new reports reached the West from the Nazi European fortress. Nazis were systematically murdering Jews—men, women, children, the young, the old, rich and poor. First guns were used; then gas because it was more efficient and cheaper.

Jan Karski, a liaison officer with the Polish underground, was sent to the West to report the genocide to the leaders of the Allies.

In the United States, he met with Frankfurter at the Polish embassy in Washington, where Karski was staying under a false name and false passport. Years later Karski recalled Frankfurter's being unimpressive in appearance and "rather nervous. But his eyes were brilliant."

When the two men were settled, the Polish ambassador with them, Frankfurter began: "I was informed that I should see you. What do you have to tell me?"

Karski answered that he was willing to answer questions. What did Frankfurter wish to know?

"Tell me," said Frankfurter, "what happens to the Jews in your country? I am interested to hear."

For fifteen minutes, his eyes closed, Jan Karski spoke. He spoke of shootings, Jews robbed of their possessions, people bundled into trains, gray clouds spiraling from smokestacks, the stench of burning flesh, murders beyond counting. Previous reports had not been preparation for the horror of the details. Felix Frankfurter did not interrupt.

Trained in the law, Frankfurter understood crime, that committed by the individual and by the state, but never before had he—or the world—confronted such crime. Throughout the 1930s he had begged leaders in the church, law, and politics to speak out against Nazism; he had implored universities to understand that to engage in a minor-level discrimination is to encourage a major-level discrimination; he had pleaded for—demanded—the return of the rule of law to the world. But he, and the others who spoke out, had rarely been heard. And now he had a glimpse, in those fifteen minutes, of the result—not in the paragraphs of a sanitized newspaper column or in a remote cablegram but in the words of one who had witnessed it.

Frankfurter rose, stared down at Jan Karski. "A man like me talking to a man like you," he said, "must be totally honest. So I am. So I say: I do not believe you."

"Felix!" the ambassador cried. "Felix, how can you say such a thing?

You know he is saying the truth. He was checked and rechecked in London and here. Felix, what are you saying?"

"I did not say that he's lying," Frankfurter replied. "I said that I don't believe him. There is a difference."

Karski said he could not forget the scene, of Frankfurter saying, "My mind, my heart they are made in such a way that I cannot conceive it," and stretching out his arms and crying: "No! No! No!"

20

Defining Patriotism

During the Second World War, the threat and the actuality, Felix Frankfurter was the Supreme Court's only foreign-born member, its only representative of that torrent of immigrants from the late nineteenth and early twentieth centuries, its only minority member. Those factors would be represented in his decisions.

The *Schneiderman* case demonstrated that.

When Germany attacked Russia, Russia became America's ally, and the Communism so abhorrent to American politicians suddenly became acceptable. Before the Court in 1942 was an effort by the government to strip William Schneiderman, a naturalized citizen, of his citizenship because he was a Communist party member. After the Russian-American alliance, the government hoped to postpone a decision, at least until the war ended. Aggravating the situation was the identity of Schneiderman's counsel: Wendell Willkie, the 1940 Republican presidential candidate.

After several arguments and rearguments, the Supreme Court met in conference on December 12, 1942, to vote. Before them was the legal situation, but outside the conference room—as each justice knew—was the political: Should the Court attack Schneiderman for adhering to Communism when Communism was a war partner's system of government and when Schneiderman was defended by the titular head of the Republican party? Could the Court gloss over the Communist aspect when Schneiderman was one of the party leaders? He had been a party member since his youth and had run for office on the party ticket.

Hugo Black wanted the decision delayed until after the war, especially because Chief Justice Stone intended to include a criticism of Communism in his opinion against Schneiderman. Reed and Douglas also suggested it be delayed.

The decision was not delayed, however; the vote was 5-3, with Robert Jackson abstaining. The majority upheld Schneiderman's right to his citizenship despite his attachment to the Communist party. "Under our traditions," said the majority decision, "beliefs are personal."

Given the record of Brandeis and Holmes during the 1920s, that is where they would have been if they had been voting, and that is where one anticipated Frankfurter would be. Frankfurter, however, voted with the minority, led by Stone, to strip Schneiderman of his citizenship.

He explained why in one of the Court's conferences. "I am saying what I am going to say because this case arouses in me feelings that could not be entertained by anyone else around this table," he began. "It is well known that a convert is more zealous than one born to the faith. None of you has had the experience that I have had with reference to American citizenship." He told about being in college when his father was naturalized, "and I can assure you that for months preceding, it was a matter of moment in our family life." He spoke of his experiences, as an assistant United States attorney under Henry Stimson, representing the government in naturalization proceedings.

And, he concluded, "as one who has no ties with any formal religion, perhaps the feelings that underlie religious forms for me run into intensification of my feelings about American citizenship."

Frankfurter conceded that "mere" Communist party membership was not a reason to disqualify an individual for citizenship but asserted that Schneiderman's involvement went far beyond that. Said Frankfurter: "American citizenship implies entering upon a fellowship which binds people together by devotion to certain feelings and ideas and ideals summarized as a requirement that they be attached to the principles of the Constitution."

Frankfurter continued to act on the Court during the war with the convert's zealousness.

He joined in the Court's unanimous 1942 decision allowing the American military to court-martial summarily eight Nazi saboteurs who had landed in the United States. They were captured while wearing civilian clothes and, by all rules of warfare, were subject to military execution. Chief Justice Stone wrote the decision refusing to take the eight saboteurs away from the military and place them in civilian custody. Frankfurter joined Stone's decision; his reasons were obvious. "Some of the very best lawyers I know are now in the Solomon Island battle," he said. He wrote a jingoist memorandum for the other justices

—"You damned scoundrels have a helluvacheek to ask for a writ that would take you out of the hands of the Military Commission and give you the right to be tried, if at all, in a federal district court. You are just, low-down, ordinary, enemy spies."

The Court upheld various military actions against Americans of Japanese descent on the West Coast, with Frankfurter in the majority. William Douglas later explained the emotionalism within the conference room this way: "The Pentagon's argument was that if the Japanese army landed in areas thickly populated by Americans of Japanese ancestry, the opportunity for sabotage and confusion would be great. By doffing their uniforms they would be indistinguishable from the other thousands of people of like color and stature." Douglas added: "It was not much of an argument but it swayed a majority of the Court, including myself." Earl Warren, then attorney general of California, where most of the Japanese-Americans were located, repeated that point in his memoirs but acknowledged that the Japanese-Americans had been subject to "a considerable amount of racial prejudice that stemmed largely from some of our farming communities." Warren had supported the actions against the Japanese.

In the first of the Japanese cases, in June 1943, the Court supported the government's power to impose a curfew on Japanese-Americans. Chief Justice Stone's unanimous decision said the Court would not review actions by those authorities charged with waging the war. In a separate concurrence, Douglas wrote: "The threat of Japanese invasion of the west coast was not fanciful but real . . . we cannot sit in judgment on the military requirements of that hour."

Frankfurter, although siding with Stone, attempted to tone down the decision, urging the Chief Justice to accept, as he did, a paragraph saying: "We do not now attempt to define the ultimate boundaries of the war power."

In a second case, the question was not a curfew but actual exclusion of the Japanese-Americans from the West Coast; the military had expelled them and placed them in "relocation" camps. Black wrote the decision upholding the government's action, again citing national defense needs. Frankfurter joined with Black, but wrote a two-page concurrence describing the government's powers as limited to wartime. "That action is not stigmatized as lawless," he said, "because like action in times of peace would be lawless."

Frankfurter's two insertions, the suggestion to Stone in the first case and the concurrence in the second, restricted the wartime excess. The first said that the Court still might step in if the war power went beyond justifiable boundaries, and the second warned that excesses allowed in war would not be tolerated in peacetime.

When the second decision came down, however, some of the justices were concerned because the actions against the Japanese-Americans had been based on their heritage and not on specific acts or evidence that acts might be committed. Justice Frank Murphy dissented, charging the case "falls into the ugly abyss of racism." Owen Roberts called the military action "a clear violation of Constitutional rights." And Robert Jackson asserted that the Japanese-American had been convicted of "an act not commonly a crime. It consists merely of being present in the state whereof he is a citizen, near the place where he was born, and where all his life he has lived."

Douglas had said those not charged with waging war should not judge the behavior of those who carry that responsibility. At the time of the military orders governing the situation in the Pacific coastal states, the United States was losing the war in the Pacific, the Japanese military was moving from island to island and rumors were rife of Japanese invasion forces near the coast.

Against that, the war's purpose had been to extend democracy, remove racism. And no comparable move had been made against Americans of German background on the East Coast. America was troubled then and has been since by its actions against the Japanese-Americans, fearing that in a moment of stress it had turned against the immigrant only for being an immigrant.

Douglas wrote years later that he regretted his decision, saying, "the evacuation case . . . was ever on my conscience" and the dissenters "had been right." Earl Warren also joined in the after-the-fact regrets "because [the action] was not in keeping with our American concept of freedom and the rights of citizens." Many other officials have since also joined in the chorus of regrets.

Two who did not express regrets were Frankfurter, who remained quiet about this issue during and after the war, and Hugo Black. In 1967, Black told an interviewer for the *New York Times,* "I would do precisely the same thing today, in any part of the country. I would probably issue the same order were I President. We had a situation where we were at war. People were rightly fearful of the Japanese in Los Angeles, many loyal to the United States, many undoubtedly not, having dual citizenship—lots of them."

Black continued: "They all look alike to a person not a Jap."

Of Frankfurter's jingoist decisions in the early 1940s, it was not the Japanese-American cases that cut him off from the liberal community but two decisions involving a requirement that school children salute the flag. "I recollect no decision of our former colleague," recalled Roger N. Baldwin of the American Civil Liberties Union, "which dismayed us more than his labored defence of compulsory flag saluting. It sealed my growing disinclination to keep up an old friendship."

The first flag-salute case involved two children named Gobitis who had declined to salute the American flag in public school because they were members of the Jehovah's Witnesses religious group. Jehovah's Witnesses consider saluting the flag an idolatrous act and compelling them to salute, they argued, violated their freedom of religion as promised by the First Amendment to the Constitution—"Congress shall make no law respecting an establishment of religion, or prohibiting the free exercise thereof." When the case reached the Supreme Court, two lower federal courts had decided for the Gobitis children against the Minersville School District in Pennsylvania.

Prior to 1940, the Supreme Court had decided that religious freedom did not include gross violations of society's rules, such as polygamy, and did not block states from imposing certain restrictions, which most of the state's citizens did not believe involved religion, upon those few of the state's citizens who did believe they involved religion. But these previous cases had not concerned school children.

When the *Gobitis* case was first discussed in conference, Hughes, then still Chief Justice, recalled the history of similar cases when the Supreme Court had said it would not interfere with such state acts. This was consistent with a policy of judicial restraint, the Thayer-Brandeis argument that the Court should not interfere with a legislative act unless it is glaringly inconsistent with constitutional rights. Many of the justices famed for their devotion to individual liberties in the 1930s and 1940s, including Brandeis, Cardozo, Stone, Owen Roberts, and Hughes himself, had accepted that premise in religious-freedom cases.

During Hughes's comments, brief and to the point as usual, since there had been no discussion, no voicing of opposition, the assumption was that the other eight justices agreed with Hughes that West Virginia should be allowed to compel its students to salute the flag.

According to Hughes's authorized biography, as the justices left the conference, the talk among themselves was that Hughes should write the opinion, that a statement from the Chief Justice would finally settle the issue. Frankfurter turned back and made the suggestion to Hughes. "No," said Hughes, "I'm going to assign it to you."

William Douglas denied that story's accuracy. "Hughes was very severe," Douglas recalled. "Frankfurter was very brash, but even Frankfurter would never have done, would never have dared do that. . . . Frankfurter, knowing of my close relationship to Hughes, called me into his office and asked if I would go to Hughes and have Hughes assign the flag-salute case to him to write." Douglas said he refused, but that Frankfurter, who "was longing to get that opinion," did get it.

There may be some truth in both accounts. Frankfurter with the convert's zealousness could have sought the decision. Hughes may have believed that the only minority member on the Court should write the decision affecting other minority members. Opinions have previously been assigned for similar reasons.

Frankfurter's decision showed sensitivity to the problems involved. "A grave responsibility confronts this Court whenever in course of litigation it must reconcile the conflicting claims of liberty and authority," he wrote. "But when liberty invoked is liberty of conscience, and the authority is authority to safeguard the nation's fellowship, judicial conscience is put to its severest test." The decision included an affirmance of religious liberty, but, said Frankfurter, "The mere possession of religious convictions . . . does not relieve the citizen from the discharge of political responsibilities." Frankfurter pitched his argument to upholding the state legislature's "judgment that such an exemption [from flag saluting] might introduce elements of difficulty into the school discipline, might cast doubts in the minds of the other children." And he reversed the lower courts—in effect, saying the Jehovah's Witnesses children must salute the flag despite their religious beliefs, on the basis of the state legislatures' making such decisions rather than courts.

The *Gobitis* decision came down in June 1940, a time when Frankfurter was deeply involved in discussions with Washington officials about the war's course. That was the spring, said Henry Stimson, that became "a nightmare" because of the "explosion of Nazi power into Denmark, Norway, Belgium, Holland, Luxembourg and France. . . . Great Britain was left alone, as the last outpost of freedom in Europe." The day of the *Gobitis* decision was the day Frankfurter met with President Roosevelt and suggested Stimson as Secretary of War. Although Frankfurter denied that the European situation had swayed him to use judicial restraint as a cover for extreme patriotism, his opinion includes this paragraph:

The ultimate foundation of a free society is the binding tie of cohesive sentiment. Such a sentiment is fostered by all agencies of the mind and spirit which may serve to gather up the tradition of a people, transmit them from generation to generation, and thereby create that continuity of a treasured common life which constitutes a civilization. "We live by symbols." The flag is the symbol of our national unity, transcending all internal differences, however large, within the framework of the Constitution.

Because of the conference discussion when the justices had remained silent, the expectation was that the decision would be unanimous, that those justices professing an adherence to liberalism would not object. The expectation was strengthened by William Douglas's comment to Frankfurter that the decision "is a powerful moving document of incalculable contemporary and historic value. I congratulate you on a truly statesmanlike job."

McReynolds only concurred, but that was ascribed to his surliness and reluctance to join anything of importance written by a Jew. Hugo Black told Frankfurter, a few days before the decision was handed down, that "Like you, I don't like this kind of law and wish we could stop it, but I just don't see that there is anything in the [Gobitis] family claim that possibly can enable us to hold this unconstitutional."

The surprise was Harlan Fiske Stone. After reading Frankfurter's draft opinion, he decided—despite his past support for the position described in the draft—not to go along with Frankfurter. When Frankfurter argued with him that the decision was "a vehicle for preaching the true democratic faith of not relying on the Court for the impossible task of assuring a vigorous, mature, self-protecting and tolerant democracy," Stone replied that he believed the case involved "the relative weight of imponderables and I cannot overcome the feeling that the Constitution tips the scales in favor of religion."

Liberals had not anticipated the Frankfurter decision. Harold Ickes said it came "to my utter astonishment and chagrin. . . . As if the country can be saved, or our institutions preserved, by forced salutes of our flag by these fanatics or even by conscientious objectors!" Twenty years earlier at Harvard, Zechariah Chafee and Frankfurter had teamed up against the Palmer raids; now Chafee said: "During the present emergency many things will be done which will be regretted later by the doers. This is one of the first of them."

Frankfurter was stung by his friends' criticism. "I am nearly 58 years old," he wrote to one, "and for certainly not less than 30 years, I think I can say with pedantic accuracy, I have been on the firing line of civil liberties. . . . Do you really think that men change their textures and their rooted beliefs over night? And you tell me that war hysteria has swept me off my feet, I would tell you in confidence that this decision was made and the opinion largely drafted weeks before the present exigencies." He then argued that Holmes and Brandeis had at times supported positions in decisions which they might personally oppose, and that, Frankfurter insisted, was what had happened to him. "Judges," he explained, "move within a framework of duty very different from that in which you happily are free to move."

One who did support Frankfurter, however, was President Roosevelt. Once at Hyde Park, when Eleanor Roosevelt criticized the decision, Frankfurter defended it, saying the Court had no business setting itself up as a local school board. The President then said he agreed with Frankfurter. He described the school board's action as "stupid, unnecessary, and offensive," but the President insisted the action was within the school board's power.

Of the eight-man majority, the first to fall away from Frankfurter was Black. Shortly after the *Gobitis* decision came down, the Court went on its summer recess. During that recess, segments of the American population turned ugly because of the decision. In Maine, when Jehovah's Witnesses refused to salute the flag, a child was wounded in the disturbances that followed, and the governor threatened to call out the National Guard if the State Police did not cope with "disorders directed at members of . . . Jehovah's Witnesses." In Illinois, sixty-one members of the Jehovah's Witnesses were hustled into jail for safe-keeping when townspeople attacked them and destroyed sixteen of their automobiles. And in California, about thirty persons who had claimed religious reasons for refusing to salute the flag were escorted from a town one morning after a riot the previous evening. These outbursts caused newspapers to reconsider the decision.

At the end of the Court recess, Frankfurter was talking with William Douglas, and Douglas said that Hugo Black would not again support a *Gobitis*-type decision.

"Has Hugo been re-reading the Constitution during the summer?" asked Frankfurter.

"No," Douglas replied, "he has been reading the papers."

Two years later, in 1942, the Court's split on the issue became public in *Jones* v. *Opelika* dealing with a city ordinance requiring vendors to be licensed. The vendor in this instance was an ordained Jehovah's Witnesses minister who sold religious material; he claimed that for the town to require him to have a license was unconstitutional because of the town's "unlimited discretion in revocation and requirement of a license."

The Court's 5-4 decision, by Stanley Reed, was against the minister, saying the city had the right to charge reasonable fees for "the privilege of canvassing."

Frankfurter was with the majority. Stone again dissented, charging that "here it is the prohibition of publication, save at the uncontrolled will of public officials, which transgresses constitutional limitations and makes the ordinance void on its face." Stone was joined by Justices Black, Douglas, and Murphy. Murphy then wrote his own dissent, joined by the other three. And then Hugo Black also wrote a dissent, the third in the case, joined by Douglas and Murphy. These three had joined the Frankfurter decision in the *Gobitis* case two years earlier. Douglas later explained the process leading to the Black dissent. "Black and Murphy and I . . . in the following term, had discussions and we were concerned about our joining the Frankfurter opinion. We thought we had been taken in and we mentioned this several times. It was, it was a matter of, that we wished we hadn't, hadn't gone along. We wished we had had a reargument. We wished we could have further consideration, and so on."

The Black dissent begins: "The opinion of the Court sanctions a device which in our opinion suppresses or tends to suppress the free exercise of a religion practiced by a minority group." He called this "but another step" in the direction pointed out by *Gobitis.* Black then added this paragraph:

Since we joined in the opinion in the Gobitis case, we think this is an appropriate occasion to state that we now believe that it also was wrongly decided. Certainly our democratic form of government, functioning under the historic Bill of Rights, has a high responsibility to accommodate itself to the religious views of minorities, however unpopular and unorthodox these views may be. The First Amendment does not put the right freely to exercise religion in a subordinate position. We fear, however, that the opinion in these and in the Gobitis case, do exactly that.

That paragraph, attacking the Frankfurter decision in Gobitis, was a personal affront to a colleague in addition to being an announcement that Black, Douglas, and Murphy, if presented with a second flag-salute case, would decide against the flag-salute requirement. Those three, plus Stone, the original dissenter, meant four against the requirement. If they gained one additional vote, the flag-salute requirement would be ended, the Frankfurter decision in *Gobitis* overturned. Their chance came the next year.

The new case, *West Virginia State Board of Education et al.* v. *Barnette et al.*, was a direct challenge to Frankfurter's *Gobitis* decision. When this West Virginia case was before the lower federal courts, Judge John J. Parker wrote a decision in favor of the Jehovah's Witnesses, referring specifically to the Black-Douglas-Murphy statement in *Opelika*, that they had changed their mind. This is the same Judge Parker who had been nominated to the Supreme Court by President Hoover in 1930 but who had not been confirmed by the Senate because of fears that he was too conservative. At the time of his decision in the West Virginia flag-salute case, he again was being considered for a Supreme Court appointment. He did not receive it.

The West Virginia case was argued before the Supreme Court in March 1943. The Committee on the Bill of Rights of the American Bar Association filed a friend of the court brief in favor of the Jehovah's Witnesses, its signatures including those of a Washington lawyer named Abe Fortas, a close Frankfurter friend named Monte M. Lemann, and Zechariah Chafee from the Harvard Law School.

This time, Frankfurter, instead of being with the majority, was with the minority. The 6-3 decision affirmed the right of the Jehovah's Witnesses to refrain from saluting the flag and overturned the Frankfurter *Gobitis* decision then only three years old. The Supreme Court had overturned previous decisions, but rarely in such a short time. In the minimum-wage decisions of the 1930s, when the Court reversed itself within one year, it tried, at least, to offer an explanation, that the Court had been asked to do something in the second case that it had not been asked in the first. But with the flag-salute case, there was no such apology; the turn against Frankfurter was blunt and brutal.

Robert Jackson, who had not been a member of the Court at the time of *Gobitis*, wrote the majority decision in this second case. He began by explaining that the Jehovah's Witnesses take literally *Exodus*, chapter 20, verses 4 and 5, prohibiting the bowing down before graven images, and that the flag to them is a graven image. As a result of adhering to this belief, Jackson said, "Children of this faith have been expelled from school and are threatened with exclusion for no other cause. Officials threaten to send them to reformatories maintained for criminally inclined juveniles. Parents of such children have been prosecuted and are threatened with prosecution for causing delinquency."

Frankfurter had argued in *Gobitis* that saluting the flag was a symbol, but Jackson pushed that aside: "To believe that patriotism will not flourish if patriotic ceremonies are voluntary and spontaneous instead of a compulsory routine is to make an unflattering estimate of the appeal of our institutions to free minds."

As Frankfurter had written at a time of stress,when Europe was being overrun by Nazis, Jackson also wrote in a time of trauma. The United States now was in the war, and had been for eighteen months; across the seas, young American men were fighting and dying. For the flag, some said. But Jackson said differently—not for the flag but for what the flag represented. "If there is any fixed star in our constitutional constellation," he wrote, "it is that no official, high or petty, can prescribe what shall be orthodox in politics, nationalism, religion, or other matters of opinion or force citizens to confess by word or act their faith therein."

The decisions, concurrences, and dissents numbered five, showing the justices felt a need to explain themselves. The six-member majority was made up of Jackson, Wiley Rutledge, Stone, Murphy, Douglas, and Black. Douglas and Black wrote a concurrence, as did Murphy. The three-member minority was Roberts, Reed, and Frankfurter. Roberts and Reed wrote a dissent, as did Frankfurter.

The Frankfurter dissent is one of the most controversial of his writings. A philosophical statement, it previews the difficulties he would have in the future. It begins:

One who belongs to the most vilified and persecuted minority in history is not likely to be insensible to the freedoms guaranteed by our Constitution. Were my purely personal attitude relevant I should wholeheartedly associate myself with the general libertarian views of the Court's opinion, representing as they do the thought and action of a lifetime. But as judges we are neither Jew nor Gentile, neither Catholic nor agnostic.

As a member of this Court I am not justified in writing my private notions of policy into the Constitution, no matter how deeply I may cherish them or how mischievous I may deem their disregard. The duty of a judge who must decide which of two claims before the Court shall prevail, that of a State to enact and enforce laws within its general competence or that of an individual to refuse obedience because of the demands of his conscience, is not that of the ordinary person.

At the Saturday conference, June 13, before the decision was to come down, Owen Roberts pulled Frankfurter aside and called the paragraphs "more and more a mistake." Frankfurter replied that he had not wished to speak so personally, but "From the time of the Gobitis case I was literally flooded with letters by people who said that I, as a Jew, ought particularly to protect minorities. . . . And when the flag salute issue again became prominent . . . I began to have a new trickle of letters telling me my duty, more particularly because I was a Jew and an immigrant." Frankfurter continued: "I therefore thought for once and for all I ought to put on record that in relation to our work on this Court, all considerations of race, religion, or antecedence of citizenship are wholly irrelevant."

On the day of the decision, a few moments before the justices took their seats, Frank Murphy also approached Frankfurter "as a friend" to say the paragraphs were too personal. Frankfurter insisted they remain, explaining they were not the result of hasty decision, but "I had thought about the matter for months."

Was Frankfurter correct? That his being a minority member and an immigrant were of no importance? Had his appointment four years earlier meant he should follow an accountancy form of law—so many points for this side and so many for that, and which side had the most? When there are two rights—that of freedom of religion and the state's interest in maintaining patriotism—and no wrongs, is there no place for experience, understanding, and emotion?

Frankfurter attempted to deal with these questions in the remainder of his dissent.

In the light of all the circumstances, including the history of this question in this Court, it would require more daring than I possess to deny that reasonable legislators could have taken the action which is before us for review. . . . I cannot bring my mind to believe that the "liberty" secured by the Due Process Clause gives this Court authority to deny to the State of West Virginia the attainment of that which we all recognize as a legitimate legislative end, namely, the promotion of good citizenship, by employment of the means here chosen.

Echoing, as he had many times before, James Bradley Thayer, Frankfurter insisted "responsibility for legislation lies with legislatures." But he had written himself into a tight corner, several of them. In one paragraph he denied that the authors of the Constitution had granted the Court "supervision over legislation" but in the next paragraph acknowledged the Court's "narrow judicial authority to nullify legislation." He spoke of the essence of religious freedom "guaranteed by our Constitution" as neutrality toward religion, no religion "shall either receive the state's support or incur its hostility," but did not speak in this case of the government's obligation to protect religious freedom.

Frankfurter was caught where he had been trapped before, and would be again. He had once said that to be a liberal on the Court "all one has to be is not to be too arrogant in setting one's judgment over against that of Congress and the state legislatures." But he also had written that judges should understand the Constitution as "a source of governmental energy no less than of governmental restriction." He would be continuously involved in that dialogue, between restraint and action.

His friends attempted to explain, if not to justify, the Frankfurter position in the flag-salute cases. "Here was a foreign boy," said one, "who comes to this loving land, does well and he loves it, and in effect says to himself, 'Why shouldn't you salute the emblem?' . . . I mean it's a very simple thing, you know law comes not out of books, it comes out of life; this was the point." But his critics leaped to attack. "Clearly Frankfurter, an interventionist even then," said one, "was emotionally swayed by martial thoughts and by hatred of Hitler. And yet, in effect, he ordered the children to 'Heil.' " On the other side, Arthur M. Schlesinger, Jr., has pointed out that at various times thirteen justices (including Black, Douglas, and Murphy) had seen nothing unconstitutional about a flag-salute law, and Schlesinger suggested that "shows at least that its status was not an open-and-shut matter."

How far Frankfurter's former liberal friends had turned against him was shown in the late 1940s when the National Consumers' League planned a fiftieth anniversary dinner. This was the League for which Frankfurter, after Brandeis had joined the Court, had worked without pay. He had represented it before the Supreme Court in the *Adkins* case, counseled it on strategy, written the New York minimum-wage law at its request. For at least twenty years he was both an intimate and vital part of the National Consumers' League.

The League's directors voted not to invite Frankfurter to the dinner.

Josephine Goldmark, who had worked with Brandeis so many years earlier in the *Muller* case and then with Frankfurter, did not tolerate the affront to him. She insisted that the directors be polled again by mail. With each ballot went a lengthy letter from Josephine Goldmark, explaining the Frankfurter contributions to the League. Her position with the League then, the respect with which she was held, her obvious anger at the slight to Frankfurter produced the desired results. The second vote on inviting Frankfurter was sixteen in favor, three opposed.

Frankfurter did not attend the dinner, explaining that the Court was in session, but only the intervention of Josephine Goldmark had saved him from the insult of not being invited.

Actually, Frankfurter had not been a complete jingoist in those early war years. If his memorandum in the saboteurs' case was extreme, it also was private and the decision was unanimous. If he did join the decisions against the Japanese-Americans, as did other justices, including Hugo Black and William Douglas, Frankfurter attempted to place some restrictions on those decisions and never used the "they all look alike" language of Black.

As the war progressed, Frankfurter lost much of the convert's zealousness he had displayed in the *Schneiderman* case. In 1944 he supported a German-American whose citizenship was challenged because of his membership in pro-German and pro-Nazi organizations. "The evidence as to Baumgartner's attitude after 1932 [time of naturalization] afford insufficient proof that in 1932 he had knowing reservations in forswearing his allegiance to the Weimar Republic."

After the Second World War ended and Frankfurter was freed of the pressures operating on him in the early 1940s, he became on the Court a forceful advocate of the First Amendment's promise of religious freedom. He was against a state law prohibiting minors (under twelve) from selling religious material on the streets, against subsidizing costs of transporting children to parochial schools, and against allowing children to be released from public school so they could have religious instruction. "I am impenitent in believing," he told a friend, "in the principle of separation of Church and State as basic to our democratic society."

As he had been criticized previously by liberals, now he was criticized by conservatives. After one decision in which he and Black had been against excusing children from public schools for private religious instruction, Frankfurter wrote Black: "And for good measure there is added some rancid Billie Graham stuff whereby we shall be reviled as atheists. But then, it wouldn't be the first time that you and I are reviled."

The major freedom-of-religion case to come before the Court was at the end of Frankfurter's tenure as a justice. The case originated in New York and involved a state's attempt to impose the recitation of a "nondenominational" prayer on students within the state. The arguments in the case centered around efforts to explain "nondenominational" and the embarrassed efforts by the lawyers for the state to justify imposing any kind of religious practice upon young people of varied religious and ethnic backgrounds. The state acted as if there had been a melting pot, as if the dozens of religions represented by the students as well as the atheism of some, had been erased and replaced with bland homilies written by committees. According to William Douglas, Frankfurter, after hearing the arguments, voted in conference against imposing the "nondenominational prayer" upon New York schoolchildren. But when the actual decision came down, Frankfurter was off the bench and so was not formally recorded.

Felix Frankfurter may have been swayed by momentary passions when on the Supreme Court in the early 1940s. In Court lore, *Gobitis* was known for years as "Felix's Fall of France Opinion." But then the fall of France and the threat to England provoked many to extremism; he was not alone. When freed of the wartime pressure, Frankfurter demonstrated he had not forgotten his Lower East Side origins, refused to tolerate attacks on the minority member, showed that still within him was a passion for justice.

21

Frankfurter versus Douglas

In 1944, when Frankfurter had visited with FDR, then in the final year of his third term, the President was tired and was going south to Warm Springs, Georgia, for a rest. He complained to Frankfurter that hardly a day passed "without pain because of this damned sinus since the first of the year." Frankfurter thought the comment odd, because, as Frankfurter told Marion, Roosevelt "was never given to self-complaint."

On January 20, 1945, Roosevelt was inaugurated for a fourth term. Marion Frankfurter, watching him take the oath, thought, "He has the look of a doomed man. He looks like a man a good deal of whom is no longer there." The next month, Frankfurter saw the President at a friend's funeral; he described FDR to Marion as a "ghastly sight."

A couple of months later Frankfurter was walking in Rock Creek Park with Lord Halifax, the British ambassador to the United States. "What do you think of the President's condition?" Lord Halifax asked. "Frankly," replied Frankfurter, "I fear the worst." The answer did not surprise Halifax. He had seen the President recently, and was "simply shocked by the change that had taken place."

That conversation took place a few minutes after 4 o'clock the afternoon of Thursday, April 12. At 4:15 that afternoon Franklin Roosevelt died. He was sixty-three years old.

The following Sunday, Felix Frankfurter attended the burial service for his friend and President at Hyde Park. "The sky was swept clean," said Frankfurter, "the Gods smiled on him at the last and there was a tang in the air that sharpened the pain."

Frankfurter was at the President's home with other members of the Supreme Court, the new President, the dead President's family and friends, co-workers, neighbors. They crowded into a small garden, enclosed by hemlock hedges planted in 1811. The service began at 10:34. The Reverend George W. Anthony, rector of St. James's Episcopal

Church in Hyde Park, where Roosevelt had been a senior warden, conducted. Reverend Anthony, seventy-eight, wore a black cassock, a white surplice, and a black skull cap. With what Frankfurter described as a voice of "unworldly authority and strangely powerful," the rector read Hymn 411 from the *Episcopal Hymnal:*

> Now the Laborer's Task is Done:
> Now the Battle Day is Past. . . .
> Father in Thy gracious keeping;
> Leave we now our brother sleeping.

Felix Frankfurter had once written Franklin Roosevelt about how "the mysterious ways of Fate" had brought together the "Dutchess County American and the Viennese American." This day, the day of his burial, Franklin Roosevelt was much the Dutchess County American, the Christian gentleman with roots deep into the community, the member of the landed gentry, the one who had enjoyed the finest education America offered as well as social benefits not available to most. Yet, for more than twelve years he had been Felix Frankfurter's President. He had opened up the presidency to the pleas and the frustrations, the needs and the passions of the foreign-born, the minority members, the poor, the working men and women. He had brought a woman into the President's cabinet for the first time, had more Jews as friends and advisors than any previous President; had met with blacks, union leaders, representatives of ethnic groups. His actions had been political, but politics is a two-way process. It gains or loses votes for a candidate, and it also tells the ethnic group, the members of a religion, the racial group, the women, that they have a friend, that government responds to them as it responds to others. Decades earlier the Irishman and the Jew had teamed up on the streets of New York to use the political process. They had learned then that, if they worked together, recognized each other's needs, brought in the immigrant and all the others who had been left out, that they could become a force to make America work for them as it had worked for others. One result had been the presidency of Franklin Roosevelt. Motivated by his own inclinations and powered by their votes, Roosevelt had given political status to the torrent of immigrants and poor who had come to the United States in the early decades of the century. If their problems had not been solved, they now were part of the process that offered solutions. The millions of Felix Frankfurters. He had been their President.

Seventeen minutes after the service had begun, at 10:51 A.M., it ended with the playing of "Taps," the soldiers' farewell to a fallen comrade.

In the years following Roosevelt's death, Frankfurter moved about official Washington, continued his many acquaintanceships. Dean Acheson, Secretary of State in the Truman administration, remained a friend, as did many others in subsequent administrations. James Reston, then Washington editor and columnist for the *New York Times,* was also a friend; and Philip Graham, a former Frankfurter law clerk, was publisher of the Washington *Post.* "He never felt on the outside of anything," said one of Frankfurter's acquaintances from that period. "He had friends in the world of the press, diplomacy. He was never an outsider." But that was not quite true. The new President, Harry S Truman, did not know Frankfurter. The White House no longer called him for advice, to work on a speech, to suggest someone for a job. With the end of the Roosevelt era, Felix Frankfurter never was as close to power as he had been in the previous twelve years.

There were, however, outside activities. One was Zionism. When he had joined the Court, Frankfurter had severed relations with all organizations, including the Zionist movement, but he had not forgotten the cause. "Certainly one does not cease to be a citizen of the United States, or become unrelated to issues that make for the wellbeing of the world that may never come for adjudication before this Court, by becoming a member of it," he once explained. He had, however, not been effective in this area in the early 1940s and was even less effective after Roosevelt's death. In 1948, he tried to arrange a meeting between Chaim Weizmann and Secretary of State George C. Marshall; Marshall refused. When the United Nations considered partitioning Palestine into Arab and Jewish states in 1947, Frankfurter lobbied in a modest way among his influential friends—suggesting they read a newspaper editorial, dropping a comment to them.

A sign of Frankfurter's failure as a lobbyist for Zionism is that Dean Acheson, perhaps his closest friend and the Frankfurter acquaintance most powerful in government, was an anti-Zionist.

Still, Frankfurter had not outlived his reputation as a power-behind-the-throne, and his efforts often were exaggerated as his past activities had been. One example involved Loy W. Henderson, a State Department official who opposed partition and saw American Jewry as attempting to coerce the State Department into accepting partition. He said that he had heard that Frankfurter and his fellow associate justice Frank Murphy "had both sent messages to the Philippine delegate to the General Assembly strongly urging his vote" for partitioning Palestine into Arab and Jewish states. When that statement was reported in the published diaries of James V. Forrestal in 1951, Frankfurter categorically denied having approached the delegate. Whether one believes Frankfurter's flat denial or Henderson's second-hand charge, the determining factors that persuaded the Philippines ultimately to vote for the creation of a Jewish state were not Frankfurter's activities but pressures from United States senators on the Philippine President and the intervention of an American civil servant who was a personal friend of the Philippine President.*

Frankfurter recommended and lobbied for the appointment of several individuals for federal court appointments, but then so did Chief Justice Earl Warren and, later, Chief Justice Warren Burger. In 1952, William Douglas attempted to persuade Harry Truman to run for reelection and even vowed to "leave the Court and stump for you"; even with FDR, Frankfurter had not gone that far. Nor had Frankfurter's relationship with FDR equaled that between Fred M. Vinson when he was Chief Justice and President Truman, who had appointed him. Vinson, while on the Court, continued to be a close advisor to the President. Late-night telephone conversations about public matters were a staple of their relationship. Vinson advised Truman specifically on the constitutionality of a presidential action certain to come before the Court.

And never, of course, had Frankfurter been in a class with Abe Fortas when he was an associate justice during the administration of Lyndon Johnson. Senator Thruston Morton of Kentucky told the story of a senator telephoning the White House to learn the President's position on a proposed change in a bill. According to Morton, a member of the White House staff took the telephone call and responded: "Well, the President is away, but Mr. Justice Fortas is here and he's managing the bill for the White House."

Frankfurter believed he had a debt to history. He designated one of his law clerks, Andrew L. Kaufman, to be the biographer of Benjamin Cardozo. And when Professor Alpheus Thomas Mason of Princeton wrote his authorized biography of Louis Brandeis, Frankfurter offered to cooperate with him. "I shall therefore be glad to talk to you about

*B. A. Murphy, in the *Brandeis-Frankfurter Connection*, p. 309, reports this incident, but says "it was the president of the Philippines to whom Henderson and *The Forrestal Diaries* claim Frankfurter sent his message, and not the delegate to the United Nations," thus negating Frankfurter's denial. Murphy misread the *Forrestal Diaries*; they refer only to the Philippine delegate.

the questions you raise in your letter," Frankfurter wrote Mason and continued in subsequent letters his offer to meet with Mason. But during the several years that Mason was working on the biography, his correspondence with Frankfurter shows that he was unable to make the trip from Princeton University to Washington. Frankfurter also participated in an oral history project at Columbia University (which he later allowed to be published) and then designated Max Friedman, a journalist, as his biographer and turned over his complete collection of personal papers to Friedman, who never finished the project because of illness.

Frankfurter's social and personal relationships continued to multiply, however. "He had his dislikes," said one who knew Frankfurter in this period, "but if he liked you, there were no stops. He wanted to know what a person was writing, saying, thinking; how he reacted to political events. . . . He seemed to be genuinely interested, and he had to know everything." Some found Frankfurter snobbish: "If you came from Houston, you might have trouble." But others believed the snobbism, if it existed, had another source: "Grace counted, whether born or acquired. It was part of FF's meritocracy."

Frankfurter, living only on his salary, could not give financial assistance as did Brandeis, but he did give a part of himself, especially when he believed he was carrying on a project or friendship begun by Brandeis. An example is the story of Donald G. Morgan. In 1939, Morgan, then a student, had visited Brandeis in Chatham to discuss doing a doctoral thesis on William Johnson, an important but overlooked Supreme Court justice during the early 1800s. "I had no trouble meeting with Justice Brandeis," Morgan recalled. "He was very responsive to young people. I remember the meeting as being a very pleasant one. He didn't waste time." Brandeis was enthusiastic and encouraging.

Morgan's advisor at college had been reluctant to have him take on the project, believing the research too difficult for Morgan, who was completely blind and had been for some years. Brandeis, in his meeting with Morgan, did not consider Morgan's blindness significant. "Did the question of your blindness come up?" Morgan was asked. Morgan thought back to that 1939 meeting with Brandeis and said: "I don't remember. He might have said something."

Frankfurter was aware of the story, and, after Brandeis's death, considered Morgan his own friend. He wrote letters of recommendation for Morgan for a wartime job, a teaching position, assisted him in acquiring the use of study facilities at the Library of Congress, and continued to be interested in his career. Morgan's thesis was published in 1954 as *Justice William Johnson—the First Dissenter* and was well received. The next year, Chief Justice Earl Warren spoke at the commencement exercises at Mount Holyoke College, where Morgan was then teaching, and sought Morgan out to congratulate him on his book. Morgan was certain Frankfurter had asked Warren to do that.

Frankfurter's generosity of spirit showed during his Court years in his relationships with his law clerks. Since he was no longer involved with large groups of students, his connection with the new generation came through the law clerks, the younger people who had been through the Second World War, had been educated in a different time, had come to maturity as lawyers when the law offered different challenges. Brandeis had used his teas to learn from the young; Frankfurter used his law clerks.

He "chose" his law clerks—there were two each year—the same way Holmes and Brandeis had chosen theirs: a faculty member at Harvard selected them. Once the clerk arrived, usually fresh from law school, he found himself an equal. "This striking egalitarianism—that was meant quite seriously. . . ." said the late Alexander M. Bickel, a clerk in the 1950s. "There was no hierarchy in this business. You were as good as he was, depending on what you had to say."

Frankfurter himself explained: "They are, as it were, my junior partners—junior only in years. In the realm of the mind there is no hierarchy. I take them fully into my confidence so that the relation is free and easy. However, I am, they will tell you, a very exacting task-master; no nonsense, intellectually speaking, is tolerated, no short-cuts, no deference to position is permitted, no yes-sing, however much some of them in the beginning be awed."

The "free and easy" relationship was oratorically sometimes near violent. "He gave it to you with both barrels," said Bickel. "He was the most unscrupulous debater alive; there were no holds barred; knees in the groin, fingers in the eyes, unfair arguments, shifting of ground; that was as it properly ought to be . . . and you'd walk away from one of these thinking, 'Oh, my God, you left a horrible impression.' . . . And he'd walk into the next room and say to somebody, 'Gee, that's a bright fellow,' you know, 'a good boy, a very good boy.' " Frankfurter thrived on intellectual combat. Once at dinner for the clerks, Frankfurter asked them to name the Court's worst opinion from the previous term. Andrew Kaufman answered with one of Frankfurter's own, and the two men thrashed the decision back and forth. "I didn't feel," said Kaufman, "the slightest compunction that I was on forbidden ground." Said another clerk: "We regarded it as part of our job when we disagreed with him."

One or both of the clerks picked him up at his Georgetown home and drove him to the Supreme Court—Frankfurter still did not own or drive an automobile. The combat began immediately. What did the clerk think of yesterday's action by the President? Of a story on page 25 of the *New York Times?* What about this and what that? The clerks thought they were used as partners in an intellectual tennis match, but Frankfurter played a higher game. He had been disappointed in the quality of the lawyers appearing before the Supreme Court: "They are really not cultivated lawyers. I have said to myself often, as I listened to these arguments, I would give a good cookie to know what this fellow has read during the last three years, besides *Time, Life,* and the higher flight of that category, *Fortune.*" Frankfurter believed the lawyer should be widely read, knowledgeable about events, and able to converse with sophistication. To assure that his clerks met those criteria, he turned those early-morning sessions into training periods for them.

The relationship continued long after the clerkship ended, the young men graduating from clerks to friends. Frankfurter remained interested in their careers, took pleasure in their successes, expressed sympathy at their defeats. His clerks became successful private practitioners, active in Democratic and Republican politics, in the government bureaucracy, and in academe—two Republican cabinet members in the 1970s and the deans of the law schools at Harvard, Yale, and Columbia in the early 1980s were former Frankfurter law clerks. Frankfurter had no religious criteria; his clerks were Protestant, Jewish, and Catholic. And one was black.

In the late 1940s, Washington continued a southern segregated city. Schools and restaurants were divided into white and black as were residential areas. In the Capitol, the Senate and House press galleries had separate sections for white and black reporters, and the National Press Club—the reporters' professional club—excluded blacks from both membership and attendance. The armed services had only recently been desegregated. According to a District of Columbia police chief, "Until the early 1950's, teletype messages calling for presidential details included the admonition 'Send white officers only.'" The Supreme Court was not immune to this; it had blacks to run errands and to clean. Christmas parties at the Court usually brought protracted discussions of whether the black personnel at the Court should be invited. No justice ever had had a black as a law clerk.

When Paul Freund of the Harvard Law School, who then selected Frankfurter's law clerks, suggested William T. Coleman, a black, in late 1947, Frankfurter replied: "I don't have to tell you that I don't care what color a man has, any more than I care what religion he professes or doesn't." When the appointment was announced in the spring of 1948, Frankfurter received a number of letters praising him for breaking a racial barrier. Frankfurter would have none of that. "Mr. William T. Coleman was named as one of my law clerks for next year precisely for the same reason that others have been named in the past," Frankfurter responded to the letters, "namely high professional competence and character. You are kind to write me, but I do not think a man deserves any praise for doing what is right and abstaining from the wrong."

Frankfurter's years on the Court coincided with the Second World War, the Cold War, the Korean conflict, Truman's Fair Deal, the Marshall Plan, the McCarthy era, the Eisenhower years, John F. Kennedy's New Frontier, the early years of the Vietnam War. The years also were the time of the triumph of the image makers, when the medium became the message, when political power began its shift from the Northeast to the Southwest; this was the space age, the television age, the time when newspapers waned. Frankfurter's life became part of the past. He had known Theodore Roosevelt, Woodrow Wilson, and Franklin Roosevelt; now people read about them in books. He had lived through Bisbee, Mooney, the Paris Peace Conference, and Sacco-Vanzetti. Some of these names were barely remembered. The first sixty years of his life—turbulent, productive, controversial—were history.

In his closing decades, Felix Frankfurter lived a new history. He was a link to the past of James Bradley Thayer, Oliver Wendell Holmes, and Louis Brandeis, and he was a modern exponent of judicial restraint. If his fellow justices had not read Thayer's essay on judicial restraint from the 1890s, Frankfurter made certain they received a copy. Although he complained often of being a Supreme Court justice—"I've been listening to the most dreary, lifeless arguments"—he relished his role on the Court, welcoming the new battle as he had welcomed the old.

Elliot L. Richardson, one of his clerks, recalled Frankfurter urging him to hurry with two citations for a draft opinion that Frankfurter wanted to circulate among the other justices before opposing views solidified. "I can still see him dancing at my desk, rocking up on his toes, down on his heels," Richardson recalled. "He said, 'This is a war we're fighting! Don't you understand? A war!' "

In conference, he did battle. When the other justices were kind, they talked of Frankfurter's "lively and animated" manner and his "storehouse of information," how he stood behind his chair when his back troubled him and lectured them with his notes and records on a book rest. When they weren't so kind, they talked about Frankfurter's indulging "in histrionics. . . . He often came in with piles of books, and on his turn to talk, would pound the table, read from the books, throw them around and create a great disturbance. . . . At times, when another was talking, he would break in, make a derisive comment and shout down the speaker."

When the Court was in session, Frankfurter continued his argumentative ways. In his own appearances before the Court in the 1910s and 1920s, he had learned that it "was a cross-examining and not merely a listening court." Some of his fellow justices and some lawyers believed his questioning went too far. One justice said that Frankfurter's questions "were often argumentative and somewhat in the spirit of a professor testing out the knowledge of his class." And Charles Burlingham called Frankfurter "the most learned man on the Court. . . . But, unfortunately, he is an awful talker."

Frankfurter, on his side, believed that too many lawyers considered the oral argument only as an opportunity to recite a set piece or to repeat points made in the previously submitted brief rather than "to get at the vitals of the issues in ways that the printed briefs do not afford."

Some lawyers did not object to his zeroing in on them, acknowledging that, if they were prepared, his questioning helped bring out the essentials of the argument. When a 1947 *Fortune* article described him on the bench as harassing attorneys, Dan Moody, a former governor of Texas, who had argued frequently before Frankfurter, winning some and losing some, said that the article "does you a gross injustice."

Once, when a former Frankfurter student was arguing before him, according to one present, Frankfurter "was pretty rough on him . . . the Justice was pretty severe—you might say professorially—with his former pupil." After the argument, however, Frankfurter sent the former pupil a note complimenting him on his argument. Another former student, Joseph Rauh, who, in arguing many cases before the Court, had often been stung by Frankfurter's questioning, wrote him, when Frankfurter retired, "It'll never be the same before the Court—much easier, I guess, but much less challenging and less fun."

Whether Frankfurter badgered or probed, he was there. John P. Frank made a study of one oral argument, an hour on each side, and found members of the Court had interrupted counsel 237 times, about two a minute; ". . . 93 were by Justice Frankfurter."

During his years on the Court, Frankfurter served with four Chief Justices and nineteen associate justices. Those nineteen included Brandeis and Pierce Butler, both of whom left the Court in 1939; James F. Byrnes, who served only one year before becoming an assistant to President Roosevelt; and Charles E. Whittaker, who served late in Frankfurter's tenure and resigned after five years because of his difficulties in handling the job. They also include Owen Roberts and James McReynolds from the Court of the 1930s. With Hugo Black, Stanley Reed, William Douglas, Frank Murphy, Robert Jackson, and Wiley Rutledge, Frankfurter was one of the "New Deal" justices who came to the bench when Roosevelt was President. Frankfurter also served with justices appointed by Presidents Truman, Eisenhower, and Kennedy, and served with one of his own former students, William J. Brennan.

But the Supreme Court during those years, from 1939 to 1962, was more than a collection of individuals who went their separate ways. In the early 1940s, when Harlan Fiske Stone was Chief Justice, it was an acrimonious group. Stone lacked the political adroitness necessary to make a collegiate body run smoothly. Frankfurter, once a Stone admirer, became his critic for that reason. In the late 1940s and early 1950s, when Fred Vinson was Chief Justice, it was a transition court, still living in the aura of the New Deal, evading rather than confronting postwar issues. Then in the period of Earl Warren's chief justiceship, from 1953 when Warren was appointed until 1962 when Frankfurter retired, the Court no longer turned from the postwar issues but dealt with them.

During Frankfurter's years on the Court, only two justices served as long as he did, Hugo Black and William Douglas. Black, a graduate of the University of Alabama, and Douglas, a graduate of Columbia, were sometimes ridiculed—"If you came from Harvard Law School," remarked a Frankfurter clerk from the 1950s, "you thought Black and Douglas were clowns." Still, because they had New Deal ties as had Frankfurter, the assumption was that the three men would work together, with Frankfurter the dominant member.

But it did not work that way. The three were not together, and if, in later years, Frankfurter and Black became friends, Frankfurter and Douglas did not. And Frankfurter never dominated either man. These personal relationships had much to do with what happened inside the Court during those twenty-three years.

Douglas and Frankfurter had known each other for years, and respected each other before their appointments to the Supreme Court. To Douglas in the early 1930s, Frankfurter was the hero of Sacco-Vanzetti. Douglas as Securities and Exchange Commissioner put into effect legislation Frankfurter had helped draft, and when Douglas was appointed to replace Brandeis on the bench, Frankfurter told a friend: "You do well to be glad over the appointment of Douglas. We shall have a man who is historic-minded about the law, but also knows that history is not a tale of dead things but part of a dynamic process."

Shortly that friendship and respect turned, on the part of both men, to a dislike so intense that, according to Douglas's biographer, "the two justices did not speak to each other for extended periods of time." One explanation offered is that Frankfurter resented Douglas's independence, but Hugo Black also went his independent ways and he and Frankfurter became friends. The explanation lies elsewhere. The two men grated on each other. Douglas was an outdoorsman, several times divorced, with an abrasive personality—few of his clerks liked him. Also, Frankfurter believed Douglas used his position on the Court for personal political gain.

In 1940, with Franklin Roosevelt's third-term plans tacitly accepted, the vice-presidential position on the Democratic ticket seemed open, and several names were mentioned, including Douglas's. Early in July, two weeks before the Democratic convention opened in Chicago, Douglas wrote Frankfurter a "Personal and Confidential" letter, scribbled while on a train to Texas. There was, he said, "considerable talk in Washington about putting me on the ticket" and "it is disturbing because I want none of it. I want to stay where I am." He added, "This line to you is to ask you, should the matter come your way, to scotch it." Frankfurter then talked down the possibility of a Douglas nomination to his friends.

The vice-presidential nomination went to Henry A. Wallace, but only after Roosevelt threatened to decline the presidential nomination unless the convention gave him Wallace. Douglas had not openly campaigned for the nomination, as he had assured Frankfurter, or perhaps he realized that the uninterested pose was best for an interested Supreme Court justice.

After Frankfurter's efforts to "scotch" the 1940 rumors about the vice presidency and Douglas, he came to believe that he had been used by Douglas to help build up Douglas's aura of political innocence. Through the years Douglas had maintained close friendships with newspapermen, who dropped items in their columns about the possibilities of Douglas for a governmental post. Once in June 1941, Frankfurter lunched with Harold Ickes, still Secretary of Interior, and expressed his suspicions about Douglas and the possibilities of a government post. "Felix believes that Bill does not have a passion for the court," recorded Ickes, "and has not fallen in line with the notion that he is wedded to his present job for life. I believe that this is true too."

Douglas, on his part, believed that Frankfurter wanted him off the Court. In September 1941, Roosevelt offered Douglas a wartime job that would have required Douglas to resign as associate justice. Douglas did not accept the position, believing there was an ulterior motive behind it. "I am quite sure that F. F. has inspired this offer—at least that he has been influential," Douglas said to Hugo Black. "It has come to me 'straight' that he thinks I am the only man. If he could get me there and you back in the Senate I am sure he would be happier."

In Washington, gossip is the currency of power. Once a story is told about a person, it spirals through Georgetown gatherings, picking up detail and innuendo. The animosity between Douglas and Frankfurter became part of this game. They were both prominent, considered influential, with powerful friends—and enemies; natural subjects for the "can-you-top-this" stories that make the teller a hero at cocktails, a king at dinner.

The Ickes diaries show much of this. Frankfurter came to lunch and complained about Douglas. Douglas came to lunch and complained about Frankfurter. At dinner parties, with neither man present, guests talked about both. Frankfurter allowed his animosity toward Douglas to push him into corners distant from where he belonged philosophically. When Douglas took a position in a decision, Frankfurter took the opposite. And Douglas was "cool and calculating and selfish and . . . deliberately putting Felix in the wrong light." And on and on the stories went.

In 1944, the vice presidency again was open. Douglas, vacationing in Oregon, wrote a letter to Chief Justice Stone, denying any interest in leaving the Supreme Court to accept the vice-presidential nomination. He did not write Frankfurter this time; the two men no longer were friends; Frankfurter would not have believed him if he had. Early in

July, Harry Hopkins sent Frankfurter a note: "I tried to get you on the phone because I wanted very much to talk to you about some things, but found you had gone for the summer, and I regret that I cannot discuss them over a Connecticut telephone line." Grabbing a pencil, Frankfurter scrawled at the bottom of Hopkins's letter: "I'm glad I was out of Washington, for I suspect that what he wanted to talk with me about was one W. O. Douglas & the V.P. ship. Tom Corcoran for months has with subterranean skill been managing the Douglas candidacy." Douglas some years later denied he was interested in elective office. "I didn't think that being on the Court was compatible with making plans to run for public office." He said, "Frankfurter used to make accusations that I was doing just that. But the truth was that I wasn't . . . that friends of mine seemed to be enthusiastic about me but I never gave them any encouragement. . . . It was only after the 1944 convention that I knew that Roosevelt had written the convention, had written the chairman of the Democratic National Committee saying that he would be happy to run either with me or with Truman."

Douglas occasionally wrote on a Frankfurter draft decision something like: "No matter what the majority may cook up, I am with you. But your speed puts a young squirt to shame." But he was unkind to Frankfurter in his autobiography and in his private remarks. Frankfurter retaliated. To friends, he said of Douglas: "He has brains, but no sense."

With Hugo Black the relationship was different. As an investigating senator in the 1930s, Black had operated in the manner of one making his own law. He once summoned a public utility executive before his committee without giving the executive warning or opportunity to prepare. As the man was about to testify, Black signaled: "Tell the boys of the press to come in. The show is about to begin." With utility executives cast as the economic villains of the 1930s, the press saw Black in heroic proportions, Jack the giant killer. Black had a number of other "liberal" credentials. In 1930 he had opposed Hughes as Chief Justice, and in 1935 had introduced legislation allowing Congress control over the Supreme Court's docket. The bill died, to the relief of many.

When appointed, Black was derided as an "Alabama hillbilly" and criticized because of an earlier association with the Ku Klux Klan. Brandeis had not joined in that criticism. Arthur Schlesinger, Sr., wrote that at the height of the attacks on Black, "Brandeis quietly remarked that from long personal acquaintance he considered the Alabaman thoroughly well qualified." Although several years later Frankfurter quoted Brandeis speaking negatively of Black, letters between Brandeis and Black show that, when Brandeis retired in 1939, the two were on friendly terms.

In the early years of Black's tenure on the Supreme Court, Frankfurter, still at Harvard, became one of his supporters. "Black as a person means nothing to me," said Frankfurter at the end of 1937, after Black had served only three months on the Court. "I have never laid eyes on him." Then Frankfurter launched into a defense of Black, who was accused of having violated constitutional rights with his subcommittee investigation. Two months later Frankfurter was saying, "I have a great deal of respect for the independence of [Black's] character that makes him indifferent to the comfort he would derive from playing with Brandeis and Stone."

In 1938, Frankfurter considered himself Black's guide and helper. He told Justice Stanley Reed "that he must not allow Black to interpose the barrier of formality" between them.

Black's first year on the Court had shown him lacking in background for the job; his Court writings were second-rate, and he himself was isolated from the other justices. Early in May 1938, a *Harper's* article by Marquis Childs said: "During his brief service on the bench Justice Black has caused his colleagues . . . acute discomfort and embarrassment. This . . . has grown out of a lack of legal knowledge and experience, deficiencies in background and training that have led him into blunders which have shocked his colleagues on the highest court." Child's source was not identified, but in Washington was known to be Black's fellow associate justice, Harlan Fiske Stone.

After the article appeared, Frankfurter was sent on a rescue mission by Brandeis. He and Marion had tea with the Blacks at their Alexandria, Virginia, home—their first meeting. Frankfurter advised Black to choose the ground for his dissents carefully and also talked with Mrs. Black privately "and she can be counted on . . . to soften and not to encourage asperities and to mitigate his feelings and habit of isolation." Frankfurter was optimistic about Black's future. "Black has, of course," Frankfurter reported to Brandeis, "the difficulties of a man who all his life has been looked at askance by the 'best people,' and in turn has been 'agin' the crowd in power. But I believe he is uncorrupted and incorruptible—maybe a touch of the crusader—for there are not many senators who acted on your wisdom and eschewed the rich and fashionable in Washington as a matter of principle because of its subtle corrupting influence."

By the end of 1939, when Frankfurter had served with Black almost a full year, he was more enthusiastic, estimating that Black eventually would become one of the Court's great justices. "Black may have had few qualifications when he went on the bench, but he has a keen mind and he is a tremendously hard worker" is how a friend quoted Frankfurter then.

Within a few years, lawyers arguing before the Supreme Court came to the same conclusion. Said one: "Yes, I know all about Black's limited record as a police judge. I know all about the hillbilly background, the Ku Klux Klan membership and the zealot's attitude as a Senate investigator. But when I went into court today I knew there were two weak spots in my argument and damned if Black didn't put his finger on both of them."

Still, years passed before Black developed the sophistication required for the Court's interpersonal relations; in the early 1940s, he feuded with many members of the Court and was largely responsible for the acrimony and discord that characterized the Court in those years. He refused to sign a draft of the brethrens' letter to Owen Roberts when Roberts resigned in 1945. Roberts's resignation was caused by the difficulties of working with Hugo Black, and after resigning Roberts never returned to the Supreme Court chamber.

Black publicly feuded with Robert Jackson. "Black at his worst," recorded Frankfurter in his diary in 1943, "violent, vehement, indifferent to the use he was making of cases." At one point, Jackson apparently came close to joining Roberts in resigning from the Court rather than continue to deal with Black. Frankfurter said he had to "really nail Bob Jackson to the wall to prevent him from resigning from the Court. He had all the steps taken to do that."

And yet in 1946 when Jackson returned from Nuremberg, where he had been chief United States prosecutor at the Nazi war crimes trial and met Black in conference for the first time after their feud had been well publicized, the two men shook hands courteously, and later "joined in a brief discussion—all in the best of quiet manners," according to one of the justices. Jackson told others that, from that moment on, he and Black had harmonious relations, as one gentleman to another. The passion had been spent.

Through the years, as Black broadened his knowledge, developed his expertise, and gained self-confidence, he became less the antagonist and more the politician within the Court and the judicial philosopher outside of it. Personally he and Frankfurter became friends, even as philosophically they grew further apart. The two men, the Harvard professor and the Alabama "hillbilly," had similar backgrounds. Frankfurter had said that Black's difficulties stemmed from being looked at "askance by the 'best people' . . . [and being] 'agin' the crowd in power." The same language fits parts of Frankfurter's life.

There was another reason for the friendship between Frankfurter and Black; theirs was the friendship of foes. Each saw in the other a worthy adversary, a partner in a dialogue, one who must be considered, not a follower but the leader of the opposing side. This philosophical debate between the two men went to the heart of the issue of what role the Court serves, how an individual decides cases, and what the American citizen could anticipate from Court decisions. In this debate, lasting almost a quarter of a century, many phrases were tossed back and forth: "judicial restraint," "due process," "liberal," and "conservative." The debate concerned how people who come to the Court attempt to deal with the conflicts they find before them. In this debate, neither Frankfurter nor Black was always consistent.

The Fifth and Fourteenth amendments to the Constitution provide citizens with protections against the state in criminal and civil proceedings; the protections are summed up in the phrase "due process of law," which appears in both amendments. In the early decades of the 1900s, Frankfurter and Brandeis objected to the Supreme Court's using the Fourteenth Amendment's "due process of law" phrase to block the legislative efforts to regulate working conditions. This was their reasonableness argument; if the state wanted to limit working hours, it should be allowed despite employers' claims that "due process of law" was being violated.

At one point, Frankfurter seemed willing to junk the phrase entirely. He wrote in the early 1920s to Holmes that he had "more and more" questions about due process, stemming from the character of judges who determine "due process." Since due process represents, as Frankfurter later quoted Learned Hand as saying, "a mood rather than a command," individual judges have considerable leeway in spelling out the details of that mood. In his letter to Holmes, Frankfurter said he would have no trouble giving the power to a Court composed of Holmes, Brandeis, Hand, and Cardozo, because then "the due process clause does serve as an articulate expression of age-old experience." But, because the Supreme Court will not have that quality of membership, Frankfurter said, "the question then becomes a balancing of gains and costs. And I must say I increasingly have me doots."

Frankfurter, still at Harvard, had his "doots" resolved in the early 1930s when seven black youths were arrested in Alabama and charged with raping two white women, the Scottsboro case. The Supreme Court reversed their conviction on the grounds that the blacks had been denied "due process of law" as guaranteed by the Fourteenth Amendment because they had not had effective legal representation at their trial. This was the first time the Supreme Court had reversed a state criminal conviction, citing unfair procedures at the trial. The opinion was written by George Sutherland, one of the "four horsemen" of the conservatives.

Only a few years earlier the Court had refused to intervene in the Sacco-Vanzetti case. Three factors probably influenced the change. One was the blatant violation of even state guarantees at the Scottsboro trial; in Sacco-Vanzetti, state procedures had been complied with. The second was the publication of the Wickersham Commission study of crime and law enforcement, its documented record of police brutality shocking the nation. Third was the growing demand both within and outside the Court for the Court to become the nation's conscience.

And Felix Frankfurter, the James Bradley Thayer disciple, the one so much against judges' making law, was part of this demand. He acknowledged that when states do not honor constitutional protections, the federal government must intervene, and the Supreme Court must assure that it does, even if it makes law to do so. "The Supreme Court," said Frankfurter in 1932 of the Supreme Court's action in the Scottsboro case, "has declared only that the determination must be made with due observance of the decencies of civilized procedure." So, from one with serious doubts about due process, Frankfurter became its advocate, at least when the "decencies of civilized procedure" were involved.

At the end of 1939, when he had been on the Supreme Court with Hugo Black for almost a year, Frankfurter attempted to explain his position in a "Dear Hugo" letter. "I, too, am opposed to judicial legislation in its invidious sense," wrote Frankfurter, "but I deem equally mischievous—because founded on an untruth and an impossible aim— the notion that judges merely announce the law which they find and do not themselves inevitably have a share in the law-making. Here, as elsewhere, the difficulty comes from arguing in terms of absolutes when the matter at hand is conditioned by circumstances . . ."

Frankfurter's problem was that he, the advocate of judicial restraint, was arguing for judicial activism. He, as well as Brandeis before him, had been caught here before, between two conflicting approaches. He attempted to defend his seemingly staring in two different directions by basing judicial activism on tradition. He told Black that he had said to Harvard students that "legislators make law wholesale, judges retail," which meant that judges "cannot decide things by invoking a new major premise out of whole cloth; they must make the law that they do make out of the existing materials and with due deference to the presuppositions of the legal system of which they have been made a part."

Hugo Black came to believe that judges should not exercise such power, either wholesale or retail. The Fourteenth Amendment had been passed, Black argued, to assure that the protections promised in the Bill of Rights reached all Americans, and he read the Bill of Rights in absolute terms—where the "difficulty" stemmed from, Frankfurter had said. "A bare majority of the members of the Supreme Court of the United States have been for a number of years assuming the right on their part to determine the *reasonableness* of State and Federal laws," Black said first in 1937, before he joined the Court, and then again after he had been on the Court a number of years. "The Constitution never gave that majority any such power." When deciding whether the Fourteenth Amendment should assist the corporation fighting the government regulation or assist the poor individual fighting the state, he insisted that judges must take the Constitution at its face value, without interpreting any "mood."

Still, in that same talk Hugo Black, at one point, sounded much like Frankfurter. "I would much prefer to put my faith in the people and their elected representatives to choose the proper policies for our government to follow, leaving to the courts questions of constitutional interpretation and enforcement."

As the dialogue continued through the years, the lines blurred, but the issues remained, the continuation of many years of struggle, the conflicts that had involved Louis Brandeis, on and off the bench, and the young Felix Frankfurter. This was the role of the judiciary in defending the individual against the state and financial behemoth.

22

The Harvard Professor
and the Alabama Hillbilly

In 1918, in *Hammer* v. *Dagenhart,* the Supreme Court refused to allow Congress to regulate working conditions in the production of goods shipped in interstate commerce even if abuse of children was involved. Holmes, joined by Brandeis, dissented, saying the law restricting child labor had been valid both from the standpoint of constitutionality and morality.

Twenty-three years later, in 1941, the Supreme Court unanimously overruled *Hammer.* The decision by Harlan Fiske Stone disallowed "distribution of goods produced under substandard labor conditions." The case was *United States* v. *Darby* and the Court's attack was without limitation, against any "substandard" condition.

To emphasize the change, the next year the Court ruled that the federal government's marketing quotas for wheat, under the Constitution's interstate commerce section, applied not only to wheat the farmer sold but also to wheat he grew for his own consumption. The government could oversee working conditions for virtually everything produced.

That case was argued in May, late in the term ending the next month, and Frankfurter urged Chief Justice Stone to put the decision over until fall, saying that more time for reflection was needed. Certain to be controversial, the decision would be stronger, Frankfurter knew, if there were no dissents. The delay worked. When the decision came down the next term, it was unanimous. Holmes and Brandeis then not only had a victory, but an overwhelming one in these two cases; a quarter of a century had been required. These cases were only the beginning, as many of the views articulated by Holmes and Brandeis in the 1920s in dissents became the law of the land in the 1940s and 1950s through Supreme Court decisions.

The nation—no longer officially tolerant of unhealthy, immoral, and dangerous working conditions—generally welcomed the change in the Court's stance. This attitude had given the worker a new authority, and from the New Deal, had come a new power. Through bloody confrontations with management, unions had demonstrated their intention to use that power. The unions had been the economic weaklings; now some were strong and showed their strength. How Frankfurter and the other justices dealt with this new strength demonstrates their attitudes toward the unions and also how individuals are caught between pressures.

In St. Louis a brewery was squeezed in a union jurisdictional dispute over construction work. When the company bowed to the machinists' union, the carpenters' union picketed the plant and organized a boycott of the company's beer; the government prosecuted the head of the carpenters' union for illegally restraining trade by means of the boycott. The Supreme Court in the 1920s, over the protests of Brandeis, had not allowed that kind of boycott in the *Duplex* and *Bedford* cases. In 1941, however, the Court accepted Brandeis's position and allowed the boycott. Frankfurter wrote the decision.

Speaking is the man who had produced the evidence showing the abuse of the workers in Bisbee, Arizona, who had stood up to Elbert Gary of the steel industry, who had demanded decent conditions for the worker during World War I, who believed that unions needed power if they were going to force management to talk with them seriously. Strife between competing unions, Frankfurter conceded, has "intensified industrial tension" but there was no reason to believe Congress had not allowed it. "So long as a union acts in its self-interest and does not combine with non-labor groups" in a conspiracy, government should not delve into the union's "wisdom or unwisdom, the rightness or wrongness, the selfishness or unselfishness."

Owen Roberts dissented; to urge union members not to buy the company's beer, he said, is a secondary boycott, and "This Court, and many state tribunals, over a long period of years, have held such a secondary boycott illegal."

With that decision, Frankfurter had strengthened his pro-union credentials, giving organized labor, so it seemed, carte blanche, the same power employers had wielded twenty years earlier. But Frankfurter was not giving anyone anything; rather, case by case, he attempted to work out guidelines, seeking direction from his understanding of the "decencies of civilized procedure." He showed this one week after the St. Louis decision. In a case involving striking milk-truck drivers in Illinois, Frankfurter wrote the majority opinion allowing a state injunction against the union because the picketing had been accompanied by violence. This decision was one of the early ones contributing to liberals' disappointment with Frankfurter. His mentors, Holmes and Brandeis, had not feared union violence in their decisions and Frankfurter himself had written the standard polemic against labor injunctions. When Black dissented from Frankfurter's decision, arguing that the violent acts of a few should not be allowed to hinder picketing rights of other union members, he was establishing his credentials with that same liberal community that was turning away from Frankfurter.

But there were elements in the case not considered by Frankfurter's critics. Holmes and Brandeis had spoken against the possibility of union or of company-inspired violence, but in Illinois there was documentation of union violence—window smashings, bombs, trucks wrecked, beatings, and stores set afire. Because of that reality, the state enjoined picketing. Frankfurter conceded the injunction invaded the right of free speech, but said, "Back of the guarantee of free speech lay faith in the power of an appeal to reason by all the peaceful means for gaining access to the mind . . . utterance in a context of violence can lose its significance as an appeal to reason and become part of an instrument of force. Such utterance was not meant to be sheltered by the Constitution." He knew his Oliver Wendell Holmes; one did not have the right to shout fire in a crowded theatre when there was no fire.

As for the injunction, Frankfurter, still the advocate of judicial restraint, said that was a state matter and there could be a rehearing to determine whether the injunction should be lifted. "If the people of Illinois desire to withdraw the use of the injunction in labor controversies," he said, "the democratic process for legislative reform is at their disposal."

Felix Frankfurter on the Court had not changed much from the Felix Frankfurter of the years before the Court, still arguing for local responsibility and against the Court's imposing its will on reasonable local action.

He showed this again, in another labor case, one from Texas. A man named Ritter hired a contractor to build a building. When the contractor used nonunion help, the carpenters' union picketed—not the construction site, however, but a restaurant owned by Ritter some distance away. The restaurant employees were union members and not involved with the dispute over the building's construction. The restaurant's business dropped 60 percent. The state courts ruled against the union, and

Frankfurter, speaking for the Supreme Court in 1942, supported the state courts.

Conceding that peaceful picketing was an exercise of free speech, Frankfurter said that "does not imply that the states must be without power to confine the sphere of communication to that directly related to the dispute." The minority decision, written by Black, joined by Douglas and Murphy, criticized Texas for frustrating the "union's objective of conveying information to that part of the public which came near the respondent's place of business."

In that case the dispute between Frankfurter and Black was visible. Black called on logic, maintaining that if peaceful picketing was an expression of free speech, guaranteed by the First Amendment, then an absolute was involved and an absolute could not be restricted. Frankfurter called on experience, arguing that the state had not lost all police power to the First Amendment—"To deny to the states the power to draw this line is to write into the Constitution the notion that every instance of peaceful picketing—anywhere and under any circumstances—is necessarily a phase of the controversy which provoked the picketing."

Three years later, the Black group had its fun with Frankfurter in *Hunt* v. *Crumboch*. A union, angered at an employer, refused to enroll his employees and then pressured his customers not to deal with him. When the union's action threatened to drive the man out of business, he sued the union. The Supreme Court upheld the union. The decision, by Black, found its justification in quoting Frankfurter's opinion in the St. Louis brewery case—"So long as a union acts in its self-interest and does not combine with non-labor groups."

Frankfurter joined a dissent written by Owen Roberts, who argued the conflict was "no part of the labor dispute but an offshoot of it; not involving wages, unionization, closed shop, hours or other conditions of work."

Brandeis had commented years earlier that the conflict between labor and capital was "a struggle of contending forces" and the "rules governing the contest necessarily change from time to time." With government protection of the rights to organize and picket, unions had gained power, if not equal to that of capital, at least comparable to it; and Frankfurter believed the Supreme Court should keep them in balance. The rules had changed.

A few years later, the issue almost went out of balance. The time was 1952, and the nation was at war in Korea—an endless, costly war without purpose, so it seemed. The steel industry was vital to the war effort, but a possible strike threatened to shut the steel mills. To prevent this, President Truman ordered his Secretary of Commerce to seize the mills and operate them, invoking general presidential powers. In 1982 a biographer of Truman reported that Truman acted only after being advised by Chief Justice Fred M. Vinson, in a private conversation, that the seizure was constitutional.

There were undercurrents, rationalizations not as visible as was the war effort argument. Nineteen fifty-two was an election year, and a Democratic President's seizure of the mills and imposition of a union-oriented settlement would go a long way toward holding union members' support for Democrats in the next election.

For the Supreme Court, however, the undercurrents pulled the other way. During the Second World War, when Hugo Black had written the Supreme Court's decision allowing the relocation of Japanese-Americans from the West Coast, he had relied on "the war power of Congress and the Executive"—powers similar to those invoked by Truman in the steel seizure. The dissents in 1944 to the Japanese exclusion case—"ugly abyss of racism," "a clear violation of Constitutional rights," "an act not commonly a crime"—had over the years grown into a chorus of doubts and moral concerns. The later apologies by Earl Warren and William Douglas represented what was in 1952 a developing national mood, a questioning: Had the United States been willing to slip into a dictatorship?

When the steel-seizure case was argued before the Supreme Court, the attorney for the steel industry was John W. Davis. He had no trouble with his case, did not even use all the time allotted for oral argument. He watched the justices jump on the government attorney: What law had the government used? What was the specific authorization?

Truman had no congressional authorization for the seizure; in the Japanese-exclusion case, the military acted under a specific congressional directive. On that basis, Truman's lack of congressional directive, the Supreme Court went against Truman, 6-3. Black wrote the decision: "The founders of this Nation entrusted the lawmaking power to the Congress alone in both good and bad times." Fred Vinson, true to his advice, was one of the three justices supporting Truman.

Frankfurter, who also had joined the majority decision in the Japanese-exclusion cases, supported Black in the steel-seizure decision but wrote a separate concurrence, making the same point. Congress, he said, had authorized presidential seizures of property at least sixteen times since 1916; and, in a fifteen-page addendum, Frankfurter offered a detailed history of those sixteen incidents. The implication was that Congress wanted the President to ask for specific authority in each seizure case rather than to assume that power on his own.

Still, the Court in 1952 had refused to allow a President unconstitutional powers in 1944, also a war period. In 1944 Frankfurter wrote that "the validity of action under the war power must be judged wholly in the context of war." In 1952 he wrote that the United States "labors under restriction from which other governments are free. It has not been our tradition to envy such governments." In 1944 Black had allowed the limitations on Congress to be broken through, explaining that "hardships are part of war, and war is an aggregation of hardships." In his 1952 decision blocking the government's grab for power, Black said that no purpose was served by recalling "the historical events, the fears of power and the hopes of freedom" that lay behind the Constitution's authors limiting the President's freedom of action. "Such a review," said Black, "would but confirm our holding that this seizure order cannot stand."

Seventy years earlier, Frankfurter's friend and mentor Oliver Wendell Holmes had written that the life of the law had not been logic but experience. Black denied this, saying the life of the law was instead a set of constitutional absolutes. But the 1952 steel-seizure case coming after the 1944 Japanese-exclusion case, after eight years of criticisms, doubts, and second thoughts, demonstrated that on occasion Black joined with Frankfurter in believing Holmes correct.

The differences between Frankfurter's and Black's interpretations of the Constitution showed starkly in their attitudes toward criminal law. Those differences were not so apparent in the final results. By one count, in cases involving state systems of criminal justice in which both men participated during the time they sat together on the Court and in which written opinions were produced, they voted together approximately 60 percent of the time. The differences showed, instead, in the different routes they traveled to those outcomes.

Black's ideas had been developed as a defense lawyer and prosecutor in Alabama; he had seen too much abuse of the individual, especially blacks, by law-enforcement agencies. Frankfurter had absorbed his ideas as a prosecutor, working for Henry Stimson, almost forty years earlier. "I do not believe any U.S. Attorney had such a successful record from the point of view of convictions and the affirmance of convictions as did Henry Stimson," said Frankfurter. "And yet he enunciated and enforced the most austere standards of conduct. . . . I have no sympathy whatever with the notion that we need third degree and wiretapping and all the other miserable business in order to be able to cope with crime. It isn't true."

There were other influences on Frankfurter. From his work with the Cleveland Crime Survey in the early 1920s, he had learned that law enforcement needs more than a cop with a blackjack in the back room of a police station. And then the vision of his uncle Solomon Frankfurter, while in his eighties, languishing in a Vienna prison, roughed up by uniformed Nazi hoodlums, was not easily erased. Such methods by police, Frankfurter said, "tend to brutalize society."

In 1928, the Supreme Court in the *Olmstead* case allowed a conviction based on wiretapping evidence, Holmes and Brandeis dissenting. Holmes had said, "I think it a less evil that some criminals should escape than that the government should play an ignoble part," and Brandeis spoke of the Constitution's authors' conferring on Americans, "as against the Government, the right to be let alone—the most comprehensive of rights and the right most valued by civilized men." A few years later the Holmes-Brandeis position became the majority position when the Court ruled wiretapping unconstitutional in a 1937 case. And then in 1939, in a second encounter before the Supreme Court involving the same incident, Frankfurter finished off what his friends had begun.

In this second case, the government sought to use material from the specific wiretapping which had been declared unconstitutional in the first case. Frankfurter, writing for the Court, said the evidence could not be used. "My Nardone opinion flowed from the first Nardone case with which I had nothing to do," he explained to a friend. "Could any self-respecting court first decide that law officers can't tap wires and then decide that they may, however, use the fruits of such tapping?"

Three years later, Frankfurter led the Court into a new area of federal law enforcement in *McNabb* v. *United States*. A federal law officer with the Bureau of Internal Revenue's Alcohol Tax Unit was fatally shot and a second officer wounded while tracking moonshiners in the Tennessee mountains. Members of the McNabb family gave police statements confessing their involvement in the crimes. Although other evidence existed, the confessions made the case against them "open and shut."

Frankfurter said no.

Although Congress required prompt arraignment before a federal magistrate and although a magistrate had been available, investigating officers had kept the McNabbs in jail for hours and then subjected them to "unremitting questioning" for several days until the McNabbs made the statements used against them. Only then were the McNabbs arraigned—and informed of their rights to remain silent and to be represented by counsel.

Frankfurter understood the ramifications of the case, acknowledging to Chief Justice Stone that involved was "our review of criminal convictions in the federal courts . . . we are moving within the federal judiciary and determining the rightness or wrongness of a conviction secured in one of our own subordinate courts." This did not deter Frankfurter. "Judicial supervision of the administration of criminal justice in the federal courts," he said, "implies the duty of establishing and maintaining civilized standards of procedure and evidence."

At Stone's suggestion, Frankfurter softened his language about the McNabbs' imprisonment in a barren cell for fourteen hours without a chair or other place to sit, and stressed, instead, the issue of unlawful detention, that in upsetting the convictions the Court was following the congressional command for prompt arraignment. Frankfurter closed the decision with two sentences that, sometimes altered, he repeated many times: "The history of liberty has largely been the history of observance of procedural safeguards. And the effective administration of criminal justice hardly requires disregard of fair procedures imposed by law."

In the chambers and hallways of the Supreme Court, there was another argument over the McNabb case, one demonstrating the differences in Frankfurter's and Black's approaches to criminal law. Hugo Black had no trouble agreeing with Frankfurter's results in the wiretapping and *McNabb* cases. But with *McNabb* Black was after more. Where Frankfurter's decision rested on congressional legislation requiring a prompt arraignment, Black wanted to reach the same results on the grounds of a denial of constitutional rights. Black discussed this with Frankfurter, saying he had talked about the case with William Douglas and Frank Murphy, and "We may be able to go along with you." The implication was that Black, then leader of the trio known as "the Axis," was speaking not only for himself but for the other two justices. Murphy also spoke with Frankfurter—"Hugo and Bill and I were talking about it, and I don't know yet what we'll do." Eventually the three did come around to Frankfurter's position. "It would all be very funny," Frankfurter wrote in his diary, "if the joke weren't on the Court."

Through the years Frankfurter's insistence that federal courts adhere to strict standards in law enforcement would not be swayed by emotionalism; his June 1946 dissent in *Fisher* v. *United States* is an example. In the District of Columbia, a black youth had struck and killed a white woman. The district court, part of the federal court system, found him guilty of first degree—premeditated—murder. Fisher's lawyer appealed, saying the district court had erred in refusing to instruct the jury to consider evidence of the defendant's mental instability. The victim had criticized the black youth's work, and then called him a "black nigger." The youth, so angered by the remark, struck her, and when she screamed, continued to strike her until she was dead.

The Supreme Court, in a decision by Stanley Reed, upheld the first-degree murder conviction, and with it the death sentence, explaining that the Court usually deferred to the District of Columbia on local law matters and "the local law now challenged is long established and deeply rooted in the District."

Frankfurter did not agree. He believed the "black nigger" phrase had set off the crime, eliminating the premeditation factor, and that the jury, if properly instructed, would have found a verdict less than first degree. To make his point, Frankfurter quoted the "black nigger" phrase in his dissent. When Reed begged him to eliminate it, Frankfurter refused; to do so, he said, is "to write *Hamlet* without Hamlet." Reed approached him again. "Of course," Reed said, "you do not employ it to stir racial feelings or to convince friends of Fisher that commutation should be sought. Those are permissible aims for a Sacco-Vanzetti protagonist after conviction but not for a judge in a case. Yet I feel sure your words will be so used by others."

Frankfurter did not yield; a federal court had erred, he believed, and as a federal judge he insisted he was obligated to speak out. "The evidence in its entirety hardly provides a basis for a finding of premeditation," wrote Frankfurter in his dissent. "He struck Miss Reardon when she called him a 'black nigger.' He kept on when her screaming frightened him. He did not know he had killed her. There is not the slightest basis for finding a motive for the killing prior to her use of the offensive phrase. . . . The justification for finding first-degree murder premeditation was so tenuous that the jury ought not to have been left to founder and flounder within the dark emptiness of legal jargon."

The next year, in *Harris* v. *United States*, the Court, including Black and Douglas, affirmed a conviction based on evidence collected by agents of the Federal Bureau of Investigation operating without a search warrant, although one could have been gained. Frankfurter dissented, going into the history of the Fourth Amendment's prohibition against unauthorized search and seizure, and said: "If the search is illegal when begun, as it clearly was in this case if past decisions mean anything, it cannot retrospectively gain legality. If the search was illegal, the resulting seizure in the course of the search is illegal."

A few days after the decision came down, Frankfurter received a letter from Learned Hand. Now well into his seventies, Hand still operated from the appellate bench. He and Frankfurter had often disagreed through the years, but Hand was completely with Frankfurter on this decision and concluded his letter: "And to have those crusaders for the underdog—Black and Douglas—go wrong! My Gods, my Gods, why have ye forsaken me?"

The most controversial insistence by Frankfurter that federal law officers use proper procedure came toward the end of his career as a Supreme Court justice; this was *Mallory* v. *United States.* Andrew Mallory, nineteen years old, of doubtful mental competency, was charged in the District of Columbia with rape, convicted in federal court, and sentenced to die. As in *McNabb,* the issue involved was the time elapsed before the suspect's arraignment. In that period, Mallory was questioned, persuaded to take a lie detector test; finally, he dictated a confession. Mallory "was not told of his rights to counsel or to a preliminary examination before a magistrate, nor was he warned that he might keep silent and 'that any statement made by him may be used against him,' " said the Frankfurter decision for a unanimous court.

Congress had commanded a prompt arraignment, said Frankfurter, and "We cannot sanction this extended delay." To allow delay, he concluded, meant allowing the "police to arrest, as it were, at large and to use an interrogating process at police headquarters in order to determine whom they should charge before a committing magistrate on 'probable cause.' " That, in fact, had been the procedure in the District of Columbia; a reported crime resulted in police making a "sweep" arrest, picking up a number of persons, usually all black, questioning and harassing them, assuming one eventually would confess.

Frankfurter's decision may have freed a rapist; Mallory was accused of that crime again before he died, shot by a policeman. But the "sweep" arrest procedure in the District of Columbia ended. "The history of liberty," Frankfurter had said, "has largely been the history of observance of procedural safeguards."

However bold Frankfurter was in extending constitutional guarantees to defendants in federal cases, he was less so in state criminal cases, arguing that, while defendants are guaranteed constitutional protections in the state courts by the Fourteenth Amendment, the specifics of those guarantees should be left to the states rather than to the federal courts. The Supreme Court could not interfere in a state prosecution unless there had been a gross violation of the "decencies of civilized procedure." Judicial restraint again. In 1937, in *Palko* v. *Connecticut,* Justice Cardozo had made the same point. Hugo Black believed the opposite, that the Fourteenth Amendment had extended the specific protections available to defendants in federal courts to those in state courts.

The names and crimes, catchwords then, have since faded. What is remembered is the dialogue between Frankfurter and Black. What they argued back and forth in their opinions, concurrences, and dissents was the essence of criminal law: How much power to the government? How much protection to the defendant? What risk is society willing to run for freedom? Should, as Holmes suggested, "some criminals . . . escape" rather than the government "play an ignoble part"?

With forty-eight states then, Frankfurter's approach meant there could be forty-eight different procedures plus the federal procedure, and whatever the judicial arguments, the arguments on the streets of America's cities were clear about justice before the local court—if one had money, one had constitutional protections. In 1931, the Wickersham Commission, formally the National Commission on Law Observance and Enforcement, had published its extensive survey of crime in the United States, its fourteen reports becoming case books for criminologists, sociologists, politicians, and lawyers for years afterward. It was a story of good intentions, shocking procedures, third-rate results, incompetence, and the policeman's investigating tool too often a blackjack. In one chapter on law and the immigrant, the Commission spoke about people who had come to the United States when Frankfurter had or in the years following. Because they had not had his opportunities, his inclinations, his standards, or, perhaps, his luck, the individuals studied in the Wickersham report were those who had ended up on the opposite side of the law from which Frankfurter operated.

The Commission interviewed 498 foreign-born prisoners in local jails, many of whom could not speak English and had to be interviewed in their native tongues. The point was money. "Not because a man is Italian, or Polish, or Russian, or some other particular nationality, as the case may be, but because he is poor he can not expect to get justice," said the report. "Or, as is frequently his desire, he can not evade justice as he sees other more affluent men do." Court-appointed lawyers? "Frequently they complained that the appointed attorney did nothing but try to persuade them to plead guilty as soon as he found out by shrewd questioning that they really had no resources and no friends who would put up a fee for them." The Commission had been told, and its members believed, that "In the United States, if you get into trouble with the law, money will get you out."

There were complaints of unfair trials and police brutality—"accusations against the police, charging the use of physical violence in an attempt to force a confession. . . . If even a small fraction of the charges made were actually true they would still constitute a grave indictment."

Although the Wickersham Commission report was comprehensive, its themes were not new. They had run through earlier studies of crime and of local and state efforts to curb it. Brandeis had been involved in one with Roscoe Pound in the 1910s and Frankfurter in the Cleveland survey in the early 1920s. As did the Wickersham report, those surveys urged eliminating politics from police and judicial systems, upgrading police work, and extending fairness to all defendants, rich and poor.

Frankfurter believed that democracy commanded the state systems to correct themselves, that interference by the federal judiciary—barring an excess—persuaded citizens not to rely on or be active in democratic government. By the 1940s, however, when the dialogue between Black and Frankfurter began, there had been little improvement by the states in their enforcement practices. As a result, defendants argued that if certain standards were required at the federal level, those same standards should be applied at the local level.

In federal court an accused person was provided with a lawyer if he or she was unable to afford one. In 1932, in the Scottsboro case, the Supreme Court had extended that right of counsel to accused in state courts but only in cases where the punishment was death. In cases involving a lesser punishment, the states were free to offer counsel or not as they chose; this was challenged in 1942 in *Betts* v. *Brady*.

Smith Betts was charged with armed robbery in Maryland. After pleading not guilty at his arraignment, Betts said he was too poor to hire a lawyer and requested the court appoint one. The judge refused; the state practice, as commanded by *Scottsboro*, was to provide a lawyer only in capital cases. Betts defended himself. It was a third-rate job at best, and he was convicted. From jail Betts appealed to the Maryland

Court of Appeals, saying he had been denied his constitutional rights under the Sixth Amendment—"In all criminal prosecutions, the accused shall . . . have the assistance of counsel for his defense." The Maryland court turned him down.

Betts then took his case to the United States Supreme Court. In a 6-3 decision by Owen Roberts, the Court ruled against Smith Betts. Roberts conceded that if Betts had been tried in a federal court counsel would have been mandatory, but argued that it was a state's prerogative to determine its own definition of fairness. Frankfurter joined in the Roberts decision, it being consistent with his understanding of judicial restraint and local responsibility.

Black dissented, joined by Douglas and Murphy—as he usually was in these cases. He repeated his belief that the due-process clause of the Fourteenth Amendment had made the Sixth, with its right to counsel, binding on the states—a direct challenge to what Cardozo had said in *Palko* v. *Connecticut*—but conceded the Court had not accepted that argument. He then wanted the Betts conviction reversed because it shocked the universal sense of justice. To deprive a prisoner of counsel because of poverty, said Black, "seems to me to defeat the promise of our democratic society to provide equal justice under law."

Frankfurter, with the majority, required more to shock his understanding of universal justice than did Black.

This again showed in another right-to-counsel case, in 1946. An Illinois state court had sustained a murder conviction when the defendant had waived right to counsel. The Supreme Court upheld the conviction in a 5-4 decision written by Frankfurter. He conceded that counsel in a capital case might be necessary at every step "from arraignment to sentencing" but that does not restrict the accused from acting in his own defense or acknowledging his guilt, after being advised of his rights. "Under appropriate circumstances," wrote Frankfurter, "the Constitution requires that counsel be tendered; it does not require that under all circumstances counsel be forced upon a defendant"—that line had been inserted at Robert Jackson's suggestion.

Frankfurter then spelled out his belief on where the federal judiciary and the state law enforcement intersect, writing: "The Due Process Clause has never been perverted so as to force upon the forty-eight States a uniform code of criminal procedure . . . the prosecution of crime is a matter for the individual States." The states then may do what they consider proper "so long as they observe those ultimate dignities of man which the United States Constitution assures."

In 1945, in *Malinski* v. *New York,* the Court had agreed about the disposition of the cases involving confessions; conviction of one individual was upheld and the other was reversed. But the journey to arrive at that point set off arguments. Frankfurter circulated a proposed concurring opinion, restating his belief that the Fourteenth Amendment's commands that no state could "abridge the privileges or immunities of citizens of the United States" or deprive persons of life, liberty or property without due process of law "are generalities circumscribed by history and appropriate to the largeness of the problems of government with which they were concerned."

Black circulated a memorandum insisting that Frankfurter's approach was "a restoration of the natural law concept whereby the supreme constitutional law becomes this Court's view of civilization at a given moment." Black said the specific case was not the proper site to debate the question, but he vowed to discuss the issue when the proper case arose.

Two years later, Black found his "proper" case, *Adamson* v. *California.* Adamson had been convicted of first-degree murder; he had not testified at his trial. California law agreed with the Fifth Amendment that no person "shall be compelled in any criminal case to be a witness against himself," but California allowed the judge to comment to the jury on the defendant's silence. This last, which would not have been allowed in a federal trial, was challenged by Adamson, saying his constitutional right against self-incrimination had been violated when the judge in the state trial spoke to the jury about his silence.

The United States Supreme Court, in a decision by Stanley Reed, upheld the conviction, using the Frankfurter argument that the adoption of the Fourteenth Amendment had not extended specific protections to state procedures. Black dissented, saying that his study of the Fourteenth Amendment shows "that one of the chief objects . . . was to make the Bill of Rights applicable to the states"; that is, the specific guarantees in the first ten amendments to the Constitution must be extended to a defendant in a state court as they were to defendants in federal court. "Conceding the possibility that this Court is now wise enough to improve on the Bill of Rights by substituting natural law concepts for the Bill of Rights," said Black, "I think the possibility is entirely too speculative to agree to take that course."

Frankfurter did not allow that to pass. He filed a concurrence, directly challenging Black. Did Congress and the states mean to extend federal protections to state legal procedures? "It could hardly have occurred to these States," wrote Frankfurter, "that by ratifying the [Fourteenth] Amendment they uprooted their established methods for prosecuting crime and fostered upon themselves a new prosecutorial system." Does the Fourteenth Amendment's due process clause summarize the Bill of Rights? "A construction which gives to due process no independent function but turns it into a summary of the specific provisions of the Bill of Rights would, as has been noted," said Frankfurter, "tear up by the roots much of the fabric of law in the several states."

Frankfurter closed by insisting that the question dealt not with violations of the Bill of Rights but with whether the proceedings "offend the canons of decency and fairness which express the notions of justice of English-speaking peoples."

Another Frankfurter victory was the 1949 case, *Wolf* v. *Colorado*. The Supreme Court, Frankfurter writing the opinion, upheld a conviction although local police had violated the Fourth Amendment's protections against unlawful search and seizure. Even Black joined this decision, but, in a separate concurrence, restated his theory about the Fourteenth Amendment making the Bill of Rights applicable to the states.

In a 1952 case, Black also wrote a concurrence to a Frankfurter decision, *Rochin* v. *California*. Here local police forced a "stomach pumping" procedure upon a subject; in the vomiting that followed, two capsules containing morphine were retrieved and the individual later was found guilty of possessing morphine. Frankfurter wrote the Court's opinion overturning the conviction because the stomach-pumping technique shocked the conscience and therefore violated due process —those "canons of decency and fairness which express the notions of justice of English-speaking peoples."

In his concurrence, Black said that "faithful adherence to the specific guarantees in the Bill of Rights insures a more permanent protection of individual liberty than that which can be afforded by the nebulous standards stated by the majority."

Frankfurter inserted a paragraph in his decision to deal with that line by Black. It reads:

. . . that does not make due process of law a matter of judicial caprice. The faculties of the Due Process Clause may be indefinite and vague, but the mode of their ascertainment is not self-willed. In each case "due process of law" requires an evaluation based on a disinterested inquiry pursued in the spirit of science, on a balanced order of facts exactly and fairly stated, on the detached consideration of conflicting claims . . . on a judgment not *ad hoc* and episodic but duly mindful of reconciling the needs both of continuity and of change in a progressive society.

Black later said that statement was "the best one ever written to justify that philosophy." He added: "Still, however, the elaborate verbal standards offered there are to me merely high-sounding rhetoric void of any substantive guidance as to how a judge should really apply the Due Process Clause."

The two men, locked in their philosophical struggle, agreed that there was a limit beyond which law officers could not go. Frankfurter spelled this out in a 1954 case, *Irvine* v. *California.* A man had been convicted of bookmaking based on evidence from a recording device secretly planted in his bedroom without a court order. The Supreme Court upheld the conviction, 5-4. Frankfurter and Black were among the four dissenters. In *Wolf* v. *Colorado,* said Frankfurter, the Court had given states discretion, but in *Rochin,* it had said there were limits to that discretion. Acknowledging that *Irvine* did not include physical violence such as the stomach pumping in *Rochin,* Frankfurter said, "We have here, however, a more powerful and offensive control over Irvine's life than a single, limited physical trespass. Certainly the conduct of the police here went far beyond a bare search and seizure." The police, he said, could hear every word said in the Irvine house for a month.

When the justices consider a case, they read briefs and hear lawyers' arguments. They do not take evidence or hear testimony; rather they deal with issues, constitutional law, legislative intentions. If the parties to a case want to hear the argument, they sit on the spectators' side of the bar, not on the Court side with the lawyers. This gives the members of the Supreme Court an above-the-battle stance. Does one of their decisions mean that a possible rapist goes free, as in the Mallory case? The brethren do not deal with that question but only with the principle of law involved. Will a man go to jail although, as in *Wolf* v. *Colorado,* if arrested by federal law officers instead of by state, he would have been freed? Again, the justices do not deal with that issue.

In one area of crime and punishment, however, a judge confronts the results of a decision. This is when the death penalty is involved.

Frankfurter opposed the death penalty. In 1929, when still a Harvard professor, he congratulated the governor of Michigan for vetoing a law to restore capital punishment in that state. Frankfurter called capital punishment "a shallow, emotional response to profoundly troublesome conditions." Twenty-one years later, he restated his opposition to capital punishment "for reasons that are not related to concern for the murderer or the risk of convicting the innocent . . . [but] when life is at hazard in a trial, it sensationalizes the whole thing almost unwittingly; the effect on the juries, the Bar, the public, the judiciary, I regard as very bad."

Whatever Frankfurter said in such public statements, he always understood a life was involved. In 1940, in a controversial Alabama case, lawyers for the condemned man had tried to reach Hugo Black to ask for a stay of execution, but Black kept himself incommunicado. Finally, the clerk of the Supreme Court contacted Philip Graham, Frankfurter's law clerk, "with the thought," recalled Frankfurter, "that I might be willing to listen to counsel, since it was a capital case." When Frankfurter heard the facts, he agreed there should be a stay of execution to allow the full Court to hear the arguments, "but I did not want to act in a case coming from Black's Circuit . . . when he was in town even tho he had kept himself incommunicado." Frankfurter finally reached Black by telephone. Black argued but finally said "that I could do what I pleased," and the stay was granted.

In 1943, the Court considered *Buchalter* v. *New York,* involving death sentences for three professional killers. When the case was first appealed to the Court, the justices refused to hear the appeal. This troubled Frankfurter; a death penalty was involved and he believed the Court should consider death-sentence appeals. To his fellow Court members Frankfurter described the convicted killers as "worthless creatures," but added that they "may invoke the protection of the Constitution is not the least of the glories of our country." When the appeal was resubmitted in another form, the Court relented and accepted it. In a 7-0 decision by Owen Roberts, the Court affirmed the convictions.

But Frankfurter's inclinations against the death penalty warred with his belief in judicial restraint. If the death sentence was a legitimate form of execution in the states, as it then was, did he have the right to prohibit that punishment? He faced the issue most bluntly in the 1947 case of Willie Francis. Francis was a seventeen-year-old black convicted in Louisiana of murdering a man in a robbery netting $4 and a watch. He was sentenced to death in the electric chair, but when the switch was thrown, the electric chair did not work, apparently because of a mechanical difficulty, and Willie Francis survived. The state set another date for his execution. His lawyers appealed to the Supreme Court, arguing that to subject Francis to a second execution attempt was cruel and unusual punishment violating due process.

The Supreme Court, 5-4, both Frankfurter and Black with the majority, allowed Louisiana a second attempt at executing Willie Francis. "I was very much bothered by the problem," Frankfurter said a few years later, "it offended my personal sense of decency to do this. Something inside of me was very unhappy, but I did not see that it violated due process of law." However he was bothered, Frankfurter acknowledged that the state had not acted with deliberate violence or callousness toward Francis, giving the Court no reason to interfere.

If as a judge Felix Frankfurter could not act to stop the second execution attempt, as a man he could. He approached a Harvard classmate, Monte Lemann, then a prominent lawyer in New Orleans. Spurred by Frankfurter, Lemann campaigned to have the governor commute the sentence—such a commutation required a recommendation from the state board of pardons. With Frankfurter watching over him and encouraging him, Lemann approached the pardon board. He offered to assist Francis's attorney. He approached the judge in the Francis case, once a student of Lemann's at Tulane Law School. Nothing worked. Francis was placed in the electric chair the second time; this time the process worked. If Felix Frankfurter had voted the other way, there would have been no execution, no death.

Some years after the Willie Francis case, a friend of Frankfurter's Alice Hamilton, criticized him for affirming the death penalty in cases coming before the Supreme Court. Frankfurter conceded to her that "few of the arrangements of our society are more repellent, more of an expression of barbarism, than is capital punishment." But should he, as Alice Hamilton suggested, "apply my 'sense of right and justice and honor' in rejecting capital punishment and vote to set aside the conviction merely because the sentence was death?" He told her: "I cannot believe that such is your view." This letter was written in 1959, after Frankfurter had been on the Supreme Court for twenty years, and more than his decisions, it summed up the passion of his position. He wrote:

Why do I take part in sending men to their death although I feel about capital punishment as I do? For a very simple reason. Let me remind you again that on becoming a Justice I did not take an oath to enforce "the sense of right and justice of Felix Frankfurter." The oath I took was to perform my duties "agreeably to the Constitution and laws of the United States." Do you really want five men who get on the Supreme Court by those fortuities by which men become Justices through the Mitchell Palmers and the Daughertys and the Brownells who advise Presidents like Harding and Coolidge to decide during the lifetime of these Judges what the powers of Congress and Presidents and the rights and duties of citizens are? That is exactly what McReynolds & Co. did for a good many years. They followed their own notion of justice and right and put it into the Constitution, and you didn't like it . . . they followed their personal private views of what was right and just.

In 1961, almost at the end of Frankfurter's tenure on the Court, he lost his fight with Hugo Black over the question of extending constitutional guarantees to state proceedings. The case was *Mapp* v. *Ohio.* The defendant had been convicted of possessing pornographic material, with evidence "unlawfully seized during an unlawful search of defendant's home." Under Frankfurter's approach, the conviction would stand, unless there had been behavior "shocking" the conscience. But the Court reversed the conviction, 6-3. Tom Clark, a former United States Attorney General, wrote the decision, saying: "There is no war between the Constitution and common sense." If the conviction was affirmed, he wrote, the local police officers would be allowed to do what a federal law officer could not, "Thus the State, by admitting evidence unlawfully seized, serves to encourage disobedience to the Federal Constitution which it is bound to uphold."

Actually the question of admitting the evidence had been raised in the briefs and arguments only peripherally and was not the basis of the original vote by the justices in conference against the state. But in the month following, so Associate Justice Potter Stewart later speculated, "the members of the soon-to-be *Mapp* majority had met in what I affectionately call a 'rump caucus' " and resolved that evidence seized in an illegal search had to be excluded from state as well as federal trials. (That was a five-man majority; Stewart concurred with their result but for different reasons, making the final vote 6-3.) By seeking out the illegal-search issue and making it the center of their decision, the five justices demonstrated that they not only wished to overrule Frankfurter's position but that they wished to do it bluntly.

Frankfurter joined a dissent by John Marshall Harlan—"a really admirable opinion," Frankfurter told his friend. The dissent charged that the Court had forgotten its "sense of judicial restraint" and was not rigidly respecting "the limitations which the Constitution places upon it."

Other decisions followed, many after Frankfurter had left the bench, one an attack on the death penalty so abhorrent to Frankfurter, another insisting that accused persons be provided counsel in state trials, until the acceptance of Hugo Black's position that the Fourteenth Amendment guaranteed Bill of Rights protections in state proceedings. Rather than experience, as Holmes had said, logic had become the life of criminal law: What people could not do on one side of the street, in the federal courts, they should not be allowed to do on the other, in the state courts. Hugo La Fayette Black, once derided as an Alabama "hillbilly," had outpointed Felix Frankfurter, the Harvard Law School professor, in intellectual combat.

23

Alger Hiss

On September 8, 1953, Fred Vinson, age sixty-three, died, after serving as Chief Justice of the United States for seven years. He had come to the Court following a career as a member of the House of Representatives, federal judge, and government official. If the Court continued faction-ridden while he was Chief Justice, it also avoided the public acrimony that characterized the Black-Jackson disagreement.

With the Frankfurter-Black philosophical dispute then being argued with full force, a question was whether Vinson's replacement would align with Black or Frankfurter.

Dwight D. Eisenhower was President of the United States, the first Republican in that office since Herbert Hoover. Frankfurter assumed Eisenhower's choice for the Court vacancy would be Earl Warren, the Republican governor of California. There had not been a westerner appointed to the Court for many years, and the political scuttlebutt was that Eisenhower had promised Warren the first Supreme Court vacancy. But Frankfurter did not believe Warren, without judicial experience, would be named Chief Justice; instead, Frankfurter anticipated that a sitting member of the Court would be elevated to the Chief Justice position and that Warren would become an associate justice. Frankfurter again hoped his friend Robert Jackson, after having been an associate justice for thirteen years, finally would become Chief Justice.

Frankfurter was naïve. The Chief Justice appointment is a major political plum for a President, and a Republican was not likely to give it to Jackson, a Democrat. The appointment did go to Warren, and it was for the Chief Justice's seat.

Little was known about Earl Warren despite his years in public life and his having been the Republican vice-presidential candidate in 1948. National political decisions then were made by easterners, who did not read newspapers published in the West or keep current with political developments there. Warren was a popular vote getter in California, and perhaps, so political speculation at the time went, Eisenhower thought the California voters would reward him in 1956 for having appointed one of their own to the Supreme Court. Other speculation suggested the appointment went to Warren (1) to pay him off for switching the California delegation to Eisenhower at the 1952 presidential convention, or (2) because Vice President Nixon and Senator William Knowland, both from California, wanted Warren out of the state and far away from controlling the Republican party there.

Eisenhower in his memoirs said "partisan politics had no place" in his search for a Vinson replacement, and "The truth was that I owed Governor Warren nothing." Also in his memoirs, Eisenhower said he wanted a nominee no older than sixty-two and then listed as possibilities John W. Davis, almost eighty; John J. Parker, who had been turned down for a Court appointment by the Senate twenty years earlier and was sixty-seven; Arthur T. Vanderbilt, sixty-five; and John Foster Dulles, sixty-five. Warren was sixty-two.

Whatever Eisenhower's reasons, Earl Warren was the new Chief Justice of the United States.

Frankfurter was impressed with Warren. "You ask whether I 'like him," he wrote a friend. "The short answer is I do and I am sure you would. . . . He has not had an eminent legal career, but he might well have had, had he not been deflected from the practice of law into public life. He brings to his work that largeness of experience and breadth of outlook which may well make him a very good Chief Justice." And to another friend: "After a good many years, indeed from my point of view since Hughes left, life promises to be extremely agreeable."

That was not to be.

Warren and Frankfurter began as more than coworkers; they leaned on each other. But eventually they grew apart. The differences between the two men—not visible at first, then edging slowly into sight, finally becoming an open dispute—showed most clearly with internal-security cases. Frankfurter, haunted by ghosts from many earlier attacks on the Supreme Court, moved slowly; Warren rushed in.

Frankfurter's attitudes toward internal-security cases were a product of many parts of his past—Sacco-Vanzetti, his intense patriotism, his being an immigrant, his personal friendships, his belief in judicial restraint, and the legacy of Holmes and Brandeis. In the 1920s those two men had risked opprobrium to speak out for the individual's claim to independent thought, to gather with one's friends and associates, to speak freely. There were changes between the 1920s and the 1950s, between the time of the Red Scare and the Cold War. Instead of disgruntled individuals and small groups of dissidents, "subversives" were seen as working, perhaps unwittingly but still effectively, with an international Communist conspiracy. Also, where many of the cases coming before Holmes and Brandeis had been the results of criminal trials, in the 1950s the cases coming to the Supreme Court had other sources: state and federal legislative investigations, loyalty programs, test oaths, and other administrative actions.

By the late 1940s, the internal-security cases were spinning a web of history. America always has had this dark side—the Alien and Sedition laws of the John Adams administration, the Know Nothings of the nineteenth century, the movement against dissidents during the First World War, Sacco-Vanzetti, the anti-Communism of the 1930s, the actions against the Japanese-Americans in the Second World War. After the war, however, the strands of that web combined into a tight cord that began choking off America's freedoms.

A major case, one that began the era, involved Alger Hiss, and with Hiss, Felix Frankfurter. It had been Frankfurter who, by designating Hiss as law clerk to Oliver Wendell Holmes in the late 1920s, had turned the young man's career toward government service. Then Frankfurter pushed Hiss into the New Deal, describing him as "first rate in every way." That was the general opinion of Hiss in the early 1930s. When William Douglas became head of the Securities and Exchange Commission, "The first man I hired was Abe Fortas . . . Abe and I decided that the next person we should hire was Alger Hiss." Hiss turned Douglas down, staying in the Agriculture Department for a while, then going to the State Department, becoming involved in the Yalta Conference, and earning for himself the plaudits of his countrymen for what seemed to be a distinguished career.

Then, in 1948, Whittaker Chambers, a *Time* magazine writer, told the House Un-American Activities Committee that he had been a Russian spy in the 1930s and that Alger Hiss had been his contact in the State Department. Hiss denied the charge and was indicted for perjury.

The Hiss case was played then, and since, on many levels in addition to that of national security. Richard M. Nixon jumped from being one of the pack in the House of Representatives to national prominence when he backed Chambers. So believe Hiss innocent, or be a Nixon man. *Time* then was the rightist bible and it supported Chambers. So believe Chambers, go along with *Time,* and be sneered at by liberals. Hiss was, by the late 1940s, the epitome of the eastern establishment —handsome, successful, a hobnobber with Dean Acheson and Felix Frankfurter—and Chambers was a fat, unkempt man who saw himself as a messianic force saving the nation from Communist devils. So believe Hiss, and be with the sophisticates.

After the Hiss-Chambers dispute began, Hiss avoided Frankfurter. "I thought it might be possibly embarrassing to him," he recalled some years later. But he did hear from Frankfurter, probably through a mutual friend, although Hiss did not remember the exact source. Hiss remembered Frankfurter's message this way: "Be sure you get a criminal lawyer. For a case like this, your corporate lawyer friends are just not equipped. This is a special branch of the law."

Two of Hiss's character witnesses were Stanley Reed and Frankfurter, both then sitting justices on the United States Supreme Court. Perhaps not since John Marshall had testified at the impeachment trial of Samuel Chase almost 150 years earlier had the nation been witness to a Supreme Court justice being sworn and interrogated on a witness stand. Reed required a summons. "I told the counsel that had charge of the trial that I wouldn't come unless I was summoned," he recalled. "If you're summoned, you're compelled to come, in a criminal trial in a Federal court. I wouldn't care to fight that. I thought he was entitled to my testimony if he really wanted it."

Frankfurter took the opposite position. "I deemed it an unnecessary formality to be formally served with a subpoena," he said. "I appeared as a witness in the trial of Alger Hiss because his counsel deemed it their duty to put my testimony before the jury. They had a right to my testimony because, under the Constitution, every accused has the right to produce evidence relevant to determining his guilt or innocence. The reputation of an accused is such a relevant matter, especially under a charge of perjury."

Frankfurter testified in the Federal Courthouse in Manhattan's Foley Square; he was questioned by Lloyd Paul Stryker, representing Alger Hiss, and Thomas Murphy, for the government. Under gentle questioning by Stryker, Frankfurter said that Hiss's reputation for loyalty to the United States and for personal integrity never had been questioned.

"And from the speech of people would you say that his reputation is good in those respect?" asked Stryker.

Frankfurter answered: "I would say it was excellent."

Then it was Murphy's turn.

As John Marshall had not performed in exemplary fashion when he testified in the Chase impeachment proceeding, Felix Frankfurter was not operating at top form when he responded to Murphy. "Didn't you hear in 1944 that [Hiss's reputation] wasn't too good, about that time?" Frankfurter said he couldn't respond to the date.

Wasn't there a rumored dispute between Hiss and Jerome Frank in the Agriculture Department in the 1930s? Frankfurter conceded "differences of opinion" existed but "that did not bear on questions of loyalty or integrity."

> *Murphy:* But you remember talking to Judge Frank about it?
> *Frankfurter:* No, I remember him talking to me.
> *Murphy:* Then I assume that you talked to him when he talked to you.
> *Frankfurter:* Well, let us not fence. All I meant to say was—
> *Murphy:* Well, you were the one that started fencing with me, weren't you, Judge? I asked you whether you talked to Judge Frank and you said that Judge Frank talked with you. Am I accurate?
> *Frankfurter:* I am trying to answer as carefully as I can with due regard to your responsibility and mine and the jury's and the responsibility of this case.

When their "fencing" finished, Murphy asked Frankfurter how Hiss became a New Deal official. Frankfurter replied that he was "not too sure" but believed that Jerome Frank in the Agriculture Department had asked him for recommendations, "and my guess is likely that Judge Frank, having been charged with the responsibility of an important headship of a law office in Washington, would ask me for suggestions, and I certainly would have recommended Mr. Hiss unqualifiedly."

Some years later, Alger Hiss recalled his reaction to Frankfurter's testimony. "I can't be objective about it," said Hiss. "I've been told it was not as effective as it could have been, because of the way Murphy treated him. I was so incensed at Murphy's hostility—and remember I was never a jury lawyer—I'm told the impact on the jury was not helpful, that the jury didn't like to see the judge get down and shake hands with Frankfurter." He paused. "From my point of view it was magnificent. I was deeply honored and touched."

The jury could not reach a verdict at the first Hiss trial, and a second trial was scheduled. Hiss changed lawyers, and Lloyd Paul Stryker stepped down. Frankfurter wrote Stryker: "Before the new trial of Alger Hiss begins, I want to say that your gallantry in undertaking the defense of a man against whom a strong popular tide was running is matched only by your gallantry in making way for another to try his chance in defending him."

Frankfurter was not asked to testify at the second trial, "because of the indignity to which he had been subjected—attacks in Congress, vulgar press," said Hiss. "And I never saw Felix again."

In the second trial Hiss was convicted and sentenced to jail. The conviction was appealed to the Supreme Court, and the first question was whether the Court would grant a writ of certiorari to hear the case. Four votes were needed to grant certiorari with a full nine-member Court sitting, but only three votes were needed when seven or six justices participated, and in the Hiss case only six justices voted—Reed and Frankfurter disqualified themselves because they had testified at the first trial, and Tom Clark disqualified himself because he had been connected with the case when he had been Attorney General.

Only Douglas and Black voted to grant certiorari. Douglas said in his memoirs: "If either Reed or Frankfurter had not testified at the trial, we would doubtless have had three to grant; and in my view no Court at any time could possibly have sustained the conviction." Douglas cited a 1945 Supreme Court decision, *Weiler* v. *United States*, stating that perjury cases required either two witnesses or one witness and corroborating evidence. This was lacking in the Hiss case, Douglas said.

Had Hiss and his lawyers considered the issue of Reed's or Frankfurter's disqualifying himself if the case came to the Supreme Court? "I feel quite sure that issue never occurred to any of us. . . ." said Hiss. "It never occurred to us there wouldn't be an acquittal. Certainly it never occurred to me." Frankfurter had faced the question of possible disqualification when he agreed to testify.

Of course [Frankfurter said], no member of the Supreme Court should needlessly disqualify himself from participation in a case that may come before the Court. But the circumstances that qualified me as a character witness at the trial would necessarily disqualify me from sitting in any case involving Alger Hiss, even if I had not been a witness in his case. As is patent from the public records, every year members of the court abstain from participation in cases because of some past relation to a party litigant or any other interested party in a litigation.

Alger Hiss went to jail, was released, and continues to profess his innocence. His case has become an industry. There have been books, one movie, dozens of articles, lawyers attempting to prove his innocence and others asserting the opposite. His story is more than a personal tragedy. His conviction persuaded Americans to accept the specter of a Communist conspiracy, to be concerned at the threat to their lives from Communists in government, in schools, and in the professions. The Hiss case was the first major battle in the postwar years, and when it was lost, liberalism came under attack and with it individualism, independent thinking, nonconformism, courage. All joined in the attack—Congress, the presidency, the government bureaucracy, the news media, the entertainment world, the veterans groups, school officials—and competed to demonstrate their own patriotism by accusing others.

Almost the only institution to challenge them was the Supreme Court.

It was an unprincipled time, called the McCarthy era after Senator Joseph McCarthy, Republican of Wisconsin, its most zealous and unprincipled leader. As a citizen, Frankfurter opposed what he saw as political oppression. "He devoted himself to encouragement of people working in the civil liberties field," said a friend from that period, "telephone calls and notes flowed over the country in a torrent." To law students at Harvard he spoke about intellectual responsibility and the Law School as a center of reason in a time when fear was exploited. "Reason and good sense can be tapped, I am sure," he said, "but it needs tappers. Our own profession is given a miserable account of itself these days." As a justice, however, he believed he had different responsibilities.

The first major internal-security case before the Court after Frankfurter testified for Hiss was *Communications Association* v. *Douds* in 1949; it involved a requirement by Congress that union officers file affidavits that they were not Communists. The Court upheld the requirement, Frankfurter concurring, although expressing fears that the act opened "the door too wide to mere speculation or uncertainty. It is asking more than rightfully may be asked of ordinary men to take an oath that a method is not unconstitutional or 'illegal' when constitutionality or illegality is frequently determined by the Court by the chance of a single vote."

The next year the Court heard *Kunz* v. *New York,* a free-speech case involving a man denied a permit to criticize groups in New York City. Osmond Fraenkel, whose civil-liberties advocacy went back to Sacco and Vanzetti, represented Kunz and thought Frankfurter "was his worst—wanted to know if [a] person couldn't be stopped from talking in front of St. Patrick's on Palm Sunday." Frankfurter accepted Fraenkel's arguments, however, holding for Kunz because there were "no appropriate standards" to guide police in issuing or denying a permit.

The case previewed Frankfurter's approach to the security issue, how he would resolve his conflict between judicial restraint and his abhorrence of McCarthyism. He was willing to allow the government to act only if its procedures were reasonable and fair. This was supported by his votes in two other cases that year, both decided the same day. One dealt with whether an organization could be declared subversive by the Attorney General without having the right to confront its accusers. The second dealt with the same question, but involved a single government employee rather than an organization. In both cases, Frankfurter was for the right of confrontation. The first case was decided against the government. In the second, the Court divided 4-4, allowing a lower-court judgment against the employee to stand. Frankfurter at one point in the oral arguments became involved in a shouting match with the government attorney. "The most important fact of this case," said Frankfurter, "is that the secret, untested, unquestioned finding by the Attorney General is not subject to review by anybody but those with power to chop off heads." Then, when he charged the government did not have adequate evidence to brand the individual a security risk, the government attorney shouted back: "That isn't so, and Justice Frank-furter should not say it is so. They had plenty of evidence. They did not disclose the evidence because that is not authorized under the presidential order. The Loyalty Review Board didn't just pull this out of the air."

A few weeks later, June 4, 1951, the Court handed down its decision in *Dennis et al.* v. *United States.* The case revolved around whether members of the Communist party could be charged with teaching and advocating "the overthrow and destruction of the Government of the United States by force and violence" or whether such a law violated the First Amendment's right of free speech and assembly. The Supreme Court decided against free speech. Frankfurter concurred separately, saying Congress had not overstepped proper bounds, but his statement seemed more a reflection of the past than the national-security implications of the present. For more than forty years he had witnessed attacks on the Supreme Court—by Theodore Roosevelt, Robert La Follette, the American Bar Association, Franklin Roosevelt—and his concerns were evident.

Throughout his forty-page concurrence, almost twice as long as the majority decision, he warned the Court against being caught in political thickets. "History teaches," he wrote, "that the independence of the judiciary is jeopardized when courts become embroiled in the passions of the day and assume primary responsibility in choosing between competing political, economic and social pressures."

Dennis shocked America's liberal community. Although this was the time, in the Cold War with Russia, of the Russian blockade of Berlin and of Russia's development of atomic weapons, the Communist party in the United States seemed a group of disgruntled, unpleasant, shrill people glorying in being attacked, elevated by the crusade against them to an importance they otherwise would not have had, to being an enemy worth concern. In the attack on the Communists, many liberals also feared, was an attack on all liberal movements.

Felix Frankfurter now was in his seventies. What had seemed clear to him for many years was confused. Judicial restraint had once been the catchword of American liberals. Now, when he advocated judicial restraint, he was attacked by those very liberals. In his earlier years, pillars of the legal community like Henry Stimson, Emory Buckner, and Charles Burlingham praised him. Now, they were either dead or silent. In the Eisenhower years, as in the Truman years, there was little White House contact. Frankfurter had never believed he was "the single most influential man" in Washington but sometimes he had enjoyed the notoriety. Now there was no more notoriety; he was only one of nine, and one under increasing criticism from those once his friends.

Early in 1952, Frankfurter refused to vote against a New York State law barring "subversives" from teaching, saying the issue should not have come to the Supreme Court—"The trial court found the interests of the plaintiffs and parents inconsequential . . . I agree"—avoiding the constitutional issue entirely. In a second case later that year, when the constitutional issue could not be avoided, Frankfurter concurred with the Court majority in overruling an Oklahoma loyalty oath for state employees. "Such unwarranted inhibition upon the free spirit of teachers . . . has an unmistakable tendency to chill the free play of the spirit which all teachers ought especially to cultivate and practice," he wrote. Douglas joined with Frankfurter—"As one professor to another, Yes—with pleasure."

In 1952 and 1953 an internal-security matter came before the Supreme Court that Frankfurter was to describe as "on the whole, the most disturbing single experience I have had during my term of service on the Court thus far." The published record of the case of Julius and Ethel Rosenberg "does not tell the story," said Frankfurter. "Indeed, it distorts the story; it largely falsifies the true course of events."

The Rosenbergs had been convicted of passing America's atomic secrets to the Soviet Union. Again, passions were aroused. Like Sacco and Vanzetti, the Rosenbergs were members of a minority. But the crime of which they were accused was not the murder of an individual but, rather, treason against their homeland. For that they were to be executed—the first execution of civilians for treason during peacetime in American history.

They had been tried in federal district court before Judge Irving Kaufman. The case went to the United States Court of Appeals for the Second Circuit, which affirmed the conviction and the death sentence decreed by Kaufman. The appeals court opinion had been written by Jerome Frank, the former New Dealer. Zechariah Chafee at Harvard wrote Frank: "I was very much impressed by the conscientious thought you gave the case. . . . At the same time I had some feeling that you were not entirely happy about the verdict and the sentences." Then Chafee asked if Frank would have any objections to Chafee's writing President Truman asking him to stop the executions. Frank replied that he believed the defendants had received a fair trial, "Indeed, it was more fair than many in which convictions have been affirmed." He then pointed out that his appellate court had no power to modify the death sentence, but if it had "I would have voted to do so." Frank was not critical of the district judge, Kaufman, as "the statute offered the judge the curious alternative of sentences of thirty years in jail or death; one can understand his reluctance to choose the former."

Against this background, the case was taken to the Supreme Court. There the two central characters were Douglas and Frankfurter.

The movements in the conferences were complicated, sometimes unexplainable. Through the summer, fall, and winter of 1952, the justices considered the Rosenberg case several times. Justices Burton, Black, and Frankfurter wanted the Court to hear arguments, but those three justices were one short of the four needed to hear arguments. Frankfurter argued that the Rosenberg death sentence was one of the few times a federal court had imposed a death sentence. If the Rosenbergs were to be executed, he did not want the shadow of an unfair proceeding hanging over the event. "I dwelt most strongly on the desirability of placing the sanction of the highest court in the land on a death sentence in a case involved in violent controversy, a case which had raised conscientious doubts in the minds of men of good will whose hostility to communism was beyond doubts," said Frankfurter. He insisted: "It was in the public interest to put such doubts to rest, and we alone could do it."

Douglas consistently voted against hearing the case. Hugo Black pub-

licly recorded his vote for hearing arguments, but Frankfurter did not
—"My oft-expressed view that dissents from denials of certiorari should
not be published kept me quiet," he explained. The press reported the
Court's decision as an 8-1 vote, the one being Black.

In March 1953, the case came to the Supreme Court again, on different grounds. Frankfurter was again responsive, saying a new issue, an
undenied charge of prejudicial behavior by a United States attorney,
was included. "I assumed that if we granted we would affirm," Frankfurter said later—that is, hearing the case would not upset the conviction. What he wanted was "a moral validation of this trial and capital
sentence." Douglas again voted to deny. The Court, however, did not
change its position; for a time Frankfurter considered expressing his
views in a memorandum to be published with the Court's decision, and
he several times requested a delay in announcing the denial. Frankfurter finally decided not to write the memorandum, believing it would
stir up needless controversy. That was early in May 1953.

On May 22, Douglas informed the justices that he had changed his
mind and wished to hear the case because he had now come to believe
that there was prejudice on the part of the United States attorney, as
the Rosenberg lawyers had charged. He planned to write a memorandum on that point, and if it was published, it would cause embarrassment for the Court—even more than Frankfurter's aborted memorandum would have done. The difference was that during the months the
Court had been wrestling with the issue four justices at one time or
another had expressed willingness to grant an appeal—Harold Burton,
the previous year but not this time on these new grounds; Frankfurter;
Black; and unexpectedly Douglas. Four is the number of votes required
to grant hearing. Robert Jackson at the conference May 23 said this was
bound to leak to the press, and the Court was required to hear the case
to avoid embarrassment. The Court then agreed to hear the case—the
four votes at that point being Jackson, Black, Frankfurter, and Douglas.
"Well, it is granted," said Chief Justice Vinson, and the talk went on to
the appropriate day for the hearing.

Douglas then announced he was withdrawing his memorandum. It
was badly written, he said, and he didn't want to embarrass anyone.
Jackson said that if the memorandum was withdrawn he would withdraw his vote to grant a hearing, and it was not granted. Later Jackson
said to Frankfurter of Douglas: "That S.O.B.'s bluff was called."

On June 12 lawyers for the Rosenbergs asked the Court for a stay of
execution. It was denied. Frankfurter, Black, Burton, and Jackson

wanted to hold a hearing on June 15, but the other justices—including Douglas—were against it. Since this was for a stay rather than to hear arguments, more than four votes were needed, and the stay was not granted.

June 15 was the final day of the term. The Rosenberg case had been before the Supreme Court for a year, Frankfurter consistently voting to hear arguments, and Douglas, with the one exception in May, opposing. After the Court had recessed and the justices were beginning their vacations, a lawyer for the Rosenbergs visited Justice Douglas and raised another legal question. Douglas believed the point had merit, and ordered the execution delayed until the district court and court of appeals reviewed the point. The Rosenbergs had been scheduled to be executed that week, but because Douglas's order was reviewable by the entire Supreme Court, it appeared to delay the execution at least until October—when the Supreme Court, after its regular session began, would decide whether to agree to the Douglas order or vacate it— unless, that is, a special session of the Court was called.

The death sentences for the Rosenbergs had come at the Cold War's height. The longer their execution date was postponed, the greater the pressure on the President to commute the sentence from death to life in prison. For a President to succumb to such pressure, however, would have earned him the enmity of those many Cold War warriors who believed the death sentence for the Rosenbergs justified. It was a decision no one wanted to make, and no one wanted to give to another to make.

The government immediately asked Chief Justice Vinson to call for a special session to vacate the Douglas order. Although such sessions were rare, Vinson scheduled a special session for June 18.

The justices hurried back to Washington. Frankfurter, planning to be away for the summer, had closed his Georgetown house. He returned June 17 for the special session the next day, and was the house guest of Joe Rauh. "Sitting on our porch that evening," Rauh recalled, "he seemed angriest at Justice Douglas whose actions at earlier stages of the case had not supported a full review of the case and now at the last minute pulled a 'grandstand' play." Frankfurter also spoke critically of District Judge Kaufman for his "unjudicious conduct" in the "manner and substance of the sentencing."

The Court met in special session in its conference room on June 18, then quickly adjourned. It returned the next morning and voted to vacate Douglas's order—Douglas, Black, and Frankfurter dissenting. The Rosenbergs were executed that night.

The ramifications of that case were many. Douglas became a hero of the liberal community for his apparent efforts to delay the Rosenberg executions, and Frankfurter never forgave him for "grandstanding." Frankfurter continued to speak ill of Irving Kaufman, who later became a court of appeals judge, to Frankfurter's chagrin. But there was a more serious result. Without a validation of the convictions by the nation's highest court, over the Rosenberg executions hangs the unresolved question of fairness. The American people were not quite certain.

The Court's internal-security cases had been decided by narrow votes; obviously the Court could be moved either way by the arrival of a new member. It was at that point that Earl Warren joined the Court. Fred Vinson, whom he replaced, had been willing to allow the Congress and state legislatures leeway in determining national security. Warren was an unknown.

Felix Frankfurter and Hugo Black buzzed after Earl Warren like bees after honey. Frankfurter had to lose the contest. There was the difference in personality between himself and Black. Black acted the courtly southern gentleman who never seemed to force his way upon another. Frankfurter was the professor who lectured to his fellow justices as if they were students in one of his Langdell Hall seminars. Warren did not take kindly to lectures. "Felix irritates; Hugo soothes," cracked a law clerk at the time.

In the spring of 1954, Warren was with the Court majority in upholding the suspension of a New York physician's license to practice because he had been convicted for failure to produce papers sought by the House Un-American Activities Committee. The New York physician had been active in liberal groups, and the records sought would have identified members and financial sources. The doctor spent six months in jail. The majority said the state had experience in regulating its physicians and should be left to its own devices. Black and Douglas dissented.

So did Frankfurter. "So far as concerns the power to grant or revoke a medical license. . . . The exercise of the authority must have some rational relation to the qualifications required of a practitioner in that profession," said Frankfurter, adding that the Supreme Court cannot "sanction a State's deprivation or partial destruction of a man's professional life on grounds having no possible relation to fitness, intellectual or moral, to pursue his profession." In other times and in other cases, Frankfurter had taken the opposite point of view, that the states—if they followed reasonable and proper procedures—could do pretty much as they wished. This dissent then represented a change for Frankfurter; the states were stretching reasonableness too far. There had been other changes in the past and there would be more in the future.

That same spring, the Court refused to grant a writ of certiorari in the case of William Remington, accused of disloyalty. Frankfurter, Black, and Douglas wanted to grant the writ, and Frankfurter believed that Jackson would go along with them to make the necessary four votes. Jackson refused, however, becoming angry at Black's announced intention to use the Remington case to attack the government in still another security case. A few months later Remington was murdered in jail. His lawyer had been Joe Rauh. When he next met Frankfurter, Rauh remembered Frankfurter squeezed his arm "as was his habit, and said: 'You and I did everything in the Remington case that human beings could do.'"

In these cases Warren had sided with the government, but in 1955, encouraged by Frankfurter, he switched. The case, *Peters* v. *Hobby*, concerned a physician denied a security clearance. Warren wrote the Court's opinion, deciding for the physician, and ordering that his records be wiped clean of any taint of disloyalty. But he did so on procedural grounds. Frankfurter had written him a memorandum suggesting language—"From its very inception, this Court has recognized, as a cardinal rule controlling constitutional adjudication, that it should not reach a question of constitutional law unless absolutely necessary to decision." In Warren's opinion are these words: "From a very early date, this Court has declined to anticipate a question of constitutional law in advance of the necessity of deciding it." Frankfurter then had contributed to Warren's moving part way from the position he had held when he first joined the Court.

Later that year, Warren joined with Frankfurter and Douglas in supporting a Black decision freeing an ex-serviceman who had been literally kidnaped by the military in Pittsburgh, Pennsylvania, and taken to Korea to stand trial there for a crime allegedly committed while in the service. The Court ruled that ex-servicemen, like other civilians, could not be denied constitutional rights. Originally the majority was with the military, but Frankfurter persuaded Black to tone down some of the language in the dissent, and gradually enough other justices, including Warren, joined Black's dissent to make it the majority decision by a 6-3 vote.

By this time, Warren was firmly on the side of the individual in internal-security cases. The question was whether he would continue to base his positions on procedure, as Frankfurter hoped, or go for the constitutional jugular, as Black hoped.

The next year, 1956, in *Pennsylvania* v. *Nelson,* Warren, supported by both Frankfurter and Black, held that federal law had preempted a state's right to prosecute an individual for attempting to subvert the national government. The effect of the decision was to free a Pennsylvania state Communist party leader convicted under state law.

Also in 1956 the Court dealt with a New York City College teacher who, with twenty-seven years' experience and tenure, was summarily dismissed. He had been called before the Internal Security Subcommittee of the Senate Judiciary Committee and asked if he was a member of the Communist party. The teacher denied current membership in the party, conceded membership years earlier, and refused to answer questions about that period of his life, saying the answers might tend to incriminate him.

Because Associate Justice Tom Clark had been the Attorney General when the Justice Department first produced a list of "subversive" organizations, the hope in the Court was that he could be persuaded to write the decision reinstating the teacher. This was consistent with the Court's traditional approach; the author of the list of "subversive" organizations could not himself be accused of being "soft on Communism." Frankfurter met with Clark and reported back to Warren that "my clear conviction is that he is anchored for reversal. . . . His ground is my ground for reversal, namely, due process." Clark did write the decision, but once he started he did not stop at due process. The Fifth Amendment denies punishment of a person who refrains from testifying on the basis of self-incrimination. "Taking the fifth" it was called perjoratively, and chairmen of congressional committees used the phrase to suggest guilt. Tom Clark, in his decision, would not allow the amendment to be attacked. Speaking for a six-member majority, including Frankfurter, Warren, and Black, Clark said: "The right of an accused person to refuse to testify, which had been in England merely a rule of evidence, was so important to our forefathers that they raised it to the dignity of a constitutional enactment, and it has been recognized as 'one of the most valuable prerogatives of the citizen.' "

In many of the internal-security cases, the Court was helped, unintentionally, by the government—officials went so far beyond what the law allowed, so grossly violated proper procedures, or prepared cases so poorly that the Court had no alternative. The 1956 case *Communist*

Party v. *Subversive Activities Control Board* is an example. The Board had required the party to register with the Attorney General as a "Communist-action" organization, using evidence from three witnesses who had perjured themselves. Twenty-eight years earlier, in a narcotics case, Brandeis had spoken to this point: "This prosecution should be stopped . . . in order to protect the Government. To protect it from the illegal conduct of its officers. To preserve the purity of the courts." Said Frankfurter in the 1956 *Communist Party* case: "We cannot pass upon a record containing such challenged testimony." The constitutional issue was not touched, and the case returned to the lower courts.

That same year, a majority opinion by John Marshall Harlan, Frankfurter concurring, said the government could not use internal-security reasons to fire employees indiscriminately; the law required first a demonstration of national-security involvement.

The next year, in May 1957, the Court dealt with two cases having to do with states' refusal to admit individuals to the bar, denying them the right to practice law. In one from California, the majority upheld the lawyer, with Frankfurter dissenting on a minor procedural matter. The second case decided that day, from New Mexico, involved an individual who had been a Communist party member in the 1930s. Although he had passed his bar examination, had endorsements of good character from his clergyman, teachers, soldiers who had served in the army with him—actually there was no derogatory testimony or evidence against him, except the admitted party membership years earlier —New Mexico denied him admission to the bar on the basis of his not having a good moral character.

The Supreme Court reversed the state. Black, writing for the majority, allowed it any standards it chose—except arbitrariness. Frankfurter concurred, for the same reason. "Refusal to allow a man to qualify himself for the profession on a wholly arbitrary standard or on a consideration that offends the dictates or reason offends the Due Process Clause," said Frankfurter. "Such is the case here."

That concurrence begins with a paragraph that says much about the lifetime love affair of the immigrant Felix Frankfurter with the law. It reads:

Certainly since the time of Edward I, through all the vicissitudes of seven centuries of Anglo-American history, the legal profession has played a role all its own. The bar has not enjoyed prerogatives; it has been entrusted with anxious responsibilities. One does not have to inhale the self-adulatory bombast of after-dinner speeches to affirm that all interests of man that are comprised under the constitutional guarantees given to "life, liberty and property" are in the professional keeping of lawyers. It is a fair characterization of the lawyer's responsibility in our society that he stands "as a shield" . . . in defense of right and to ward off wrong. From a profession charged with such responsibilities there must be exacted those qualities of truth-speaking, of a high sense of honor, of granite discretion, of the strictest observance of fiduciary responsibility, that have, throughout the centuries, been compendiously described as "moral character."

By the late 1950s the split between Warren and Frankfurter edged into the open. In 1957, Warren wrote the Court's decision in *Watkins* v. *United States,* upholding the right of an individual to refuse to answer certain questions before the House Un-American Activities Committee. Involved was the power of Congress itself and the Court's right to limit that power. Warren had no difficulty finding against the Congress. "We cannot simply assume, however," he wrote, "that every Congressional investigation is justified by a public need that overbalances any private rights affected. To do so would be able to abdicate the responsibility placed by the Constitution upon the judiciary." Frankfurter concurred, for the same reasons that motivated Warren, that "the questions must be put with relevance and definiteness" to the witness. But his language was not nearly as strong as that of Warren, who seemed anxious to take on the House committee for its free-wheeling ways. "Investigations conducted solely for the personal aggrandizement of the investigators," said Warren, "or to 'punish' those investigated are indefensible."

A related case, decided at the same time, was *Sweezy* v. *New Hampshire.* Since there was so much publicity about "subversives," the New Hampshire legislature determined to discover if there was any in that state and directed the state attorney general, Louis C. Wyman, to seek them out. He questioned a teacher about membership in the state Progressive party and other "subversive" matters. After the teacher refused to answer questions put to him by Wyman, by a state legislative committee, and then by the state court, he was convicted of contempt. Warren related the case to *Watkins,* saying they both dealt with the extent of legislative power. Then in the majority decision he found against the state, saying: "The sole basis for the inquiry was to scrutinize the teacher as a person, and the inquiry must stand or fall on that basis," and that academic and political freedom had been infringed upon. Frankfurter concurred, saying that academic freedom had been infringed upon by the state. Once he had believed that a state should be allowed to make its own mistakes, but he could not hold to that in the face of the sweeping attack on independent thought in the name of a war on subversion. The Constitution would not allow it. Judicial restraint went only so far.

There were two other internal-security cases that day. One involved leaders of the Communist party in California, convicted for conspiring to teach and advocate overthrow of the government by force or violence. The Supreme Court, Warren and Frankfurter joining the decision of Justice John Marshall Harlan, overturned the convictions, saying only actions rather than "mere advocacy" were a basis for conviction. This was a restatement of Holmes's "clear and present" danger doctrine.

The second case that day was *Service* v. *Dulles,* and it demonstrates Frankfurter's willingness to believe his closest friends wrong. John Stewart Service had been a respected career foreign service officer for sixteen years, stationed for most of that time in China. He reported honestly and made forthright recommendations. When China fell to the Communists, he became one of the scapegoats and on December 14, 1951, he was summarily fired by Secretary of State Dean Acheson.

By this time Acheson and Felix Frankfurter were as close as two men can be in Washington. Stories of the two men striding through Georgetown each morning debating the weighty issues of the day were legion. Because of the manner in which Acheson had fired Service, the Court's decision would reflect on him. The decision by Harlan did just that, charging Acheson had not followed proper procedure. The decision was 8-0, with Frankfurter one of the eight.

During the next several years, the intensity of the cases increased. In 1959, in *Barenblatt* v. *United States,* the Court upheld the conviction of a recalcitrant witness before the House Un-American Activities Committee; Harlan wrote the decision and Frankfurter joined him. All procedural requirements had been met, the majority said, and "So long as Congress acts in pursuance of its constitutional power, the Judiciary lacks authority to intervene on the basis of the motives which spurred the exercise of that power."

Those sentences, written by Harlan, were vintage Frankfurter; he had, in fact, helped shape them. They said what Holmes and Brandeis had been arguing for decades, that the Supreme Court should not become a superlegislature, should not go to the wisdom of the act. The position was not accepted that day by Black, Douglas, and Warren— "The fact is that once we allow any group which has some political aims or ideas to be driven from the ballot and from the battle for men's minds because some of its members are bad and some of its tenets are illegal, no group is safe."

That same month, June 1959, the Court faced the loyalty-security issue again in *Greene* v. *McElroy*. Warren wrote the majority decision reinstating an employee of a government contractor, saying, "Without explicit action by lawmakers, decisions of great constitutional import and effect would be relegated by default to administrators who, under our system of government, are not endowed with authority to decide them." Warren used some twenty pages to attack the government's procedures. Frankfurter concurred in a brief statement, saying that unauthorized procedures had been used in discharging the employee.

Earl Warren had come to view the Constitution as a document of ethics; "But is it fair?" he demanded of the lawyers before the bench. Given the issues dominating the Warren Court—civil liberties, desegregation, and law enforcement—that question was answered better with Black's sweeping view of the Constitution as a list of prohibitions placed on government, federal and local, rather than with Frankfurter's view of the Constitution as a limited document to be extended only cautiously. "The basic ingredient of decision is principle," Warren wrote later, "and it should not be compromised and parceled out a little in one case, a little more in another, until eventually someone receives the full benefit. If the principle is sound and constitutional, it is the birthright of every American, not to be accorded begrudgingly or piecemeal or to special groups only." Frankfurter believed the opposite. When a columnist friend had written that Frankfurter "likes" to avoid deciding constitutional issues, Frankfurter conceded the accuracy of the remark and added: "There 'likes' does refer to a conscious process. But the consciousness is not that of making a personal choice. It is an alert effort to obey the rules of adjudication which we all profess."

The two men became acknowledged opponents, lashing out verbally from the bench and in conference at each other. In 1960, Frankfurter declined to give the Holmes lectures at Harvard, believing forthright comments about the Supreme Court would cause too many difficulties with Warren. He explained in a "confidential" letter:

If the giving of the Lectures had arisen in the time of Hughes, C. J., I would have felt no problem whatever, and while both Stone and Vinson were extremely touchy, their sensitiveness derived from and related to self-love and did not generate personal friction arising out of differences in doctrinal views. And so in their days I would not have felt barred from dealing with the kind of problems with which I had planned to deal in the Holmes lectures. The situation now is quite different.

For the nation and the Supreme Court, the 1950s had been a roller-coaster, extreme after extreme, each higher than the other. Still shuddering from the McCarthy era, the nation could not come to grips with the black civil-rights movement, did not understand its role as a world power, longed for another time when the responsibilities were not so great, the threats not so ominous, the tomorrow not so questionable. The Supreme Court came under constant and heavy attack—"Impeach Earl Warren" said the billboards, strip the Court of its power said the congressmen. Legislative proposals would have restricted the Court's power to review practices of congressional committees, national security and state subversive cases; state regulations having to do with teachers and admission to the state bars would virtually have undone everything the Court had done in the decade. Several times Federal Bureau of Investigation agents guarded both Warren and Frankfurter because of threats to their lives.

Frankfurter, now in his late seventies, having had one heart attack, his wife almost a complete invalid, felt increasing fear for the Supreme Court, the institution he loved. Through all of his public life, he had believed the best defense against attacks on the Court was judicial restraint. Constantly he harked back to James Bradley Thayer's article seventy years earlier calling on the courts to limit their role. Against that background, in 1961 Felix Frankfurter dealt with the case that summarized the McCarthy era, that climaxed the time of the witch hunters—*Communist Party* v. *Subversive Activities Control Board.*

The case involved the government's efforts to brand the Communist party a physical threat to the United States. When the case had come to the Court earlier, Frankfurter's opinion sent it back to the lower courts because the government had used perjured testimony. Now the perjured testimony had been eliminated.

Writing for the Court majority in 1961, Frankfurter found for the government, against the Communist party. In a decision running 111 pages, Frankfurter relied heavily on judicial restraint:

We cannot in this case say that the Board—and, in affirming its order, the Court of Appeals—has misapplied the Act. . . . The role of the judiciary in a government premised upon a separation of powers . . . precludes interference by courts with legislative and executive functions which have not yet proceeded so far as to affect individual interests adversely. . . . The Party would have us conclude that the Act is only an instrument serving to abolish the Communist Party by indirection. But such an analysis ignores our duty of respect for the exercise of the legislative power of Congress.

But there was more to his decision than judicial restraint. Frankfurter had accepted the government's claim that the United States was under siege from a Communist conspiracy.

"No doubt, a government regulation which requires registration as a condition upon the exercise of free speech may in some circumstances affront the constitutional guarantees of free speech," Frankfurter acknowledged, but continued:

Where the mask of anonymity which an organization's members wear serves the double purpose of protecting them from popular prejudice and of enabling them to cover over a foreign-directed conspiracy, infiltrate into other groups, and enlist the support of persons who would not, if the truth were revealed, lend their support . . . it would be a distortion of the First Amendment to hold that it prohibits Congress from removing the mask.

In other decades those who became the Communists in the 1950s and 1960s had been the Wobblies and the radicals. Frankfurter had risked much to defend them from an overbearing government and to allow them the rights promised in the Constitution. In the 1961 Communist party case Frankfurter had the opportunity again to be guided by Oliver Wendell Holmes—"if there is any principle of the Constitution that more imperatively calls for attachment than any other it is the principle of free thought—not free thought for those who agree with us but freedom for the thought that we hate." But Frankfurter chose not to be so guided.

Frankfurter's critics charged the decision represented the climax of his growing conservatism, which had begun, they claimed, when he had first joined the Court. But perhaps the man who had come to the United States as a twelve-year-old immigrant could not have done other than he did when he believed his adopted country was under attack. It was a war, and—as it had been with the school-prayer decisions, the German saboteurs, and the Japanese exclusion cases—"all bets are off."

The internal-security cases, climaxed by the Communist party case, came for Felix Frankfurter in the last decade of his public career, one that spanned almost sixty years. Those cases, however, were not the climax of his career. Because, in the end, the McCarthy era was a blip on the American scene—frightening, ugly, dangerous—but it passed, a victim of its own excesses as much as of judicial courage, and remains a reminder of the threats a democracy constantly faces.

Frankfurter's achievement in that decade came in another area, one a continuing part of the American scene: the black civil-rights movement.

24

Brown v. Board of Education

When the South defended school segregation before the Supreme Court in the 1950s, its chief lawyer was John W. Davis. Almost eighty, he had been prominent in public affairs and law for almost half a century and was considered by many to be the ablest advocate before the Court and certainly was the most active advocate before it. Between 1913 and the desegregation case in 1954, Davis's last, he argued 141 cases before the Supreme Court. No other lawyer in the twentieth century had equaled that figure, and only two lawyers in the nineteenth century, Daniel Webster, and Walter Jones, had surpassed it.

His personal attitudes toward blacks and black civil rights were mixed. In 1915, as Solicitor General, Davis had supported the blacks' cause before the Supreme Court and in 1924 had courted black support when he ran for President. But, according to his biographer, his "heart was really with the white social order . . . he privately defended poll taxes, never criticized the exclusion of blacks from Democratic primaries, and never commented, privately or publicly, on the nation's dual system of justice."

The lawyer leading the attack on segregation was a big, burly black man named Thurgood Marshall. He was assisted by graduates from the law school at Howard University, the black institution in the District of Columbia, who had been sharpening their skills for years in preparation for this case, as well as by lawyers representing groups supporting the end of segregation. Also, there was one lawyer who was with them that day but whose name was not mentioned. Louis Brandeis.

In 1908, Brandeis had introduced the "Brandeis brief," the concept that law must acknowledge experience, and law had responded. "What we know as men," the judges had said, "we cannot ignore as judges." And one by one, before this new concept, relationships in American life had changed, changed between employer and employee, utility and state, governed and government. And now that concept, enunciated by Louis Brandeis and passed on to Felix Frankfurter, would meet its greatest test: the cleavage between the races.

As Brandeis had done in *Muller,* Thurgood Marshall went beyond the law. He submitted with the formal briefs an appendix titled "The Effects of Segregation and the Consequences of Desegregation." It had been prepared by Kenneth Clark, an associate professor of psychology at City College in New York; Stuart Cook, chairman of the graduate Psychology Department of New York University; and Isidor Chein, director of research for the Commission on Community Interrelations of the American Jewish Congress. The appendix also was signed by thirty-two social scientists and psychiatrists with expertise in race relations. Marshall was attempting to force upon the judges the understanding that they could not ignore as judges what they knew as men.

John Davis was scornful of Thurgood Marshall's material—"I can only say that if that sort of 'fluff' can move any court, 'God save the state!' " and "I ran across a sentence the other day which . . . described much of the social sciences as 'fragmentary expertise based on an examined presupposition.' " The paths of Davis, Brandeis, and Frankfurter had crisscrossed for almost fifty years. This one additional time they intersected again, the lawyer as technician, the hired gun using the law to defend the status quo—"The lawyer as a lawyer does not build or erect or paint anything," Davis once had said. "He does not create"—versus the lawyer using the law as a means of dealing with the experience of the state and of the people.

From the early 1800s the Supreme Court had had ambivalent attitudes toward the slave and toward the freed black. When John Marshall was Chief Justice from 1801 to 1835, the Court treated blacks as property with status equal to that of a parcel of land or a draft animal. However, toward the end of his career, Marshall wrote for the Court that the slave trade being "contrary to the law of nature will scarcely be denied," and of slaves, "That every man has a natural right to the fruits of his own labour, is generally admitted; and that no other can rightfully deprive him of those fruits, and appropriate them against his will, seems to be the necessary result of this situation." This judicial trend against slavery, however slight, was blunted by the Court's Dred Scott decision in 1857, which strengthened slavery; and the nation's refusal to accept that decision helped precipitate the Civil War. When the war ended, the United States adopted the Thirteenth, Fourteenth, and Fifteenth amendments to the Constitution. The Thirteenth outlawed slavery; the Fourteenth defined citizenship to include blacks; and the Fifteenth upheld the right of black citizens to vote.

But soon the nation shrank from the promises in those amendments, and blacks went to the Supreme Court to have their rights enforced. The Court in the 1890s backtracked and upheld, in *Plessy* v. *Ferguson,* a separate but equal concept, in effect, allowing segregation. John Marshall Harlan, the grandfather of the John Marshall Harlan who sat on the Supreme Court with Frankfurter, dissented: "Our Constitution is color blind, and neither knows nor tolerates classes among citizens." Few, however, accepted that three decades after the Civil War.

Blacks had slowly been moving to the North in the closing decades of the nineteenth and early decades of the twentieth centuries, a move accelerated by the need for laborers in northern plants and mills during the First World War. Northerners, favoring racial equality until the blacks came in large numbers, became less certain. Blacks found themselves victims of an acknowledged segregation in the South and de facto segregation in the North. They again turned to the Supreme Court for help.

The Court seesawed. It upheld the rights of blacks to fair procedures in criminal trials but seemed uncertain how to deal with other racial questions without a large body of precedent to guide it, uncertain how the public would react or whether the public would obey sudden reversals of practice.

Under Chief Justice Edward White, a former Confederate soldier, the Court outlawed the "grandfather clause"—one could register to vote only if one's grandfather had been registered to vote; i.e., blacks could not register to vote; this was the 1915 case when John W. Davis as Solicitor General had argued the blacks' cause. In 1927, the Court dealt with a case involving public-school segregation. A Chinese-American family, living in Mississippi, sent its daughter to a public school where she was classified as nonwhite and directed to a school for blacks. Her family challenged the order but did not attack segregation, only the designation of the daughter as nonwhite. "The white, or Caucasian race, which makes the laws and construes and enforces them," said the lawyer for the family, "thinks that in order to protect itself from the infusion of the blood of other races its children must be kept in schools from which other races are excluded." Whites in Mississippi levy "taxes on all alike to support a public school system," the argument continued, "but in the organization of the system it creates its own exclusive schools for its children." Chief Justice Taft's decision supported the state's interpretation of "colored" children as including "brown, yellow and black races." The decision was unanimous, Brandeis included.

In 1935, in *Grovey* v. *Townsend,* the Court confronted the white primary, the replacement for the grandfather clause to disenfranchise blacks. In Texas, as in other southern states, the Democratic party called itself a private club and operated the primary as a nonpublic affair. Because the Democratic nominee in those then-one-party states was invariably the winner in the election, if one did not vote in the primary, one did not possess an effective vote. Blacks were excluded from the "club." When they sued for their right to an effective vote, the Supreme Court unanimously ruled against them, agreeing that a political party was, as the southerners claimed, a private club allowed to exclude anyone it chose.

By the late 1930s, however, American blacks were forcing the Supreme Court to re-examine its position. Missouri had "separate but equal" college facilities for blacks but not a separate law school. When Lloyd Gaines, a black, was denied admission to the University of Missouri Law School, the state offered to pay his expenses to any out-of-state school. Arguing that an out-of-state school would not fulfill his need for an education in Missouri law, Gaines sued for admission to the local law school; he did not attack the separate-but-equal doctrine of *Plessy* v. *Ferguson* but said that doctrine had not been adhered to. The Court ruled in his favor. Brandeis was with the majority; only McReynolds dissented.

When Felix Frankfurter joined the Court in 1939, he already had a history of supporting black civil rights. In 1929, Walter White of the National Association for the Advancement of Colored People—NAACP —had asked him to become a director. Frankfurter refused; he could not attend board meetings, and "I have strong convictions against dummy directors." But he did offer to serve on the NAACP's national legal committee, and "I am at all times ready to serve on specific legal issues for which you think I can be of use."

In 1932, when the Supreme Court ordered a new trial for the seven blacks charged with rape in the *Scottsboro* case, Frankfurter defended the Court's action in the *New York Times.* "I was under great pressure," said Frankfurter, "and my wife said that when I have seven things to do I take on an eighth. But . . . I felt in the nature of a public duty to yield to the request of the Times." Frankfurter became "mentor and exemplar" to Charles H. Houston, early black civil-rights lawyer. In 1938, when William H. Hastie, a former Frankfurter student at Harvard and a black, became a federal judge in the Virgin Islands, Frankfurter sought Harlan Fiske Stone's help in having Amherst College, from which both Hastie and Stone had graduated, award Hastie an honorary degree. Stone refused.

Frankfurter resigned from all outside activities, including the NAACP's legal committee, when he joined the Supreme Court, but there was no doubt at NAACP headquarters that Frankfurter remained a friend. Thurgood Marshall, then a young lawyer handling many of the NAACP's civil-rights cases, noticed then that Frankfurter's name still appeared on the organization's letterheads. "I think this should be corrected at the earliest possible moment," he said, to avoid Frankfurter's disqualifying himself in any NAACP case. "It would be quite a tragedy for us," said Marshall, "to have Mr. Felix Frankfurter disqualified on any case in which we are interested."

Walter White continued to be a Frankfurter friend and Frankfurter once arranged a dinner to bring him together with younger people in Washington, primarily from the South. "He just thought it would be a good idea to expose these young southerners to Mr. White," said one who attended the dinner.

Frankfurter was not naïve about the problem of civil rights for blacks; he called it "the most complicated and baffling of all our social problems, which means that it requires more humility and gentleness and forbearance on the part of everyone who has concern for our national well-being than any other problem." He frequently discussed it with his southern colleagues on the bench and with southern lawyers. He hoped that, with the end of the Second World War, a new liberalism would move through the nation, including the South. "I thought it very important," he wrote in his diary, "to give those liberal forces full play and not to make their efforts more difficult by a smug attitude on the part of the Northerners regarding Southern backwardness and Northern righteousness."

In 1944, after Frankfurter had served on the Supreme Court for five years, the Court was again faced with the white primary, which had been accepted in *Grovey* v. *Townsend*. Although only nine years had passed since that decision, a dramatic new element had been introduced into the equation: blacks were being drafted into the American military with whites. The NAACP, particularly vociferous, criticized the Roosevelt administration for not filing an *amicus curiae* brief in the new case. Francis Biddle, then Attorney General, had advised against filing the brief, telling Roosevelt: "The Supreme Court have not asked

our help (as they often do) and don't need it. The question is purely
political. . . . If we intervened it would be widely publicized and Texas
and the South generally will not understand we are not taking sides."
His memorandum was dated October 30, 1943, one year and a few days
before the next presidential election.

The Court voted on the case, *Smith* v. *Allwright*, in conference on
Saturday, January 15, 1944; it decided to outlaw the white primary,
reversing *Grovey* v. *Townsend*. Shortly after the conference, the assignments came down from Chief Justice Harlan Fiske Stone, and Frankfurter was assigned the decision.

That afternoon, Robert Jackson visited Frankfurter. The two men's
friendship dated back to the late 1930s and was strong enough for blunt
talk. As Frankfurter recalled the conversation, Jackson

> thought that it was a very great mistake to have me write the Allwright opinion.
> For a good part of the country the subject—Negro disenfranchisement—was in
> the domain of the irrational and we have to take account of such facts. At best
> it will be very unpalatable to the South and should not be exacerbated by having
> the opinion written by a member of the Court who has, from the point of view
> of Southern prejudice, three disqualifications: "You are a New Englander, you
> are a Jew and you are not a Democrat—at least not recognized as such."

Jackson made the same points to Stone, who took the case from
Frankfurter and gave it to Stanley Reed, a Kentuckian. Frankfurter did
not like Reed's opinion. It lacked "aggressive candor," said Frankfurter,
and "Reed had his own notions of appeasement which are bound to
fail."

When Reed could not be moved to write a stronger opinion, Frankfurter wrote a concurrence. "No mere individual preference but only
a compelling regard for the Constitution as a dynamic scheme of government," Frankfurter wrote, justified reversing *Grovey* but, he continued, the justices on the present court "cannot forego our responsibility" because judges at another time decided differently, and "We
cannot escape this duty."

A few days before the opinions were to come down, Jackson again
approached Frankfurter, asking him if he planned to issue a concurrence. When Frankfurter said yes, Jackson said: "I think that would be
a great mistake for the same reasons that led me to think it would be
a mistake [for you] to write the Court's opinion." Frankfurter, acknowledging the force of Jackson's argument, agreed not to issue the separate
concurrence, and it was never published. Still, he could not agree to

what he considered the "pussyfooting and the pettyfogging" of Reed's opinion, and so merely concurred in the result without joining in the opinion.

In 1950, in *Cassell* v. *Texas*, the question before the Court was whether to uphold a murder conviction of a black because of systematic and deliberate exclusion of blacks from grand-jury panels. The Court, calling the actions "intentional exclusion that is discrimination," reversed the conviction. The decision was a command to end segregationist jury practices throughout the South.

Frankfurter agreed with the result, but in a separate concurrence made three additional points. First, he insisted that the grand-jury panels be representative of the community but argued that quotas were not needed—"The prohibition of the Constitution against discrimination because of color does not require in and of itself the presence of a Negro on a jury. But neither is it satisfied by Negro representation arbitrarily limited to one." Second, he was stronger in denouncing the local discrimination than was the Court's decision—"the law would have to have the blindness of indifference rather than the blindness of impartiality not to attribute the uniform factor to man's purpose."

The third point was his respect for local judges. In a five-and-one-half-year period, the jury commissioners had chosen twenty-one grand-jury panels with only one black on each. Evidence "clearly indicates," said Frankfurter, that this was a deliberate act of the jury commissioners. Associate Justice Tom Clark did not accept that, saying there was no evidence in the record placing the blame on the commissioners. Frankfurter replied that either the commissioners submitted panels with only one black or that the local judges, choosing the grand juries from the panels, selected only one black. One of those two, the commissioners or the judges, was discriminating, and, said Frankfurter, "I cannot attribute such discrimination to the trial judges of Texas." Clark, himself a Texan, remained unconvinced and filed a separate concurrence.

In the late 1940s and early 1950s, the Court again faced the question, as in *Gaines* a decade earlier, of whether separate-but-equal was truly equal. In a case involving the University of Oklahoma Law School, the Court ordered a black admitted because the school was the only state-supported law school in Oklahoma. Two years later, in a Texas case, the Court sided with a black who refused to attend a Jim Crow school, claiming it was not on a par with the white school.

To this point the attacks before the Court had been isolated challenges in specific communities, but the black community was changing.

Spurred by their experiences in World War II, educated by the G.I. Bill, strengthened by their understanding of American history, young black people were organizing, challenging discriminatory practices, demanding equal educational opportunity. They were ready for a new step.

In the early 1950s, seventeen southern and border states plus the District of Columbia had mandatory segregated public elementary and high school systems, and four other states allowed such systems. This system of segregated education became the blacks' target.

Decades pass, and old passions are replaced by new longings, disappointments, emotions. The insistence by white southerners on segregation of the races in schools becomes difficult to remember or to understand. Clothed in rhetoric from another time, it was powerful, and its power generated fear, anger, and potential for violence. Within the Supreme Court, Hugo Black, Stanley Reed, Tom Clark, and Chief Justice Fred Vinson had come from southern states, had grown up in segregated societies. They understood the passions.

Frankfurter understood them also. The veteran of Bisbee, Mooney, and Sacco-Vanzetti knew how hatred, fear, and ignorance could sweep through a people. This understanding cautioned him, when he moved forward, to do so slowly. "The ugly practices of racial discrimination should be dealt with by eloquence of action but with austerity of speech," he told fellow justice Wiley Rutledge in 1947. "By all means let us decide with fearless decency, but express our decisions with reserve and austerity." In a case before the Court dealing with a black's drive for equality of graduate education, Stanley Reed had suggested language to Chief Justice Vinson saying, "These are handicaps to an effective education." Frankfurter, reviewing the suggestion, believed the time too soon for an apparent general attack on separate educational facilities and suggested the sentence speak only of handicaps "to graduate instruction." The decision, *McLaurin* v. *Board of Regents,* says: "The result is that appellant is handicapped in his pursuit of effective graduate instruction."

The southern segregationists long had been aware they were not living up to their promises of providing educational opportunities for blacks equal to those provided for whites. They also understood the legal movement in process, and while blaming the movement on "northern agitators," they knew they had to get busy. When James Byrnes was sworn in as governor of South Carolina in 1951, he asked the state legislature for a massive infusion of state funds for schools for blacks and for anti–Ku Klux Klan laws. This is the same James Byrnes who had served on the Supreme Court for one year, had been an assistant to President Roosevelt during the Second World War, and was almost FDR's running mate in 1944. Now his job was to head off the civil-rights movement, to buy off the blacks by giving them what they had been promised, but denied, for almost a century. The blacks would not be bought off.

The black strategists believed that to attack "separate-but-equal" on a school-by-school basis, as had happened with the graduate-school cases, would require decades to end segregation. Instead, they decided to attack the principle of segregation itself, arguing there could be no such thing as separate but equal, that the phrase was a contradiction in terms. Their plan to move through the federal courts brought the issue before the Supreme Court in the early 1950s. Of the five school-segregation cases the Supreme Court agreed to hear, one was from South Carolina, one each from Virginia, Delaware, the District of Columbia, and Kansas; this last was *Brown* v. *Board of Education.* When Thurgood Marshall and his staff prepared their briefs, they kept Felix Frankfurter in mind, certain that if they could answer his questions they could deal with all questions.

Frankfurter's role in the hearing and deciding the segregation cases is shrouded by the biases of the participants. "Felix Frankfurter was not the stage manager of the desegregation decision," said William Douglas to an interviewer some years after Frankfurter's death. "He opposed it." Chief Justice Warren, also some years after Frankfurter's death, evaluated Frankfurter's role this way: "No more, no less than everybody else. It was the most self-effacing job ever written there. Everyone was so conscious of the importance of it."

The justices were reluctant to issue an order bluntly commanding a change in the way of life for people living in one third of the states in the union. Would the order be obeyed? How could it be implemented? Would it be followed by violence? "Nothing is more important," Hugo Black commented once in conference, "Than that this court should not issue what it cannot enforce." Philip Elman, a former Frankfurter law clerk then working for the Justice Department, was involved in the case and said that in 1952, "There weren't five votes."

Robert Jackson spoke of the problems the justices faced: "What are we going to do to avoid the situation where in some districts everybody is perhaps held in contempt of court almost immediately because that judge has that disposition, and in some other districts it is twelve years before they get to a hearing?" This troubled other justices; some feared a massive resistance and others believed only a blunt order for immediate action would suffice. All were uncertain. "How to say and do as little as possible is my present desire," said Black in one conference discussion. Douglas said the Court should "not rush pronouncements." Frankfurter told Dean Acheson some years later that he had worked to block a too-early confrontation in the Court on desegregation, "which would, he thought, have produced a decision the other way," Acheson said.

Frankfurter's law clerk in the 1952–53 term, Alexander Bickel, recalled: "The main danger that [Frankfurter saw] was a decision which would be disobeyed, which would be the beginning rather than the end of a controversy. . . . His main purpose in the whole operation was to try to so devise things so that could not happen, or that that would happen in minimal fashion."

The Court heard three days of arguments in December 1952, and then the justices kept their silence until June 1953. Then the Court asked for rehearings, with arguments directed at five specific questions. Frankfurter had urged the rehearings, and his memorandum to Chief Justice Vinson, June 8, 1953, has the tone of the professor making certain that the student has prepared everything as planned. The five questions deliberately mystified.

Three were directed at whether the Fourteenth Amendment had intended to outlaw school segregation, to please the South; and two were directed at how a desegregation order would be implemented, to please the blacks. "Counsel were to be asked to address themselves to specific questions, concerning both merits and remedy," Frankfurter wrote Vinson. "By looking in opposite directions, the questions would not tip the mitt." The Attorney General would be invited to appear, and on and on. With each delay, there was time for more thought on implementation, more time for the concern within the Court to give way before the necessity for unanimity, more time for the nation to understand the decision was coming.

In September 1953, before the rearguments, Earl Warren replaced Vinson. Warren, unburdened by the concerns of the southerner and with a strong political background, understood immediately the need for unanimity in a decision as far-reaching as the desegregation decision promised to be. Using the goodwill that comes to any new Chief Justice and his own powers of persuasion, he determined that the Court would, in fact, end segregation, and do so unanimously. He found a Court in agreement that segregation should be ended but without a formula the justices could agree on, a formula that held out hope their decision would be a solution to a controversy, not the beginning of a new one.

"Only for those who have not the responsibility of decision is it easy to decide these cases," Frankfurter wrote in December 1953 after the rearguments. The comments were in a private memorandum, apparently his attempt to sort out his thoughts. There was something of the martyr in that sentence; others could not know the pain, only the judges. Still, he felt the pain; it was not imagined. He saw the necessity for separating the legal issue from the social and political issues. "It is not our duty to express our personal attitudes toward these issues however deep our individual convictions may be. The opposite is true. It is our duty not to express our merely personal views." But could a judge determine that blacks are inferior and segregation is proper? "To attribute such a view to science, as is sometimes done," Frankfurter scribbled, "is to reject the very basis of science."

The data from the social scientists, the psychologists, the educators produced by Thurgood Marshall had added up to a damning indictment of the impact of segregated education on the black child.

But what was the Court's justification for acting? For Frankfurter the answer came from Holmes and Brandeis. The first had talked about experience being the basis of law and the second about reasonableness being a proper test. Those two themes melded in Frankfurter's mind as he wrote the final paragraph of his thoughts.

The quality of laws enshrined in a constitution which was "made for an undefined and expanding future, and for a people gathered to and gathered from many nations and of many tongues" . . . is not a fixed formula defined with finality at a particular time. It does not reflect, as a congealed summary, the social arrangements and beliefs of a particular epoch. It is addressed to the changes wrought by time and not merely the changes that are the consequences of physical development. Law must respond to transformation of views as well as to that of outward circumstances.

He closed his memorandum to himself with these words:

The effect of changes in men's feelings for what is right and just is equally relevant in determining whether a discrimination denies the equal protection of the laws.

One month after the rearguments, in January 1954, Frankfurter sent a memorandum to the other justices. These were his own ideas, he said, but he hoped that "sometimes one's thinking, whether good or bad, may stimulate thoughts in others." First, he insisted that the Court not achieve integrated schools by lowering educational standards. Any decision for integrating the schools must be "promoting a process of social betterment and not contributing to social deterioration." He then argued that the Court could not "in a day" change a deplorable situation to an ideal one. The Court, said Frankfurter, "does its duty if it decrees measures that reverse the direction of the unconstitutional policy so as to uproot it 'with all deliberate speed.' "

The phrase "with all deliberate speed" had been used by Holmes in one decision, by Frankfurter in three decisions and then by Philip Elman in the government's *amicus curiae* brief filed in the desegregation cases. It meant that lower courts could adjust decisions to local conditions; it allowed school districts, supervised by local federal courts, to devise their own plans. The test of compliance would be good faith evidenced locally and not a time schedule set in Washington. This satisfied those who feared an order demanding immediate desegregation with its ensuing turmoil and those who objected to an order without a time limit with its possibility of being avoided. The bringing of the "all deliberate speed" formula was the major contribution of Felix Frankfurter to the desegregation process.

On May 17, 1954, at 12:49 P.M., in the Supreme Court's chamber, Chief Justice Warren began to read the *Brown* v. *Board of Education* decision. "Does segregation of children in public schools solely on the basis of race, even though the physical facilities and other 'tangible' factors may be equal, deprive the children of the minority group of equal educational opportunities?" Warren asked.

For the Supreme Court, he answered: "We believe that it does." The decision was unanimous.

To substantiate the Court's belief, Warren quoted the social scientists: "To separate [black schoolchildren] from others of similar age and qualifications solely because of their race generates a feeling of inferiority as to their status in the community that may affect their hearts and minds in a way unlikely ever to be undone . . . this finding is amply supported by modern authority." What we know as men, we cannot ignore as judges, the line once said in response to Brandeis, was said again this day.

One year later, on May 31, 1955, the Court issued its implementation decree. The first decision had been for the black schoolchildren; this second decision was for the school boards. They were allowed every consideration—public and private needs, administrative and physical plant problems, transportation and personnel, and others having to do with running a successful school system—in drawing up their plans for desegregating their schools. They were not allowed, however, any consideration that would thwart the intent of the 1954 *Brown* decision. They could not use racial criteria, gerrymander the districts for racial reasons, be influenced by "psychological factors." And the school boards must act "with all deliberate speed." This decision also was unanimous.

In effect, the Supreme Court had issued a two-part decision: the first in 1954 had branded segregation in public schools as unconstitutional and the second in 1955 said that the local school boards must act in good faith to end the practice, but that, given good faith, they could do it in their own time. That approach was aimed at producing compliance. There would be time for gradual change, education, public understanding of what was happening.

At first, compliance seemed possible, that the anticipated good faith would appear in the South. "I quite agree with you that Jimmy Byrnes has shown more good sense after the event than before it," Frankfurter wrote to Warren less than three months after the Court handed down its 1954 decision. Byrnes and Frankfurter had been close friends ever since Byrnes's one-year stint on the Supreme Court, and they had a long talk. "I have hopes," said Frankfurter of that talk, "that the sobriety of thought that he showed in his talk with me will continue to guide him in what is ahead of us." Frankfurter also was hearing from some of his lawyer friends in the South, especially through Monte Lemann in New Orleans. Lemann, said Frankfurter, "has been taking the lead in stirring a sense of responsibility on the part of leading Southern lawyers."

The reports were encouraging because if compliance was to happen the politicians and the lawyers must lead the way, explaining to the South that the law must be obeyed.

But there were negative developments also. "In the primaries of some of the state, segregation is exploited as a political issue," said Frankfurter.

The demagogues took over. Shouting "massive resistance," men whose names which were among the most distinguished in the South appealed to the worst of the southerners' prejudices and fears. Senator Harry F. Byrd of Virginia, perhaps the most respected of southern politicians, led that part of the nation against the desegregation order. Following the lead of Byrd and other admired southern politicians, new people, hoping for a vote in the next election, a quick trip to power and fame, shouted their opposition, vowed to block desegregation by standing in the schoolhouse door; some preached violence. Southern senators signed manifestos against the order. The news media in the South attacked it. State legislatures enacted resolutions "interposing" their sovereignty against that of the federal government. Southern lawyers generally were quiet or joined in preaching defiance of the law. The Supreme Court had avoided the blunt, frontal attack demanding immediate desegregation, hoping that, by allowing the all-deliberate-speed formula, the South would respond to the law with good faith. That did not happen, and the years following the desegregation decisions became America's worse time; promises denied, law scoffed at, educational institutions destroyed.

The south developed a variety of techniques to thwart the Supreme Court's decision. Public schools were abolished. Tuition grants for students attending private segregated schools were authorized. School district lines were redrawn. Legislation was enacted contradicting the Court. Schoolchildren were allowed "freedom of choice" in their school assignments, meaning whites could attend "white only" schools.

As the virulence of the southern opposition increased, the North became concerned. When Learned Hand made his concerns the theme of a lecture, Frankfurter wrote his old friend, "you cannot scare me," continuing:

I doubt very much whether in the end you would have held out against the decision in the *Segregation Cases*. On the basis of some of the activities that he manifested during the short single term that Jimmy Byrnes was on the Court, I am bold enough to believe that even Byrnes, had he stayed on the Court, would no more have dissented than Reed and Tom Clark dissented.

Behind it all was disrespect for the law. This bred violence. Going to an integrated school in the South for a black meant walking a gauntlet of jeering, threatening members of a mob.Obscenities were plentiful, school buildings destroyed, people's lives threatened. The nation was in the midst of a double revolution, a legal one brought on by the civil-rights activists and a violent one by those who refused to obey the law.

A turning point came in Little Rock, Arkansas, in the fall of 1957 when nine black students attempted to integrate the high school. "Where are the niggers? Let them try to get in," cried members of the mob around the school. "Oh, God," said one, "the niggers are in the school." Another howled: "The niggers are in our school!" Central High School in Little Rock eventually was integrated that fall, but only with federal troops standing guard. This was the first time since the Reconstruction Era after the Civil War that federal troops had gone into the South to protect the rights of black citizens. Southern politicians blustered, ranted, and threatened. But the troops stayed. The segregationist game was over.

The segregationists would not give up. Urged on by Governor Orval Faubus of Arkansas, they had created controversy and consternation, and the Little Rock school board attempted to push the situation away. In June 1958 an obliging federal judge called a halt to the school integration because of the "unfavorable community attitude." Two months later the case was argued before the Supreme Court, sitting in special session. Richard C. Butler, arguing for the school board, said integration was not working. Frankfurter seized on that statement.

Frankfurter: But what I want to know is if that plan was frustrated or obstructed not by any educational experience or, to the extent that there was educational experience, tension, etc., the causative factor, the real reason, was not anything due to the plan of the Board or the experience gained thereunder, but what happened through outside forces, isn't that correct?

. . . at no point is there any document in which they said, "We have now had experience, educational experience, and the plan which we matured and which began to be operative in the school year of '57, experience now shows us that educationally speaking, this is not a sound plan."

Butler: . . . the School Board was faced with certain realities.

Frankfurter: Yes, but those realities are attributable—if you are going to trace them to their causes, it wasn't any educational experience, it wasn't the feeling that you couldn't have colored children with white children, educationally speaking, but because of the intervention of outside force, forces were brought into play which obstructed that which they had so carefully planned. . . . You can't teach if you are going to have troops in the classroom. . . . But it wasn't the School Board that interjected the armed forces, was it?

Butler: No, sir. The School Board didn't ask for them.

At another point, Butler said that desegregation should be postponed until establishment of a clear national policy. That was too much for Frankfurter. "Why," he asked, "aren't the two decisions of this Court a national policy?"

Earl Warren joined in. "Suppose," he asked, "every other school board in the South said the same thing: 'We'll postpone this thing until the law is clarified.' How would it ever be clarified?" He continued: "Can we defer a program of this kind merely because there are elements in a community that will commit violence to prevent it from going into effect?" Violence or law. People must choose.

The Supreme Court ruled against any delay. In a decision, stronger than the original desegregation decision in 1954, the Court refused to accept the claim by Governor Faubus and the state legislature "that there is no duty on state officials to obey federal court orders." The Court conceded that desegregation might not be immediate in all localities, but where it was not, under the all-deliberate-speed approach, there should be arrangements "pointed toward the earliest practicable completion of desegregation." Constitutional rights, the Court insisted, "are not to be sacrificed or yielded to the violence and disorder." And to assure that local officials understood exactly what the Court meant, it added: "No state legislator or executive or judicial officer can war against the Constitution without violating his solemn oath to support it."

The decision, filed September 29, 1958, was signed by all nine justices, a unique act. Customarily in unanimous decisions, only the actual author of the decision signs it. But here the justices wanted to stress their unanimity, their agreement that the law must be obeyed—by governors, state legislators, school board members, everyone. Frankfurter had suggested the procedure.

Frankfurter filed a separate concurring opinion. This concerned his fellow justices because they feared it might detract from the Court's decision. To placate them, Frankfurter delayed a week before issuing his concurrence, until October 6.

He began by stating his "unreserved" support of the Court's decision but said he deemed it appropriate "to deal individually with the great issue here at stake." His separate opinion, much of it, retraced what the Court had said the week before. But, as Frankfurter later explained, he was now writing to a different audience: "the lawyers and the law professors of the South, and that is an audience which I was in a peculiarly qualified position to address in view of my rather extensive association, by virtue of my 25 years at the Harvard Law School, with a good many Southern lawyers and law professors." Frankfurter believed that the legal profession in the South had to lead that area out of the morass where it was wallowing.

Felix Frankfurter was now almost seventy-six years old; his public career spanned half a century. He had been many things in that career —activist in civil-liberties causes, gadabout in government, teacher of the law, adviser to presidents, fierce debater, judge. But those parts of his life faded as he spoke through his decision, and the years slipped away, leaving not the justice, not the professor, not the assistant secretary, but only the Jewish immigrant from Vienna walking down the gangplank of the S.S. *Marsala*, to a new world from an old one.

To bow to the request for postponing desegregation, Frankfurter wrote in his concurrence, means "that law should bow to force. To yield to such a claim would be to enthrone official lawlessness, and lawlessness if not checked is the precursor of anarchy." Didn't they understand, he seemed to be saying, that they wanted the way of the old world, the way of violence, of bloodshed, of might making right; the way of solving problems on the battlefield, of the taking of lives?

"Criticism need not be stilled," he wrote. "Active obstruction or defiance is barred. Our kind of society cannot endure if the controlling authority of the Law as derived from the Constitution is not to be the tribunal specially charged with the duty of ascertaining and declaring what is "the Supreme Law of the Land.' " Didn't they know their history? he seemed to be asking. Europe was a story of monarchies crumbling, of nations warring, of peoples caught between drives for power and possession. There was no cohesive force, and peoples trembled and ran before the threats of their more powerful neighbors. But in the United States there was a cohesive force. Law.

"The Constitution is not the formulation of the merely personal views of the members of this Court," continued Frankfurter, "nor can its authority be reduced to the claim that state officials are its controlling interpreters. Local customs, however hardened by time, are not decreed in heaven." Didn't they realize how law developed? Holmes had said it was experience. Brandeis had spoken of reasonableness. It was those two elements, plus a third which the Supreme Court had enunciated in the desegregation decision. That was decency. The three elements had come together not from the fantasies of the moment but from the traditions of the past. Frankfurter understood what happened when decency did not intertwine with experience and reasonableness. He had the example of Nazism, when law had been jettisoned by society, the example of his uncle Solomon Frankfurter and of the tragedy of the destruction of six million of his fellow Jews.

"The responsibility of those who exercise power in a democratic government," said Frankfurter, "is not to reflect inflamed public feeling but to help form its understanding." Did they not appreciate the choices before them? Frankfurter had written of the lawyer as the guardian of civilization: "The bar has not enjoyed prerogatives; it has been entrusted with anxious responsibilities . . . all interests of man that are comprised under the constitutional guarantees given to 'life, liberty and property' are in the professional keeping of lawyers. It is a fair characterization of the lawyer's responsibility in our society that he stands 'as a shield' . . . in defense of right and to ward off wrong." Lawyers must exercise those responsibilities, to speak up for the law, for nonviolence, for civilization. The Jewish immigrant perhaps better than anyone understood the alternative.

Frankfurter's role in the desegregation-decision process, as one of nine justices, was not sufficient to regain him his status with the liberal community, especially because of the position he took in the reapportionment cases. Where segregation was the social and moral scandal of the United States in the post–World War II years, malapportionment was the political scandal. Congressional and state-legislature districts were drawn to give power to sparsely populated areas at the expense of heavily populated areas. In 1946 voters in Illinois had sued to block a congressional election, saying they were denied the full effect of their vote because of malapportioned congressional districts. The districts had been established in 1901 on the basis of the 1900 census and their congressional representation had never changed, although the population of the areas had changed radically. Writing for the majority, Frankfurter said the Supreme Court would neither block the congressional election nor require the state to redraw the districts.

"It is hostile to a democratic system to involve the judiciary in the politics of the people . . . " he wrote. "Authority for dealing with such problems resides elsewhere." His critics charged he overlooked that "elsewhere" was the state legislature, which had consistently drawn the malapportioned congressional districts. Still, Frankfurter insisted, in one of his best-known lines, "Courts ought not to enter this political thicket."

In 1960, in a case dealing with districts malapportioned for racial reasons, to dilute the black vote, Frankfurter supported reapportionment, writing the Supreme Court's decision. As he worked on the decision with his brethren, Frankfurter stressed that the case was being decided on the racial aspect, and that he was not leading the Court into any "political thicket."

The following year, in *Baker* v. *Carr*, the Court entered that political thicket, and Frankfurter stayed outside. In Tennessee, the state legislature had not been reapportioned since 1901 although the population in the districts had shifted. The result was that urban voters were not properly represented in the rural-dominated legislature and efforts to have that legislature redistricted had failed. In a decision written by

Associate Justice William Brennan, once a student of Frankfurter's, the Supreme Court demanded that legislative and congressional districts be equal in population size. Across the nation, political lines were redrawn and political power shifted from rural to urban and suburban areas.

Frankfurter would have none of it and grumbled privately that the Court had held "a little judicial pregnancy is permissible." In conference, said Douglas, Frankfurter "felt very fervently that the remedy was at the political level, the level of legislative action, election of a Governor who would stand for those reforms and building up of the pressure on the legislature through public opinion, and so on, to do something about it." In his dissent, Frankfurter said, "Appeal must be to an informed, civically militant electorate. In a democratic society like ours, relief must come through an aroused public conscience that sears the conscience of the people's representatives."

So Frankfurter, the judicial activist in the desegregation cases, reverted to being the advocate of judicial restraint in the apportionment cases. Perhaps it was because he realized that the desegregation cases required a unanimous court. Perhaps because of his involvement in the 1946 Illinois case, he believed he was too identified with judicial restraint on the apportionment issue to change. Perhaps it was because while individuals may live by symbols—as Frankfurter enjoyed quoting Holmes—they should not become, as Frankfurter also said, captives of slogans, and because desegregation was the kind of issue that commanded new loyalties.

Whatever the reason, Frankfurter's position in *Baker* v. *Carr* was the position he and Brandeis had taken throughout much of their judicial lives: "The Court's authority—possessed of neither the purse nor the sword—ultimately rests on sustained public confidence in its moral sanction. . . . There is not under our Constitution a judicial remedy for every political mischief, for every undesirable exercise of power." Once that plea for judicial restraint had been a powerful liberal call, a plea not to have life dictated by a James McReynolds, a Pierce Butler, a George Sutherland.

But judicial restraint had passed out of favor, replaced by judicial activism, and Frankfurter, judicial restraint's most powerful exponent in the postwar years, passed out of favor with it. But, as attitudes changed once, they may again. In the late 1970s and early 1980s, a politically conservative Supreme Court charged in with its notions of right and wrong, going to the "wisdom of the act," in James McReynolds's phrase. Perhaps as that Court is judged and the nation has the opportunity to experience, as it did in the 1920s and 1930s, the other side of judicial activism, Felix Frankfurter's philosophy of judicial restraint—*"as judges we are neither Jew nor Gentile, neither Catholic nor agnostic . . . on becoming a Justice I did not take an oath to enforce 'the sense of right and justice of Felix Frankfurter' . . . there is not under our Constitution a judicial remedy for every political mischief"*—may come back in favor and Frankfurter with it. Perhaps.

Death did not come gracefully to Felix Frankfurter, nor did it come swiftly without pain and suffering. It squeezed from him more of the juices of life each day. He, being who and what he was, resisted. In November 1958 he had suffered a "mild heart disturbance" but, after a period of recuperation, returned to the Court. Almost four years later, on Thursday, April 5, 1962, at 4:30 in the afternoon, he was stricken while he was working at his office desk and rushed to George Washington University Hospital. The official announcement said he had suffered a mild stroke but his condition was more serious than that. On April 30, his doctors said that Frankfurter would not return to the Court that term, but "It is still anticipated that he will return for the next term."

A friend, the playwright S. N. Behrman, visited him in the hospital in May and reported: "He talked a blue streak and wonderfully as ever, but his diction is slightly impaired. He said that his doctors told him that the question of his survival will depend on him—on his will to live—that he must not think about the Court. He said that he will have to ' . . . reeducate certain muscles'—don't you love that phrase?"

Frankfurter, at seventy-nine, realized he soon would have to decide about his future on the Court. He was at home in the summer, and, according to his secretary, "His biggest thrill comes with a trip down to the dining room for breakfast and the morning paper. All of which is good therapeutics, of course." The "reeducation" process, however, did not progress well.

On Thursday, July 26, 1962, President John F. Kennedy visited Frankfurter in the garden of his Georgetown home. Frankfurter was excited about the visit but feared it was "an inspection." It was not; Kennedy came, he said, to seek Felix Frankfurter's advice "on the general trend of affairs." Frankfurter said his response had developed from the "many conversations which he had had during his illness with nurses, orderlies, doctors, and attendants at the hospital." And for forty-five minutes, as President Kennedy listened, the ailing, aged Felix

Frankfurter was once again advisor to presidents and bureaucratic swashbuckler cutting through the layers of Washington officialdom.

On August 22, Frankfurter wrote to a friend: "You will want to know that I have never worked harder at anything in my life than I have at the task toward recovery." It was not sufficient. In a letter dated August 28, 1962, Felix Frankfurter retired "from regular active service as an Associate Justice of the Supreme Court of the United States."

The President announced the resignation at his news conference the next day. There was an audible gasp from the reporters; a public career lasting more than half a century had ended. "Few judges have made as significant and lasting an impression upon the law," said President Kennedy. "Few persons have made so important a contribution to our legal tradition and literature."

A year later, President Kennedy notified Frankfurter he was to receive the Medal of Freedom, the highest civilian honor the nation can bestow. Frankfurter replied that it is "only by trying to convey to you my feelings about America and how they came to be almost religious feelings in their nature that I can tell you how deeply I feel the honor that you have bestowed on me."

On November 22, 1963, John F. Kennedy was assassinated and Frankfurter in a wheelchair attended the funeral. On December 5, 1963, President Lyndon B. Johnson wrote Frankfurter; "I need your help—I need your mind." Frankfurter, barely strong enough to hold a pen, scrawled in reply to his President: "Whatever strength is left in me is at the disposal of my country and therefore at your disposal."

Frankfurter lingered on. Sometimes strength returned and he insisted on having a dinner party for a friend passing through town or dictating a lengthy letter to Hugo Black about a pending case. But, each time his friends visited him, he seemed weaker than the last. His spoken English, in these last days, picked up the sound of his native Vienna. Garson Kanin, the playwright and director, was a close Frankfurter friend and wrote: "Now and again, for a few seconds, one could hear (perhaps even see?) that avid immigrant lad in the New York City of 1897 wandering about his new world, haunting the Cooper Union reading room, asking, asking, always asking, cultivating English as though it were a living thing to be wooed and won."

Marion Frankfurter, ill for some years, had rarely gone out of the house, often she did not leave her bedroom. Before his own illness, Frankfurter had been an attentive husband, refusing to go out in the evenings—"I leave her to normal loneliness at night only on the rarest occasions." After his retirement, they spent even more time chatting and having their meals together. On special days, they would go on an outing, and the driver recalled: "They'd sit there, y'know, riding along, and holding hands, these two lovely, I mean loving people—and he'd point things out like as she were a tourist and him a guide—he'd get all excited, y'know, the way he did—all *involved*— and she'd—well, you know, she'd make all the right sounds. Some fine days, he'd be like a little boy looking things over—every time like the first time—the Justice could do that, y'know."

Toward the end, when both were too weak to go outside, they had moved to an apartment where there were no stairs. In different rooms, they had to scrawl notes back and forth. Frankfurter wrote his "Darling Marion" that "If the Census Bureau had to make a census of the people who loved you, I'm sure their count would run into the hundreds." That "unceasing song" that he and Marion Denman had begun almost fifty years earlier still continued.

On February 21, 1965, Frankfurter was stricken again and taken to George Washington University Hospital. A few minutes after five o'-clock the next afternoon, George Washington's birthday, Frankfurter turned to an aide who had worked for him since he had joined the Court and said: "I hope I don't spoil your Washington's birthday." Then Felix Frankfurter turned his head and died. He was eighty-two.

As an associate justice, Felix Frankfurter had written 263 opinions, 171 concurrences, and 291 dissents. But his contribution was not in numbers. Said Earl Warren: "While so many others who are born here accept freedom as their birthright and fail to appreciate the necessity of guarding it zealously, he acted always as a sentinel on watch."

The memorial service was held in the apartment where the Frankfurters had been living. A hundred people attended, including the Supreme Court justices and the President of the United States. Paul Freund, Brandeis law clerk and Frankfurter friend, read, as Frankfurter had done at the service for Louis Brandeis, the section from *The Pilgrim's Progress* that speaks of the death of Mr. Valiant-for-Truth: "My sword I give to him that shall succeed me in my pilgrimage, and my courage and skill to him that can get it. My marks and scars I carry with me, to be a witness for me that I have fought his battles who now will be my rewarder."

Felix Frankfurter had never forgotten his Jewish origins and had specifically requested that a Jewish prayer be said at his death. "I came into the world a Jew and I want to leave it as a Jew," he insisted. Louis

Henkin, a former law clerk and orthodox Jew, read the Mourner's Prayer in Hebrew. The prayer has no words about death, none about a loved one's passing. Rather, the prayer speaks about the glory of God's name and asks, "May His great name be blessed forever and to all eternity." With this prayer, Jews affirm life, even in the midst of adversity.

The two readings said much about Felix Frankfurter's life, and that of Louis Brandeis. Despite "marks and scars," they had affirmed life, their lives. They had not denied their origins but reveled in them; turning from the melting-pot concept, they were among those who insisted, as Frankfurter said, that the United States "is the only country without a racially homogeneous population rooted to a particular soil. We represent a confluence of peoples who derive their bond of union from their common, intrinsic human qualities." They not only insisted on that statement's truth, but demonstrated that the United States was strengthened by that confluence.

And also despite "marks and scars," they had seized opportunities for service. However that service is evaluated—and given the length and impact of the Brandeis and Frankfurter careers, constant evaluation is required—one point is beyond question: They understood the responsibility of society. With Theodore Roosevelt and Charles Evans Hughes, Hugo Black and Al Smith, Franklin Roosevelt, and many others, they understood that government must respond to the needs of people, the wealthy and the poor, the native-born and the immigrant, the members of the established society and the outsider; that law, experience, and need must shape America.

That was their legacy to future generations, the task they imposed upon those who follow them—"My sword I give to him that shall succeed me in my pilgrimage, and my courage and skill to him that can get it." The specifics of their decisions and acts may not be the guides for the future, but behind the specifics are watchwords: restraint, experience, reasonableness, decency: watchwords important in the future as in the past. Present minorities will have new problems. There will be new minorities, continuing conflicts, new challenges. There always will be a need for the Louis Brandeis and the Felix Frankfurter.

Afterword

Louis Brandeis's wife, Alice Goldmark Brandeis, died in 1945. Both husband's and wife's ashes are interred beneath the steps of the Law School at the University of Louisville. Small plaques mark the spot. Their daughter, Susan Brandeis Gilbert, died in 1975, after a career as a lawyer in New York City; she had been a special assistant to the United States Attorney for the Southern District and a member of the State Board of Regents as well as being in private practice. Their second daughter, Elizabeth Brandeis Raushenbush, was, in 1983, living in retirement in Madison, Wisconsin, after a career as an economist at the University of Wisconsin.

Brandeis University at Waltham, Massachusetts, was founded after Justice Brandeis died as a means to remember and honor him. In the city of Louisville, where he was born and lived his early years, and at the University of Louisville, to which he contributed so much, there are no memorials to Louis Brandeis.

Marion Frankfurter, after her husband died, lived her remaining years in a nursing home. In 1972 news stories revealed that her husband had indeed, as he had promised his mother, never committed "vealth." His disdain for money had left his wife unable to pay her bills, and his former law clerks were contributing funds to prevent her from becoming a welfare case. As a result of that publicity Congress enacted a law giving widows of Supreme Court justices the first increase in pensions (from $5,000 to $10,000 a year) since 1937 and also liberalized their pension benefits to bring them in line with those available for widows of lower federal court judges. Marion Frankfurter died in 1975.

Acknowledgments

At Harper & Row Erwin A. Glikes suggested this book to me in 1979. Ann Harris nurtured the project, and Aaron Asher helped bring it to completion. My copy editor was Margaret Cheney. The late Frieda Fishbein was my agent.

The following persons read this book either in part or in its entirety, in one or more of its several forms, and offered suggestions, comments, and criticisms: David Baker, Liva Baker, J. Leonard Bates, Lawrence Bernstein, Frank Freidel, Dennis J. Hutchinson, James R. Ingram, Kenneth C. Judd, Morton A. Lebow, and David Wigdor.

Sara Baker, Charles H. Ball, Leonard P. Curry, and Marsha Rozenblit assisted me with my research.

The following persons allowed me to see the material cited: Mary Clark Dimond, the Grenville Clark papers at the Baker Memorial Library at Dartmouth College; Grant Gilmore, the Oliver Wendell Holmes, Jr., papers at the Harvard Law School; Ruth Gordon, her papers in the Manuscript Division at the Library of Congress; Gerald Gunther and Norris Darrell, the Learned Hand papers at the Harvard Law School; Robert P. Bass, Jr., the Robert P. Bass papers in the Baker Memorial Library at Dartmouth College; the Trustees of Columbia University in the City of New York, material from the Columbia Oral History Collection; Paul A. Freund, the Felix Frankfurter and Louis D. Brandeis papers at the Harvard Law School; the Harvard University Archives, the A. Lawrence Lowell papers; Stanley F. Reed, Jr., the Stanley F. Reed oral history at Columbia University.

The staff at the libraries and manuscript repositories listed in the sources were always helpful as well as gracious. In addition I would like to thank at the Library of Congress the staffs of the Research Facilities Office and the Law Library.

Sources

Interviews

Benjamin V. Cohen, Washington, DC; February 16, 1981
Norman Dorsen, New York; March 5, 1982
Philip Elman, Washington, DC; February 25, 1981
Fred N. Fishman, New York; May 7, 1981
Osmond K. Fraenkel, New York: May 5, 1981
Paul A. Freund, Cambridge, MA; July 17, 1981
Henry J. Friendly, New York; May 7, 1981
Ruth Gordon, New York; May 12, 1982
Erwin N. Griswold, Washington, DC; July 21, 1982
Louis Henkin, New York; May 6, 1981
Alger Hiss, New York; May 26, 1982
Garson Kanin, New York; May 12, 1982
Andrew L. Kaufman, Cambridge, MA; July 6, 1981
Harry K. Mansfield, Boston; July 22, 1981
John H. Mansfield, Cambridge, MA; July 21, 1981
Donald G. Morgan, Mount Holyoke, MA; August 18, 1981
Joseph L. Rauh, Jr., Washington, DC; March 10, 1981
Gerald D. Reilly, Washington, DC; May 13, 1981
Elliot L. Richardson, Washington, DC; August 17, 1982
David Riesman, Jr., Cambridge, MA; August 7, 1981
Albert J. Rosenthal, New York; May 6, 1981
Seymour J. Rubin, Washington, DC; February 18, 1981
Albert M. Sacks, Cambridge, MA; July 10, 1981
Frank E. A. Sander, Cambridge, MA; August 5, 1981
Albert E. Stephan, Seattle, WA; December 5, 1980 (by telephone)
Donald T. Trautman, Cambridge, MA; August 4, 1981

Manuscript Collections

American Jewish Archives, Cincinnati, OH
  Adath Israel Congregation
  David Werner Senator
  Jacob H. Schiff

American Jewish Historical Society, Waltham, MA
  Louis D. Brandeis
  Stephen S. Wise

Brandeis University, Special Collections Department; Waltham, MA
  Louis D. Brandeis

Catholic University of America, Mullen Library, Department of Archives and Manuscripts; Washington, DC
  John A. Ryan

Dartmouth College, Baker Library; Hanover, NH
  Robert P. Bass
  Grenville Clark

Filson Club, Louisville, KY
  Louisville Male High School Records
  Joseph Rauch

Franklin D. Roosevelt Library, Hyde Park, NY
  Governor's Papers/Private Correspondence
  President's Official File
  President's Personal File
  President's Secretary's File

  Adolf A. Berle, Jr.
  Francis Biddle
  Mary Dewson
  Gardner Jackson
  Henry Morgenthau, Sr.
  Samuel I. Rosenman
  Rexford G. Tugwell
  Louis Brandeis Wehle

Harvard Law School, Cambridge, MA; Archives Division
  American Bar Association Bill of Rights Committee
  Louis D. Brandeis
  C. C. Burlingham
  Zechariah Chafee
  Grenville Clark (Felix Frankfurter addenda)
  "Conversations between L. D. B. and F. F.," in Brandeis Papers:
    114 (7–8), unpaged
  Herbert B. Ehrmann
  Felix Frankfurter
  Harvard Law School Association
  Oliver Wendell Holmes, Jr.
  Calvert Magruder
  John M. Maguire
  Roscoe Pound
  Thomas Reed Powell
  Pow Wow Club
  Austin W. Scott
  Charles Wyzanski, Jr.
  Meyer A. Zelig

Library of Congress, Washington, DC; Manuscript Room
  Joseph and Stewart Alsop
  Ray Stannard Baker
  Wendell Berge
  Hugo L. Black
  Louis D. Brandeis
  Harold H. Burton
  Homer S. Cummings, Diaries
  Josephus Daniels
  William R. Day
  William O. Douglas
  Herbert Feis
  Walter L. Fisher
  Felix Frankfurter
  Felix Frankfurter Family Collection
  Felix Frankfurter/Zionist File/Hebrew University (microfilm)
  Emanuel A. Goldenweiser
  Pauline D. Goldmark

Ruth Gordon
Thomas Watt Gregory
Charles S. Hamlin
Benjamin W. Huebsch
Charles Evans Hughes
Harold Ickes, Diaries (manuscripts)
Garson Kanin
John A. Kingsbury
La Follette Family
Ben B. Lindsay
Archibald MacLeish
Agnes Meyer
Eugene Meyer
George Middleton
Henry Morgenthau, Sr.
Victor Murdoch
National Association for the Advancement of Colored People (NAACP)
National Consumers' League
Reinhold Niebuhr
Gifford Pinchot
Donald R. Richberg
Theodore Roosevelt
Wiley B. Rutledge
Harlan Fiske Stone
George Sutherland
William Howard Taft
Huston Thompson
Willis Van Devanter
Carl S. Vrooman
Charles Warren
William Allen White
Woodrow Wilson
Robert W. Woolley

National Archives, Washington, DC
  Justice Department, Bureau of Investigation
  War Labor Policies Board

Princeton University, Princeton, NJ; Seeley G. Mudd Manuscript
Library
  American Civil Liberties Union
  John Marshall Harlan
  David E. Lilienthal

Radcliffe College, Cambridge, MA; Schlesinger Library
  Elizabeth Glendower Evans

University of Louisville: University Archives and Records
  Louis D. Brandeis
  Jewish Community Center
  Israel T. Naamani

University of Virginia, Charlottesville, VA; Alderman Library,
Manuscript Division
  Homer S. Cummings

John Knox, "Experiences as Law Clerk to Mr. Justice James C. McReynolds"
James C. McReynolds
Yale University, New Haven, CT; Sterling Memorial Library, Manuscripts and Archives
Jerome N. Frank
Edward M. House
Walter Lippmann
Henry L. Stimson
Harry Weinberger

Oral Histories

American Jewish Archives
Bernard A. Rosenblatt
Columbia University
George W. Alger
Paul H. Appleby
Thurman Arnold
Roger Nash Baldwin
C. C. Burlingham
Marquis W. Childs
James Freeman Curtis
John W. Davis
William H. Davis
Guy S. Ford
Felix Frankfurter
Edward S. Greenbaum
Learned Hand
Quincy Howe
Gardner Jackson
Robert H. Jackson
Alvin Johnson
Nicholas Kelley
Arthur Krock
James M. Landis
Chester T. Lane
Herbert H. Lehman
John Lord O'Brian
Robert Lincoln O'Brien
Stanley F. Reed
Bernard G. Richards
George Rublee
Walter E. Sachs
William Jay Schieffelin
Rexford Tugwell
James T. Williams Jr.
Franklin D. Roosevelt Library, Hyde Park, NY
Adolf A. Berle, Jr.
Lyndon B. Johnson Library, Austin, TX
Thruston B. Morton
Princeton University, Princeton, N.J.; Seeley G. Mudd Manuscript Library
William O. Douglas

University of Louisville, University Archives and Records Center
  Doni Greenebaum
  Suzanne Hamel
  Clarence F. Judah
  Charles Tachau
  Eric Tachau

Other Unpublished Sources

Letters to the author from James E. Bond, Keith E. Eiler, John P. Frank, Gerald Gunther,
          Willard Hurst, Lewis H. Weinstein, and Elizabeth Weiss.
Liva Baker, author of *Felix Frankfurter,* published in 1969, made much of her research
          available to me.
James K. Hall of the Federal Bureau of Investigation provided me with the material in
          the Bureau's files about Felix Frankfurter, following my request under
          the Freedom of Information Act.

Published Materials

ABA *Journal,* Chicago, IL
Acheson, Dean. *Morning and Noon,* London edition, 1967.
————. *Present at the Creation,* NY, 1969.
————. "Reminiscences of a Supreme Court Law Clerk," *Pittsburgh Legal Journal,* Pitts-
          burgh, PA, January 29, 1955, pp. 3–9.
Adams, J. Donald. *Copey of Harvard,* Boston, 1960.
Adler, Cyrus. *Jacob H. Schiff: His Life and Letters,* NY, 1928.
Adler, Jacob. "The Morgenthau Mission of 1917," *Herzl Year Book,* NY, v. 5, 1963.
The American Hebrew, NY.
The American Review of Reviews, NY.
Anderson, Mary. *Woman at Work,* Minneapolis, 1951.
Andrews, Fannie Fern. *The Holy Land Under Mandate,* Boston, 1931.
Auerbach, Jerold S. *Unequal Justice,* NY, 1976.
Baker, Leonard. *Back to Back—The Duel Between FDR and the Supreme Court,* NY,
          1967.
————. *Days of Sorrow and Pain,* NY, 1978.
————. *John Marshall—A Life in Law,* NY, 1974.
————. *Roosevelt and Pearl Harbor,* NY, 1970.
Baker, Liva. *Felix Frankfurter,* NY, 1969.
Baruch, Bernard M. *The Public Years,* NY, 1960.
Berle, Adolf A., Jr. *Navigating the Rapids 1918–1971—From the Papers of Adolf A. Berle,*
          NY, 1973.
Bernick, Michael. "Benjamin Cardozo: A Judge Most Eminent," ABA *Journal,* May 1979,
          p. 718.
Boston *American,* Boston, MA.
Boston *Globe,* Boston, MA.
Boston *Herald,* Boston, MA.
Boston *Post,* Boston, MA.
Bowen, Catherine Drinker. *Adventures of a Biographer,* Boston, 1959.
Black, Hugo L. *A Constitutional Faith,* NY, 1968.
Black, Hugo, Jr. *My Father: A Remembrance,* NY, 1975.
"Brandeis and Lamont on Finance Capitalism" (Paul B. Abrahams, ed.), *Business History
          Review,* Spring 1973, pp. 72–94.

Brandeis, Frederika Dembitz. "Reminiscences of Frederika Dembitz Brandeis," privately printed.

Brandeis, Louis D. *Business—A Profession,* NY, 1971, ed.

———. *The Curse of Bigness* (Osmond K. Fraenkel, ed.), NY, 1934.

———. "The Harvard Law School," *The Green Bag,* 1889, pp. 10–25.

———. "The Living Law, *Illinois Law Review,* February 1916, pp. 461–71.

———. *Other People's Money,* NY, 1932.

———. "True Americanism," Boston, 1915.

———. "Workingmen's Insurance—The Road to Social Efficiency," *The Outlook,* June 10, 1911, pp. 291–94.

Brennan, William J., Jr., *An Affair with Freedom,* NY, 1967.

Brewer, David J. "The Nation's Safeguard," *Report of the New York State Bar Association,* January 1893.

Broderick, Francis L. *Right Reverend New Dealer—John A. Ryan,* NY, 1963.

Brown, John Mason. "The Uniform of Justice," *Saturday Review,* October 30, November 6, November 13, 1954.

Burns, James MacGregor. *Roosevelt: The Lion and the Fox,* NY, 1956.

Byrnes, J. F. *All in One Lifetime,* NY, 1958.

Cardozo Law Review, NY.

Carter, John Franklin. *The New Dealers,* NY, 1975 ed.

Chafee, Zechariah, Jr. "Thirty-Five Years with Freedom of Speech," *University of Kansas Law Review,* November 1952, pp. 1–36.

Chamberlain, John. "The Nine Young Men," *Life,* January 22, 1945, p. 76.

Childs, Marquis W. "Minority of One," *Saturday Evening Post,* September 20, 1941.

———. "The Supreme Court Today," *Harper's,* May 1938, pp. 581–88.

———. *Witness to Power,* NY, 1975.

Choate, Joseph H. *Abraham Lincoln and Other Addresses in England,* NY, 1910.

Clapper, Raymond. "Felix Frankfurter's Young Men," *Review of Reviews,* January 1936, pp. 27 ff.

Clark, Kenneth. *The Other Half,* NY, 1978.

Collins, Ronald L. and Friesen, Jennifer. "Looking Back: *Muller* v. *Oregon* Seventy-Five Years Later," ABA *Journal,* March 1983, author's ms.

Cotter, Arundel. *The Gary I Knew,* Boston, MA, 1928.

Cox, Archibald. *The Role of the Supreme Court in American Government,* NY, 1976.

———. *The Warren Court,* Cambridge, MA, 1968.

Cuff, Robert D. *The War Industries Board,* Baltimore, 1973.

Danelski, David J., and Tulchin, Joseph S., editors. *The Autobiographical Notes of Charles Evan Hughes,* Cambridge, MA, 1973.

Daniels, Josephus. *The Wilson Era: Years of Peace,* Chapel Hill, NC, 1944.

———. *The Wilson Era: Years of War and After,* Chapel Hill, NC, 1946.

Dash, Joan. *Summoned to Jerusalem—The Life of Henrietta Szold,* NY, 1980.

Dawson, Nelson L. *Louis D. Brandeis, Felix Frankfurter, and the New Deal,* Hamden, CT, 1980.

Deering, Richard. *Louisville: Her Commercial, Manufacturing and Social Advantages,* Louisville, KY, 1859.

De Haas, Jacob. "Brandeis," *The Jewish Outlook,* November 1936.

———. *Louis D. Brandeis,* NY, 1929.

Dembitz, Lewis N. "Jewish Beginnings in Kentucky," *Proceedings of the American Jewish Historical Society,* 1893, pp. 99–101.

De Toledano, Ralph. *J. Edgar Hoover,* New Rochelle, NY, 1973.

Donovan, Robert J., *Tumultuous Years,* NY, 1982.

Dorough, C. Dwight. *Mr. Sam,* NY, 1962.

Douglas, William O. *The Court Years,* NY, 1980.

———. *Go East, Young Man,* NY, 1974, paperback ed.

Duffus, R. L. "Felix Frankfurter: The Man Behind the Legend," *NY Times Magazine,* January 15, 1939, p. 3.

Dugdale, Blanche E. C. *Arthur James Balfour,* London, 1936.

Dunne, Gerald T. *Hugo Black and the Judicial Revolution,* NY, 1977.

Ehrenfried, Albert. "A Chronicle of Boston Jewry," 1963 (typescript in Library of Congress).

Ehrmann, Herbert B. *The Case That Will Not Die,* Boston, 1969.

Eisenhower, Dwight D. *Mandate for Change,* NY, 1963.

Eliot, Charles W.; Storey, Moorfield; Brandeis, Louis D.; Rodenbeck, Adolph J.; and Pound, Roscoe. "Preliminary Report on Efficiency in the Administration of Justice," Boston, 1914.

Elliott, Sheldon D. "Court Curbing Proposals in Congress," *Notre Dame Lawyer,* August 1958, p. 597.

Evans, Elizabeth Glendower. "People I Have Known—Louis D. Brandeis, Tribune of the People," *La Follette's Magazine,* December 1926.

———. "The Story of Louis D. Brandeis," *The Jewish Advocate,* November 13, 1931.

Fehrenbacher, Don. *The Dred Scott Case,* NY, 1978.

Forcey, Charles. *The Crossroads of Liberalism,* NY, 1961.

Frank, John P. "The Legal Ethics of Louis D. Brandeis," *Stanford Law Review,* April 1965, pp. 683–709.

———. *Marble Palace—The Supreme Court in American Life,* Westport, CT, 1972 ed.

"Felix Frankfurter—Talks in Tribute," Cambridge, MA, 1965.

Frankfurter, Felix. *The Case of Sacco and Vanzetti,* NY, 1962 ed.

———. "The Conditions for, and the Aims and Methods of Legal Research," *Iowa Law Review,* February 1930.

———. *Felix Frankfurter Reminisces,* NY, 1962.

———. "Hours of Labor and Realism in Constitutional Law," *Harvard Law Review,* February 1916, pp. 353–73.

———. "The Job of a Supreme Court Justice," *NY Times,* November 28, 1954, VI, p. 4.

———. "The Law and the Law Schools," *Report of the American Bar Association,* 1915, pp. 365–73.

———. *Law and Politics,* NY, 1962 ed.

———. "Memorandum on 'Incorporation' of the Bill of Rights into the Due Process Clause of the Fourteenth Amendment," *Harvard Law Review,* February 1965, pp. 746–83.

———. *Mr. Justice Brandeis,* Yale, 1932.

———. *Mr. Justice Holmes and the Supreme Court,* NY, 1965 ed.

———. "The Palestine Situation Restated," *Foreign Affairs,* NY, April 1931.

———. "Report of the President's Mediation Commission to the President of the United States," Washington, DC, January 9, 1918.

———. "The Supreme Court in the Mirror of Justices," *Vital Speeches,* May 1, 1957.

Freedman, Max, ed. *Roosevelt and Frankfurter,* Boston, 1967.

Freidel, Frank. "Election of 1932," in *History of American Presidential Elections 1789–1968,* NY, 1971.

———. *Franklin D. Roosevelt: Launching the New Deal,* Boston, 1973.

Freund, Paul A. "Felix Frankfurter (1882–1965)," written for the *American Jewish Year Book,* reprint courtesy of P. A. Freund.

——. "Justice Brandeis: A Law Clerk's Remembrance," written for American Jewish History, copy courtesy of P. A. Freund.

——. "Mr. Justice Brandeis: A Centennial Memoir," *Harvard Law Review*, March 1957, pp. 769–92.

Friedman, Leon, and Israel, Fred L., eds. *The Justices of the United States Supreme Court 1789–1969*, NY, 1969.

Fuchs, Lawrence H. "Election of 1928," in *History of American Presidential Elections 1789–1968*, NY, 1971.

Fuess, Claude M. *Joseph B. Eastman—Servant of the People*, NY, 1952.

Gal, Allon. *Brandeis of Boston*, Cambridge, MA, 1980.

Gary, Elbert H. "Looking Forward by Looking Backward Twenty Years," January 1923.

Gengarelly, W. A. "The Abrams Case," *Boston Bar Journal*, March 1981, pp. 19–24.

Gilbert, Martin. *Winston S. Churchill*, London, 1975.

Gilbreth, Frank B. *Primer of Scientific Management*, NY, 1912.

Gilkey, Royal C. "Felix Frankfurter and the Oregon Maximum Hour Case," *University of Missouri at Kansas City Law Review*, Winter 1967, pp. 149–56.

——. "Felix Frankfurter's Role as a Progressive," *The University of Missouri at Kansas City Law Review*, Summer 1965, pp. 265–75.

——. "Felix Frankfurter's Years of Preparation," *The University of Missouri at Kansas City Law Review*, Summer 1964, pp. 322–28.

——. "Frankfurter's Career as a Law Officer," *The University of Missouri at Kansas City Law Review*, Winter 1965, pp. 61–67.

Goldmark, Josephine. *Fatigue and Efficiency*, NY, 1912.

——. *Impatient Crusader—Florence Kelley's Life Story*, Urbana, IL, 1953.

——. *Pilgrims of '48*, NY, 1975 ed.

——. and Hopkins, Mary D. "Comparison of an Eight-Hour Plant and a Ten-Hour Plant," *Public Health Bulletin* No. 106, Washington, DC, February 1920.

Gunther, Gerald. "Learned Hand and Felix Frankfurter: Their Correspondence, Relationship—and Personality Differences," a lecture, April 20, 1977, courtesy of G. Gunther.

Gwynn, Stephen. *The Letters and Friendships of Sir Cecil Spring Rice*, Westport, CT, 1971 ed.

Hamilton, Walton. "Preview of a Justice," *Yale Law Journal*, March 1939, pp. 819–38.

Handlin, Oscar. *The Uprooted*, Boston, 1951.

Hapgood, Norman. *The Changing Years*, NY, 1930.

——. "Justice Brandeis: Apostle of Freedom," *The Nation*, October 5, 1927, pp. 330–31.

Harbaugh, William H. *Lawyer's Lawyer—The Life of John W. Davis*, NY, 1978, paperback ed.

Harlan, John Marshall. *Manning the Dikes*, NY, 1958.

Harvard Law Review, Cambridge, MA.

Harvard Law School *Bulletin*, Cambridge, MA.

Hays, Samuel P. *Conservation and the Gospel of Efficiency*, NY, 1969 ed.

Hellman, George S. *Benjamin N. Cardozo—American Judge*, NY, 1940.

Hirsch, H. N. *The Enigma of Felix Frankfurter*, NY, 1981.

A History of the Jews of Louisville, KY, New Orleans, LA, undated but circa 1900.

Hofstadter, Samuel H. "Louis Dembitz Brandeis," ABA *Journal*, October 1961, pp. 978–80.

Holmes, Oliver Wendell, Jr. *The Common Law*, Boston, 1882.

Hoover, Herbert. *Memoirs*, NY, 1951–52.

Hourwich, Isaac A. *Immigration and Labor*, NY, 1912.

House, Edward Mandell. *The Intimate Papers of Colonel House*, Boston, 1926.

Howe, Mark DeWolfe, ed. *Holmes-Laski Letters,* Cambridge, MA, 1953.

———, ed., *Holmes-Pollock Letters,* Cambridge, MA, 1941.

Hughes, Charles Evans. *The Supreme Court of the United States,* NY, 1966, paperback ed.

Hutchinson, Dennis J. "Felix Frankfurter and the Business of the Supreme Court, O.T. 1946–O.T. 1961," *Supreme Court Review,* 1980, pp. 143–209.

———. "Unanimity and Desegregation: Decision Making in the Supreme Court, 1948–1958," 68 *Georgetown Law Journal* 1.

Irons, Peter H. "Fighting Fair," *Harvard Law Review,* April 1981.

Isenburgh, Max. "Frankfurter as a Policymaker," *Yale Law Review,* December 1975, pp. 280–98.

Jackson, Robert H. *The Supreme Court in the American System of Government,* Cambridge, MA, 1955.

Jacobsohn, Gary J. "Felix Frankfurter and the Ambiguities of Judicial Statesmanship," *New York University Law Review,* April 1974, pp. 1–44.

Jaffe, Louis L. "The Court Debated—Another View," *NY Times,* VI, June 6, 1960, p. 35.

Johnson, Hugh S. "Think Fast, Captain!" *Saturday Evening Post,* October 26, 1935, p. 5.

Johnson, Walter, ed., *Selected Letters of William Allen White,* NY, 1968 ed.

Josephson, Matthew. "Jurist," *The New Yorker,* NY, November 30, December 7, December 14, 1940.

Kahn, Harry J. "Zionism Before and With Brandeis," *B'Nai Zion Voice,* November 1936, pp. 4–5.

Kallen, Horace M. *Of Them Which Say They Are Jews,* NY, 1959.

Kanin, Garson. "FF Toward the End," *Virginia Law Review,* v. 51, number 4, typescript courtesy of Garson Kanin.

———. "Trips to Felix," *Atlantic Monthly,* Boston, March 1964, typescript courtesy of Garson Kanin.

Katz, Irving. "Henry Lee Higginson vs. Louis Dembitz Brandeis: A Collision Between Tradition and Reform," *New England Quarterly,* March 1968, pp. 67–81.

Kerney, James. *The Poltical Education of Woodrow Wilson,* NY, 1926.

King, Willard L. *Melville Weston Fuller,* Chicago, 1967 ed.

Kluger, Richard. *Simple Justice,* NY, 1976.

Konefsky, Samuel J. "Justice Frankfurter and the Conscience of a Constitutional Judge," *Brooklyn Law Review,* April 1965, pp. 213–19.

Korn, Bertram W. *American Jewry and the Civil War,* NY, 1970.

———. "German-Jewish Intellectual Influences on American Jewish Life, 1824–1972," B. G. Rudolph Lecture in Judaic Studies for 1972.

Kraut, Benny. *From Reform Judaism to Ethical Culture: The Religious Evolution of Felix Adler,* Cincinnati, OH, 1979.

Kurland, Philip B., and Casper, Gerhard, eds. *Landmark Briefs and Arguments of the Supreme Court of the United States: Constitutional Law,* Washington, DC, 1978.

La Follette, Belle and Fola. *Robert M. La Follette,* NY, 1953.

Landis, J. M. "The Legislative History of the Securities Act of 1933," *George Washington Law Review,* October 1959.

———. "Mr. Justice Brandeis and the Harvard Law School," 55 *Harvard Law Review* 184.

Lash, Joseph P. *Eleanor Roosevelt—A Friend's Memoir,* NY, 1964.

———, ed., *From the Diaries of Felix Frankfurter,* NY, 1975.

Levy, David W. "The Lawyer as Judge: Brandeis' View of the Legal Profession," *Oklahoma Law Review,* November 1969, pp. 374–95.

———— and Murphy, Bruce A. "Preserving the Progressive Spirit in a Conservative Time: The Joint Reform Efforts of Justice Brandeis and Professor Felix Frankfurter, 1916–1933," *Michigan Law Review,* August 1980.

Lewis, Anthony. *Portrait of a Decade: The Second American Revolution,* NY, 1964.

Lief, Alfred. *Brandeis,* Freeport, NY, 1971 ed.

————, ed., *The Brandeis Guide to the Modern World,* Boston, 1941.

————. *Democracy's Norris,* NY, 1939.

Link, Arthur S. *Wilson: Campaigns for Progressivism and Peace 1916–1917,* Princeton, NJ, 1965.

————. *Wilson: Confusions and Crises 1915–1916,* Princeton, NJ, 1964.

————. *Wilson: The New Freedom,* Princeton, NJ, 1956.

————. *Wilson: The Road to the White House,* Princeton, NJ, 1947.

————. *Wilson: The Struggle for Neutrality 1914–1915,* Princeton, NJ, 1960.

Lipsky, Louis. "Early Days of American Zionism, 1897–1929," *Palestine Year Book,* NY, v. 2, 1945–46.

————. *A Gallery of Zionist Profiles,* NY, 1956.

————. *Thirty Years of American Zionism,* NY, 1977 ed.

Louisville *Courier-Journal,* Louisville, KY

Love, Albert, and Childers, James Saxon. *Listen to Leaders in Law,* Atlanta, 1963.

McAdoo, William G. *Crowded Years,* Boston, 1931.

McKay, Robert B. " 'With All Deliberate Speed'—A Study of School Desegregation," *New York University Law Review,* June 1956, pp. 990–1090.

McKelway, A. J. "Child Labor in the South," *Annals of the American Academy of Political and Social Science,* Philadelphia, PA, January 1910.

McLean, Joseph E. *William Rufus Day,* Baltimore, MD, 1946.

McLellan, David S. and Acheson, David C., eds. *Among Friends—Personal Letters of Dean Acheson,* NY, 1980.

MacLeish, Archibald. "Felix Frankfurter: A Lesson of Faith," *Supreme Court Review,* 1966, pp. 1–6.

————. "Mr. Justice Frankfurter," *Life Magazine,* NY, February 12, 1940.

Manuel, Frank E. *The Realities of American-Palestine Relations,* Washington, DC, 1949.

Marcus, Maeva. *Truman and the Steel Seizure Case,* NY, 1977.

Martin, Albro. *Enterprise Denied,* NY, 1971.

Martin, Kingsley. *Harold Laski,* NY, 1953.

Mason, Alpheus Thomas. *Brandeis—A Free Man's Life,* NY, 1946.

————. *The Brandeis Way,* Princeton, NY, 1938.

————. *Bureaucracy Convicts Itself,* NY, 1941.

————. *Harlan Fiske Stone: Pillar of the Law,* NY, 1956.

————. "Louis Dembitz Brandeis: Tempered Boldness in a Stand-Pat Society," *University of Pittsburgh Law Review,* March 1967, pp. 421–46.

————. *The Supreme Court from Taft to Burger,* Baton Rouge, LA, 1979 ed.

————. *William Howard Taft: Chief Justice,* NY, 1965.

Mayer, Martin. *Emory Buckner,* NY, 1968.

Mendelson, Wallace. *Felix Frankfurter: A Tribute,* NY, 1968.

————. *Justice Black and Frankfurter: Conflict in the Court,* Chicago, 1961.

Merwick, Donna. *Boston Priests, 1848–1910,* Cambridge, MA, 1973.

Middleton, George. *These Things Are Mine,* NY, 1947.

Moley, Raymond. *After Seven Years,* NY, 1972 ed.

————, (assisted by Elliot A. Rosen). *The First New Deal,* NY, 1966.

Morgenthau, Henry. *Ambassador Morgenthau's Story,* NY, 1918.

Morison, Elting E. *Turmoil & Tradition,* NY, 1966, paperback ed.

Morison, Samuel Eliot. *Three Centuries of Harvard,* Cambridge, MA, 1946 ed.

Morris, Edmund. *The Rise of Theodore Roosevelt,* NY, 1979.

Morris, Jeffrey B. "The American Jewish Judge: An Appraisal on the Occasion of the Bicentennial," *Jewish Social Studies,* Summer-Fall 1976, pp. 195–223.

Murphy, Bruce A. *The Brandeis-Frankfurter Connection,* NY, 1982.

———. "Elements of Extrajudicial Strategy: A Look at the Political Roles of Justices Brandeis and Frankfurter," *Georgetown Law Journal,* October 1980, pp. 101–32.

Nathan, Maud. *The Story of an Epoch-Making Movement,* NY, 1926.

The Nation, NY.

National Commission on Law Observance and Enforcement (Wickersham Commission), *Reports,* Washington, DC, 1931.

Neuberger, Richard L., and Kahn, Stephen B. *Integrity—The Life of George W. Norris,* NY, 1937.

The New Palestine, Washington, DC.

The New Republic, Washington, DC and NY.

New York Times, NY.

Norris, George W. *Fighting Liberal,* NY, 1945.

Nutter, McClennen & Fish—The First Century 1879–1979, Boston, 1979.

Oppenheimer, Robert. "Niels Bohr and Atomic Weapons," *New York Review of Books,* December 17, 1964, pp. 6–8.

The Outlook, NY.

Paper, Lewis J. *Brandeis,* Englewood Cliffs, NJ, 1983.

Parrish, Michael E. *Felix Frankfurter and His Times: The Reform Years,* NY, 1982.

Parzen, Herbert. "Brandeis and the Balfour Declaration," *Herzl Year Book,* NY, v. 5, 1963.

Paschal, Joel Francis. *Mr. Justice Sutherland,* NY, 1969 ed.

Peabody, James B., ed., *The Holmes-Einstein Letters,* NY, 1960.

Penick, James L., Jr. *Progressive Politics and Conservation,* Chicago, 1968.

Pepper, George Wharton. *Philadelphia Lawyer,* NY, 1944.

Percy, Eustace. *Some Memories,* London, 1958.

Perkins, Frances. *The Roosevelt I Knew,* NY, 1964 ed.

Pinchot, Gifford. *Breaking New Ground,* NY, 1947.

Portland *Oregonian,* Portland, OR.

Pringle, Henry F. *The Life and Times of William Howard Taft,* NY, 1939.

———. *Theodore Roosevelt,* NY, 1931.

Pritchett, C. Herman. *The Roosevelt Court,* NY, 1948.

"Proceedings in Honor of Mr. Justice Frankfurter and Distinguished Alumni," Cambridge, MA, 1960.

Pusey, Merlo J. *Charles Evans Hughes,* NY, 1951.

Radcliffe Quarterly, Cambridge, MA.

Rauh, Joseph L., Jr., "Felix Frankfurter: Civil Libertarian," *Harvard Civil Rights–Civil Liberties Law Review,* Summer 1976, pp. 496–520.

Raushenbush, Paul A. "Starting Unemployment Compensation in Wisconsin," *Unemployment Insurance Review,* April-May 1967, pp. 17–24.

Ritchie, Donald A. *James M. Landis,* Cambridge, MA, 1980.

Roberts, Owen J. *The Court and the Constitution,* Cambridge, MA, 1951.

Robinson, Edgar Eugene. *The Presidential Vote 1896–1932,* Stanford, CA, 1934.

Rodell, Fred. "Felix Frankfurter, Conservative," *Harper's Magazine,* October 1941, pp. 449–59.

Rodgers, Daniel T. *The Work Ethic in Industrial America 1850–1920*, Chicago, 1978.

Rosenfield, Leonora Cohen. *Portrait of a Philosopher: Morris R. Cohen in Life and Letters*, NY, 1962.

Rosovsky, Henry. "From Periphery to Center," *Harvard Magazine*, Cambridge, MA, November–December 1979.

Rostow, Eugene V. "The Democratic Character of Judicial Review," *Harvard Law Review*, December 1952, pp. 193–224.

Rublee, George. "The Original Plan and Early History of the Federal Trade Commission," *Proceedings of the Academy of Political Science*, January 1926.

Russell, Francis. " 'The Case of the Century' Fifty Years Later," *Harvard Magazine*, Cambridge, MA, July–August 1977.

Rutledge, Wiley. *A Declaration of Legal Faith*, Lawrence, Kansas, 1947.

Ryan, John A. *Social Doctrine in Action: A Personal History*, NY, 1941.

———. *Social Reconstruction*, NY, 1920.

Sachar, Abram L. and Goldsmith, William M. "Guide to a Microfilm Edition of the Public Papers of Louis Dembitz Brandeis in the Jacob and Bertha Goldfarb Library of Brandeis University," Waltham, MA, 1978.

Sachar, Howard Morley. *The Course of Modern Jewish History*, NY, 1977 ed.

———. *A History of Israel*, NY, 1976.

Sayre, Francis Bowes. *Glad Adventure*, NY, 1957.

Schlesinger, Arthur M., Sr. *In Retrospect: The History of a Historian*, NY, 1963.

Schlesinger, Arthur M., Jr. *The Coming of the New Deal*, Boston, 1959.

———. *The Crisis of the Old Order*, Boston, 1957.

———. *The Politics of Upheaval*, Boston, 1960.

———. "The Supreme Court: 1947," *Fortune*, 1947, reprinted in H. M. MacDonald, et al., *Outside Readings in American Government*, NY, 1949.

———, and Israel, Fred L., eds. *History of American Presidential Elections 1789–1968*, NY, 1971.

Schwartz, Bernard. "Felix Frankfurter and Earl Warren: A Study of a Deteriorating Relationship," *Supreme Court Review*, 1980, pp. 115–42.

———. *Super Chief*, NY, 1983.

Shapiro, Yonathan. *Leadership of the American Zionist Organization 1897–1930*, Chicago, 1971.

Sherwood, Robert E. *Roosevelt and Hopkins*, NY, 1948.

Shulman, Harry. "Mr. Justice Brandeis," *Yale Law Journal*, March 1939, pp. 717–18.

Simon, James F. *Independent Journey—The Life of William O. Douglas*, NY, 1980.

Simon, Julius. *Certain Days*, Jerusalem, 1971.

Smythe, William E. "Justice Brandeis in Palestine," *American Review of Reviews*, December 1919, pp. 609–15.

Soviv, Aaron. *Louis D. Brandeis*, NY, 1969.

Spaeth, Harold J. "The Judicial Restraint of Mr. Justice Frankfurter—Myth or Reality," *Midwest Journal of Political Science*, February 1964.

Sparks (published by the Rotary Club of Louisville, KY).

Steel, Ronald. *Walter Lippmann and the American Century*, Boston, 1980.

Steffens, Lincoln. *The Autobiography of Lincoln Steffens*, NY, 1931.

Stein, Leonard. *The Balfour Declaration*, NY, 1961.

———, ed., *The Letters and Papers of Chaim Weizmann*, Volume III, Series A, Jerusalem, 1975.

Steinberg, Stephen. *The Ethnic Myth*, NY, 1981.

Stierlin, Ludwig. *The State of Kentucky and the City of Louisville with Special Consideration of the German Element*, Louisville, 1873.

Stimson, Henry L., and Bundy, McGeorge. *On Active Service in Peace and War,* NY, 1948.

Strauss, Lewis L. *Men and Decisions,* NY, 1962.

The Survey, NY.

Sutherland, Arthur E. *The Law at Harvard,* Cambridge, MA, 1967.

Sykes, Christopher. *Crossroads to Israel,* NY, 1965.

Tarbell, Ida M. *The Life of Elbert H. Gary,* NY, 1969 ed.

Thayer, James Bradley. "The Origin and Scope of the American Doctrine of Constitutional Law," *Harvard Law Review,* October 1893, pp. 129–56.

Thomas, Helen S. *Felix Frankfurter—Scholar on the Bench,* Baltimore, MD, 1960.

Tierney, Kevin. *Darrow—A Biography,* NY, 1979.

Todd, A. L. *Justice on Trial,* NY, 1964.

Tuchman, Barbara W. *Bible and Sword,* NY, 1956.

———. *Practicing History,* NY, 1981.

U.S. Bureau of the Census, *Historical Statistics of the United States,* Washington, DC, 1960.

U.S. Congress, Senate, 61st Congress, 3rd Session, *Investigation of the Interior Department and the Bureau of Forestry,* 1911.

U.S. Congress, Senate, 64th Congress, 1st Session, *Nomination of Louis D. Brandeis,* parts 1 and 2, 1916.

U.S. Congress, Senate, 76th Congress, 1st Session, *Nomination of Felix Frankfurter,* 1939.

U.S. Department of State, *Foreign Relations of the United States,* 1917, Supplement 2, v. 1, 1932.

Urofsky, Melvin I. *American Zionism from Herzl to the Holocaust,* NY, 1975.

———. *Big Steel and the Wilson Administration,* Columbus, OH, 1960.

———. *Louis D. Brandeis and the Progressive Tradition,* Boston, 1981.

———. *A Mind of One Piece,* NY, 1971.

——— and Levy, David W. eds., *Letters of Louis D. Brandeis,* Albany, NY, 1971–77.

Vose, Clement E. "The National Consumers' League and the Brandeis Brief," *Midwest Journal of Political Science,* Detroit, MI, November 1957.

Warner, Emily Smith. with Daniel, Hawthorne. *The Happy Warrior,* NY, 1956.

Warren, Earl. *The Memoirs of Earl Warren,* NY, 1977.

Warren, Samuel D., and Brandeis, Louis D. "The Right to Privacy," *Harvard Law Review,* December 15, 1890, pp. 193–220.

Washington *Post,* Washington, DC.

Washington *Star,* Washington, DC.

Wehle, Louis B. *Hidden Threads of History—Wilson Through Roosevelt,* NY, 1953.

Weizmann, Chaim. *Trial and Error,* NY, 1966 paperback ed.

Werner, M. R. *Julius Rosenwald,* NY, 1939.

Westin, Alan F. "When the Public Judges the Court," *NY Times,* May 31, 1959, VI, p. 16.

White, G. Edward. "Allocating Power Between Agencies and Courts: The Legacy of Justice Brandeis," *Duke Law Journal,* April 1974, pp. 195–244.

———. *Earl Warren,* NY, 1982.

White, Theodore H. *In Search of History,* NY, 1978 paperback ed.

Wigdor, David. *Roscoe Pound,* Westport, CT, 1974.

Wilson, Jerry. *Police Report,* Boston, 1975.

Wise, Stephen S. *Challenging Years,* London, 1951.

Wittke, Carl. *We Who Built America,* Cleveland, OH, 1964 ed.

Woollcott, Alexander. *The Letters of Alexander Woollcott,* Westport, CT, 1972 ed.

Wyzanski, Charles E., Jr. "Brandeis," *Atlantic,* November 1956, pp. 66–72.

Yale, William. "Ambassador Henry Morgenthau's Special Mission of 1917," *World Politics,* April 1949, pp. 308–20.

Yale Law Journal, New Haven, CT.

Yale Law Review, New Haven, CT.

Yater, George H. *Two Hundred Years at the Falls of the Ohio,* Louisville, KY, 1979.

Yeomans, Henry Aaron. *Abbott Lawrence Lowell,* Cambridge, Ma, 1948.

Zangwill, Israel. *The Melting Pot,* NY, 1914 ed.

Notes

PAGE

ix   **"Suppose [Brandeis] . . ."** "**There will be . . .**": McLellan and Acheson, pp. 113, 275.

BOOK ONE: KNIGHT ERRANT

Chapter 1. Before the Supreme Court

3   **"very slender"**: Danelski and Tulchin, p. 161.
4   **"The question"**: 208 U.S. 412, Muller brief, p. 31.
4   **"Our case"**: BU/LDBP: III.
5   **"pitiable"**: Pringle, *Taft,* p. 530.
5 ff.   **See generally**: Friedman and Israel, and King; Kluger, pp. 102–3; Brewer, p. 37.
7   **"The life of"**: Holmes, p. 1.
7   **"The Fourteenth Amendment"**: *Lochner* v. *New York,* 198 U.S. 45, 76.
7   **"We are at"**: Holmes to LDB, 1/19/1908, BU/LDBP: 24.
8   **"woman who had"**: Goldmark, *Crusader,* p. v.

8   "There is no": 155 Ill. 98.
8   One such law: 189 NY 131; Vose, pp. 283–84.
9   "I have never": Kerney, pp. 41–42; "If there are": Pringle, *Roosevelt,* pp. 478–79; also Choate, p. 178.
10   There was another: Author's visit to Naumkeag, 7/11/1981.
10 ff.   See generally: Goldmark, *Crusader,* pp. 151–53; F. Kelley letter, *Survey,* 5/13/1916, pp. 191–92.
11   Louis Brandeis was: Goldmark, *Crusader,* pp. 69–70.
11   "If you look": LC/FFP: 127 (002648).
11   Brandeis listened: Goldmark, *Crusader,* pp. 154–55, 143; Vose, pp. 282–83.
11   When Elbert H. Gary: UL/LDBP: 57 (NMF 43-4c).
12   The Supreme Court had: *Holden* v. *Hardy,* 169 U.S. 366, 397; *Lochner* v. *New York,* 198 U.S. 45, 57.
12   He had argued: *Wisconsin Central Railroad Co.* v. *Price County,* 133 U.S. 496.
12   relishing the tough: Middleton, p. 108; "Remember, to": Radcliffe/Evans: 28a.
12   "same old hue": 208 U.S. 412, Oregon brief, pp. 9, 10.
13   When he had: Goldmark, *Crusader,* pp. 155–58.
13 et. seq. And so he began: 208 U.S. 412, Brandeis brief, pp. 1, 9–10, 16, 24, 42, 44, 47, 48, 62, 92, 104.
15   "very little to do": FF, *Reminisces,* p. 121.
15   Muller's legal team: 208 U.S. 412, Muller brief, p. 13.
15   Cases of national: King, pp. 333, 379.
15 et. seq. "The two sexes": 208 U.S. 412, 423, 421, 419.
16   "will have the": Collins and Friesen, p. 19.
16   "may put heart": *Outlook,* 3/21/1908, pp. 618–19.
16   After *Muller:* Vose, p. 284; Goldmark, *Crusader,* p. 169.
17   "subject to the": *Ritchie* v. *Wayman,* 244 Ill. 509, 512, 521.
17   "thoroughly hated": COHP/Alger: 283, 211.

Chapter 2. Origins

18   "When you look": Goldmark, *Pilgrims,* p. 202.
19   "Another attraction for": Wittke, pp. 186–87, 188, 192, 200; Deering, pp. 22–23.
19   Adolf went into: Goldmark, *Pilgrims,* pp. 2–4–5; UL/Naamani: "Louisville Lore," *Jewish Frontier,* Apr. 1955, pp. 8, 13; *History of the Jews in Louisville,* p. 41; Louisville *Courier-Journal,* 2/27/1916.
19   In 1856, Adolf: Louisville *Courier-Journal Magazine,* 10/28/1956, pp. 7–8; de Haas, "Brandeis," p. 36; Filson Club: Louisville Male High School Records (BI M245).
20   Louis Brandeis's family: Goldmark, *Pilgrims,* pp. 284, 227–28; Louisville *Courier-Journal,* 2/27/1916.
20   By the 1860s: Stierlin, p. 77, 95–96; UL/LDB: 233 (1); Louisville *Courier-Journal,* 1/29/1916.
21   For a high school: Filson Club: Louisville Male High School Records (BI M245).

21   **There were in:** Stierlin, pp. 59, 79; L. N. Dembitz.

21 et. seq.   **In Europe Frederika's:** F. D. Brandeis, "Reminiscences," pp. 27, 24, 25, 8–9, 19, 32–34.

22   **Her brother Lewis:** Ibid., p. 47.

22   **However tenuous:** Frequent references to the Brandeis family are found in AJA/Adath Israel Records, Microfilm #2609; UL/Jewish Community Center Records; and Louisville *Courier-Journal*, 1/23/1906, p. 5.

22   **During and after:** F. D. Brandeis, "Reminiscences," p. 29; E. G. Evans, "People I Have Known," p. 188.

23   **"One night":** J. Goldmark, *Pilgrims,* p. 286.

23   **Louis Brandeis entered:** Sutherland, pp. 168, 180; UL/LDBP: 233 (1); LDB to W. B. Douglas, 1/31/1878, Urofsky and Levy, v. 1, p. 222.

23   **"Believing that law":** LDB, "Harvard Law School," p. 19; see also Sutherland, pp. 162, 167, 175, 177; Harvard Law School *Bulletin,* Spring 1981, p. 16.

24   **"to name one":** FF, *Reminisces,* p. 347.

24   **Brandeis also learned:** Urofsky, *A Mind of One Piece,* pp. 53–54; LDB to Alfred Brandeis, 6/28/1878, Urofsky and Levy, v. 1, pp. 24–25.

24   **"the leader of":** E. F. McClennen memorandum, UL/LDBP: 21 (21-14a).

24   **He did remarkably:** Landis, pp. 184–86; Evans, "People I Have Known," p. 188.

25   **"The law as a":** LDB to C. Nagel, 7/12/1879, Urofsky and Levy, v. i, p. 39.

25   **Still, Brandeis:** LDB letter in St. Louis *Post-Dispatch,* and S. D. Warren to LDB, 11/9/1878, LC/FFP: CF (Brandeis).

26   **"not afraid":** S. D. Warren to LDB, 5/5/1879, LC/FFP: CF (Brandeis).

26   **Brandeis accepted the:** S. D. Warren, 5/22/1879, 5/28/1879, 6/18/1879, LC/FFP: CF (Brandeis); LDB to S. D. Warren, 5/30/1879, Urofsky and Levy, v. 1, p. 35.

26   **"Warren and Holmes":** LDB to A. Brandeis, 7/31/1879, Urofsky and Levy, v. 1, p. 45.

27   **"I have read":** Urofsky and Levy, v. 1, p. 34, note 2; Holmes to LDB, 3/9/1881, UL/LDBP: Box Addendum 1 (1–2).

27   **Financially he also:** UL/LDBP: NMF/Box 7 (7–15d).

27   **But that kind of:** *Nutter, McClennen & Fish,* pp. 2, 3, 4, 6, 7, 11–12, 13.

28   **One young lawyer:** FDRL: Berle OHP, pp. 21–23.

28   **"The expected hours":** *Nutter, McClennen & Fish,* pp. 15, 11–12; E. F. McClennen, 11/12/1941, UL/LDBP: 21 (21-14a).

29   **"Of course, a lawyer's":** COHP/Burlingham, p. 30.

29   **"is valuable as a":** UL/LDBP: Addendum Box 4 (4-3).

29   **"The attitude Brandeis":** FF, *Reminisces,* p. 157.

29   **"This is the":** COHP/Kelley, p. 55.

30   **"The lawyer as a":** Harbaugh, p. 23.

30   **"The Right to Privacy":** Warren and Brandeis, pp. 193–220; LDB to Warren, 4/8/1905, and Warren to LDB, 4/10/1905, UL: LDBP: 27 (NMF 13-3).

30   **"nothing less than":** Pound to W. E. Chilton, 2/18/1916, LC/FFP: 128 (002652).

30   **Brandeis continued his:** HLS/Harvard Law Association: 1 (2, 5); Sutherland, p. 197; in UL/LDBP: C. W. Eliot to J. B. Thayer, 6/12/1891, in 233 (4); LDB's overseer appointment in 36 (NMF 22-2); and C. W. Eliot to LDB, 3/23/1894 in 1 (NMF 1–2b).

31 **I have seen:** LDB to E. G. Evans, 8/7/1887, Radcliffe/Evans papers: 2 (28a).
31 **"That you have":** Warren to A. Goldmark, 9/1880, LC/FFP: CF (A. T. Mason).
31 **"I long for":** LDB to A. Goldmark, 12/4/1880, Urofsky and Levy, v. 1, p. 95.
31 **"Never once":** Fola La Follette remarks, 5/15/1945, Filson Club/Joseph Rauch Papers: A R1412.
32 **"You know":** COHP/Landis, p. 97.

Chapter 3. Brandeis versus the President

33 **"Whatever the theories":** J. Goldmark, *Crusader,* p. 123; A. M. Schlesinger, Jr., *Crisis,* p. 22.
33 **In Birmingham:** Dunne, pp. 94–95.
34 **Charles Evans Hughes:** *NY Times,* 1/10/1919, p. 1; Hughes, p. 205.
34 **Elizabeth Glendower Evans:** From her "People I Have Known," p. 188.
35 **The mentally ill:** Urofsky and Levy, v. 1, p. 120, note 1.
35 **"After the Homestead":** *NY Times,* 2/14/1939, p. 3.
35 **"One wondered at":** Learned Hand in ABA *Journal,* 2/1943, p. 67.
35 **In Boston:** Fuess, pp. 43–44; **"The ability to":** LDB to L. F. Abbot, 7/1/1907, Urofsky and Levy, v. 2, pp. 3–4.
36 **"If we cannot have":** LDB to R. M. Easley, 7/16/1907, Urofsky and Levy, v. 2, p. 13.
36 **"Financial depravity":** LDB, *Curse of Bigness,* pp. 3–9.
37 **"Our insurance":** LDB to A. Brandeis, 1/17/1907, Urofsky and Levy, v. 1, p. 516. See also LDB to A. E. Pinanski, 3/12/1909, Urofsky and Levy, v. 2, pp. 228–29, and numerous LDB letters urging support in UL/LDBP: Levy (2).
37 **The bill became:** LDB to R. G. Hunter, 11/10/1908; LDB to L. Steffens, 12/10/1908, both in Urofsky and Levy, v. 2, pp. 214, 303; *Jewish Advocate,* 7/2/1937, in UL/LDB: 119 (119 (I-9-1c); O. K. Fraenkel in LDB, *Curse of Bigness,* p. 2.
37 **"waged a battle":** Fuess, p. 43.
37 **In one month:** Letters in UL/LDBP: 2.
38 **In another matter:** LDB to W. H. Lincoln, 4/28/1903, UL/LDBP: 23 (NMF 8-1a); LDB to R. W. Pullman, 12/3/1910, Urofsky and Levy, v. 2, p. 392.
38 **"had to be looked":** Hapgood, *Changing,* pp. 130–31; **"to suggest":** LDB to E. A. Grozier, UL/LDBP: NMF 9 (9-29-a).
38 **"headline seeker":** Fuess, p. 44.
38 **Another strength:** LDB sketch in LC/FFP/127 (002648); *NY Times,* 12/4/1910, V, p. 1.
39 **Brandeis did collect:** ICC clerk to LDB, 9/12/1914, UL/LDBP: 75 (NMF-1d); *NY Times,* 12/4/1910, V, p. 1.
39 **"If a man were":** Urofsky and Levy, v. 2, p. 92.
39 **In the early:** Harbaugh, pp. 83, 56–57.
39 **Brandeis often was:** Rosenfield, pp. 71–72; LDB, *Business,* pp. 317, 321, 326, 327.
41 **One of these:** Letter to author from Elisabeth Weiss, "Israelitische Kultusgemeinde Wien," 11/8/1982.
41 **If the Jews in:** Josephson, p. 36; Boston *Globe,* 1/8/1939; *Marsala* passenger list, LC/FFP: 18.
42 **"It was P.S.":** FF to Burlingham, 11/23/1948, LC/FFP: CF.
42 **He was graduated:** LC/FFP: 234 (004181), 200; FF, *Reminisces,* pp. 17–18.

43	**Frankfurter went on:** D. Acheson, 328 U.S. xxi.

43   **Frankfurter went on:** D. Acheson, 328 U.S. xxi.

43   **[T]his College was":** FF address, 9/30/1942, LC/FFP:198.

44   **"The students came":** FF, *Reminisces,* p. 42.

44   **"was at liberty":** Sayre, p. 20.

44   **"I was the":** "Proceedings," pp. 38–39.

44   **"I remembered how":** Love and Childers, p. 11.

44   **"and I heard":** A. W. Scott to FF, 8/31/1962, HLS/Scott: Frankfurter file. **"My vivid memory,"** COHP/Sachs, p. 16; FF, *Reminisces,* p. 49.

44   **Frankfurter particularly:** FF, *Reminisces,* p. 44; FF, *Law and Politics,* p. 3.

45   **"discliplined, highly":** FF, "Mr. Justice Brandeis," LC/FFP: 200.

46   **The New Haven:** LDB to L. F. Buff, 2/3/1908, Urofsky and Levy, v. 2, pp. 70–71; UL/LDB: Addendum 2 (2-2); LDB to A. Brandeis, 6/5/1908, Urofsky and Levy, v. 2, p. 175.

46   **The New Haven argued:** LDB to W. Taussig, 6/18/1908, Urofsky and Levy, v. 2, pp. 188–89.

47   **With his statistics:** LDB, *Curse of Bigness,* p. 189.

47   **When the merger:** LDB to J. Goldmark, 6/14/1908, and LDB to A. Brandeis, 6/15/1909, in Urofsky and Levy, v. 2, p. 186, pp. 282–83.

47   **"Of course":** HLS/Ehrmann: 21 (16).

47   **Brandeis did not:** LDB to M. C. Fleming, 1/23/1905, Urofsky and Levy, v. 1, p. 276.

48   **"Standard Oil men":** *NY Times,* 10/11/1912, p. 6.

48   **"When you increase":** *NY Times,* 11/13/1938, IV, p. 6.

48   **"absentee landlordism":** LDB, *Curse of Bigness,* pp. 77, 72.

48   **"believes that the":** *NY Times,* 6/4/1939, VII, p. 10.

48   **In 1913 Brandeis:** "Brandeis and Lamont."

50   **"sole effective means":** LDB, *Curse of Bigness,* pp. 43–44.

50   **Sometimes, however, it:** Boston *Herald,* 12/5/1902; COHP/Curtis, p. 60.

50   **"The important question":** Boston *Post,* 2/6/1905.

51   **"This is unnecessary":** LDB, *Curse of Bigness,* p. 41.

51   **"Have been here":** 7/31/1910, UL/LDBP: 216 (Md-3b).

51   **"In the entire":** J. H. Cohen, 7/27/1910, UL/LDB: 46 (NMF 33-1a).

52   **For Brandeis:** Boston *American,* 11/12/1911; *NY Times,* 11/7/1926, IV, 8; COHP/Schieffelin, p. 60.

52   **"These demands":** LDB, *Curse of Bigness,* pp. 51, 48–49.

52   **"Will you be":** T. Roosevelt to LDB, 6/14/1907, LC/T. Roosevelt Papers, Series 2.

53   **women's suffrage:** LDB, 1913 statement, UL/LDBP: 17 (17-10).

53   **"Alaska; the Land":** LDB to R. M. La Follette, 7/31/1911, LC/La Follette Family Papers: B-66.

53   **Brandeis joined Roscoe:** C. W. Eliot, LDB, et al., "Efficiency in the Administration of Justice," pp. 7 et seq.

53   **Not only was:** See UL/LDBP: 233 and NMF: 9(29a); LDB to E. G. Graves, 10/18/1907, Urofsky and Levy, v. 2, pp. 26–27.

53   **"My course in":** LDB to A. Brandeis, 10/19/1907 and 11/4/1908, Urofsky and Levy, v. 2, pp. 31, 213.

55   **"We cleaned out":** Hapgood, *Changing,* p. 168.

55   **"said they":** U.S. Congress, *Brandeis,* pp. 454–55.

56   **"but it required":** Hapgood, *Changing,* p. 186.

56   **"There is nothing":** LDB to A. Brandeis, 5/1/1910, Urofsky and Levy, v. 2, pp. 332–33.

56   "probably the most": U.S. Congress, *Interior,* p. 4906, 4923.
57   **George Wharton Pepper:** Pinchot, pp. 469–70; Pepper, p. 86; see also La Follette, p. 288.
58   "a lawyer of": Pepper, p. 85.
58   "Aside from the": U.S. Congress, *Interior,* p. 5005.
58   "keen, persistent": *NY Times,* 12/4/1910, V, p. 1.
58   "Louis is enjoying": Alice Brandeis to A. Brandeis, 4/11/1910, UL/LDBP: 216 (M3-3a).
58   "Don't you snap": *NY Times,* 5/11/1910, p. 3.
58   "I was sitting": Rublee to FF, 7/2/1946, LC/FFP: CF.
59   "They are": LDB to A. Brandeis, 3/27/1910, UL/LDBP: 216 (M3-3a).
59   "Theodore may not": Pringle, *Taft,* p. 507.
60   "I was sorry": Pringle, *Taft,* p. 512.
60   "It remained for": Pringle, *Taft,* p. 513.
60   "It was the lying": Hapgood, *Changing,* p. 190.
60   "In view of the": U.S. Congress, *Interior,* p. 5013.
61   "Your interpretation": 6/24/1910, UL/LDBP: 43(NMF 29-4b).
61   "Ballinger has ostentatiously": LDB to M. Sullivan, 6/4/1910, Urofsky and Levy, v. 2, pp. 340–41.
61   "from the path": Paschal, pp. 61–62.
62   "My friend Gifford": COHP/Williams, p. 958.
62   "It occupied the": COHP/Rublee, pp. 60–61.

Chapter 4. Melting Pot

63   "I was a Jew": FF, *Reminisces,* p. 56.
63   "We were both": E. Root, Jr., to Marion Denman, 11/22/1919, LC/FFP: CF.
64   "Follow the dominant": "Proceedings."
64   "I came to feel": Stimson and Bundy, p. xxii.
64   "People spoke of it": Quoted by D. Acheson, 328 U.S. Reports, xxiii.
64   "on many a": FF to H. H. Burton, 6/1/1953, LC/Burton Papers: 86.
64   "eager, ardent youth": Gunther, "Learned Hand."
65   "I am fortunate": LC/FFP: Diary, 10/20/1911.
65   "there is evidence": Gunther, "Learned Hand."
65   "Just at present" and "May it please": LC/FFP: Diary, 11/21/1911.
65   "Supreme Court Justices": FF, *Reminisces,* p. 82.
65   Frankfurter almost became: FF to C.C. Burlingham, 10/3/1952, and FF to H. Brownell, LC/FFP: CF.
66   "In the early": FF to H. Rosenwald, 10/13/1947, LC/FFP: CF. Percy, pp. 40, 22.
66   "He reminded me": Percy, p. 199.
67   "Please send me": LDB to FF, 11/15/1911, LC/FFP: CF.
67   "It is the first": FF to LDB, 8/24/1912, LC/FFP: CF.
67   "He is thoroughly": LDB to P. P. Wells, 7/21/1913, Urofsky and Levy, v. 3, p. 146.
67   "has a faculty": LDB to R. B. Hull, 1/31/1914, Urofsky and Levy, v. 3, p. 242.
67   "Brandeis has a depth": LC/FFP: Diary, 10/20/1911.
67   "Most of the time": Holmes to FF, 8/17/1915, HLS/Holmes Papers: 29(3).
67   "Long afterwards": FF, *Mr. Justice Holmes,* p. 18.
68   "From time to time": FF to W. A. Harriman, 2/8/1960, LC/FFP: CF.

68	**"if you promise":** Mayer, p. 61.
68	**"a year of complete":** E. R. Buckner to FF, 1/2/1913, LC/FFP: CF.
69	**"You know what I":** W. T. Denison to E. H. Warren, 6/12/1913, LC/FFP: CF.
69	**"I would let those":** Quoted in COHP/FF, p. 317.
69	**"the center of things":** FF to Stimson, 7/1913, LC/FFP: file 002174.
69	**"There is no reason":** FF to W. E. Meyer, 9/25/1913, LC/FFP: CF.
69	**The Wyman vacancy:** Sutherland, p. 217.
70	**"All discussions of":** FF to W. E. Meyer, 9/25/1913, LC/FFP: CF.
70	**"I should like":** FF to LDB, received 7/12/1915, UL/LDBP: 60 (NMF 47-3b).
70	**"Your son":** LDB to E. W. Frankfurter, 11/14/1916, Urofsky and Levy, v. 4, p. 265.
70	**"There is a cause":** Wise, pp. 112–13.
70	**He spoke the then:** LDB to A. Brandeis, 11/29/1905, Urofsky and Levy, v. 1, pp. 386–87.
70	**"in recognition of":** LDB to L. Pickert, UL/LDB: NMF/9 (9–29d).
71	**"definitely agnostic":** Gal, p. 72.
71	**"Here the homes":** E. G. Evans, "Story of . . . Brandeis," p. 2.
71	**"I enquired of":** W. Denman address, in UVA/Homer S. Cummings Papers: 81.
71	**"He was very handsome":** COHP/Burlingham, p. 31.
71	**"sort of whispered":** COHP/Richards, p. 37.
72	**Healy and Early quotes:** Merwick, p. 217, n. 96; p. 185.
72	**"By the way":** LDB to A. Brandeis, 10/16/1914, Urofsky and Levy, v. 3, p. 330–31.
72	**"It seems to me":** LDB to Pound, 11/27/1914, Urofsky and Levy, v. 3, p. 373.
73	**"He . . . pondered long":** De Haas, *Louis D. Brandeis,* p. 50.
73	**"a noble Jew":** De Haas, "Brandeis."
73	**"It was":** LDB to C. A. Cowen, 4/6/1916, Urofsky and Levy, v. 4, p. 152.
73	**1910 interview:** Reprinted in *New Palestine,* 11/8/1940, p. 8.
73	**"You cannot possibly":** LDB to A. Brandeis, 12/8/1914, UL/LDBP: 216 (M4-1b)
74	**"Thank you, Dr.":** AJA/Rosenblatt OHP, unpaged.
74	**"My sympathy with":** LDB to B. G. Richards, 2/2/1911, Urofsky and Levy, v. 2, p. 402.
74	**"Saturday at dinner":** LDB to A. Brandeis, 1/7/1912, Urofsky and Levy, v. 2, p. 537.
74	**In the United States:** See Lipsky, "Early Days," pp. 447, 463; Lipsky, "Thirty Years," p. 66; Shapiro, pp. 24, 53; Manuel, pp. 117–18; Urofsky, *American Zionism,* pp. 120–21; COHP/Richards, p. 42.
75	**"We were actually":** Kahn, pp. 4–5.
75	**"the two men":** Wise, p. 13.
75	**"He seemed to have":** Lipsky, "Early Days," p. 463.
75	**"became a Bar Mitzvah":** COHP/Richards, p. 41.
75	**"I have signed":** Wise, p. 89.
76	**"not an orthodox":** FF, *Reminisces,* pp. 336–37.
76	**Around the Passover:** FF to M. Denman, 4/6/1917, LC/FFP: CF.
76	**"Frankfurter we used":** COHP/Richards, pp. 258, 104.
77	**In contrast to:** LDB to A. Brandeis, 10/25/1912, UL/LDBP: 216 (M 3-3d); LDB to Mrs. J. Fels, 6/14/1915, UL/LDBP: 147 (Z/p 7-2b); LDB to A. Brandeis, 3/6/1915, Urofsky and Levy, v. 3, p. 466.
77	**His letters went:** Letters are in UL/LDBP; 147 (Z/p 7-2b) (Z/p 7-2c).

77   **He had not:** FF to LDB, 7/31/1915, and R. S. Baker, 8/11/1915, both in UL/LDBP: 148 (Z/p 7-3a).

77   **"I can never":** C. Adler, II, p. 309.

78   **"America is God's":** Zangwill, pp. 33–34.

78   **"fellow-Americans":** "The American Hebrew," clipping in LC/T. Roosevelt Papers, Series 1.

78   **"The first way":** B. W. Korn, "German-Jewish," p. 2.

79   **"Judaism was not":** Steel.

79   **"This is the only":** FF, "Democracy and False Shibboleths," *Radcliffe Quarterly,* p. 9.

79   **"My approach to Zionism":** LDB, *Curse of Bigness,* p. 209.

80   **"The Jewish State":** LDB to L. E. Kirstein, 9/10/1915, UL/LDBP: 148 (Z/p 7-3c).

80   **"Obviously":** LDB, *Curse of Bigness,* p. 218.

80   **"Many of those":** LDB talk fragment, UL/LDBP: 144 (Z/P 4-2a).

80   **"We can scarcely":** LDB, *Curse of Bigness,* p. 218.

80   **"Wer Nichts wagt":** LDB to J. Billikopf, 1/25/1915, Urofsky and Levy, v. 3, p. 412.

Chapter 5. With Woodrow Wilson

81   **"just the man":** LDB to S. Bonham, 1/16/1912, Urofsky and Levy, v. 2, p. 539.

81   **"There has been":** LDB to R. W. Pullman, 7/17/1912, Urofsky and Levy, v. 2, p. 651.

82   **"particularly his discussion":** LDB to N. Hapgood, 7/3/1912, Urofsky and Levy, v. 2, p. 633; see letters in Urofsky and Levy, v. 2, for that period and in UL/LDBP: 65 (NMF 53-2a).

82   **"With Wilson nominated":** LDB to FF, 7/12/1912, LC/FFP: CF.

82   **"The raucous voices":** FF, *Law and Politics,* pp. 305–6.

82   **"What I really":** FF to T. Roosevelt, 1/15/1912, LC/T. Roosevelt Papers, Series 1: FF to H. F. Armstrong, 10/21/1963, LC/FFP: CF.

82   **"a very unfair":** FF to L. Hand, 9/23/1912, HLS/FFP: 198 (10).

82   **"The sacrosanct notion":** LC/FFP: Diary, 10/27/1911.

82   **In 1910 Roosevelt:** Pringle, *Roosevelt,* pp. 543–67.

83   **In its platform:** Schlesinger and Israel, v. 3, pp. 2187–88.

83   **"and I should":** FF, *Law and Politics,* pp. 3, 6, 7.

84   **"Every big crooked":** in Link, *Wilson . . . White House,* pp. 475–76, 472–73n., also pp. 487–89.

84   **When Wilson was:** Kerney, p. 106.

84   **"Was very favorably":** LDB to unknown, 8/29/1912, UL/LDBP: 216 (M 3-3c).

84   **"did not share":** R. S. Baker/LDB interview, 3/23/1929, LC/Baker Papers: 102.

85   **"The two parties":** LDB to Wilson, 9/30/1912, LC/Wilson Papers, Series 2.

85   **Once Wilson accepted:** See LDB to W. G. McAdoo, 10/2/1912, Urofsky and Levy, v. 2, pp. 697–98.

85   **"You were":** Wilson to LDB, 11/19/1912, Urofsky and Levy, v. 2, p. 709, n2.

86   **Democratic politicians:** LDB to A. Brandeis, 9/15/1912, Urofsky and Levy, v. 2, p. 673.

86   **Thayer comments:** LC/Charles S. Hamlin Diary, v. 2, p. 2.

86   **But it was not:** Katz, pp. 76–78.

86   **Norman Hapgood then:** Hapgood, *Changing*, pp. 190–91; Wise, p. 100; see also UL/LDBP: 63 (NMF 50-5a, 5b, 5c); Link, *Wilson . . . Freedom*, pp. 10–15.

86   **"And in Mr. Brandeis' ":** Unpaged clip in UL/LDBP: 65 (NMF 50-5b).

87   **"I thank you":** LDB to FF, 3/6/1913, UL/LDB: 65 (NMF-lg); LDB to G. Middleton, 3/12/1913, LC/La Follette Family Papers: B-73.

87   **"Had a good":** LDB to A. Brandeis, 3/10/1913, Urofsky and Levy, v. 3, p. 42.

87   **Both inside and:** See C. McCarthy to LDB, 2/7/1913, LC/Wilson Papers, Series 2; LC/Charles S. Hamlin Diary, v. 1, pp. 9–10; and in UVA, James C. McReynolds Papers; in 1, LDB to W. C. Redfield, 6/12/1913, and in 3, Lane to McReynolds, 1/30/1914.

87   **"more than a lawyer":** House to Wilson, E. M. House, *Intimate Papers*, v. 1, p. 91.

87   **"McReynolds will make":** LDB to M. Leon, 2/28/1913; LDB to Gardner, 3/5/1913; LDB to M. E. Clapp, 3/5/1913, all in Urofsky and Levy, v. 3, pp. 35, 39.

87   **"In deciding upon":** LDB to McReynolds, 3/5/1913, Urofsky and Levy, v. 3, p. 41.

88   **Once when McReynolds:** LC/Charles S. Hamlin Diary, v. 2, pp. 18–19.

88   **"is very tired":** LDB to Alice Brandeis, 3/18/1913, Urofsky and Levy, v. 3, p. 224; also UL/LDBP: 69 (NMF 58-1d, e).

89   **"power to issue":** LDB to Wilson, 6/14/1913, LC/Wilson Papers: Series 2.

89   **Late in 1913:** LDB to F. K. Lane, 12/12/1913, Urofsky and Levy, v. 3, pp. 218–21; LDB to A. Brandeis, 1/23/1914, UL/LDBP: 216 (M4-1a).

90   **"These definitions":** Rublee, p. 116.

90   **"We had our":** COHP/Rublee, pp. 100–14.

91   **at Wilson's request:** LDB to Wilson, 6/10/1914, LC/Wilson Papers, Series 2.

91   **"a man of":** Boston *Globe,* 1/30/1916.

91   **"I am in excellent":** LDB to A. Brandeis, 1/14/1910, UL/LDBP: 216 (M3-3b).

91   **"Away from the":** E. F. McClennen to A. T. Mason, 12/1/1944, UL/LDBP: 21 (14b).

92   **Brandeis's secretary:** Boston *Post,* 1/29/1916.

92   **McClennen once described:** McClennen memorandum, 10/20/1941, UL/LDBP: NMF 21 (21-14a).

92   **He was also generous:** See LDB to A. Brandeis, 1/3/1914, UL/LDBP: 216 (M4-1a); to N. Hapgood, 7/15/1913, 7/23/1913, 9/23/1913, and to J. R. Smith, 2/2/1914, in Urofsky and Levy, v. 3, pp. 137–38, 147, 176, 224–25, 243.

92   **to ask him to:** LDB to G. Sutherland, 11/6/1915; G. Sutherland to LDB, 11/8/1915; LDB to G. Sutherland, 11/18/1915, LC/Sutherland Papers: 2.

93   **"You are evidently":** LDB to H. Hurwitz, 4/3/1916, UL/LDBP: NMF 16 (16-12c).

93   **"It would seem":** FF letter, 1/19/1915, LC/FFP: CF (A. Bickel).

93 et seq.   **The admissions committee:** W. B. King to FF, 2/15/1915; FF to W. B. King, 2/23/1915; E. Thayer to FF, 3/3/1915, all in LC/FFP: CF.

94   **On March 15, 1915:** Notification in UL/LDBP: 83 (NMF 73-4a).

94   **"We had faith":** LDB, "True Americanism."

95   **At the beginning of 1916:** LDB, "The Living Law," *Illinois Law Review,* 2/1916, pp. 461–71.

Chapter 6. Mr. Justice Brandeis

97   "It is fairly certain": W. Van Devanter to W. H. Sanborn, 1/17/1916, LC/Van Devanter Papers: 10.

97   "I never thought": LDB conversation, notes, 9/15/1939, UL/LDBP: 216 (M2-5).

97   Attorney General Gregory: E. M. House to F. W. Buxton, 4/8/1936, LC/FFP: 127 (002649).

97   "the wisest that": Wilson to R. L. Owen, 2/7/1916, in Link, *Wilson . . . Crises*, p. 357, and p. 324.

98   "I am not": LDB to A. Brandeis, 1/28/1916, UL/LDBP: 4.

98   "I had some misgivings": Alice Brandeis to A. Brandeis, 1/31/1916, UL/LDBP: 216 (M4-2).

98   "Weather miserable": LDB to Alice Brandeis, 2/2/1916, BU/LDB Papers: 7.

98   "How they howl": FF to Holmes, 1/27/1916, LC/FFP: 115 (Buckner file).

98   "Judges of little": *NY Times*, 1/29/1916, p. 8.

99   "If Mr. Wilson": G. J. Karger to W. H. Taft, 1/29/1916, LC/Taft Papers: Reel 162.

99   Attorney General Gregory: E. F. McClennen to LDB, 2/3/1916, UL/LDBP: 86 (NMF 76-1a).

99   "It is terribly": FF to J. W. Mack, 1/31/1916, LC/FFP: CF (Mack file, attached to 1926 letter).

99   Brandeis publicly: LDB to M. Berlin, 2/10/1916; to S. R. Stern, 2/10/1916; to S. S. Wise, 5/18/1916; to N. Hapgood, 2/1/1916, all in Urofsky and Levy, v. 4, pp. 38, 42, 192, 32.

100   "I venture": Taft to G. J. Karger, 1/31/1916, LC/Taft Papers: Reel 537.

100   A 1971 account: Shapiro, pp. 66–67.

101   Jacob Schiff praised: C. Adler, p. 72; LC/Morgenthau Papers: Diary 5/3/1916.

101   Nathan Straus, another: A. Brisbane to LDB, 4/25/1916, UL/LDBP: 6; Straus to LDB, undated, UL/LDBP: 158 (Z/P 16-1f).

101   appointed a Jew: Kerney, p. 120; *NY Times*, 1/29/1916, p. 1; G. J. Karger to W. H. Taft, 3/3/1916, LC/Taft Papers: Reel 162.

101   "For the first": A. L. Todd, p. 85.

101   A. Lawrence Lowell, president: *NY Times*, 6/6/1922, p. 2.

102   Edward McClennen, Brandeis's: E. F. McClennen to A. T. Mason, UL/LDBP: 21 (14b).

102   "The heart and": FF to E. Buckner, 3/3/1916, LC/FFP: 115.

102   The President was aware: La Follette, p. 568; P. F. La Follette to LDB, undated, Urofsky and Levy, v. 4, p. 38.

102   "You may say": Link, *Wilson . . . Crises*, p. 362. See N. Hapgood to J. Tumulty, 2/1/1916, LC/Wilson Papers: Series 4, Case #3156.

103   "all of us": W. Lippmann to LDB, 2/18/1916, Yale/Lippmann Papers: 4 (182).

103   "I plead guilty": FF to T. R. Powell, 3/2/1916, LC/FFP: CF.

104   "What a commotion": LDB to R. W. Woolley, 2/11/1916, LC/Woolley Papers: 2; LDB to C. E. Russell, 2/10/1916, Urofsky and Levy, v. 4, p. 41.

104   "Brandeis did not": E. F. McClennen memorandum, 10/20/1941, UL/LDBP:21 (21-14a); LDB to R. Pound, 2/24/1916, Urofsky and Levy, v. 4, p. 91; LDB to A. Brandeis, 2/12/1916, UL/LDBP: Levy, Box 6.

105   On February 1: LDB to N. Hapgood, 2/1/1916, Urofsky and Levy, v. 4, pp. 27–29.

105   "I succeeded yesterday": F. J. Henry to LDB, 2/1/1916, UL/LDBP: Levy, Box 6.

105   "Of course there": LDB to A. L. Weil, 2/8/1916, LDB to H. Emerson, 3/17/1916, Urofsky and Levy, v. 4, pp. 36, 128.

105   There were hundreds: Many letters are in UL/LDBP: 85 (NMF 75); UL/LDBP: Levy, Box 6. R. Pound to W. E. Chilton, 2/8/1916, LC/FFP: 128 (002652).

105   "has not the": Katz, p. 80.

105   "I imagine most": McClennen to Nutter, 2/14/1916; Nutter telegram to McClennen, 2/15/1916; Nutter to McClennen, 2/15/1916; in UL/LDBP: 86 (NMF 76-1c).

106   "Frankfurter has evidently": Taft to G. Wickersham, 2/7/1916, LC/Taft Papers: Reel 537.

106   "I think Taft's": LDB to N. Hapgood, 3/14/1916, Urofsky and Levy, v. 4, pp. 118–19, n. 4.

106   "a pompous": FF, *Reminisces,* p. 60.

107   "It is important": McClennen to LDB, 2/18/1916, UL/LDBP: 86 (NMF 76-1d).

107   "to act for": U.S. Congress, *Brandeis,* v. 1, p. 171.

107   Brandeis's public stance: See letters LDB to McClennen, Urofsky and Levy, v. 4, pp. 39–141.

107   "the Supreme Court": LDB to FF, 3/1/1916, Yale/Lippmann Papers: 4 (182).

107   The hearings reviewed: U.S. Congress, *Brandeis,* v. 1, p. 707, v. 2, pp. 365–67.

107   He was criticized: U.S. Congress, *Brandeis,* v. 1, p. 25; Frank, "Legal Ethics," p. 686.

107   Brandeis's role in: U.S. Congress, *Brandeis,* v. 1, pp. 116–34.

108   "Mr. Pound, one": U.S. Congress, *Brandeis,* v. 1, p. 280.

108   Sometimes this tactic: U.S. Congress, *Brandeis,* v. 1, pp. 338, 344.

108   In another instance: U.S. Congress, *Brandeis,* v. 1, p. 299.

109   "the episode is": Frank, "Legal Ethics," p. 706.

109   "the latest news": De Haas, "Brandeis," unpaged.

109   "Austen Fox and": LDB to H. J. Laski, 5/9/1916, Urofsky and Levy, v. 4, p. 182.

109   "By the way": LDB to E. F. McClennen, 4/5/1916, Urofsky and Levy, v. 4, p. 150.

109   "It really is not": LDB to FF, 4/6/1916, Urofsky and Levy, v. 4, pp. 153–54.

110   "Delays are not": LDB to E. F. McClennen, 4/14/1916, Urofsky and Levy, v. 4, p. 166.

110   "We are all": Quoted by F. La Follette, 10/15/1945, Filson Club/Joseph Rauch Papers: A R141 2.

110   "did not believe": LDB to Gregory, 4/14/1916, Urofsky and Levy, v. 4, pp. 165–66; Gregory to T. J. Walsh, 4/17/1916, UL/LDBP: 6.

110   "No decent person": LDB to E. S. Meredith, 11/1916, UL/LDBP: 97 (SC 2-1d).

110   "Things look well": McClennen to Nutter, 3/4/1916, UL/LDBP: 86 (NMF 76-1e).

110   "I am inclined": Nutter to McClennen, 3/10/1916, UL/LDBP: 86 (NMF 76-1f).

110   "after a shampoo": McClennen to Nutter, 3/15/1916 and 3/28/1916, UL/LDBP: 86 (NMF 76-1f).

111 **William E. Borah:** Wise, pp. 101–2.

111 **Borah's vote became:** McClennen note, 4/5/1916, UL/LDBP: 86 (NMF 76-1g).

111 **Frankfurter understood:** See FF correspondence, LC/FFP: 28 (002652, 002653).

111 **"Two men have":** FF to Root, 3/17/1916, LC/FFP: 002176.

112 **"seems to draw":** Root to FF, 5/3/1916, LC/FFP: 128 (002653).

112 **"Law practice presents":** FF to Stimson, 3/18/1916, LC/FFP: 002176.

112 **In 1910, Stimson:** Stimson to LDB, 6/14/1910, Yale/Stimson Papers: 20 (8).

112 **"I am sure":** Adams, p. 280.

112 **"He always left":** Holmes to L. Einstein, 5/14/1916, in J. B. Peabody, p. 128; FF to C. E. Clark, 1/17/1930, LC/FFP: CF.

113 **"were doing all":** LC/Charles S. Hamlin Papers: Diary, v. 3, pp. 200–201.

113 **"We regard it":** U.S. Congress, *Brandeis,* v. 2, p. 306.

113 **"It will not do":** Ibid., p. 251.

113 **"The real crime:** U.S. Congress, *Brandeis,* v. 2, p. 234.

114 **However, when a Boston:** COHP/O'Brien, pp. 31–32.

114 **"This gives us":** LDB to Baker, Urofsky and Levy, v. 4, p. 177.

114 **But there were:** E. D. Peabody to McClennen, 5/1/1916, UL/LDBP: 86 (NMF 76-2a); FF to W. Lippmann, 5/4/1916, LC/FFP: 128 (002654).

114 **"Brandeis confirmation may":** Link, *Wilson . . . Crises,* p. 357.

114 **Wilson waited three:** McClennen to LDB, 5/2/1916, 5/4/1916, UL/LDBP: 86 (NMF 76-2a).

115 **The arrangement worked:** C. A. Culberson to Wilson, 5/5/1916, LC/Wilson Papers: Series 7a.

115 **prepared in Boston:** Unsigned memorandum, LC/Wilson Papers; Series 2.

115 **"probably" his most:** Wilson to C. A. Culberson, 5/5/1916, LC/Wilson Papers: Series 2.

115 **George Nutter, working:** Nutter to McClennen, 5/10/1916, UL/LDBP: 86 (NMF 76-2b); see also Nutter to Robert P. Bass, 5/20/1916, Dartmouth/Bass Papers: 13 (with Brandeis papers).

116 **Senate subcommittee hearings:** U.S. Congress, *Brandeis,* v. 2, pp. 241–42.

116 **Shields had served:** See McClennen to LDB, 4/15/1916; McClennen to Nutter, 4/19/1916; both in UL/LDBP: 86 (NMF 76-1i).

116 **"I feel that":** Morgenthau to Wilson, 5/18/1916, LC/Wilson Papers: Series 4, Case #3156.

117 **"the dangerous state":** *NY Times,* 1/1/1920, p. 10.

117 **On Thursday, June 1:** U.S. Congress, *Congressional Record,* 6/1/1916, p. 9032.

119 **Three telegrams from:** McClennen to LDB, 5/26/1916, 6/1/1916, 6/5/1916, UL/LDBP: 86 (NMF 76-2c).

119 **"Welcome":** Holmes to LDB, 6/2/1916, UL/LDBP: Levy (Box 6).

119 **"Greetings and what":** FF to LDB, 6/1/1916; FF to LDB, 6/6/1916, UL/LDBP: Levy (Box 6).

119 **"a new era for":** FF to Alice Brandeis, 6/8/1916, BU/LDBP: 27.

119 **"Needless to say":** A. G. Brady to A. Brandeis, 6/2/1916, UL/LDBP: 6.

119 **He resigned his:** UL/LDBP: 83 (NMF 73-4b).

119 **His partnership in:** W. H. Dunbar to LDB, 7/13/1916, UL/LDBP: 19 (19-18a); also see UL/LDBP: Warren and Brandeis bound volumes, #64.

120 **"It has been my":** LDB to E. D. White, 6/29/1916, Urofsky and Levy, v. 4, pp. 241–42.

120   "the most critical": Link, *Wilson . . . Progressivism,* p. 141.
120   "**In law also**": FF, *Mr. Justice Holmes,* p. 9; FF, *Law and Politics,* p. 115.

BOOK TWO: THE ONE ABOVE THE CLOUDS

Chapter 7. On the Court

125   "**Have just**": BU/LDBP: XI.
125   "**went hard**": HLS/"Conversations between L.D.B. and F.F."
125   "**No one can**": FF, "Supreme Court in the Mirror of Justices," p. 434.
125   "**Had 1½ hours**": 11/27/1916, Urofsky and Levy, v. 4, p. 267.
126   *Van Dyke* v. *Geary:* 244 U.S. 39, 46.
127   *Sutton* v. *New Jersey:* 244 U.S. 258, 260.
127   Brandeis wrote six: 244 U.S. 261, 266, 368, 377, 383, 617.
127   "**Technical rules**": 244 U.S. 377, 380.
127   "**has the approval**": 244 U.S. 261, 264.
128   Pierce Butler . . . "vanity": HLS/"Conversations between L.D.B. and F.F."
128   "**a good deal**": Hellman, p. 257.
128   "**an appeal to**": Hughes, pp. 68, 67.
128   "**I have concluded**": 5/20/1918, HLS/Holmes Opinions: 1917.
128   "**I was rushed**": HLS/"Conversations between L.D.B. and F.F."
128   "**I can understand**": to A. Bickel, 12/8/1955, HLS/Magruder Papers: 33 (7).
128   "**in order not**": FF to T. C. Clark, 11/6/1951, LC/FFP: CF.
128   "**One can say**": Holmes to H. Laski, 8/16/1924, Howe, *Holmes-Laski,* pp. 646–47.
128   "**I dissent from**": *NY Central Railroad Co.* v. *Winfield,* 244 U.S. 147, 154.
129   "**Actually he decides**": J. M. Landis to FF, 1/12/1926, LC/FFP: CF.
130   *Adams* v. *Tanner:* 244 U.S. 590, 597.
130   That 1916–17 term: 244 U.S. 170, 205, 255, 310, 499.
130   "**Now I am**": Holmes to Laski, Howe, *Holmes-Laski,* p. 68.
131   "**the almost intrinsic**": FF to J. B. Reston, 6/21/1963, LC/FFP: CF; B. V. Cohen interview, 2.17/1981.
131   "**believed that these**": Acheson, *Morning and Noon,* p. 58.
131   "**His opinions remind**": LC/Burton: Diary, 3/12/1946.
131   It had been Brandeis: Landis, p. 186.
132   "**master of formulas**": Friedman and Israel, v. 3, p. 1948.
132   "**the highest general**": To FF, 4/22/1921, McLellan and Acheson, p. 14.
132   "**Grandfather Brandeis**": Undated, HLS/LDBP: Addendum Box 4 (4-a).
132   "**The Chief was**": 3/1/1917, Urofsky and Levy, v. 4, p. 274.
132   "**our Court**": Acheson, *Morning and Noon,* p. 59.
132–134   The Supreme Court: Leonard Baker, *John Marshall,* pp. 10, 91, 382 et seq.
134   "**The provisions of**": *Gompers* v. *U.S.,* 233 U.S. 604, 610.
135   Taft quotes: *Tyson* v. *Benton,* 273 U.S. 418; Taft to G. Sutherland, 9/10/1922, LC/Sutherland: 4.
135   Thayer quotes: Thayer, 135, 144, 156.
135   Brandeis has been: Sachar and Goldsmith, pp. 1–2.
135   "**The felt necessities**": Holmes, p. 1.
136   "**The purpose was**": Acheson, *Morning and Noon,* p. 83.
136   "**if you could**": 1/13/1918, 1/16/1918, 6/16/1928, Howe, *Holmes-Laski,* pp. 127, 675, 1066.

136	"There were two": Boston *Herald*, 11/11/1956, p. 13.
137	"sits above the": LC/Baker: 102.

Chapter 8. In World War I

138	**Since the National:** LC/NCL Papers, 13th report, p. 26.
138	**Brandeis had continued:** Goldmark, *Crusader*, pp. 170–71.
138	**"With women you":** FF, *Reminisces*, pp. 122–23.
138	**"The public issues":** FF to G. M. Brown, 3/10/1916, LC/FFP: 128 (002665).
138	**"can we do anything":** Goldmark to FF, attached to J. D. Maher letter, 10/14/1916, LC/FFP: 128 (002665).
139	**"Since there are":** FF to G. M. Brown, 10/17/1916, LC/FFP:CF.
139	**"I have always":** G. M. Brown to J. N. Teal, 10/19/1916, LC/FFP: 157 (003146).
139	**"A matter of":** LC/FFP: 183 (003522).
139	**FF/White meeting:** FF, *Reminisces*, pp. 123–27.
140	**"trench warfare":** FF to G. M. Brown, 1/27/1917, LC/FFP: CF.
140	**"Anyone who looked":** *Nation*, 3/15/1917, p. 320.
140	*Bunting* v. *Oregon:* 243 U.S. 629; *Stettler* v. *O'Hara, Simpson* v. *O'Hara,* 243 U.S. 629.
141	**"I have never known":** Cited in FF to L. Henkin, 1/23/1963, LC/FFP: CF.
141	**"After he had":** HLS/Ehrmann: 21 (9—pp. 12-4).
142	**"It is the":** 3/9/1912, Rosenfield, pp. 240–41.
142	**"almost magical":** FF, "The Law and the Law Schools," p. 367; and see FF, "The Zeitgeist and the Judiciary."
142	**FF/*The New Republic:*** COHP/Johnson, pp. 132–33.
143	**"One after-dinner":** Josephson, 12/7/1940, p. 39.
143	**"born to their":** FF to M. R. Cohen, 10/3/1916, Rosenfield, p. 248.
143	**"big business dominated" and following:** FF to J. G. Palfrey, 1/31/1917, LC/FFP: CF.
144	**LDB/Mexican Commission:** LDB to R. Lansing, 8/9/1916; LDB to Wilson, 8/14/1916, in LC/Wilson Papers: Series 2; LDB to White, undated, UL/LDBP: 128 (C-1-1); FF to P. A. Freund, 1/22/1957, LC/FFP: CF.
144	**"I can't get":** To H. Feis, 4/18/1917, LC/Feis Papers: 11.
144	**Eugene Meyer's job:** LC/Meyer: 1 (Diary, 11/18/1917).
145	**Some of Brandeis's efforts:** Mason, *Brandeis,* pp. 519–20; B. A. Murphy, *Connection,* pp. 50–51 (which relies on the Mason account); *NY Times,* 2/14/1982, p. 1; Hoover, v. 1, p. 248; 255 U.S. 81, 88; 255 U.S. 98.
145	**Brandeis's advice was:** LC/Woolley: 44 (ch. 38, pp. 11–13); LC/Hamlin: Diary, v. 10, pp. 15–16.
146	**Wilson often sought:** Mason, *Brandeis,* p. 525; Wise, p. 107; Fuess, pp. 81–82; LC/Woolley: 44 (ch. 38, pp. 15–17).
146	**"We are not":** FF and Stanley King memorandum, 4/30/1918, LC/FFP: Zionist file (Reel 1).
146	**"I'm sorry but":** FF to LDB, 12/12/1917 (telegram), UL/LDBP: 122 (WWI-1g).
146	**In dealing with:** LDB to E. M. House, 1/9/1918, Yale/House: 18 (0586); see Urofsky, *A Mind of One Piece,* pp. 124–25; Urofsky, *Big Steel,* p. 174.
147	**"I only rejoice":** 3/5/1917, HLS/Holmes: 29 (4).
147	**"I learned":** FF to N. D. Baker, LC/FFP: 189 (003604).
147	**"Felix seems to":** 9/5/1917, Howe, *Holmes-Laski,* p. 98.

147 Frankfurter's move to: A. L. Lowell to N. D. Baker, 10/1/1917, UL/LDBP: 126 (WW 8-1a).

148 "interests are conflicting": FF, "Utilities Bureau," unpaged copy in LC/FFP: 194.

148 The Commission's first: FF, "Mediation Commission," pp. 3–8.

149 "You said it all": 10/20/1917, UL/LDBP: 122 (WW1-1e).

150 "Keep at it": 11/12/1917, LC/FFP: CF.

150 FF/T. Roosevelt relationship: See their letters, 1911–1917, LC/Roosevelt: Series 1 and 2.

150 "conscientious purpose": 1/7/1918, LC/Roosevelt: Series 1.

151 "in no wise": FF to E. R. Buckner, 11/20/1917, LC/Roosevelt: Series 1.

151 "on behalf of": Roosevelt letter, 12/19/1917, LC/Roosevelt: Series 3A.

151 "as in the copper": FF, "Mediation Commission," pp. 9–17.

152 "fine beyond anything": 12/25/1917, LC/Wilson Papers: Series 2.

152 "ugly—no other": 11/28/1917, UL/LDBP: 122 (WWi-1f).

152 Frankfurter's next Washington: WLPB records, LC/FFP: 189, 190, 191.

153 Mary Anderson, working: Anderson, pp. 102–3; WLPB report, 7/12/1918, LC/FFP: 191 (003644).

154 "grand seigneur": Cotter, pp. 33, 34.

154 "The number allowed": Gary, p. 12.

154 "The crucial fact": FF, *Law and Politics,* p. 204.

155–157 FF/Gary meeting: Drawn from letters, memoranda, verbatim accounts in NA: RG 1: 16; LC/FFP: 190 (003638); FF, *Reminisces,* pp. 169–72; Gary, pp. 10–12. Also Cotter, pp. 45–47; Cuff, p. 273; Urofsky, *Big Steel,* pp. 84–85, 272–78.

157 "What American business": FF, *The Survey,* 12/7/1918, pp. 291–93.

157 "American industry must" and following: *NY Times,* 12/15/1918, p. 8.

158 LDB/Wilson exchange: LC/Wilson, LDB to Wilson, Series 2, and Wilson to LDB, Series 3.

Chapter 9. The Balfour Declaration

159 In the first half: See correspondence, UL/LDBP: 158 (Z/P 16).

159 "On the East Side": Lipsky, *Thirty Years,* pp. 51–52.

159 The American Jewish: Minutes, 7/12/1915 meeting, UL/LDBP: 157 (Z/P 15-2a).

160 "that we are Jews": Werner, p. 176.

160 After Brandeis's confirmation: See LDB, "Jewish Unity and Congress," in LDB, *Curse of Bigness,* p. 233–36.

160 were repeated in: *NY Times,* 7/18/1916, p. 23.

160 Brandeis believed his: To Hugo Pam, 7/21/1916, UL/LDB:159 (Z/P 16-3b).

160 "Jews in America": FF to Louis Marshall, 6/23/1916, AJA.

161 "After he had": Transcript, Jewish Agency meeting, 10/15/1941, LC/LDBP.

161 "And Jerusalem is": 12/1917, UL/LDBP: 122 (WW1-1g).

161 "The work for": to R. W. Goldmark, 12/20/1917, UL/LDBP: 216 (M3-4).

161 "a country exhausted by war": From first official report of British administration of Palestine, Andrews, v. 1, p. 327.

162 "in childhood imbibing": Dugdale, v. 1, pp. 433–35.

162 "You know, Dr.": Dugdale, v. 2, p. 226.

162 "Surely it is in": Dugdale, v. 2, p. 217.

162   "essentially a psychological": FF, "Palestine Situation," p. 411.

164   "You may tell": Stein, ed., *Weizmann,* pp. 346–47.

164   "Unless the . . . Jews": 4/23/1917, Stein, ed., *Weizmann,* p. 373.

164–165 "I met Balfour": To de Haas, 4/24/1917, Urofsky and Levy, v. 4, p. 283.

165   LDB/Wilson meeting: Stein, ed., *Weizmann,* p. 406, n. 6; LDB to J. de Rothschild, 5/15/1917, UL/LDBP: 165 (Z/P 22-3a); Dugdale, v. 2, p. 231; LDB to de Haas, 5/8/1917, Urofsky and Levy, v. 4, p. 289.

166   "[Secretary of War] Baker": FF to "Dear Brandeis," undated, UL/LDBP: 165 (Z/P 22 3c).

166   "a policy of expelling": Stein, ed., *Weizmann,* p. 437, n. 5.

166   In England: Weizmann, p. 195.

166   "there is still": Stein, ed., *Weizmann,* pp. 436–38.

166   "It was midsummer": Weizmann, p. 198.

167   Accounts of meeting: U.S. Dept. of State, *Foreign Relations,* 1917, Supplement 2, v. 1, pp. 120–22; "Minutes of Conference at Gibraltar," LC/FFP: 155 (003127); Weizmann to Sir Ronald Graham, 7/6/1917, Stein, ed., *Weizmann,* pp. 460–61.

167   "If Brandeis knows": De Haas, *Brandeis,* p. 83.

168   "The views outlined": Yale/House Papers: Diary, v. 11, p. 290, 9/23/1917.

168   "From talks I have": 9/24/1917, Urofsky and Levy, v. 4, p. 310.

168   Brandeis telegraphed Weizmann: 9/24/1917, Urofsky and Levy, v. 4, p. 311.

168   "Our Jewish opponents": 10/7/1917, UL/LDBP: 165 (Z/P 22-3c).

168   "It is essential": 10/9/1917, Stein, ed., *Weizmann,* p. 530.

168   Wilson, however, did: Wise, pp. 120–21.

169   "Joyous congratulations": 11/9/1917, Urofsky and Levy, v. 4, p. 321.

169   "He thought": Gwynn, v. 2, pp. 421–22.

169   'Let no Jew': 12/6/1917, Urofsky and Levy, v. 4, p. 327.

170   "William C. Bullitt": 11/28/1918, Urofsky and Levy, v. 4, pp. 366–67.

170   "sailing on a": Steffens, p. 778.

170   "My months at": FF to T. R. Powell, 10/5/1954, LC/FFP: CF.

170   Against this background: FF/Feisal meeting and letter texts, FF to LDB, 3/3/1919, LC/FFP: CF; FF to M. W. Weisgal, 12/3/1929, and Feisal to FF and FF to Feisal, all in LC/FFP: 161 (003218).

171–172 FF/Wilson exchange: FF to Wilson, 5/8/1919; Wilson to FF, 5/13/1919; FF to Wilson, 5/14/1919; Wilson to FF, 5/16/1919; FF to Wilson, 5/20/1919; G. F. Close to FF, 5/21/1919, all in LC/Wilson Papers: Series 5B.

172   "I don't know": Sent by FF, 5/22/1919, LC/Wilson Papers: Series 5B.

172   "A packed week": FF to M. Denman, 7/31/1919, LC/FFP: CF.

172   The United States and: See Yale/House Papers: Diary, v. 15, p. 113 (3/26/1919) and 180 (4/29/1919); FF to LDB, 5/25/1919, LC/FFP: CF.

173   "Weizmann is": To Alice Brandeis, 6/22/1919, Urofsky and Levy, v. 4, p. 404.

173   "to the Champs": LDB to Alice Brandeis, 6/24/1919, Urofsky and Levy, v. 4, p. 405.

174   "My interview with": To Alice Brandeis, 6/25/1919, Urofsky and Levy, v. 4, pp. 406–7.

174   July 1, 1919: LDB to Alice Brandeis, 7/1/1919, Urofsky and Levy, v. 4, p. 409.

174   LDB in Palestine: See Smythe; de Haas, *Brandeis,* pp. 116–17; LDB to Alice Brandeis, 8/1/1919, 8/8/1919, Urofsky and Levy, v. 4, pp. 420, 421.

175   **Back in London:** Julius Simon, pp. 93–95.

175   **"his big frame":** *American Hebrew,* 11/13/1936, p. 523.

175   **"transfigured":** To Laski, 10/5/1919, Howe, *Holmes-Laski,* p. 212.

176   **The time was:** LDB to Wilson, 2/3/1920, Urofsky and Levy, v. 4, pp. 446–47; Manuel, p. 256; LDB to Mack, 2/9/1920, Urofsky and Levy, v. 4, p. 447.

176   **"I have heard":** To E. Percy, 6/26/1916, UL/LDBP: 165 (Z/P 22-3b).

176   **"We must, to":** to Julius Simon, 12/26/1917, Urofsky and Levy, v. 4, p. 331.

177   **On the boat:** Minutes, caucus of American delegates to London conference, 7/14/1920, in Julius Simon, pp. 345–47.

177   **"Chaim," Simon said:** Julius Simon, p. 100.

178   **"Felix and Brandeis, I":** 7/18/1920, Howe, *Holmes-Laski,* p. 271.

178   **The World Zionist:** Julius Simon, pp. 100–105, 344; Manuel, pp. 261–66; *NY Times,* 7/8/1920, p. 7; Urofsky, *American Zionism,* pp. 129, 277; Urofsky and Levy, v. 4, p. 475–76; Lipsky, *Thirty Years,* pp. 67–69. Also, LDB to J. E. Farber/11/7/1920, AJA.

180   **"resulting from differences":** LDB to A. Brandeis 4/23/1921, UL/LDBP: 217 (M4-4b); B. V. Cohen interview, 2/17/1981.

180   **LDB's donations to Zionism:** Mason, *Brandeis,* p. 692.

180   **A law clerk:** H. J. Friendly interview, 5/7/1981.

181   **"The banks and waters":** *NY Times,* 2/25/1923, VII, p. 12.

181   **Until his death:** Much of the LDB Zionist contribution records are in UL/LDBP: 100 (SC 5-2c); also see "An Index to the Correspondence of Judge [sic] Louis D. Brandeis, Reels 13–31," AJA.

181   **"I understand that":** LDB to J. W. Mack, 10/20/1923, LC/FFP: CF.

Chapter 10. Holmes and Brandeis Dissenting

182   **"The tension is":** LDB to R. W. Goldmark, 11/17/1918, Urofsky and Levy, v. 4, pp. 363–64.

182   **Having many of:** A. E. Stephan interview, 12/5/1980; FF to P. A. Freund, 3/20/1945.

182   **Reading and "Brandeis":** LC/Agnes Meyer Papers: Diary, 3/4/1919.

182   **"the Stoneleigh so":** LDB to Alice Brandeis, 10/14/1917, Urofsky and Levy, v. 4, p. 316.

182   **"I am very":** To H. Feis, 5/18/1919, LC/Feis Papers: 11.

183   **This social life:** Pepper, p. 158.

183   **"The whole question":** LC/Meyer Papers: Diary, 1/16/1918.

183   **"Louis' friends":** LC/Meyer Papers: Diary, 3/4/1919.

183   **"All the time":** COHP/Landis, pp. 77–78.

183   **"The bed he":** H. J. Friendly interview, 5/7/1981.

183   **"Some industrial":** LDB to FF, 8/25/1921, Urofsky and Levy, v. 5, p. 8.

184   **"Nothing down":** Freund, "Justice Brandeis," p. 5.

184   **"I never":** H. F. Stone to FF, 6/22/1945, LC/Stone Papers: 74.

184   **"I do not":** G. W. Anderson to T. W. Gregory, 7/16/1924, LC/Gregory Papers: 2.

184   **"I'm not":** To Laski, 1/12/1921, Howe, *Holmes-Laski,* p. 304.

185   **"infinitely more":** Acheson to FF, 3/2/1921, LC/FFP/CF.

185   **The entertainment form:** COHP/Landis, pp. 67–68; B. V. Cohen interview, 2/17/1981; Wyzanski, p. 67.

185   **Acheson, by now:** Acheson, *Morning and Noon,* p. 47.

185   Those Republican scandals: LDB to FF, 5/20/1924; FF to E. R. Buckner, 6/12/1924, in LC/FFP: CF.

186   "I am told": To Laski, 5/9/1925, Howe, *Holmes-Laski,* p. 738.

186   "particularly unfit": NY *Sun,* 10/23/1924.

186   "well and cheerful": To Laski, 12/17/1925, Howe, *Holmes-Laski,* p. 806.

186   "Refuse to accept": LDB to R. W. Bruere, 2/25/1922, LC/FFP: CF (Brandeis).

187   "would floor me": Acheson to FF, 11/26/1921, LC/FFP: CF.

187   With his family: Family correspondence in BU/LDBP.

187   "There is much": To FF, 11/21/1927, Urofsky and Levy, v. 5, p. 313.

187   "there are no": Wyzanski, p. 66; LDB to E. B. Raushenbush, 6/3/1931, Urofsky and Levy, v. 5, p. 478.

188   "You do not": 5/23/1936, BU/LDBP: 21.

188   "You turn the": 11/12/1926, HLS/Holmes Papers: 38 (4).

188   In honor of: LDB to FF, 11/15/1926, Urofsky and Levy, v. 5, p. 245, *NY Times,* 11/27/1926, p. 17.

188   Since the Brandeis: LDB to Alice Brandeis, 12/4/1918, Urofsky and Levy, v. 4, pp. 370–71.

188   "He thinks much": Pringle, *Taft,* pp. 970-71.

189   "I must stay": W. H. Taft to Horace Taft, 11/14/1929, in Pringle, *Taft,* p. 967.

189   "Impossible!": Acheson, *Morning and Noon,* p. 88.

189   "a man who is": FF, *Reminisces,* p. 109.

189   "a benevolent": HLS/"Conversations between L. D. B. and F. F."

189   FF's Holmes story: FF to L. Hand, 3/22/1960, HLS/FFP: 199-13.

189   "I hate facts": To L. Einstein, 5/22/1919, Peabody, *Holmes-Einstein,* p. 187; to Laski, 1/6/1923, Howe, *Holmes-Laski,* p. 469.

189   In 1922, after: LDB to Holmes, 12/8/1922, HLS/Holmes Papers: 38 (4); LDB to Holmes, 5/18/1925, Urofsky and Levy, v. 5, p. 173. Also see Howe, *Holmes-Laski,* p. 268; *NY Times,* 1/16/1927, IV, p. 12.

190   "In the middle": HLS/"Conversations between L.D.B. and F.F."

190   John Hessin Clarke: Clarke to G. Sutherland, 10/4/1922, LC/Sutherland Papers: 5; Clarke to Wilson, 9/9/1922, Mason, *Taft,* p. 167; LDB to FF, 10/2/1922, Urofsky and Levy, v. 5, p. 73.

191   Brandeis thrived on: Acheson, "Reminiscences," p. 6.

192   "We've had some": HLS/"Conversations between L.D.B. and F.F."

192   "we disposed of": To Laski, 10/13/1925, Howe, *Holmes-Laski,* p. 790.

192   "our regular Saturday": To Einstein, 3/10/1916, Peabody, *Holmes-Einstein,* p. 125.

192   Usually the conference: See Holmes to Laski, 2/22/1929, Howe, *Holmes-Laski,* p. 1135; HLS/"Conversations between L.D.B. and F.F."

192   "The statement that": Acheson to FF, 4/6/1920, LC/FFP: CF.

193   Because Brandeis put: LDB to W. H. Taft, 11/3/1923; W. H. Taft to LDB, 11/4/1923, LC/W. H. Taft Papers: Reel 258.

193   "What can we": Wyzanski, p. 67.

193   The work was: Acheson, "Reminiscenses," p. 4.

193   "The court has": to W. A. White, 2/15/1927, LC/White Papers: C-119.

193   Even the law: See Wyzanski, p. 71; Acheson, *Morning and Noon,* p. 81; Freund, "Justice Brandeis," pp. 6–7; Acheson to FF, 3/15/1920, LC/FFP: CF; D. Riesman to FF, LC/FFP: CF (Brandeis folder); various case files at

HLS; H. J. Friendly interview, 5/7/1981, all for general background on
LDB's work habits.

194   "Herewith is some": Robert Page ("R. G. P.") to LDB, 4/27/1927,
HLS/LDBP: 52 (5).

194   "You'd have to": H. J. Friendly interview, 5/7/1981.

194   Acheson story: Acheson, "Reminiscences," p. 5.

194   "I have a": 10/24/1920, HLS/Holmes Papers: 29 (5).

195   "bother us in" Mason, *Taft*, p. 211.

195   "I suppose it": HLS/LDBP: 58 (4), 16 (2).

195   "It relieves me": HLS/LDBP: 20 (1), 57 (10).

195   "I think you": HLS/LDBP: 24 (8).

195   "While I voted": HLS/LDBP: 43 (5).

195   *Hamilton:* 251 U.S. 146, 149.

195   The decision was: HLS/"Conversations between L.D.B. and F.F."; Acheson,
Morning and Noon, p. 60.

196   "I heard that": 12/27/1919, McLellan and Acheson, p. 4.

196   *Myers:* 272 U.S. 52.

196   William Howard Taft: Pringle, *Taft*, pp. 1023–25; Mason, *Taft*, pp. 225–27.

196   Brandeis had several: For LDB/Wilson 1920s relationship and "document"
letters, see LC/Wilson Papers: Series 2, Wilson to LDB, 6/20/1921; LDB to
Wilson, 6/20/1921; Wilson to LDB, 11/6/1921; LDB to Wilson, 11/8/1921;
Wilson to LDB, 12/6/1921; LDB to Wilson, 12/8/1921; LDB to Wilson,
12/28/1921; Wilson to LDB, 4/9/1922; LDB to Wilson, 4/11/1922; LDB to
Wilson, 4/15/1923; Wilson to LDB, 12/23/1923; in Series 12, Wilson to F.
I. Cobb, 4/18/1923; in Series 14, file 10, LDB to T. L. Chadbourne,
6/27/1921.

197   "as thorough a": COHP/Landis, pp. 38–39.

197   "exercised continuously": 272 U.S. 52, 250, 291; also see LC/Hamlin Papers:
Diary (12/9/1926), v. 12, p. 163.

198   Child labor was: Hourwich, pp. 27, 298, 318–23, 383.

198   "I think children": McKelway, p. 161.

198   Senator Albert J. Beveridge: Harbaugh, p. 63.

199   In Boston in: LDB to J. A. Sullivan, 1/31/1907, Urofsky and Levy, v. 1, pp.
520–21.

199   Quickly challenged: *Hammer* v. *Dagenhart*, 247 U.S. 251, et seq.

201   In 1922, Brandeis: *Pa. Coal Co.* v. *Mahon*, 260 U.S. 393 et seq.

201   *Burns:* 264 U.S. 504, 513, 533, 520, 534.

201   "But Van Devanter": HLS/"Conversations between L.D.B. and F.F."

202   "Let any disinterested": FF, *Law and Politics*, p. 15.

202   Following the First: Acheson, *Morning and Noon*, pp. 100–101.

203   His hostess at: LC/Agnes Meyer Papers: Diary, 2/6/1922.

203   "We cannot go": Acheson, *Morning and Noon*, p. 101.

203   *Hitchman Coal and Coke Co.* v. *Mitchell:* 245 U.S. 229, 249–50.

203   "no such thing": Acheson, *Morning and Noon*, p. 85.

204   Brandeis caught the: 245 U.S. 229, 271.

204   In the town of: *Truax* v. *Corrigan*, 257 U.S. 312.

204   With Pitney's switch: Mason, *Taft*, p. 242.

205   If the picketers: 257 U.S. 312, 331, 343, 354, 357.

205   Brandeis's criticisms: FF, *Law and Politics*, pp. 219–21.

205   In 1928, Frankfurter: G. W. Norris to FF, 5/5/1928; 6/2/1928; 11/25/1929;
in LC/FFP: CF.

205   In 1932, Frankfurter: FF, *Law and Politics,* pp. 223–27.
206   *United Mine Workers:* 268 U.S. 295.
207   "I determined to": Mason, *Taft,* pp. 194, 202–3.
207   "will take from": HLS/"Conversations between L. D. B. and F. F."
207   "Why I had no idea": Mason, *Supreme Court,* p. 53.
207   "hugger-mugger of": Pringle, *Taft,* p. 1040.
207   *Duplex Printing Company:* 254 U.S. 443, 480, 486, 488.
208   *Bedford Cut Stone:* 274 U.S. 37, 54, 55, 58, 59, 65.
208–209   On Sutherland's opinion: Paschal, p. 86.
210   *Weeks:* 232 U.S. 383.
211   *Bureau:* 256 U.S. 465, 475, 477.
211   *Ziang:* 266 U.S. 1, 13, 14, 17.
212   "Yes sirree": HLS/LDBP: 30 (12).
213   *Casey:* 276 U.S. 413, 418–19, 421–25.
213   "I have much": Holmes memorandum, HLS/LDBP: 45 (6).
213   *Olmstead:* 277 U.S. 438.
214   In Brandeis's office: H. J. Friendly interview, 5/7/1981.
214   "It will be": 277 U.S. 438, *amicus curiae* brief, p. 8.
214   "Some of our number": 277 U.S. 438, 466.
214   "We have to choose": 277 U.S. 438, 470.
215   Taft was furious: Mason, *Taft,* p. 227; Holmes to F. Pollock, 6/20/1928, Howe, *Holmes-Pollock,* v. 2, p. 222.
215   Brandeis believed that: H. J. Friendly interview, 5/7/1981; 277 U.S. 438, 477–85.
216   "You may have seen": W. H. Taft to G. Sutherland, 7/25/1928, LC: Sutherland Papers: 5.
216   "some reviewer of": LDB to FF, 6/15/1928, Urofsky and Levy, v. 5, p. 346.
217   *Southwestern Bell:* 262 U.S. 276, 292, 304, 312.
218   "Count me in": HLS/LDBP: 65 (5-280 U.S. 234).
218   *McCardle:* 272 U.S. 400, 423–24.
218   *St. Louis:* 279 U.S. 461, folders in HLS/LDBP: 55.

Chapter 11. The Jew at Harvard

220   "We have got to": FF to R. Pound, 2/4/1912, LC/FFP: CF.
220   "There is also": to F. Pollock, 4/5/1919, Howe, *Holmes-Pollock,* v. 2, p. 8.
220   "real effort in": 4/20/1919, Howe, *Holmes-Laski,* p. 196.
221   LDB/Pound meeting: LDB to R. Pound, 5/28/1919; LDB to Alice Brandeis, 6/14/1919, both in Urofsky and Levy, v. 4, p. 395–96, 400–401.
221   "are too guileless": 10/31/1919, UL/LDBP: 99 (SC 4-2c).
221   "he will be": Urofsky and Levy, v. 4, pp. 458–59.
221   But that same: HLS/Pound Papers: 25 (10); Pound to LDB, 4/24/1920, UL/LDBP: 99 (SC5-1b).
222   "Let me know": To R. Pound, 4/27/1920; HLS/Pound Papers: 67 (18); FF to Holmes, 5/15/1920, HLS/Holmes Papers: 30 (12).
222   "The result is": 5/15/1920, UL/LDBP: 99 (SC 5-1b).
222   "not infrequently on": Mayer, p. 4.
223   In 1916, Harold: 11/7/1916, Howe, *Holmes-Laski,* p. 35; LC/Agnes Meyer Papers: 1 (Diary, 12/20/1918).
223   FF/M. Denman correspondence: Undated, LC/FFP: CF.
224   "I wonder if": FF to M. Denman, 7/20/1918, 12/27/1918, LC/FFP: CF.

224 **"Please tell Mrs.":** 9/24/1916, Howe, *Holmes-Laski,* p. 25.

224 **"Why should I":** FF to M. Denman, 7/18/1919, LC/FFP: CF.

224 **"Felix is safe":** To Holmes, 5/9/1919, Howe, *Holmes-Laski,* p. 219; LDB to M. Denman, 11/3/1919, LC/FFP: CF.

224 **"Have you forgotten":** 12/9/1919; 12/1919, LC/FFP: CF.

225 **"Felix and Marion":** 1/14/1920 (but mismarked 1919), Howe, *Holmes-Laski,* p. 233.

225 **"Sweetheart—I'd":** 7/7/1925, 11/28/1924, LC/FFP: CF.

225 **"Graduate work":** FF, "The Conditions for . . . Legal Research," p. 297.

225 **"The control of":** FF, "Task of Administrative Law," p. 231.

226 **"Frankfurter took us":** COHP/Lane, p. 153.

226 **"We were not":** E. J. Brown, *Harvard Law Review,* June 1965, pp. 1523–24.

226 **"all of these":** E. N. Griswold, Harvard Law School *Bulletin,* 3/1965, p. 3.

226 **"bounced" into his:** J. L. Rauh, Jr., interview, 3/10/1981.

226 **"Let [a student]":** NY *Globe,* 6/26/1932, in LC/FFP: 229 (oo4143).

227 **"the bright boys":** F. Rodell, p. 453.

227 **"In the course":** FF to Wyzanski, 6/24/1930, LC/FFP: CF.

227 **"He was a":** COHP/Landis, pp. 36–37; FF to "Dear Joe," 11/19/1925, LC/FFP: CF (Landis); FF to H. Croly, 1/8/1925, LC/FFP: CF.

228 **"You may have":** 5/19/1933; 1/28/1936, LC/FFP: CF.

228 **"National and international":** Schlesinger, Sr., *In Retrospect,* p. 82.

228 **"merely the manifestation":** G. Gunther.

228–229 **FF/family relationships:** See LC/FF Family Collection.

229 **In 1919 there:** *Lampoon,* 1/16/1920; K. Martin, pp. 34–35; Holmes to FF, 2/11/1920, HLS/Holmes Papers: 29 (5).

229 **Harvard had first:** S. E. Morison, pp. 57–58, 198, 422; Rosovsky, p. 82.

230 **Lowell biography:** Yeomans, pp. 209–16.

230 **"If every college":** A. L. Lowell to A. I. Stix, 6/9/1922, HLS/FFP: 191 (18).

230 **"Lowell had also":** Rosofsky, p. 89.

230 **"from New York lawyers":** to J. W. Mack, 5/29/1922, LC/FFP: CF (Mack).

231 **"I do not":** 6/14/1922, LC/FFP: CF (Mack).

231 **Lowell/FF letters:** From 6/19/1922 to 6/29/1922 (five letters), LC/FFP: 126 (002620).

231 **"I do not regard":** R. Steel, p. 194.

231 **Stix/Lowell letters:** From 6/6/1922 to 7/24/1922 (eight letters), HLS/FFP: 191 (18).

232 **At times the:** C. W. Eliot to FF, HLS/FFP: 191 (19).

232 **The committee of thirteen:** Report in LC/FFP: 126 (002626); Rosofsky, p. 89.

232 **"Of course, Margold":** 12/8/1926, LC/FFP: CF.

232 **On February 21, 1928:** Meeting memorandum, HLS/FFP: 186 (17).

233 **"Pound opposed":** T. R. Powell to FF, 2/8/1930; HLS/Powell Papers: A (A9).

233 **Harvard was not:** M. R. Cohen to H. A. Overstreet, 12/9/1937; L. C. Rosenfield, p. 106; Pound to FF, 7/25/1922, LC/FFP: CF; LDB letter quoted in FF to C. E. Clark, 11/4/1929, LC/FFP: CF.

233 **"is fifty per cent":** to E. M. Morgan, 1/31/1930, LC/FFP: CF (Buckner).

234 **"I assume that":** To E. R. Buckner, 4/1923; FF to D. R. Hawkins, 1/8/1931, LC/FFP: CF.

234 **"lacking too much":** to G. Parsons, LC/FFP: CF.

234 **"Why is it":** "Proceedings . . . Frankfurter," p. 48; FF to C. Magruder, 6/23/1933, HLS/Magruder Papers: 34 (2).

234   "withdrawing children from": *NY Times,* 7/31/1922, p. 10.
235   **Harold Laski once:** To Holmes, 7/20/1925, Howe, *Holmes-Laski,* p. 766.
235   **His "infinite sense":** FF, *Law and Politics,* pp. 3–7.
235   **"Let's stop being":** to C. C. Burlingham, 2/14/1924, HLS/Burlingham Papers: 4 (8); Harbaugh, p. 242.
235   **"Marion is dead right":** 4/6/1924, Urofsky and Levy, v. 5, p. 123.
235   **La Follette, in his:** Schlesinger and Israel, v. 3, p. 2520; La Follette, p. 1128.
236   **"slaughtering . . . social":** *New Republic,* 10/1/1924, pp. 110–13; Urofsky and Levy, v. 5, p. 141.
236   **Frankfurter endorsed Smith:** FF, *Law and Politics,* pp. 321–24.
236   **During the First:** Hillman to FF, 3/29/1920; FF to Hillman, 3/30/1920, LC/FFP: CF; FF, *Reminisces,* pp. 204–6.
236   **Frankfurter's next project:** See Sutherland, pp. 271–72; FF/Moley correspondence and Mack/Lowell correspondence, Feb. and March 1922, LC/FFP: CF (Mack).
237   **"Felix has always":** G. Kanin, "Trips to Felix," p. 16; G. Kanin, "FF Toward the End," p. 2.
238   *Adkins:* 261 U.S. 525.
238   **"It is beyond":** FF to B. Flexner, 2/16/1921, LC/FFP: CF.
238   **Determined to educate:** M. W. Dewson to E. M. Johnson, 11/21/1922, LC/FFP: 153 (003094).
238 , **"We are in the last":** F. Kelley to A. A. Berle, Jr., 1/31/1923, LC/NCL Papers.
238   **"unless transgression of":** 261 U.S. 525, FF brief, p. ii.
238   **"If this act is":** 261 U.S. 525, Ellis brief, pp. 4, 5.
239   **Brandeis did not:** J. Goldmark, *Crusader,* p. 173; COHP/*Frankfurter,* p. 166.
239   **The decision is credited:** W. H. Taft to Holmes, 4/4/1923, HLS/Mr. Justice Holmes Opinions: 1922; 261 U.S. 525, 558, 559, 560; Holmes dissent, p. 568; Sanford/Taft dissent, p. 562.
239   *Adkins* **was handed:** Minutes, 4/19/1923 conference, LC/NCL Papers.
240   **"As to my":** F. Kelley to FF, 5/26/1923, LC/FFP: 157 (003148).
240   **There was talk:** J. H. Clarke, ABA *Journal,* 1923, pp. 691–92; F. Kelley to C. F. Amidon, 10/26/1923, LC/NCL Papers.
240   **"I don't think":** E. N. Griswold interview, 7/21/1982.
241   **Although Brandeis lived:** LDB to FF, 11/19/1916; LDB to FF, 11/25/1916; Urofsky and Levy, v. 4, pp. 266, 267. LDB to FF, 5/3/1917, LC/FFP: 26.
241   **"Of course, he":** LDB to de Haas, 4/7/1920, Urofsky and Levy, v. 4, p. 458.
241   **In the early 1920s:** LDB to Mack, 1/12/1922; LDB to FF, 1/3/1923, also LDB to FF, 1/6/1923, LC/FFP: 26.
242   **Brandeis's biographer, reported:** Mason, *Brandeis,* p. 692.
242   **For Brandeis the:** LDB to B. Perlstein, 2/16/1916, 6/1/1916; Brandeis to N. Sokolow, 7/7/1918, Urofsky and Levy, v. 4, pp. 62, 208, 347.
242   **LDB to A. Brandeis:** 9/16/1921, Urofsky and Levy, v. 5, pp. 13–14.
242   **Brandeis gave funds:** See LDB to FF, 12/19/1922, LC/FFP: CF; LDB to FF, 2/3/1922, Urofsky and Levy, v. 5, pp. 43–44; "President and Fellows of Harvard College" in UL/LDBP: 110 (SC 22-1e); Landis, pp. 184–90.
242   **"It is a task":** 2/18/1925, LC/FFP: CF (Brandeis folder).
243   **" 'The Fine Arts Library' ":** 2/17/1925, LDB to R. A. Kent, 1/27/1936, Urofsky and Levy, v. 5, pp. 162, 564.
243   **"the more freely":** In UL/LDBP/NMF: 20 (20-2b).
243   **"I am glad":** LDB to FF, 2/24/1925, LC/FFP: 26.

243   **An account was:** FF to E. L. Malloch, 10/7/1925; Alice Brandeis to E. L. Malloch, 1/11/1939, UL/LDBP: Series X (Warren and Brandeis/Brandeis, Dunbar & Nutter [WB]) microfilm. Comptroller of the Currency records.

243   **"Frankfurter told our":** L. H. Weinstein to author, 7/14/1982.

244   **Brandeis also discussed:** LDB to E. M. McClennen, 10/30/1932, UL/LDBP: NMF/20 (20-2a); LDB to J. W. Mack, 3/11/1934, UL/LDBP: Z/P 58 (1d).

244   **John P. Frank, who:** Frank to author, 5/24/1982.

Chapter 12. Sacco and Vanzetti

245   **"And here let":** *Debs.* v. *U.S.* 249 U.S. 211.

246   *Schenk:* 249 U.S. 47.

246   **"there was a":** Holmes to F. Pollock, 4/5/1919, Howe, *Holmes-Pollock,* v. 2, p. 7.

246   **"I had not then":** HLS/"Conversations between L.D.B. and F.F."

247   *Abrams:* 250 U.S. 616; W. A. Gengarelly, pp. 19–24.

247   *Schaefer:* 251 U.S. 466.

248   **In the next internal:** 252 U.S. 239.

249   **"Please count me":** To LDB, HLS/LDBP: 4 (2).

249   *Gilbert:* 254 U.S. 325.

249   **"any flaw in":** LDB to FF, 12/6/1920, LC/FFP: 26.

249   **When Brandeis planned:** Acheson memorandum, 11/19/1920, HLS/LDBP: 5 (12).

249   **laws in Nebraska:** *Meyer* v. *Nebraska,* 262 U.S. 390; *Bartels* v. *Iowa,* 262 U.S. 404.

250   **At Harvard, Frankfurter:** FF to L. Hand, 6/5/1923, HLS/FFP: 198 (12).

250   *Gitlow:* 268 U.S. 652.

250   **"The last day of":** To Laski, 6/14/1925, Howe, *Holmes-Laski,* p. 752.

250   *Whitney:* 274 U.S. 357; HLS/LDBP: 44 (7).

251   *Fiske:* 274 U.S. 380.

251   **"clear and present danger" argument:** Gunther, p. 9; Chafee, p. 8.

252   **How anxious the:** *U.S.* v. *Schwimmer,* 279 U.S. 644; Harbaugh, p. 285.

253   **Given his inclinations:** COHP/Baldwin, p. 211.

253   **Frankfurter joined:** FF to J. W. Mack, 5/12/1921, HLS/Chafee Papers: 29 (21).

253   *Colyer:* 265 F. 17 (D. Mass. 1920).

254   **"Could you take":** HLS/Lawrence G. Brooks Papers: 3/21/1920.

254   **Attorney General Palmer:** Palmer statement, correspondence, LC/FFP: 204 (003758).

255   **"Word comes of":** LDB to Z. Chafee, 5/19/1921; LDB to FF, 5/20/1921, Urofsky and Levy, v. 4, pp. 558–60.

255   **"The Trial at the Harvard Club" accounts:** Yeomans, pp. 317–27; FF, *Reminisces,* pp. 209–11; Irons.

256   **"Gentlemen, I had":** Z. Chafee to U. Sinclair, 9/19/1922, HLS/Chafee Papers: 24 (19).

257   **"I am not as":** 11/22/1923, HLS/FFP: 198 (12).

258   **Frankfurter's involvement often:** COHP/Jackson, p. 180; Lash, *Frankfurter,* p. 80.

258   **"the art of":** to H. Laski, 9/23/1926, LC/FFP: CF.

259   **"blind spot":** J. M. Maguire to G. A. Gordon, 2/22/1927, HLS/Maguire Papers: 14 (3).

259   "blue-penciled myself": E. Sedgwick to J. McReynolds, 3/23/1927, UVA/
McReynolds Papers: 3; also COHP/Howe, pp. 81a–82.

259–260 **Quotes on Sacco and Vanzetti:** FF, *Sacco and Vanzetti,* pp. 3, 8, 104,
63.

260   "Your flaming zeal": B. N. Cardozo to FF, 3/10/1927, HLS/FFP: 196 (10);
Douglas, *Go East, Young Man,* p. 167.

261   "Wigmore was a": quoted by FF to R. H. Montgomery, 2/20/1958,
HLS/FFP: 208 (14).

261   "I can remember": E. N. Griswold, *Harvard Law Review,* Nov. 1962, p. 8;
interview, 7/21/1982.

261   "had the condemned": Harvard *Crimson,* 4/29/1927, in LC/FFP: 245
(004250).

261   "a more important": to P. L. Sayre, 3/5/1948, HLS/FFP: 197 (21a).

261   "I fully realized": E. Sedgwick to J. McReynolds, 3/23/1927, UVA/
McReynolds Papers: 3.

261   **Had Frankfurter violated:** S. Williston to FF, 10/31/1927; FF to S. Williston,
10/31/1927, LC/FFP: CF.

262   **Lowell reaction:** Liva Baker, *Frankfurter,* p. 121.

262   **There were personal:** FF to W. F. Smith, 1/3/1928; to L. Sharfman,
3/10/1927; to H. S. Shattuck, 4/28/1927, in LC/FFP: CF.

262   "Those two so-called": to A. E. Cohn, 4/12/1927, HLS/FFP; 196 (13);
COHP/Ford, pp. 465–66.

263   "I did not go": Liva Baker, pp. 126–27.

263   "I think a": FF to W. A. White, 5/19/1927, LC/White Papers: C-120.

263   **From the beginning:** C. H. Moorman to FF, 5/12/1928, HLS/FFP: 207 (13).
COHP/Jackson, p. 280.

264   "Convinced that we": Ehrmann, pp. 485–86.

264   **Lowell had been:** Yeomans, p. 488.

264   "but when I came": A. L. Lowell to R. N. Hale, 8/15/1927, HLS/FFP: 197
(1); see also A. L. Lowell to W. H. Taft, 11/1/1927, sent by A. Bickel to FF,
3/8/1960, in FDRL/Gardner Jackson Papers: 19 (FF folder).

264   **FF/Hill:** FF, *Of Law and Men,* p. 314.

265   **Frankfurter tried for:** See tapes of FF telephone conversations, 8/13/1927
and 8/18/1927, HLS/FFP: 215 (5), (6).

265   "I'm afraid that": Telephone conversations, FF/M. Frankfurter, 8/18/1927;
FF/Buller, 8/15, 1927, HLS/FFP: 215 (6).

265   "This is quite": Telephone conversations, HLS/FFP: (5), FF/G. Jackson,
8/14/1927; (6), FF/Mears, 8/16/1927.

266   **Even he did not:** HLS/FFP: 215 (5).

266   "What are the": FF/Barso telephone conversation, 8/9/1927, HLS/FFP:
215 (5).

266   **Holmes was the:** Holmes to Laski, 8/18/1927, Howe, *Holmes-Laski,* p. 971;
also NA: RG 267, No. 32919, at 467–8; Holmes to L. Einstein, 8/14/1927,
Peabody, p. 272; Holmes to FF, 9/9/1927, HLS/Holmes Papers: 29 (11).

267   "The views a": To L. H. Winters, 7/1/1959, LC/FFP: CF.

267   "I speak without": Telephone conversation, FF/Hill, 8/20/1927, HLS/FFP:
215 (6).

267   **Brandeis had followed:** LDB to FF, 11/8/1925; 3/9/1927, Urofsky and
Levy, v. 5, pp. 193, 275; LDB to FF, 4/12/1927, 4/20/1927, LC/FFP: CF;
LDB to FF, 8/5/1927, Urofsky and Levy, v. 5, p. 299; LDB to FF, 6/2/1927,
LC/FFP: 27.

268   **In 1921, when:** LC/Hamlin Diary, v. 14, pp. 21–22: 8/23/1927; Lief, *Brandeis,* p. 437; LDB to FF, 1/7/1927, LC/FFP: CF.

269   **LDB encounter:** Telephone conversations, FF/G. Jackson, 8/20/1927, 8:55 PM; 8/21/1927, 1 AM; FF/Sherman, 8/21/1927, noon, HLS/FFP: 215 (6) (7); *NY Times,* 8/22/1927, p. 1.

269   **"It is a most":** Telephone conversation, FF/G. Jackson, 8/21/1927, 3:45 PM, HLS/FFP: 215 (7).

269   **Learned Hand saw:** COHP/Hand, p. 101; H. R. Morse to FF, 9/14/1927, HLS/FFP: 207 (23).

270   **"What he did":** FF to P. Weiss, 10/27/1927; FF to Pound, 8/23/1927, LC/FFP: CF.

270   **Frankfurter never lost:** to R. W. Hale, 9/4/1927, LC/FFP: CF; HLS/Ehrmann Papers: 21 (9-p. 34).

270   **Marion, with Gardner:** COHP/Jackson, pp. 295–97; HLS/FFP: 210 (1).

270   **The case and:** Russell, p. 45.

270   **For Felix:** FF to J. M. Harlan, 5/29/1963, LC/FFP: CF.

271   **"Thompson and I":** HLS/Ehrmann Papers: 21 (9-pp. 35–7); W. G. Thompson to LDB, 6/28/1932, UL/LDBP: 131 (G-6-1a).

271   **In reporting:** *NY Times* 6/23/1932, p. 23.

271   **"I think the":** Boston *Herald,* 6/24/1932, p. 1.

271   **"You know me":** to J. W. Mack, 6/21/1932, LC/FFP: CF.

271   **Frankfurter said he:** FF to W. Lippmann, 7/12/1932, LC/FFP; 120 (002502); FF to A. E. Cohn, 7/18/1932, LC/FFP: CF.

BOOK THREE: THE MOST INFLUENTIAL SINGLE INDIVIDUAL

Chapter 13. The New Deal

275   **Of the nation's:** Fuchs, p. 2608; Freidel, "Election of 1932," p. 2738; Robinson, pp. 29, 103, 277.

275   **Then the depression:** U.S., *Historical Statistics,* pp. 73, 116, 139.

276   **When FDR was:** *NY Times,* 12/14/1928, p. 10; Freidel, *Franklin D. Roosevelt,* p. 400; FF to FDR, 10/9/1928, Freedman, p. 38.

276   **"Tell Frank Roosevelt":** FF to C. C. Burlingham, 3/24/1931, FFP: CF.

277   **"are still":** FF to C. C. Burlingham, 2/10/1932, HLS/Burlingham Papers: 4 (10).

277   **When FDR was:** FF/FDR conversation, 7/2/1932, memorandum by FF, Freedman, pp. 73–77.

277   **Finally, Bernard Baruch:** Baruch, pp. 245–46.

278   **"Why I Am":** FF, *Law and Politics,* p. 331.

278   **Between Roosevelt's:** Freidel, *Franklin D. Roosevelt,* p. 106; FF to FDR, 11/12/32, Freedman, p. 94; FF, *Reminisces,* pp. 154–55.

278   **"play of wit":** COHP/Childs, pp. 112–13.

279   **"integrity and":** FF to L. Hand, 10/15/1931, HLS/FFP: 198 (16); see also COHP/Stimson: 20–21; Stimson and Bundy, pp. 289–92; FDR to Stimson, 12/24/1932, Yale/Stimson Papers: 112(16).

279   **"to remould":** *New State Ice Co.* v. *Liebmann,* 285 U.S. 262, 311; Berle, p. 82.

279   **"Aunt Alice and":** LDB to Fannie Brandeis, 7/11/1932, Urofsky and Levy, 5, p. 505.

279   **FDR/LDB meeting:** FF, *Reminisces,* p. 281; FF to FDR, 10/26/1932, Freedman, p. 91; FF to M. LeHand, 11/10/1932, LC/FFP: CF; LDB to FF, 11/17/1932 and 11/19/1932, LC/FFP: CF. For LDB's reaction, LDB to FF, 11/24/1932; LDB to E. G. Evans, LC/FFP: CF.

280   **"I had a most":** FDR to FF, FDRL/PPF 140: 1.

280   **"life in Washington":** LDB to Alice Goldmark, 1/11/1934, Urofsky and Levy, v. 5, p. 531.

280   **"somebody in there":** Moley, *Seven,* p. 123 n.

280   **"I hear you":** to FF, 2/25/1933; to Thacher, 2/27/1933, in LC/FFP: 180 (003646).

280   **"took me":** FF memorandum, LC/FFP/CF (Roosevelt); also FF to FDR, 3/14/1933, LC/FFP: 183 (003515); E. N. Griswold interview, 7/22/1982; Holmes to Laski, 11/23/1932, Howe, *Holmes-Laski,* p. 1421.

282   **"Felix is a":** Josephson, p. 28.

282   **FF/Hoover account:** Stone to FF, 4/14/1933; FF to Stone, 4/17/1933, HLA/FFP; 171 (13); also FDRL/OF: 10 (10b); Moley, *Seven,* p. 77; de Toledano, pp. 99–101.

283   **"Typically, F. F.":** Berle, pp. 83, 73.

283   **"a package too":** Freidel, *Franklin D. Roosevelt,* pp. 341.

283   **What easterners like:** Dorough, p. 335.

283   **FF/securities legislation:** FF/Rayburn and FF/FDR correspondence in LC/FFP: 182 (003498); LC/FFP: Diary, 5/8/1933; Berle, p. 86; Landis, "Legislative History."

285   **"Felix Frankfurter":** Moley, *Seven,* p. 130.

285   **"Drop me a line":** Eugene Meyer to FF, 2/16/1932, LC/Eugene Meyer Papers: 22.

285   **E. N. Griswold coming to Washington:** E. N. Griswold interview, 7/21/1982.

285   **"Do you know":** FDR to FF, 5/19/1930, FDRL/Governor's Papers: Private correspondence.

286   **"I don't know":** COHP/Tugwell, p. 45.

286   **Felix Frankfurter didn't:** COHP/Appleby, pp. 29–30.

286   **"You know the":** LC/Ickes Diaries: 3/23/1933 (mss.); Margold to FF, 3/27/1933, LC/FFP: 149 (003019).

286   **"He is first":** FF to Margold, 5/11/1933, LC/FFP: 149 (003019); A. Hiss interview, 5/26/1982.

286   **"a person of":** FF to M. LeHand, 9/24/1933, FDRL: OF 1560.

286   **"to get his friends":** Undated memorandum to D. R. Richberg, LC/Richberg Papers.

287   **"I would likely":** Rauh, pp. 496–97.

288   **"Anyone who":** *Harvard Law Review,* 11/1962, pp. 23–24.

Chapter 14. The German Jews

289   **"send [him] back":** FF to F. W. Buxton, 9/8/1933, LC/FFP: CF.

289   **"the controlled experiment":** FF to C. Magruder, 9/28/1933, HLS/Magruder: 34 (2).

289   **"I felt about":** FF to B. N. Cardozo, 11/24/1932, LC/FFP: CF (A. L. Kaufman folder).

289   **"sniff at the new":** FF to Holmes, 10/30/1933, HLS/OWHP: 30 (18).

289   **"What was truly":** Lord Evershed, *Harvard Law Review,* 11/1962, p. 4.

290 **Between semesters he:** FF to T. R. Powell, 1/25/1934, HLS/Powell Papers: A (A6).

290 **FF/Shaw encounter:** H. J. Laski to Holmes, 2/3/1934, HLS/Holmes Papers: 30 (18); FF to T. R. Powell, 2/20/1934, HLS/Powell Papers: A(A6); FF to C. C. Burlingham, undated, HLS/Burlingham Papers: 4 (12); Kanin, "Trips to Felix," p. 12.

290 **"In England, happily":** LC/FFP: 197.

291 **Frankfurter became a:** See, for example, Freedman, pp. 194–95, 214; FF to FDR, 4/25/1924, FDRL/PSF: 150.

291 **"There is no doubt":** FF, "Persecution of Jews in Germany," LC/FFP: 197.

291 **"I assume Felix":** LDB to J. M. Mack, 3/11/1934, UL/LDBP: Z/P(58).

292 **"Pesach in Jerusalem":** undated postcard, LC/FF Family Collection.

292 **"a most":** FF to FDR, 4/14/1934, Freedman, p. 211.

292 **Once when visiting:** Julius Simon, p. 96.

292 **"the reclamation of":** FF to Holmes, 5/7/1934, HLS/Holmes Papers: 30 (18).

292 **"I suspect there":** FF to M. L. Avner, 4/2/1935, LC/FFP: CF.

292 **"in order that":** FF to C. Magruder, 10/19/1933, HLS/Magruder Papers: 34 (2).

292–293 **Marion's illness:** See G. R. Girdlestone correspondence, LC/FFP: CF (A. E. Cohn folder).

293 **"It was all":** FF to T. R. Powell, 1/25/1934, HLS/Powell Papers: A (A6).

293 **"refreshment and new":** Laski to LDB, 5/21/1934, UL/LDBP: 105 (SC 14-1d).

293 **"He could listen":** Baruch, pp. 259–60.

294 **"I am by temperament":** FF to A. M. Schlesinger, Jr., 6/18/1963, LC/FFP: CF.

294 **"One objective":** Corcoran to FF, 4/22/1934, LC/FFP: 116.

294 **LDB/Hughes:** LDB to FF, 4/1/1930, LC/FFP: CF.

294 **"Hughes ought to":** HLS/FFP: 198 (4); FF to W. Lippmann, 2/5/1920, LC/FFP: CF.

295 **Holmes retirement:** Danelski and Tulchin, p. 299; Hughes to H. F. Stone, 1/11/1932, LC/Stone papers: 75.

295 **"I wish":** FF to E. R. Buckner, LC/FFP: CF.

295 **When the Holmes:** See FF/H. F. Stone; FF/S. S. Wise, and FF/H. L. Stimson correspondence for this period in LC/FFP: CF and LC/Stone Papers: 13; Yale/Stimson diaries, 1/19/1932, 1/22/1932.

296 **Hoover/LDB meeting:** LDB to FF, 4/1/1930, LC/FFP: CF.

Chapter 15. Powers Behind the Presidential Throne

297 **"The secret of":** J. F. Carter, p. 307.

297 **Newspaper accounts:** H. L. Varney, Albany *Times-Union,* 11/1/1936, p. 4-A; J. P. Pollard, *NY Times,* 1/28/1934, V, p. 4; F. R. Kent column, 9/15/1934, LC/FFP: CF (Brandeis); H. J. Johnson, "Think Fast, Captain," *Saturday Evening Post,* 10/26/1935, p. 5.

297 **Dorothy Thompson:** Thompson to FF, 10/15/1936, LC/FFP: CF; G. Clark to FDR, 7/4/1936, FDRL: PSF/Box 140.

297 **"Mother tells me":** M. Frankfurter to FF, circa 1935, LC/FFP: CF.

298 **Another point ignored:** Burns, *Lion and the Fox,* p. 204.

299 **"During this whole":** F. R. Kent column, 9/15/1934, LC/FFP: CF (Brandeis).

299   "Frankfurter radicals": W. R. Hearst letter, reprinted in *NY Times,*
           9/21/1927, p. 1.
299   "When I see you": 5/30/1934, LC/FFP: 117 (MA).
300   "beginning to assume": F. M. Isserman to FF, 1/13/1936, FF to Isserman,
           1/14/1936, LC/FFP: CF.
300   "I cannot recall": M. Childs, *Witness,* pp. 33–34.
300   In 1934, 1935: Mason, *Brandeis,* p. 692.
300   "I would say": COHP/Childs, pp. 66–67.
300   William Douglas, then: Douglas, *Go East, Young Man,* pp. 441–42, 307.
300   "I could almost": COHP/Burlingham, p. 32.
301   "He kept up": John Sapienza, in COHP/Reed, pp. 341–42.
301   In the early days: See J. J. Burns to FF, 3/1/1935, LC/FFP: CF; M. Lerner,
           NY *Herald Tribune,* 3/17/1935, p. 6.
301   At times Brandeis: Berle, p. 95; "B.V.C." memorandum, LC/FFP: CF (Bran-
           deis).
301   But at other: H. Shulman memorandum of meeting with LDB, 12/8/1933,
           LC/FFP: CF (Brandeis).
301 et seq. In 1932, Wisconsin: Drawn from Perkins, pp. 188–89; Raushenbush, pp.
           21–23; LDB to J. Gilbert, 1/22/1936, BU/LDBP: 21; T. Corcoran and B.
           Cohen to FF, 6/18/1935, LC/FFP: CF; LDB correspondence in UL/LDBP:
           105 (SC 14-a) and 216 (M2-7); Freund, "Justice Brandeis," p. 10; Wyzanski,
           p. 69; Freund interview, 7/17/1981. Supreme Court case referred to *Mellon*
           v. *Florida,* 273 U. S. 12.
303 et seq. The second area: Drawn from "Memorandum on Public Works," LC/FFP:
           226 (004135); LC/FFP: Diary, 2/10/1933; Moley, *First New Deal,* pp. 274–
           76.
304   "many of the": R. Wheeler, "Extrajudicial Activities," pp. 126, 128.
305   "If I thought": W. Van Devanter to H. Thompson, 2/16/1918, LC/Van
           Devanter Papers: 11.
306   "If I had": 7/19/1924, Urofsky and Levy, v. 5, p. 135.
306   In June 1916: Yale/House Papers: Diary, 6/17/1916, 6/19/1916.
306   "was the strongest": Pringle, *Taft,* p. 1043–44; also Mason, *Taft,* p. 172.
306 et seq. Perhaps the most: See in LC/Van Devanter Papers, in Box 12: W. Van
           Devanter to W. H. Sanborn, 10/11/1922; to J. W. Davis, 10/28/1922; to W.
           H. Sanborn, 11/2/1922; in Box 13, to W. H. Sanborn, 10/31/1922. Also see
           Mason, *Taft,* pp. 168–69; Harbaugh, p. 192.
307   *New State Ice Co.:* 285 U.S. 262, 273, 287, 311.
307   "whether the business": Mason, *Stone,* p. 322.
307   "We may not forget": HLS/LDBP: 76 (2).
308   The Supreme Court in 1928: *Quaker City Cab Co.* v. *Commonwealth of Pa.,*
           277 U.S. 389, 403–11.
308   *Liggett Co.:* 288 U.S. 517, 536, 541–80, 586.
309   "The only difficulty": 2/28/1933, HLS/LDBP: 81 (1).
309   "a very powerful": 3/18/1933, LC/FFP: CF.
309   "I think you": 3/1/1933, HLS/LDBP: 82 (12).
309   *Nebbia:* 291 U.S. 502, 537, 556.
310–311   *Frazier-Lemke:* 295 U.S. 555, 580.
311   *Schechter:* 295 U.S. 495, 500, 505.
312   "any court that": Princeton/OHP/Douglas, p. 255.
312   FF/Corcoran communication: Corcoran telegram to FDR, 4/4/1935,
           FDRL/140: FF file.

312   **After the Court:** COHP/Krock, pp. 25, 28; FF to A. E. Cohn, 1/1/1935, LC/FFP: CF.

312   **Baruch on Johnson:** Perkins, p. 200.

312   **Johnson/LDB:** F. R. Kent column, 9/15/1934; NY *Herald Tribune,* 9/26/1934, LC/FFP: CF (Brandeis).

313   **"The Herald Tribune's":** LDB to FF, 9/25/1934, LC/FFP: CF (Brandeis).

313   **Brandeis felt so:** P. A. Freund interview, 7/17/1981; H. S. Johnson statement, undated, LC/FFP: CF (Brandeis); Johnson to LDB, 1/1/1935 (with note of LDB's response), UL/LDBP: 230 (M17-1b); see also FF to A. E. Cohn, 10/30/1935, LC/Stone Papers: 13.

313   **Johnson and Brandeis:** LDB to FF, 9/22/1934, LC/FFP: CF (Brandeis).

313   **"I can only":** Stone to FF, 10/2/1934, LC/FFP: CF.

313   **When the Court:** HLS/"Conversations between L.D.B. and F.F."

313   **third case:** *Humphrey's Executor* v. *U.S.,* 295 U.S. 602.

314   **"Hot Oil":** *Panama Refining Co.* v. *Ryan,* 293 U.S. 388.

314   **Gold-clause cases:** 294 U.S. 240, 330, 217.

314   **Railroad Retirement Act:** 295 U.S. 330, 374.

314   **Agricultural Adjustment Act:** *U.S.* v. *Butler,* 297 U.S. 1, 88.

315   **Tennessee Valley:** *Ashwander* v. *Tennessee Valley Authority,* 297 U.S. 288.

315   **minimum wage:** *Morehead,* 298 U.S. 587.

315   **"In our day":** FF, *Law and Politics,* pp. 240, 351.

315   **"The point is":** Fuess, p. 193.

315   **In 1932, Frankfurter:** FF to B. L. Young, 10/18/1932, LC/FFP: CF: Perkins, pp. 248–49, 255, 265.

316   **"ultra free markets":** Berle, p. 79.

316   **"no doubt":** Moley, *Seven,* p. 307.

316   **"It was suggestive":** Ibid., p. 316 n.

316   **"When I got":** LC/Ickes Diaries: 8/6/1935 (mss.)

316   **Frankfurter spent much:** Schlesinger, Sr., *In Retrospect,* p. 137; J. L. Rauh interview, 3/10/1981.

316   **"not one of them":** Burns, *Lion and Fox,* p. 153.

316   **FF gold clause message draft:** See LC/FFP: 256 (004321), and message as delivered, *Public Papers and Addresses of Franklin D. Roosevelt,* v. 4, p. 287. See FF draft, tax revision message, LC/FFP: 214 (003967), and as delivered in *Public Papers,* v. 4, p. 270.

317   **"I would add":** FF to FDR, 5/22/1936, FDRL/PSF: 150.

317   **There was time:** M. H. McIntyre to M. Frankfurter, 10/25/1934; F. Frankfurter to McIntyre, 10/27/1934, FDRL/PPF: 140.

317   **"It's the storm":** 7/10/1935, LC/FFP/CF.

318   **In exchange, Frankfurter:** FF to LDB, 6/14/1935, 8/31/1935, undated but circa 1934–35, in UL/LDBP: 134 (G-9-2c).

Chapter 16. Pack the Supreme Court

319   **A few minutes:** Leonard Baker, *Back to Back,* pp. 33–34.

320   **As early as 1935:** Memorandum and correspondence, UVA/Cummings Papers: 199.

320   **"They seem to be":** Hughes, p. 75.

321   **"After March 4, 1929":** Leonard Baker, *Back to Back,* p. 108.

321   **At the White House:** FDRL/PSF: 76 (Homer Cummings 1935–1936 file); LC/Cummings Diary: 3/19/36.

321   **Cummings developed:** See LC/Cummings Diary: Nov. to Dec., 1936; Leonard Baker, *Back to Back,* p. 134.

321   **"As I read this":** LC/Cummings Diary: 12/26/1936.

322   **"esteem it a":** E. L. James to LDB, 2/8/1937, UL/LDBP: 39 (G-14-1a).

322   **"Whom did F. D.":** LDB to FF, 2/6/1937, LC/FFP: CF.

322   **Brandeis's law clerk:** W. Hurst to author, 7/1/1982.

322   **In subsequent years:** Schlesinger, Sr., *In Retrospect,* p. 125.

323   **"Brandeis valued":** R. H. Jackson, quoted in L. Baker, *Back to Back,* p. 35.

323   **"Very confidentially, I":** FDR to FF, 1/15/1937, LC/FFP: CF.

323   **"What about it":** Liva Baker, p. 183.

323   **"conscious moulders of":** *New Republic,* 1/25/1922, pp. 236–38.

323   **"In all governments":** *New Republic,* 10/1/1924, pp. 110–13.

324   **"real grievances and":** to H. L. Stimson, 10/6/1924, LC/FFP: CF.

324   **Then propose a":** FF to FDR, 5/29/1935, LC/FFP: CF.

324   **In 1936, Frankfurter:** See LC/Cummings Diary: 1/13/1936; FF to H. F. Stone, LC/FFP: CF; LC/Ickes Diary: 5/22/1936 (mss.).

324   **"And so it was":** FF to FDR, 2/7/1937, Freedman, pp. 380–81.

324   **"I am awfully glad":** FDR to FF, 2/9/1937, LC/FFP: CF.

325   **"disregarding all":** FF to FDR, 2/18/1937, LC/FFP: 256 (004326).

325   **With all of his:** Holmes to FF, 9/9/1921, HLS/Holmes Papers: 29 (6); H. F. Pringle, *Taft,* p. 1000.

325   **"There is no":** FF, *Law and Politics,* pp. 28–29.

325   **"wholly without foundation":** FF to R. M. Remick, 6/26/1935, LC/FFP: CF.

325   **"Lawyers, above all":** FF to H. M. Brune Jr., 2/10/1937, LC/FFP: CF.

326   **"I am not satisfied":** 3/4/1937, LC/FFP: CF (Burlingham folder).

326   **"Why don't I":** 3/6/1937, LC/FFP: CF.

327   **Frankfurter never wavered:** Request, E. K. MacColl, 8/18/1952, LC/FFP: 181 (003480).

327   **"Frankfurter never went":** COHP/Landis, pp. 49, 302.

327   **"there was no doubt":** F. Buxton, unpublished mss., LC/FFP: 256 (unpaged).

328   **"Some foolish folk":** 3/30/1937, Freedman, p. 392; FF to FDR, 7/20/1937, FDRL/PSF: 150.

328   **"They showed me":** P. A. Freund, "Justice Brandeis," pp. 3–4; Frank, *Marble Palace,* p. 110; Childs, "Majority," p. 45.

329 et seq.   **Hughes letter account:** Drawn from Danelski and Tulchin, pp. 304–5; Childs, "Minority," p. 45; Childs, "Supreme Court Today," pp. 587–88; Leonard Baker, *Back to Back,* pp. 153–64; C. C. Burlingham to FF, 6/8/1937, LC/FFP: CF; FF to C. C. Burlingham, 6/9/1937, Freedman, pp. 401–2.

330 et seq.   *Morehead,* 298 U.S. 587, 619; for Roberts's actions, Leonard Baker, *Back to Back,* pp. 173–76.

332   *West Coast Hotel:* 300 U.S. 379; Leonard Baker, *Back to Back,* pp. 173–76.

332   **FF/LDB exchange:** LDB to FF, 3/29/1937; FF to LDB, 3/31/1937, LC/FFP: CF.

333   **"After today":** FDRL/PPF: FF 150.

333   **Cardozo's reactions:** J. L. Rauh, Jr., *Cardozo Law Review.*

333–334   **LDB's possible retirement:** Acheson to R. E. Lee, 4/23/1937, McLellan and Acheson, p. 32; HLS/"Conversations between L. D. B. and F. F."; FF to H. Laski, 5/25/1937, LC/FFP: CF.

334   **Van Devanter retirement:** COHP/Childs, p. 70; B. V. Cohen interview, 2/17/1981; Leonard Baker, *Back to Back,* pp. 225–31.

335   "The Supreme Court": FF to FDR, 8/10/1937, memorandum, Freedman, pp. 404–6.
335   Another effect was: B. V. Cohen to FF, 10/11/1937, LC/FFP: 28; LC/Ickes Diary: 7/16/1938 (mss.).
336   "they were in": FF to C. C. Burlingham, 10/4/1939, HLS/Burlingham Papers: 5 (1).
336   "your talk with": B. V. Cohen to FDR, 10/24/1938, FDRL/PSF: 140.
336   "Its ghosts will": FF to H. F. Stone, 6/2/1936, LC/Stone Papers: 13.

Chapter 17. Against Adolf Hitler

337   May 11, 1933 talk: Text in FDRL/PSF: 150.
338   "I guess the Jews": LDB to FF, 4/29/1933, LC/FFP: CF; Wise, pp. 158–59.
338   "seems not to": Julius Simon, pp. 242–44.
338   Negotiations had begun: Urofsky, *American Zionism*, pp. 361–63; FF to J. Mack and J. de Haas, 10/3/1929, LC/FFP: CF; LDB to FF, 10/5/1929, Urofsky and Levy, v. 5, pp. 398–99.
339   In 1929 the: LDB, *Curse of Bigness*, pp. 255–57.
339   The Brandeis theme: FF, "Palestine Situation Restated," pp. 414, 424, 434.
340   "I think I": Laski to Holmes, 9/30/1930, Howe, *Holmes-Laski*, pp. 1298–99.
340 et seq. LDB/Lindsay meeting: LDB memorandum, 6/1930, LC/FFP: CF.
341 et seq. Hull/LDB meeting: LDB to Wise, 5/11/1933, LC/FFP: 137 (002820); "Memorandum of Conversation with Raymond Moley . . . Sunday, May 14th," LC/FFP: 187 (003584); Freund interview, 7/17/1981.
343   "a conglomeration of": Leonard Baker, *Roosevelt and Pearl Harbor*, p. 121.
343   "For once in my": FF to C. Hull, LC/FFP: 137 (002820).
343   Frankfurter had received: FF to FDR, circa 5/1933, LC/FFP: 137 (002820).
343   FF/Hull dialogue: Hull to FF, 5/6/1933, LC/FFP: 137 (002820); FF to Hull, 5/23/1933, LC/FFP: CF; W. Phillips to FF, 6/2/1933, LC/FFP: 137 (002820).
343   Roosevelt did raise: Freidel, *Franklin D. Roosevelt*, p. 396; Freund, "Justice Brandeis," pp. 15–16.
344   Brandeis and Frankfurter: *NY Times*, 5/12/1933, p. 7; LC/FFP: 134 (002759).
344   Frankfurter began a: FF to C. C. Burlingham, 4/28/1933, in LC/FFP: CF; 5/2/1933, LC/FFP: 137 (002820).
344   *The Wave of the Future:* By Anne Morrow Lindbergh, NY, 1940.
344   "I happened to have": FF to E. Sedgwick, 11/19/1920, LC/FFP: CF.
345   "That things should be": FF to J. G. McDonald, 5/8/1933, LC/FFP: 187 (003583).
345   Frankfurter and Brandeis: LDB memorandum, 10/17/1933; FF memorandum, 11/19/1933, LC/FFP: 117 (McDonald folder).
345   "The general description": A. E. Cohn to J. G. McDonald, 1/9/1934, LC/FFP: 117 (McDonald folder).
345–346 McDonald's statement: Leonard Baker, *Days of Sorrow and Pain*, p. 225.
346 et seq. Pound/FF clash: Wigdor, p. 250; "Memorandum of conversations with Pound and Conant," LC/FFP: CF (Pound).
347   If Harvard gave: FF to J. B. Conant, 10/4/1934; J. B. Conant to FF, 10/8/1934, LC/FFP: CF.
347   "What was done": FF to G. Clark, 3/3/1936, LC/FFP: CF (C. C. Burlingham folder).

348 et seq. **FF/Coffin exchange:** Excerpt from Warren will, H. S. Coffin to FF, 1/16/1936; FF to H. S. Coffin, 1/21/1936, LC/FFP: CF; H. F. Stone to FF, LC/FFP: CF; S. E. Morison to FF, 1/23/1936, LC/FF: CF (FF's response, same date and citation, shows he took Morison's comments seriously).

349 **"It is a common":** In Rosovsky, pp. 89–90.

349 **Not all American:** Steel, p. 373; FF to Lippmann, 11/28/1936, LC/FFP: CF.

350–351 **Solomon Frankfurter details:** A. Lippe to FF, 10/23/1941; FF to A. Lippe, LC/FFP: 123 (002554); NY *Post*, 1/24/1939, p. 4.

351–352 **FF/Lady Astor exchange:** To Lady Astor, 3/22/1938; to FF, 3/24/1938; to FF, undated, to Lady Astor, 4/7/1938, 6/2/1938, LC/FFP: CF; Washington *Star*, 10/23/1941, unpaged clipping, LC/FFP: 233 (004171).

352 **Laski's messages:** Laski to FF, 1/20/1937; 8/8/1938, LC/FFP: CF.

352 **"London felt like":** FF to F. W. Buxton, 9/24/1938, LC/FFP: CF.

353 **The President suggested:** B. V. Cohen to Missy LeHand, 10/13/1938, FDRL/PSF: 140.

353 **". . . The White House":** *NY Times*, 10/15/1938, p. 1.

353 **Brandeis found the:** LDB to FF, 10/16/1938, Urofsky and Levy, v. 5, p. 503.

353 **"the liquidation of":** Leonard Baker, *Days of Sorrow and Pain*, p. 229.

354 **In the United States:** Leonard Baker, *Roosevelt and Pearl Harbor*, p. 120.

354 **A few days later:** Memorandum, 11/18/1938, signed "A.S.F.," HLS/LDBP: 113 (10); B. V. Cohen to FF, 11/21/1938, LC/FFP: CF.

Chapter 18. Mr. Justice Frankfurter

356 **July 6 cabinet meeting:** LC/Cummings Diary, 7/6–7/9/1938.

356 **Boston *Herald* editorial:** In LC/FFP: 197.

356 **On Monday, October 3:** J. Knox, "Experiences as Law Clerk . . . ," pp. 872–73; LC/Cummings Diary: 12/19/1938.

357 **They also heard from:** *NY Times*, 8/16/1938, p. 3.

357 **"In the ordinary":** Pringle, *Taft*, p. 239.

358 **"No, the country would":** LC/Cummings Diary: 11/18/1938.

359 **"Will not his":** To P. Kellogg, 9/16/1938, W. Johnson, pp. 389–90.

359 **Prominent American Jews:** LC/Ickes Diary: 9/18/1938 and 12/3/1938 (mss.); Lash, *Diaries of Frankfurter*, p. 64; Freedman, pp. 481–82.

359 **Even the western:** Corcoran/Norris material, LC/Norris Papers: 280 (1938–39 folder); *NY Times*, 8/9/1938, p. 3.

360 **"The movement":** *NY Times*, 8/18/1938, p. 3.

360 **Another boost came:** *NY Times*, 9/23/1938, p. 15.

360 **Still Roosevelt dallied:** LC/Cummings Diary: 9/18/1938.

360–361 **FF/FDR October meeting:** *NY Times*, 10/8/1938, p. 8; HLS/FF interview with G. Gunther, 9/15/1960, 2nd tape, pp. 8–11; *NY Times*, 11/15/1938, p. 14; FF to FDR, 11/17/1938, FDRL/PSF: 150.

361 **At the end of the month:** Cummings to FDR, 11/30/1938, FDRL/PSF: 77 (Cummings folder).

361 **After Krystallnacht:** LC/Cummings Diary: 12/18/1938.

361 **Brandeis had turned eighty-two:** B. V. Cohen interview, 2/16/1981; J. Alsop and R. Kintner, *NY Times*, 11/17/1938, p. 2; LC/Ickes Diary: 1/1/1939 (mss.).

362 **"He has a real":** LC/Ickes Diary: 1/2/1939.

362 **On Wednesday, January 4:** LC/Ickes Diary: 1/7/1939 (mss.).

362–363 **FF appointment:** HLS/FF interview with G. Gunther, 9/15/1960, 2nd tape, pp. 8–11; FF to C. C. Burlingham, 7/8/1942, LC/FFP: CF; FF, *Reminisces,* p. 334.

363   **The appointment was:** LC/Ickes Diary: 1/15/1939 (mss.).

363   **"I think Felix's":** FDR to Laski, 1/10/1939, FDRL/PSF: 53.

364   **LDB congratulations:** LDB to FF, 1/15/1939, LC/FFP: 120 (002508).

364   **Other justices, liberals:** A. L. Lowell to FF, 1/17/1939, LC/FFP: 121 (002518); letter, unsigned to FF, 1/26/1943, LC/FFP: 114 (1943–44 folder); F. W. Buxton to FF, 3/3/1939, LC/FFP: CF.

364–365   **Ryan letter to FF:** 1/7/1939, Catholic University, Ryan Papers.

365   **Buxton letter to FF:** 1/5/1939, LC/FFP: CF.

365   **Frankfurter himself said:** FF, *Reminisces,* pp. 333–34.

366   **Acheson quotes:** Acheson, *Morning and Noon,* p. 201; to G. Rublee, 1/17/1939, McLellan and Acheson, p. 37.

366   **"Why not an American":** U.S. Congress, *Frankfurter,* p. 6.

366   **The subcommittee members:** Acheson, *Morning and Noon,* p. 202–3.

366   **Felix Frankfurter was:** R. L. Fuffus, "Felix Frankfurter," *NY Times Magazine,* 1/15/1939, p. 3.

367   **"He did a superb job":** to G. Rublee, 1/17/1939, McLellan and Acheson, p. 37.

367   **McCarran/Frankfurter exchange:** U.S. Congress, *Frankfurter,* pp. 125–26.

367   **There was a luncheon:** Acheson, *Morning and Noon,* pp. 208–11.

367   **The morning of:** *NY Times,* 1/19/1939, p. 6.

368   **Classroom events:** S. J. Rubin interview, 2/18/1981; Washington *News,* 1/18/1939.

368   **"That fellow":** Boston *Post,* 1/19/1939, p. 1.

368   **Franklin Roosevelt had:** FF to FDR, 1/16/1939, LC/FFP: CF; *NY Times,* 1/20/1939, p. 2.

369   **The Supreme Court:** HLS/Powell Papers: A(A7).

369   **"Dear Frank":** Freedman, pp. 485–86.

370   **In November of 1938:** *NY Times,* 11/13/1938, IV, p. 9.

370   **On January 7, two:** *NY Times,* 1/10/1939, p. 20.

370   **During the remainder:** LC/Ickes Diary: 2/4/1939 (mss.); FF's handwritten note on A. Bickel to FF, 7/1/1955, HLS/FFP: 205 (7); H. F. Stone to FF, 2/10/1939, HLS/FF: O. T. 1938, bound volume, Paige Box 10.

370   **LDB's letter of resignation:** LC/FFP: 127 (002649).

370   **Brandeis wrote his:** FF to L. Hand, 2/16/1939, HLS/FFP: 199 (1); Alice Brandeis to Mrs. W. Wilson, 3/1/1939, LC/Wilson Papers: Series 9.

371   **FDR to LDB:** 2/13/1939, Urofsky and Levy, v. 5, p. 610.

371   **LDB on Douglas:** See LDB to J. H. Holmes, 4/4/1939.

371   **Brandeis in the:** FF to C. C. Burlingham, 10/4/1939, HLS/Burlingham Papers: 5 (1).

371   **Politics continued to:** FF to FDR, 7/29/1940, FDRL/PSF: 150; Acheson, *Morning and Noon,* p. 222.

371   **What strength Brandeis had:** Acheson to G. Rublee, 1/17/1939, McLellan and Acheson, pp. 36–37; Acheson, *Present at the Creation,* p. 169; see considerable FDR/LDB correspondence regarding White Paper, refugees, and Palestine in FDRL/PSF: 64 (Palestine folder) and in FDRL/PPF: 2335; Douglas, *Go East, Young Man,* p. 443. Also see LDB to D. Ben-Gurion, AJHS/LDBP, p. 248; transcript, Jewish Agency meeting, 10/15/1941, LC/LDBP.

372   **On the evening of:** FF to C. Magruder, HLS/Magruder Papers: 34 (5); Freedman, p. 618.

372   **That being the end:** Urofsky and Levy, v. 5, p. 655; *New Palestine,* 11/14/1961.

372   **"I should not mourn":** to D. Lilienthal, 10/28/1941, Princeton/Lilienthal Papers: 96.

372–373   **Memorial service remarks:** LC/Middleton Papers.

BOOK FOUR: A SENTINEL ON WATCH
Chapter 19. In World War II

377   **Felix Frankfurter told:** FF memorandum, 1/30/1939, LC/FFP: 226 (004126).

377   **His first written:** *Hale, Chairman, et al.* v. *Bimco Trading, Inc.,* 306 U.S. 375, 380.

378   **That same day:** *Milk Control Board* v. *Eisenberg Farm Products,* 306 U.S. 346, 351.

378   **Also, on February 27:** *Kiefer & Kiefer* v. *Reconstruction Finance Corp.,* 306 U.S. 381, 389.

378   **Mass. tax case:** *Texas* v. *Florida, et al.,* 306 U.S. 398, 431.

378   **Frankfurter wrote several:** *Graves* v. *NY,* 306 U.S. 466, 491–92.

378   **Another time:** *Driscoll* v. *Edison,* 307 U.S. 104, 422.

379   **Black murder case:** *Pierce* v. *Louisiana,* 306 U.S. 354.

379   **In the second case:** *Lane* v. *Wilson,* 307 U.S. 268.

379   **"Fifteen pertinent":** *NY Times,* 4/2/1939, IV, p. 7.

379   **Chief Justice Hughes:** "Remarks of Felix Frankfurter at the Law School–Graduate School Alumni Day, June 13, 1956," LC/FFP: 200; FF to R. M. Perkins, 5/12/1958, LC/FFP: CF.

380   **"There was something":** H. Black, Jr., p. 224.

381   **Two weeks after:** FF to L. Hand, 2/19/1939, LC/FFP: CF; to A. M. Hand, 3/30/1958, HLS/FFP: 198 (8).

381   **FF/Alpaca coat story:** COHP/Landis: p. 90.

381   **"I have known":** FF to C. C. Burlingham, 6/4/1941, LC/FFP: CF.

381   **"a simon-pure":** MacLeish, "Mr. Justice Frankfurter," p. 53.

381   **The key word:** M. Josephson, 11/30/1940, p. 25; LC/Ickes Diary: 3/24/1940 (mss.).

382   **He never tired:** L. Henkin in COHP/Hand, p. 105.

382   **"He loves the touch":** MacLeish, "Mr. Justice Frankfurter," p. 54.

382   **The Gridiron Club:** Newspaper clipping, unidentified, LC/FFP: 233 (004171).

382   **"Quietly aloof":** Washington *Times-Herald,* 3/13/1939.

383   **"The Doctor thought":** FF to H. F. Stone, 2/24/1939, HLS/FFP: 171 (18); O. J. Roberts to FF, 8/30/1944, HLS/FFP: 171 (2); H. Mansfield interview, 7/22/1981.

383   **Felix and I:** M. Frankfurter to FDR, Christmas, 1939, FDRL/PSF: 150.

383   **Roosevelt continued to:** LC/Ickes Diary: 6/8/1941 (mss.); FF to A. T. Mason, 5/22/1953, LC/FFP: CF; Pusey, pp. 787–88; Mason, *Stone,* pp. 566–67.

384   **In September 1941:** Leonard Baker, *Roosevelt and Pearl Harbor,* pp. 242–43.

384–385   **Hopkins/Churchill:** Ibid., pp. 49–50.

385   **FF/Lend-Lease:** Ibid., p. 76; Liva Baker, pp. 249–50.

385   A legend has grown: Lash, *Diaries,* p. 74; quoted in Liva Baker, p. 253.
386   Whatever assistance he gave: LC/FFP: Diary, 2/3/1943, 1/10/1943, 4/21/1943; FF to R. Niebuhr, 2/21/1940, LC/Niebuhr.
386   "It will seem": Rauh, "From the Diaries . . ."
386   "I thought the": FF to F. W. Buxton, 3/12/1941, LC/FFP: CF.
387   "arsenal of democracy": FF draft in LC/FFP: 256 (004329); compare with text as delivered, *Public Papers and Addresses of F.D.R.,* 1940, p. 633.
387   "two or three matters": FF to Missy LeHand, 2/4/1941, Freedman, p. 580.
387   FF/Hand: FF memorandum, 12/3/1942, LC/FFP: FDR (1942 folder); LC/Ickes: Diary, 4/3/1943 (mss.); COHP/Hand, pp. 148–49; see also A. N. Hand to FDR, 11/13/1942, HLS/FFP: 199 (1), indicating others also pushing L. Hand.
387   "Felix cannot talk": LC/Ickes: Diary, 6/2/1940 (mss.)
388   "Felix Frankfurter appears": HLS/FFP: 203 (16).
388 et seq. FF/Bohr: Oppenheimer, p. 7; V. Bush, "Memorandum of Conference," 9/22/1944, Dept. of Energy Archives; Yale/Stimson: Diary, 6/12/1943, v. 67, p. 172; L. R. Groves to FF, 9/6/1962, LC/FFP: 121 (002530).
390 et seq. "I think Felix": LC/Ickes: Diary, 4/20/1941, 9/28/1941 (mss.); letters to FDR, FDRL: OF 1560; Princeton/OHP: Douglas, Cassette No. 13, p. 282.
390   Frankfurter still had: Acheson, *Present at the Creation,* p. 43; Berle, pp. 345, 358, 362, 377, 405, 406.
391   "the Jewish group": Berle, p. 342.
391   Rankin: L. S. Dawidowicz, "American Jews and the Holocaust," *NY Times Magazine,* 4/18/1982, pp. 47 ff.
391   Lindbergh speech: Leonard Baker, *Roosevelt and Pearl Harbor,* pp. 263–65.
392   "The President asks": G. Tully to FF, 7/17/1942, LC/FFP: FDR.
392n   Roosevelt had not: Byrnes, p. 242.
392   "The use that had": to E. I. Kaufman, 10/20/1944, LC/FFP: CF.
393 et seq. FF/Karski: Statement by J. Karski, "The Impact of the Holocaust on Judaism in America," American University, 3/23/1980.

Chapter 20. Defining Patriotism

395   *Schneiderman* v. *U.S.:* 320 U.S. 115.
395 et seq. Hugo Black wanted: see LC/FFP: Diary, 3/12/1943, 3/13/1943; FF to H. F. Stone, 3/31/1943, HLS/FFP: 170 (13); W. O. Douglas memorandum to "Dear Frank," 6/14/1943, LC/Douglas Papers: 228; FF to F. Murphy, 5/31/1943, LC/Stone Papers: 74.
396   Saboteurs case: *Ex parte Quirin* 317 U.S. 1; FF, memorandum, 9/25/1942, LC/Stone Papers: 69.
397 et seq. The Court upheld: Douglas, *Court Years,* p. 279; Warren, *Memoirs,* p. 147; *Hirabayashi* v. *U.S.,* 320 U.S. 81, 93, 106; FF to Stone, 6/4/1943, HLS/FFP: 172 (3): *Korematsu* v. *U.S.,* 323 U.S. 214, 225, 233, 225, 243.
398   Douglas wrote years later: Douglas, *Court Years,* p. 280; Warren, p. 149: *NY Times,* 9/26/1971, p. 76.
399   "I recollect no": COHP/Baldwin, p. 258.
399   Flag-salute case: *Minersville School District* v. *Gobitis,* 310 U.S. 586.
399   According to Hughes's: Pusey, pp. 728–29; Princeton/OHP: Douglas, cassette #3, p. 47.
400   The Gobitis decision: Stimson and Bundy, p. 317; see FF to A. Hamilton, 6/21/1940, HLS/FFP: 178 (11).

401   "is a powerful": Douglas comments on back of decision, and Black comments, FF to Stone, HLS/FFP: O.T. 1939, Paige Box 10.

401   FF/Stone exchange: Stone to FF, LC/FFP: Mason (1946–51 folder).

401   Liberals had not: Ickes, *Diaries*, v. 3, p. 199; Chafee to G. Clark, 6/5/1940, HLS/ABA Bill of Rights Committee: 3 (3).

401   "I am nearly 58": FF to A. Hamilton, 6/21/1940, HLS/FFP: 178 (11).

402   One who did: Lash, *Eleanor Roosevelt*, p. 159n.

402   Of the eight-man: *NY Times*, 6/11/1940, p. 27; 6/17/1940, p. 17; 12/25/1940, p. 20.

402   FF/Douglas exchange: HLS/FFP: O.T. 1939, Paige Box 10.

402   *Jones:* 316 U.S. 584, 624.

403   "Black and Murphy and I": Princeton/OHP: Douglas, Cassette #3, p. 47.

404   *West Virginia:* 319 U.S. 624, et seq.

405   At the Saturday conference: LC/FFP: Diary, 6/13/1943, 6/15/1943.

406   Frankfurter was caught: FF to E. Sedgwick, 2/10/1932, LC/FFP: 164 (003529); FF, *Law and Politics*, p. 91.

407   His friends attempted: Liva Baker interview with Morris Ernst, 12/5/1968; F. Rodell, "Frankfurter," p. 457; A. M. Schlesinger, Jr., "The Supreme Court: 1947," p. 427.

407   NCL story: Letters in LC/NCL Papers: 1949; D. McAllister to FF, 11/12/1949; FF to D. MacAllister, 11/14/1949, LC/FFP: 157 (003150).

408   "The evidence as to": *Baumgartner* v. *U.S.*, 322 U.S. 665, 677.

408   After the Second: *Prince* v. *Mass.*, 331 U.S. 158; *Everson* v. *Board of Education*, 330 U.S. 1; *McCollum* v. *Board of Education*, 333 U.S. 203; FF to C. C. Burlingham, 4/13/1951, LC/FFP: CF: FF to H. L. Black, 5/5/1952, LC/Black Papers: 313.

408   The major freedom: *Engel* v. *Vitale*, 370 U.S. 421.

409   According to William Douglas: Princeton/OHP: Douglas, Cassette #3, p. 339.

Chapter 21. Frankfurter versus Douglas

410   In 1944, when: FF to A. L. Richards, 5/1/1945, LC/FFP: CF.

410   A couple of: FF to C. C. Burlingham, 4/24/1945, LC/FFP: CF.

412   "He had friends": P. Elman interview, 2/25/1981.

412   "Certainly one does not": FF to W. Millis, 1/19/1953, LC/FFP: CF.

412   Weizmann/Marshall: FF to G. C. Marshall, 3/10/1948; Marshall to FF, 3/15/1948, LC/FFP: CF.

412   *Henderson story:* Forrestal, Diaries, pp. 348, 357–58; FF to W. Millis, 1/19/1953, LC/FFP: CF; *NY Times Magazine*, 11/21/82, p. 100.

413   W. O. Douglas to H. S. Truman, received at the White House, 7/5/1952, Washington *Post*, 11/7/1982; "Earl Warren: The Governor's Family" (an Earl Warren oral history project in the Law Library, College of William and Mary), p. 25. Truman-Vinson: *NY Times*, 9/9/1953, p. 26; Israel and Friedman, v. 4, p. 2658. Fortas story: LBJ Library/T. Morton OHP, p. 22.

413–414 FF/Mason correspondence: LC/FFP: 83.

414   "He had his dislikes": D. Trautman interview, 8/4/1981.

414   "If you came from": N. Dorsen interview, 3/5/1982; D. Riesman, Jr., interview, 8/7/1981.

414 et seq. Morgan story: D. G. Morgan interview, 8/18/1981; B. Wright, Jr., to FF, 2/7/1944, LC/FFP: CF.

415	"This striking egalitarianism": A. Bickel to Liva Baker, 2/20/1968.
415	"They are, as it were": FF to W. C. Warren, 5/22/1945, LC/FFP: 41.
415	The "free and easy": A. Bickel to Liva Baker, 2/20/1968; A. L. Kaufman interview, 7/6/1981; confidential source.
416	"They are really not": "Proceedings in Honor of Mr. Justice Frankfurter," p. 16.
416	"Until the early": J. Wilson, *Police Report,* p. 190.
417	FF/Coleman: FF to Freund, 12/18/1947, HLS/FFP: 214 (13); FF to J. W. McCormack, 4/30/1948, HLS/FFP: 176 (21).
417	"I've been listening": FF to C. C. Burlingham, 4/22/1952, LC/FFP: CF.
417	Elliot L. Richardson: E. L. Richardson interview, 8/17/82.
418	In conference, he: H. L. Black, "Mr. Justice Frankfurter," p. 1521; T. Clark, ABA *Journal,* 5/1965, p. 331: Douglas, *Court Years,* p. 22.
418	When the Court: FF to C. C. Burlingham, 2/8/1944, HLS/Burlingham Papers: 5 (5); COHP/Burlingham, p. 23.
418	Moody comment: To FF, 1/7/1947, LC/FFP: CF.
418	Once, when a: C. Fahy to Liva Baker, 11/6/1967; Rauh to FF, 9/3/1962, LC/FFP: 70.
419	Whether Frankfurter badgered: Frank, *Marble Palace,* pp. 104–5.
419	"If you came from Harvard": N. Dorsen interview, 3/5/1982.
420	Douglas and Frankfurter: Early FF/Douglas correspondence in LC/Douglas Papers: 4, 16; FF to C. E. Wyzanski, Jr., 3/22/1939, HLS/Wyzanski Papers: 1 (12).
420	Shortly that friendship: James F. Simon, p. 217.
420	"considerable talk in": Douglas to FF, 7/2/1940, HLS/FFP: 169 (12).
421	"Felix believes that": LC/Ickes Diary: 6/8/1941 (mss.).
421	"I am quite sure": Douglas to Black, 9/8/1941, LC/Black Papers: 59.
421	"cool and calculating": LC/Ickes Diary: 5/3/1942 (mss.), see also 9/26/1942 (mss.).
421	In 1944, the: Douglas to Stone, 7/12/1944, LC/Stone Papers: 74; Hopkins to FF, 7/10/1944, HLS/Burlingham Papers: 5 (5); Princeton/OHP: Douglas, Cassette #8, p. 178.
421	Douglas occasionally wrote: HLS/FF: O.T. 1940, bound volume, Paige Box 10 (on back of Sibbach v. Wilson); Kanin, "Trips to Felix," p. 3; Kanin interview, 5/12/1982.
422	Hugo Black background: Dunne, pp. 152, 156, 143, 165.
422	When appointed, Black: Schlesinger, Sr., *In Retrospect,* p. 125: Lash, ed., *Diaries,* p. 174; LC/Black papers: 58.
423	In the early years: FF to G. Clark, 12/16/1937, HLS/Clark Papers/FF addenda: XXV; FF to Burlingham, 2/2/1938, HLS/Burlingham: 4 (16).
423	In 1938, Frankfurter: FF to FDR, 5/18/1938, Freedman, p. 457.
423	Childs article: "Supreme Court Today," p. 582 et seq.
423	After the article: FF to LDB, 5/20/1938, LC/FFP: CF.
424	"Black may have had": LC/Ickes Diaries: 12/3/1939 (mss.).
424	"Yes, I know all": J. Chamberlain, "Nine Young Men," pp. 82–84.
424	Still, years passed: HLS/FFP: O. J. Roberts to FF, 11/12/1944: 171 (2); copy of brethren's letter to Roberts: 172 (6); Stone to FF, 8/13/1945; FF to brethren, 8/25/1945; FF to Stone, 8/25/1945: 187 (11).
424	Black publicly feuded: LC/FFP: Diary, 4/19/1943; HLS/FF interview with G. Gunther, 9/15/1960, 2nd tape, p. 23; LC/Burton Papers: Diary (10/10/1946).

424   **At one point:** FF to Holmes, 4/18/1921, HLS/Holmes papers: 30 (16); FF, *Law and Politics,* pp. 191–94.

426   **At the end of 1939, when:** FF to Black, 12/15/1939, HLS/FF: O.T. 1939, Paige Box 10 (with Jackson case).

427   **Hugo Black came:** Black, *Constitutional Faith,* pp. 24–25, 11.

Chapter 22. The Harvard Professor and the Alabama Hillbilly

428   *United States* v. *Darby:* 312 U.S. 100.

428   **To emphasize the change:** *Wickard* v. *Filburn,* 317 U.S. 111; FF to H. F. Stone, 5/26/1942, LC/Stone Papers: 74.

429   **In St. Louis a:** *U.S.* v. *Hutchinson,* 312 U.S. 219, et seq.

429   **Milk-truck drivers case:** *Drivers Union* v. *Meadowmoor Co.,* 312 U.S. 287.

430   **Ritter case:** *Carpenters Union* v. *Ritter's Cafe,* 315 U.S. 722.

431   *Hunt* v. *Crumboch:* 325 U.S. 821.

432 et seq.   **A 1982 Truman biography:** Donovan, pp. 386–87; *Youngstown Sheet and Tube Co.* v. *Sawyer,* 343 U.S. 579; Harbaugh, pp. 462–68; LC/Burton Papers: Diary, 4/9/1952 to 6/2/1952; see M. Marcus for comprehensive account of the case.

433   **The differences between:** From a paper delivered by Liva Baker, 11/19/1982, FF centennial observance, Harvard Law School.

433   **"I do not believe":** FF to C. C. Burlingham, 5/19/1952, LC/FFP: CF.

434   **"tend to brutalize":** FF to H. H. Burton, LC/Burton papers: 86.

434   **Wiretapping cases:** 302 U.S. 379, 308 U.S. 338.

434   **In this second case:** FF to C. C. Burlingham, 12/19/1939, LC/FFP: CF.

434 et seq.   *McNabb:* 318 U.S. 332: FF to H. F. Stone, 11/6/1942, LC/Douglas Papers: 228; FF to H. F. Stone, 2/20/1943, LC/Stone papers: 74; LC/FFP: Diary, 2/26, 1943.

436 et seq.   *Fisher:* 328 U.S. 463; Reed to FF, 6/2/1946; FF to Reed, 6/14/1946, LC/FFP: CF.

436 et seq.   *Harris:* 331 U.S. 145, 167: Hand to FF, 5/10/1947, HLS/FFP: 11 (12).

437   *Mallory:* 354 U.S. 449.

438   *Palko:* 302 U.S. 319.

438   **The Commission interviewed:** National Commission, v. 10, pp. 177, 180, 181.

439   *Betts:* 316 U.S. 455.

440   **This again showed:** *Carter* v. *Illinois,* 329 U.S. 173; Jackson to FF, 11/23/1946, HLS/FFP: 10 (16).

441   *Malinski:* 324 U.S. 401: Black memorandum to brethren, 12/23/1945, HLS/FFP: 7 (17).

441   *Adamson:* 332 U.S. 46.

442   *Wolf:* 338 U.S. 25.

442   *Rochin:* 342 U.S. 165, 172.

443   **Black later said:** Black, *Constitutional Faith,* p. 30.

443   *Irvine:* 347 U.S. 128.

443   **Frankfurter opposed:** FF to F. W. Green, 5/18/1929, LC/FFP: CF; FF, *Of Law and Men,* p. 81.

444   **Whatever Frankfurter said:** *Vernon* v. *Wilson,* HLS/FFP: O.T. 1940, inserted in bound volume, Paige Box 1.

444   *Buchalter:* 319 U.S. 427; FF statement, 3/11/1943, HLS/FFP: O.T. 1942, Paige Box 11.

444–445   Francis case: *Francis* v. *Resweber,* 329 U.S. 459.
445   "I was very much": FF, *Of Law and Men,* pp. 98–99.
445   If as a judge: See FF/Lemann correspondence, LC/FFP: CF. Also correspondence and memoranda in LC/Burton Papers: 67, 138, 171.
446   *Mapp:* 367 U.S. 643.

Chapter 23. Alger Hiss

448   Dwight D. Eisenhower: G. Clark to H. Tweed, 9/14/1953, HLS/FFP: 184 (2), describing a meeting with FF.
449   Eisenhower in his: *Mandate for Change,* pp. 226, 228.
449   "You ask whether": To Oliver Gates, 10/29/1953, LC/FFP: 23.
450   "The first man I": Douglas, *Go East, Young Man,* p. 259.
451   "I thought it might": A. Hiss interview, 5/26/1982.
451   "I told the counsel": COHP/Reed, pp. 189–90.
451   "I deemed it": *NY Times,* 7/21/1949; FF sent clipping to H. L. Blumgart, 10/27/1949, as accurately reflecting his feelings, HLS/FFP: 216 (2).
451   Frankfurter testified in: Trial transcript, HLS/Meyer A. Zelig Papers, pp. 1569–80.
452   "I can't be": A. Hiss interview, 5/26/1982.
452   "Before the new": 11/10/1949, LC/FFP: CF.
453   Only Douglas and: *Go East, Young Man,* pp. 378–80; *Weiler* v. *U.S.,* 323 U.S. 606.
453   Had Hiss and: A. Hiss interview, 5/26/1982; *NY Times,* 7/21/1949.
454   "He devoted himself": Rauh, "Felix Frankfurter," p. 520; FF to C. E. Wyzanski, Jr., 2/22/1951, LC/FFP: CF.
454   *Communications:* 339 U.S. 382.
454   The next year: 340 U.S. 290; diary entry, courtesy of O. Fraenkel.
454   The case previewed: *Joint Anti-Fascist Refugee Committee* v. *McGrath,* 341 U.S. 123; *Bailey* v. *Richardson,* 341 U.S. 918; *NY Times,* 10/13/1950, p. 14.
455   *Dennis:* 341 U.S. 494, 518.
456   Early in 1952: *Adler* v. *Board of Education,* 342 U.S. 485, 498; *Wieman* v. *Updegraff,* 344 U.S. 183, 195–96; HLS/FFP: 67 (9).
456 et seq.   Rosenberg case: HLS/FFP: in 65 (2) FF memorandum, 6/4/1953; FF's "Addendum," 6/19/1953; FF to H. H. Burton, 5/23/1953; FF "Memorandum for the Conference," June 15; SC record of sessions, 6/18/1953–6/19/1953; FF memorandum of Black dissent, undated; in 65 (7) FF memorandum to conference, 5/20/1953; Douglas memorandum, 5/22/1953, and FF's memorandum in response, same date; in 179 (12) FF statement, 11/17/1952; and in 179 (11–14) see correspondence to FF. HLS/Chafee papers: 35 (21) Chafee to Frank, 11/14/1952, and Frank to Chafee, 11/18/1952. HLS/Burlingham Papers: 5 (12) FF to Burlingham, 6/24/1953. LC/Burton Papers: Diary 6/15/1953. D. Troutman interview, 8/4/1981. *NY Times,* 6/23/1953, p. 1; Rauh, p. 515. Douglas, *Court Years,* pp. 237–38; J. F. Simon, pp. 298–307.
460   "Felix irritates": Confidential source.
461   In the spring of: *Barsky* v. *Board of Regents,* 347 U.S. 442, 467.
461   That same spring: 347 U.S. 913; Rauh, p. 513.
461   *Peters:* 349 U.S. 331, 338; FF memorandum, undated, HLS/FFP: 80 (17).
461   Later that year: *Toth* v. *Quarles,* 350 U.S. 11; FF to Black, 10/26/1955, HLS/FFP: 89 (11).

462   *Pennsylvania:* 350 U.S. 497.

462   **Also in 1956:** *Slochower* v. *Board of Higher Education,* 350 U.S. 551; FF to Warren, 3/13/1956, HLS/FFP: 84 (1); FF to Clark, 5/21/1956, HLS/FFP: 88 (9).

462–463   *Communist:* 351 U.S. 115; see FF's memoranda to conference, HLS/FFP: 84 (5) and 84 (2).

463   **That same year:** *Cole* v. *Young,* 351 U.S. 536.

463   **California case:** *Konigsberg* v. *California,* 353 U.S. 252.

463   **New Mexico case:** *Schware* v. *Board of Bar Examiners,* 353 U.S. 232, 247.

464   *Watkins:* 354 U.S. 178, 198, 216.

464   *Sweezy:* 354 U.S. 234, 249.

465   **California case:** *Yates* v. *U.S.,* 354 U.S. 298.

465   *Service:* 354 U.S. 363.

465   *Barenblatt:* 360 U.S. 109, 132, 150.

466   *Greene:* 360 U.S. 474, 507, 508.

466   **"The basic ingredient":** E. Warren, *Memoirs,* p. 6.

466   **"There 'likes' does":** To M. Lerner, 5/17/1952, LC/FFP: CF.

466   **"If the giving":** FF to Griswold, 9/23/1960, LC/FFP: 53.

467   *Communist:* 367 U.S. 1.

Chapter 24. *Brown* v. *Board of Education*

470   **Between 1913 and:** Harbaugh, pp. 531–35.

470   **His personal:** Ibid., p. 493.

471   **"I can only say":** Ibid., p. 506.

471   **From the early:** Leonard Baker, *Marshall,* pp. 725–29. 10 Wheat. 66.

471   **Dred Scott decision:** 19 Howard 393.

472   *Plessy:* 163 U.S. 537, 559.

472   **"grandfather clause":** *Guinn* v. *U.S.,* 238 U.S. 347.

472   **1927 segregation case:** *Gong Lum* v. *Rice,* 275 U.S. 78.

473   *Grovey:* 295 U.S. 45.

473   **By the late 1930s:** *Missouri ex rel. Gaines* v. *Canada,* 305 U.S. 337.

473   **When Felix Frankfurter:** FF to W. White, 11/6/1929, LC/NAACP Papers: I-C-64.

473   **In 1932, when:** *NY Times,* 11/13/1932; FF to H. F. Stone, 11/18/1932, LC/Stone Papers: 13; Kluger, p. 115; FF to Stone, 2/16/1938, LC/FFP: 37; Stone to FF, 2/17/1938, LC/FFP: 38.

474   **Frankfurter resigned from:** FF to W. White, 1/24/1939, LC/NAACP Papers: 1-C-64; T. Marshall memorandum to "Secretary," 1/16/1939, LC/NAACP Papers: I-A-69.

474   **"He just thought":** Liva Baker interview with Adrian Fisher, 8/31/1967.

474   **"the most complicated":** FF to S. Reed, 4/25/1944, LC/FFP: 32; LC/FFP: Diary, 11/20/1942.

474   **In 1944, after:** *Smith* v. *Allwright,* 321 U.S. 649; Biddle to FDR, 10/30/1943, FDRL/PSF 77 (H. Cumming 1938–1939 folder).

475 et seq.   **That afternoon, Robert:** FF memorandum, 4/10/1944, HLS/FFP: 6 (17); FF to H. F. Stone, 3/17/1944, LC/FFP: 38; FF's unpublished concurring opinion is in LC/FFP: 206. Also, Mason, *Stone,* pp. 614–16; "Philips" memorandum, 8/1957, LC/FFP: 30.

476   *Cassell:* 339 U.S. 282; Clark to FF, and FF response, 3/14/1950, HLS/FFP: 33 (3).

476   **In the late 1940s:** *Sipuel* v. *Oklahoma,* 334 U.S. 641; *Sweatt* v. *Painter,* 339 U.S. 629.

477   **Frankfurter understood them:** To W. Rutledge, 1/2/1947, LC/FFP: CF; FF to Vinson, 5/19/1950, LC/FFP: 40; 339 U.S. 641.

477   **The southern segregationists:** Harbaugh, pp. 488, 496.

478   **When Thurgood Marshall:** Harbaugh, p. 503.

478   **Frankfurter's role in:** Liva Baker interview with Douglas and with Warren, 4/16/1968.

478 et seq. **Notes, conference:** 4/16/1955, LC/FFP: 219; P. Elman interview, 2/25/1981; Kluger, p. 675; Hutchinson, "Unanimity," p. 92; Acheson to A. Bickel, 9/13/1965, McLellan and Acheson, p. 274.

479   **"The main danger":** A. Bickel to Liva Baker, 2/20/1968.

479   **Frankfurter had urged:** LC/FFP: 40.

480   **For Frankfurter, as for:** FF memorandum, undated, HLS/FFP: 72 (14).

480   **One month after:** FF memorandum, LC/Burton papers: 263.

481   *Brown:* 347 U.S. 483; 349 U.S. 294.

482   **"I quite agree":** 8/17/1954, HLS/FFP: 172 (12).

482 et seq. **"has been taking":** FF to Warren, 7/21/1954, LC/FFP: CF.

483   **"I doubt very much":** FF to L. Hand, 2/13/1958, LC/FFP: CF.

483 et seq. **A turning point:** A. Lewis, *Portrait of a Decade,* pp. 51, 68; transcript, special term, 8/28/1958, LC/Burton Papers: 325.

484   **The Supreme Court ruled:** *Cooper* v. *Aaron,* 358 U.S. 1.

485 et seq. **He began by stating:** 358 U.S. 1, 20; FF to Burlingham, 11/12/1958, LC/FFP: CF.

487   **Illinois case:** *Colgrove* v. *Green,* 328 U.S. 549, 554, 556.

487   **1960 case:** *Gomillion* v. *Lightfoot,* 364 U.S. 339; FF to Warren, HLS/FFP: 136 (4).

487   *Baker:* 369 U.S. 186, 267, 270.

488   **Frankfurter would have:** FF to A. Bickel, 4/4/1962, HLS/FFP: 206 (11); Princeton/Douglas OHP, Cassette #7b, p. 151.

489   **"It is still":** *NY Times,* 5/1/1962, p. 28.

489   **A friend:** Behrman to Ruth Gordon, 5/15/1962, LC/Ruth Gordon Papers: 1.

489   **"His biggest thrill":** Elsie Douglas to J. M. Harlan, 7/24/1962, LC/FFP: CF.

489   **On Thursday, July 26:** Kanin, "Trips to Felix," p. 24; Acheson memorandum, 7/26/1962; E. Douglas to J. M. Harlan, LC/FFP: CF.

490   **"You will want":** FF to F. W. Buxton, 8/22/1962, LC/FFP: CF.

490   **The President announced:** *NY Times,* 8/30/1962, p. 1. The author was present at the news conference.

490   **A year later:** FF to J. F. Kennedy, 7/5/1963, LC/FFP: 152 (003087).

490   **On November 22:** L. B. Johnson to FF, 12/5/1963; FF to Johnson, 12/7/1963, LC/FFP: CF.

490   **Frankfurter lingered on:** H. Black, Jr., *My Father,* p. 237; Kanin, "Toward the End," pp. 9, 1, 7; FF to J. R. Wiggins, 1/30/1962, LC/FFP: CF.

491   **"Darling Marion":** FF to M. Frankfurter, undated, LC/FFP: CF.

491   **"I hope I don't":** E. Richardson, Harvard Law School *Bulletin,* 3/1965, p. 3.

491   **As an associate justice:** 328 U.S. xliv.

491   **Felix Frankfurter had never:** Freund interview, 7/17/1981; L. Henkin/A. J. Rosenthal interviews, 5/6/1981; Kanin, "Trips to Felix," p. 30; Freund, "Felix Frankfurter," p. 36.

Index